MW01064816

Fifty-two "SUNDAYS" ON THE BLUE ROADS

U. GRANT BROWNING

Cold Tree Press

To Betty whom I have deeply loved for 55 years and who admits to loving me for 54 years. We confirmed our love to each other when we were married over 50 years ago.

Grant

Acknowledgements

"And in accepting this award I would like to thank all the people who helped make this dream come true" are words we hear many times when awards are being presented and received at the Tony and The Oscar awards each year. But these words are rehearsed by the far more losers than they are actually ever spoken by the eventual winners.

I however want to say these words, even before my far too many words are actually printed, because whether they are ever printed or not I owe a great debt of gratitude to several people.

First and foremost among this group is my wife Betty. For a full year she got up far too early for her on Sunday mornings to go with me, first to breakfast (the easy part), and then to a religious service some-where. I am not at all sure Betty ever felt this was such a grand idea, but, of course, she would never, ever say so. Betty is a trooper, and never a party-pooper. This was my party and my parade. She is not the type to beat the drums, but she will march with the band until the last float has passed the reviewing stand.

Years ago, when Betty and I were doing some serious and extended blue-road traveling, she agreed to go along and allow me to set the tone for the whole trip. She signed on as my first-mate and allowed me to be the captain. This was the only trip out of many which we had made together where I had made all the plans. And she went along in a sup-porting role. She readily acknowledged that the 52 "Sundays" journey was also my parade, my trip, my adventure. All year long she went along, helping me to finish this project which I had decided I wanted to do. And she helped a lot. She read all my manuscripts carefully, correcting my spelling and punctuation and generally advising me with proper grammar. You know, helping me with the correct tenses, pronouns, and dangling participles. And she never complained even when my verbs were far too many, and incorrectly conjugated.

"And next I would like to thank …" At this point the award recip-ient would pull out a piece of paper and read off a list of names so that they would not forget anyone. I will not have this problem because my

list is very short. The second person I am grateful to is Mary Louise Barrack who was at one time a court reporter and then for a few years worked as my assistant in my real estate business, until she grew up and got a real job. But when I wanted someone to do the technical work on this manuscript for me she was my first and only choice. The fact that she already had gone through several years of trying to read my writing was no small part of this decision. And I have always liked the way she does things. She is so neat and precise. And I am not. She transposed my sloppy manuscript to a floppy disk and kept helping me improve the nearly finished product every week of the year.

There are several other people whose assistance I wish to acknowledge. Frank Sutherland, the editor of The Tennessean *newspaper*, helped me by reading my first scripts, and did not advise me to quit after he had read the first few chapters for which I am grateful, but I had to promise him two more strokes in our regular golf games. He is a tough editor and an equally tough negotiator on the first tee. Frank also introduced me to Brian Lewis, the religion editor of The Tennessean, who made some valuable suggestions regarding some of the churches I attended.

Then there was the valued opinion of Gary Fistkejohn who is an editor with the Alfred C. Knopf Press. He also did not advise me to quit after he had read several chapters even though I suspected that both he and Frank, in their heart of hearts, felt I really should have quit – just a hunch. Gary did, however, advise me to shorten my book by perhaps re-titling it "A Month of Sundays." And then, Jan Wells, an old friend from high school and college days, read much of my script and gave some valuable advice. Sonya Watson gave extremely valuable graphic design assistance and my editor Madison Gray managed to sandwich a noble effort in terms of time and energy between working at her "day job" and working on yet another graduate degree. Lastly, I would like to thank Bob DuLany, of Hendersonville, Tennessee, who did a wonderful job photographing the historic Hendersonville Presbyterian Church for the front cover and Cold Tree Press, my publisher, who stayed the course and were able to design, format and deliver my book in a timely fashion, while making it a pleasant experience throughout.

That's all folks. And if I forgot someone it was because the dog ate my list. I don't even have a dog, but that's my story and I'm sticking to it.

Table of Contents

Introduction

Table of Contents

Introduction

In the year that followed "9-11-01" people spoke of a religious awakening taking place in the United States, and perhaps even in the whole world. Church attendance was reported to be up substantially. And the strong sales of religious and gospel music, despite a downturn in music sales generally, supported the notion that perhaps there actually was a trend towards inner consciousness or spiritual awakening in America. Always in times of crisis, the minds and hearts of people tend to turn inward.

In a post 9-11 world, the search for answers, meaning and direction dominated the thoughts and conversations of many Americans. They turned to ask God why all of this was happening even as fears and anxieties took root in their lives. 9-11 was a call to 9-1-1 from all Americans — a genuine emergency! It was a call that left most individuals shocked, hurt, offended and rudely shaken awake. And it was a call that left most individuals with troubling questions: how do we defend ourselves from future terrorist acts; what will terrorists do next; and, will biological terrorism or some other weapon of mass destruction soon be used against us?

The aftermath of 9-11 also forced us to consider why the tragedy occurred at all. What could cause anyone to be filled with such hatred toward our nation and our citizens as to justify such malicious extremes against innocent civilians? We, along with the majority of the world, define the perpetrators as "terrorists" while they call themselves "martyrs." The difference in perception is staggering. The simple fact that we are Americans precludes our being "innocent" in their eyes. Our very "Secular" Westernism pronounces us guilty in the courts of their minds — "Death to America and Americans" is their cry, their religious chant. Selected parts of the Muslim religion have been whipped into a jihad, a religious war, against "American infidels."

Our collective education in post 9-11 has included the important point that the multitude of Muslims who have such hatred for

Americans are extremely vocal, extremely active but definitely a small minority of Islam. Many millions of Muslims dislike, and disrespect, the United States because of its relationship with and its support of Israel, a relationship which they perceive as unjust and blind. Still other Muslims focus on the secularist nature of our country in their disapproval. But we have found that those who expand these negative feelings into violent, hate-based action are truly a numerical minority. Hate-based minorities exist in most religious populations. We are painfully aware of a small minority of Christians who would still support the Klu Klux Klan or the bombing of abortion clinics. These are certainly fundamentalist Christian "jihads" against those they perceive as being sinful unbelievers. In most religious traditions, including Christian and Muslim, the adherents range from the most liberal to the most rabid fundamentalist.

Readings on the history and traditions of Islam by noted scholars reveal that these great variations surely exist in modern Islamic culture. Most Americans, religious or not, recognize America as a "Christian nation" with numerous divisions, denominations and sects of the Christian faith. Those same Americans, however, have come to think of Islam as being a monolithic religion. However, the undisputed fact is that the number of varied Muslim traditions may come close to equaling the number of varied traditions that exist in Christianity.

My early religious studies made me keenly aware of the variations existing within the major religions of the world. My personal post 9-11 questioning of "why?" and "how?" created a strong desire to find out, first-hand, more about the varied religious traditions in America. I wanted to know what the people were feeling and saying as they came together to worship, regardless of their religion. I wanted to know how 9-11 was affecting how Americans were feeling and speaking — both about themselves and about those who might seem so different, so foreign.

I chose a very simple way to learn more about religious life in America post 9-11. I wanted to experience the reawakening of American spiritual life for myself. I decided to put aside the books I was reading about such matters and actually visit 52 different religious services. This would be a year's worth of worship as my personal lesson plan. I confess that as I started out on my journey into the faith of America that I wondered if anything was being said about 9-11 in our places of worship. What if nothing was being said? I would be there to "hear nothing" on this subject if this was the case.

After visiting 52 different religious services during the period between September 11, 2002 and September 11, 2003, I found that 9-11 was rarely a topic in the worship services. I felt certain that in the first year after 9-11 the issue of terrorism had been addressed often; during the second year after 9-11, however, the prayer book in the 52 different religious services I attended was primarily closed on this subject. On only a few occasions were oblique references made to 9-11. These references generally took the form of asking God to bless our country as it faces the new and dark days ahead. We were often reminded to "remember the victims of 9-11 in our prayers." Occasionally we were asked to remember and to pray for the soldiers risking their lives on foreign soil "in these dark days."

So then, was my journey all for naught? This was the question I was left with after a year of travel and fellowship. Certainly not. That Americans were saying very little about 9-11 during their weekly worship was, in and of itself, something. The "sound of silence" on 9-11 was important to take note of and consider. Perhaps it spoke to the human capacity for healing and moving on. Or perhaps noting the silence challenged me to hear instead what Americans really were talking about during their weekly worship.

My 52 week journey was never intended as a singular search for the answer to a singular question. I was open to whatever I heard, to whatever I saw, on this set of visitations. The "sound of silence" was found only with regard to 9-11, the catalyst in many ways for this personal journey. The only answers offered to you, my reader, with regard to what Americans *were* discussing during their worship services are the stories shared on the following pages. These stories speak to the different ways religious Americans seek answers to their questions about life. These stories also speak to, simply and directly, the ways different American congregations approach God in their search for faith and in their practice of worship.

Setting the Mood

Sixteen years ago, I left Nashville on a trip that lasted for 10 weeks. My wife, Betty, accompanied me as an "invited guest." She is referred to as a "guest" because the 10 week trip was to have been "my trip." I had been thinking about and carefully planning for this adventure for some time. I wanted to see America "up close and personal" and had planned the trip with this goal in mind. I worried a bit that Betty would not enjoy a trip designed strictly to suit my individual tastes. Knowing from experience her preference for fine hotels and restaurants, I invited her to go with me as a "guest." I made certain she understood that the RV, along with wayside bed and breakfasts, and "greasy-spoon" restaurants would be the foundations of this travel experience. We also agreed that she was not signing on for the entire trip; she was welcome only so long as she could travel with ease under these guidelines. I was not at all sure she would care to travel by my "rules of the road." I suspected that she might well get fed up with this type of travel after a few weeks and pictured waving to her as a Greyhound bus pulled out of a bus station to take her home. Wrong, completely wrong!

Betty loved the "up close and personal" way of traveling, almost as much as I did. To her credit she good naturedly accepted the travel rules and became "first mate," allowing me to truly be the captain of my ship. "For this trip only," she emphasized. I believe one of the reasons she enjoyed the trip so much was the first mate requirement of deferring to the captain. She was not called on to make any decisions at all. She just relaxed and enjoyed the trip. And as captain I enjoyed her companionship.

The rules of this journey years ago were very simple: (1) the "blue roads" on the map would be our path; (2) the RV would be our "home" on the road, with the option of any country inns or bed and breakfasts that crossed our path; (3) there would only be a direction, never a destination; and, (4) there would never be a sense of hurry or rushing. And for the most part these guidelines went unchallenged during our travels. The few exceptions to these guidelines are explained later on. Right now, however, let's consider more fully how each of these propositions operated to set the tone for the stories that follow.

1. The blue roads. We traveled only on the "blue roads," never on the interstates or major highways. William Least Heat Moon, in his intriguing book *Blue Highways*, describes planning a trip on which he would not travel on major highways, colored red and green on most maps. Instead, Moon planned to travel only on the back roads of America, colored black and blue on most maps, and calls his choice of paths the "blue highways." We kicked his concept down a notch for our purposes and embraced the idea of "blue roading." When we traveled on a red or green highway, it was only as a means to access the next blue road.

2. *Home on the road.* We stayed only in country inns or bed and breakfasts. If no such accommodation was available, we slept in SCOLTA, the family name for our RV. Patterned after the name SCUBA (Self Contained Underwater Breathing Apparatus), I had named our touring vehicle SCOLTA (Self-Contained Over Land Touring Apparatus). Self-contained, indeed! SCOLTA guaranteed a fine bed if no suitable wayside inns were able to accommodate us. Be it large or small, each inn or bed and breakfast was something unique and not just another place to sleep.

3. *Direction, not destination.* We had no destination, only a direction. We simply went northeast. Guided only by direction, there was no need to constantly check the map or highway signs; when going "nowhere" in particular it is impossible to be on the "wrong" road. We needed only a compass to head northeast towards the Northeastern U.S. And since we had SCOLTA, we had no need for hotel reservations which would have meant dastardly destinations.

4. *"Do Not Pass."* The last guiding principle demanded a definite change from how I typically travel. Anyone who knows me would testify that I tend to crowd the speed limit, and that I depend on the unwritten understanding between highway patrolmen and would-be speeders allowing for a 5–7 mile per hour lagniappe between the posted speed limit and the speed at which the red lights go on. The notion of not-hurrying seemed distinctly profound as a result. Without a set destination, however, the concept of an estimated time of arrival fell away. The clock was, for all purposes, thrown away; our eyes were kept on only the compass.

Betty and I held ourselves to the guideline of not-hurrying, every day and all day. In an attempt to make this profound change from hurrying to non-hurrying, I adopted the "Do Not Pass" sign seen on the back roads of America as the motto for our journey. We did not pass anyone on the road, anytime or anywhere. We hoped that if we got in anyone's way that they would come on around. We took our good ol' time, literally. Those behind us going somewhere on the same day we were going nowhere uttered, I suspect, a few choice words before passing SCOLTA and leaving the non-hurrying Brownings in their wake.

Surprisingly however, not everyone hated us — even when they actually had a destination. One beautiful day while somewhere-going-nowhere, I was zipping along at the breakneck speed of about 30 miles an hour when I pulled up behind a tractor pulling a trailer load of wood. The farmer was outdoing me at slowness, poking along at about 10 miles-per-hour. SCOLTA fell in line behind him. Instead of passing him, I continued listening to a very fine tape with my foot properly propped up on the dashboard. I, the 30 miles an hour speed demon, was content to slow down and follow "Farmer Brown" to wherever he was going. I was, after all, somewhere-going-nowhere and singing "do not pass" as my travel song.

Farmer Brown, my new friend on the road, had some trouble accepting the presence of the large SCOLTA behind him as non-threatening. As I drove behind him, he looked anxiously over his shoulder time and time again. He did not understand why I was not taking any one of a number of opportunities to pass his tractor. I imagined him wondering, "What is wrong with that fool?" and "Why don't they keep those dang RVs off the roads?" And I wondered about all the times in the past I had perceived tractors like his as being an annoyance on this same road we now traveled together. We traveled like this for several miles.

Gradually Farmer Brown came to accept SCOLTA as some kind of protection from other vehicles racing up from behind. He was probably questioning my sanity, but at least I was some measure of a buffer, protecting his tractor from some other hurrying city slicker who would have to destroy my RV before damaging his vehicle. He started to think differently about SCOLTA and its unknown driver. Perhaps it was the foot on the dash; the tip of my jogging shoe on the dash must have told him that I wasn't going anywhere and, since I wasn't going anywhere, I was in no hurry. The anxious looks over his shoulder became less frequent and then ceased altogether. Without any verbal communication Farmer Brown and I had a pleasant, relaxed conversation. He started it with a "Welcome, friend, and thanks for covering my rear."

The non-conversation between Farmer Brown and me touched on what a nice day it was and how great it was not to be in a hurry. For about 8 miles we continued our wordless chat until he came to his destination. Carefully and courteously Farmer Brown signaled with his arm that this was his farm and thanked me for blue roading along with him. I told him that I had enjoyed our talk about how people are in too much of a hurry these days. My new friend then turned, slowly of course, onto a dirt road and pointed to a farmhouse visible in the distance. He wished me a fine trip to nowhere. He said he wished he could go along with us but he needed to go unload his wood. He was going to go back for another load before the day was done and hoped to find another friend driving a SCOLTA. He wanted to congratulate me for finding the right way to travel and to live. He told me I would enjoy life more and would probably live longer because I had stopped, or at least slowed down, to smell the roses. Or, in this case, the newly cut firewood he was hauling. All of these things were shared with the most beautiful non-verbal words I have ever not heard. I waved goodbye to my forever new friend as he stood up on the seat of his tractor and slightly bowed in my direction, giving me the okay sign with his thumb and curved forefinger. And as I sped off at about 25 miles an hour, I found myself looking rather wistfully for another farmer pulling a load of wood.

The four guiding propositions set forth above provided the key to enjoying a trip that was markedly different from the norm. I encourage the reader to give it a try. Proceed with caution though; these travel guidelines may be addictive. You might find yourself forevermore shying away from the routes indicated in red and green on the maps, unless of course, you find yourself going somewhere. And if that is the case, my friend, you have my sympathy; I hope you find your way back to the blue roads sooner rather than later.

A New Journey

I decided that these four keys, or guidelines, we had developed 16 years ago for our trip to the Northeastern part of the country would be followed as nearly as possible as we started our new journey in September of 2002. For the most part these guides to blue roading were the actual method used to "find" 52 different religious observances in churches, synagogues, temples and mosques as we meandered. We followed these guidelines religiously even though each of these 52 trips would be short ones. On Sunday mornings Betty and I would head out of town, from wherever we found ourselves. We set off on blue roads in differing directions confident that a place of worship would be found. The directions would branch out in different sub-directions, especially from our home in Nashville. By choosing a different direction each week, we covered the whole area of Middle Tennessee. If we found ourselves in another area or state on any particular weekend, we followed the same guidelines for traveling to find a religious service to attend. As adherents to the compass we kept true to the blue roading guideline of "no destination, only direction."

On short trips we left early Sunday morning from wherever we were to give us plenty of time. We created enough time to "shop" for a church to attend, using the time to consider several possibilities before investing this Sunday or Sabbath time as casually as possible. We found that the more time we had to do so, the more it suited the blue road mood of those mornings. This relaxed pace kept true to the blue roading guideline of "do not pass."

The blue roading guideline of "home on the road' led us to seek out different types of worship services to visit. During our *Fifty-Two "Sundays" on the Blue Roads* we visited a wide variety of churches, synagogues, temples and mosques and other religious gathering places. Regardless of location, we joined Americans in their weekly worship. No place of worship was chosen or rejected because of its size, too large or too small. Blue roading on these 52 short trips, much like the longer blue roading trips, led us to a wide variety in the types of services we attended. They were "found" as we traveled by blue roading guidelines instead of being "sought out" as high profile places of worship.

Exceptions

There are always exceptions I suppose. And there would be on our fifty-two Sundays traveling the blue roads. In some cases spontaneity was purposefully and consciously compromised as a step toward increasing the level of variety in the types of services attended. A few special places were sought out, and certainly without regret. These special places needed to be sought out or else they would have been missed altogether. Planning was required in order to experience the worship services in a Jewish synagogue, a Muslim mosque, Hindu and Buddhist temples and others such as the Seventh Day Adventists and the Mormons. And "Sundays" became Fridays or Saturdays when different religious traditions called for worship on these days.

Although such exceptions were happily made, for the most part we traveled the country roads, entering small villages and feeling the pulse of religious worship in these out-of-the-way places. Perhaps here, I hoped, I could find if and how the heart of America truly reacted to the world events such as 9-11. Perhaps here I might discover what Americans really believed and felt as they turned inward in an attempt to answer questions about life in the modern world. While the more notable and pre-selected religious services we attended were perhaps more dramatic examples of the changing religious moods, the salt-of-the-Earth churches we visited on the blue roads might just be a better, or more nearly accurate, indication of how America has really changed in the post 9-11 era, if it has at all.

Food for Body and Soul

Searching in a relaxed mode on these Sunday mornings, we decided we would eat breakfast on the blue road most Sundays. The whole morning's experience, including starting out in some direction without a specific destination, the interlude of a relaxed breakfast somewhere along the blue roads and the finding and experiencing of a religious worship service, would complete the full Sunday morning blue road experience.

What I found along the way of the travels, the worship services we attended as well as the blue road restaurants we visited, is shared in *Fifty-Two "Sundays" on the Blue Roads.* The descriptions of our dining experiences, both of the atmosphere and of the food, are not intended to pass as those of a food critic. I do love good food, as any casual observer of me would readily notice, but I do not offer a professional critique of the blue road establishments, except perhaps with regard to biscuits. I am a better-than-average critic of biscuits, mainly because I have eaten far more than my share of these beloved southern blue road loaves.

Similarly, the descriptions of the worship services attended are certainly not the words of a theologian or religious scholar, nor are they fashioned from any particular theological basis. When I left the active pursuit of all things theological and strictly academic back in 1964, I left them behind forever. My recollections of what I saw and what I heard are hopefully as objective as a man's recollections ever can be. This is not a serious attempt at anything other than sharing a few stories from the blue roads. I hope you enjoy reading these accounts of my 52 weekly journeys half as much as I enjoyed my time blue roading into the heart of America.

Fifty-two "Sundays" on the Blue Roads

U. GRANT BROWNING

Chapter 1

Centerville United Methodist Church
Centerville, Tennessee
September 15, 2002

I was excited on the morning of September 15, 2002. It was the first of the 52 weekend trips Betty and I were planning, and a reunion of sorts. We were connecting our days and mode of blue roading of 16 years ago with these new weekend trips. We left our home in Nashville, Tennessee at about 8:30 a.m. In the introduction I stated that we left "early" on our trips. Well, 8:30 is early for me. Being self-employed has allowed me to live like the bears in the woods. I go to bed when I get sleepy and get up when I am rested. And generally I am not refreshingly rested until 8:00 a.m. most mornings.

Come to think of it, the ability to sleep until I am rested may be the prime benefit of being self-employed. To be sure, I had not planned on being self-employed but I have been since 1964, the year I left the ministry. I had served three Presbyterian churches while I worked on a graduate degree in philosophy and theology. Neither topic, I came to find out, prepared me for the job market. I applied for employment as president of National Life, as president of Life and Casualty Insurance Companies, as CEO at the then Third National Bank and as CEO of the First American Bank. I'm still waiting to hear back from them. Sometimes I wonder if I should re-apply to the new parent companies which have acquired the original institutions to which I applied. I have always wanted someone to hire me to an important position. But as of today I am still looking.

I am also considering re-submitting my application to the Belle Meade Country Club. My application must have been misplaced. How disappointing that the club's lack of management systems would allow the misplacement of my application which was submitted to them back in 1967. Since we have a new governor in Tennessee, a member of my own party, I'm thinking of asking him to push a bill through which would automatically approve any club applications to which there had been no return communication for more than 30 years. I wonder if my club application would suddenly reappear if I became CEO of the Sun Trust Banks. If my application comes through approved, I think I'll not communicate back with them for 35 years; I'll just "lose" their letter of acceptance. That'll teach them!

My self-employment has other benefits. For example, it allows me to be snooty to snooty clubs. I just love that! It also keeps me from having to concern myself with the weighty problems of wealth preservation. Some of my very gainfully employed friends are constantly worrying about maintaining their wealth. Self-employment has allowed me to while my time away in relaxed adventures such as fifty-two Sundays of blue roading. Some friends spend their weekends walking and sweating on tennis courts while playing with often obnoxious CEOs.

I feel richer as time goes by. And I felt truly rich the Sunday morning Betty and I tooled out on Highway 100, going west towards Centerville, a town that lies about 50 miles from Nashville. Beyond Centerville Highway 100 proceeds westerly, in a back roads way, and eventually meanders into Memphis. I soon realized that I hadn't been very far out this blue road in several years. Once upon a time we had traveled this road frequently to dine at several country restaurants which we had discovered on other blue road excursions. As the first of our fifty-two blue roading adventures began, we decided to retrace some old steps down this blue road from the past. It was a beautiful late summer morning and one of our favorite blue road restaurants, remembered for weekend country breakfasts, was only 30 miles in the direction of this morning's trip. Betty's mother, Elizabeth Meggs, had been known to most of her family and friends as Nannie. She had lived with us for eight of the last nine years of her life and loved the Silver Leaf and Beacon Light restaurants out on Highway 100. Nannie had actually discovered these great blue road spots years ago while antiquing in the area. It became a treat to take a Saturday or Sunday drive to one of these spots, especially when Nannie would go with us. We normally went to the Silver Leaf for lunch or brunch because of its fabulous buffet. We favored the Beacon Light for its exceptional breakfasts, especially the truly outstanding biscuits and preserves. At 8:31 a.m. on this particular day, one minute into the trip, I began to think about those delicious biscuits. Please try to remember that I am something of an amateur expert in this area of country culinary art.

This was a beautiful sunny, late-Summer/early-Fall day that made for a beautiful drive. Driving "SCOLTA-like," we took leisurely notice of all the churches and restaurants as we traveled along. Many choices, both for breakfast and church, were presenting themselves. Although we were open to any which might strike our fancy, I have to admit that the Beacon Light had an edge in the restaurant category.

Another fabulous, heavy-duty blue road restaurant that lies near the newly completed Nashville leg of the Natchez Trace Parkway had to be considered. The Loveless Café, a favorite with many Nashvillians for several decades, was owned as of this beautiful day by the McCabe family. Hopefully blue roaders traveling the beautiful Natchez Trace Parkway will find this gem of an eating experience for years to come. The Loveless Café, as usual, was so crowded that it was an easy choice to pass up their biscuits and gravy. We would wait for a few more miles to pass for the same type of fare at the Beacon Light. Both restaurants serve, almost as soon as you are seated, a whole basket or plate of biscuits (actually both serve all you can, or care, to eat) with plenty of preserves.

A few minutes after passing The Loveless Café we were comfortably seated in the cozy Beacon Light dining room. With its décor reminiscent of an early 1900s country home, and a warm relaxing fireplace, the dining room's atmosphere leaves one convinced that surely it was created by a devoted Christian family. The walls are lined with biblical pictures of Jesus and the disciples, copies of the sweet Sunday school type images of years past. After being seated at a table in the middle of the main room, our friendly waitress soon brought us a basket containing about a dozen delicious and hot biscuits, served just as I had remembered. Sitting and savoring our "appetizers," we noticed another part of the Beacon Light tradition — The Promise Box. The Promise Box is a small plastic box shaped like a loaf of bread and filled with small, multicolored cards, each printed with verses from the Bible. Several people read from the little promise cards while waiting patiently for another cup of coffee.

My mother used to say, "Don't fill up on bread." It always proved impossible for me to follow that instruction at the Beacon Light. After devouring several of the biscuits, we ordered our standard blue road restaurant breakfasts. Betty asked, as usual, for two scrambled eggs with bacon. I ordered three eggs over-easy with bacon, hash browns and gravy, my favorite breakfast.

The waitress and I had a discussion about whether I should order my eggs over-easy or over-medium. I wanted the whites of my eggs cooked but the yokes warm and "runny," not fully cooked. I know, I know! Some say the eggs should be thoroughly cooked to avoid the possibility of salmonella. But give me a break. I was on the blue road and wanting a real blue road breakfast. And somehow runny yellows just said "blue road" loud and clear to me. The waitress and I finally agreed the eggs should be fried over-medium, leaving me the risk of having the yokes cooked too much and perhaps getting salmonella as well. Those eggs turned out to be as near to perfect as possible — almost as good as the biscuits — and I have yet to suffer from salmonella.

I asked the waitress about where the owner attended church. She surprised me by saying that she did not know. I had assumed because of the overtly religious décor that the owners were people who talked constantly, with their employees, their customers, and anyone who would listen about their church experiences.

The "Beacon Light Tea Room," the official name on the menu, was so named for a beacon light which had been constructed just across the road in 1931. The light had guided the old mail planes flying between Nashville and Memphis. On the menu of the Beacon Light were written these words:

> *Thank you for coming. The desire of our heart is that we serve you in such a way that when you leave, you are happy and content and will want to tell your friends. Our prayer is that God our Father would grant you an ever increasing measure of His presence, and may He fill you with peace, love and joy, feeding your spirit and soul, as well as your body.*

By the way, the "promises" Betty and I pulled from The Promise Box read: "*John 6: 35* I am the bread of life. He that cometh to me shall never hunger." and, "*Proverbs 11: 30 (a.)* The fruit of the righteous is a tree of life." Our bodies had certainly been fed in a truly delicious way that morning. We left the Beacon Light in search of a church to attend in hopes of seeing if some particular pastor would be feeding his flock spiritually as well as our bodies had been fed at this truly fine blue road restaurant.

After breakfast we continued west on Highway 100 and passed several Baptist churches and Churches of Christ, considering them all. We drove into the parking lot of an Assembly of God church which announced on its marquee, "A Holy Ghost Revival coming soon." The service there did not start until 11:00 a.m.; it was only 10:20 a.m. With forty minutes still to shop for a church, I made a mental note that sometime during the next fifty-one Sundays I would like to come back and visit this church if possible. We continued moving west and ended up in Centerville at about 10:45 a.m. We took a lap around the square, down a couple of nearby streets and soon saw what could well have been a Norman Rockwell painting — a United Methodist Church just one block off the square, the members gathering to worship on a beautiful Sunday morning. Right off we knew this was it, and proceeded to find a parking spot. I wore a jacket over a sport shirt with the top button buttoned. A tie might be too much but this would be okay in most places.

Betty and I were greeted warmly by several members of the church as we entered. They knew instantly that we were visitors because this was a relatively small church, making visitors easy to spot. We felt immediately that we were welcome. One of the individuals who greeted us tempered his welcome with an apology. Their minister and a group of members were somewhere in North Carolina volunteering on a church mission. So, the apology went, we were not to meet their minister David N. Spencer, "but we are still very pleased to have you here visiting with us today."

While we were sorry that the minister was away, we witnessed some of the fruits of his ministry, most importantly a warm, friendly and active church. The church bulletin was full of announcements about the activities of the congregation. A sign outside the church entrance reminded all to "Pray for the victims of 9-11;" an announcement in the printed church bulletin noted that the senior-youth group had recently participated in remembering 9-11 by "lighting the square;" and, the printed bulletin shared that the junior-youth group had washed the fire trucks for free, announcing proudly: "What a great group of young people we have."

The service began with piano music softly playing "This is my story, this is my Song…" as the choir assembled. The choir had no robes and consisted of one man and ten women. A lay reader welcomed visitors and invited members of the congregation to introduce their visitors for today. Betty and I were introduced as the Brownings by a man who had met us earlier. He said how pleased he was that our Sunday morning trek had brought us to their church.

Two girl acolytes, somewhere between the ages of eight and ten and dressed in white robes, marched down the aisle. Their tiny hands shielded the flickering candles as they led a lay speaker, the eighty-year-old Don Carpenter, to the pulpit. Many announcements were made by Mr. Carpenter: acolyte training, birthdays, church meals, prayer lists, etc. The choir director led both the choir and the congregation in singing *Morning has Broken*. Then a group of young children, probably between the ages of ten and twelve, gathered in the front to sing three songs. One of the songs was a rap song with no instrumental music and was sung to the tune and beat of *"Hambone."* This image before me also seemed vintage Norman Rockwell, as if it might have been printed on the cover of The *Saturday Evening Post* sixty years ago. I estimated that there were about seventy-five people gathered in the church this morning.

The worship service continued with the reading of the Scriptures. The Old Testament reading was *Exodus 14: 19 – 31* and spoke of the parting of the Red Sea for the Israelites. The New Testament reading included *Romans 14: 1 – 12* as well as a Gospel reading from Matthew about an unforgiving servant whom Jesus exhorted to forgive others even as much as 70 times 70.

Don Carpenter, the elderly gentleman serving as the lay speaker, read a favorite poem by an unknown author entitled "Give and Do" with at least two lessons in it: (1) Someone you know needs a friend; and, (2) "When God measures a man he puts the tape around the heart and not the head." He then shared a number of personal stories. One of the stories was about their house catching fire while the seven-year-old Don Carpenter and his mother were listening to the radio. His mother had shouted, "Go tell your father." Young Don ran to tell his father. His father, however, was busy talking with a customer and scolded, "Don't interrupt me when I am with a customer." Don was told to sit and wait. And so he obediently took a seat and waited. When his father was finally finished with the customer, he turned to Don and asked, "Now, son, what was so important that you felt you had to interrupt me when I was with a customer?" Don said, "The house is on fire." Fortunately, his mother had not waited before seeking help from a neighbor. The fire had been put out.

The next story Mr. Carpenter told involved a minister asking a farmer several probing questions that the farmer answered creatively. Finally the minister asked, "Are you ready for the resurrection?" "I don't know. When is it?" asked the farmer. "We don't know," said the minister, "It may be today, tomorrow or another day." The farmer pleaded, "Please don't tell my wife or she'll want to go all three days." While I never quite understood how this story related to the rest of Mr. Carpenter's remarks, I must say that I enjoyed hearing it as I did all his remarks this day. He concluded his portion of the service by offering two personal stories as an illustration of his belief that God had guided his life.

The first story was that Don Carpenter was stillborn when he arrived in the world. His family tried to urge him into life through the power of prayer. The whole family prayed. His mother prayed while she put him, swaddled in a blanket, next to the stove in an attempt to warm him. Suddenly the family heard a cry. The infant Don had moved his hand, brushing it against the stove. The eighty-year-old Don raised his hand slightly to show us the scar still present on his skin. He believed, he said, that God heard his mother's prayers and caused him to move his hand against the stove.

The second story was when Don Carpenter was a soldier in World War II in the fight against the Japanese. In one battle all of his companions had been killed. He pulled the pin out of a grenade and rolled over on it, a young man who thought his time had come. He had been prepared to die that day so long ago, prepared to rest among his dead friends, if a Japanese soldier came and turned him over. The Japanese soldiers did come. But they assumed he was dead and left him untouched. He believed, he said, that God saved him by making him "invisible to his enemies." These experiences,

Carpenter concluded, were evidence of God's hand in his life and in the life of all God's followers.

The beautiful and simple service ended with the congregation singing *Lord, I Want to be a Christian in My Heart*. Mr. Carpenter gave the benediction and was led out of the worship by the two cherubic acolytes as they had led him in, tiny hands shielding flickering flames on the candles and tiny stifled grins as the flames struggled for life.

Pastor Spencer may have been away but the remaining church members worshiped very well without him, indeed. Don Carpenter and the other members of the church that remained in Centerville performed admirably even without Pastor Spencer's direct leadership. This says two things to me. First, the pastor had done a fine job of encouraging his church leaders to carry on in his absence. Second, the pastor would be well advised, in the interest of job security, to not allow his church leaders to carry on too often in his absence. Get my drift, Brother Spencer?

Chapter 2

Cumberland Presbyterian Church
Dickson, Tennessee
September 22, 2002

Once again we left Nashville "early" at about 8:30 and headed, also once again, west toward Memphis. Our blue road of choice for this day, however, was Highway 70 West. We drove out through Bellevue and passed the Bellevue Community Church on our left. Several policemen were directing traffic at the church's entrance. While the church itself could not be seen from the highway, the beautiful entrance prompted a comment that perhaps we would visit there the next time our blue roading would take us west on Highway 70.

We meandered through White Bluff and, then a few miles later we passed the entrance to Montgomery Bell, a beautiful state park with an 18-hole golf course and a motel and meeting facility that was new. We remembered the restaurant at Montgomery Bell well from previous trips. It served a better than adequate buffet lunch on Sundays but we decided to keep blue roading on toward Dickson since it was well before 10:00 a.m. We hoped to find another one of our favorite blue road restaurants in Dickson, only a few miles farther west.

As we approached the outskirts of Dickson we began to see other restaurants which we had visited in times past. The High Point Restaurant on the eastern edge of Dickson was duly noted as one of our possible choices but we decided to drive on into Dickson since it was still early. Of the several churches we saw, the Cumberland Presbyterian Church seemed as if it might be the one where we would attend services today. Then we drove on further to see if one of our favorite restaurants, the East Hills Restaurant, was still open in the center of town. Sadly, it was not. This one-time landmark restaurant had been torn down. As progress would have it, a new CVS Pharmacy had gobbled up what had been a truly great blue road restaurant on this prime piece of property. And the Brownings, at least, will surely miss it for many years to come.

After a moment of silence to honor the memory of one of our truly favorite blue road eating spots, now departed, we drove on to a tea room that Betty had visited with friends once before on a Sunday. It was closed as well but happily not in a permanent sense. While I had never eaten there, Betty assured me that I would have enjoyed it. Becoming a little impatient now, we drove on. We proceeded toward I-40 to see what else we could see of Dickson. While a plethora of mobile home sales lots were to be found there in this area, there were no blue road restaurants that suited us.

One thing Dickson did have which was new to us was the truly remarkable new Renaissance Center. It had been built with a gift of $35 million by a foundation funded by the Late Dr. Jimmy Jackson, a gentleman who made $103 million by selling the Goodlark Regional Medical Center to Hospital Corporation of America in 1995. The Renaissance Center has, among other things, a space exhibit and a theater for many kinds of cultural events. Today the Center was announcing the upcoming performance of the "Louisville String Quartet." Betty and I were quite impressed with this new cultural center and its activities. It is certainly a fine addition to the social and cultural life of Dickson that was all made possible by the generous gift of Dr. Jackson.

After a few more minutes of driving around, at about 10:00 a.m., we decided to eat at the High Point restaurant back on Highway 70 east of Dickson toward Nashville. We also decided that we would go to the 11:00 service at the Cumberland Presbyterian Church.

The High Point has no real distinguishable design characteristics other than its appearance as a clean, functional blue road restaurant. Ambiance and notable architecture are certainly not parts of its main draw. We were reminded why we had been there a couple of times before — good food! Betty ordered the High Point breakfast special with two eggs scrambled, sausage, and coffee ($3.35). I ordered the Country Boy special: three eggs, bacon, hash browns and biscuits ($4.55). I had the same discussion with the waitress, as I had with others before, about whether I should order my eggs over-easy or over-medium. Again, we agreed on over-medium. The breakfast was good but not as good as the Beacon Light of last Sunday. The biscuits fell far short of the biscuits served at both the Loveless Café or the Beacon Light, mainly because the High Point biscuits apparently had been heated in the microwave rendering them "spongy." Remember now, I have laid some earlier claims to being an authority on the subject of biscuit quality.

The few pictures on the walls were a feeble attempt to bring some sense of history to the place. One was a framed copy of an old newspaper article about "Dr. Bell opening an office at the station" and announcing that "he would be connected with the Dickson County Hospital."

The menu addressed the availability of side items and noted a time limit: "Bowl of Grits – $ .90"; "Bowl of gravy – $ .80"; and, "Breakfast is served until 11:00 a.m." And on a wall in an anteroom a sign read:

Coffee Rules

– One cup of coffee	$ .70
– Half morning	$2.00
– All morning	$2.50
– All day	$3.00

* *$3.50 allows you to go home for lunch and return.*

As we were leaving the High Point three state troopers arrived. The presence of police officers in a restaurant usually tells me something good about a restaurant. But in reality it can mean one of several things: (1) the food is good; (2) the owner is a good ol' boy; (3) the coffee is hot; or, (4) the waitress is hot.

At 10:45 a.m. we headed to the Cumberland Presbyterian Church to attend the 11:00 service. The Cumberland Presbyterian denomination split off from the Presbyterian Church primarily because there had not been enough pastors to go around. In order to solve this shortage problem some churches lowered the educational requirements for minister, and this became one of the main reasons the Cumberland Presbyterians split off from the main body of Presbyterianism.

The marquee of the church displayed, "The Offer Still Stands. John 3: 16." As we entered on the ground floor, we were greeted by several of the church members as they were leaving Sunday school.

Still others welcomed us as we entered the sanctuary on the top floor. *Amazing Grace* was being played on the piano as we found a place to sit. The choir, already seated, wore light-blue robes with royal-blue sashes, and the acolytes wore royal-blue robes with light-blue trim.

Announcements were made: Ms. Debbie Thomas would speak Wednesday night about the terrorist tragedy and 9-11; a young man announced that there would be a family retreat the following week. The church had an interim minister, The Reverend Michael Duke, which was perhaps an indication that the old problem of too few ministers was a continuing matter of concern as it now is in many different denominations. He announced a baptism of a Mr. Clifton to be held that afternoon in a creek near the Clifton house. I could not help but think that it was going to be rather chilly to be immersed today. It would have been far more comfortable for Mr. Clifton if the Cumberlands had rejoined, at least for today, the "regular" Presbyterians where sprinkling is the normal chosen mode of baptism.

Next was the delivery of the children's message by Mary Bell. She told a story of two men walking down a busy street in New York City. There was much noise and confusion as everyone rushed by. One of the men, an American Indian said, "I hear a cricket." The other man said in amazement, "I can't hear it." The Indian replied, "You hear what you listen for." He demonstrated the point by stopping to drop a quarter. Suddenly, amidst all the noise, some twenty people stopped to look for the quarter they had heard drop. Ms. Bell summarized the meaning of the story for the children: "We only hear God if we listen for Him." She then asked the children to pray with her: "Dear God, I love you so much. Thank you for talking to me. Amen."

The Reverend Mr. Duke then offered a number of prayers. He called for prayers for the pastoral search committee. The next prayer began with a moment of silence before he prayed, "We pray for ourselves, our needs, and then for the needs of others, those dismayed by sickness." Then he prayed for the retreat, "Please be with us in the retreat. You will be with us, won't you?" And finally he led the congregation in *The Lord's Prayer*.

The interim minister then read the scripture lesson, the basis for his sermon, *Isaiah 40 :28 – 31*: "He gives strength to the weary. Those who wait for the Lord will mount up with wings of eagles. They shall run and not be weary, walk and not faint." His sermon began by saying that this scripture has four promises: (1) We shall have new strength; (2) we shall mount up with wings of eagles; (3) we shall run, not be weary; and, (4) we shall walk and not faint. These promises served as the format for the sermon. The minister said, "But to get these promises we must *WAIT* on the Lord," and that "We have been waiting for a pastor for eight months." He was telling the congregation to be patient and to wait on the Lord, and that the Lord would then lead them to a new pastor in His own good time.

Next the minister shared several biblical references that called for waiting on the Lord. He asked that we should not just say to God what we want to say during prayer but that we should also ask God to speak to us. He said that God wanted us to "soar with the eagles and not just hop along with the chickens." And that after you soar with the eagles you can "run and not be weary and walk and not faint." The title of the sermon was printed in the bulletin, *How the Sore Can Soar*. After completing the sermon he invited anyone in need of prayer to come to the altar and wait on the Lord. But no one came.

The worship service concluded with the acolytes leading the Rev. Mr. Duke out of the sanctuary after the benediction.

The whole worship service was one of a concerned community. The sheer number of the printed prayer requests made it seem as if almost the entire congregation was sick. The prayer requests were quite specific in most cases: "Robert Clark – Holly's cousin, cancer"; "Robert Monteville, leukemia"; "Amber Mifsud, diabetes"; "Marie Adcock, stroke." There were a total of 82 printed requests for prayer. The bulletin also stated that on the previous Sunday fifty-one people attended the 8:30 service and eighty-six people attended the 11:00 service. I estimated the number during the 11:00 service on that day to be about eighty-five — about the same number for whom prayer was being requested.

I left this Church with the hope that they could find a full-time pastor very soon. A young and strong pastor, more specifically. He would certainly need to be both in order to make the trips required of a pastor to the hospitals, to the nursing homes and to the residences of the overwhelming church members who were listed as ill in the bulletin. A bit of advice to the search committee — don't leave any loose bulletins lying around when a prospective minister comes to visit. The sheer number of sick people might scare him away completely.

Chapter 3

Smithville Church of God
Smithville, Tennessee
September 29, 2002

On Saturday, September 28, 2002, we went to our little getaway lake cottage at Silver Point, Tennessee. Silver Point is about 10 miles from Smithville, the county seat of Dekalb County. Our "lake cottage" would be more appropriately described as a cottage in the woods with Center Hill Lake nearby. This naturally beautiful lake is located about 60 miles east of Nashville. Over the past few years the trees have grown up to completely block the view of the lake during most of the year. In a way, though, this makes the atmosphere of the cottage a little more relaxing. The busyness of boating on the lake cannot be seen until we are actually on our boat. Most of my family would prefer a view of the lake but I don't know...

We were at the lake on this weekend with our daughter Beverly and two good friends, Jim and Jan Wells who had been schoolmates with us at Trevecca College in the early '50s. We spent several hours after dinner that evening watching movies, including *A Beautiful Mind*. Since I had seen the movie before, I retired earlier then usual to watch TV in bed. I did not watch long though because sleep came soon and easily. It always seems to be this way for me when I am at the lake.

The saying "early to bed and early to rise" was true for me on this occasion. I awoke the next morning at about 5:30 a.m. and went to the kitchen to make coffee. Since I was up I began making early preparations for a true blue road breakfast at our home away from home. Now, what to make? I started with leftover mashed potatoes from the night before. I baked another potato in the microwave to supplement the potato quantity to be sure there would be enough for everyone. After getting the potatoes together, I added three eggs and mixed them together along with salt, pepper and a

15

little flour. We called such epicurean delicacies "potato cakes" back in West Virginia, where I was born and raised until the age of 15. I fried the cakes in hot vegetable oil until they were good and brown — so brown, in fact, that the smoke set off the alarm, waking everyone including the security alarm people. They called to see if we were still alive.

After assuring the security company that everything was well, I prepared the next item for our home cooked Sunday breakfast — pork tenderloin. I had cut the tenderloin into pieces, pounded them thin and seasoned them with salt and pepper the night before. I fried these in hot oil as well. No alarm this time though! I had placed a cloth over the alarm. While cooking the tenderloin I was also preparing a pound of bacon, good and crisp, in the microwave.

No biscuits today. It is shocking to not have a breakfast biscuit report from a biscuit connoisseur. "How can this be?" you ask. I'll tell you. I set aside my unyielding lust for biscuits in order to enjoy a sacred bread product from my hometown of Logan, West Virginia — "Tony" bread. This delicious bread is made from a secret recipe kept in Logan only. I have this baker ship me a dozen loaves whenever I am getting low and keep them in a freezer in our storeroom. The consistency of this bread makes the best toast I have ever eaten. It is almost as good as biscuits. I sliced some "Tony" bread, spread butter on it and sprinkled some of Emeril's Original Seasoning on it. I then held the bread aside for a ten-minute toasting time at 380 degrees just before eating.

Two more items completed the breakfast. First, I beat eighteen eggs with salt and pepper and scrambled them gently in butter. No over-easy or over-medium eggs today. That would be too much work for me! And last, but hardly least, I created my own concoction. It does not have a name yet. I mixed about two cups each of chopped celery, red seedless grapes, and English walnuts. To this I added about one-half box of currents and one box of mission figs, which I cut into smaller pieces. Just before I served the nameless concoction I put one can of pears with the juice into the blender and "mushed it up." To the pear mush I added three packs of sweet-n'-low and one cup of milk, although half-and-half would have worked better. The chopped items were put in a small serving bowl with three to four tablespoons of the pear mush over them. At the very last minute I added about four tablespoons of a crunchy cereal mix over it all. Well look, you try it. You'll like it! I promise.

After enjoying such a satisfying home cooked blue road breakfast, Jan Wells and I were the only ones willing to venture out in search of a worship service. We headed south on the Highway 56, a fine blue road, and looked for a church. We passed several Methodist and Baptist churches before we reached Smithville and turned west on Highway 70 where very soon on the left we spotted the Smithville Church of God. We stopped, took a couple of pictures and entered the sanctuary at about 10:45 a.m.

A few people greeted us as we entered. We sat on the last pew while an adult Sunday-school class wound down. The pastor, The Reverend Donnie Kelly, introduced himself as the Sunday school lesson was ending. He was dressed in a medium-gray suit with a light blue, mock-turtleneck knit shirt. He appeared to be between thirty-five and forty-five years of age and he had beautiful blond hair and wore glasses. He warmly welcomed us to the worship service.

The church building itself was a contemporary design with a vaulted ceiling that was paneled. The sanctuary also had matching supporting beams that were arched. A large mural of pastoral scene was behind the choir with an American flag to the left of the pulpit. There was another flag to the right which obviously had some significance to the congregation. Four truncated columns were topped with plants. And prompter screens were located in three locations: to the right, to the left, and in the back. The screens were apparently new since they were not functioning all that well today. Early in the service, though, prayer requests were successfully displayed on these screens.

Instrumental music was played between the Sunday school and the worship service — piano, organ, guitar and drums. The pastor played the organ himself. The choir consisted of eight men and fifteen women. The music director welcomed all visitors before making several announcements. Birthdays were recognized enthusiastically with a happy-birthday song. Instead of "Happy birthday, dear (John, Jane, Jim)," the song went "Happy birthday, God bless you." The music was lively and inspired much hand clapping and waving.

The pastor then took over the service. More announcements

about ministers' meetings and meetings of ministers' wives were made. The singing continued with *Look What the Lord Has Done* and *I Feel Jesus in This Place*. Both were sung repeatedly until a man, apparently of Indian descent, was introduced by the pastor and he gave a sermonette that lasted about ten minutes. He was dressed in a brown suit with a yellow shirt and a brown striped tie. The scripture he read was *Luke 18: 10 – 14*. He spoke about prayer and then took prayer requests from the congregation before offering a long "pastoral prayer."

The congregation next returned to music with a rendition of *There's Going to be a Meeting in the Air*, and much exulting was demonstrated by waving and clapping. After this portion of the service concluded the choir departed from the choir loft to join the congregation. The choir director called for the offering and a member of the congregation was called on for a pre-offering prayer. Velvet maroon sacks were passed by the ushers who were all dressed informally in short-sleeved shirts. Only three or four suits or jackets were evident in the entire congregation. And mine was one of them.

The minister read from *Psalms 103* and prayed a pastoral prayer with many "Lords" throughout — "And, Lord, we thank you Lord." It was 11:45 a.m. when he started preaching, microphone in hand. He spoke of God's ability to help and to heal. He told a story of Rex Hombard at whose service a prostitute was sitting in the front row. Some members of the congregation began to complain but Rex told them that he wanted the woman there to show what God can do.

The minister insisted that God could heal all of us. He called for a show of hands from those who had witnessed God's healing. Many hands were raised. He spoke of Jesus' paying the ransom for us. Like kidnappers demanding a ransom, he said, the devil had kidnapped mankind until Jesus paid the ransom to set us free. The minister then walked toward the piano and sang an invitational hymn to invite anyone to come forward to offer a prayer. No one came.

The minister closed the service by calling on a congregation member to offer the benediction. As the benediction was offered the minister exited to the back of the church. This service had been of a 'structured informality' in which church members felt free to worship God individually and together with the entire congregation. Their worship indicated that they felt certain that God was reaching them in this service.

Jan and I felt certain that God was not reaching the slothful souls we had left languishing at the cottage. They said they were worshipping but we returned only to find them gathered around the television watching some godless movie. We should have requested prayer for them.

Chapter 4

First Baptist Church
Gallatin, Tennessee
October 6, 2002

T he direction for this Sunday's blue road adventure was a given because we had accepted an invitation to watch the Tennessee Titans football team play the Redskins that afternoon. Our hosts, Jim and Jan Wells, had visited with us at our lake cottage the previous weekend. They live on Old Hickory Lake in Hendersonville and have a real lake house from which you can actually see the lake. In order for us to be able to accept their invitation to eat lunch and to watch the game we needed to be in the vicinity of their house after the church service.

We left our home in Nashville once again at 8:30 a.m. and drove east on West End Avenue toward the Cumberland River and First Avenue. It was an absolutely fabulous day with a clear, blue sky and a temperature of 70°. West End Avenue becomes Broadway at 17th Avenue and we continued on toward the entertainment center of Nashville — lower Broadway. Unfortunately it is not as much of an entertainment center today as it was a few years ago. The closing of the Opryland theme park drastically cut down the number of tourists visiting Nashville. Surely the owners of Opryland now realize that closing the park was a huge mistake, both for them and for all of Nashville. Several "hot spots" had already closed, including Planet Hollywood. The grand opening of this restaurant had included much fanfare with Bruce Willis and his celebrity entourage attending the event. The "Planet" sign is no longer there. This spinning replica of the planet Earth had caused a fuss in the City Council because it violated various city codes. Eventually Planet Hollywood had received the variances required, probably because many had hoped it would be an anchor of the revitalization of downtown Nashville as a tourist attraction. The 'anchor,' however, had pulled loose when the hot area lost much of its sizzle.

The area of Lower Broadway in the downtown area of Nashville still has some grand attractions. The Gaylord Entertainment Center hosts the Predators hockey team, Amy Grant's holiday concerts every Christmas, and the concerts of other luminaries from the "planets" of L.A. and New York, such as Barry Manilow and Jimmy Buffet. The Titans are ensconced in the $200 million new Adelphia Coliseum. Oops, it's just "the Coliseum" now that Adelphia has fallen on hard times along with Enron and WorldCom. Even so, there are still more restaurants and entertainment centers which are closing in the area rather than opening. Mere Bulles, NASCAR, O'Charley's, and several others have all closed. The Hard Rock Café, The Big River Brewery and Merchants are still open, however.

The activity level of the Lower Broadway was already picking up at this early hour on this morning. Die-hard fans and vendors were prepared for the clash of the Titans and the 'Skins. The traditional scalping and buying of last-minute tickets had already begun. In addition, several hundred tailgaters had long been set up hoping that the Titans would stop their own bleeding and that the hemorrhaging of the Redskins would continue. But the Titans lost again. Regardless, I believe that 100% of the tailgaters will be back in place on the next game day. They are rock-hard, died-in-the-wool fans, win or lose. At least for this season.

As we drove across the Main Street Bridge we noted that it was already busy with hopeful walkers on their way to the stadium. Several dozen police and police cars were there to see that all went well. We wondered who paid for the security involved in hosting the NFL game in the city. The Titans or the city of Nashville? Just wondering...

We passed the East Branch of the Nashville Library housed in its old and beautiful building. We also passed the East High Magnet School before continuing on out Rt. 31 East, also known as Gallatin Road. Before long we turned, almost instinctively, onto Iverson Avenue. My wife Betty had lived at 1005 Iverson when I first met her. Her home had been a cozy stone house at the far end of the street. Golly, gee, this street had seemed so much longer when I was seventeen. After a date I would stay at her house until the last possible minute and then run as fast as I could to catch the last bus back to town. The dean of men at Trevecca College gave me great latitude on the lights out policy because of his great admiration of Betty.

Moving further north on Gallatin Road we began to look for a blue road restaurant for breakfast and a church to visit. Resisting the temptation of several donut shops, we continued to search for true blue road soul food for breakfast. Near the corner of Gallatin Road and Old Hickory Boulevard, a memory hit me. There had been a "greasy-spoon" restaurant or meat-n'-three nearby where my friend Roy DeSha had taken me several years ago. After a quick turn around the block I found the "Madison Restaurant" still sitting on the corner of a small strip center at 201 South Gallatin Road. Alongside of Brad's Barber Shop, Madison Hair and Beauty Supply, and a video store we found this place which is a true plain-Jane, blue road restaurant for sure.

The Madison Restaurant was double plain. So plain it hurt: green vinyl (asbestos, I'll bet) floors, a cork menu board on the wall, and no expense-given décor. The plastic-coated menu read, "A Family Place to Eat." Breakfast, it said, was served until 11:00 a.m. daily and until 12:00 p.m. on weekends. A sign on their mostly bare walls read:"I can only please one person a day and today ain't your day. Tomorrow ain't looking too good either." Another read: "As soon as the rush is over, I'm going to have a nervous breakdown. I worked real hard for it and nobody's going to deprive me of it."

Betty ordered oatmeal, toast and coffee — $2.25. I ordered three eggs over-easy with my usual instructions to the waitress about how to interpret "over-easy." The proper interpretation is whites done and yellows runny. It seems as if the servers in meat-n'-three restaurants tend to be mostly waitresses and rarely male waiters. I also ordered bacon, hash browns with biscuits and coffee — $4.80.

The yellows of the eggs were "runny" and the bacon crisp, the grits simply perfect, and the slab-style hash browns unappetizing to the eyes but quite tasty. The crowning part of the breakfast were the biscuits — excellent!! I tell you, I know exceptional biscuits when I taste them.I thought surely they must have been made with lard, like the biscuits served at the Loveless Café on Highway 70. The owner of the restaurant, however, told me the biscuits was individually frozen Pillsbury biscuits which now can be bought at almost any grocery store. The secret, she said, was to crisp the bottoms without burning them. She baked the biscuits at 425° on "fresh Teflon" baking sheets. We'll see. I'll try this as soon as I get a new Teflon-coated baking sheet.

After eating we started to shop for a place to invest our Sunday testing of the religious temperatures of places of worship on the blue road. We passed several likely prospects: Methodist, Presbyterian, Churches of Christ, Baptist and community churches. At 10:50 a.m. we settled on the First Baptist Church, located near the center of Gallatin. We had not visited a Baptist church yet and that was part of our rationale for our choice today. There are, of course, many different types of Baptist Churches but the First Baptist Church was Southern Baptist.

Baptists emphasize the "priesthood of all believers," the right of individuals to interpret the *Bible* under the direct guidance of the Holy Spirit. Baptists also believe in baptism by immersion only and are evangelistic in the proclamation of their faith. They are autonomous and have no allegiance to any other church except on a voluntary basis. Many of the Baptist Churches, however, do join together voluntarily to support missionaries and other projects. The forefathers of all modern day Baptists were the Anabaptists. The Anabaptists were so called because they re-baptized other Christians who had been baptized during their infancy because they did not consider baptizing of infants to be efficacious. John Smyth of England and Roger Williams of Rhode Island are generally considered the founders of the Baptist movement.

After entering through the side door of the handsome old Baptist Church, we quickly found restrooms to deposit the coffee we had rented earlier. We then entered the sanctuary and took a place in the empty back right-corner pew. The sanctuary was a beautiful traditional design with white pews and walnut trim placed on a theater-style floor, gently sloping from back to front. Five beautiful stained-glass windows lined each side of the space. The burgundy carpet and matching pew cushions were rich and new. The church bulletin announced Dr. Jim Fitch as the pastor.

The members of the congregation were respectfully dressed. Almost everyone had on Sunday clothes — men in suits and ties and women dressed in their "Sunday best." You know what I mean. Only the young people wore sport shirts and pants. I saw no jeans. I felt slightly underdressed in a sport coat and slacks with a short-sleeved shirt, the top buttoned. On the first three Sunday visitations I had felt slightly overdressed wearing the very same type of clothing which I was wearing today. The unwritten dress codes present in different congregations was beginning to be a major interest for me. I decided to think more on the matter. I think something theological is going on here.

Beautiful organ music played with a piano accompanying it. The choir, fifteen women and six men, wore blue robes with white sashes. The pastor and the two ministers of music were not wearing robes. Two of them were nicely dressed in suits and ties. The minister of music wore a suit with a black ministerial collar.

The first part of the service listed in the order of worship was the "Deacon Installation." The pastor explained that this was not an ordination service because these men were already deacons. It was simply an installation service as active deacons on the board of directors rotated off and other deacons took their place. Dr. Fitch presented each deacon rotating off with a plaque honoring faithful service to God and the church. He had something appropriate to share about each individual's specific service.

The next part of the service began with the congregational singing of the hymn *Praise Him, Praise Him*. The hymn was followed by a thoughtful pastoral prayer by Dr. Fitch about the state of the country and the hope that God would help peoples of the world learn to live together. I took this to be a prayer, in part, for Muslims and Christians to learn how to live together in peace. He then prayed for all in need of help and for all who were suffering for whatever reason. His "Ah-men" was more Presbyterian than Baptist with the accent on the "Ah" — different from the softer "A" sound as in "A-men, brother."

Ed Collins, the minister of education, welcomed the congregation and visitors. The congregation was then encouraged to take a few minutes to greet each other and the visitors. Invited to move about the sanctuary, people were free to greet friends wherever they were. Several people greeted us. Unlike some of the other churches we had visited, they did not introduce themselves by name in a manner that would have encouraged us to respond by saying, "Hello, I am Grant and this is Betty." I estimated that the service was being shared by a hundred and fifty individuals that morning. The period of greetings was directly followed by the singing of *All Creatures of Our God and King.*

The scripture reading was by a young man named Jimmy Bartlett, perhaps of high-school age. He was dressed in wash slacks and wore a long sleeved blue shirt without a tie or jacket. He read from the Psalms Chapter 8. Next in the order of worship was the "Choral Worship" by the adult choir. The choir beautifully sang *The Majesty and Glory of Thy Name.* The pieces were obviously well rehearsed with several trained voices adding to the singing of this formal worship anthem.

The order of worship in the church bulletin then called for *The Gathering of <u>God's</u> Tithe and <u>Our</u> Offerings* (underlining added). The wording was an unveiled lesson that the "Tithe" that was being brought in already belonged to God and that the voluntary amount of "Our"offerings were to be over-and-above the tithe. Betty and I did not tithe. Instead, we gave our usual $5 offering to participate in the service. Lynn Shoulders, a member of the choir, sang a solo entitled, *Jesu, Joy of Man's Desiring.* Because the service seemed somewhat informal, I interpreted the performance of another anthem by a beautifully trained vocalist as a slight bow to a liturgically ordered worship service.

The pastor then gave his sermon. He immediately began to move freely away from the pulpit, one hand in his pocket. Apparently this strategy was designed to bring the sermon to a conversational level with the members of the congregation and to dispel the preaching-to-the-people feeling. He delivered his message comfortably and effectively. He shared a quote from his college days: "Don't let your faith insult your intelligence and don't let your intelligence insult your faith." Then he interpreted this quote as the point that everything is not to be taken literally, even in the *Bible.* God doesn't always intend for us to do literally what is said, he offered. As an example he noted the Bible's instruction, "If your hand offends you, cut it off." He told us that this message is not meant to be followed literally and neither was "If your eye offends you, pluck it out."

The pastor read from the scripture in *Matthew 6: 25* and emphasized the words, "Seek first this kingdom and His righteousness and all these things will be added to you." He used that scripture to make a point about the vote on the state lottery which would be coming up on November 5th. Some people justify the lottery by saying that it will help the state financially, he said. He argued against this point because he felt it would not help the state financially at all. He made references to the state of Georgia which had a lottery experience to back-up his position. His main point, however, was that even if there were some financial benefit, which he seriously doubted, the main reason to vote against the lottery was that the lottery is not putting the Kingdom of God first. He felt that if we put God's Kingdom first the rest would take care of itself. He did not believe that voting for the lottery was a way to put God's Kingdom first. He said that he was going to vote against it and hoped that the members of the congregation would vote against it also. He stopped short of saying one could not be a good Christian and vote for the lottery. But he did seem to be saying that one would be a better Christian by seeking first God's Kingdom (and perhaps voting against the lottery).

Dr. Fitch also discussed the rationality of "investing" in a lottery. The purchase of 100 one-dollar tickets per week from the time a person was 18 until the age of 75 would total an investment of $295,000 yet only a 1-to-100 chance of winning. He also rejected the idea that we should all have the freedom to buy a lottery ticket because the positives associated with such a "freedom" do not outweigh the negatives associated with the lottery. And he said that the next logical progression after allowing a lottery would be allowing the operation of casinos, which would be an undesirable outcome in his opinion. He stated that five percent of those exercising the "freedom" to play a lottery become addicted, thus losing that "freedom." Dr. Fitch pointed out that "hoped-for" riches don't necessarily provide the "hoped-for" life that those who play the lottery are actually seeking.

The pastor stressed that he was not an "aginer." He did not want to be thought of as "against" everything. He was for anything good for the state but that in terms of the lottery he said, "I just don't think this is one of them." He stressed emphatically, "I ain't for it." He then prayed: "Thank you for your Book where we find direction and promises. Give us wisdom and insight to look for that, which will be a, help rather than a hindrance. Amen." The Amen was pronounced "A-men," with a soft "A." Baptist style this time.

After his sermon he returned to the order of worship which called for "opportunities for service." He invited everyone to meet him at the altar if they wanted to find an answer to a problem in their lives or a place for service to God. Three people accepted his invitation. The first was a young man named John who announced his desire to follow a call into the ministry. Next was Ms. Ella Burns, a senior citizen and a lifetime Baptist, who wished to become a part of the fellowship after a recent move into a retirement place located near the church. Last was a young girl, about eight years old, who wished to make a public profession of her faith. She was accompanied by her father, who the pastor said had been encouraging her about this decision to commit her life to God. The pastor then turned to the congregation and asked, "Will you help them and pray for them?" The congregation, with one voice, responded: "Amen," once again with a soft "A." I suppose they will baptize her later.

The worship service concluded with the congregation singing a closing song, *"O' Victory in Jesus, My Savior Forever, He sought me and bo't me with his redeeming blood: He loved me ere I knew Him and all my love is due Him. He plunged me to victory, beneath the cleansing flood."*

We left the worship service by slipping out the side door and proceeded to our friends' house where we watched the Titans lose to the Redskins. As we watched "our team" sink further and further in terms of the game score, people began wondering if the Titans' move to Nashville had actually been a good thing for the city. Was the euphoria of a couple of years worth the depression during the years before and after the team's move to Nashville? Just as Dr. Fitch had questioned the economic value of the lottery, many also now openly question the economic value/cost relationship to Nashville and Tennessee of the Titans' move. My concern was the spiritual value. I question whether the euphoria of two years ago outweighs the spiritual depression we now suffer.

Perhaps for the first time, I heard someone at the party say, "I think it is time for the Titans to look for a new running back and a new coach."

Do I hear an "Amen" out there among the devout followers of the Titans? Use either soft or hard "A." Your call.

Chapter 5

Church of Christ
Silver Point, Tennessee
October 13, 2002

*A*t one time only a few years ago the Browning family, my brothers and sisters and my mother, would have a "gathering of the clan" once a year at a selected vacation spot. The 'vacation spot' was chosen primarily to entice our children and grandchildren to the "Old-Folks' Reunions," as I am sure the younger Brownings called them.

My sister Janice died in 1994. Since her death a "gathering of the clan" has not been held except for a partial one in 1999 at the funeral of my youngest brother Latelle. Yet even at this gathering some members of the family were not able to be there. Age is certainly taking its toll. I've missed the times we have had together as a family. Such occasions always give me insights into my family history through new stories which often come into the light during late night bull sessions.

The weekend of October 11, 2002, was one I looked forward to for several weeks because my brother Joe and I had "cooked up" a mini-clan gathering. Joe and I talked our older brother Drurrey, who lives in Florida, into coming to Tennessee for a visit. We also got our youngest sister Pixie (Margaret Jane, all of 4'11") to come along with her husband "Pig" (Boyd, to all non-family members.)

Drurrey arrived in Nashville on a Southwest Airlines flight from Orlando at 2:40 p.m. He said it was an uneventful flight, which is what we all like to hear these days. Uneventful, except for all the passengers making rather urgent calls on their cell phones. These calls would have been disconcerting if anyone thought the passengers were reporting some suspicious character or activity. In reality, the passengers were calling friends to share the news that Sam Donaldson was on the flight. Sam Donaldson flying on Southwest? Probably his presence was not so unusual with the reported recent low earnings of most television news divisions.

Dru and I concluded that Sam probably needed to get to Nashville in the worst way, thus explaining his choice of Southwest. Or he could have had an insatiable appetite for peanuts. More than likely, the networks are giving all their traveling personnel a flat rate or per diem expense account. Such a policy will get employees to use Southwest every time. Other than seeing Sam Donaldson, Dru had been happily bored and crowded. He was pleased to have paid only $240.00 for his round-trip ticket, rather than the $1000 or more on another airline that would have guaranteed a more exciting trip with cashews, instead of peanuts. Upgrades are expensive.

Dru and I had a chance to visit pretty much to ourselves for the first few days. He arrived on Friday afternoon. Joe and Pixie and their spouses were not due to arrive until Sunday afternoon. Pixie lives in Bristol, Tennessee while Joe lives in Sparta, North Carolina near the Blue Ridge Parkway. Joe and his wife Jetta planned to pick up Pig and Pixie on the way to the "lake" cottage on Center Hill Lake near Smithville, Tennessee. There they would meet up with Dru, my wife Betty and me.

"Lake" cottage is a tongue-in-cheek reference, remember? The lake is hidden by the tops of the trees now. We would cut some of the tops of the trees but I can't sing and Betty can't dance. At least not enough for us to trade these retarded talents for time in jail like country singer Alan Jackson did. A few years ago he cut some trees in front of his lake place, a few miles from our place, in order to enhance his view. He now has to play annual concerts on the lake, for God-only-knows how long, as penance for his Paul Bunyon exploits.

On Friday evening Dru and I told stories and lies while Betty opted for an early bedtime. Our daughter Barbara and her friend David came by before Betty retired so that Barbara would have a chance to pay her respects to Uncle Dru, with whom she would have no other chance to visit during this mini-gathering time. The next morning, I cooked a traditional Saturday morning breakfast of eggs, potatoes, bacon, sausage, and biscuits. It was a typical Browning West Virginia breakfast. Browning West Virginia breakfasts were those at which the numbers of eggs, bacon, sausage or potatoes were not counted. With a family of eight children and one mother, one father and one grandmother, the Brownings cooked by the pound rather than by the piece. Betty, an only child on the other hand, was trained to cook by the piece. Breakfast for three at her family's house meant three pork chops and six eggs. And that's a bit of a stretch because her family never had pork chops for breakfast. Browning West Virginia breakfasts were "kosher" only in the sense that it was not "kosher" for anyone to eat a third pork chop until everyone else had already eaten two. After that all bets were off. No rules, just right. I think some restaurant uses that line.

After breakfast Dru and I drove to see our other daughter Beverly at her new house, which had just been finished being built. After visiting with her for awhile, we packed all the food for the weekend and left for Center Hill. Included in the food were several pounds of Bar-B-Q from the Bar-B-Cutie in Nashville. Brother Joe planned to smuggle this contraband back across the border into North Carolina after the mini-reunion. The restaurants in North Carolina apparently have no clue about Bar-B-Q, at least according to Joe and a few fortunate neighbor friends with whom he shares the delicacy when he successfully gets it past the North Carolina border guards. Joe believes the FDA would classify Bar-B-Cutie Bar-B-Q as a drug if its addictive qualities were ever exposed.

Sunday morning at the lake I made a pot of Kona Mountain coffee, a rich, delicious coffee Betty and I found with friends on a trip to Hawaii last year. We had visited a coffee plantation and brought back several pounds of the roasted beans. It may not actually be as good as its $25 a pound price but it sure seems like it. Maybe the delicious times we had in Hawaii were transferred to Tennessee via the medium roast Kona peaberry coffee.

After coffee with Dru, I set out alone to find a blue road breakfast and a worship service to attend. Dru declined my gracious invitation to come along because he did not have a suit coat with him. Leaving the lake cottage without a view, I turned east on Highway 96 and headed instinctively toward the Rose Garden Restaurant, about four miles from the cottage. I passed Blackberry Hill and Captain's Point where our friend Ray Danner's son, Roger, has a place with a lake view as well as a helicopter pad to minimize his commute time from Nashville.

I pulled into the Rose Garden and looked at the menu for no reason at all. I know it by heart. Want me to quote it to you?

Probably not, but I could. I can especially quote the section about the fried catfish fillets and the home-baked pies — coconut, chocolate, and pecan. It was breakfast time, however. The eggs, bacon, grits and biscuits were the quote my stomach was waiting to hear. I quoted my order to the attractive, neatly dressed and coifed waitress who is always there. Sometimes she is there with her young, petite and attractive daughter. The daughter is only a waitress part-time here because she has another full-time job. I bet they love her where she works full time just as we do at the Rose Garden. They are both always pleasant and efficient. The mother was especially efficient today and brought my eggs pronto. Over easy, you all. Whites done and yellows runny. Crisp bacon, grits and super delicious biscuits. Most restaurants have good biscuits now that Pillsbury has filled the grocery stores with individually frozen, home-style biscuits. The health department, or some department, should shut down any restaurant without good biscuits. There's just no excuse anymore. Maybe we should have a new Bureau of Biscuits to act as the official watchdog.

After paying $6.46 for a fine blue road breakfast, I looked for a church where members would soon gather to feed their spirits. I would have said "souls," except I am not as sure we have souls as I am sure we have spirits. Is there a difference? But my theology, or lack of the same, is not the point of this quest. I wanted to witness those gathering to have their souls or spirits fed. I saw the Silver Point Church of Christ. I couldn't miss it. It's just across the road from the Rose Garden, the name of which always makes me remember Lynn Anderson's *"I Never Promised You a Rose Garden."* But it was only 10:30 a.m. Church did not begin until 11:00 a.m. so I had 25 minutes to drive around. I went west on Rt. 246 or Wolf Creek, which parallels I-40 between two exits to Center Hill Lake. I drove by a Presbyterian church, a couple of Baptist churches and another Church of Christ about one mile west of the larger Silver Point Church of Christ. I turned around at about 10:50 with the decision made to attend services at the Silver Point Church.

I took a note pad and a tape recorder into the church with me. I found a vacant seat in the pew near the back on the right side. I am a right-handed church and movie-goer. The congregation was apparently not surprised to have a visitor. I suspected that it probably has a plethora of visitors, especially during the boating season. No one introduced him or herself to me or inquired about my status. I settled almost unnoticed into a pew that was padded on both the seat and the back.

The sanctuary was simple and neat with pine wainscoting on the walls and pine paneling surrounding the pulpit area. A large glass window separated the foyer from the sanctuary, probably a baby-crying protective barrier. The Hymnal titled *Songs of the Church* was divided into sections, such as *God's Praise and Love* – 1-59; *Savior's Sacrifice* – 58-130; *Savior's Praise* – 131-181; *Savior's Leadership* – 182-215 on down to *Special Songs* – 613-650, which included *Love Lifted Me and Tell Me the Old, Old, Story*.

There was animated visitation among the members of the church until a shirt-sleeved leader, without a tie, arose to begin the service. He welcomed both members and visitors. He noted the songs on a listing board located to one side in the front of the sanctuary: 284, 244, 297-601, 163, 511. He then segued into some announcements: a costume party, Brother Burke's message at 6:00 on "The Divided Kingdom and the Beginnings of the Arab People," and the continuation of Burke's message on Wednesday, "The Modern Jewish State." Also, the West End Church of Christ had cordially invited the Silver Point congregation to its 2:00 p.m. service later in the day.

When I first noticed the two churches of the same denomination so close together during my earlier search, I had surmised that some friction or faction had caused the separation of a larger congregation into two bodies. The "cordial" invitation nixed that idea. There was at least one difference, however. The West End congregation's Sunday-go-to-meeting clothes were much more formal. By contrast, I seemed to be the only one wearing a jacket in the Silver Point service. The worshipers here were all dressed casually. Even the minister and the elders serving communion wore shirtsleeves. Three of the five elders wore short sleeves and two of the three had their shirtsleeves rolled up like 'Hell's Angels" bikers. If only Dru had known! He would have fit right in here. The minister, whose name I never did get, wore an olive shirt with a necktie but with no coat.

An announcement board to the left of the pulpit offered the following information: Attendance today 160, Attendance last

Sunday 158, offering today $26.63, offering last Sunday $37.97. I took these statistics to be based on the Sunday-school classes since an offering had not yet been taken and recorded. I figured there were somewhere between a 100 and 125 people in the church service on this Sunday.

The preacher began his sermon unceremoniously by announcing that it would be about stewardship and about "prioritizing your life." He wanted to challenge the ownership concept with the stewardship concept. He said the more stuff we have or own, the more concerns we have and the more we worry. He said if we have an old "rust bucket" of a car we do not worry about it as we would worry about a new car. Boy, do I know about this. I drive a 1990 Jeep Laredo with 210,000 miles on it. I don't worry at all!

The preacher spent several minutes stressing the man's responsibility in providing for the family and leaving the wife to care for the children. He walked a little softly here as if he knew some of the congregation did not fully agree. Next he quoted *Matthew 6: 24*, "No man can serve two masters. We will serve God or our money." He said it is the pagans who seek after the things of this world,"We must seek first the Kingdom of God...then all these things will be added to you." He briefly summarized his own life and relationship with money. He had made more money at each church than he had made at the church before — yet it was never enough. He always spent more than he made. He had left the ministry to make more money — only to find, yet again, that it was not enough. He was now back in the ministry and trying to practice real stewardship. He and his wife always paid God first before attending to all the 'other obligations.' He suggested that we should all try it out between now and Christmas. He said that if we pay God first — "Seek Ye first...then all these things will be added to you." — we would find that God will care for us as "the birds of the air and the lilies of the field."

The elders passed the plates for the offering after the sermon. I participated with my customary $5 offering. The offering was immediately followed by the Sacrament of the Lord's Supper. The elders offered trays of "Bread" (large pieces of cracker wafer). Seated members of the congregation would break off a piece and eat it reverently before passing the tray on to the next person. I declined to participate without drawing attention to myself. When the "wine" (grape juice) was passed to "represent the Blood that was shed for us," I noticed that my non-participation had been noticed because I was not offered "the Cup," in the form of individual glass demi-cups. The elders partook of both the bread and the wine after serving the congregation while standing in the aisles.

The simple service ended with the singing of a song a capella, as were all the songs during the service. Most Churches of Christ do not use instrumental music in the church. They believe that if we are not explicitly instructed in the *New Testament* by Jesus or the disciples to participate in a practice during worship that we should not participate in such a practice. In other words, they believe that instrumental music was not mentioned in the New Testament and, therefore, should not be used in the modern church. Other denominations simply believe that if a practice is not strictly prohibited that the practice is permissible. Fundamental difference or splitting of hairs? The debate continues. This was the first religious worship service I attended without accompanying instruments. It seemed strange, of course. Instruments seem to help worshipers sort of stay on tune and also to soften missed notes. It was obvious during this service that different members of the congregation were trying to sing three- and four-part harmony — most of the time rather unsuccessfully.

At the end of the service I felt that the people belonging to the Silver Point Church of Christ believed strongly that they worship as God had instructed. Concern about others not following God's instructions was evident in the announcement regarding the Sunday and Wednesday services offered by Brother Burke which focused on the Arabs and the Jews.

Later that day my brother Joe and my sister Pixie, along with their spouses arrived and a fine time was had by all for the next three days. I wish you all could have been there. I'd like to share the details of my extended weekend with my family but my publisher insists that I save them for my next book. Sorry.

Chapter 6

First Baptist Church
Charlotte, Tennessee
October 20, 2002

*A*lthough I had lived in Middle Tennessee for some fifty-five years, I had never been to Charlotte, Tennessee. It is off the beaten path. That is, you don't often go through Charlotte on your way to some other place. I am originally from Logan, West Virginia. Once after informing someone that I was from Logan, my new acquaintance said, "Oh, yes, I went through there one time." I responded, "I don't think so. Logan is not on the way to any place. You have to plan to go there." Charlotte reminds me of Logan in that respect. You might go through Logan to get to Mud Fork or Cow Creek, and you might go through Charlotte to reach Dull or White Bluff. But that's about it. Generally, however, you don't just accidentally go through either Logan or Charlotte. You must make plans to each or otherwise you will never get to visit these out of the way places.

Betty and I went to Charlotte on this day because we intended to go there. To get there you must go by the blue roads. We left Nashville on blue road 70, commonly referred to as Highway 70, and headed west toward Memphis. At White Bluff we turned north onto Highway 47. I had often seen a sign at White Bluff that point-ed north to Charlotte. Several weeks ago, however, I realized that I had never actually been there. Years ago Betty had visited the town with her mother and some other friends to explore antique shops. She remembered it being ten to fifteen miles from White Bluff. This early autumn morning was misty and foggy as we traveled pur-posefully to Charlotte in order to find a blue-road breakfast and a blue-road church.

About two miles north of White Bluff we passed a sign that read "Paw Paw's Restaurant." We kept going for about a mile before I turned around and drove back. I had realized that this uninviting blue-road eatery was the only restaurant we had seen open since having left Nashville. Would this be the only restaurant we would see before church time at 11:00? All churches have services at 11:00 a.m. on Sundays, don't they? It would. And, no, they don't.

There it was, "Paw Paw's — A Family Restaurant." The very plain metal building seemed to have been constructed for a hay barn or a feed store but certainly not for a restaurant.The unpaved parking lot held eight or ten cars neatly lined up in two rows — just as if the parking lot were lined off. We parked the car in a vacant spot up front that appeared to have been reserved just for us. Several rustic benches made of rough sawn tree limbs and wood slabs lined the porch; they did not look any more comfortable than did the restaurant look inviting. Not wanting to risk our stomachs rumbling in church, however, we pressed on through the doors.

The interior of the building was not much more inviting. The cavernous barn-like building had concrete floors painted a light gray and had rough sawn paneled walls. And I really mean, "rough sawn" — boards never intended for use as paneling which were nailed up vertically to point at the white plastic covered exposed insulation serving as the ceiling. The heat and air ducts were also exposed, of course. At one end of the "hay-barn building" a band-stand stood that fit in very well. Although we did not ask, it certainly appeared ready for a square dance. Except square dances are not held on a Sunday, are they? Okay, maybe it was permanent — a jamboree every Saturday.

We sat down at the Formica-topped table with 1950s-type chairs. Betty quickly ordered a ham and cheese omelet which was for her a bit of a switch. I wondered if she knew something. I ordered my usual — three eggs, over-easy with bacon, hash browns and grits. Also as usual,I took a moment to explain the runny-yellow require-ment to the waitress. Biscuits and coffee rounded out the order for both of us.

We did our usual people watching while waiting for the order to come up. Three men, rough as the paneling, sat near the door in what was probably their usual spot. Six or seven other customers were seated at a long community-type table and were joined by two breakfast stragglers who received a warm welcome even though the early arrivals were well on their way to topping off breakfast with dessert — jelly on the biscuits.

The people watching continued. The most intriguing customers of all sat in the middle of the dining room, although a bit closer to a wall. Here was another rough sawn pilgrim in his early-to-mid-thirties with a neatly trimmed beard and clean painter-like overalls, bibs buckled. After all, it was Sunday. Right? On his knee sat a one-and-a-half to two-year old daughter, no doubt. Their breakfast was being eaten in a back and forth manner — a bite for him and an "airplane" bite for her.

The analyzing soon began by Dr. Browning. I thought, "He's probably divorced and this is his week with Katie or Samantha or Jenny Sue" or "His wife is a nurse working the weekend." Father and daughter finished their meal and walked out the door hand-in-hand. I hoped that my last analysis was nearer to the real truth and that Big Jim had taken Jenny Sue out for breakfast so that wife Sally could sleep late. And in my imagination the complete family spent the rest of the chilly, rainy afternoon sitting around a wood fire popping popcorn and reading fairy tales to Jenny Sue. Or Katie. Or Samantha. Or whatever her name was.

I had mesmerized myself with this warm family image when my bacon and eggs arrived. Big Jim and his family's plans for the rest of the afternoon faded quickly from my mind and were replaced by the aroma of coffee and bacon. The smell of bacon and eggs has ended many sweet dreams for me over the years.

My eggs were cooked perfectly. The hash browns were commercially grated but home fried and close to the quality of the first baked, then peeled, then cut up and finally griddle-fried potatoes of the Pancake Pantry in Nashville. Close, but not quite. The bowl of grits was oversized so I shared them with Betty. I did not share my potatoes, however. Sharing grits is one thing. Sharing nearly perfect fried potatoes is another thing altogether.

Betty's departure from the usual while ordering had proved a fortunate one. Her omelet was the best breakfast she had eaten during the last few weeks on the blue roads. The biscuits were just okay. They would have been better had they not been microwaved — better cold or room temperature biscuits any day than nuked sponge balls. Although the taste was there, the consistency had been sabotaged by the kitchen terrorist on duty, who had apparently smuggled in a microwave from Iraq or North Korea, or some other terrorist stronghold. Microwaves should be illegal in blue road kitchens. The jelly and the honey partially saved the biscuits. We realized that our only choice for this blue-road Sunday, Paw Paw's, had been a great choice overall — $11.23.

After breakfast we had forty-five minutes to find a church. With certainty that it's still a law that all churches have services at 11:00 a.m. we were comfortable with that time frame. We were sure that no church would risk their tax-free status by fooling with the mandated 11:00 a.m. service time, even if the Titans do play at noon when in town. God mandated somewhere in the Bible that all Christian churches were to meet at 11:00 a.m. in worship of the God of the Titans, the Rams, and the Redskins alike, didn't He? I'll look up the scripture as soon as I can. And if the 11:00 service commandment is not in the Bible, it should be. But there are unwritten laws and traditions that are sacred too. Surely in "historic, proud, progressive Charlotte" as the sign read, a good and strong tradition would lead the good people of Charlotte to keep the written, or unwritten, Law of God with regard to the sacred 11:00 a.m. hour.

Charlotte proved more 'progressive' than we had imagined. The Cumberland Presbyterians announced on the church sign: Worship 9:30, and, Sunday school 10:30. I guess this schedule gives Bubba and the boys time to reach Nashville to see the Titans play if they leave the rest of the family at Sunday school. The Church of Christ held its worship service at 10:00, finishing at 11:00 sharp! This schedule was pushing it, but it did give their fans, uh, members a chance to make it — probably missing the kick-off but not the whole first half. Maybe not, the way the team had been playing that season.

We felt desperate. The Titans had screwed everything up and they were not even playing today. They were nursing their wounds with a week off and hoping that next Sunday God would reward their last win over Jacksonville with another win over the Bengals. Suppose God was punishing the righteous for a lack of reverence for traditions by jacking around with the sacred hour? Could be.

We wondered. Could one righteous congregation be found in all of Charlotte? Would God save the Titans if we found a righteous congregation who kept the sacred 11:00 worship hour? With one last prayer, and an excursion down a narrow side street off the square, we found a church with an 11:00 worship service — The First Baptist Church, "One Spencer Alley, one block above the square." Maybe, just maybe, God will vanquish all the Rams, the Raiders and the Cowboys in the name of the Titans just because one righteous congregation was found in Charlotte, Tennessee.

At the very least, Pastor Keith Curd and his congregation saved this blue road Sunday for Betty and me. We arrived just in time for me to arrange the tape recorder in my pocket for maximum reception and to get my note pad and pen out of my briefcase. I still would not risk going into a strange church, even a righteous one such as this, with a briefcase in my hand. I guess I'm a little paranoid but better safe than sorry. With the recorder, pen and pad in my pocket and the briefcase bomb safely resting on the back seat of the car, we entered the church at 10:58 a.m.

Entering the small sanctuary and seating ourselves in the "right-handed" section near the back, I read the church statistics sign: Sunday school enrollment – 45. Attendance today – 31. Attendance last Sunday – 25. Offering – $271. The little sanctuary would burst at the seams if 100 people attended. I imagine that God would surely feel obligated to take the Titans to the Super Bowl again if it were full every Sunday!

The ceiling of the church was 10-feet high. I could determine the height accurately from the paneling. Two-foot high pieces of pre-finished, quarter-inch thick, four-by-eight paneling rested atop each full piece of paneling, a neat and inexpensive material choice for the church. The piano played religious mood music as Deacon Curd introduced himself and his wife and offered us a warm welcome. Deacon Curd was one of three men in the sanctuary wearing a coat and tie. And these three men equaled about 30 percent of the males in this righteous congregation.

There were choir seats and a baptismal pool secluded by burgundy curtains. Alas, there was no choir for this day's service. A choir could not be afforded with only twenty-five or so righteous souls in attendance — in addition to two breakfast-stuffed and grateful wayfarers. Brother Jimmy Gossett, wearing the second of the three jackets with tie, invited the congregation to stand and sing Hymn No. 15, *Come Thou Fount of Every Blessing*. He then led us in singing Higher Ground. *"Lord Lift Me Up to Higher Ground."*

After we were lifted higher, Pastor Curd prayed the prayer of invocation. He wore a pale yellow sport coat and a blue tie, making him No. 3.

Brother Gossett then made several announcements about future events in the church, including a Sunday evening service at 5:00 p.m. — he stressed, "Not 6:00," as if this were a change. He then invited Pastor Curd back to the pulpit and presented him with a gift in recognition of "Pastor Appreciation Month." I wanted him to open the gift. I wanted to know how much they appreciated him. But he didn't open the gift.

After accepting the gift, Pastor Curd, a genteel man with a noticeable, but not painful, stutter, read the scripture from *Matthew 5: 13 – 16:* "Ye are the salt of the Earth" and "Ye are the Light of the World." Brother Gossett then led the congregation in singing No. 340, *He Hideth my Soul.* Pastor Curd then arose to deliver the sermon for today. It was entitled "A Life Damaged by Wrath" and referred to the life of Moses. He told of the times that anger overcame Moses, another of God's servants with a speech impediment. The pastor said that although anger is a powerful force we should always bury our anger because the Bible says "Vengeance is Mine, I will repay sayeth the Lord."

The bespectacled, sincere and humble-seeming preacher continued by detailing the events in Moses' life when he let anger get the best of him. The first example of Moses' anger was at the Pharaoh for refusing to let the people of God go, even after God had visited several plagues upon the Egyptians. Pastor Curd then stopped in the middle of the sermon to offer a short prayer for God's guidance for the rest of the sermon and the remainder of the service. He then continued in his soft stutter to share more stories exhibiting Moses' anger. Moses became angry when the children of Israel complained in the wilderness about the short supply of food and water. He then became exceptionally angry when the people disobeyed God's instructions on how to use the manna provided daily by God. Moses also became angry when the people criticized Moses and Aaron. Moses became perhaps the angriest when he returned from the mountains with the Ten Commandments on plates of stone. He was so angry that he threw them to the ground and broke them.

According to Pastor Curd it was the last fit of anger that did Moses in. The people had been fussing again about water. This time God asked Moses to take his rod and "touch the rock" but Moses, in his extreme anger, "smote the rock." Pastor Curd said that because of this exhibition of anger God told Moses he would not be allowed to go into the Promised Land. He was only allowed to go to the mountain top to see "the land that flowed with milk and honey," but because of his anger that led to his disobedience, he would not be allowed to cross over.

The Pastor offered a closing prayer and humbly asked God's forgiveness for forgetting to write a scriptural reference in his sermon notes. Because he had forgotten to write the reference down he could not, therefore, share the reference with the congregation. He prayed, "God, please forgive me for misplacing the scripture reference this morning. I wanted to read directly from Your word this lesson to Your people." His open and humble act of contrition was the most effective part of his sermon to me, and, I imagine, to all the others present. The people of the First Baptist Church of Charlotte are indeed fortunate to have such a thoughtful, humble man leading them as he attempts to follow in the footsteps of Jesus. The service closed with hymn No. 35, *I Have Decided to Follow Jesus*.

After we left, we drove "through" the remainder of Charlotte, on through Ashland City and on into the land of the Titans. We did not turn back and Betty was spared turning into a pillar of salt. Actually, she was spared for two reasons. The first, of course, was because we did not turn back but proceeded forthwith and straightway toward the land of the would-be Titan giants. Secondly, because one righteous congregation had been found that would not bow to those refusing to worship at the sacred hour of 11:00 on Sunday mornings. Betty and Charlotte were, therefore, spared. Amen!

Chapter 7

Christ Community Church
Franklin, Tennessee
October 28, 2002

W e were quite ambivalent about which direction from Nashville to take on the blue road search this morning — a search for how different blue road restaurants feed the bodies of their customers and a search for how different blue road churches feed the souls of their members. We had been to Centerville, Dickson, Gallatin, Smithville, Silver Point and Charlotte. Would we go out today toward Lebanon, Nolensville or Franklin? It may have been because we came first to Hillsboro Road as we left home at 8:30 a.m. that we pointed our vehicle in the direction of Franklin. Franklin is a truly beautifully historic town about 20 miles south of Nashville. And Hillsboro Road took us right into Franklin on this overcast but pleasant Sunday.

We traveled south on Hillsboro Road passing several potential church stops. But important things had to be taken care of first. We had not yet had a fine Sunday blue road breakfast. So we moved on and made mental notes of several potential future churches we might visit.

One thing for sure, there are more blue road churches than blue road restaurants. We passed the Woodmont Christian Church and Calvary Methodist Church, both imposing edifices on two blocks of valuable real estate in the Green Hills section of Nashville. The only restaurants in this area were the Donut Den or McDonald's. I am not above, nor beneath, eating at either. I love the apple and Hawaiian fritters at The Den. And I love the Egg McMuffin or the egg, bacon and cheese biscuits at The Mac. The blue road, however, beckoned to us. We passed the Church of Latter Day Saints, a Mormon congregation that occupies the location of the former Green Hills Church of Christ. We then passed the Covenant Presbyterian Church, a congregation that has moved to an impressive new facility at the top of Burton Hills and across from St. Paul's United Methodist Church on Hillsboro Road. The St. Paul's congregation prides itself on a conservative tradition in contrast to what some of their members have perceived in the past to be an overly liberal Methodist brotherhood in the Nashville area. Maybe we would visit one or all of these churches at some point, but not today.

We pressed onward toward Franklin and passed the Hillsboro Presbyterian Church — of America, not of the Southern Presbyterian Church, you all. We also passed the impressive Forest Hills Baptist Church at which I had given a eulogy a few years ago for my departed very good friend Bill Granstaff. Next, and literally in the shadows of the Baptist church, was the quaintly beautiful Harpeth Hills Presbyterian Church — of the USA, as Southern as grits. The Harpeth Hills Presbyterian Church sits on the banks of the meandering, peaceful Harpeth River. In times past, the Harpeth River would turn less peaceful and overflow its banks, making the historic church literally an island. Probably out of respect for another deceased friend, the former pastor of the sometimes island church, The Reverend Mr. Priestly Miller, I wanted to return to the Harpeth Hills Presbyterian Church some Sunday. I remember him fondly as a former fellow Presbyterian minister in another life that seems a lifetime ago, the late '50s and early '60s. But respects for Priestly also needed to wait. A blue road restaurant somewhere was beckoning to me like a beautiful siren out of the mist and calling, "Come to me, come to me."

Did I say blue road? This may be the last year I can conscientiously call Hillsboro Road a blue road. Certainly, the cartographers will change this blue road to green or red by the next time we take the road out to Franklin. Patches of the road are turning green as the planners of the roads insidiously eat the 'blue' off the maps of the beautiful pike, mostly at major intersections and in almost spider-like ways. Its real name is Hillsboro Pike because many years ago it was a turnpike for travelers between Franklin and Nashville. Travelers on the Pike were obligated to pay a toll to the farmer whose land the wagon trail crossed. Many years ago probably several tolls had to be paid to several different farmers when traveling between the two frontier towns. Nowadays the only toll pilgrims pay to travel the historic route is the cost of the patience needed to handle the long delays caused by construction "progress." Me thinks the planners are sneaking up on us. One day soon all the construction spots will be connected by a fell swoop of the T-DOT budget director's pen that makes all blue roads suddenly into red ones. The churches seem to sense the change too. They are all enlarging to make room for the red roaders speeding by the church spires. It seems as if the only way to get their fair share of wayfaring sinners is to make the spires higher and, by all means, lighted to catch the attention of late-night pilgrims.

For our purposes here, however, I decree Hillsboro Pike to still be a blue road, not a red one. Since blue roading is technically my word, I use it where and when I want. And on that particular day I wanted to go blue roading on Hillsboro "Pike," or Hillsboro "Road" to newcomers to the area.

Nearing Franklin, we approached Christ Community Church. It is a new and impressive church with a modern design and a spire that needs a sign on it to let passers-by know it is a spire. It is really more nearly a spike but I did not create the words "spike," nor "spire," and I did not build it. I suppose the congregation can call it whatever they wish. At any rate, we decided to take a look and found two worship services offered, at 9:30 and 10:45 a.m. We thought we wanted to come back at 10:45 — after breakfast, of course.

The concern now was where to find breakfast on this fast-fading blue road. And I suppose now is the time to confess something. The sin to which I must confess is one of omission. I omitted earlier that the real reason for turning toward Franklin this morning was my memory of Dotson's Restaurant. Dotson's is located on the far side of Franklin from the route we took into the town. This, however, as we say back in West Virginia, is no step for a climber. I would simply drive on toward Franklin and meander around the square of this beautiful old town before turning north on Franklin Pike, the distance of one block to Dotson's.

We drove past Franklin High School, which now apparently houses two separate congregations' worship services: Graceland Community Church and Franklin Community Church. In and around the square of Franklin we saw the historic Franklin Presbyterian Church, the Franklin Cumberland Presbyterian Church and the

Episcopal Church. In addition, the square hosts the sprawling, and also quite historic, First United Methodist Church which was established in the late 1700s. While we had found the First Methodist Church of Centerville to be a "Norman Rockwell" type church, Franklin proper is a Norman Rockwell type of town with beautiful old churches, historic courthouse and street after street of historic houses, both quaint and handsome. The town is a real treasure for history buffs. When our meandering was completed we meandered into Dotson's parking lot.

A friendly parking space in the front of a crowded front parking lot was found. And we walked into the restaurant at 9:05 a.m. The menu subtitle under Dotson's read, "Pure Country Cooking" and read:

– 2 Eggs	*$3.10*
– Additional eggs	*$ .60*
– Plain Omelet	*$3.50*
– Sausage/bacon, 2 eggs	*$4.25*

Betty ordered 2 eggs scrambled with sausage, home-fried potatoes and biscuits. I ordered 3 eggs over medium, after consultation with the helpful and friendly waitress, with potato-cheese casserole and grits. Once again, biscuits and coffee rounded out the order for both of us.

The coffee was hot and promptly served. It was also kept hot and refreshed throughout the meal. As we waited for breakfast, we discovered more information on the menu. Dotson's is open Monday through Fridays from 7:00 a.m. – 8:30 p.m., Saturdays 7:00 a.m. – 2:30 p.m., and Sundays 8:00 a.m. – 2:30 p.m. It also gave a 'Gary Morris Special.' I think Gary Morris is a country-music star. At the very least the man knows how to eat country and may be huge. The special named for him included:

– 2 Chicken Breasts	
– 2 Eggs	
– Biscuits, Gravy and Grits	*$8.00*
– $2.00 less with one Breast	

The menu warned that those ordering the special, including Gary, should expect a fifteen-minute cooking time.

Looking for something to fill the space between the last fill-up of coffee and the arrival of the salvation of a Sunday morning, I began to observe the rapidly filling restaurant. When we had arrived at 9:05 a.m. we had a choice of ten to fifteen tables. At 9:30 a.m. the restaurant was full. The crowd was a mixture of sophisticated suburbanites. There were three ladies having a leisurely Sunday morning breakfast. There was a young couple with two young daughters that were probably on the way to church when they left at about 9:20 a.m. Next to us was a woman with a daughter about six-years-old. I wondered where the father was. I named the father "Chad" in my head. Were they divorced? I hoped not. I hoped he had worked the night shift at the Saturn plant the night before and was catching up on his sleep. I let Chad sleep on though because I didn't finish the story in my mind. The "Wall of Fame" had immediately distracted me.

There was a wall to my left which was a wall full of pictures, mainly of celebrities who had visited there. I walked over to see if my picture, snapped by paparazzi, was on display. I guess it is still in the darkroom but I did see pictures of fellow-celebrities: Vince Gill, Alan Jackson, The Judds and George W. Bush. George W's photo came out of the darkroom quicker than mine apparently. He had only been in Nashville a few days prior campaigning for Lamar Alexander and Van Hillary, his fellow Republicans, trying to get them elected to the U.S. Senate and to the governor's office. I hoped the president had enjoyed his meal but that his political efforts would fail. I wanted Bob Clement and Phil Bredesen elected to those offices.

My mental politicking ended the moment my eggs arrived prepared just as I had ordered them. I'm getting good at explaining to the waitresses — remember there are no male waiters in blue road restaurants — how to get the kitchen staff to cook the whites until done while leaving the yellows runny. The four pieces of bacon were sort of twisted around and stuck together but they were crispy. The potato and cheese casserole was gunky yet tasty. I suppose gunky is the right consistency for potato casseroles. The grits were excellent and had a great nutty after-taste. "Great nutty after-taste" makes it sound like I have been reading my friend Frank Sutherland's wine column.

The biscuits, while obviously homemade and tasty, had been

pulled out of the oven about five minutes too soon to suit me. They were a little too soft and doughy with no real crusts, top nor bottom. Even without perfection in the form of biscuits, the breakfast was topped off superbly with a few bites of breakfast desserts — biscuit pieces topped with spoons of grape and cherry jellies and jams. Our complete breakfast cost $11.83.

When we left the restaurant at 10:00 a.m. there was a line of some twenty-five people waiting to be seated. We had apparently arrived there at the perfect time. With 45 minutes before church, we drove around Franklin for a few minutes more looking at the beautiful homes and quaint shops. After this post-breakfast tour we went on to Christ Community Church. They don't play up the "Presbyterian" part of the name. As a matter of fact, they tend to hide it as if it is a parenthetical matter. And it probably is.

I noted that the church bulletin given out as we entered the church provided no "order of worship," which typically guides the eventual flow of the service. Obviously, the "flow" could be more "fluid" without it. The bulletin did give a lengthy list of eight pastors including John Patton, the pastor for youth and their families. John is a handsome young man who grew up in the same neighborhood with our children. There was also a list of sixteen other staff members. Running the church looked like big business.

As we arrived, we came into a foyer literally full of young families. Everyone was milling around several coffee, punch and cookie islands. We found out later that a reception was being held for about sixty-five new members at the church. We squirmed our way through the crowd and found the restroom before moving on to the sanctuary. I don't believe that I have ever seen such a young persons' church before. Young children swarmed like locusts. I have absolutely no doubt that we were the oldest people there. Then again, we are getting to a point in life where we are the oldest people wherever we go. Here, I suspected, they card people appearing over the age of forty. We must have eluded the age profilers when we slipped into the restroom.

I also suspected that it was against the law to wear a coat or tie here. We were given a light sentence because I had a coat but no tie. Thank God, I did not wear both or I could still be incarcerated. One can't dress nicer than the pastor and he was dressed like a mailroom assistant clerk. He wore dark wash jeans, a light blue shirt with no tie, of course, and sleeves rolled up to the elbow as if he were ready to sort mail or perhaps chop wood. Black and white tennis shoes completed the outfit of Scottie Smith, listed as the senior pastor. "How could he be a senior pastor and only be twenty-nine?" I asked myself. I felt certain that Betty was asking herself the same question.

Music started in the large and open sanctuary. It was of a modern design with tiered seating. We sat in the farthest back, most right-handed seat in the place. The seats were individually upholstered on fiberglass frames with some sort of connectors to stabilize them, effectively making them into pews. The band-like stage was large and roomy. It had the pulpit for the pastor and plenty of room for him to move around freely. Which he did. The music was provided by a lively band of piano, drums, bass and guitar and two singers, one of whom also played a guitar. Suddenly, as we stood to sing, I felt more relaxed, because there, about 30 rows in front of us, I could now see a man with a tie, although no coat, and another maverick with a jacket, although no tie. They would, no doubt, be my cellmates. I suppose if we swore that we would never, ever dress up again we might get off with probation. And with good behavior, wearing only sandals or tennis shoes from then on, we might be released on our own recognizance if we promised not to bring any other old people with us. At any rate, I felt comfortable that public stoning was probably not the punishment meted out to infidels who offended God with such worldly dress in His place of worship.

Senior Pastor Scottie (age 29?) made several announcements, emphasizing the tree in the foyer with small cutout trees hanging on it. The small trees offered the name of and suggested gifts for missionaries and their families. Pastor Scottie had just come back from a trip to the "mission fields" of Italy, France and the Netherlands.

We're now sending missionaries back to the very place from which missionaries were first sent to make America into a Christian nation? This struck me as like someone taking "coals to New Castle." But mine is not to question why. Then again, is not our great commission as Christians to go to the places where the gospel has not even been heard? Or is it to go to places where the gospel has been heard but where people may not have gotten the finer points of the gospel as straight as we have? I don't know. But I wonder if this is not misguided enthusiasm for some deeply held Christian beliefs in God's divine plan for all of history and the strategic place of modern American Christians in that plan. What about converting the heathen? Or are the French and the Italians heathen? Maybe it is just easier to convert the "Christian" heathen than those who do not know anything about the gospel. Perhaps one gets more credit for reforming or re-saving Christians of a slightly different persuasion than for saving Hindus or Buddhists. Maybe it's just a numbers thing.

But I digress. This was Reformation Sunday according to a large screen above the pulpit stage. Pastor Scottie gave a Reformation sermonette about how we know God. He said we know God in four ways: (1) through His creation; (2) through His word; (3) by grace and through faith; and, (4) through Christ alone. He concluded with part of the Presbyterian catechism about how "the chief end of man is to glorify God and to enjoy Him forever." Pastor Scottie, with no obvious notes, delivered his message pleasantly and effectively, a good communicator and fervent believer in God's plan for salvation for all of mankind.

The pastor than called on the musicians, who were unknown to me, and any visitor, to lead the congregation in singing *Come As You Are To Worship*. Everyone sang along enthusiastically with the overhead words prompter. A few people in the congregation waved their hands and arms in praise. Then the congregation sang "Can it be? Can it be that God shouldest die for me...amazing love. How can it be that my God shouldest die for me?" The song leader, a member of the duo, commented on the words of the songs and offered a prayer of praise and thanks. He then led in a prayer of silence.

The service continued the singing of *The King of Love, My Shepherd Is*. During the next song, *He Is Exhalted on High*, Senior Pastor Scottie praised God by raising his arms and waving them gently side by side. During the pastor's arm praising about twenty timid souls became brave enough to join him in praising God in the same manner. One tiny young mother of three, sitting with her family two rows in front of us, continued her praising of God during the remainder of the singing, freely and unselfconsciously waving her arms in a veritable in-place body dance to the rhythm of the music. During the singing I spotted two other visitors. They were dead giveaways because they were wearing sport jackets.

The pastor next prayed an informal, yet thoughtful prayer ending with an "Ah-men," rather than an "A-men." He then called a young couple with a baby to come forward to the sacrament of Covenant Baptism. He said the baptism was more than a dedication because two believing parents accompanied the child, who was also a child of the covenant. He also said that God would relentlessly pursue this child from this day forward until the child accepted Christ because this is God's promise and covenant to His children. The pastor then "sprinkled" the child — baptizing him in the name of the Father, Son and Holy Spirit. The congregation then sang together, "Jesus loves me this I know, for the Bible tells me so. Little ones to Him belong…"

Following the baptism the pastor gave a pure exegesis of the scripture lesson from *Romans 12: 3 – 20.* He said the scripture spoke of God's commitment to reach the whole world. And that Paul told the people of the church in Rome that God expected them to live in such a way that He would be glorified through the way they lived, day by day. Pastor Scottie stated that God gave each individual a spiritual and particular gift. He encouraged everyone to identify the gift that God has given to him or her and to find a way to use it to glorify Him. When the gifts are identified and used so, he said, our individual gifts would be woven into a beautiful tapestry as the body of Christ. The pastor exhorted the congregation to practice hospitality, to live in harmony and to show the beautiful tapestry of the body of Christ, the Church, to the world.

Three songs of the prayer of St. Francis were sung as the offering was taken: "Lord make me an instrument of thy peace…Where there is hatred, let me sow love; May I seek not so much as to be understood as to understand…for it is in giving that we receive;and, It is in pardoning that we are pardoned."

It was 11:58 a.m. A short closing prayer meant we would miss only the Titans kick-off on the radio while driving home. Just then Pastor Scottie came back to the missionaries in Europe! He especially emphasized progress that had been made in Italy. He said that Franco, an ex-priest of the Vatican, had been converted to true Christianity and was now exuberantly witnessing his new found joy. He said Franco earlier had made thousands of dollars selling candles in the churches before Mass. But Pastor Scottie said that Father Franco had been converted and was now preaching the new Gospel of his newfound faith. He had been converted from Catholicism to Protestantism.

At 12:05 the preacher was still going. Maybe next Sunday they should start the worship service at 10:40 instead of 10:45. Now it was 12:10. Can we move the start time back to 10:35? This is certainly not a "BBL" church as we used to call a church I attended years ago. "BBL" church? Beat-the-Baptist-to-Lunch church. It was now 12:20. The Baptists were all out swarming over every biscuit and buffet in town. Senior Pastor Scottie called for a song, "Take my life and let it be...consecrated Lord to thee. Take my hands...take my feet." The service finally concluded with a beautiful and, thankfully, rather short prayer after one more song, *Spirit Fall On Us.* It was 12:25 p.m. when we left the sanctuary. Betty and I finally found our way out of the catacomb maze of schoolrooms. We fought our way through a mass of strange little creatures that seemed to have more energy than any earthly creatures I had ever known. Or perhaps I had just forgotten the energy that comes with being a child.

At any rate, by the time we reached the car the Titans were down 14 – 0 to the Bengals. We began to think that God had perhaps forgotten his promise to the faithful church in Charlotte that meet at 11:00 a.m., as the scriptures surely require, and disperse at 12:00 a.m., as the holy tradition taught. Surely, a good God would not forsake the faithful. And, indeed, He did not. His might and power stopped the Bengals in the last minute at the goal line of the righteous Titans. God had saved the jobs of coach Jeff Fisher and running back Eddie George and, perhaps more importantly, the day for true tail-gaters.

The job of Senior Pastor Scottie (age 29?), however, remained in question. Obviously a righteous man full of conviction, he needed to get his priorities straight. Bad habits can form. A church service from 10:45 a.m. to 12:25 p.m., even in celebration of the re-conversion of all Europe, can be forgiven. But when the Titans are here? Forget it. God will certainly punish those who are proud of their "much speaking," don't you think?

What about Afghanistan, Senior Pastor Scottie? Any plans for sending missionaries to Afghanistan? Maybe missionaries should be kept in a safe place like Europe where the "heathen" are more "Christian." Or maybe sending missionaries to Europe is following the wise, if not great, commission of "Physician, heal Thyself."

At the very least, Senior Pastor Scottie, aged twenty-nine years at the most, please do not send any new missionaries to Afghanistan or Europe or anywhere until after the Super Bowl. The congregation probably can't take long missionary sermons during NFL season. Please. And thank you.

Chapter 8

United Methodist Church
Spring Hill, Tennessee
November 3, 2002

When things don't please me perfectly about my wife Betty, a seldom occurrence thank God, I refer to her among close friends as "my present wife." And that is how I thought about her on a chilly, rainy and blue Sunday morning while driving the blue road alone. Things had not gone perfectly this gray fall morning. My present wife had not gotten up until after 8:00 a.m. Her late start was probably a result of having too much fun the night before. A large group of friends had joined us for dinner and the evening had not ended until very late. There would be no way she could get up and get ready to leave at 8:30 a.m. for a blue roading excursion. No way.

How someone so naturally beautiful needs well over an hour to get ready to go anywhere has always puzzled me. Me? I can get ready to leave the house in five minutes, if necessary. And no one has ever accused me of being beautiful. Thirty seconds to brush teeth. Sixty seconds to shave. Thirty seconds to wet, thus making it appear that I had showered, and combed my hair. A full three minutes left to dress, not including a tie, and leave. If you think that's fast, I can be out of my clothes and sitting on the sofa with the TV on in 50 seconds flat after returning home in the evening. Any evening. Every evening.

Betty was easily convinced that I should not wait for her to join me in a search for a blue-road restaurant and a blue-road church. It was a natural stay-at-home type of day for her, partially because the funeral of the mother of some close friends was to be held at 1:00 p.m. If she went out this morning she would end up being pushed at both ends. But not me! Five minutes and I was on my way to I-did-not-know-where. The five minutes include a fake shower, of course. I've heard it said that too much bathing will weaken you anyhow.

Out I went, alone, south on Woodmont Boulevard and across
Hillsboro Pike. I turned onto Granny White Pike still going south
and still not knowing where I would wind up. I passed a Church of
Christ. It was no trouble to find a Church of Christ because they
are everywhere in this area. Baptists, too. I came to a corner at Old
Hickory Boulevard and Granny White Pike that holds the Bethel
World Outreach Community Church. A small church just a short
time ago, the church had grown dramatically in recent years. The
new facility was of a size that indicated large crowds. Three morning
services were held on Sundays, including one at 10:00 a.m. and one
at 11:45 a.m. This was truly new — a service at 11:45! What would
the god of the Titans think? Obviously they do not believe that
God and the god of the Titans are one and the same. At any rate, I
took note of the 11:45 a.m. service for future reference. We could
attend that particular service some other sleep-late Sunday when I
was willing to wait for Betty. I could take her there with me and
introduce her as my wife — past, present and future.

I kept moving. I drove north on Old Hickory and then south
on Franklin Road, State Route 31, passing through the old established business district of Brentwood. The enormous Brentwood
Methodist Church looked inviting but I had not yet had a blue-road
breakfast. There just are not enough blue road breakfast joints. At
least, not enough joints open on Sundays. There was the City Grill
in the Brentwood Kroger Center, a blue-road "meat and three," but
it was not open. I pressed onward, a hungry blue-road pilgrim in
search for country nourishment. Nothing. I drove for miles into
Franklin. I drove around The Factory, an interesting antique-infested
shopping center that occupied the old Jamison Bedding factory.
There were several restaurants inside but none was open. There was
a sign pointing to a community church. Community churches are
everywhere. Why? What does the proliferation of community
churches mean? It was a topic I would continue to think about.

I pressed on southward. I had the internal fortitude to pass
Dotson's restaurant where we had eaten last Sunday. I was not
above eating in the same blue-road restaurant, especially Dotson's,
two Sundays in a row. But I felt that I could find something acceptable or perhaps better if I pressed on. I passed through Franklin and
continued south on Rte. 31 toward Columbia. I was soon in true

blue-road country. It won't be blue-road country for much longer. Expensive subdivisions are sprouting up nearly everywhere in this area like mushrooms. I came upon the community of Thompson's Station, the home place of the late Jerry Thompson, a former reporter for the Tennessean. Jerry had been so very proud of the 'country-ness' of the Thompson's Station area. Rest in peace, Jerry. But hurry and get your rest now because Thompson's Station is becoming a 'burb. We just don't know whether it is a 'burb of Franklin or Spring Hill. Perhaps both.

I had gone without coffee the entire morning. I stopped at a BPS station to fill up with gas and find some coffee in the "grocery" section. The establishment was labeled the "Country Corner" and served as pitiful evidence of Jerry Thompson wannabes wishing to hold onto something country, even if only in name. It was not a blue road Paw Paws like the one near Charlotte. There were four or five "Green Acre" would-be farmers sitting around inside this mini-market that had no more country character than any of the other 7-11 stores I had ever been in. The "farmers" had on bib overalls and "John Deere" caps. They sat on white plastic Wal-Mart chairs waiting for something country to happen or something country to be said. One tobacco-chewing, would-be farmer, probably a worker in Nashville or at the Saturn plant in Spring Hill, was using a Styrofoam cup as a spittoon. An aspiring Tennessee farmer, he was trying to act country and to feel country. But I'll double-dog guarantee you that his country credentials were being challenged more and more every day.

Anyhow, I bought city-tasting coffee in the 7-11 masquerading as a "Country Corner" and continued to travel south. I noted a large Baptist church across the road from the Country Corner which held a 10:30 a.m. service. But I was called onward in hope of having a true blue-road breakfast first, and soon. And soon it was. After just a few more minutes and miles I sat in front of Early's. Early's real name is "Early's Honey," a mail order country foods place near Spring Hill. They ship country hams, sausage, bacon and other country goodies all over the world. Early's was not a restaurant and it was not even open. But I had just remembered that the Poplar House restaurant was just ahead. What a great country meat and three that had been. And within minutes I was in the heart of downtown Spring Hill, the home of General Motors' Saturn plant and the Poplar House Restaurant.

What a comfortable feeling, like coming home to a warm house and a comfortable pair of slippers. I had not thought of the Poplar House restaurant in years but memories returned as I walked in.The restaurant was nothing unusual. No great atmosphere to the place. As a matter of fact, quite the opposite. It was just like any storefront café — big glass aluminum framed windows, dark pan-eled walls and three game machines stationed in one corner. There was a very large TV in one corner and a smaller one near the area where the waitresses sit and the 'regulars' seem to hang out. I paid my proper respects by not encroaching upon the farmers' fraternal corner. There were four farmer-types gathered there. You know, in future 'burbs you can't really be sure who wears bibs these days — hip-hops, not withstanding. But these four looked roughly the farmer-type with farmer-like shoes and the camouflage design and "name" caps.

The tables held one young couple, a single young man and a single spinster-type older woman. Over near the "farmers forum" was a big talking-type would-be farmer. Think Cliff the mailman on the popular TV series *Cheers.* "Big talking" means that he spoke as if he knew everything. He looked like country music's whispering Bill Anderson except, of course, that this country cousin did any-thing but whisper. It was not that he talked so overbearingly loud. But he had a strong voice that made him heard throughout the entire restaurant and made him sound like he "really ought to know," the very reason Tavia in "Fiddler on the Roof" wanted to be rich. Tavia felt that when rich people talk others listen because "you really ought to know," being rich and all. If the big-talking farmer didn't actually know what he was talking about, the tone of his voice insisted that he really did know — and that maybe he was rich.Everybody listened. We had to. It wasn't mandatory;it was just invasive. As he talked on and on, I shifted my attention hopefully to the menu.

The Sunday menu read:

Meat and three eggs   *$5.50*
Chicken and dressing
Salisbury Steak

Cream Style Corn   *Green Beans*
Pinto Beans   *Mashed Potatoes*
Baked Apples   *Stewed Cabbage*
Pears and
    Cottage Cheese   *Cole Slaw*
Tossed Salad

Cornbread or Rolls

But it was breakfast time. The menu said breakfast was served daily 6:30 – 11:00 a.m.and from 2:00 – 8:30 p.m.,Monday through Thursday.

Some choices for breakfast were:
  – *Biscuits and Gravy* $1.75
  – *2 Pancakes*   2.95
  – *3 Pancakes*   3.65

  – *Country Ham Breakfast $6.95*
  – *Center-cut Ham*
  – *Two eggs – Potatoes*
  – *Biscuits*

  – *Rib Eye Steak Breakfast $6.95*
  – *2 Eggs – Potatoes*
  – *Biscuits*

I ordered the country ham breakfast. The blue-road discrimination against male waiters continued as a friendly waitress assured me that 'over medium' meant the way I like my eggs. She was right. They were perfect and the home-fried potatoes were prepared by a true country-gourmet cook. And the 'center cut' slice of ham was from a hog, not a pig. The size of the cut was enormous, covering the entirety of the small platter. And its flavor was excellent. Country ham is like peanuts to me. I don't eat them often but the salty tastefulness is addictive. Half of the cut was more than enough but I couldn't quit. Bite after bite I thought about quitting but I didn't. I could not until the moment came — "I can't believe I ate the whole thing."

The country biscuits showed telltale evidence of having been homemade, no beautiful preciseness here giving the signs of a factory-cutting machine. The biscuits, the size of cat heads, were irregularly handsome, delicious and had a delicate crustiness. I finished the last bit of the biscuits with bits of jelly hidden beneath the lids of individual factory-filled mini-tubs. The jelly may have looked unappetizing but it tasted sweet. My bill came to $9.26. It was 10:30 a.m. when I pressed on in search of a church.

I needed a righteous congregation in Spring Hill that obeyed the eleventh commandment to meet for worship at 11:00 a.m. on Sundays. I found two — the United Methodist Church and the Presbyterian Church. Choosing between the two was difficult. The Presbyterian Church was a quaint historic white-frame church that was at first my choice because I had not yet been to a 'real,' or regular, Presbyterian church. The Cumberland Presbyterian Church previously attended had separated from the Presbyterian denomination in the 19th century, partially due to differing views on the ordination of ministers. I had also visited the Christ Community Church in Franklin, which apparently was only parenthetically Presbyterian.

I ended up going to the Methodist Church because it had a woman minister. Or at least so I thought. I had misread the bulletin board outside the church:

Rev. Don Noble, Pastor
Rev. Kathy Noble, Deacon

I had not read the word "Deacon" at the bottom. And so I went to the Methodist Church because it seemed an opportunity to hear a female minister for the first time in my life. By the time I realized my mistake, I was already seated in a curving pew, in the back right-hand section of the sanctuary. The church bulletin revealed that the ministerial situation was a team matter. The Reverend Don Noble was the pastor and <u>The</u> Reverend Kathy Noble, presumably his wife, was a deacon. While both were ordained as ministers, The Rev. Kathy Noble would not be speaking today according to the order of worship in the church bulletin.

The handsome and historic church was divided into three sections separated by two middle aisles. The floor gently sloped toward the chancel at the front. There was a pipe organ to the right, which would not be used this day, and a piano to the left, which would accompany the music during this worship service. The chancel colors were shades of dated avocado green. The ceiling was coffered with handsome wood beams and three beautiful stained-glass windows lined each side of the space. A white banner hung above the choir loft had painted leaves and inscribed words, "The Colors of God's Love."

Two small acolytes, a boy and a girl, about six-years-old came down the aisle dressed in white robes to light the chancel candles as The Reverends Noble entered from the right side of the chancel. The Reverend Don Noble, a bearded gentleman with glasses, walked using a cane. He moved with great difficulty, with much trepidation and with very small steps. I made a note to concentrate on taking much larger steps now that I am 71. I can at least appear strong and virile. The Reverend Kathy Noble walked with no apparent difficulty. They both appeared to be in their sixties. They were also dressed alike in long white, priestly robes and colorful sashes around their necks.

As the Nobles entered, a choir of four, two men and two women, took their seats. The lady directing the choir and congregation seemed both cheerful and unselfconscious as *O How I Love Jesus* and *Jesus Remember Me* were sung. The Reverend Don Noble announced several prayer requests. He asked for prayer requests from the congregation at large and received requests from two women. Then he led a prayer divided into several parts. First, the *Prayers of the Community* offered prayers for those in the immediate community, then for those around the world and lastly for any "special situations." Second, the *Prayer of Confession* allowed the congregation to confess their sins. Next, the *Word of Grace* announced God's forgiveness for those who truly confess their sins. Finally, the *Lord's Prayer* followed by the singing of the *Gloria Patri* —"Praise God from whom all blessings flow."

At this point in the service a lady of the congregation called all the young children to the front of the chancel for a 'Message for Young Christians.' The message was about leftover food. While we might be tempted to complain about having to eat leftover food, she said, there are those who would love to have any food, even the leftover kind. She encouraged the young people to ask their parents to buy extra food and extra supplies for the poor. The food drive in progress was in need of donations. She then prayed, "Thank you,

God, for everything. For food, for family, and for Jesus Christ."

The pastor then called the youngsters that were 12-years-old and teenagers to the front. He delivered a sort of Halloween sermonette, which seemed a bit awkward both for the minister and for the five teenagers. The teenagers had marched self-consciously to the front to receive the child-like sermonette and then back to their seats again afterwards.

The special "Cherub Choir" provided music next. They came to the front to sing *Jesus Loves Me* and received hearty applause from the congregation. The congregation then sang *Tell Me the Story of Jesus.*

The Reverend Don Noble read the scripture lesson for the day, *Matthew 23: 1 – 12.* It was about the Scribes and the Pharisees who do not practice what they preach and whose deeds are done "to be seen by others." The Reverend Mr. Noble pointed out that the Pharisees thought that their way of thinking was the *only* way to think. His point, of course, was that there are other ways of thinking that may not coincide with ours "but there is only one Judge, Jesus Christ." He also said, "Jesus judges only the heart." The minister then shared his belief in healthcare for children and Section-8 housing programs. He concluded with the thought that by supporting these and other good causes we can be good servants together.

The Reverend Kathy Noble then took the lead in preparing the Sacrament of Holy Communion for the congregation. The congregation numbered about 75 people who were for the most part casually dressed. She invited the congregation to come to the altar to partake of "the body and blood of Christ." Members, and visitors, were directed to come by two ushers who allowed about 15 people at each "table" to kneel and receive the Sacrament. There were four such "seatings." During this period The Reverend Kathy Noble came out into the congregation in order to serve those who could not go to the altar to be served. The two ministers then served each other.

The congregation then sang *This Is My Father's World* which was followed by the benediction given by The Reverend Mr. Don Noble. The acolytes came to the front to light their candles and then extinguish the chancel candles. They took the lighted candles "to the world" as the Reverend Mrs. Nobel exited to the rear. The

Reverend Mr. Noble exited to the side with short and painful steps, walking very carefully with his cane. And that concluded the service.

The contrast between this church service and last week's church service at Christ Community Church in Franklin was so dramatic that the two churches seemed to belong to two different religions altogether. The only commonality was the acknowledgment of Jesus Christ as Savior. One church was open, aggressive and modern; the other was traditional, patterned and ordered. The youthful senior pastor Scottie Smith, all of twenty-nine years perhaps, contrasted with the aging Reverend Don Noble, sixty-nine years perhaps. The two figures could not have been more different. The youthful man presented himself as a part of a worldwide evangelistic effort to change the way the world worships God. The elder Reverend Noble presented himself as dedicated to helping the few pilgrims gathered in his church to keep the faith they have and allowing others the world over to keep theirs.

I rushed to my car to call Betty and assured her I would be home by 1:00 p.m. We would then go together to what would be the second funeral-type service I would attend that day. In the first, the congregation remembered the death of Jesus by partaking in the Sacrament of Holy Communion. In the second, the life of Mrs. Ruth Hawkins would be remembered. Mrs. Hawkins was the mother of JoAnn and Barbara, both friends of our family for many years. Mrs. Hawkins had led a loving life of simple deeds including working at Cain Sloan's, washing and ironing and cleaning out closets — mostly for Barbara.

At the risk of seeming sacrilegious, I "enjoyed" the funeral of Mrs. Hawkins more that the church Communion service. The first one concentrated on the death of Jesus; the second one concentrated on the life of a dear mother. The first remembered the death of Jesus for the world while the second remembered the life and efforts of Mrs. Hawkins for her children and her grandchildren. Maybe it was the specificity. Maybe it was the time element; Jesus died 2000 years ago and Mrs. Hawkins died in 2002 AD. Regardless, Mrs. Hawkins' religion was her family. And those attending her funeral felt good as they considered the depth of love manifested in a life of mundane tasks performed selflessly for the benefit of those whom she believed God had given to her care.

Christians celebrate the birth of Jesus explicitly only once a year at Christmas while many celebrate his death at least once a week. In remembering Jesus' death all Christians are following his instructions to do so. Do Christians think that Jesus would be offended if His followers celebrated His birth, and life, just as deliberately? And just as often? Christmas every Sunday! Something for Christians to think about.

Chapter 9

Covenant Fellowship: A Church of the Nazarene
Mt. Juliet, Tennessee
November 10, 2002

O n November the 9th I received a letter that had been mailed to my previous address several days earlier, returned to the sender and then re-mailed to my office address. The letter was a welcomed surprise from a longtime friend and acquaintance, McCray Holmes, with whom I had spent one year at Trevecca College in 1954. I had not heard of nor from McCray since 1954. He was returning to Trevecca, now Trevecca Nazarene University, to appear in a performance of a singing group of men.

I received the letter after returning home from a Saturday of golf with my good friends Jim Neal, John Seigenthaler and Frank Sutherland. Our wives' joining us for dinner at Richland Country Club topped off the day. Frank and I were in high spirits having just won fifteen dollars each from Jim and John. We celebrated the occasion with a brief ceremony of the "Crossing of the Palms" and with the vanquished paying proper respects to the victors. Fifteen dollars is a hard won sum of money when mined out at $1.00 per hole over an eighteen-hole course. We had beaten them badly! The fifteen dollars topped the record amount ever won in our foursome. And I had an ominous feeling that the stage had been set for fierce negotiations over the number of handicap strokes for many months to come.

Jim's illustrious career as an attorney put him in good stead for the haggling surely to take place over the next week on the first tee. And John, a word merchant for many years, would no doubt be exercising his first amendment right to freedom of speech if his golfing partner allowed him to take the stand. The one thing they might both lobby aggressively against would be freedom of the press if Frank made any attempt in his role as editor of The Tennessean to print the newsworthy story — "Utter Humiliation of Heretofore Proud Men." It would make a nice headline.

The day's activities had kept me from receiving McCray's letter until late in the evening on my return home. In the letter my old Trevecca friend reminded me that the first time he had played golf in his entire life was with me back in 1954. Golf has been a passion since 1944 when I was only thirteen years of age and worked as a weeder of the greens at Logan Country Club in West Virginia. McCray also spoke in the letter about our times playing basketball and working for a local TV sales company.

Needless to say, I was sorry to have missed McCray's group performing. The letterhead on the paper was for "Musical Ministries, Inc." A division of the organization was "The Singing Men of America" and listed McCray Holmes as Vice President – Public Relations Coordinator. Immediately I made a few calls in an effort to reach him while he was still in Nashville. I had fifteen dollars in my pocket and wanted to brag about it to one of my earliest golfing partners. Although I could not find him that night I did discover that his group was scheduled to sing the next morning at the Covenant Fellowship, a Church of the Nazarene in Mt. Juliet, Tennessee.

The new turn of events helped me decide the blue road of choice for that weekend's journey. Betty and I traveled east on West End Avenue until we reached the Cumberland River. At that point we turned right onto First Avenue and started out toward Donelson, Hermitage and Mt. Juliet. We talked about all the property development that will probably happen in this area during the next decade. The first development would probably be the move of the Nashville Sounds to the site of the Nashville Thermal Plant, currently sitting on several acres of prime property at First Avenue and the Cumberland River. Always thinking like the real estate developer I am, I made note of the large amount of land in this area that could be easily developed. I also made a few prognostications about future projects that would no doubt occur on the various properties we passed on the way out to Donelson. Betty, my permanent wife that morning, dutifully agreed with my amazing foresight into the future of Nashville development. She only wishes this uncanny ability to predict the future could have produced something other than "mind money."

My mind-money games were so vivid that I actually forgot to look for a blue road restaurant. The smell of sure money to be made faded as my appetite was awakened at the sight of the most famous of all blue road restaurants — McDonald's. On blue, green or red roads, the thought of McDonald's bacon, egg, cheese biscuits will awaken my appetite anytime. I resisted the urge to be a pushover for the first breakfast that captured my attention.

We drove on. In Donelson, on the right, we passed the Nashville School for the Blind. Betty noted that I knew precisely the location of this longtime important Nashville service to the blind and near blind. Betty reads a lot. Too much for my liking. She even reads while we are driving on the blue roads sometimes — a sacrilege if there ever was one. Her ability to appreciate my brilliant insights as we drive along is often inhibited by her reading material. I threatened to visit the School for the Blind in search of a pretty volunteer to accompany me on the next long blue road trip. It was my hope that such a volunteer would not be so inclined to read all the time and, thus, could pay a proper amount of respect to my observations regarding nothing in particular. Betty kept on reading.

As we exited Donelson we felt amazement at how beautiful the drive was and noted that Andrew Jackson had certainly picked the most beautiful area of Nashville in which to build his stately home, The Hermitage.

But I was looking for a "country" restaurant — something different. We passed an interesting looking restaurant at 14841 Lebanon Road called "Elmo's Country Buffet." That did it. Country Buffet! To be honest I was not so keen on the 'buffet' part of the name but was quite taken with the idea that Elmo thought it was country. It was. And it wasn't.

We entered an unimaginative square dining area with a large buffet island surrounded by plastic sneeze guards. The guards should be called 'food guards' because they sometimes make the food impossible to reach. But we could reach enough. Actually, too much. I carried a plate of scrambled eggs, bacon, sausage and biscuits to the vinyl-covered table and sat on a vinyl-covered chair. Vinyl is always country, although not always by intention. It just happens. It happens because it is the cheapest material to use and country restaurants need to keep costs down because the average check is generally quite low. For example, the breakfast buffet was $7.50 a person.

I passed up the continental bar part of the buffet because the fruit was either too country or not country enough. I don't know which. But the sweet rolls were not country at all. Unless the Kroger's store from which they were purchased was a rural one. I'm not complaining, mind you. Some of the best food comes out from underneath a Sarah Lee see-through plastic wrapper. I just wanted country cookin' today. I knew what Pepperidge Farms and Chiquita Banana could do. I had come to see what Elmo could do.

Elmo did all right. He's on the right track. The owner's name is Elmo Patterson. The waitress-cashier said that Elmo had been a cook in many restaurants throughout the states and even in Germany. I wondered if he had been in the service cooking for the military in Germany. Anyway, she told us this was his first restaurant. God bless him. He's in the toughest business in the world. I know. I tried it once. Come to think of it, I have tried about everything — and failed at plenty. Particularly in my efforts to please the palates of Nashvillians.

Back at the vinyl covered country table Betty was waiting for fresh eggs and bacon to arrive, which they soon did. I ate what was before me and asked no questions. Well. I did ask if the biscuits were homemade in an effort to confirm my suspicion that they were. And they were! They were delicious. I ate three including one that I decorated with country sausage gravy at the bar as part of a strategic plan to hit the vinyl eating. Betty could wait if she wanted. The shopped-over eggs and bacon were fine for me. And they were good. It's almost impossible, however, to ruin eggs for me. When ordering in a restaurant, I always order them over-easy or over-medium after discussing the cook's proclivities. But however they are cooked I will like them. I may have my preferences but I like them almost any way — hot or cold, or in the refrigerator several days old.

We ate with religious music playing over a radio or sound system near the cashier's desk. *I need Thee, oh, I need Thee* played as we were seated. Maybe this was the Sunday worship ritual for these blue road waitresses. *And He Walks with Me* played as we walked out the door. Elmo had provided a better than average blue road breakfast in a less than average country-feeling, blue road restaurant. I could not help but say, "Good luck, Elmo" with no one but Betty to hear. I wish him good fortune. He deserves it. It's a hard job and blue road country cooking restaurants are an endangered species.

We set out to find the Covenant Fellowship Church in Mt. Juliet.I had been told it was located at 101 Falkner Lane, just across from the high school. Since we found it with no difficulty and were early, we decided to drive the ten miles or so out to a subdivision I had developed several years before called Pointe Barton. It was on Old Hickory Lake and had come about from one of my forward thinking investments that turned out to be too far forward. I seem to be ahead of my time or at the end of the line mostly. Pointe Barton was so far ahead of my time that a few lots are still for sale in this beautiful subdivision on Cole's Ferry Pike near Lebanon. Perhaps one of my millions of readers will want one. If so, please call. You can get the number off the signs that are still there. Thank you for your patronage.

Covenant Fellowship Church seems to be a parenthetical-type church, "Covenant Fellowship, A Church of the Nazarene." See what I mean? The name seems to indicate a desire to be a community church first and a something else church second. Would it not be named "Covenant Fellowship Nazarene Church" if the Nazarene portion was more than just a subtitle? This trend towards paren-thetical subtitles can be seen in most community-type churches proliferating in America. Two weeks ago, for example, we attended "Christ Community Church (Presbyterian Church of America)" near Franklin, Tennessee. The name is as presented in its own printed material. It's like saying "We are Presbyterian, you all, but that's not an important thing to us." The naming trend may be a move to emphasize the "core" elements of the Christian faith rather than the identifying elements of a particular denomination's doctrines.

So I'll call it "Covenant Fellowship" and they'll approve. I had wanted to get there early to hopefully speak with my handsome, dark-haired friend McCray Holmes before the service started. But my investigation of the ahead-of-time investment caused us to get to the church at 10:50 while the service started at 10:45. I had to guess which of the men in the choir McCray was. I had not seen him since he was twenty-two years old and he was now seventy-two. Still, I thought I might be able to pick him out.

As we entered the sanctuary, *Nothing Is Impossible With God*

73

was being directed by an enthusiastic song director as if it were a symphony before him. In actuality he was leading a band of several pieces and a large choir of talented voices. The pulpit, choir and band were located in a side, pushed-out area of the gymnasium-type building. The same area could be used as a spectator section during a basketball game.

Covenant Fellowship is apparently a forward-thinking congregation. They had built an exposed metal beam building with gym-type lights and exposed whitish, vinyl-covered insulation in the ceiling. The basketball goals respectfully knelt upwards toward the ceiling as if in worship themselves. The seats were connectable and mauve colored — the type that can be moved quickly before and after athletic events.

Next, the choir sang *Come Let Us Bow Down* to the full congregation, somewhere between 200 to 300 people. Most people were comfortably dressed in the current informal uniform of the typical community church. During the singing many of the congregants waved their arms and applauded, particularly after singing *All Hail the Power of Jesus' Name.*

The pastor of this lively congregation was an articulate fellow by the name Jon Gray. He announced that the service would be dedicated, in part, to the celebration of Veterans' Day, the holiday honored on the following Monday. A full page of the church bulletin read in large, bold letters:

Celebrate Jesus!
Celebrate America!
Celebrate Our Veterans!

Pastor Gray said that we certainly all should be proud to be Americans. He noted proudly that in several recent elections held in our land of freedom not a single candidate received 100 percent of the votes cast — a not-so-subtle reference to the lack of freedom of the Iraqi people as indicated by Saddam Hussein's 100 percent victory in the last election. The pastor then prayed for the soldiers currently serving in dangerous locations to protect freedom, even the freedom to not vote for someone.

The church bulletin did not offer an order of worship. Instead it offered only announcements of various activities and notice that the *Singing Men of America* would be in concert today singing hymns, spirituals and gospel songs. The pastor said, "Please forget the time," as a forewarning to the congregation that the service would go well beyond 12:00 p.m. His dramatic wink, recognizing that the 'sacred' quitting time would not be abandoned forever, was more or less a prayer for forgiveness for a hopefully pardonable sin, especially in the light of the distinguished group of singers that would be soon singing.

Pastor Gray then introduced the "Charlotte Chapter of the Singing Men of America." He said there weren't any other chapters of the group yet but, by faith, there would be others in the future. *The Singing Men* were seventeen distinguished senior men of the average age of sixty-five. They all wore gray pants, white shirts and blue blazers with American flag neckties. Their rich, well-trained voices offered *Rise Up, Oh, Men of God* which the director later referred to as the group's theme song.

One of the choir members stepped out of the choir to share a story about his grandfather missing the Titanic by fifteen minutes. He felt that God's timetable had saved his grandfather, thus allowing him to be born and to father his own son. God had been looking way down the road on His own time schedule when He saved his grandfather, he said, because his son was now planning to be a missionary in Japan where only a small percentage of the population was Christian. Then the men's choir sang *God Is On Time Every Time For Me*, a lively and entertaining song that received warm applause from the whole congregation.

During this whole time I looked for my friend McCray among the seventeen gray and balding men in the choir. Six of the men had beards. Eleven of the men had glasses. It was impossible. I would not be able to pick him out from the choir members. I started to think that perhaps he did not actually sing with the group. But it turned out that he did.

Pastor Gray then recognized several retired veterans in the congregation. He invited Sgt. First Class Delbert Powell share his experiences in the service from 1948 to 1968. Powell had served in Okinawa, Korea and Germany. He informed the congregation that over 900,000 Americans had died in all the American wars, including more than 200,000 during the Civil War. A survivor of Pearl Harbor then led the congregation in reciting *The Pledge of*

Allegiance. Afterwards he spoke of his remembrances of Pearl Harbor and concluded with the humble thought,"I hope you were not too bored." The congregation assured him that they had not been bored at all by giving him perhaps the biggest round of applause of the day.

The Singing Men of America then returned to finish the concert, giving me another chance to try to spot McCray. They led the congregation in singing the *National Anthem* and *America the Beautiful*. One of the group's members then offered a solo, *We Want America Back*. He sang, "Where are the men who once stood for right...we want America back...This nation is like a runaway train...running down the wrong track...We want America back." Then, in a Johnny Cash type talk song, he said, "sometimes our schools are like war zones...with the TV bombarding our senses telling us what is wrong is right...We can pass out condoms at our schools, but the Gideons cannot pass out Bibles...but the Bible says, what is wrong is wrong ...We want America back."

The entire group then sang "Jesus is calling America...calling her back to the fold, calling her young and her old...Back to the ways of our fathers...Jesus is calling America back. Won't you answer His loving call...this may be His last call."

The strong-voiced group was unabashedly calling Americans back to solidarity and old-fashioned patriotism. A member of the group with long curly hair, pigtail-like, came forward to sing Lee Greenwood's, *I'm Proud To Be An American*: "I'm proud to be an American...where at least I know I'm free...There ain't no doubt I love this land. God bless the USA." The red, white and blue road, all-American song brought forth a rousing round of applause from the congregation. The patriotic feelings of the congregation had been called forth by the *Singing Men of America*.

The pastor invited us all to stay for "dinner on the grounds" before leading us in prayer, "God is Great. God is Good. Let us thank Him for our food. " And with that the service was concluded. Yet I still had not spotted McCray. I asked the man in the control booth who ran the lights and the sound for the concert if he knew McCray Holmes. He pointed to a gray haired man a few rows in front of us, "He is the man with the white hair." I said, "You mean the man with the gray hair?"McRay, according to the control booth fellow, made a practice of assuring people that his hair was white, not gray. And I had to agree as I walked over to say hello. It was so gray it was white — every strand of it. But McCray, even with the gray-white hair, was just as handsome as the dark haired, would-be golfer friend I had known 50 years ago. We reminisced for a few minutes about life and then talked about the singing group. McCray is now 72 years old and,semi-retired, serves as the director of music at a small Baptist church near Charlotte, North Carolina. The members of the group were from many denominations including Moravian, Methodist, Church of God, Baptist, Nazarene and Presbyterian. The all-volunteer group was made up primarily of retired men from many walks of life, mostly businessmen.

The men obviously enjoy these concerts almost as much as the people to whom they sing. The Charlotte Chapter of The Singing Men of America is the only chapter active as of today. My prognostication is that with the religious and patriotic themes they carry, the group will inspire other groups to follow in their footsteps "from the lakes of Minnesota to the hills of Tennessee" by helping "Call America back." This prognostication, unlike my future-gazing of the past in investments such as Fantiques and Pointe Barton, is a no-brainer given the present atmosphere in America.

And, thanks, McCray. Seeing you again rekindled many fond memories of schooldays nearly fifty years ago. Hit 'em long and straight, old friend.

Chapter 10

Cornerstone Church
Madison, Tennessee
November 17, 2002

F all is my favorite season. It had arrived early this year with today being a capstone of sorts on the fabulous season of colors. The peak of the fall colors had passed during the preceding week but had been partially obscured by several days of heavy rain. Yesterday the weather front had passed through the area and delivered today as a harbinger of the approaching winter season. It was still fall, mind you, and ample evidence of the season remained, including a number of tree-lined streets that were magnificent with a verital rainbow of leaves. We left home on Woodmont Boulevard at 7:45 a.m. on a vacillating day — one minute a perfect fall day, the next a chilly almost-winter day. The temperature that morning was 30 degrees, a fair warning that winter was close by.

There was not a perceptible cloud in the fall-winter sky as we hurried to the car and made "smoke" with our breath, perhaps for the first time this season. Betty, impatient because of the cold, reached over to start the car motor in an unveiled attempt to chide me for being too slow in trying to coax a little early warmth out of our car's heating system. The novelty of the cold weather felt great to me. I put my hand gingerly to the steering wheel for the first few blocks, alternating warming my hands by rubbing them against my pants leg. Betty was not as receptive to the seasonal challenge but I loved every minute of it. I loved the tingle of the cold as I warmed one hand on the gabardine and then held the other hand close to the heater vent of the gradually warming winter-cheating-thermal-touring-apparatus.

The crisp, germ-killing, pre-seasonal and invigorating cold snap had me feeling like driving all day as we started out. We went north on White Bridge Road, the natural extension of Woodmont Boulevard immediately after crossing Harding Road until we came to Charlotte Avenue. Charlotte Avenue is the namesake for Charlotte, Tennessee, the town I discovered for the first time several weeks ago. Charlotte was home to the 'righteous' little Baptist Church in this Titans dominated, Middle Tennessee Sodom and Gomorra. I recognized the righteousness of the little church from its steadfast refusal to bow to the Titans' schedule and its commitment to follow the Biblical tradition of holding worship services at 11:00 a.m. Had we taken a left onto Charlotte Avenue, we could have had a return visit. Instead, we took a right onto Charlotte Avenue and headed east. We were also headed directly toward the Titans' coliseum where late arriving Titan fans were often threatened with being fed to the Bears or the Jaguars.

We were about twenty-five minutes earlier leaving home today than we typically are on our Sunday journeys. Winter was definitely a little impatient on this day as we turned off Charlotte onto James Robertson Parkway, which leads to the Main Street Bridge. The bridge crosses the Cumberland River, which is actually a moat protecting the Titans' fortress from those seeking easy access to the slaughtering ground of many opposing teams in recent years. Not as many fans had gathered early today to see the death of the enemies as we had seen on previous game days. What a difference 30 minutes makes! And what a difference a small dip on the thermometer reading makes on the enthusiasm of tailgaters in Nashville. That said, neither the time nor the temperature slowed down the efforts of scalpers selling tickets to those wishing to witness the mayhem today. Already out in great force at every intersection once we crossed the bridge, the scalpers held their undying signs in support of the Titans reading, "I need tickets!"

We had no business to transact with these entrepreneurs. We had nothing to sell of interest to them, nor were we seeking to negotiate with them for access to the contest between the Titans and the Pittsburgh Steelers. The game was surely an evenly matched battle between two sets of warriors with similar records. The Titans needed all the support they could get for the looming battle between one ancient tribe and one modern army, but, alas, I could not be of help today. A fine Sunday breakfast was calling but from whence I knew not. I was determined to follow the call of the breakfast sirens who were performing their beautiful morning temptations. These temptations can drive all of the men (and half of the women) of the world delirious after a single step toward them is made.

Our first step toward temptation was making a U-turn in order to head back parallel to the Main Street Bridge before turning right onto Dickerson Road. The Titans police, also smarting at the bite of the early morning chill, had not yet arrived to witness my driving infraction and penalize me.

This part of Dickerson Road badly needs the help of Mayor Purcell in this area. In fact, no other area of the city needs a boost more to get it back on the right track. Block after block one finds as much evidence of urban decay as is found in Nashville. The rows of seedy motels give credence to the cries of the people who live in the high crime area brought about primarily through the illegal trafficking of drugs and prostitution, both effortlessly incubated in these cheap motels. One lowlife business taking root and nourishing the prurient interests of denizens of this moral desert in Nashville was the "PLEASURE PALACE." The Pleasure Palace occupies what had apparently been a service station at one time. With gold-covered windows to prevent unpaid voyeurism, the establishment apparently 'serviced' the pleasure needs of those who, in desperation, come to think of any place offering some relief from loneliness as a "pleasure palace."

The blight along Dickerson Road did not continue forever. Soon after we crossed Trinity Lane a dramatic change was evident. Here was evidence of the hard won triumph of free enterprise and entrepreneurship. Businesses begin here to blossom and grow as the unwanted advance of criminal activity is thwarted by the just efforts of citizens and the police. And Betty and I were happy for the united front between the citizens of the area and law enforcement officials that has created a safe haven for successful businesses out this way. Especially for one of our new favorite breakfast 'pleasure places' in Nashville — Jay's Family Restaurant. Jay's is a well-maintained business located at 3037 Dickerson Road. It attracted our attention immediately although we almost passed it before realizing that the breakfast sirens were calling from inside this attractive restaurant. We were able to 'brake' quickly enough to pull in off this busy road without causing a pile-up and pull into the only remaining parking space. A full parking lot is a good sign already since those inside probably know something about the quality of the food to be found inside. They have surely been here before. Certainly not all of them were out blue roading and just happened to find this place as we had. Comforted by the sight of the full parking area, we followed the other 'sheep' inside. Were we being led to the slaughter? Happily, we soon discovered that we had not been.

Jay's Family Restaurant was obviously just that — a restaurant serving good country cooking to families of the area. We found out that the good food at Jay's actually was prepared and served by members of a family, along with some very dedicated employees and friends. The interior was arranged to allow comfortable and efficient service to the customers. One obvious sign that great numbers of nearby residents regularly eat here was the customer-control lanes in the foyer. The airport-type controls were needed on "Dinner-Special" nights, each Wednesday and Friday. On these nights they advertise "all you can eat"spaghetti and catfish on respective nights. Apparently the crowds line up to wait for a table.

We stood in line only a few seconds before a friendly hostess ushered us to a booth on one wall. Directly across from our booth was another line of booths already full of happy customers. We were served hot coffee and given a few minutes to 'look at the menu.' It had some of the following items for breakfast:

– *2 Eggs, Bacon or Sausage, gravy or grits*   *$2.75*
– *2 Eggs, 2 Pork Tenderloin, gravy or grits*   *5.75*
– *3 Egg Western Omelet*   *5.85*
– *3 Biscuits and Gravy*   *2.45*

Betty ordered a two-egg cheese omelet with grits and toast for $3.65. I bravely ordered three eggs over-easy with bacon, grits, biscuits and home fries for $4.65. While we waited impatiently for the food, I read the rest of the menu and decided I wanted to come back for lunch or dinner soon. I had a gut feeling that the sirens had led me to the right place. They served five different entrees each day with two new items added daily. The three constant items served every day are roast beef and gravy, steak and gravy, and grilled ham. The 'floating' items include chicken and dumplings, fried chicken livers, meatloaf, stuffed peppers, salmon patty, beef tips and noodles, and chicken with dressing. Each day there were 15 different vegetables or side orders, with white beans, corn, fried potatoes and turnip greens as constant offerings. Good choices! The menu warned customers that an assortment of pies and cobblers was always available for $1.65 per serving.

Our breakfasts were teetotally perfect. The brave move to order my eggs over-easy without consulting with the waitress as usual created some trepidation on my part. As it turned out, my fear was not justified. The bacon was crisp. The grits had that elusive nutty flavor. And the biscuits were true winners — crisp on the bottom and baked to a light golden brown on top, just perfect. They were just like the Beacon Light and the Loveless Café, only different; just like the biscuits from the other two breakfast spots in that they were truly delicious, but still they were somehow different. You'll have to try all three to see what I mean.

In case I haven't made it clear yet, we loved our breakfast. And I found the secret as to why our breakfast was so delicious. Her name was Fran. Fran, who is about 70-years-old, is the chief cook at Jay's. (My only worry is that Fran is about as old as I am. How long are both of us going to be around to create and enjoy her cooking?) If Fran worked at Mario's she would be called the "chef." But if they called her the chef at Jay's they would have to pay her more. She almost refuses to take a day off according to a "mole" that shared some of the secrets to Jay's success. Fran did all the cooking with the help of just a few good men and women. I told my informant that the owner should call the place "Fran's" or at least give her equal billing; how about "Jay and Fran's?" I like it. Short of that, Jay, what about a raise for Fran? None of my business? I think it is. From my perspective you really need her. At the very least, I want you to thank her for me. And thanks to you as well for providing Nashville with a great blue-road stopover.

It was now about 9 a.m. Our bodies had been delightfully fed, probably slightly overfed, and we were now looking for a place where good people go to have their spirits fed. We meandered out Dickerson Road contentedly. Nothing caught our eyes as a clarion call to join people who would soon be gathering to worship. At just a little past nine, we had plenty of time to shop for a church. We turned right onto Old Hickory Boulevard and headed toward

Madison. Here, there were several choices to be considered: the Cumberland Presbyterian Church, McFerrin Missionary Baptist Church, the Madison Church of Christ and the Cornerstone Church, a church we had heard about from several friends. The Cornerstone Church had worship services on television, parts of which we had watched on one or two occasions. But it was now only 9:30 a.m.Their worship service was at 10:00 a.m. Would God be pleased with this? Was this genuflecting ever so slightly at the altar of the Titans? Maybe they just like long services.

We drove past the few churches between I-65 and Gallatin Road on Old Hickory Boulevard. After we crossed over Gallatin Road we saw a Seventh Day Adventist church and a church called "The Turning Point, A Pentecostal Experience." Perhaps some day we could come back to one of these two churches but since it was getting close to 10:00 a.m., we decided to go back to the Cornerstone Church. We had heard that it was a Pentecostal church but nothing on the sign, or later on the church's literature, directly says that it is Pentecostal. Was this in the way of the community church wave? No entangling alliances, maybe?

We pulled into an enormous parking lot which would make the Titans envious — both of its size and definitely of its organized, efficient parking attendants. As we drove in, a sign read "Visitors blink your lights." I did not know how to blink the lights in Betty's car. She has automatic lights and prefers that no one "fool with them." Nevertheless, I stopped at the polite attendant standing helpfully near the 'blink' sign. "Are you visitors?" he asked courteously. Upon confirmation that we were, and noting Betty's handicapped sign in the car (she has had both hips replaced, thankfully very successfully), he used his "Nextel" or some similar walkie-talkie to tell the men on down the line that we were visitors with a handicapped person on board. We moved on to be received by attendants waiting to pass us on to the next friendly attendant until finally we were comfortably parked about 50 yards from the front door of the church. Very friendly, very impressive!

We were greeted at the door by another friendly soul, this one nearer our own age. He invited us into a large open foyer in which there were about two hundred new arrivals. Betty and I both opted to go to the restroom. (Do I need to remind you we are 70-plus-years-old? All that coffee at Fran and Jay's was kicking in.) We then rendezvoused at the entrance to an enormous, cavernous sanctuary. We later guessed that the sanctuary had a seating capacity of about 3,000 people. The space was impressive with its massive size, cleanliness and relative newness. We wandered our way through hundreds of congregants and worked our way to the very last pew in the center-right section of this modern-day tabernacle.

As we were seated, we began to appraise the totality of the premises. This was the largest church building that I had ever seen up close. There was a stage at least 100 feet wide hidden by an enormous green theater-type curtain. Shortly after we were seated, the curtain dramatically opened to the music of a well-rehearsed band or orchestra and the voices of an extremely large choir of perhaps a hundred or more. The choir was dressed in green robes with yellow sashes. Everything was very crisp and very contemporary. The choir was singing, "Lord, let the Holy Ghost come on down," over and over as they awakened the congregation to lively worship. And the congregation stood in response.

Next the choir and the song director (who wore no robe but was dressed in a dark suit as were all the other ministers) led the still-standing congregation in singing *Victory in Jesus* — "He sought me and bought me with His redeeming blood." The words to the hymn were transcribed sequentially across two very large screens located on each side of the pulpit. Each of the screens appeared to be at least 20 feet square. The music called forth a spirited response from many in the congregation. Hundreds were waving their arms and swaying to the rhythm of the music and to God. The dignitaries who would lead the various parts of the service were in the 'Bull Pen' to the congregation's left while the band was front and center with the choir also centered behind them.

The congregation was totally mixed in terms of ages — not just a youth movement here. We did not feel at all out of place. Many young people were there to be certain. But Betty and I had no fear that we would perhaps be asked if we wanted a lift to the old folks' home or to a separate service for old folks, similar to the children's services held in many churches. I should not offer that thought out of fear that it might give too many churches too many ideas. If I believed these words would be read by anyone other than a few loyal friends, I would indeed keep such seditious thoughts to myself. Another thing, there were more than a few men wearing suits. The older ones primarily, to be sure, but suits or jackets were worn freely, nonetheless.

We continued to stand for a full fifteen minutes from the first song until completing a song about how the Lord has "Fire in His eyes and a sword in His hands." In the song the Lord rides on a white horse and He asks, "Will you ride with me?" The congregation answered by singing "We will ride with the Army of the Lord and with the Armies of Heaven we will fight. Yes, Lord, we will stand up and fight." The song director and the choir led the congregation to sing over and over many times "rekindle the fire in me, Lord, once again," and the congregation responded gratefully with much exultation and praise for the Lord. We were then given a respite and a seat before the pastor read the scripture lesson for the day.

The Senior Pastor was a real honest-to-goodness senior-looking man named Maury Davis. He was a mature, trim man somewhere in his 50s and he wore a neatly fitted black suit. Pastor Davis asked members of the congregation whether they had brought their Bibles to the service. "If you did bring your Bible," he said, "please stand and let us read together." Almost all the congregation stood. I did not stand because I did not bring my Bible. I spotted some cheaters, however, who stood even though they did not hold Bibles. I considered tattling but decided against doing so; I never liked a snitch. Regardless, God knows who the cheaters are, we are told.

The distinguished and articulate pastor then invited the congregation to partake of the sacrament of the Lord's Supper. He said one need not be a member of the Assembly of God (the only reference to a denomination, either printed or spoken) and that all one needed to know was God and to be a Christian. He added that even if you were not currently a Christian but had decided to know God that you should partake. A simple ceremony to invite these new converts into the family of God could be held later on. The ushers were then instructed to pass trays holding some wafers of bread and cups of wine. Pastor Davis did offer a warning however. No one should eat or drink unworthily lest they be "guilty of the body and blood of Christ." His point was that one should partake with care and only with the knowledge that one is truly a Christian.

While the elements of the sacrament were being offered, the song director sang, "I can only imagine." Encouraging all those communing at the Lord's Table to pray as well, the pastor then offered a prayer, "Lord, I confess that Jesus Christ is Lord of my life. I receive you as my Lord. I receive you as my Father." He asked the members of the congregation to "take this bread" and "take this cup ...for as often as you do eat this bread and drink this cup you do proclaim His death 'till He comes." The song director said, "Just relax, stand if you wish, but just relax and sing...there is nothing like the presence of the Lord."

Then the pastor began his sermon and a question that was also the title of the sermon, "Are you naked, yet?" The church bulletin offered:

> Some of you are here because of the sermon title, which was intended to titillate your mind and get you in a frame of mind where I can really put the Word in you. You are going to leave here differently. And, this week if someone tells you how bad their life is, just ask them the great question: "Are you naked, yet?"

The pastor, one of ten including two pastors emeritus, then directed our attention to Job, a man of God in the Old Testament. Job was a very righteous man but the devil and the crowd said, "Of course, Job is a good man who serves God. Sure, he is good, but just look at him. He is wealthy. It is easy for Job to be righteous because he is rich." The senior pastor then shared what he described as the only joke he would tell during the service. The joke was from the *Readers Digest*, a publication second only to the Bible for many according to the pastor. I suspect the pastor himself did not feel that the joke was really worth telling. I did not and therefore will not repeat it here. My editors thank me, I am certain.

Pastor Davis, "Maury" as he referred to himself, offered that one is born naked. He said that you were once warm and comfortable in the womb until someone said, "Get out of there." And that someone then "smacked you on the butt and made you cry as you came into the world." He believed that many newborn Christians will remain as babies or "ninny" Christians. These are the people who disagree a lot and go around saying, "I have a right to my opinion." These are the people who go around "ninny, ninny, ninny," whining because everything does not go to suit them. He called them "baby Christians" and "immature Christians." Then he read *Hebrews 5: 12*, which says that there are those Christians who always are babies, who always need milk and cannot eat the real meat of the truth. These are "milk addicts" who do not want the real meat of adult Christians. "These people need to grow up," he said.

He then spoke about what it means to be a real adult Christian. They are the ones who do not "have" to go to church and who do not "have" to pay their tithes. Instead, they are the ones who "love" to go to church and who "love" to pay their tithes. If you have the spirit in you, he said, it will change you and "you will have a passion to serve the Lord." We need to learn to grow up and be mature Christians — "To learn to wear clothes." He said the hard part of growing up is that "you have to stay grownup" and will have to do things you do not like to do. He said, "I am grown up but I still hate raking leaves and stacking wood." He said that when you are grownup you will be discouraged and depressed. He noted that the great Englishman Winston Churchill suffered from depression and sixteen million Americans are said to be depressed. But, he said, when you are an adult Christian and encounter discouragement and depression, "Don't blame God. Keep your mouth shut." He said, "I have been in a lot of trouble in my life caused by a lot of things, caused by sin, caused by friends, caused by recession, but I did not blame God." He said, "When Job was troubled he did not complain to God, he turned to God." He concluded, "When we are troubled we should turn to God, to Jesus Christ."

He then asked the congregation to bow their heads for prayer. But before praying he asked those in need of prayer or in need of Jesus Christ to raise their hand. Many people raised their hand and he asked them to come to the altar so that he could pray with them. About 125 people went forward; the pastor then prayed, asking every one of them to repeat this prayer from their hearts, "Heavenly Father, in the name of Jesus Christ, I ask for forgiveness." He also asked them to repeat: "I pray that you will answer my prayer and I believe that my prayer will be answered." Then he asked them to return slowly to their seats as the song director sang: "I can only imagine." More and more people stood, waving their arms in the air, as the director sang over and over again, "I can only imagine." Then, for the first time in my life, I heard a woman near the front begin to speak in tongues. Her utterances were offered in a strange and haunting manner that intrigued me. It only lasted for a few seconds which was disappointing. I wanted to hear more. It was a sound the like of which I had never heard before.

Pastor Davis then asked the ushers to take the offering. He said that he had changed the order of worship a bit but, to be honest, I was wondering if he had perhaps forgotten the offering where it had originally been scheduled in the service. It's okay, senior pastor, no harm done. No threat to your status as senior pastor. Just don't do it again. The congregation, you see, had begun to think that they would be out of there real soon and without having to pay. The pastor also noted the time, 11:37 a.m., saying that the Titans would not begin playing for another 23 minutes. He shared with us that on the last game day he had not left for the stadium until well after 12:00 p.m. yet arrived at the game before the end of the first quarter. It was a perfect time to go, he said. No lines. No crowds at the food stands. He said, "Don't ever go early and fight that mess." Me thinks he protesteth too much; what doth thou thinketh?

Pastor Davis mentioned a Toyota dealership which would give $100 to the church when a member bought a car — obviously a commercial. He then invited a couple who had become missionaries to Kenya at their own expense onto the stage. They wanted to return to Kenya but were out of money. He asked the congregation to give a "love offering" while leaving the sanctuary in support of their loving effort. After they spoke a few words about their call and their work, we were dismissed to go hear the kick-off on our car radio.

The Steelers received the kick-off just before we got in our car. According to the radio announcer the Steelers had run for a touchdown on the first play after the kick-off. The Steelers were ahead, 7 – 0, after only 15 seconds of play. Was this a sign of retribution to this congregation for forgetting the sacredness of 11:00 a.m.? Or a warning to Senior Pastor Davis for forgetting the sanctity of 12:00 p.m.? Senior Pastor Scottie at the Christ Community Church had surely been warned a few weeks ago. On that occasion God allowed opponents of the Titans an early 14 – 0 lead while Pastor Scottie, servant of the Lord, forgot that God is not impressed by the "much speaking" of even well-meaning desecraters of revered religious traditions. Some of these traditions started as far back in history as the late 1990s when the Titans moved to Nashville from Houston.

Senior Pastor Davis probably did not lose his job which he says he really loves. He had plans to make it up to the congregation by hosting a great big Titans' tailgate party the very next Sunday when the Titans were out of town. Guess we came here on the wrong Sunday. Oh, well, maybe we'll have better luck next time. At least I was not a baby about it. I did not "ninny, ninny, ninny" just because I had not been told about the upcoming tailgate party early enough to make plans. I tried to act like a grownup about it. Senior Pastor Maury will be happy that someone got the message today.

Chapter 11

Bellevue Community Church
Bellevue, Tennessee
November 24, 2002

S ome trees never give up, but the diehards were very few at
the end of November. Almost all the leaves had disappeared
in the wake of a cold snap and fall was becoming less and less
colorful. Do the trees with remaining leaves hold on for fear of the
unknown months of cold ahead? Or do they hold on because they
are "never-give-up-till-the-fat-lady-sings" trees? Maybe some of
both. The realistic trees had already "bitten the bullet" and had
"bought the farm" for the winter months ahead.

In spite of the lack of color, it was a remarkably cheerful looking day. The atmosphere was clear, crisp and fresh, but not cold
enough for "smoking breaths" as Betty and I walked to our car at
8:15 a.m., heading out for another blue-roading Sunday. Now, however, is as good a time as any to fully clarify what a "blue road" truly
is. It's not a cut-and-dried matter at all. "Blue roads," generally, are
the back roads that are either blue or black by some capricious
decision of the cartographers. I imagine these fellows probably sit
in some dark and dank, smoke filled room somewhere unimportant
deciding, in god-like fashion, the "importance" of the various
branches of the road system which they were drawing that day.
Considering the roads they are mapping one day they probably say,
"This one is a grand, heavily traveled super highway. So, let's bestow
upon it the grand and regal color of red, and this other one richly
deserves the friendly color of green." They probably feel as if they
have just given birth to a grand scheme which will guide weary
traveling pilgrims on the way to true highway bliss. Considering all
the rest of the roads they are mapping they probably say, "Let's just
let all the others be blue or black according to the availability of the
supply of ink at the friendly printers," as if these "left over" roads
have no real significance.

The cartographers probably should have chosen purple for this day's chosen routes. Betty says that the color purple is a combination of both red and blue. We live on Woodmont Boulevard in Nashville. Only a year or two ago Woodmont definitely was a jet black or midnight blue road. It has changed from the blue-black road it was only months ago and seemed a nearly red purple road, if the volume of traffic has anything to do with influencing the mind of the coloring cartographers of Nashville, Tennessee. But Woodmont this day had temporarily reverted back to basic blue as we started our trek. There were very few pilgrims traversing our trail. In the midst of a busy city, we were leisurely blue roading as soon as we left our home even though Woodmont is definitely a true purple road for at least five days a week.

West End or Harding Road, a four to five lane road that was a greenish red road on most other days, was accommodating our blue roading desire on what was a beautiful day. We turned west on this receptive route, which only two days earlier, would have been consti- pated with cars as if it were a NASCAR event under a yellow flag. With a respite from this five-day event, we were respectfully allowed to meander at a leisurely pace west on West End/Harding Road/Highway 100/Highway 70 all balled into one blue road. It was as if God had hung a great sign at every intersection reading, "Sunday: No Race Today!!" With only ladies and gentlemen drivers allowed behind the wheel, we found ourselves acknowledging a silent "Good morning, hope you have a great day" attitude which seemed to emanate from the smiling face of every driver. Everyone seemed to be going no place in particular on a marvelous blue-road Sunday.

The day's blue roading experience was going to be a rather short one today because of other commitments I had made for early afternoon. But the day had turned out to be an absolutely perfect day for a long and leisurely back-road pilgrimage. I hate it when I make plans that alter the potential for relaxed and spontaneous adventures. At times like this I revert back to what the Greeks called "Kyros" time instead of "Kronos" time. Kyros time is meaning-filled time. In Kyros mode, then, chronological time is compressed or expanded according to the circumstances. Today we needed to compress a lot of meaning into a relatively short period of chrono- logical time. And we did.

After passing St. George's Episcopal Church on Harding Road at the intersection of Belle Meade Blvd., just a few blocks from home, we began to wonder how many of the very wealthy Belle Meade residents would make it to St. George's that morning. According to the number of neatly parked vehicles, many wretched souls were seeking the answers to life's many perplexing questions —among which were probably some of the most constant ones such as: Is it really easier for a camel to pass through the eye of a needle than for a rich man to enter the kingdom of heaven?; Will the recent surge in the market allow us to catch up on our tithes before the end of this tax year?; and, Will Vanderbilt be able to break a twenty-year losing streak to the Tennessee Volunteers?

While the communicants at St. George's, which is clearly in the city limits of Belle Meade, meditated on these and other soul-wrenching almost imponderables, we moved west on Harding Road, passing on the right, and 'across the tracks,' the congregation of the Belle Meade Methodists. Hopefully those attending this service were confessing their sins, including surely the sin of envy as evidenced by the congregations' masquerading as BelleMeaders even though their place of worship is clearly across the railroad tracks and out-side the city limits of the fifth-richest city in the United States. We had visited both churches in the past for weddings and funerals but never for worship services. We were hoping to visit them again sometime in the future — especially before the hopefully good-natured members of the congregations have a chance to read these words. I was struck by the fear that their membership rolls includ-ed those individuals who have it within their power to call due each and every one of my bank loans.

While the members of these churches were possibly considering calling my loans, I began to hear the not-so-faint call of my stomach as a reminder that no man's financial life should end on an empty stomach. Luckily, we just happened to be near one of the reportedly best breakfast places in the city, LePeep. Granted, this 'Class A' breakfast restaurant was located on the purplish blue roads inside the City of Nashville. But my stomach was warning me that it was not time to get technical. As if struck by a blinding light — not unlike the one which blinded Paul on his way to Tarsus — I saw the sign of the Le Peep Restaurant. I surrendered and went peacefully into what might have been my last meal in a life out of bankruptcy, especially if an insider mole somehow revealed these secret words to my banking enemies. (Are bankers ever truly friends? I mean, come on now.) That's right. My banking enemies masquerade as members of St. George's Episcopal and Belle Meade Methodist. "Good" banks encourage their employees to pretend to be real people, joining churches and Lions Clubs and letting their kids play in the little leagues. Anything to cause us to think that they are real, that they actually have a cardiovascular system.

Inside LePeep, I saw several of them. I decided to eat with the enemy for my last meal outside debtors' prison. They did not know me but I recognized a couple of them. They were with wives and children but really they were lurking to see how many of the customers were paying their checks with borrowed money. And from the prices on the menu, I knew I was going to have to borrow money from Betty or I might end up in debtors' prison even today, long before my revealing words would fall into the hands of my enemies. Actually, the prices were not all that high compared on an item-by-item basis with other true blue road breakfast locations. But LePeep also had many choices not offered in most blue-road places and the prices of these items were slightly higher. My ample proportions tell any bystander that I am a pushover for the best and the richest food available. And since this was going to be my last meal...

The menu at Le Peep revealed that if this was a country, blue road restaurant, it was a country French, blue-road restaurant with contemporary appointments. This French roadhouse's menu was divided into three sections: Le Breakfast, Le Brunch, and Le Lunch. Le Breakfast and Le Brunch had le items that Le Brownings found interesting. Under the heading of Le Breakfast there were selections from Bagel and Shmear (a.k.a., cream cheese) for $2.95 all the way to Steak and Eggs for $7.95. In between, there was a Breakfast Banana Split with bananas, strawberry compote, yogurt, pineapple and granola for $4.25 and Aspen Fruit Crepes for $5.25. There was also a section called "The Benedicts," which in my mind was a thinly veiled attempt to honor one of the bankers emeritus of a leading bank in Nashville. Betty decided to ignore this possibility and ordered Eggs Benedict for $7.50. I ordered a full breakfast, The Lumberjack, which included three eggs over-medium, bacon, peasant potatoes, biscuits and three pancakes. This started out at $7.85 but with the add-ons who knows what it ended up costing and who cares? It's borrowed money anyhow.

The waitress (my theory still holding true about the obvious discrimination against male waiters here) brought coffee tout suite as we continued to marvel at the many selections on the menu. I wondered how they could prepare all this many dishes and keep the quality up. I will give them credit for trying at any rate;I admire all those who will make the effort.Efforts like this in restaurants are sort of like a dog playing checkers; we are not surprised if they do not do it well because we're just amazed that they try it at all. I was amazed that they offered "Pampered Eggs" with almost any vegetable and/or meat and "The Great Lite Way" featuring egg whites with a whole variety of vegetable and meat items to accompany them. There were also numerous selections of pancakes with berries, wheat germ or granola. In addition, French toast, Belgian waffles, combinations of several items under (what else?) Les Combos, a whole array of omelets and "Panhandled Skillet Dishes" were also available. Perhaps now you see more clearly what I meant about a dog playing checkers.

The LePeep Pups, however, played a fine game with us — not perfect, but nearly so. Betty's Eggs Benedict were excellent. And my eggs and bacon were beautifully prepared and couldn't have been better. But the biscuits and potatoes needed some help. The biscuit did not "hold up" under the pressure of a real hungry man eating his last meal in freedom. And the potatoes were held after cooking a little too long and were of a leathery texture. Now the pancakes were superb and enormous! They would be a real treat for a very hungry man , whether on the ways to the gallows or not, but I had designed this part of my breakfast as a dessert.As a result, half of one of the three pancakes was all I could handle. They were very light and almost as good as those found at the Pancake Pantry. But not quite.

The Le Peep in the Belle Meade Galleria Shopping Center on Harding Road is located in the middle of the shopping area. The décor is simple yet sophisticated.A couple of large paintings on the walls depicted aristocrats in formal evening clothes and one lady holding opera-type glasses set the tone for how much the patrons probably think of themselves when they are not in their banking clothes. Bankers don't just go to church, you know. They eat, too. I guess you don't have to have a cardiovascular system to eat. But bankers have a stomach for anything. Know what I mean?

Our check came to $28.75, an amount double to triple the bill in most blue-road Les Brownings restaurants. It was well worth it to Les Brownings, without a doubt. We paid our check (with a credit card, of course) and got out of there before they realized that we probably were not entitled to be there; we actually don't live in Belle Meade even though we live in the same zip code. Anyhow, I did not feel up to defending this point and left a generous tip so that the waitress would not reveal our secret. (I am sure she knew. Waitresses have a way of finding out things, you know?).

It was about 9:30 a.m. when we left the restaurant and found our way out onto Highway 70 headed towards Dickson and Memphis. After a few miles we passed St. Henry's Catholic Church and then the Jewish Community Center, both within a gunshot of Belle Meade. I am sure they all probably refer to themselves as being "in the Belle Meade area." And they are, but they are not. Close, but no cigar, lady! That's the way the cookie crumbles. Them's the breaks of the game. If you live in Belle Meade, you earn tremendous bragging rights and you pay for them through the nose. Just a few blocks more and we were at Nine Mile Hill, a dividing line between the Belle Meade area and the Bellevue area. The line has faded a little since Catherine Darnell of *The Tennessean* quit Bellevue bashing a few years ago. The top of the hill, for all practical reasons, is the gateway to Bellevue, a thriving comfortable community which has experienced amazing growth in the last decade.

The churches have also grown right along with Bellevue in the post-Darnell era. In the heart of Bellevue, we turned right, or north, onto Old Hickory Boulevard to see the West Meade Fellowship, which bills itself as an "International Church." I was interested in attending this community church but the times of service were not posted. We drove back to Highway 70 and continued west again, passing several relatively new churches or churches with relatively new facilities: The Bellevue Presbyterian, The Bellevue Baptist, The Bellevue Church of Christ, and The Bellevue Grace Assembly of God.

We soon passed under I-65 and continued west on Highway 70. We kept marveling at the tremendous growth of a once sleepy little blue-roads village only ten to twenty years ago. A mile or so farther out of Bellevue we came to the Bellevue Community Church on the left. We had passed the BCC a few Sundays ago and were intrigued at the number of cars coming and going. But we had not seen the actual church facilities, only the entrance. The sign announced that services were held at 8:30, 10:00 and 11:30 a.m. It was now about 9:45 and so we decided that the BCC would be our church for today. We turned into an inviting entrance and soon we realized why we had not actually seen the church facilities;they are located on a large church campus about one-half mile from Highway 70 on a very attractive, well kept entrance road.

As we neared the church, there were hundreds of cars in the multiple parking lots with the 8:30 people leaving as the 10:00 people arrived.Active traffic controllers directed us hurriedly on to a parking space, making certain that we did not miss one minute of the service. Betty put her "handicapped" sign on the rearview mirror and we were ushered to a spot about 50 yards from the building, just as we were last Sunday. The main building is a red brick con-temporary facility that looked as much like a school as a church, and maybe it is. There were also several temporary-type out buildings indicating a need for more future permanent facilities. Some of these had signs that read, "Kids Place, 1 – 2 – 3 – A fun place to learn about God."

At about 9:50 a.m. we entered the auditorium or sanctuary as you please. I am not sure how the church members refer to it, but it was certainly more auditorium looking than most other church facilities. It reminded me of two other large community-type churches we had visited in the last few weeks; each one had a very large, contemporary, open space with a theater-type ceiling from which hung all sorts of air conditioning ducts, lights, and speakers. Also, like the others, the BCC had three large screens hanging across the "stage," as one minister called it. (His terminology, thus, was part of the reason for thinking of the building as more of an auditorium, than a traditional sanctuary). Band equipment was placed all across the stage ready for something to happen. Identical banners, hung from the ceiling on each side of the stage, offered the following words: "Unmet Needs, Unresolved Anger, Unfinished Business, Unwanted Pain, Unrealistic Expectations, Unexplained Goodness, Unshared Values."

The church bulletin introduced the senior and founding pastor, Dr. David Foster. He founded the church in 1989 after graduating from the Free Will Baptist Bible College, Mid America Baptist Seminary and Reformed Theological Seminary. The bulletin spoke to Foster's vision to "to build a dynamic community of faith, which encourages and empowers people to grow and stretch to the maximum of their God given potential." We were informed that the pastor would not be there this day but were given greetings from him by the "Chief of Staff," Randy Thompson.

The screens began to scroll down the time countdown to the beginning of the service 3:00 minutes, 2:59, 2:58, 2:57. With 1:30 left to go the band began to gather. There was a piano/keyboard, two sets of drums, four guitars, one violin and three singers. Precisely at: 01 the band began to play, what was to me, rock-style music. Almost magically, the whole auditorium was now completely filled. A man walked down the aisle with a pigtail and a leather cap still on, sat on the front row and then, finally, removed his hat. How strange. Some faiths believe no one should worship with uncovered heads. Most Christians, however, believe it shows disrespect to God when a man enters a sanctuary with a hat on his head. Yet the same concept does not apply to women in the same setting.

While the band played a lively and pulsating rhythm, Jeff Wood led the congregation in a performance-style direction of several gospel rock songs. The congregation stood, rhythmically swaying and clapping just as one would expect at a rock concert.

The difference between the BCC and the other community churches I had recently visited emerged at this point. At the other two community churches the animated motions of the congregation consisted of heavenward lifting of the hands in a seeming act of praise to God. The swaying and the clapping of hands of the BCC congregation, however, seemed to be more about keeping rhythm with the band and song leader Jeff Wood. The emphasis, so it seemed, was as much on the beat of the music as it was on the words.

Some of the words included, "I feel His presence. It's become my passion...All I want to do is please Him...When I do, what I do in this life is not for me, but for Jesus" and "I will sing to my God with my dying breath...If I'm rich or if I'm poor...I'll sing a song to praise the Lord." The lights then dimmed with theatrical precision as Jeff Wood sang, "Holy, Holy, Holy, Lord God Almighty," a new rock-style arrangement. The congregation was 99 and 44/100% pure young people who were uniform in their casual dress. There were no ties. Zero. Zilch. I spotted three sport coats out of the 1000 – 1500 or so in attendance. I wish I'd known. I, too, prefer to dress informally and do so 99 percent of the time. But I'm learning.

Some of the words to another song were, "God's bigger than the air that I breathe...All we do is change the old to the new...God will save the day." During the song the lights were raised as the music-oriented congregation resumed clapping and swaying enthusiastically to a beat that struck a chord in most of their beings. The singer/leader then segued back into, "The world is shaking with the love of God." and "God is greater than the air that I breathe."

At this point Randy Thompson, who identified himself as the "Chief of Staff," made several announcements. He was dressed in a long-sleeve, crew-neck shirt and sleeveless sweater with some kind of identification badge hanging on the front of his sweater. He then led an offertory prayer before reminding the congregation that there would be no mid-week service because of the upcoming Thanksgiving holiday. "If you are bored with your in-laws," he said, "you can tell them you are going to church and you can just come up here and drive around the campus for a while to break the boredom."

Thompson announced that Ed Holland, the guest speaker today, would be on "the stage" in just a few minutes. Jeff Wood then sang a rousing rock song entitled *Like Paper, Like Fire.* The song spoke of the misspent lives of a young man and young woman whose days would burn up "like paper and fire." At the end of the song the curtain dropped as a stage hand brought out a stool and a simple music-stand type pulpit.

Ed Holland then strolled out onto the stage, left hand in his gray pants pocket in a motivational speaker type gait, and said he was going to speak today about "Unresolved Anger." As he walked back and forth, "warming up the audience" in his most collegiate demeanor, dressed in a long-sleeve sweater over an open-necked shirt, he told us that the day's topic had been assigned to him by the senior pastor. He gave no such indication that, "God laid this message on my heart today." He simply said that he was given the topic by Dr. Foster in a way that emphasized he had no choice but to follow the senior pastor's instructions.

He began by pointing out that we have all hurt someone and have all been hurt by someone because of anger. And that this hurt causes estrangement between us and our fellow human-beings. He used Adam and Eve's relationship with God as an example. "God," he said, "created us so that we could choose to love Him back." Adam and Eve chose otherwise and became estranged from God. But God did not give up; He pursued Adam and Eve as He pursues all of us. Ed identified the root of anger as "ruptured relationships," just as it was for Adam and Eve. Ed then called for a clip from the recent movie *Changing Lanes* in which the characters of Ben Affleck and Samuel Jackson become angry over a fender-bender. Then they allowed their anger to grow into deep anger that resulted in attempts at vengeance. His point was that this is the way things will grow if we allow our relationships to be ruptured by anger.

Ed also said another root of anger was broken promises. He shared his experience of living in Southern Florida, the hot bed of "hanging chads," where he witnessed so many sad and lonely older people. They were sad because of the promises their families had broken to continue to love and to visit them during their last years. The promises were not kept and many, many of these people are old, alone, sad and angry. He then pointed out that many people in the audience were sad and angry because of similar broken promises. He told a story about Ronald Reagan being saddened by a broken relationship with Jane Wyman. Reagan apparently said that he was hurt because he had no one to love him back.

Speaker Ed then identified another root of rage and anger as "splintered egos." He said, "God wants us to be emotionally healthy. To do this we must love ourselves, accept ourselves." He continued by saying that God has given us worth and we need to let our splintered egos be healed in the light of God's love. Next he identified even another root of anger as "unfulfilled expectations." He told us that things often do not turn out as we expect and we experience hurt and anger as a result. He cited the great expectations we all have about marriage. The hurt and anger that follow a divorce come from the expectations and hopes for the marriage that have gone unfulfilled.

Ed noted that while we should have "righteous indignation" when wronged we should not have anger. This is a very thin line to walk. To have righteous indignation toward someone who has hurt us sounds very suspiciously like anger toward that person instead of at the devil who caused the "brokenness" to begin with. He told us that the journey toward freedom over anger comes when our anger can be directed in positive ways. And that the reward is when we rebuild our relationships.

He ended this "Power of Positive thinking" type sermon with a prayer and asked us to pray with him: "Dear Heavenly Father...I have hurt others." He then asked us to pray for God's help in building back our broken relationships and our relationship to God.

As if he were leaving a lecture hall, the speaker said, "Thank you all for coming and have a great day." Thus, the service concluded abruptly. The parking attendants began to helpfully rush us out in order to make room for the next service. The members of the next audience were probably somewhere nearby contractually agreeing to hear the speaker of the day as the price to be paid for getting to sing along with the gospel rock music — directed by the star of The Jeff Wood Show. They seemed to be saying, "Move quickly now, please. The next show starts in ten minutes. Thank you. Please come again."

Chapter 12

New Life United Pentecostal Church
Smithville, Tennessee

December 1, 2002

S ometime during the last three weeks of November our weekend home in the woods had become a lake home again, a miracle that happens at approximately the same time every year. Mother Nature strips all the deciduous trees of unbelievably beautiful foliage in order to craft a warm blanket for the new seeds and shoots bedded down for the coming winter months. And, voila, the lake suddenly appears. It is as if Seigfried and Roy have dramatically pulled away the veil of spring, summer and fall to reveal the fabulously blue waters of Center Hill Lake to those sitting in the "cheap seats" of the surrounding lake area.

Once again, those of us with weekend homes on Hurricane Hill Drive can see with our own eyes that the lake has reappeared. Those sitting in the "club seats" around the lake are not privileged to see this magic trick performed by the touring team of Mother Nature masquerading as the "Vegas magicians." From lofty and snooty perches atop high and mighty hilltops, their senses are dulled by the over indulgences of their optical senses. They "think" they see the real lake all year long but, in fact, they never see the "real lake" at all. They are not aware, as Plato was, that "their lake" is just like the shadows on the walls of their caves. The real winter beauty of the deep blue waters framed by the grayish beige of the sleeping trees and the aging rocks along the shoreline can only be seen by those whose eyes have not been blinded by looking too long on the summer-like flames from the fires of their commodious caves.

Those around the lake whose precious vision has been spared, thanks to nine months of peering through the shadowbox of comfortable trees and foliage at the eclipse of the lake, could now see clearly with the magic of wintertime upon the lake. During the winter season we have the best seats in the house as the lake becomes a beautiful part of the winter-world, but not our whole world. If this seems like "cheap seat, lake-spin" at least we have come to believe it. Beauty is in the eye of the beholder and "behold!," the lake appears for the first time in months. Thanks Seigfreid and Roy, whoever and wherever you are.

Betty and I arrived at our lake winter wonderland on November the 27th, the day before Thanksgiving, in order to get things ready for the holiday dinner the next day. Our daughters Barbara and Beverly, as well as Barbara's friend Dave Kazmarowski, were coming for Thanksgiving the next day. It was to be a cooperative family affair. Beverly was making cornbread dressing and a squash casserole. Barbara was preparing a twice-baked potato casserole and bringing the ingredients to make a blueberry crisp pie. Betty and I were bringing a 15-pound double turkey breast to roast and making a salad with new broccoli, onion, raisins and sunflower seeds. I also brought two Amaretto cream pies and some brownies that I had made. Maybe I am telling you more than you want to know, but I just had to tell somebody.

Barbara, Beverly and Dave arrived at the scene of the magical happening around noon on Thanksgiving Day. The turkey was in the G.E. fiery furnace and well on its way to its expected and appointed time of resurrection at 1:00 p.m. After popping the two casseroles into the oven to warm there were three images in the "furnace." The salad and cranberries waited impatiently among all five of us now. At 12:45 a.m. Sister Schubert's rolls were added to 'leaven' the meal. We unanimously joined the clean plate club, not because of the poor hungry children in China but because we did have a very fine Thanksgiving feast. We all truly had so much for which to be thankful.

After the holiday meal we progressed to the real reason the pilgrims started Thanksgiving. Football. The true wishes of our fore-fathers were honored as we dutifully watched football for the remainder of the afternoon. Please don't give me a pop quiz on the outcome or the score. Give me a break. Not one of us could probably even remember what we dreamed about as we alternately watched the flames dance off the beautifully warm fire, and the football bounce crazily to the delight of millions of pilgrims around the country on Thanksgiving Day.

After the football game we watched a couple of movies before Dave headed back to Nashville. He was the sacrificial lamb sent back into the work force while the rest of us stayed behind for a couple of replays of the Thanksgiving dinner. The possibility that the poor people in China would eat turkey leftovers from the Brownings' Thanksgiving dinners was thereby further reduced. And, of course, more movies had to be watched. We had already paid for them, after all, in the expensive package we had contracted for with Direct TV.

Friday morning we had the usual "Thanksgiving Day After" breakfast consisting of scrambled eggs, bacon, toasted fruit and nut bread from Alpha Bakery in Bellevue and cantaloupe. The only new item was potato cakes made from Barbara's leftover twice-baked potatoes. There was also superb pear preserves on some leftovers from Sister Schubert's contribution to the Thanksgiving dinner. After breakfast everyone watched a couple more movies before taking a shakedown drive around the lake on Thanksgiving, Jr. day. Sadly for mom and pop, Barbara and Beverly then had to return to Nashville for more celebrating with their extended families of friends.

Betty and I enjoyed a marvelous day blue roading most of Saturday and then watching movies, each with his/her favorite companion in the whole world for the past 49 years. Sunday morning we got up and left our now lake-view house at 8:10 a.m., driving south on Hwy. 56 toward Smithville. About nine miles later we turned right and drove around the Smithville square, a comfortable county seat. It finds its "comfort" primarily thanks to the fifteen or so miles separating it from I-40. Any closer and it would have been too close for comfort. As it was, the distance was just right. And it couldn't have been any nearer right than it was on Thanksgiving Day, III.

We drove past the "twin churches" located near the square — Methodist and Baptist churches which appear to be identical twins. They look to be the same age and of the same parentage from an architectural standpoint. They also appear to be about the same size and are located on the same block, just across a narrow street from each other. I could only hope that the two were as close to each other in every other way as they seemed to be from the outside. Of course, there were differences. There always are, even between twins. But I just hoped that, as they grew older together, they would realize more and more that their true similarities were much more substantial than any superficial ones. We did some blue roading around several of the back streets of this non-'burb of any man's city. We then turned south again onto Broad Street, also Highway 70, to begin the search for a place to have our Thanksgiving III breakfast.

As noted at least once before, many blue road breakfast places are closed on Sundays. Many of those that do open on Sundays delay opening until about 11:00 a.m., officially past the mystical breakfast period according to notable authorities on the subject such as McDonalds, Burger King and Hardee's. Those places incarcerate employees if they broker an egg biscuit after 10:30 a.m. any day. Any unsold biscuits as of 10:29 a.m. are packaged and sent to China. Never mind the poor hungry Americans who happened to sleep late that particular day. The slow boat to China must be leaving in a hurry. But luck was with us. We found Cathy's Café, a real all-American blue road breakfast place. Cathy's Café had decided to let the pinko Chinese communists eat rice because they served breakfast foods to customers all day long, as long as they were open or until they ran out of eggs. They open at 5:00 a.m. every morning, a fitting time for any self-respecting 15-miles-from-the-interstate-country restaurant. When we entered at 8:45 a.m., the attractive waitress who came to our table had already worked almost half of an eight-hour shift. She would be on her way home at 1:00 p.m. if the bureaucrats at OSHA have their way about the matter.

Betty noticed right off that our waitress had braces on her teeth. She said she felt sorry for her because her boyfriend would probably drop her. Betty firmly believes that she and I broke up one time when we were dating during our school years because she started wearing braces. I assured her that I had thought braces were cool ever since I could remember; I thought anyone who wore braces was rich. My first girlfriend, in my mind, Jenny Mae Brewster back in West Virginia wore braces as a cheerleader and I have liked girls in braces ever since. But Betty will not be dissuaded. She still thinks we broke up because she started wearing them. I really did like them. Even the metallic taste.

We were still debating the issue of braces when our dentally-challenged waitress brought the first cup of coffee and took our order. Betty ordered two eggs scrambled, bacon and toast. I ordered three eggs over easy/medium, my new way of ordering eggs. Of course I also ordered bacon, grits and biscuits, too. With gnashing of braces, which I found fetching, she assured us the order would be out very soon. We had just enough time to psychoanalyze a few of the people there before having to concentrate on our meal. The patrons were mostly men. Cathy's Café was obviously a coffee hangout for men who like their women in braces. Or perhaps it was the neat, tight fighting overalls with bibs that were sort of the uniform for the waitresses. I liked them almost as much as I liked the braces.

While noticing two men talking, I noted to Betty that I could tell the level of friendship or acquaintance between people when I see them speaking without hearing a word being said. The two men I had noticed were not really close friends. How did I know? The man speaking was using wide gestures as if trying to convince his breakfast companion of something. Also, a sort of nervous grin often crept across the speaker's face as if the points being made were done so in an obsequious manner not required when one speaks to a close friend. With close friends, we relax more, do not feel pressure to impress and do not feel nervousness when talking about anything. Thus, one man's silent speaking revealed that they were acquainted, but not close friends.

A man and a wife were not speaking at all. What was their problem? They came in, ordered and never looked at each other. They never spoke a word but did not appear to be angry with each other because their faces were relaxed. They seemed just bored. I felt sorry for them. It was a beautiful day and they could find absolutely nothing they wished to share with each other. They were both dressed in nice Sunday morning, not-going-to-church clothes. His car keys indicated that he drove a Lexus. He wore cowboy boots and his pants and shirt were both nicely pressed. He also wore an expensive cowboy hat which he kept on the entire time they were in the restaurant, apparently following local custom because all the other men also wore their own particular style of headgear while eating. One pilgrim had on a nice brown Saturday/Sunday morning sport coat, a buttoned cotton shirt and a white painter-type cap. Several other men wore hunting caps. But the cowboy and the cowgirl were not going to the next square dance. At least, not together. Breakfast had to be eaten somewhere and, so, why not go together? It wasn't going to hurt either one of them; they knew that. But life is too short to go to dances with either boring or ugly people. So, the barn dance is out, partner. And it's not because you are ugly.

Jenny Mae (I'll call the waitress after my first "girlfriend" in honor of her braces) brought our breakfasts and, smiling unselfconsciously through her braces, asked if she could bring us anything else. Still feeling sorry for her, Betty politely said, "Just a little more jelly, please." Betty could not believe that the pitiful little dab of jelly which had been served was for two obviously still-growing adults. I reminded Betty that for $2.25 each, we could not be too choosy. Jenny Mae soon returned with another dab even smaller than the first one. Well, Jenny Mae was a cheerleader, not a waitress anyhow. We remembered the $2.25 and pressed the point no more.

The food was just as tasty as the décor in Cathy's Café, which was neat, clean, and the reflection of a proud owner's personal taste. It was obvious that the country-like items had been carefully chosen and placed neatly, both in the no-smoking room and in the main dining room where smokers and friends who wanted to be friendly gathered. Cathy gets an A+ for her effort on everything but the biscuits. With Pillsbury frozen biscuits available at Kroger's, there's no reason for a C- in biscuits when Kroger gets a B+, and maybe even A-. Cathy, in this open letter, I tell you as a new friend — go to Kroger's and nuke the nuke box. Just the one you use for biscuits, not the one that heats your gravy. You'll thank me for telling you. And all the $2.25 paying customers will thank you. It might even get the cowboy and cowgirl so happy that they might smile at each other again, maybe even go dancing.

I didn't want to offer my suggestion to Jenny Mae, what with her braces and all. After the two dabs of jelly matter, I was afraid she would come to us and ask like the worldly wise, gum-chewing waitress asked four overly critical women customers: "Ladies, is anything all right?" Believe me, Cathy, I like your place, your food and your friendly two-dab service but 86 the present biscuits and serve only toast until you can, at the very least, wean your kitchen staff off the microwave.

I left my Jenny Mae a nice tip to help her pay for her braces before we left to search for a church to attend. It was 9:15 a.m. as we drove east on Highway 70 toward the Sligo area of the lake. We spotted several possible smaller churches, doubled back and then turned south again on Highway 56 towards McMinnville, the plant-nursery capitol of the area. After only a few blocks we saw the New Life United Pentecostal Church on the left and determined that, since we had not yet been to a Pentecostal church, it would be our choice for the day.

The service began at 10:00 a.m. but I determined that, at about 75 miles away from Nashville, the church was probably outside the TADI, "Titans' area of Dominant Influence." In other words, the choice of the 10:00 a.m. hour probably had nothing to do with the 12:00 a.m. game time of the Titans. And just maybe they had some explanation as to why they ignored the scriptural 11:00 a.m. worship hour. I gave them the benefit of the doubt that the time of the service was not a blatant rejection of what is right and proper. Anyhow, that's between God and them, right? At 9:50 a.m. we entered the church and made a beeline to the right-hand side of the back pew, which was comfortably padded with a pleasant medium green upholstering — both the seats and the backs of the pews. Some worker bees intercepted the beeline flight; they pleasantly greeted us, "Welcome to our church. Praise the Lord." The only variation on these words of genuine welcome was a reversal in the order of the words, "Praise the Lord. Welcome to our church." Our location became a veritable beehive as numerous members of the congregation made sure we felt welcome. The pastor and his wife also stopped by to erase any possible doubt about our being welcome to worship with them.

The church is a new contemporary brick building. Its sanctuary has a white cathedral ceiling and walls with neat paneled wainscoting about four feet high around the whole worship area. A band with two guitar players and one drummer was placed to the right of the pulpit area with a piano and organ on the left. In the center was a baptismal font, directly behind a single row of choir pews.

Suddenly, without any introduction, the band and choir began to perform a lively song entitled *Praise the Lord*. Most of the 75 or so members within the sanctuary (designed to seat some 200 individuals) offered considerable hand waving, clapping and rhythmic body movement. For the most part the members of the church were dressed in their Sunday finest clothes. Next a young man in a white shirt, tie and suspenders led the congregation in singing song Number 261: *He Took My Sins Away*. He had the most animation I had witnessed in the few months I had been attending different worship services. This young leader, who had difficulty keeping on tune, then led the congregation in singing, "Oh, I want to see Him ...Oh, I want to see Him, look upon His face, there to sing forever of His saving grace. On the streets of glory let me lift my voice, home at last, home at last, ever to rejoice."

Pastor Sanders then invited those with birthdays during the past week to stand; a lively *Happy Birthday* was sung to them. The pastor then recognized a woman from the congregation who went forward to invite the pastor's wife up to the pulpit in order to receive a birthday gift from the women of the church. The gift was a check for $150 in recognition for her loving hard work. She was instructed not to let Brother Sanders "have any of it."

Next, Sister Denise Flick came forward to report on a recent youth retreat in Nashville. However, she reported primarily on the level of giving from the congregation as it compared to all the other churches making up the entire denomination. She proudly reported that the Smithville congregation was first in per capita giving and second in dollar giving for the entire denomination. After the report Brother Sanders presented gifts of $150.00 and $200.00 to her, and her husband, in recognition of their work and achievements in raising the level of giving so dramatically.

The pastor then asked the ushers to pass the plates for the offering. While that was being done the choir of six women led the congregation in a lively singing of *We Will Worship the King*. Again, most of the congregation joined together in clapping hands and waving arms. The offering was followed by announcements from the pastor about choir practice, youth meetings and about the congregation's efforts to collect food for Christmas baskets and small toys for children.

The pastor asked us to stand for a prayer during which all members of the congregation prayed aloud individually while the pastor voiced his prayer. A solo followed by one of the members of the choir. Some members of the congregation joined her in singing at some points during the solo. Then the pastor welcomed everyone and, again, welcomed the Brownings in worshipping with his congregation.

Just before the pastor began to preach, a young girl brought a glass of water and put it on the pulpit next to him. He began by reading the scripture lesson from *Exodus*, Chapter 3. He started with Verse 7, where the Lord says that He had seen the affliction of His people and had heard their cries. The pastor said that the Hebrews had been in Egypt for 400 years, but Egypt was not their destiny and not their destination. He said God had promised them more — a land that flowed with milk and honey.

Brother Sanders announced the title of the sermon, "Disturbed into our Destiny." He said we should not become too relaxed, too comfortable in the world because this world was not our destiny. Microphone in hand, the pastor moved freely about the entire front of the church. He told how Pharaoh became worried about the growing number of Israelites in Egypt's midst. He began to make life hard for them and the oppression caused the Israelites to pray and the Lord "heard the cries of His people." They were disturbed and became aware that Egypt was not their destiny, the pastor declared. As he spoke he walked down to the level of the congregation, sitting on the level of the pulpit, and continued as if visiting in a living room.

The pastor said we were complacent until 9-11. He warned us to not become complacent again because it was going to happen again because so much sin was in the world. He said there was going to be chemical and biological warfare and that we would be seeing our children dying. He wondered if we were prepared for what is ahead with perhaps 10,000s upon 10,000s of body bags dominating the field of our vision.

He offered a story about how eagles build their nests carefully — first with large rough sticks, then with straw and lastly with feathers to make the nest comfortable as well as strong for the baby eagles. When it is time for the eagle chicks to leave the nest, however, the mother eagle removes the comfortable straw and feathers from the nest, thus making it uncomfortable. She then nudges the young eagles out of the nest time and time again until they are flying after having been disturbed into their destiny. He then said that God would do whatever it takes to disturb us and to show us our true destiny.

At 11:27 a.m. the pastor asked the congregation to stand. He continued preaching as we stood and walked over to sit on a chair on the pulpit level. He continued to speak about how God wanted to disturb us "out of our comfortable nests." God would show us the wickedness of men if He must in order to disturb us. He was still preaching, saying that we should not wait for something tragic to bring us to our knees, at 11:35 a.m. The pastor continued to warn that God would do whatever it took to disturb us and asked if anyone was "disturbed enough this morning to know that he needs the Lord." He invited anyone who needed prayer to come to the altar and pray with him. "What will it take to disturb you to your destiny?" he continued to ask. It was 11:40 a.m.

The pastor then offered a short prayer, said "Amen" followed by "God bless you, and you are dismissed." And, with that, the service was unceremoniously over just as it had unceremoniously begun. We walked out of the church at 11:41 a.m. with the full under-standing that its 10:00 a.m. worship hour was not a bow to the Tennessee Titans. Instead, the early hour was designed to give Brother Sanders a running start toward trying to disturb us out of our complacency. He required plenty of time for his full game plan — including leisurely time-outs as he took a seat, taking all the time he needed to get his people disturbed enough to seek their true destiny with God.

Chapter 13

Bethel World Outreach Center
Brentwood, Tennessee
December 8, 2002

My wife and I have loved each other since she was 16 and I was 17 — over fifty years. And we have grown to love one another even more and have become more and more alike. Yet,in many ways, we are quite different. With regard to some of these differences we both say "viva la difference," if you get my drift. Even though the differences between us cause occasional friction, I am basically still glad that we do not always agree. One of the ways in which we both agree we differ is in the approach we take to weekends and social activities. Maybe it is just a simple extension of the male-female thing. Could it be that this is just the way we have evolved? Whatever. At any rate, to put it simply, Betty is a planner while I am more spontaneous. She wants to plan our social activities far ahead of time; she prefers to invite friends over for dinner or some activity many weeks in advance, planning it all out very carefully. In contrast, I want to wait until an hour before-hand and then invite some friends over for a hamburger or pizza, to watch a football game on TV or to just sit around and talk big.

This is the way it goes most of the time. I am sure she wishes I would not be so impulsive in the way I go about these things, putting her on the spot by her having to rush around and be sure the proper hand towels are neatly laid out in the powder room. And, of course, I wish she would not want to commit us so far in advance for some activities when I have no clue as to what my mood will be at that particular time. So do I wish she would change and be like I am? Not really. Without her long-range planning we would certainly miss out on many interesting events and situations. Another thing — because she is the way she is I can always count on her having things right. I know she will have the right color of candles to go with the occasion or season. It goes deeper than that, of course. She sees that we do not forget certain social obligations and other events that are both important and interesting to both of us.

The events of the 7th of December are some indication of how Betty's planning proclivities have rubbed off on me during the past 49 years. Should I note here that I don't think my impulsiveness has affected her at all? Anyhow, on the late evening of the 7th I actually made some plans for where we would go to eat breakfast the next morning and where we would go to church afterwards. Actually the decisions were almost tied together. A few weeks earlier I had decided that I wanted us to go to another one of the now ubiquitous community churches in the Nashville area — The Bethel World Outreach Center (BWOC) located on Granny White Pike at Old Hickory Boulevard. In order to do so we needed to have breakfast somewhere in the area of the BWOC. Now, this is how Betty's planning tendencies had rubbed off on me. When I had decided that the BWOC would be one Sunday's destination, I also decided that I needed to have a good blue-road restaurant in mind for that day's experience. For the past few weeks I had been saving what is one of the best breakfast restaurants we have ever visited for the BWOC Sunday — "The Pancake Pantry" in Hillsboro Village.

There you have it — a blatant violation of at least two of the rules of the blue road. The first rule we broke was in planning at all. When we are truly blue roading, we have no destination — only direction. Today we had no direction, only destination. No direction? Right. I had no idea which blue road to take to get to the Pancake Pantry. I could go east on Woodmont and turn north onto Hillsboro Road back towards Hillsboro Village. Or I could go east on West End and turn south onto 21st Avenue past Vanderbilt towards the Hillsboro Village area. I chose the first route and we left our home on Woodmont at 8:30 a.m.

The second blue-road "rule" we broke was perhaps not broken at all. If all city streets can be declared to be blue roads, no rule was broken here at all. Without objection the blue-road rules will be amended to so declare. Since these are my rules, there can be no objection. Motion carried. There are destinations worthy of doing some planning to visit, even if it requires the suspension of our own rules.

By 8:40 a.m. we had arrived at the Pancake Pantry. And we were already too late! What was I thinking? It was the weekend and, of course, there would be a line at this great breakfast place. And the temperature was about 30 degrees. There were no parking spaces close to the entrance either. I had volunteered to sacrifice myself by going to stand in the line and letting Betty stay in the car; she could watch and join me when I burst through the first set of doors to the relative warmth of the "inner line." But because we had to park so far away Betty had to join me and the twenty-some others already waiting in the line. David Baldwin, the genial and handsome owner of this popular spot, is not thoughtless with regard to such brave hearts. He always places a large pot of coffee outside to offer some measure of warmth for pancake pilgrims.

With coffee in hand, a sort of badge of courage, we waited and struck up conversations with all who wanted to talk about what fools we were for being there at all. Several Titans fans were present to get a "pancake fix" before going to see the Titans play the Indianapolis Colts at the coliseum. The kick-off was only 3 hours away. We secretly wished that they would hurry on to a tailgate party and leave their spots in line for us. This would save us a few freezing minutes. David has so much weekend business that I am going to suggest banning all Titan tailgaters on Sundays. Let them insulate themselves with beer instead of pancakes. It's only right. Either that or he should open a new location for non-Titan season ticket holders. I'll settle for either one. I'm not unreasonable.

Back to the line itself. One man in line with his family was originally from St. Louis. Born there, he was educated in Texas before moving to Nashville in 1989. He bemoaned a recent study published in *The Tennessean* just a couple of days prior that St. Louis was now the most dangerous place to live in the U.S. among all cities with a population greater than 500,000. St. Louis had gained the dubious "honor" by pushing out Detroit, which had headed the list the year before. Now hear this! Nashville was listed as number seven. Someone on the line concluded that one of the main reasons Nashville had so many deaths or near deaths pushing them "UP" on the list had to do with the Pancake Pantry line — the number of pancake pilgrims who froze to death in the line and the bodily harm done to those trying to break in the line on extremely cold days.

Betty and I were about to have a near death experience from hypothermia when a miracle happened. As if by divine providence we were "plucked" out of the line by a female floor manager who seemed to fear neither God nor man as she braved the hostility of the cold and the hungry. She came to nearly the back of the line and invited us to come on in and be seated. For a brief moment I thought that David or someone had finally come to respect me for the man of power and influence I always wanted to be. I was disappointed when I found the truth — they had a table for two. Betty had heard the manager come outside and raise her fingers signaling "two." Thankfully, most tailgaters are at least four. Braving boos and hisses we were ushered to the warm, inviting place reserved for non-tailgaters. We were about to sing "Warm at Last. Warm at Last. Thank God Almighty, I'm warm at last." when a no-nonsense waitress pushed menus into our hands. Efficient yet friendly, she asked, "Coffee? Are you ready to order?" I answered, "yes" and "yes," while Betty was still looking at the menu. I ordered what I always order here:3 eggs over easy/medium, bacon,hash browns, toast and a short stack of pancakes ("for the table," I told myself). Betty then ordered "pigs in a blanket," sausage rolled in pancakes and smothered with butter.

As far as I am concerned there are only two reasons that the Pancake Pantry is not a "five star" restaurant: (1) they do not serve biscuits and (2) they are not open for dinner. Their toast is great but biscuits are biscuits! Not open for dinner? What an egregious violation of the patrons' realization that the Pancake Pantry taste "is not just for breakfast anymore." Me thinks some pancake pilgrim blackballed the establishment from the "five star" list while suffering from pancake withdrawal. Said pilgrim was probably deprived of a fix of pancakes during the time David and his staff were comfortable at home with a private stash of pancakes and syrup and emitting heinous laughter at the plight of poor "hooked" souls with no means of withdrawal assistance. I should say "No mean *known* to David" because I am on my own Pancake Pantry "methadone." I learned from a very reliable source, whom I promised not to identify, how to make the establishment's syrup which is 75 percent of the secret of the pancakes. I don't have it down perfectly yet but it can tide me over during after-hours until the restaurant re-opens. I've also searched high and low for a pancake mix close to the mix used by the Pantry. Again, not the real thing but it will do till the real thing re-opens. I will give you the information about the substitute pancake mix but not the recipe for the homemade syrup — not upon threat of death by freezing in a long line in the middle of February. The faux pancake flour is Carbon's Malted Pancake Flour, telephone 1-800-253-0590.

I have also learned how to closely duplicate the Pantry's world class hash-brown potatoes. You simply bake the potatoes first and then peel them, cut them up into random sized pieces and brown them very fast on a very hot, very thick griddle. You don't have a very thick gas grill? Neither do I. But I come close by frying smaller amounts (one serving at a time) in a very hot, thick skillet for just enough time to get them brown and crispy. Salt and pepper to taste. These potatoes can also help hold you over until 6:00 a.m. in the morning when the Pantry finally opens.

In an amazingly short time our food was on the table. Just as we ordered it! Now that should not be so exceptional except that the waitresses here take all the orders verbally. No notes. No pads. Nothing. But there it was. And there it was for 108 other people at various stages of gorging themselves, helplessly and unashamedly.

David's staff was obviously well trained because, although he arrived at the restaurant just as we were driving up, the restaurant had already been open for about three hours. After I caught his eye he came over to the table. I told him I was trying to "knock-off" his recipes — especially the potatoes. He said, "Good luck, but you can't succeed unless you get a 1 1/2 – 2 inch thick heavy gas grill." Well, if I must, I must. I suppose we'll just have to get rid of our dining table. Maybe I could then serve everything "Kobe Steak House" style at home from now on. David also told me that he had won a weekend at our Center Hill Lake house at a recent wine auction; we had contributed the weekend to the charity event last fall. He was worried about meeting the deadline of the 31st of March for using the weekend. I graciously told him not to worry about the deadline because I would extend the deadline to suit his needs. I also told him that he could use my boat and that the house was available to him during the week, not just the weekends. Stay tuned! I may get the name of the pancake mix yet. Read all about it in the sequel to this book. The working title is *52 Ways To Get Secret Recipes*.

We left the Pancake Pantry at 10:00 a.m. By then the line to get in was wrapped around the corner and stretched about one-third of the way down the block. If my plan works and I get the recipes I want from David, I am going to put in a bid for the next available restaurant spot and open a pancake restaurant that will be open 24 hours a day. I can raise the needed capital any weekend just by planting some "Scalpers" in the Pancake Pantry line to sell their place in line. Sorry David. Nothing personal. It's only business. With your recipes, my Pillsbury biscuits and being open to meet the needs of the customers, my restaurant is certain to get a "five star" rating. And thanks for your help.

We headed south on 21st Avenue, which becomes Hillsboro Pike when it crosses over I-40. We passed the Belmont Methodist Church, Trinity Presbyterian, Woodmont Baptist, Woodmont Christian and Calvary Methodist all on the right. We turned left onto Graybar Lane, passing the Second Presbyterian Church on the corner of Graybar Lane and Belmont Boulevard. We then turned south onto Granny White Pike. From there we drove about five miles until reaching the Bethel World Outreach Center located at the corner of Granny White Pike and Old Hickory Boulevard. The BWOC is one of the "community type" churches proliferating in the Middle Tennessee area and, I understand, all around the country. I had become interested in this relatively new phenomenon on the Christian religious scene. At 9:50 a.m. we pulled into the enormous parking lot and were guided along by the energetic parking assistants. They kept the traffic moving. They have no choice but to do so. The church holds three worship services each Sunday: 8:15 a.m., 10:00 a.m., and 11:45 a.m. The service schedule leaves no more than fifteen minutes to empty and refill the parking lots in between services.

By 9:55 a.m. we were seated in the back pew on the left side. The right side of the church was already full, and soon the left side was as well. It was standing room only. The church is a contemporary structure as have been each of the community type churches we have visited. The comfortable padded pews were arranged in semicircle tiers pointing to a very large platform. The platform held the orchestra/band on the left and the choir, dressed in beige robes with red and green sashes, in the center. There were two large screens (about 12 feet by 12 feet), one over the platform and another to the rear of the sanctuary. An energetic black song leader who wore glasses welcomed the congregation to worship in the spirit. "Some people look stupid trying to look cool while everyone else is looking and acting stupid," he said, "Since we all look stupid one way or the other let's all let go and act stupid and sing." And thus the service began.

In the "Christian Rock" tradition, a hallmark of the community churches we have visited, the leader and the choir led the congregation in singing *Faith Is the Substance of Things We Hope For*. The BWOC's congregation, the most racially and chronologically diverse congregation of the three community churches we had visited, was also the most diverse in the matter of dress code. There absolutely was none. It appeared that perhaps the split was about 50/50 between those who wore "Sunday clothes" and those who were casually dressed. The ministers all wore coats and ties, but this did not seem to be a "signal" as to how the congregation should dress. If it was meant to be such a signal, 50 percent of the congregation had not yet deciphered the code.

The congregation clapped hands and swayed back and forth (another common thread of the community churches) while singing, "Now is the time for all people from every land to come together...Now is the moment for worship...Gotta open up our mouth and give Him praise." Some 1,500 voices joined a female leader to sing, "Fill this place with the praise of the God of all grace ...God is here. Fill this place with praise." Next, the congregation sang *Whenever I Call You Are There, Redeemer and Friend*. Up to this point none of those directing the service had identified themselves. The bulletin we had been given as we entered the church offered no assistance on this matter. There were ten pastors and associate pastors listed in the literature, including the senior pastor, Rice Brooks, who apparently was not there for the service. The bulletin had a picture of him and a woman I presumed to be his wife; they are both very young and very attractive.

The bulletin gave the "Number one priority" of the church — "to produce a people that are pleasing to God." It also told of the Bible school and Victory Leadership Institute, which provides training by "world class ministers and theologians." The pastor was quoted in the bulletin;he expects, through the efforts of the church, a "harvest of lives transformed into a mighty army of men and women who will not only shake this city, but also shake the world for Christ in their lifetime." The bulletin also explained that the church was a part of the "Morning Star International" family of churches and ministries, which has churches in 35 nations.

The bulletin also told about the "U. Church" that is basically for university students and young adults. It is housed in the building formerly known as Planet Hollywood at 322 Broadway in downtown Nashville. Numerous other activities, prayer groups, and "The Church of the Nation" meetings were also listed. Actual services were scheduled on Saturdays, Sunday mornings and evenings, Wednesdays and Friday evenings. There were re so many activities I actually felt tired just reading about them. Somebody's got a lot of work to do.

At 10:20 a.m. we were still standing and singing just as we had been at the beginning of the first song. It was then that a young black man identified himself as "Pastor Morgan" (as I understood him to say but the name was not listed in the bulletin) and began to exhort us to brotherhood. He said, "Within this Congregation we have a covenant relationship. Together we can serve God, whereas alone we can only serve ourselves." He led us in prayer. With so many pastors and assistants, I prayed that the Senior Pastor Rice would make a requirement that, for the sake of visitors, all participants in a service would introduce themselves. Like they say at Titans games: "You can't know the players without a program." Think about it, Pastor Rice.

At 10:28 a.m. we were all invited to greet those in the pews near us before being seated. The simple act of finally being seated pleased me greatly. Next a young white man with glasses welcomed all visitors and invited all visitors to meet with him at a reception following the service. I would thank him for the invitation but, unfortunately, I do not know his name either. He also introduced the offering as a part of the service. During the offering a young guitarist (let's call him John Denver Doe) sang and played an absolutely beautiful and inspiring rendition of *The First Noel*.

The next pastor actually introduced himself as "Paul Barker, one of the pastors here." Thanks, Pastor Paul, for introducing yourself.

I would vote for them to put your name on the printed roster of pastors as well, but perhaps you do not have tenure yet. It's expensive printing all those blank bulletins. Pastor Paul was dressed in a handsome light suit and tie. He was bald and wore a smallish beard and mustache. He read the scripture lesson from *Acts 6: 1 – 7* and announced that his sermon topic was "Divine Physics." He presented each member of the congregation with a one-page syllabus to follow and fill in the blanks at appropriate places. I was scared to death there would be a quiz at the end of the service and, while I do believe he intended to give one, providentially he ran out of time.

The first part of Pastor Paul's sermon was a reintroduction to Sir Isaac Newton's first law of motion, which, simply stated, holds that "an object in motion tends to stay in motion unless acted upon by another object." He went through the strife and divisions of the early church between the Hebraic Jews and the Hellenistic Jews, telling about how this adversely affected their early efforts. These dividing forces hindered the work of the church, he said. One body was acting against another. After several minutes of delving into early church history, he thought that some members of the congregation were probably asking, "Pastor, that is a good Bible story and we're glad you exegeted this for us...but what does that have to do with me today?" What it means for us, he said, was that we had to guard from both internal and external pressures, and divisions, which lead to broken relationships. He said that it is inevitable that offenses will come but that we must put them behind us. We are different and have different tastes. There are those who like vegetables and those who don't. There are those who love beef liver and those who don't. He admitted, however, that he was not at all sure that liver lovers would go to heaven. I wanted to answer him that liver lovers were already in heaven when it is prepared like it is at Arnold's, another one of my favorite meat-n-three's in Nashville.

At 11:20 a.m. he was still preaching and I began to relax; there would not be enough time for a quiz before the next service. Summarizing, he said that God has "joined us in a covenant relationship and we must never quit...We should never let anything divide us." He said that disagreements and gossip would divide us and thwart the motion of the spirit within us. He exhorted us to "participate in the Divine Physics" by refusing to let divisiveness and gossiping divide us, and divert us, from allowing God's spirit to move in and through our lives.

Pastor Paul then prayed and he asked God to "safeguard our hearts against schemes of the evil one." He said, "Some here may have allowed the spirit of gossip to invade their hearts...and I pray for them." He hurriedly concluded the prayer as if he felt the evil spirit of the restraint of time or the watchful eye of Senior Pastor Rice, the giver of all good and valuable tenures, upon him.

Another unnamed pastor then invited anyone who felt a divisive spirit in their lives to come to the front to pray, worrying I was sure, what he would do with those seekers if anyone actually did come forward. A new crowd was already gathering; a new service was about to begin. I believe this pastor was somewhat relieved when no one arrived at the front in need of prayer. He then said, as if ending a classroom discussion, "You are dismissed." For a brief moment I felt anxious as if I was back in college and had to rush to my next class; at the same time I felt relief as if a long-winded teacher had not left enough time for the quiz. If there had been a little more time left, I would have wanted to ask the professor, I mean pastor, a question for future reference — If we do not pass the written tests, can we do some kind of make up work such as singing in the choir or paying extra tithes or something? I'm good at parking cars. Maybe I could help organize a valet service.

Chapter 14

The Congregation Micah: Jewish Synagogue
Brentwood, Tennessee
December 13, 2002

T his would be the first time when my title, *Fifty-Two Sundays on the Blue Road*, would be open to question. In the introduction I noted that the "Sundays" should more accurately be "Sabbaths." From the very beginning I had planned for a year in which I would visit religious services of many different faiths. An inherent part of the plan, then, was attending the services of different faiths on the day on which their traditional days of worship are held. The Jewish Sabbath goes from sundown Friday until sundown Saturday. It was the 14th week out of the year. So, including my attendance on the Jewish Sabbath on this night, a more accurate title of this book might be *13 Sundays and One Friday on the Blue Road*. I was again invoking what I will henceforth call my "Mohonk – Charlotte" amendment to my blue roading experiences. My visits to the Lake Mohonk Mountain Retreat and The Charlotte Inn on Martha's Vineyard had been slight deviations from the master plan I had developed for blue roading a number of years ago. The main rule suspended on the "Mohonk – Charlotte" parts of a blue road trip is the "no destination" rule. Once upon a time I had really wanted to visit these two marvelous blue road inns and made specific plans to search them out. While true blue roading is an experience in relaxed meandering and experiencing what the travels of the day deliver to you, on this Friday I had a destination in mind — the Congregation Micah. I had planned my visit to the Synagogue about three weeks prior to this day.

The long story of planning to visit the Congregation Micah in its shortened version (my editor will be very happy about this) is simply that the plan was a result of the confluence of two currents. First, my friend Bill Moran had called three weeks ago about coming to Nashville on this particular weekend. He wanted us to visit some of his local real estate investments with which I had assisted him, to my financial gain, in the past. Okay. I had acted as his real estate broker and received nice commissions for doing so. Bill has lots of money. And I might get some more of it if I played my cards right and understood the "golden rule" —he who has the gold rules. Bill wanted to come to Nashville; he holds the gold. Get my drift? Of course I would pick him up at 10:30 p.m. Friday at the airport and spend Saturday working with him. So, the "Golden Rule" in the first confluent current helped to re-channel my weekend plans. The second current was my love of golf. Bill wanted to play golf with me on Sunday. Now you get the picture — Sunday was out for blue roading on the 14th week as well as Saturday.

Now, what to do? Aha! My friend David Green, the managing editor of *The Tennessean* newspaper, was a member of Congregation Micah. He had told me that the Congregation's worship services were held on Friday evenings at 7:30 p.m. And Bill would not arrive until 10:30 p.m. Perfect. God works in mysterious ways.

Dave volunteered to meet Betty and me at Friday's service in the newest Jewish congregation in Nashville. Congregation Micah is sort of located on the blue road. At least it was not on West End or in Belle Meade, but it is close to Belle Meade in concept. Congregation Micah is located in the Brentwood area, the next most affluent section of Nashville. Aren't there any Jews in Bordeaux or Smyrna?

Now, in order to salvage the concept of *Fifty-two Sundays on the Blue Road*, I needed to eat "breakfast" somewhere. The total concept was close to being shattered. I had already broken the "no destination, only direction" rule. I had changed Friday into Sunday. I was also calling Old Hickory Boulevard, the silk stocking area of Brentwood, a "blue road." And now I was forced to make "supper" into "breakfast." Doing so would be simple. I could just go to a Waffle House, open 24 hours a day, and eat anything that I please. I could eat anywhere I pleased and eat whatever I pleased and call it whatever I pleased. Now that is the real power of the plan. And I loved it.

So, intoxicated with the power of changing Friday into Sunday and night into day, I set out to change supper into breakfast at any restaurant I chose. On the mission to achieve this last miracle, Betty and I left our home on Woodmont Boulevard at 6:10 p.m. Thanks to my poetic license, under which I had recently decreed all residential streets to be blue roads, I could call Woodmont Boulevard a blue road. Traffic on our personal blue road was backed up for about a mile; other Nashville pilgrims were progressively making Woodmont the choice route for the journey home each work day. Only on the Jewish and Christian Sabbaths is any relief found from the onslaught of traffic bearing those whose theme song is *Show me a way to go home*. It was a cold and rainy night and we were thankfully going in the opposite direction of the traffic. I spitefully told myself that I was going to take my car and help make some traffic in someone else's backyard. "I'll show them," I said to no one other than myself in a personal version of road rage, "I'll go do it to the people on Old Hickory Boulevard. And I'll eat in one of their restaurants, too. Tit for tat."

We were soon part of someone else's traffic after going north on Harding Place and then turning south onto Franklin Road. We were soon in the old section of Brentwood. Betty and I were trying to decide where to perform the miracle of changing supper into breakfast — Shoney's, Captain D's or the Wild Iris. We chose the Wild Iris because we had fallen in love during the last few months with The Yellow Porch restaurant located on Thompson Lane. We had heard that the Wild Iris was owned by the same person and thought this was the best clue we could get about the quality of the food. Unfortunately, it wasn't as good a clue as we had hoped. The food was okay, maybe even good, but not as good as that of The Yellow Porch. Consistently at the Yellow Porch we left feeling that everything we had eaten had been superb, no matter how many times we ate there.

The magic just didn't happen at the Wild Iris. Perhaps I should have gone one step further and performed another miracle, or magic trick, by making the better-than-acceptable meal into a gourmet's delight the likes of which we had experienced at its "sister's place." Betty ordered the shrimp scampi and lobster sauce over fettuccini. Shrimp and pork are two items that Orthodox Jews refrain from eating because of their Kosher Laws. I ordered the lamb chops truly because I wanted to honor the occasion of my going to a Jewish service by eating traditional Jewish foods. The chops were served with goat cheese, semolina dumplings and asparagus. The chops were cooked to order and very tasty but the asparagus and the dumplings were almost tasteless — not bad or good, just tasteless. Betty's shrimp scampi was better than average but just not perfect in the way we were convinced the dish would have been at The Yellow Porch. Maybe it was the yuckish night and the rain distorting our taste buds. We plan to go back with the hope we won't need to spend one of my precious miracles on just making the food a little better. We ordered only water with the meal and after I had changed it to wine I felt worn out. Miracle performing takes so much out of you, don't you think?

At 7:00 p.m. we were back out on Old Hickory Boulevard on the way to meet Dave Green at 7:10 p.m. at the Congregation Micah synagogue. Dave had offered to meet us, introduce us to the Rabbi and show us around the beautiful new synagogue. The synagogue had been designed to generally allow 300 to worship but the architect had also designed movable partitions to allow the worship area to be expanded to accommodate as many as 1,100. Before the beautiful and commodious new synagogue had been built they had worshiped out in Bellevue in a building which, at different times, had been a restaurant, a bar, and (back at its very beginning) a golf course clubhouse and pro shop.

As it so happened, some partners and I had owned that building and the one-time golf course several years earlier. We had bought the land and building after the golf course failed and we had changed the zoning to allow for its present uses — one of which had been as a temporary synagogue. Dave introduced me to Rabbi Kanter. I could see immediately by his open countenance that he possessed a remarkable sense of humor which gave me the courage later on to say to him, "I used to own a synagogue." I pressed the point a little further by adding, "I think everyone should own one." I then explained my past ownership of the once temporary location of the synagogue. As expected, the Rabbi laughed heartily. We enjoyed a few minutes of easy conversation which made Betty and me feel completely and warmly welcome.

I only wish that I owned the present synagogue. It is a beautiful facility sitting on several acres of equally beautiful land located on Old Hickory Boulevard just east of Hillsboro Pike. We were fortunate to be given a verbal tour of the synagogue by Rabbi Kanter, a man both easy to like and equally easy to listen to. He spoke about several of the architectural features of the facility which came to life as he explained their significance and functions. The large opaque windows did not perfectly diffuse the light as had been intended but they did serve the purpose of allowing the naturalness of the area to be a part of the worship. The seven rows of soft green color on the beautiful seats represented the seven days of the week and complimented the natural feeling initiated by the windows. The semicircular seating arrangement created an intimate feeling between the worship leaders and the congregation.

The pulpit area was raised only 14 inches above the floor of the congregation. According to the Rabbi, this was done purposefully in order to convey a feeling that the Rabbi was on the same "level" as the members of the congregation and to help erase any possible feelings that the Rabbi was in an exalted position over them. In his role as a teacher, the Rabbi does not "preach down" to the congregation.

In the center of the pulpit area was a circular enclosure containing the semblance of the "Ark of the Covenant" which symbolizes the presence of God. This was the focal point of the entire sanctuary. The double doors of the enclosure are opened only twice, for a very few minutes, during the service for brief acts of dedication and devotion. The ark appeared to hold the same level of reverence by the congregation members as the Communion table does in Christian churches. The large handsome doors to the Ark of the Covenant were made of three-eighth inch thick panels of solid copper and had been handsomely sculptured in Israel for this congregation. Emanating from the top of the ark were the main architectural structures which represent the tree of life. At the center of the top of the ark is a piece of sculpture from which a light continuously shines.

The Congregation Micah was formed about 10 years ago. And it was assisted financially in expediting its formation by at least one very wealthy Jewish family in Nashville. The family had a daughter engaged to a man who was not of the Jewish faith. As it turned out the Rabbi of the Jewish Temple belonged to the more fundamental school of Judaism which forbade the marriage of Jews to those outside the faith. Within the context of this personal history, the wealthy family joined with others of like minds to finance the formation of a more liberal synagogue.

There are three basic branches of Judaism. The Orthodox branch is the most fundamental of the three "sects"within the faith. They observe the Sabbath very strictly by refraining from work, travel,business, and even the carrying of money on the day of worship. They keep separate pews for men and women in the synagogue and use only Hebrew in prayers and ceremonies. They also follow very strict dietary (Kosher) laws. Another "sect"is Conservative Judaism. They see Judaism as an evolving religion allowing them to change in ways not in direct conflict with the spirit of the Jewish law. They allow minor changes in dietary practices and allow the language of the culture in which they find themselves to be used in their services. They also allow Friday evening services after sunset. Reform Judaism is the third "sect" of Judaism. It is even more liberal. They feel that the faith should be rational and withstand the scrutiny of science and reason. They use both English and Hebrew in services and do not require the separation of the sexes during worship. Reform Jews permit the marriage of Jews to non-Jews, allow the ordination of women as rabbis and are not strict followers of kosher laws. If I had thought this through very carefully, I could have had pork chops instead of lamb chops for my "breakfast" dinner because the Congregation Micah is very definitely in the reform tradition of Judaism. Changing water to wine is one thing. But changing lamb chops into pork chops would require more religious capital than I could afford.

I have always considered myself something of a liberal and immediately felt at home among the most open minded worshipers of the Jewish community. As we entered the service, we were given an "Order of Service" and a prayer book entitled *Gate of Prayer for Shabbat and Weekdays*. Shabbat is the Hebrew word for Sabbath. Under the title was written, "A Gender Sensitive Prayer Book" which was a sure sign that we were in a reform synagogue. As we took a seat Joyce and Joel Cutler were chosen to light the two beautiful, tall Shabbat candles. The Cutlers were celebrating what I understood to be their 25th wedding anniversary and were being honored among some other "Pulpit Guests and Participants." Rabbi

Kanter welcomed everyone to the service and set a relaxed tone for the evening. He presided over the service and, as the "Master of Ceremonies," led the congregation from one part of the service to the next with ease.

Lisa Silver was the Cantorial Soloist for the service and Michael Ochs was the pianist. Lisa, who also played the guitar at times, was the director of the music and, in the style of the late John Denver, created a worshipful mood with seeming ease. The "Order of Service" indicated that we would use Shabbat Evening Service I. The first part of the service flowed smoothly between prayers and songs starting with:

> *"Source of mercy, continue your loving care for us and our loved ones. Give us strength to walk in your presence on the paths of the righteous, loyal to your Torah and steadfast in goodness and keep us far from all shame, grief and anguish; fill our houses with peace, light, and joy. O God, Fountain of Life, by your light shall we see light."*

The congregation sang and read prayers from the prayer book in a fashion not unlike the responsive readings read from the back of most Christian hymn books. Next the congregation was seated. We then had another reading:

> *"You shall love your eternal God with all your heart, with all your mind, with all your being. Set these words, which I command you this day, upon your heart. Teach them faithfully to your children, speak of them in your home and on your way, when you lie down and when you rise up. Bind them as a sign upon your hand; let them be symbols before your eyes; inscribe them on the doorposts of your house, and on your gates...I am your eternal God who led you out of Egypt."*

Rabbi Berk, a young woman, gave a sermon that lasted about 15 minutes on the subject of "Faith." Rabbi Berk and Rabbi Kanter both attended the Hebrew Union Seminary in Cincinnati, Ohio (the Reform branch also has seminaries in Los Angeles and New York). She spoke of her days in the seminary and, in particular, of a classmate by the name of John who constantly fretted and worried over his grades even though he was an excellent student. He fretted that he might not make all A's. She shared that she had once heard John's father, telling him not to worry so much, say, "a little faith, Rabbi."

During the thoughtful sermon Rabbi Berk also told a story about a family whose daughter had been kidnapped. The family prayed and prayed for her safe return and it happened in this case that the daughter was returned. The family credited her safe return as the result of their faith in God. But, the Rabbi said, not all prayers are answered affirmatively. Sometimes the answer does not come in the manner we wish. And it is then when we need real faith.

Rabbi Berk then told of the story of Joseph, sold into slavery by jealous brothers. Through his faith Joseph became the second in command in all of Egypt, rising above all his misfortunes and coming to a place in Egypt so that God could use him in a better way in service of His people. God does not want us to just pray in demand that God answer our prayers and thus make us happy, she pointed out. God expects us to "get up" and cooperate with God to help bring about goodness to His people like Joseph had.

During Rabbi Berk's sermon I realized that it was the first sermon I had ever heard by a woman. And I was by no means disappointed. She blended into the service so effortlessly that it became a seamless fabric from beginning to the end. She had been with the congregation for only two and a half years but she and Rabbi Kanter shared the sermonizing on a fairly equal basis. Sermons are only given during the Friday evening services; there are apparently no sermons delivered during the Saturday services.

Before the service came to a close Rabbi Kanter invited the pulpit guests to join him in celebrating the milestones of their lives by offering the "Kiddush," the prayer of thanksgiving to God for the wine, and the "Motz," the prayer of thanksgiving to God for the bread. Thus, the simple service, which had begun with the lighting of the Sabbath candles, came to an end with a non-scripted, informal moment during which the Rabbi and other pulpit guest led the Congregation in recognition of God as the giver and sustainer of life.

After the service the congregation was invited to enjoy refreshments and a reception in the large open room located next to the sanctuary. The reception was sponsored by Melissa and Scott Farrar, members of the congregation. Betty and I visited a few minutes with both Rabbis and then with our friend Dave Green but decided not to enjoy the refreshments and the fellowship of the reception; it was time for me to get back on the wet and cold blue roads in order to take Betty home and then pick up my friend Bill Moran at the airport.

Bill had been the proximate reason we visited a congregation that worshiped on Friday night, thus allowing us the time to visit and play golf on the following Saturday and Sunday. But Bill only helped change the schedule to this Friday rather than at some other Friday in the near future. Yet we were grateful to him. It was the first time I had attended a worship service at a synagogue — a memorable experience. Betty and I both agreed that it had been a sweet service in which the oldest monotheistic religion in the world was related to the descendants of Abraham in a new day in a new synagogue, a piece of whose history I used to own. Maybe my past ownership gave me some kind of associate membership rights at the Congregation Micah. I think I'll ask Rabbi Kanter about it.

I was raised in a nominal Christian family and taught early that we were a part of the Judeo-Christian tradition. Why, then, was I a bit surprised that the beautiful Sabbath service had not been significantly different from the many Christian services I had attended on Sunday mornings? Both traditions worship the same God. The only differences I noticed were that prayers were not ended with the words, "In the Name of the Father, the Son and the Holy Spirit" and that all the prayers were ended with "Amein," rather than "Ahmen" or "Amen." These differences weren't much different than the differences existing among the beliefs of different sects within the Christian faith itself. In fact, I read somewhere about a Jewish leader who refers to Christianity as a temporarily very successful Jewish sect. I'm thinking about trying to get the two religions reunited. I am working on the development of an anti-theological hair splitting serum. The serum, when injected into those of either faith, would ward off an outright rejection of the reunion concept. I am assured a Nobel Prize if I can achieve the desired result. Would it be awarded for medicine or the peace? Maybe both. A similar serum that I developed to unite the Baptists and the Church of Christ ran into several serious setbacks. Pray for me.

Chapter 15

First United Methodist Church

Smithville, Tennessee

December 22, 2002

"*I*t is 7:49," Betty proudly said to me as we got in the car to leave home on yet another beautiful December morning. She wanted to be certain that I knew we were leaving several minutes before 8:00 a.m. because I had told her that I wanted to leave a little before 8:00 a.m. She knew full well that I had not expected her to actually comply with my request. So her "It is 7:49" was a triumphal statement of her victory over the devil morning clock. Maybe not a total victory but Rome wasn't built in a day, so they say. One step at a time. We beat the clock by eleven minutes. Next week we might be fewer than eleven minutes late at the time of departure. It's something we'll just have to keep working on. Know what I mean? Anyhow, like a friend wanting to encourage a struggling alcoholic in sobriety, I congratulated her on a first step in the battle with the clock demon. I wanted her to know that I would be with her on this new journey toward chronological sobriety and that together we could lick this thing.

As soon as I had congratulated her on this small victory in the battle of the Bulovas I tried to get her mind off the nagging life-time problem. I switched the topic as quickly as I could by focusing on something light and fluffy. "Look at that beautiful sky," I said in an effort to get her mind on a more positive subject. I saw some soft billowy multicolored clouds randomly decorating the far distant sky and seized upon the opportunity they presented: "Those little clouds are so beautiful, just like a group of young children running out to play. And the two or three slightly larger ones are teen-aged brothers and sisters their mothers sent out to sort of watch over them.Isn't that sweet?"And it worked marvelously. Our concentration was immediately shifted away from the only problem that our two daughters and I have ever been able to detect in the otherwise totally unblemished fabric of my nearly perfect wife. When a life is so close to perfection, however, one little zit on its countenance seems like a disaster. There was a beautiful smile on her face and a lilt in her voice as she began to count the cloud children. The rest of the day seemed guaranteed to be free of all weighty, mundane problems. Free, that is, unless my slight fear that a woman so relieved of the only weight on her soul could just drift away into the heavens to be with the angels. There are angels, aren't there?

I decided that no theological or philosophical problems were going to blemish the day, now as sweet and fluffy as cotton candy. "If she goes, she goes." And since I helped remove the only weight on her soul, I am sure God would provide me with someone else equally as sweet for my remaining few years, wouldn't he? There is a God, isn't there? " Now stop that," I said to myself. No theology — no hairsplitting — today. No sir. Just a light and beautiful fluffy day. More and more children were coming out to play in the eastern sky. It looked like a birthday party or something, and on Sunday too. That's why they were all dressed so pretty.

Soon we started talking about other subjects. When free, you are free indeed. We began to talk about food and churches. Back on solid ground, we were. We were on Route 70 which is also known as Lebanon Road if you're going toward Lebanon. I guess it is known as Nashville Road if you are going in the opposite direction. That's hairsplitting of a sort so we'll just call it Lebanon Road. As we started to look for restaurants and churches, we realized how very much many banks look like churches, or is it that churches look like banks? Hairsplitting again? Anyhow, it's a fact. Many banks look so very religious. I think that's their ploy. "Trust us," they seem to be saying, "See how religious we look? Of course, you can trust your money with us. Our bank officers are just like your deacons. As a matter of fact some of your deacons are our bank officers." That last statement might be pushing the analogy too far. I have known some deacons I would not trust with your money, much less mine.

It might be the other way around. Maybe the churches are trying to look like banks. Maybe the churches are built to look like banks so that they seem to say to possible new members, "Come on in. We are pillars of the community. We are solid as a bank. As a matter of fact, some of our members are officers at some our most prestigious banks." Churches need to be careful not to draw the comparison with banks and bankers too closely. You know as well as I do the reasons that so many bankers go to church: (1) because they are prospecting for more depositors and (2) because they need forgiveness more than almost any other single group of sinners. (My God. I love writing. I've wanted to say something like this publicly for many years.)

Anyhow, banks and churches have started to look alike and that troubles me. As we travel and look for different churches to attend, we slow down to read the name of the church and the times of services. More than a few times we see a prospective church and, lo and behold, the sign reads, "First National Bank." Banks invite all new prospective depositors to come in and get a "free toaster with each new account." If I ever see one open on Sunday, I will go in and open a new account — especially if they offer a free Mr. Coffee. My toaster is okay but I need a new coffeemaker.

In Lebanon we read church signs and times of worship. The First Presbyterian Church had no times announcing its services. Maybe they wanted you to come in and ask what time services were held. If one did go in and ask, the conversation might have gone something like a would-be Vanderbilt football spectator's conversation would go with the Vandy ticket office: "You got any tickets left for the game?" the fan asks. "Yes we do. What game?" the hopeful ticket agent asks. "The Alabama game," the fan replies. "Yes, we have some left where would you like to sit?" "I'd like the 50 yard line about 20 rows up." "Let me see, yes we have those, how many do you want?" "Oh, just two, but what time is the game?" "What time could you get here?" the agent asks hopefully. Maybe the First Presbyterian Church would be so happy to have new faces in attendance that they would start the service at anytime the new prospects requested. Maybe not? Maybe the reason they did not have a sign announcing service times was that they required you to personally come in and fill out a request form for written permission to attend on some future date. This may all be totally wrong but I'm just trying to figure out why the bank, I mean church, did not announce the hours it was open for business. Betty and I are official members of a Nashville Presbyterian church. Or at least we were the last time we were there. I hope they have not given our member-ship positions to some more frequent depositors. I mean worshipers.

The First Baptist Church, proudly and notoriously, announced that its service was at 11:00 a.m. And proud they should be. They met at 11:00 a.m. and were clearly in the TADI (Titans Area of Dominant Influence). Over sixty percent of the fans attending Titans games travel into Nashville from outside Davidson County. A neighboring county, Lebanon was clearly in the TADI but the Baptists would not bow to the god of the Titans; they obeyed the 11th Commandment that all churches hold a worship service at 11:00 a.m. in order to meet the needs of all blue-road pilgrims.

The College Street Church of Christ apparently also did not require pre-registration to attend its services, openly announced as beginning at 10:45 a.m. I do hope that God overlooks this 15-minute deviation from His 11th and, by far, most important commandment. What's 15 minutes to eternity? I would vote to overlook it but I don't think God looks favorably on democratic principles when it comes to His relationship with mankind (and womankind). I think He is more liberal on how churches organize themselves politically. But, in general, God leans toward a type of monarchical theocracy. So the 15-minute leeway possibility was, for all practical purposes, probably out. Since all Churches of Christ are very careful about the letter and the spirit of God's will, I'm going to advise them that God is probably negative on the 10:45 a.m. thing. Titans or no Titans, long-winded preachers notwith-standing, the church had better consider a change, pronto, because I had seen a sign earlier which read "Jesus is coming soon."

It was now about 8:50 a.m. We still had plenty of time to find a blue-road restaurant and a righteous, God-fearing congregation that meets at 11:00 a.m. With faith in that fear, we planned the remainder of the morning on that theocratic principle. Invigorated with new faith, primarily and probably because we were getting to be quite hungry, we began to intensify the search for a real blue-road restaurant. I would like to point out to all owners of blue-road restaurants that restaurants, as well as churches, come under the theocracy. Blue road restaurant owners seem to believe that the Sabbath day of rest includes them. False and self-serving restaurant teachers must have masqueraded as servants of God and distorted

God's expectations of those who feed the souls and those who feed the bodies of His children. All restaurants and churches are required to selflessly serve those needs. Why are there not more sermons on the subject from the God-fearing church ministers of our day? Especially those who understand the 11:00 a.m. service Commandment? Surely they know that the multitudes that Jesus fed also need nourishment on Sundays.

We passed the righteous people at the Cracker Barrel, Shoney's and the Waffle House. These fine establishments have understood for years what may well come to be known as the 12th Commandment, "Feed my sheep — and that means on Sundays too." We still had a few more minutes to look for those who righteously keep the 12th Commandment and continued east on Highway 70. Once we crossed over I-40, Highway 70 immediately and miraculously changed into Sparta Highway. The good people of Smithville probably resent the oversight; Smithville lies about half way between Lebanon and Sparta. Like a bolt out of heaven, there it was — "Uncle Pete's Restaurant and Truck Stop," a Phillips 66 truck stop. It had to be a winner. Truckers love to eat and get gas at the same time. I was reminded of two friends, Don Sheffield and Sam Causey, and a gift they had given me when a restaurant venture of mine opened in 1978. The gift was a self-made picture of Don and Sam dressed in their most authentic good ol' boy "get ups" and eating in a restaurant whose sign read, "U. Grant's Restaurant and Filling Station — eat here and get gas."

Don't tell anyone but I already had a full tank of gas. All I wanted from the righteous Uncle Pete was food. He might be breaking all eleven of the First Commandments but he was obeying the 12th one. And how! It was a blue road restaurant. I walked into the restaurant with Betty trying to do the truckers' strut. Not Betty, me. Betty just followed along. Anyhow, the strut is sort of a blend of humble obsequiousness and the look of someone who holds and puffs a cigarette as if fearing neither God nor man. It's necessary to learn the look as soon as possible when you have to stop for a one-hour nap at truck rest stop spots in the middle of the night. The look tells everyone that you are a loner and "don't want to bother nobody" while at the same time, and with the same breath, says simply: "Don't tread on me."

I did the trucker strut over to a table as if I was a regular, took a seat and sat back as if I was in my own domain. I don't think the waitress was really convinced that we had just parked a rig outside and were coming in for breakfast before continuing the haul to Knoxville. Finally, she did come over. She gave us a couple of menus and asked if we wanted something to drink. ("Something" to drink? Doesn't she know that all truckers drink coffee?) We said, "Sure, bring us two cups," but then Betty blew our cover by adding, "de-cafe." For a minute I thought she was going to ask us to leave but then she gave me a look as if saying, "Your secrets are safe with me, good buddy." Or did she say "granddaddy?" I wasn't sure. Anyhow, she brought the de-cafe and took our orders just as if we were real people.

Betty ordered a ham and cheese omelet with grits and wheat toast ($5.99). I ordered "Uncle Pete's Breakfast" ($8.88), still trying to keep up the charade. We had made a strategic mistake, now a dead giveaway, by not selecting a booth along one of the three walls. It was obvious now. The booths held individual telephones allowing the truckers to "check in." Some of them were "checking-in" for considerable lengths of time while we were there.

Another mistake we made was not having a thermos bottle for a coffee fill-up before the next leg. Well, you don't just become a "good buddy" over night. But I took all this in so that we won't make the same mistakes next time. And next time I'll order the "Trucker's Delight," whether I want it or not. With it you get ham, fried fish, chicken or pork chops along with sliced tomatoes, gravy or grits. I really liked the special notation on the menu which read "HOME-MADE BISCUITS" as if they were proud of the fact. If they're proud, I'm proud with them. They also had four kinds of potatoes: french fries, tater tots, hash browns and home fries. I chose home fries with my order because is sounded more "trucker like."

As we waited for our food, we began to notice the "others" who had made Uncle Pete's their breakfast truck stop. There was a big black man with a black leather cap who weighed about 400 pounds. I think he only used his rig to haul himself around. He left, probably to haul his precious cargo home to his mom's for some true country cooking. And I wanted to go with him — he looked so happy and content. He didn't have to do the truckers' shuffle. He was the kind of guy that caused the other truckers to learn the shuffle.

There were three good ol' boys in camouflage outfits that were probably going rabbit hunting. Or maybe they were in some secret militia. I couldn't tell if they were skinheads because they all had on camouflage hunting caps. There were several single, Clint Eastwood types who looked long, lean and completely self-sufficient. There was a "community table" with people just drifting in and out; the main-stay at the table was a couple dressed as if they had gone or were going to go to church. Perhaps it was this couple, later identified by us as perhaps the owners, who appealed to the waitress to let us stay.

I saw a man with long, pretty, and female-looking hair. It would have been pretty on most women but on him it was just country looking. Know what I mean? The owner, or manager, came around and handed out nice little pocket calendars and then his wife (we thought) came through on a good-will tour. She sort of personally assured us with her demeanor that no one was actually going to ask us to leave. We began to feel that a certifiable membership in this truckers club required you to be driving either an 18-wheeler or a car that could hold 400 gallons of diesel.

There was a bar-like table for loners who just hoped someone would sit at the bar and speak to them. Of course, these individuals were lightweights who drove only smaller rigs. The floor was garish — red and white, 12"x 12" ceramic tile. The remainder of the décor consisted of hundreds of coffee mugs of every description lining shelves throughout the restaurant.The restaurant was divided from the gas and merchandise store by only a walkway. Several framed certificates hung on the wall in honor of the man I assumed was the owner. Two of the certificates were from governors McWherter and Alexander, a democrat and a republican, and named Haywood P. Norman IV as an honorary Colonel on their staffs. He was also "appointed" as an honorary staff member of Lt. Governor John Wilder and "Aide-De-Campe" of State Senator Robert Rochelle of Lebanon. I suspected that the "P." stood for Pete if the restaurateur and the politician were one and the same. An U.S. Army School of Aviation diploma also hung on the wall, which explained several pictures of aircraft displayed in the restaurant.

The several male/female trucker teams inhabiting the booths were also interesting. They might have been just like Betty and me though except they had already learned the ropes of acting like real truck drivers, like where to sit and how to hold a cigarette. One "wife" sitting with a man spent the entire time talking on her wall phone, the booth serving as an oversized phone booth with food service. She reminded me of one of my soon-to-be-recorded (according to my agent's assurances) country songs entitled, My Telephone Bill. The lonely traveler in my song has to call his/her mate throughout the day, everyday. She/he makes so many calls that his/her telephone bill is out of sight leaving him/her with no choice other than to sell bits and pieces of his/her car (luggage rack, spare tire, jack, radio, etc.) just to get enough money to keep making the calls. The lady on the wall phone seemed to be heading down the same path. Maybe my song could be a warning to her. Look for my other songs soon-to-be-in-record-stores-everywhere: *Emergency, Emergency – Heart Trouble, I Want To Be Somebody Else In Some Other Place, Now I Lay Me Down To Weep*, and *Don't Give Me Time to Think It Over*. I don't expect to sing my own songs for some time yet — not until I am at least as old as Willie Nelson.

The food came quickly and was good, as expected. Truckers would have it no other way. They talk more on their CBs about good food stops than they do about "rubber ducks." You have to be a trucker to understand and, frankly, I don't have the patience to explain it to those of you who don't hold a chauffeur's license. Now back to the food. My eggs were perfect. The potatoes had a great taste, probably due to the amount of grease left in them. But the pork chops, ordered to prove my trucker's credentials, were not as good as those at the Waffle House. Now there was a partnership to be made. Are you ready for this? Gas at Waffle Houses or, better still, a major gas company could buy the Waffle House franchise rights at major intersections. Believe me the idea's a winner. Let me know if any of my readers pick it up; I expect some significant options for the tip. By the way, that's the best idea I've had since Fantiques, my failed restaurant venture in 1978. (I didn't say Fantiques had been operated right. I just said it had been a good idea.)

I said that the food at Pete's was good, and it was. But it was not perfect. The biscuits had the telltale consistency of having been nuked. Although beautiful and tasty, they had lost their crustiness and had been bombarded by electrons, or some sort of invisible heat missiles, inside those biscuit destroying machines from hell. But, hey Pete — the Waffle House doesn't even try biscuits at all. Keep improving on your pork chop frying and trash the nuke box. I'll be back with all the rest of my good buddies.

As we left, I noticed that the lady, who had been on the phone in her booth for a solid hour, was still talking. From the expressions crossing her face she had to be speaking with her lover. I felt sorry for her but not nearly as sorry as I felt for her husband; he had to just sit there and get eggs all over his face while she made out on the phone. It was 10:00 a.m. and time to find a place where "The saints of God are fed." We continued east on the Smithville-Sparta Highway in search of a church with an 11:00 a.m. service that did not require an advance application in order to attend.

After passing through Watertown and finding only two Baptist churches, we wondered if the Baptists had euthanized all members of the Church of Christ to create a total lock on Watertown. We were hoping to attend a church of a group that we had not yet visited. Finding new groups was getting harder and harder in Middle Tennessee where it seemed that 75 percent of all churches were Baptist, Methodist or Church of Christ. We then passed "by" Alexandria, not "through" Alexandria, and saw no churches on the highway. It was now 10:33 a.m. and we were in no man's land. Should we go back to Lebanon or press on towards Smithville? Smithville won the internecine battle in my mind between Lebanon and Smithville. And with that we were on our way to Smithville. Prepare Ye the way of the Lord and be sure to have a church with an 11:00 a.m. service.

It was about 10:38 a.m. when we crossed the line into Dekalb County. I realized a congenital flaw that exists in the concept behind *Fifty-two "Sundays" on the Blue Roads*. Here it is plain and simple. Blue roading, by my own definition, means "no destination." But we were faced with the destination of a church although not a particular church — technically, that let us slide by the "no destination" rule. But any conceivable destination means some kind of constraint. We needed to be in church and 11:00 a.m. was the final tolling of the bell for churches on Sunday mornings. Now there's the rub. The clock was a major factor. We were now racing to beat the clock by finding a church before 11:00 a.m., even if it was one of the same denominations we had already visited. Now this was another real point of conflict. We were in a hurry with slow-moving traffic in front of us yet we had to be in a seat in church by 11:00 a.m. Remember the "Do Not Pass" rule of blue roading? Out the window! We passed two slow-moving cars that truly were blue roading. As we were zipped along, trying to salvage the "52" part of the endeavor, I broke the "Do Not Pass" part. Decisions, decisions. Just an integral part of life. Moments after passing the cars I saw a roadside sign, "Prepare to Meet Thy God." If I was not more careful, I thought, I would end up meeting Him even before 11:00 a.m.

We made it to Smithville at 10:52 a.m. and drove up to the square where, weeks before, I had seen the "twin churches," a Methodist church and a Baptist church. "Let's go to the Baptist," I said. We had been to two Methodist churches but only to one Baptist church. We got out of the car and suddenly saw a sign that was certainly an affront to us, if not to God, "Worship Service 10:00." It was too late to do anything but go to the other church. The Methodist church, perhaps self-righteously, announced on its front sign that they worshipped, as the 11th Commandment says, at 11:00 a.m. So in we went to find two of the last seats left; that's the way it is on Christmas and Easter. You can count on both of these holidays to fill Christian churches.

We slipped into comfortable white pews with maple trim and soft green cushions. We may have been stealing the two seats from far more deserving members since we were here by default; but possession is nine-tenths of the laws, even in churches. The church looked like a church. It had a mossy green carpet, light green walls with white trim and seven stained-glass windows, including one behind the chancel. A beautiful Christmas tree, about fifteen feet tall, stood to the right of the chancel and was decorated with various Christian symbols. At *exactly* 11:00 a.m. the choir came in and the service began. It really was a God-fearing congregation — 11:00 a.m. sharp. The choir of eighteen was dressed in burgundy robes with white trim, eight men and ten women. There was a piano on one side of the chancel and an organ on the other. Two ministers, an older balding one dressed in a suit and a younger bearded one in a black robe with a purple sash, were seated in the chancel area in front of the choir. The older minister, Glen Hendrixson, was listed as the "liturgist." He stood and gave a general welcome to all in the congregation to the worship service. He then made a couple of announcements before acolytes came forward to light the chancel candles. The lighting of the candles was followed shortly by the printed responsive reading, a choral call to worship, and "The Lighting of The Advent Wreath" by three young boys of the congregation.

After a hymn sung by the congregation, *O Come, O Come Emmanuel,* the young bearded minister, identified in both the bulletin and the order of worship as the Reverend. Mark C. Pafford, asked the congregation to remain standing. He then asked the members to greet each other by saying "The Peace of Christ be with you." He also instructed everyone to respond with "And also with you." Although the people seemed to get into this in a big way, I stood there feeling like a truck driver pretender in a truck stop. I always feel a little ill at ease in situations like this. It's like when a mother says to a child, "Say hello to the nice man, Suzy" but Suzy just wants to hide behind mamma's dress. The service proceeded with a reading of the scripture from *Luke 1: 47 – 55* followed by a pastoral prayer and then the *Lord's Prayer.* The Methodists say, "forgive us our trespasses" while the Presbyterians say, "forgive us our debts." This is about as far as the differences go in Methodist and Presbyterian services so far as this pilgrim can tell.

There would be no sermon; the real program was *Bringing Christmas Home* by the chancel choir. The Reverend. Mr. Pafford was the narrator and Sherry Bush was the director. The songs by the choir were interspersed with bits of what sounded like a story from the pastor's life. He told, in the song-story pattern, of his early life with his brother, Jim. He spoke about how close they were, about how they competed with each other in many ways and about how they went their separate ways after growing up. Pastor Mark went into the ministry while Jim's life and marriage was troubled. Then, after a separation of five years, Jim called wanting to spend Christmas with Mark and his family. Mark was happy to have him come but did not know what to expect. Jim shared his troubles with Mark and his feeling that if he could be with his brother for the holiday that "things would be just like they used to be." After dinner Mark asked Jim to read the Christmas Story. Jim hesitated but started to read. He was okay until the part where the angels

143

said, "Do not be afraid." He stopped there saying that he wanted them to pray, right there in the living room, for God to come back into his life.

The narrator, and brother of Jim, said that this was a true example of bringing Christmas home. The choir then sang *Bringing Christmas Home* as the finale of the choir for the Christmas service. The acolytes then lighted their candles again and walked back down the aisle in the "Sending Forth" part of the service, which symbolically sends out the light of Christ into the world. A "Choral Benediction" and a postlude followed before the service ended at 12:00 p.m. sharp.

The pastor truly understood both the commandment to begin at 11:00 a.m. and the strong admonition, if not still another commandment, to end the service at 12:00 p.m. Let's keep it as part of the requirement to meet at 11:00 a.m. Everybody knows that all services are supposed to last for only one hour, else God would have made man's attention span longer than an hour. If we are not careful here, however, a theological debate might begin with the growing recognition of the need for a 10-minute worship service.

Did I hear someone say, "Leave the theologians alone. A little debate never hurt anybody?"

Chapter 16

Trinity Missionary Baptist Church
Cookeville, Tennessee
December 29, 2002

Christmas day had come on a Wednesday and, as usual, our family had spent several days together at the lake cottage near Center Hill Lake. Barbara and Beverly, our daughters, had returned to Nashville two days later for more Christmas festivities while Betty and I stayed on at the lake cottage for the rest of the week. We had decided to stay longer for two reasons. First, we were about out of firewood. A friend, Wayne Williams, and his crew, Dennis, Stan and James, were coming on Saturday with a trailer load of wood from Nashville. We were hoping that the load might be sufficient to last us the rest of the winter but I doubted it. There were still ten weeks of winter left. We spend much of the fall-winter and early spring at Center Hill and we love to sit in front of a beautiful wood fire eating popcorn, cookies and a lot of other good weekend-lake kinds of things. The chances of Wayne and his crew needing to make yet another mercy mission load of firewood were certainly better than 50/50.

Second, I had made a mess trying to clean up a mess on carpet on the steps at the cottage and felt it was my job to take care of the situation. So what did I do? I called Buck, of course. Buck is James Buck, an integral part of our support system whether in Nashville or in Center Hill. What Wayne and his team can't do, Buck can. Buck is one of those people that even the most ardent opponents of human cloning would seriously consider making an exception if such a helpful, talented, considerate and gentle man could successfully be cloned. Buck said he could be at the cottage around 4:00 p.m. on Saturday. I told him to bring a toothbrush. I would cook dinner and we could watch movies late into the night after he finished fixing my boo-boo. Three hours of Buck's efforts had me back in the good graces of my family.

While we watched two movies and enjoyed some brownies and ice cream, I told Buck about my *Fifty-Two Sundays* project. I asked if he had any reason to hurry back home the next morning and, if not, if he would like to go with us for a blue-road breakfast and a blue road church service somewhere in the area. He liked the idea and so, at 8:30 a.m. the next morning, Betty, Buck and I left the cottage in search of blue-road institutions catering to the nourishment of body and soul.

We drove Buck around "our" area of the lake for a few minutes before heading north on Highway 56 towards Baxter and Cookeville. There is a very good reason that some flexibility in the rules of blue roading is necessary. Although driving on a "red" road, or Interstate, is an anathema to all true blue-roaders, we had no choice in this case. Somewhere in the warped and twisted minds of the Tennessee Department of Transportation officials, the routes of State 56 and I-40 had been irresponsibly merged together for about five miles on the trek from Smithville to Baxter. I felt like I was betraying all of what was sacred about blue roading as I pressed on toward Baxter on 56/I-40 during these few miles of merger mania; I felt sort of dirty all the while. We abandoned I-40 as soon as 56 extricated itself from I-40's snare, which obviously had trapped many hundreds of mindless pilgrims who had been lured by the endless stretches of highway into going nowhere quick and back again as soon as possible.

After that ordeal was over, I felt freer and cleaner by the moment as we eased back into the relaxed mode of true blue roading. We were now also free to look for a blue-road restaurant — one that caters to Sunday wayfarers on their search for Sunday morning fulfillment. And it's not easy; the blue law advocates of years gone by, which at one time forbade all commercial ventures from being open on Sunday, have left a mark on far too many restaurant owners. I have threatened to expose several restaurants' disregard for the traveling public in not being open at least for Sunday morning breakfast. Churchgoers should be able to worship on Sunday with a full stomach, just as those who worship on other "Sabbaths." It borders on religious discrimination. I'm thinking of filing a class-action suit against them. I am going to start a petition and get the ball rolling. Please sign the petition when you see it in your area.

We can stamp out this conspiracy, which causes millions of worshipers to miss the true religious experience enjoyed by others who can worship so much more freely and completely on a full Sabbath stomach.

The search was on for one righteous restaurant owner who believed that all true worshipers should be allowed to worship in spirit and in truth without fear of hunger pangs. As if by answer to prayer, we came upon Odie's Drive-In Restaurant which had several cars parked in front. The wheels of the car skidded to a stop in the loose gravel of the road shoulder as I backed up to pull in the parking area of the unlikely breakfast place. The Odie's Restaurant sign was obviously a form of payola provided by Coca-Cola, the two red "Coke" offerings dominated the black and white name of the restaurant. Even if they were only serving hot dogs and onions rings, they were open. And we were hungry. In we went, not willing to wait to see if some carhop would dash out of the past to take our order and attach a tray to the car's window. Mustering all our Sunday faith,we pressed through the windbreak into the restaurant and hoped there would be actual tables inside, to which a waitress would come offering a full breakfast menu.

The name was "Odie's Drive-In Restaurant," but as I stepped through the door and peered inside I almost instinctively did a double take. What an unexpectedly pleasant surprise! Here was a clean and comfortable restaurant, which says that the person who owns and manages the restaurant really cares. There was an open room with seats for about fifty people spread among tables that could sit two to six each. The tables were covered with fresh, cheerful blue and white "oil cloth" tablecloths. The floor was a clean 4 x 4 gray tile; the walls and ceilings were white. The white walls were decorated with antique farm implements and tools including a two-man crosscut saw. And there was a Dr. Pepper clock in direct competition with the sign provided by Coke on the outside. There were also displays of rolling pins, teapots, pitchers and decorative jars of canned fruits and vegetables.

A friendly waitress quickly brought menus that confirmed immediately that they had more than barbecue sandwiches. There it was in bold letters, "Breakfast Menu." We felt immediately at home, assured that Odie's was a place where souls are fed and where we would soon be able to worship contentedly. While pursuing the menu selections we saw a sign which read, "Friday Special — All you can eat. Catfish $6.50." There was also a one-time salad bar, which had been decommissioned for the occasion by the captain of the ship; in place of brunch selections on the salad bar stood a little Christmas Village scene far too elaborate to be easily moved by brunch time. Perhaps the salad bar will be reconsidered after the New Year.

Betty and Buck ordered two scrambled eggs with bacon. I ordered three eggs over-easy (I was getting brave) with country ham as well as three pancakes "for the table." We all ordered coffee and biscuits. With the coffees custom-creamed and sugared, we were content to do some blue-road restaurant gazing. These words were on the menu, "Odie's Drive In Restaurant — Gary Sudham, owner." There also was a black and white picture near the cash register, "Odies's Drive In — 1951." Black and white evidence that Gary was not the first owner. The first owner was Odie someone. I wanted to say, "Thank you, Odie, wherever you are," because the 1951 picture took me back many years. Odie's Drive In reminded me of "Stewart's Root Beer" place in Logan, West Virginia. Stewart's had been a drive-in restaurant where we would go in the 40's and early 50's to get root beer and hot dogs and just hang out hoping for something "neat" to happen. It never did, but Odie's made me realize that the time I had spent with my friends at Stewart's had been neat. And I wanted to thank Odie for taking me back for a few minutes.

Now in a real warm and nostalgic mood, I looked around the room hoping to see Junior Smith and Mickey Gordon and Cordy Wilson and some of the other gang I remembered seeing when going to Odie's. I mean, Stewart's. They were not there but I did see a warm Mayberry-type scene with different Sunday morning blue-roaders coming in as we first drank our coffee, then leisurely ate our breakfasts. Two tables each held one man who was slowly and deliberately eating his morning meal with white "ad" cap in place, as if the caps were a part of their blue road worship vestments. At another table, two men were eating together that apparently belonged to the same congregation of the two men eating alone. At least their blue road yarmulkes were properly in place as they reverently feasted in Odie's blue road, soul food sanctuary. The owner, as the priest of the sacramental morning feast, came by to bless all his paying parishioners with fresh refills of coffee — the nectar of the early morning gods. At another table a small private congregation of five — three men and two women — were praising The Creator of the pancakes and sausages in their own obvious but private ways. And two fearless trucker-types appeared humbled at the sight of the full breakfasts being served to them.

By now Gary, the present titular head of Odie's offerings, and his choir of kitchen angels had presented us with plentiful platters of pancake accompaniments. These were the answer to our own individual breakfast prayers. And we three kings and queens of country cuisine attended to the affairs of the state of Sunday morning hunger by pondering where to begin. I found the answer to this question by moving my biscuits and gravy to the left side of the plate leaving the full center-cut slice of country ham exposed in all its sacrificial glory; my personal feast began. The ham was succulent and was very near salt-cured perfection. I, by now, had massacred the three over-easy eggs and was ready to build three layered bites of ham, potatoes and eggs. Just about perfect. That is, if I didn't count the biscuits in on the bites. I tried to ignore them. They had been handled by a nuclear nazi masquerading as one of Gary's kitchen angels. And they bombed. Sponge ball bombs despite the fact they were congenitally well-bred biscuits; they had the genetics and the great molecular structure of the high-born Pillsbury clan. But they had mutated into something unfit to be served even at a table of storm troopers, much less the table of the descendants of King Odie's aristocratic breakfasters.

When Marie-Antoinette was told that her subjects were restless, she was given a reason for their unrest — the people had no bread. "They have no bread?" asked the queen, "Then let them eat cake." The breakfast was so great that it deserved great biscuits and these were not. So I say to Gary, and to all the descendants of the Odie's of the world, "If you don't have good biscuits, then serve cake with your eggs. Anything! But make it good. If you can't serve great biscuits to go with your great breakfasts then serve your customers great toast." While you're at it, Gary, study how the Pancake Pantry in Nashville does its fried potatoes; you will be on your way to letting Odie rest in peace.

Once on a blue-road trip to the western part of the U.S., I saw a sign in a little western version of a southern meat-n-three, "In case of an atomic attack, pay your bill...and then run like hell." There had been a nuclear attack on the biscuits at Odie's but, thank God, the bomb was a "Smart" bomb; a direct hit was made only on the biscuits. We happily paid our bill but felt no urgency to "run like hell," but Gary should and as soon as possible — to the first Pillsbury doughboy biscuit class he can find. His food is too fine to be sabotaged by a small tactical nuclear weapon such as a microwave. Any certified Pillsbury biscuit baker would tell you that!

We left Odie's at 10:00 a.m. to find a blue-road church to join others seeking food for their souls. We passed the Trinity Missionary Baptist Church with an announced service time of 10:45 a.m. This was a possibility; we had not yet been to a "Missionary" Baptist Church. We had attended the First Baptist Church in Gallatin, Tennessee but not a Missionary Baptist Church. However, we still had 45 minutes to shop. We decided to use the time and drove on. We went east on Highway 70 and turned north onto South Willow Street. We passed several large churches and then turned west onto 290, traveling several miles out that direction. We passed a Jehovah's Witness Church but their "Public Talk" service was at 10:00 a.m. We made a notation because I wanted to attend one of their services at the first opportunity. We also passed a Free Will Baptist Church and also noted it as a future possibility. It was now 10:30 a.m. and we decided to return to the Missionary Baptist Church located on Highway 70, west of Cookeville at W. 4th Street. The Minister was Pastor Earl Dirkson.

We arrived at 10:40 a.m. and left the car in a nearly empty parking lot. We entered the relatively neat brick church, which apparently had only recently been built. We entered the church near the end of the Sunday School service. The Sunday School superintendent called on the secretary to read the minutes, which noted the attendance for each class, the offering of each class, and then the totals for both along with some other comments and announcements. Then the superintendent called for a motion to approve the minutes. Motion made, seconded and approved as read. The superintendent ended the Sunday school service.

We seated ourselves at the next to the back row (the back row was reserved for the ushers). The neat and new church had a vaulted ceiling, burgundy carpet and new pews with white end caps and burgundy upholstered seats. The Sunday School superintendent, an African-American, introduced himself as John Jackson. He was a handsome man, confident and reserved, who had been a member here all his life, His father founded the church in 1946 after graduating from the American Baptist Seminary in Nashville. The new church building was the third one on the same location and was built in 1996.

By this time there were only about 15 or 20 people in the church. The members were predominantly African-American although three other white men were in attendance — plus the three of us who were visiting. Almost every one of the church members came by our pew and warmly welcomed us to the service. John Jackson, the Sunday School superintendent and also a deacon, brought us a hymnal. I noticed that it was *The New National Baptist Hymnal*, a hymnal I had a part in developing. It's a long story but the late Dr. T.B. Boyd Jr. was head of the National Baptist Publishing Board (NBPB) about 25 years ago. At that time I helped arrange for a builder friend to contract to build their new headquarters. It turned out that the builder went bankrupt and providing the funds to finish the building fell on me. Dr. Boyd, in gratitude, offered me the opportunity to make back some of my lost money by arranging for me to publish a new hymnal. I formed a company with three parts: (1) my company; (2) John T. Benson; and, (3) T.B. Boyd III (Dr. Boyd's young son who, at the time, was about 24 years old.) In honor of the three parts we chose the name, "Triad Publishing Company." The hymnal, I noticed, still recognizes my friends John T. Benson and Don Sheffield, as well as me, as among the individuals who helped to publish the hymnal.

The service began slowly. Deacon Jackson led the singing and selected hymns from the hymnal I had assisted in publishing. The first hymn was No. 79 — *At The Cross*: "At the Cross, at the Cross where I first saw the light and the burdens of my heart rolled away." There was an organ to the right of the pulpit and a piano and a set of drums to the left. The organ was not used during the service.

As we began to sing, five men gathered and sat on the right

front pew. I assumed these were the church deacons because Deacon Jackson was among them. As the pastor finally entered, the congregation stood in honor of his arrival (just as those in a courtroom stand when the judge comes in), and remained standing until he was seated. Pastor Earl Dirkson was dressed in a beige suit with a dark brown shirt and tie. The pastor sparked the real beginning of the service. He welcomed everyone and said, "We're all glad to be here at the last service of this year. Some started but did not finish. I'm glad I made it. Do I hear Am<u>a</u>n? Am<u>a</u>n."

The five deacons knelt, facing the congregation, and sang, *In That Land Where I'm Bound.* At this point a white drummer joined the piano as part of the instrumental musical accompanying the congregation. The song continued, "Don't you want to go to the land where I'm bound?" One of the five deacons, still kneeling and facing the congregation, then passionately offered a 15 minute extemporaneous prayer with members of the congregation and the pastor saying "Amen" and "Uh, huh." The deacon prayed "Lord, stop by here this morning. You are the Father to the Fatherless and the Mother to the Motherless " and also prayed for the sick, the sinner, the congregation and the world.

The pastor then called for everyone to stand during the procession of the choir, entering from the rear of the sanctuary. The choir consisted of 15 members, mostly black women, two black men and one heavily overweight white man; the choir did not wear robes. The choir gently swayed in rhythm as they sang *We're going to see the King.* Everyone in the congregation and the choir clapped and swayed as they continued to sing. After the hymn the pastor said, "We're going to see the King. Aman? Aman."

A different deacon read two passages of scripture from *1st John* and from *Isaiah Chapter 40.* Then another deacon led a prayer while kneeling with the other deacons facing the congregation. This deacon was a tall and handsome man wearing a royal blue suit with a Nehru collar. He prayed, "Father, thank you for taking us through the valley to the mountain." He prayed for about five minutes for those in nursing homes and all those in need, with "Yes, Jesus" encouragement coming from the pastor, over and over. Then still another deacon stood and led the congregation in a responsive reading of the scripture.

Pastor Dirkson then offered a spirited prayer:
*"Thank you, Lord. You've been so good. You saved my soul,
that's why we raise our hand (everyone seated raised their
hands) and I just want to thank you, Jesus. That's why we
stand and raise our hands (the congregation stood and
raised their hands) and say thank you Lord."*

The deacons acted as cheerleaders throughout the service, ready to
support the pastor at his every move and word.

At this point the offering was taken. The choir and the congregation sang while every worshiper marched to the altar to make an
offering instead of an usher passing a basket from aisle to aisle. The
church secretary made a report including several announcements
and then asked for any visitors to stand and introduce themselves.
I stood and introduced Betty, Buck and myself as visitors from
Nashville; the entire congregation again welcomed us warmly. The
congregation was encouraged to visit with each other and to welcome each other in the name of the Lord for a few minutes. The
congregation acted as if it was a family reunion; everyone greeted
and hugged each other. Most of the church members came to our
pew to hug us and truly welcome us, over and over again. Then the
pastor started singing. Gradually, the visitation came to an end and
everyone went back to his or her seat.

A tall black man in a red coat had been playing an acoustical
guitar to augment the music program. As they arrived different
musicians would just start "sitting in" with the others and adding to
the spirit of the music. There were about 50 or 60 people in the
entire congregation, including the choir of 15. The members of the
congregation were respectfully dressed in a manner in which, in the
not too distant past, all churchgoers of all denominations were
accustomed to dressing when going to church. The pastor asked
those with a birthday in December to stand; he personally took a
birthday greeting card to each one while the congregation sang
"Happy birthday everybody, happy birthday to you." Then the pastor asked young people under the age of 12 to come forward for
"Children's church." A young woman went with the pre-teens to
the front and asked them, "Do you know how to worship the
Lord?" She continued, "We all know how to act when we are happy

and this is the way we should be when we worship the Lord." The children then stood in a circle holding hands while saying the *Lord's Prayer*. Each of the children then made an offering just as each of the adults had done.

Pastor Dirkson then called the congregation to the "Altar Prayer." Most of the members of the congregation gathered at the altar to pray with each member telling what they wanted to pray for. Like one large family, everyone joined hands while the pastor prayed,"Thank you Lord,for allowing us to come for the 52nd time this year to join in worship. Father thank you for looking down on this piece of clay. Thank You who can be everywhere at the same time." He prayed for the needs of the congregation, the president, secretary of state, secretary of war and for the congress; he also prayed that they would know that their power is limited. He prayed, "Bless everyone holding hands around the altar who has needs ... You can do anything but fail" and continued in a beautiful, passionate, rhythmic prayer for the needs of the congregation, "Come on, Jesus. Let us feel you one more time. In the name of Jesus, in the mighty name of Jesus, and all the people say, Aman. Aman." A deacon started to sing, "One more time...we are all allowed to come together one more time."

The pastor kneeled at his seat on the pulpit while the choir and soloist sang, "Hold My Hand," with enthusiastic swaying and clapping. The congregation then picked up the song, which continued,"Now I can cry all night long, hold my hand...When I can't see ...hold my hand." Then the pastor sang, "I've been born again... makes me feel so good right now."

The pastor then read *Matthew 2:3 – 6* with the whole congregation reading along. The scripture was about "the wise men who missed Jesus," and was the topic of his sermon. He said that the shepherds saw Jesus, but the wise men did not. The deacons said: "Well all right," "Uh huh," "Come on preacher." One deacon stood during the entire sermon, cheering the pastor on: "Well all right, preacher,""Uh huh,""Yes, preacher,""Yes, sir," and, "Amen, preacher."

The pastor continued the sermon, "The wise men knew the location but they missed the incarnation...They knew the scriptures but did not know the Savior." He said, "We cannot be saved by the Christmas story only." He said God must turn us around.

The deacons played a supporting role and contributed:
"All right, preacher."
"Come on, preacher."
"Come on now."

By now the preacher was on a roll. He said:
"I wasn't there when Jesus was born,
but I'm wise enough to know:"
"That He came for me,"
"That He is my all and all,"
"That His name is Jesus,"
"That He is my Savior."

"But it's not enough to know," the pastor continued, "We must do something about it." Then, as if on cue, two deacons pulled out an altar seat and the pastor moved directly to an altar call. The pianist went to the piano. Five people, including one white man, went forward for prayer. Others came to pray with those who came for prayers.

Sometime during the service a new drummer and guitarist had replaced the original musicians. It seemed as if the last team was the "A" team and the original players had just been warming up their spot until they arrived at their own pace.

With the altar prayer proceeding, the choir and a choir soloist, the original guitarist, sang over and over again:
"Don't you know that Jesus can hear me:"
"Late at night"
"Late at night"
"Late at night"
"Late at night"
"Jesus, Jesus"
"Jesus, Jesus"

A woman at the altar and a woman in a pew began to shout. Both convulsed almost helplessly and female ushers administered to them. Two deacons at the altar literally kept one seeker from injury by not allowing her to fall to the floor.

Those who came forward to the altar were asked to testify which they did, one at a time, with the encouragement of the pastor.

Then a deacon made a motion that these seekers be admitted to the church. The deacons and the pastor all joined hands. The pastor touched those at the altar by placing his hand on them. He said, "Thank you, Lord for adding to the church...Holy, Master, we pray for them. Shower them with your blessing." The pastor again touched each of them and said, "In the name of the Lord." The prayer service at the altar wound down and the service was over — after three hours, 10:45 a.m. – 1:45 p.m. We were tired just from being there. But the emotionally draining service must have left the pastors, the deacons and the other lay leaders emotionally drained.

A three-hour service and the Titans playing! Don't these people know that this is Titan country? The truth is that the Missionary Baptist Church lies totally outside the TADI — the Titans Area of Dominant Influence. The Titans are a total non-entity at the church. The members of the church certainly would say they are God-fearing people who take religion seriously and worship in triple doses. Three hours worth at a time. Time for lunch Pastor Dirkson. Aman? Aman.

Betty, Buck and I all agreed that the worshipers had not been at all concerned with the length of the service. Pastor Dirkson was in no danger of losing his job for going past the 12:00 p.m. termination time of most other congregations. If anything, the pastor was in for a healthy raise. His direction of the emotional, spirit-filled services kept the church members here not because of the church's distance from Nashville, but because Sunday is their time for worship — Titans or no Titans, clock or no clock. For such devout worshipers Sunday is the day for worship; Monday night is for football. Everybody knows that.

Chapter 17

Clarksville Family Bible Church
Clarksville, Tennessee
January 6, 2003

etty and I left our home in Nashville at 8:00 a.m. We took
Woodmont Boulevard until it turned into White Bridge Road
and, even farther along, into Briley Parkway. It was a pleasant
day, slightly overcast yet clearing. We had decided to go toward
Clarksville, Tennessee, a city of more than 100,000 people located
near the Kentucky border. Clarksville is in the environs of Ft.
Campbell, a well-established military institution with a base population of about 25,200 military personnel and about 4,250 civilian
employees.

There was considerable attention on Ft. Campbell at this time
because of the brewing crisis in Iraq; the U.N.'s inspectors had
recently been sent to Iraq, primarily to check out its potential
threat in terms of weapons of mass destruction. The U.N. inspectors
had been sent at the request of President Bush. Bush had charged,
through our ambassadors, that Saddam Hussein violated a U.N.
agreement by which Iraq would not build and store weapons that
could be used for mass destruction. But, to many U.S. citizens, it
seemed there were also other political reasons that President Bush
was "spoiling for a fight" with Iraq. Whatever the other underlying
reasons might have been, there was a great probability that war
between U.N. forces and Iraq would soon be a reality.

Any new war in today's situation always brings Ft. Campbell
into play with its 101st Airborne Division. The 101st is composed
of about 23,000 men and women who are highly skilled and
trained to assist in air warfare, which any war with Iraq would
undoubtedly call upon very heavily. Thus, at times like this, the
whole Ft. Campbell/Clarksville area is full of nervous excitement:
Will it happen? When will it happen? How many of the troops
from Ft. Campbell will be needed? And for how long?

So, in spite of the present situation, which the Democrats call a recession and the Republicans call a downturn in the economy (which, they say, of course, started during the Clinton/Gore administration) the Clarksville area seemed a beehive of activity. Betty and I were eager to let our blue roading experience partake of Clarksville's atmosphere as much as possible for just a few hours. We turned off Briley Parkway onto Clarksville Pike (or 41-A) at about 8:20 a.m. and figured we would be in Clarksville (about 50 miles away) about 9:30 a.m. We were blue roading, remember? No real hurry. Just get there leisurely, find a place for breakfast and then find a church to complete the Sunday morning experience.

Within a few miles we were in a little community which we later learned was Joelton. So that is where Joelton is. From now on I'll have a better sense of recognition when I hear a weather report that includes "Storm front moving in through Joelton," often the case. You know, if there was no threat there was no mention at all of these "name" spots for storm trackers. As we passed through Joelton, we saw two churches: the "House of Righteous Endeavor" and the "Calvary Bible Church." Both would be good to keep in mind for the future.

Zipping along at about 45 miles per hour we were soon in Pleasant View and, within a span of a very few miles, we noticed three Freewill Baptist Churches: Goodsprings, Oaklawn and Head's. A curiosity. Why were these churches bunched so close together? Maybe one or the other's free will was too free. We decided to come back if possible during the fifty-two week, self-limited period to seek an answer to this question. We also noticed that Pleasant View had a fine looking blue-road attraction that would certainly make another Sunday morning visit to their area possible and, hopefully, pleasurable; its sign said that the Pleasant View Café was open from 6:00 a.m. – 2:00 p.m. on Sundays.

Of course, there were "regular" Baptist churches all along this highway, too — not "Freewill Baptists" — just "Baptists." I guess these are the Baptists who are "Predestination Baptists" instead of "Freewill" ones. Actually, and technically, I understand any Baptist church can believe and teach anything they wish since each congregation is totally autonomous. It may be that if they do or do not believe in certain things they may not be able to join certain other strictly voluntary groups or associations but they could still, pre-sumably, call themselves Baptists. I suppose a Baptist church could be a Baptist church and not believe in Baptism or in immersion. I guess they could, but why not just get another name if that is the case? I'm going to ask some of my Baptist friends. Surely they would not reject me as a friend for just being ignorant of some of the finer points of their beliefs.

As we neared the city limits of Clarksville, we saw a Mormon church (Church of Latter-day Saints). We drove in just as a service was about to begin apparently because several people were driving in and parking at the same time. I was disappointed because the very discreet sign only gave the name of the church but no service times. I drove all around the building and still saw no notice of times of service. I wondered if the public was invited to come or if it was by invitation only. I only have one or two acquaintances that are Mormons but I decided to ask them about it and, if necessary, get an invitation to attend one of their services.

There was a more urgent matter to be considered though. It was about 9:15 a.m. I remembered from a previous visit to Clarksville that most of the restaurants were located on the by-pass around the southern part of the city and along the banks of the Cumberland River. So, for now, theological questions and invita-tions to churches would have to be postponed to a later date. Betty and I had to seek out an invitation to a breakfast club of some sort where we could discuss weighty matters such as the age old ques-tion of whether eggs are to be ordered over-light (or over lightly, to be grammatically correct) or over-medium. (Over mediumly?) I usually evade the grammatically correct issue by asking for over-easy or over-medium. There were also the questions about the legality of heating biscuits in a microwave and the integrity of the taste of potatoes compromised least by the cooking process, hash-brown vs. home-fry, to be considered. I could not wait to enter into such intellectual discussions with some culinary consultant at a greasy-spoon restaurant. And it would be soon.

Should we choose to have the discussion with the consult-ant/waitress at Shoney's, McDonalds, Burger King (proudly now proclaiming their new status of being breakfast certified) or G's Pancake House? The decision was easy. As Jesus said:"The poor you have with you always." I transposed this by saying "Shoney's, McDonalds and Burger Kings are everywhere, but G's Pancake House was obviously a local institution." At G's I might get the benefit of hands-on cuisine quality from the proprietor. At 9:35 a.m. we entered G's, were seated immediately, given a "Cuisine Curriculum" and signed up for the course immediately. Betty chose the non-thinking person's "basket weaving" type of course — "Pigs In The Blanket" — for the registration fee of $3.75.

I chose the "College Prep" course — a thinking man's breakfast — one in which there were many questions to be asked and answered. I answered all my consultant's questions correctly and ordered three eggs over-medium, pork tenderloins, home fries, gravy and "grilled biscuits." The last part of the exam took my consultant by surprise. And she was impressed that I knew the sure way to keep the biscuits out of the hands of kitchen Nazis and out of the nuke box — "grilled biscuits." At home I call my crispy biscuits "toasted biscuits," but I did not want to seem too learned right at first. Oh, and I also ordered eight silver-dollar pancakes for extra credit.

While waiting for the results of the entrance exam, I took some time to look over the other "students." Many were from Ft. Campbell, of course, and several knew each other. One friendly black man wore a Titans jacket and a proud "go to hell" hat. He was conversing with his other soldier buddies around the restaurant and keeping everyone in a fun-friendly mood. One of the tables with which the friendly man was conversing held a family of three: a wife nicely dressed as if she were going to church and a husband and son who were dressed so that they would not be summarily rejected. They were politely talking with the other military people in the room. Were they expecting a call from the Commander-In-Chief at any time? There was a friendly somberness on all their faces — friendly and brave with a hint of worry on their brows.

The table I noticed mostly housed a very large man, perhaps 6'4", who was with, apparently, his three-year-old son. The son was a handsome little soldier and as well behaved as a buck private in front of a drill sergeant. Father-son, father-daughter breakfasts like this always intrigue me. Rarely do I see mother-daughter, mother-son breakfasters. I guess mothers tend to stay at home and cook, but when fathers have the responsibility it is to a restaurant they head most of the time. And here they were. But where was mom? Could she already be in Iraq? Was he going soon? Was he taking his little tenderfoot out to breakfast for the last time perhaps for a long time? As the big bear of a man and his little cub walked out, somehow I hoped that this was just a routine treat; a treat for a young son whose father is just a loving father who manages the PX at the base and will not be going anywhere soon — at least not to Iraq.

Betty flunked her quiz because her "pigs in the blanket" turned out to be a "pig in a poke" — an unpleasant surprise. They were too heavy and the syrup was too coarse. They were not light and delicate like the pigs in the blanket served at the Pancake Pantry, the seminary for all truly righteous pancake students. I felt sorry for her and let her eat half of my "extra credit" order, which were much better. (I get extra credit from Betty when I am generous with her and let her "cheat" in "class" like this.)

I passed, but not "summa cum laude" because of my failure to answer the question about potatoes as precisely as I should have. While I had correctly assumed that "home fries" was the correct answer among the multiple choice of French fries, hash browns or home fires, I failed to finish the essay part of the question. I should have told my consultant that I knew that all home fries must be fried to a golden brown and crisped at least on one side and the edges. I deserved to be "marked down" because I knew better than to leave this part unanswered. I was so ashamed of my failure that I did not complain about the grade of my potatoes.

Everything else I ordered could not have been prepared more precisely to my specified taste. Great eggs, great tenderloin (properly pounded into submission before frying) and the coup de gras of it all were the grilled biscuits. The biscuits were so great that I recommend they change the biscuit question on the entry exam to, "do you think your biscuits would be better served nuked, grilled or toasted?" If anyone answers this question by saying "nuked," he or she should be expelled forthright into an undergraduate class for those devoid of taste buds altogether.

After "evaluating" my extra credit order of silver dollars, I left a few pieces of "change" swimming in syrup; Betty and I left to go to a church. There was a "community type" church I had seen just a few blocks from the restaurant that I decided we would attend.

But we had to hurry. I had noticed that the worship service started at 10:30 a.m. and it was now 10:20 a.m. But no sweat. Surely we could find a righteous congregation that worshipped at 11:00 a.m. if we were too late for our chosen destination. All was well. We were there in two minutes. We walked into "Clarksville Family Bible Church" at 10:25 a.m. The church was a one-time twin movie theater, rather well recycled. The theater to the right was the "children's church" while the one to the left was the "adult church," the one we felt came the closest to us. If there had been a third auditorium labeled "senior citizens' church," we would have felt obligated to "fess up" and go into that show.

The recycling of the theater into a church got me thinking about how we effectively recycle many things in life. I remember going away to "Bible School" when I was only 15, partially to please my sweet mother who dearly wanted to have at least one "preacher son" out of the four which she had still living. When I left home, I recycled clothes my older brother had used, probably before he had totally finished with them. I think my mother conscripted his favorite sport coat and a couple of pairs of pants, placing them in the work of the Lord and into my single suitcase. I looked really nice for the first time in my life. I don't know what my brother Dru did. Probably without. After all, I was the one chosen, perhaps conscripted, to be our mother's "preacher boy." Dru probably rejected her efforts so she took his favorite sport coat and recycled it on me. And off I went.

After we left the twin theater recycled into the Clarksville Family Bible Church, we noticed several other recycled buildings; it delighted me because, as a real-estate man, I had often been turned down for a requested loan because a bank considered my proposal to be a "single-purpose" building. There probably was no such thing in Clarksville — a Shoney's building was now a China Star restaurant, a Central Park drive-through restaurant was now being used as a credit and check cashing office, a Shakey's Pizza was now being used as a Subway Sandwich Shop, a Beefy's Hamburger place was now a "Wok and Roll" Chinese takeout place, and several service stations were now being used as car lots. These car lots were selling mostly smaller sports type cars, obviously catering to the younger clientele from Ft. Campbell.

It was almost a religious experience for me to help recycle a piece of real estate that my bankers would have classified as a single purpose theater building. Hallelujah brother, we have those moneychanger bankers on the run. Let's convert other theaters into churches and give all our mortgage business to diatech.com.

Anyhow, back to the movie. I mean, church. We entered the "auditorium," which seemed an appropriate name considering both what it had been and how it had been set up for its recycled purpose. The seats were comfortable, padded chairs without arms that were connected in a theater like arrangement. There was a center aisle and aisles both to the left and the right. The theater's sloping contour, high in the back and low in front, gave every seat a "ringside" view. The walls and ceiling were painted white. The upholstery was green and the carpet was of a muted tone. Band instruments were spread across the entire stage including two keyboards, three sets of drums, one saxophone and microphones for four singers. There was a 10-ft. by 10-ft. screen above the pulpit, which was a single Plexiglas stand located in the middle of the stage and in front of the band.

Just before the service started, four black women walked down the far-left aisle, arms extended heavenward, shouting praises to God. They were singers and part of the "Worship Team," as the pastor later referred to them.They took their place in the center of the band section and continued to praise God as the music director, a white woman with blonde hair, began the service. The congregation, numbering about 125 worshipers, was about 40 percent black and 60 percent white and made up of mostly military-age people. About 20 percent of the congregates were children apparently truant from the children's church in the other theater.

The first rousing song was *My God is Good*, which was sung over and over again, "My God is good. Yes He is. Yes He is. Yes He is. He sets my feet to dancin'. Yes He does. Yes He does. Yes He does." Many members of the congregation shouted, waved and clapped.The song director jumped and bounced up and down with the beat on each repetition of "Yes He is" and "Yes He does," which went on for at least 10 minutes.

The minister, Pastor David Cook, made his first appearance after the worship team had "warmed up"the congregation for about

20 minutes. He was a white man about six feet tall and dressed in a tan sport coat with brown pants, white shirt and multicolored tie. After he welcomed everyone to the service, the worship team led the congregation in another song. The song leader prayed in praise of God before beginning the next rousing song. Again with several minutes of repetition, the congregation sang, "I just came to tell you that I love you…that you are worthy of my praise." The four "back-up" singers clapped and praised the Lord while the band's drummer, an African American gentleman with a large drum set and a whistle in his mouth, led the beat and the exultation.

The pastor then called on the ushers to serve communion. They passed trays of cracker pieces and white wine or grape juice. This was the first time I had ever seen white wine representing the blood of Jesus, serviced in the sacrament of the Lord's Supper. Things are changing so rapidly in forms of worship that I can almost imagine an order of worship announcement at some churches (probably starting first in California) saying something like: "The wine served in the sacrament today is a delightful fruity Merlot from the Napa Valley. We know you will enjoy it." The thought was encouraged by the sight of some members of the congregation enjoying a bottle of water or a cup of coffee in an insulated cup during the entire service. Maybe the progressive, ever ready to adapt and please pastor would add: "If you wish us to serve a wine of your choosing please let the tasting commit-tee know. Blind tastings are held monthly in the fellowship hall. All members are invited to come. Reservations are helpful. Many of our ladies will be happy to know that at the next communion we will be serving a light refreshing Kendall Jackson Grand Reserve — 2000."

The pastor paced nervously back and forth across the stage as the communion elements were served to the congregation. Then he read from the scriptures of the Lord's Supper and added the scrip-tural words "By His stripes we *were* healed." Then he said that if we "were" healed we "are" healed today and gave the assurance that physical healing was passed to us through the life and death of Christ. Then he said, "Ahmen," as if the Lord's Supper called for a more liturgical sound. For the rest of the service the pastor used the less "high churchly" pronunciation of "Amen."

The offering was then taken during the singing of "Blessed by your name, God Almighty...you are worthy, Lord." After the song and the offering, the "worship team" of the singers and the band left the choir area to join the congregation. One of the four singers joined a single African American man who was sitting directly in front of us whom we had sadly thought had come to church by himself (a serviceman, I assumed).

The pastor then read the scripture lesson from *III John 1: 1 – 4* and gave his sermon title, *God's Best Will Be In 2003*. He asked the members of the congregation to raise their Bibles and repeat after him, "This is my Bible. What it says I have, I have. What it says I am, I am...It is the eternal indestructible...seed of God." Then he went back to the scripture lesson that he quoted: "I am praying that your body is healthy as I know your soul is." Another translation went more like, he said, "I pray that you are well and that you are winning in every area of your life and that your bodies and souls are healthy."

During the rest of the sermon the pastor said, over and over, that God does not expect us to be poor and sick. He said it is an untruth that sickness and a lack of money will make you more spiritual. He asked: "How does it make God look if His children are always struggling? God is no different than we are and we do not want our children to be poor, ill clothed and sick all the time." He continued by saying that God wants us to be victorious in all parts of our lives. He quoted *Psalms 35: 27*: "Let the Lord be magnified who has pleasure in the prosperity of His servants." The congregation kept responding:

"Amen"
"Uh Huh"
"Yes Lord"
"Yes, That's right"
"Praise the Lord"

"There's nothing attractive about a Christian always being down and out," continued the pastor. And the members agreed:
"Amen, Glory"
"Bless God"
"Yes, Lord"

The pastor, spurred on by his cheering section said:"God does not get pleasure out of the failure of his saints." Like dueling preacher and praisers the support came right back:
"Praise God"
"Amen"
"That's the Word"

The pastor responded: "The poorer you are the less effective you will be in reaching others for Jesus."
"Hallelujah"
"My, my, my"

The pastor then said he was going to tell us of some "laws" which could make us successful for the Lord. He said the laws of God were as real as the law of gravity, a law that must be respected and obeyed. And it is the same with God's laws. He said there were 10 laws that he would be preaching about for the rest of this month. The "Laws" were:

(1.)   *"It is God's will that we be winners and prosperous and that we desire wealth and success."* The pastor said that God needs successful people to help with the finances of His church. While salvation is free, it has been "paid for" because someone paid their tithes and helped bring His word of salvation to us.

(2.)   *"Make God your partner in life."* He said that God is the originator, designer, and owner of the universe; He knows everything. *"What a partner,"* he said. *"Wall Street would go crazy over such a partner."*

(3.)   *"Get into life's work that you are best suited for."* He said we should ask our doctor if he likes what he is doing before letting him operate on us.

(4.)   *"Develop a strong living faith in God."*

(5.)   *"Don't be afraid to venture out."*

(6.)   *Follow certain business principles found in the Scriptures such as God's desire for us to be the best at what we do.*

(7.)   *"Follow the Golden Rule."* The person who does this is a very attractive person, he said.

(8.) *"Seek First the Kingdom of God and His ways of*
doing things and you will be prosperous in every area."
(9.) *"Always be a giver."*
(10.) *"Honor the Lord with your substance and your titles."*
He said we should put God's 10 percent first since it
really is all His anyway. Some of his flock responded:
"That's exactly right."
"That's good preachin'."
"That's right."

The preacher, determined to have the last word on the subject, gave a closing benediction that came a few minutes after 12:00
noon. As we left the church and headed back to Nashville, we read
from the church's statement of faith summarized as follows:

(1.) *Scriptures — The inspired word of God; the New*
Testament is the infallible guide in matters of conduct
and doctrine.

(2.) *The Godhead: God is one but manifested in three*
persons who are eternal: The Father, the Son and the
Holy Spirit.

(3.) *Man, His Fall and Redemption: Man was created*
in the image of God but fell through Adam's
transgression. It is through the sacrifice of His Son
that we are redeemed.

(4.) *Eternal life and now birth: Repentance is the*
beginning of the new life and the new birth that leads
to eternal life.

(5.) *Water Baptism is by immersion only.*

(6.) *Baptism in the Holy Ghost is subsequent to being*
born again. It is accompanied by the speaking in
other tongues.

(7.) *Sanctification is a definite yet progressive work of Grace.*

(8.) *Divine Healing: Wrought by the power of God through*
faith and by the laying on hands, it is the privilege of
every member of the church today.

Clear enough pastor, thank you. But I cannot determine from
the materials we were given to read if there is any official connection

between your church and other religious bodies or groups. Perhaps your church is just like most of the other community churches, which are parenthetically connected to other groups or denominations. It seems so from what I have heard and read. Not that it seems to matter. Most new "community" churches seem to place far more emphasis on their independence than their connectedness. I guess a "no name" congregation has more success in drawing new members from other churches and religious groups. It certainly seems to be working.

Chapter 18

Mt. Zion Baptist Church
Nashville, Tennessee
January 12, 2003

Betty and I lived in a home on Tyne Boulevard in Nashville for thirty-five years. Being in the real estate and construction business, we overbuilt our means considerably when we constructed our Tyne Boulevard house, but we were always glad we had done so because we never felt a need to "move-up" as our financial picture improved over the years. We sold the Tyne Boulevard house two years ago and moved from a house with about 7000 square feet, and over three acres of land, to a condominium with about 3000 square feet. We had actually helped to develop the condominium complex some twenty years earlier and had kept three of the condos as investments. When we sold our house, we combined two of the three condos and remodeled the space to accommodate our "move down" in square footage. It was a temporary move because we were planning to design and build a new house to accommodate our needs for the "next 35 years."

The story of our move to the "double-wide" condo would be incomplete without telling you that Betty did not want to move into a condominium — any condominium, but especially one that did not have a garage. Even for a short period of time the absence of a garage was objectionable to her. To make things worse, we moved into the condo in November, the beginning of the cold winter months. Feeling a little guilty about pressing and winning the case for a temporary move into a condo which we already owned rather than moving into a rental from someone else, I would go out on very cold mornings to scrape the ice off the windshield of Betty's car and warm the car up for her. And it worked! Or something did because Betty has come to love condo living. I guess that is sort of providential because we still live in the condo two years later and the "new" house is still not under construction.

It was 8:30 a.m. when we walked out from our double-wide and got into the car. The blast of cold winter air reminded me immediately that I had not gone out and warmed up the car while waiting patiently for Betty to proudly present herself to me in the living room and have her to announce that we were leaving "on time." The biting cold in the car was a testimony to my failure in itself but, even so, I did verbally confess my failure to Betty. Better for me to confess than for Betty to make the charge that I had not accomplished my "manly duty." Not that she would have said anything, but it was understood that I had failed, of course.

It was so cold in the car as we started out that I used my knees to stabilize the steering wheel while on a straight course and touched it only with my finger tips when turning. Trying to humorously deflect my noticeable guilt, I said, "Look, Betty. I can drive with no hands." The attempt at humor in an otherwise "chilly situation" worked. Betty responded, "I know you can. I have known it since we were first dating and the policeman stopped us because you were attempting to drive with no hands." She reminded me that the policeman had given me a warning ticket "for paying too much attention to your girlfriend." I don't know, but I think I was paying just the right amount of attention. My no hands (on the wheel) trick helped lead to a marriage of over 49 years. The defense rests, your honor.

After a few minutes both the situation and the car warmed considerably. We traveled on White Bridge Road and its natural extension of Briley Parkway on our way to a more legitimate blue road for our Sunday morning trek. We turned west onto Ashland City Highway, indeed a blue road, and traveled for a couple of miles before turning north onto Old Hickory Boulevard. Now don't let the term "Boulevard" throw you here. Old Hickory Boulevard, a circumferential road around Nashville, is many things. A few weeks ago we were on Old Hickory Boulevard, in an entirely different part of town, while visiting the congregation Micah and I had to perform a "minor miracle" in declaring it to be a blue road. Today I would have no trouble at all doing so. Old Hickory in this part of Nashville is true blue — bluer than blue. It is so blue that the cows trying to break through the ice on a frozen pond were blue with cold. We were almost amazed that an area "this rural," called

Scottsboro, still existed in Davidson County. It doth appear to me, Mayor Purcell, that we still have plenty of land on which to expand the tax base out here on this blue road. Keep the taxes down but expand with a few McDonalds and Burger Kings out here, and some condos, too.

After a few miles of enjoying the true blue of Old Hickory Boulevard, we came to Clarksville Pike. Remember this one? This was the road we took blue roading to Clarksville last Sunday. Had we turned west at this intersection we could have been eating toasted biscuits at G's Pancake House in about thirty minutes. Remembering G's got Betty and me to thinking — we were hungry and could also use some gas. Voila! There on the corner of Old Hickory and Clarksville Pike stood Brenda's Market and B.P. station. Betty is never going to buy gas anywhere but a B.P. station. She has it figured out; B.P. gives a three percent discount on gas purchased at B.P. locations on a B.P. card. She cried out, "There's a B.P. station." We filled up on a "free gas card" which Betty proudly presented to me. After this I proudly announced to Betty that Brenda's Market was a fine looking possibility for breakfast. We went inside to investigate and to use the facilities which two senior citizens on diuretics always spot first in any establishment. Our breakfast investigation was conducted far more leisurely after we checked out the other facilities.

Brenda, and her employees, displayed perhaps the most beautiful biscuits that I had ever seen behind a glass lighted "sneeze guard" type of case. The biscuits had multicolored hues of light yellow, light gold and brown rippling across the surface of each homemade, medium to large biscuit. The colors were enhanced with ample combinations of bacon, ham, sausage, cheese and eggs peering out between the middle of some of the biscuits. The biscuit sandwiches had been prepared, wrapped in cellophane, and presented ready for the palates of Sunday morning blue road breakfasters. They were gorgeous! Betty's decision was simple. She wanted "One of those," pointing to a large golden brown biscuit with more than ample portions of pork tenderloin, egg and cheese pressing against the edges of the cellophane wrapping and the sneeze guard. "Are you sure?" I asked, thinking perhaps she wanted to think about it some more. "Take your time," I said to no one but myself. "This is a serious blue-road decision." Not serious enough to cause her to think twice however. The beauty of the biscuit had sealed the deal for her and so I placed her order.

My order was not going to be made so quickly. "This may be the last breakfast of your life. It could be. So take your time," I counseled myself. I inquired further as to the possibilities. "Could you fry some eggs over-medium for me?" I asked the jovial round-faced male attendant whom we will name Daryl. Darlene, the cook, answered back immediately. Daryl then told Darlene to fry two eggs over medium. I amended this order, increasing the cholesterol dosage to "three eggs." Daryl concurred and relayed the amendment to Darlene. I tacked on one more amendment — only after the first amendment passed for fear that I would spend too much blue-road political capital too soon — asking, "Can you put some bacon on that order?" Darlene cheerfully said "Sure," and I was on my way to having a complete breakfast bill passed. Almost as if my next move was not a real request for another amendment, but merely a question, I nonchalantly asked, "Do you have any kind of potatoes?" Daryl said, "We have some potato wedges." I said, "That's great. Put some of those on the plate." And as slick as that I had run a rider through almost unnoticed.

Betty and I waited for our order on two of the four wicker bottom bar stools at the condiment and coffee bar at Brenda's Market. After drinking a half of a large cup of fresh coffee, I called out to Daryl, "Would you put a piece of tenderloin on one of my biscuits?" "Two biscuits with that egg order, one with a piece of tenderloin, okay?" Daryl carefully asked the cook. "Sure, no problem," answered Darlene. At that point I had ordered everything I could think of. Soon Darlene came out with Betty's order in her left hand and balancing an overloaded Styrofoam takeout type of box with my order in her right hand.

Every bite of the breakfast was delicious. Betty said she had never had a better sandwich in her life. She noted that, "Even the microwaved biscuit is delicious." I told her that the biscuit had not been microwaved. Instead, the cellophane wrapper traps some of the heat. As the cooling process occurs, it allows some of the interior moisture to collect on the surface of the biscuit. Lord, how I love to talk technical talk and make Betty think how smart I am to know all these important scientific facts.

The most important fact about my breakfast was its perfection. The eggs, the strips of bacon, the wedge potatoes and the biscuits, and the tenderloin biscuit, could not have been better. I asked Darlene about how she made the biscuits. She revealed that she uses a buttermilk biscuit mix from Robert Orr, a restaurant supply outlet in Nashville. Darlene said, "All I do is add buttermilk and bake." Note to self: "Get some of the buttermilk biscuit mix at Robert Orr and try it out at home."

After discussing with Daryl and Darlene how exciting last night's Titans game had been (Darlene had gone to the game, paying $46 for the ticket which she said she could have sold at game time for $125) and thanking them for a great breakfast (only $11.09), we headed out. We left this "city farmer's" paradise with a parking lot full of pickup trucks with mud on most of the tires and fenders. A couple of drivers chewed on breakfast toothpicks in an attempt to dislodge the last morsels of tenderloin as their last bite of breakfast.

We continued north on Old Hickory and looked for a fitting blue-road church to cap off a great blue-road breakfast. We passed several Baptist churches and Churches of Christ, including one whose sign read "Calvary Church of Christ — Oneness Pentecostal Service." We found that sign intriguing and wanted to be sure to check it out some day — if not today. The enormous Mt. Zion Baptist Church stood across the street from the Calvary Church of Christ. Some friends had discussed this predominantly African-American church as probably the largest church in Nashville and recommended that we should definitely go there some time. It was now 10:00 a.m. and services at Mt. Zion did not start until 10:45 a.m. Although we thought that perhaps we would come back to Mt. Zion, we continued our blue-road investigation.

We went on toward Dickerson Road, passing the Church of God of Prophecy, another Baptist church and another Church of Christ. We then turned onto Dickerson Road and then onto Broadmoor where we saw the First Apostolic Church, subtitled "Broadmoor Family Worship Center." We had recently noticed a growing trend to name churches "Family worship centers." The trend was an attempt, we surmised, to broaden a congregation's appeal to the community by making it appear somehow more ecumenical.

It was 10:28 a.m. when we decided to attend the 10:45 a.m. service at Mt. Zion. We should have started back to the church a little earlier because the parking lot for this 5000-seat church was enormous. Because Betty had neglected to bring the handicapped tag for her car, I dropped her off at one of the entrances while I parked the car in the lower Slobovia parking lot. This gave her time to scope out the rest rooms. By the time I got to the church Betty was ready to get in her line at the rest room, and I was ready to get in my line. While I was in the men's room, I overheard someone who had been at the earlier service sort of complaining about one part of the pastor's sermon with which he disagreed. He was saying that the minister said things which would just "cause pain and confusion in the minds of the people." He said that if they followed everything the minister taught them their lives would be unnatural and boring and they would have to give up gambling and a lot of "natural activities." He certainly felt that the preacher had quit preaching and had started meddling, as we used to say.

I reconnoitered with Betty before going into the sanctuary. We went to the first of two balconies which provided us a panoramic view of the congregation. It was 10:43 a.m. when we took our seats, and the sanctuary was about two-thirds full. The other one-third doubtlessly were still trying to park the car because by 11:00 a.m. the church was full — about 4000 people in the main sanctuary and perhaps 1000 more in the overflow room.

The sanctuary was a spectacular cavernous auditorium which was more like a theater than a church. The entire space was finely finished, complete with completed ceilings instead of the exposed steel beams and ductwork arrangement which we had seen in some of the "community type" churches. The sanctuary itself was fully equal to the quality of Jackson Hall at the Tennessee Performing Arts Center. There were beautiful contemporary appointments throughout. Three beautiful discreet stained glass windows lined each side of the worship area and were located high on the exterior walls up and next to the ceiling. The pulpit floor had two types of patterned hardwood inlays and, at the right, a set of six free floating upholstered dignitaries' chairs. On each side of the pulpit area was a large screen. But the screens did not carry the words of the hymns as had been the case in all the other churches we had attended. A sunken orchestra area in the center section of the chancel held a choir of about seventy. An "auxiliary" orchestra area held musicians with instruments to supplement those in the center orchestra. All the choir and orchestra members wore either black or orange shirts.

Early in the service a handsome young deacon gave a short pep talk about membership responsibility. He was dressed in a light tan sweater. His name was not listed in the bulletin. He then read the scripture lesson from *Psalms 92*, "for thou, Lord, hast made me glad through thy work: I will triumph though the work of thy hands." The scripture lesson was followed by a prayer during which he addressed God every few words, "We thank you, God, because, God, you are good, God, and we praise you, God." When he finished the rousing prayer of thanks and praise, there was a wave of enthusiastic shouts of praise and clapping which led into "A period of praise and worship," as listed in the bulletin. A middle-aged black woman dressed in a dark suit led this portion of the service. With a very strong voice, and an even stronger presence, she directed both the choir and the congregation. She sang and the congregation responded: "Because of who you are," over and over again.

The next part of the service was listed in the bulletin as "The Welcome Ministry." A senior woman, obviously widely known by most of the congregation, welcomed all visitors to the service and asked all visitors to stand. Obediently, Betty and I stood with 20 or 30 other visitors. We were all warmly welcomed — first from the pulpit and then by many of the people in the balcony area in which we were sitting. The members near us welcomed us with well wishes and warm hugs. I truly felt welcome. And I appreciated the warmth of such a sincere welcome by the congregation, particularly because we were the only white people we had seen in the sanctuary. The choir and the congregation followed up with a sweet song that repeated, "Welcome, we love you."

Next a young woman dressed in a knee length white coat began her section of the service by saying, as did all the participants, "Good morning, Mt. Zion." To which the congregation responded courteously, "Good morning." She made some announcements and emphasized that the pastor, Bishop Walker, was to give the prayer in a few days at the inauguration of Tennessee's new governor, Phil Bredesen.

Another attractive young woman then introduced herself as speaking on behalf of the young singles of the congregation. She then said immediately, "How about those Titans?" Her question was in reference to the narrow victory of the Titans the night before in the NFL playoffs. It occurred to me that perhaps one of the greatest benefits of the Titans being in the community is in race relations. All members of all walks of life in Nashville now share something strong in common to cheer for — the Titans.

The pastor, Bishop Walker, a dynamic man who appeared to be in his late 40's or early 50's, came to the pulpit to talk about "Ministry Reflections" as listed in the bulletin. His primary focus was the new Antioch location of Mt. Zion's extended ministry. He spoke about the growing crowds at the extended area of the ministry and said that at the service there today many "gave their lives to the Lord." Dr. Walker is a busy man. He has a 7:30 a.m. worship service here at Mt. Zion, a 9:00 a.m. service at Glencliff, and then a 10:45 a.m. service back at Mt. Zion. No wonder I had not seen the pastor during the early minutes of the service.

At one point in the service a young lady read the mission statement of Mt. Zion:

The Mount Zion Baptist Church is a Word-centered ministry designed to evangelize the lost at any cost, equip and empower the people of God, and provide holistic ministry to our community as well as the world.

Seeking to minister to the total person, we are a multi-ethnic, multi-cultural ministry impacting the world in which we live with the uncompromising message of Jesus Christ.

Committed to the Spirit of Excellence, we are striving to become an oasis of hope within the Nashville community by promoting and providing education, awareness, as well as financial independence.

We believe that God must be worshiped in spirit and in truth. We embrace freedom in worship because the Word says, "Where the spirit of the Lord is there is liberty." Our foundation is the Word of God and we believe it in its entirety. We believe we can do

what it says we can do, be who it says we can be,
and have what it says we can have.

I liked very much the "multi-ethnic, multi-cultural ministry" part of the mission statement. The Mt. Zion congregation has a great opportunity to be a part of the glue that helps hold Nashville together amidst its diversity.

The congregation then was directed to a time of fellowship among the people. There was much moving around with warm greetings, introductions and hugs. Again, Betty and I were greeted and hugged by many members in our section of the church. And, again, I had a genuine feeling of warmth and inclusion, if only for this one service.

At this point the order of worship announced the "Ministry of Music: The Mt. Zion Mass Choir." The director was a spirited man in charcoal pants and sweater. He directed eight women singers each with individual microphones. The remainder of the choir sang, "Alleluia, Alleluia" in a very rousing anthem that moved the congregation to the highest emotional level to this point in the service. He then led them in a soft beginning of another song, "I learned how to sing, standing in the rain" repeated over and over and then several times, "I thank you for my song." The song rapidly reached a crescendo that left most of the congregation standing and shouting while the choir concluded with many repetitions of the phrase, "Worthy is the Lamb."

The order of worship next announced: "Word of God: Bishop Joseph H. Walker, III." The pastor read the scripture lesson from *Deuteronomy 12: 10 – 12* and said that the title of his sermon was *It's Been a Long Time Coming.* Then he said, in a very powerful and effective way, "Get ready. God's about ready to do something in your life."

The pastor offered a rhetorical question, "What did God remind His people of?" And then he answered by saying that God said, "I have given you a promised place" and that God would fulfill His promise. He pointed out that God said in *Deuteronomy,* "When you go over into Jordan...Not if you go over." He said that God's promise was that He would bring them up out of Egypt into a land that flows with milk and honey. The pastor said that he didn't

care what the devil said to us. You can say "But God will deliver me." He said we should believe and say:
"When I get this job"
"When I graduate"

Not *"if"* but *"when,"* because "God has promised deliverance." The congregation agreed:
"Amen"
"All right"
"Yes, yes"

The whole congregation waved and applauded both Bishop Walker and God at the same time.

The preacher noted God's words, "When you cross over Jordan." He said that until that happened God said we shall "rest" and "dwell in safety." God had promised His people a place that was already occupied. The preacher then said that Moses sent spies over to see the situation and brought back reports that there are "Giants in the Land." But the preacher said that God still told His people to go on in because "The God who delivered them out of Egypt, across the Red Sea was going on before them." Bishop Walker was saying that God's people would not face any "giants" without His presence.

The preacher declared that if God promised you a job and there is someone else in the job (if the land is occupied) just relax and wait; God will deliver the job to you. God's desire is to bring you to the land of "more than enough." He wants you to prosper. He wants you to be healthy. The pastor then said that a lot of people have a problem with this. He pointed out that God said, "When you go you shall bring *all* that I command you to bring." He then started talking about people taking gambling trips to Tunica to play the numbers and foolishly waste their money. But God said, "Bring your tithes and offerings into the storehouse." He said that God said "Bring it *all*." He was saying *all* of it, not just the part leftover after you waste it by gambling foolishly. The pastor observed, "A lot of people start getting suspicious when the preacher starts talking about money and the church."

I think this must have been the part of this service the church member in the restroom before this service had been complaining about. He had said that the preacher was trying to dehumanize the people and take all the fun out of life. The preacher was right. Some of his members would not agree with him on this point. But most of the members did. They shouted encouragements to the preacher all along. And many members had begun to walk down the aisles to leave money and envelopes on the steps leading to the pulpit.

The pastor said everyone has a "need" and "seeds." He said if we sow some seeds, God will fill our needs:

"Okay"
"Yes, yes"
"All right"
"Amen, Amen"
"C'mon Bishop"

The pastor then said, somberly, "When I prepared this sermon God gave me a prophetic announcement." (I wondered if the "Bishop" pastor might now be claiming to be a "prophet.") He continued. God told him to tell the congregation that "God is going to let something dramatic happen in the next 90 days, so get ready." He said, "I feel deliverance is on the way." The whole congregation was on its feet again, shouting and praising. The preacher continued, "It's going to happen so fast, it is going to blow your minds. Halleluiah." and "You should stop letting carnal people talk you out of God's blessings...It is <u>when</u> God is going to get you a job. It is <u>when</u> God pays your tuition."

"When it is a long time coming," the preacher said, we should say "I don't have it yet, but..." Again nearly the whole congregation was standing, praising God and cheering the preacher. It was like a football game when you have to stand to see the touchdown by looking over the excited fans. The "fans" were excited and so we had to stand to be able to see the preacher.

The preacher invited people to come forward for prayer if they needed God to become a part of their lives. The invitation continued for about fifteen minutes while the choir sang *He Will Bring Me Out* and *I Surrender All*. The 50some people who came to the front for prayer were led by other church members to prayer rooms to pray together.

The pastor then announced that the tithes and offerings would be taken. Ushers stood at the top of all aisles with large straw baskets while other ushers guided us all in filing past the baskets in order to place our offerings in them. This was the same way offerings were collected at the missionary Baptist Church in Cookeville. As we filed past the basket Betty, the "treasurer" in our family, deposited our usual $5 offering. I felt we should have made it a $10 offering just to pay our part of what must be an enormous heat bill here at Mt. Zion. It was still cold outside and in our car. And I might have to drive with my knees again for the first few blocks.

After depositing our $5 offering we did not return to our seats but instead exited the church. Our strategy was to get to the car fast and beat the crowd to the exit but it did not work as planned. Apparently we were not alone in that strategy; it still took us 30 minutes to get out of the parking lot.

My message in an open letter to Mt. Zion follows:

We loved your church, your music and your powerful preacher. But most of all we loved your warm welcome to two white blue-road pilgrims on a cold Sunday morning. One friendly bit of advice: Send some spies into the land of some other giants (churches, that is) and learn how they expedite the traffic into and out of their parking lots. A real giant in the traffic directing department is the Cornerstone Community Church at the corner of I-65 and Old Hickory Boulevard. You will love their parking system almost as much as we loved the warm hugs of welcome we received in your church.

> *With love,*
> *The Brownings*

Chapter 19

St. Matthew Catholic Church
Franklin, Tennessee
January 19, 2003

I t had been a humbling week for me. Surgery always produces a blush of recognition — the recognition of one's own mortality. Over the past 13 years I have had surgery three times. And each time I faced my own mortality in different ways and to different degrees.

The first surgery required facing up to the fact that my health situation called for surgery and to realize that it was serious enough that I might die. The second surgery, about five years after the first, was the result of an illness that had me in so much pain that, at times, I wished I could hurry up and die. The third surgery had been on Tuesday of the past week.And I was so embarrassed by the cause of it that I thought I would die.

The first surgery, by far the most serious, was the one during which I had all rights to come to grips with my own mortality. The threat of death lay in my heart's congenitally small heart arteries; they might not be able to accept the six bypasses that the doctors would perform. My personal recognition of mortality was profound. It was so profound, in fact, that I wrote my own funeral service. I wanted to relieve my family of any concern about how to conduct the funeral of one with a non-traditional worldview. What evolved during that process of my writing was actually not so much a funeral at all. I wrote that my remains were to be given to Vanderbilt Medical School with any final remains cremated and disposed of by the crematorium — no ashes, no nothing. My funeral "service," then, was to be a simple recognition of death. The main point here is that I really thought there was a real possibility that I might die during the surgery. Obviously I didn't. I could not tell you about surgeries number 2 and 3 if I had died of the six bypasses that Dr. Petracek performed on me in St.Thomas Hospital back in 1989.

Surgery number 2 snuck up on me one day while I was playing golf. I had to quit on the ninth hole because I thought I was surely having a heart attack. I wasn't. I was in, however, such pain that I demanded some kind of surgery. If nothing else I could find relief from the horrendous pain during the period of warm, sweet sleep given so lovingly by one of the greatest branches of medicine — anesthesiology. I think the doctors ended up flipping a coin to decide what to operate on. Heads, gall bladder. Tails, appendix. It was heads. I think about the removal of my gall bladder as a mercy killing of sorts. And I am comforted that I saved my appendix as a future sacrifice for the next time severe pain shows up. Anyhow, the same pain which I had before surgery number 2 came back after the surgery; it had not been a gall bladder attack at all. I went to a new internist, a young man by the name of Dr. John Shaw. During my first visit I told him my symptoms and in a matter of seconds, not minutes, he said, "You've got 'GERD."

It was the first time I had heard the word "GERD" and it sounded worse than cancer. "GERD? My God," I asked, "Can it be cured?" Dr. Shaw said, "You will not have this pain tomorrow." I asked, "Are you sure you know what this is? Could you be mistaken?" After all, I had already given a perfectly good gall bladder during the search for a surgical cure. "I am positive. Just take one of these pills a day and you will have the pain no more." I did take the pills and I don't have the pain anymore. As an end result, I find myself in love with all anesthetists of the world, my cardiologist Dr. Bart Campbell, my heart surgeon Dr. Michael Petracek, my internist Dr. John Shaw, and Prilosec. Those little purple pills are like my American Express card; I never leave home without them. The tales above have been attempts at delaying the tale of surgery number 3. After 3 surgeries, boy, was I ever getting to have a personal glossary of medical terms. I had been hobbling around for two or three weeks with what I thought was a simple, yet painful, case of hemorrhoids. Dr. Shaw referred me to a proctologist (a new glossary addition) by the name of Dr. Richard Howerton. Dr. Howerton's diagnosis provided a new term for permanently implantation in my glossary — "anal fistula abscess." He also provided an appointment for surgery to correct the problem.

During the two weeks before the surgery I explained my

problem to "friends." "Friends" are in quotation marks because of the way some of them handled the information. It was just too much of a temptation to my "friends." For example, Jim Neal seems compelled to nickname his friends in ways that sort of caricaturize their least attractive physical attributes. Jim's latest nickname for me had been "little Jelly" but my weight loss on a successful diet had put him on the search for a more scorching and more accurate nickname. The hole near my anus caused by the fistula was just the inspiration Jim needed. Within 24 hours of hearing the news about my poor unfortunate condition, my "friend" Jim started calling me "double A," a caricature of my anus and its new unwanted satellite. He was actually using common vernacular while calling me "double A," street language for anus. Within another 24 hours he had other accomplices, such as John Seigenthaler and God-only-knows-how-many others, in the crime of, dare I say, caricature assassination.

I had checked into the outpatient surgery clinic at Centennial Hospital at 6:00 a.m. and by 11:30 a.m. Betty was driving me home. I basked in the afterglow of a miracle drug injected into my IV tube by one of the new love heroes of my life. Once upon a time Mickey Mantle and Willie Mays had been my heroes. Now I say, "Hey!" in my friendliest voice to doctors and nurses. I hope to add Dr. Richard Howerton, my proctologist, to my Valentine's list. My God, I hope he makes the list. I hope he moves near the top but to get there he would have to topple three anesthesiologists and the inventors (whoever they may be) of Prilosec and Norgesic Forte.

Whoever said getting old is not for sissies surely must have had "AA" surgery at some point. The surgery causes one to gain total respect for simple things such as hot tub baths, prunes, All-bran cereal and Metamucil. After five days of gorging myself on those goodies I was the cleanest recovering "AA" in town. And I was also making enough post-op progress to continue my *Fifty-Two Sundays on the Blue Road* as long as the blue roads were kept short and sort of purplish blue.

Three days earlier the city had a heavy winter snow storm by Nashville standards. The weatherman had predicted a "few inches" of snow, but the snow gods rode in on a Trojan horse dumping 8 inches on an area expecting maybe 3 inches. What a pretty snow it was! It made my involuntary confinement much easier to take.

Most people still suffer from a puritanical ethic which makes us feel guilty when we are "forced" to stay home and rest for a few days. Add a beautiful snow to an embarrassing surgery, however, and the guilty feeling vanishes. By Sunday morning most of the snow and ice had been cleared from the main roads around Nashville. Only the true blue roads remained impassable. Thus our blue roading was slightly tempered by my "AA" condition and the weather condition in mind; a short route was called for if true blues were to be kept at a minimum.

We left Woodmont Boulevard after some "rocking the boat" action (reverse — forward, reverse — forward, reverse — forward) finally freed the car from its near ice-coffin condition. Woodmont was clear and we turned west onto Harding Road. We continued west on Highway 100 to our blue-road restaurant for today — the Loveless Café. Only a few years ago the place was still known as "The Loveless Motel and Café." But the motel had long since lost its battle with the planning and codes departments of Nashville. Now it's just "Loveless Café." Just Loveless? Just about the best blue road country restaurant in the country! Maybe even the world. Pretty high cotton for a humble little roadhouse restaurant.

The little roadhouse that is The Loveless Café was just a house once upon a time but it has expanded room by room over the years. It makes no pretense to be anything other, anything fancier than what it offers — good country food. Yet it does find itself in high cotton so far as clientele. It is famous worldwide with such notables for clients as Princess Anne. And the Brownings. We have come here for years because it was one of Nannie's (Betty's mother) favorite places ever. Nannie wanted to eat at The Loveless Café almost every Saturday and someone in the family always came with her. We credit her with the find. Nannie was good at finding good country places to eat.

The Brownings, who have developed into self-professed biscuit critics, arrived here at 8:45 a.m. for a biscuit-breakfast feast for the first time since Nannie died in 1997. And we ordered quickly because we both knew exactly what we wanted. Betty ordered two scrambled eggs with bacon and biscuits. $6.95. I ordered three eggs over-medium, with complete assurance that only the whites would be not runny. I also ordered bacon, home fries, grits and biscuits.

The total bill came to $21.00. Coffee was served immediately by a friendly waitress. (Newsflash! Major victory for men everywhere at The Loveless Café — "Male Busses Tables." He was not a waiter, true, but as men we need every small step toward parity with the dominant position waitresses hold in blue-road restaurants.)

We people watched while waiting for our breakfast. The restaurant was nearly full even though it was such a lousy day to be out anywhere, a real tribute to the restaurant's drawing power. There were three tables holding two men each whom I assumed were in the music business, a supposition later confirmed by the cashier. The Loveless, along with the Pancake Pantry and Dotsons in Franklin, is a hot spot for celebrities in the music business in this area.

There was only one child in the restaurant. McDonalds this is not. Then again, all the meals at The Loveless Café are happy meals. I've never seen a customer who was not completely happy here. We certainly were. Betty said that her scrambled eggs were excellent and "almost as good as yours," ever mindful not to offend the source of 99 % of all the scrambled eggs she had eaten during her life. The bacon was truly outstanding — thick and crispy. And the grits were prepared perfectly. The only places where The Loveless Café could improve at all would be the potatoes and the preserves. They might try to copy the Pancake Pantry's baked-then-grilled potatoes and to steal the Beacon Light's recipe for preserves.

The raison d'étre of the Loveless is the unmatched quality of their biscuits. They are homemade and it shows. The biscuits were all individually beautiful, totally crispy brown on the bottoms and elegantly browned with waves of tan across the tops. The secret? There is no secret, per se. One reason the biscuits are so nearly perfect in every aspect is the use of pure lard for shortening. The lard gives these works of art their crispy brown bottoms as they fight for room in a pan full of biscuits, creating individual shapes. The hues and colors created on the tops of the biscuits are as varied as snowflakes. And biscuits are baked fresh throughout the day.

While we "topped off" our breakfast feast, a man came in and sat at a table that had been recently vacated by four people who had just finished a breakfast including "everything but the kitchen sink." The lone customer asked the waitress for suggestions and said it was his first time to eat here. He had on a CAL sweatshirt and I commented on how different the winter weather must be from the weather in California. He confirmed the difference for sure but told us that more recently he was from Illinois. It turned out that he was working on a six month consulting contract with HCA. I recommended that he check out the Pancake Pantry also while he was in town, and he told me he had already been there. He was obviously a breakfast connoisseur, too (a claim I obviously make for myself). He ordered some red-eye gravy, among other things. The waitress explained that it was made of country ham pan drippings, coffee and water. He wanted to try several things and I admired his adventuresome palate. As we were getting ready to leave I asked how he had heard of the Loveless Café, and he said that he read about it in the American Airlines *In Flight* magazine. The "better mousetrap" theory is alive and well, the bait in this instance of The Loveless Café being the best biscuits in the world. And the world is obviously beating its path to the little roadhouse café located just west of Nashville, near the terminus of the Natchez Parkway.

The two blue-roading pilgrims, one who felt like a Native American had shot him in the anus with a poisoned arrow, moved on to look for a blue road church which hopefully offered divine healing. We turned back toward Nashville and saw the Pasquo Church of Christ. We knew that if we got stuck in the ice and snow on Pasquo Road we could attend worship services there. But since we were in the neighborhood of a Catholic Church we would try to attend its service which we had learned would begin at 10:30 a.m. It was 9:30 a.m. as we turned south onto Pasquo. An icy hill at the intersection of Highway 100 and Pasquo was treacherous but we carefully and barely negotiated it. Soon we turned east onto Sneed Road, the scene of one of my earliest subdivision developments over 30 years ago.

We pulled out into very little traffic. As we traveled east on Sneed, we saw the Holy Trinity Evangelical Lutheran Church. It was now about 9:40 a.m. and its sign said the worship service was at 9:30 a.m. Obviously the TADI (Titans Area of Dominant Influence) included this area of Williamson County. St. Matthew Catholic Church was located at 533 Sneed Road and we were quickly in front of it. Both the Lutheran and Catholic churches were new congregations to the area. It was still 45 minutes before the beginning of the Catholic service so Betty and I continued east on Sneed with the sole purpose of scouting it out as a possible way home after St. Matthew's service. There is a large hill between St. Matthew and Hillsboro Road. If we could get to the top of the hill, we would be able to go on home this way after the service. We could not make it. About two-thirds up the hill we turned around, put the transmission in low gear, made it safely back down the hill and then into St. Matthew's parking lot. We waited in the car until 10:20 a.m. at which time I got my tools of the *Fifty-Two Sundays* trade out of my briefcase. We entered the foyer of the very attractive, contemporary new church. The foyer was inviting, an open area with much light shining onto tiled floors and beautiful brick walls.

As we entered a friendly man greeted us, "I like your collar. It looks like you could be doing the mass today." He laughed freely as he referred to my white mock turtle shirt which was mostly covered by a charcoal gray sweater. Come to think of it, my choice of clothes did have sort of a priestly look. I think the friendly greeter thought I was a communicant at St. Matthew's.

While I waited for Betty to emerge from the restroom I looked at several of the cast plaques that honor many of the Saints of the Church, including, of course, St. Matthew. As soon as Betty emerged rested from the restroom, we claimed what we had come to think of as our rightful place in all churches — the back pew in the far right hand section. The church was about half full when we were seated at about 10:25 a.m. and by the time the service had been proceeding for no more than five minutes it was totally full. As the communicants entered they would reverently kneel at the entrance to the pew section and solemnly make the sign of the cross before continuing on to a seat.

Houses in the surrounding parts of Williamson and Davidson counties are owned primarily by young families, and the congregation was a true reflection of the area's demographics. There were a few people our age, but not many. Nearly all the worshipers there today were warmly, tastefully and casually dressed — sort of what we refer to as "Belle Meade casual," I think.

The sanctuary was constructed in a manner that gives a feeling of simple and strong elegance. The floors were tile. The walls were brick accented by dark walnut wood trim. The pews were darkly-stained solid oak that gave the feeling of strength and substance. The coffered ceiling was supported by heavy wood beams that were all painted white. At the back and high above the chancel was a crucifix showing Jesus hanging on the cross, still beautifully robed. I liked the depiction of the crucifixion more than the disturbing and probably more realistic ones that emphasize the more gruesome aspects of the scene.

The service began with a young female communicant welcoming all visitors and making several announcements including a new member who would be baptized today. She said the service would begin by the introduction of this part of the service at the baptismal font at the back, or the entrance of the church. She invited us to stand, turn to the rear and participate as witnesses in the preamble to the child's baptism. The priest, Father Mark Deckman, wore a green clerical robe and was assisted by a middle-aged ordained deacon who wore a white robe with a green sash. The parents and Godparents of baby Frances were gathered at the baptismal font. They were asked to attest to their faith in God and to make a sign of the cross on the baby. Each of them then pledged to bring up baby Frances in the faith of the church.

The preliminary part of the baptismal service concluded with the procession of the priest and the deacon to the chancel. The deacon held a large white Bible high above his head, apparently as a symbol of their worshiping the God of the Scriptures. After the priest and deacon were seated at the chancel another young woman read from the scriptures from *I Samuel 3: 3 – 10.* The scripture concerned Samuel not recognizing that it was God who had spoken to him. Eli told Samuel that when he heard the voice again that Samuel should say, "Speak, Lord, for Thy servant heareth."

Following the Scripture reading, the congregation stood and sang, "I have waited for the Lord...Come do your Will." A small, informal choir group was gathered around the organ to, more or less, direct the congregation in singing the hymns. The level of congregational participation in singing was noticeably quite low. It may have been the selection of the hymns or the lack of effectiveness of the group "leading" the congregational singing.

After the first hymn, a young man (perhaps in his early thirties), read from the *New Testament* scriptures of *I Corinthians 6: 13 – 15, 17 – 20*. He was handsomely dressed in a black mock turtle neck sweater and a dark brown sport jacket with a bold crucifix hanging around his neck. The worshipers then sang "The Gospel Acclamation...Alleluia" just before Father Mark rose to read from *John 1: 35 – 42*. The scripture lesson told how some of Jesus' disciples spent a leisurely day following Jesus, even going to His house to see where He lived. Father Mark pointed out that it was important often to just "waste a day with our families and with God." His point was that sometimes we are just too busy and too preoccupied and that we need to change our pace, slow down and "waste" a day with our families and with God.

Father Mark spoke of a beautiful custom held by many people from India. When someone comes to a home, the owners take time to wash the feet of the visitors when they first enter. Then they spend about thirty minutes of getting acquainted with each other and ministering to each other before going about the business at hand. Father Mark suggested that we need to do the same with God's people and with God. "Waste more time with each other in the community of faith and with God," he said. He then referred to Scripture reading from *I Samuel* where Samuel said, "Speak, Lord, for your servant listeneth." With real warmth and feeling, he said, "We, too, need to listen to God."

Father Mark spoke freely, without notes, and with great concern as he descended from the top level of the chancel to stand speaking from the first step leading to the chancel. His words were calm and assuring as he spoke casually to the congregation. He stood almost in our midst in an attempt to bring his message to where the people live. He said, "During these snow days I hope you are wasting some time with your family and friends."

After the brief but warm and meaningful lesson on how we should slow down and waste some important time with others, Father Mark invited the congregation to, again, turn their attention to the rear of the sanctuary. He completed the service of Baptism of baby Frances at the baptismal font. Frances was sound asleep and Father Mark said that she was sleeping as soundly as Samuel was before God awakened him. The congregation responded with a polite, warm laughter. Then the priest began a prayer by saying:

"Mary, Mother of God, Pray for us"
"St. Peter, pray for us"
"St. John, pray for us"
"St. Francis, pray for us"

And he continued to pray for God's love and guidance in our lives. Father Mark continued and turned to the parents and asked, "Do you wish Frances to be baptized in the faith of the church?" After an affirmative answer he said "Frances, I baptize you in the faith of the church." He said, "Receive the light of Christ," as he lit a special candle for her. Then baby Frances was welcomed "into the faith of our community" by warm applause of the congregation

Next the congregation sang the hymn "Jesus, Jesus, you are the way" during which the offering was taken. The Brownings, being equal opportunity givers, put our customary $5 in the plate which was then taken by young people to the chancel to present the offering to God.

Father Mark then began the Eucharist by saying: "May we celebrate this Eucharist with love." The congregation knelt together as one as Father Mark prayed "You so loved the world that in the fullness of time you sent us your son and...He gave Himself to die for us...Father may Thy Holy Spirit sanctify these offerings." He continued by quoting the scriptures: "While they were at supper He took bread and said...this is my body...and in the same way He took the cup and gave it to His disciples and said, "Drink ye all of this... this do in remembrance of Me."

As a continuation Father Mark prayed: "Father, we celebrate this memorial of redemption...Please remember the Pope, the bishops...and all your children." Then he raised the cup high, presented it to God, sang a song in Latin and concluded it by saying, "Ahmen, Ahmen, Ahmen." He then led the congregation in the *Lord's Prayer*. A difference between the Catholic version of the "Lord's Prayer," from the way it is in many Protestant churches, is that the Catholic prayer is not concluded by the words: "for Thine is the kingdom, the power and the glory, forever. Ahmen." Father Mark continued this part of the service by saying, "May the peace of the Lord be with you," and the congregation responded, "And with you." Then the congregation sang: "Thou who hast taken away the sin of the world...grant us Your peace."

Father Mark first served the bread and the wine to the members of the choir and others who were assisting in serving the Lord's Supper. Then, row by row, the members filed out of the pews and up to the chancel to be served the bread and the wine. The piano softly played while the choir sang No. 429, the Communion song, *Be Not Afraid*. At 11:27a.m. the mass ended by the benediction of Father Luke, "Lord you have nourished us with bread from heaven ...Ahmen."

Father Mark encouraged each member to buy a Kroger gift card for buying groceries. Those doing so had helped St. Matthew to raise over $15,000.00 to date. He also spoke about a church sponsored ski trip and asked for nominations for the St. Matthew School Board.He then announced an upcoming mass at St. Henry's for the 41 million lost to abortion last year

The service concluded with hymn No. 374, "Take the word of God with you as you go. Take the seeds of God's word and make them grow." The congregation dispensed as the song was sung, mostly by the small choir standing around the piano.

As we left, we met Mary Snyder Neifhoff, a friend of ours in the real estate business. She introduced us to Father Mark who was as personable in person as he had been during his sermon while exhorting us all to "waste some time." I almost told him that telling me to waste time is like preaching to the choir. Wasting time is one of my best things. I have developed it into an art form.I thought for a moment about offering to put on a seminar for his congregation on this subject, but I decided to wait until I know him a little better. In the meantime, I give lessons on the subject several times a week on the golf course at Richland Club. You can register at the pro shop. Registration is $70.00 plus golf cart and lunch.I'll call Father Mark.

Chapter 20

Union Presbyterian Church
Belfast, Tennessee
January 26, 2003

We left our home on Woodmont Boulevard at 8:10 a.m. on a chilly overcast Sunday morning. Middle Tennessee had experienced two significant snows during the past ten days. The first snow, about ten days before, had been truly beautiful. The seven to eight inches of snow that fell made everything look clean and pristine. Such snowfalls call forth several kinds of emotions that are not always easy to explain. A part of the feelings I associate with snowfalls certainly relates to the beauty of the purifying whiteness as if all the dirty sins of the world, for a brief period, are washed "as white as snow."

Other parts of the feelings I associate with snowfalls relate back to my childhood when snow simply meant "no school today." It always was an expected and welcome mini-vacation. Then, of course, there were the opportunities for new types of play, also a relief from the ordinary. At this point in my life I don't play in the snow as I once did. I don't get out of school, I don't build snowmen, and, I don't ride down the hills on a piece of cardboard. Regardless, snow still brings some kind of lagniappe to my life. Even at my age there is still the tendency to feel some level of guilt when I just stay home and do nothing. But snow days miraculously wash away such guilt. On a snow day I can just stay home and do nothing. I can sit in front of a beautiful warm wood fire and read or watch television. I can also eat absolutely anything I want. A real snowfall brings forgiveness to me for my sins of laziness and gluttony.

Snow also makes us into better neighbors and just better people. We offer a helping hand to the neighbor whose car doors are frozen. We get out of the car and risk life and limb to help someone stuck on the highway knowing full well we absolutely will never see them again. I like all of these side effects of snow.

This second snow had only been about two inches — still enough to cover my sins. I stayed home and claimed it as a real snow. I kept continuous fires going during the entire period. I thought I had stored enough firewood to last the remainder of the winter, but by the end of this period I had just about depleted my winter's supply. I made a note to call my friend Wayne Williams and have him bring another load of wood the next day. The second snow had come on Thursday and it was now Sunday morning. Most of the snow was gone and what snow was left rested in dirty little patches beside the roads and in the ditches. The temperature was 30 degrees. The cloudy sky cast a pall over what had been a week of cheerful cleansing with home fires burning. Sunday morning brought us back to grim reality. The charitable, warm friendliness of the past week would now fade away as we returned to the rogues we all are in real life. A motorist's problems would now again be his own. Righteousness would now turn back into road rage. I wanted the snow to come back. My excuse for doing absolutely nothing had melted away with the snow.

I had decided to take Highway 431 south of Nashville toward Lewisburg. To get there we followed Woodmont Boulevard east until it became Thompson Lane somewhere along the route. Streets change names quite often this way in Nashville. Along the Woodmont-Thompson Lane trek we passed the Universalist Unitarian Church which I wanted to visit in the next few weeks. On the way to Nolensville Pike, which is Highway 431, we passed the Woodmont Bible Church and the Faith Fellowship Seventh Day Baptist Church located on Hopkins Street right off Woodmont. We turned south on Highway 431 and began blue roading for sure.

Nolensville Pike holds both bitter and sweet memories for me. My partners and I had developed several properties along the Nolensville corridor, all of which were successful in their own right. Unfortunately, in one development a partner had to file for bankruptcy and, by default, an out of state bank became my new partner. You might think that a bank would make a great partner. It has all that money and should be able to simply hold onto the property until the right situation comes along, right? Wrong. The right time for a bank to sell anything held as an asset is today. Period. And they work by the "golden rule" which is simple: he that has the most gold rules. They ruled that we had to sell the property. Not next month but right then. And so the property was quickly sold. This left the new owner with the golden opportunity to make many millions of dollars which we should have made.

That left a bitter memory. A sweeter memory resided back in 1959 when I was doing graduate work at Vanderbilt in philosophical theology. I had received my B.D. (Bachelor of Divinity degree — now called M.Div. degree for Master of Divinity) in 1958 and was in graduate school working toward an advanced degree that would allow me to be either a teacher of theology or a minister. While working on my M. Div. Degree I was, for a short time, a supply pastor at a small Presbyterian church in Clifton, Tennessee. After commuting to Clifton for two years I was asked to be the supply minister at the Union Presbyterian Church in Belfast, Tennessee, just a few miles south of Lewisburg.

Beginning in January of 1959 I made the 60-mile trek from Nashville to Belfast for several months until the church built a cozy brick ranch house for us. I reversed my commute and traveled to school daily, rather than commuting to the church only on weekends. Betty and I lived in Belfast with our first daughter, Barbara, born in 1956. I learned the Highway 431 route so well that I could almost just point my car and sit back and snooze until arriving at Vanderbilt. I loved the drive. When I wasn't snoozing, I would rehearse my class notes from that day or the day before.

Betty taught the first grade in Lewisburg while we lived in Belfast. Before we moved there from Nashville she had taught at Maplewood Junior High School. One of her students there had been Brenda Lee, a little bombshell of a country music singer who was already becoming quite the sensation. One of our requirements for making the move to Belfast was Betty's ability to get a job teaching school. This was when I first learned the power of politics. Even though no new teachers were needed in the county, Betty was given a job teaching first grade in Lewisburg. She was not trained to teach elementary school, but there she was teaching anyway — proving that "it's not what you know but whom you know." Whom did we know? Well, we knew several members of the Session of the Presbyterian Church. And those individuals knew some of the school board members or, more than likely, knew of some dirt on some of the school board members.

Betty and I today were retracing our many trips between Nashville and Belfast. I had decided that, assuming we did not find another church between Nashville and Belfast which would compel our attendance, we would revisit the Union Presbyterian Church for the first time since June 1963. That was the year that I had returned to Belfast to officiate at the funeral of Paul Tate — a true gentleman, a pillar of the community and the clerk of the Session of the church. He had probably been chiefly responsible for getting Betty a teaching job.

I resigned as the minister of the Belfast Church in 1961 to be the pastor of another church. And the funeral of Paul Tate was one of the few times I had ever gone back. Until now. This would be the first time I had been back for a worship service in about forty years. We only lived in Belfast for a couple of years in the nice little manse the church built for us. I had always felt a little guilty for only staying a couple of years in the lovely home those wonderful people had built for us. And I had always sort of wanted to apologize for moving to the Presbyterian Church in Hendersonville, Tennessee, a move which cut my commuting time to Vanderbilt in half.

It was 30° according to the car's thermometer. We remarked on how our bodies adjusted quickly to temperature. Just before the 2° weather a few days ago we would have felt that 30° was very cold, but now it felt like a heat wave. Just before turning onto Nolensville Pike, we passed the newly remodeled Krispy Kreme Donut Shop. We would have to return soon to taste the very best donuts I had ever eaten. I had not been to this Donut Shop since the regional donut chain had created a national feeding frenzy during the past few years.

We passed the large, very active Radnor Baptist Church thinking that we would like to visit it before our 52-week period ended. Then we passed the Hi Fi Buys store which we developed about 30 years ago and had to sell because of another problem regarding another partnership. The trip turned bitter again for a few short minutes as I mulled over what had been a partnership disappointment for me. Oh well, let bygones be bygones. I focused on relishing the sweet memories of a trip made many times over 40 years ago.

Soon we passed the Tusculum Hills Baptist Church. Then we passed a sign which read, "We Buy Ugly Houses." And we soon saw why that sign was placed on this blue road. As a true blue road Nolensville Road sometimes is deep blue with its mixture of scattered, rundown old farm houses and house trailers. It is the type of blue road that gives the term its meaning. But, even on Nolensville Road, subdivisions were encroaching and soon suburbanites would be trying to change the zoning laws to prohibit the aborigines of the area from living in the ubiquitous house trailer.

We passed through Nolensville proper and took note of the Nolensville Church of Christ, Nolensville United Methodist Church and then the Cumberland Presbyterian Church. We passed on through Arrington and Triune. Triune is where the largest growth will be for the area in the future because of the SR 840 interchange. SR 840 passes through Triune on its way to I-65 and to I-40 and, eventually perhaps, to all around Nashville. We passed the Primitive Baptist Church before coming to an intersection where the left fork goes over toward Shelbyville while the right fork goes over toward Lewisburg. The right fork also took us through College Grove, into and out of Rutherford County and Williamson County, and finally into Marshall County before arriving in Chapel Hill.

By now the sun was trying to come out, making the day not quite as bleak. Things began to look a lot brighter at about 9:00 a.m. in Chapel Hill when we came to a true country blue-road restaurant boasting the name "Country Diner." We had seen no hope of finding a blue-road restaurant up until this point, so we turned quickly into a pothole-riddled parking lot. We found encouragement in the number of pilgrims that had already waded to shore through the gravelly mud holes to the blue metal building. The building appeared to have been a garage of some type before the Country Diner opened its doors.

We walked into a small room which could seat about 30 people with another anteroom which could seat perhaps 20 more hungry souls. The name of the establishment said it all. It truly was a "country" diner with Formica-topped tables and green vinyl chairs. The furnishings probably had been bargained for in a used restaurant equipment auction. A young woman and a middle-aged woman, possibly the mother of the younger one, were the only two work-ers in the restaurant.They were frantically busy trying to take care of the 20 or so customers; the customers were waiting fairly patiently for breakfast or a refill of coffee. In addition, people would occasionally come in for a takeout order.

One couple was sharing the morning paper over their last cup of coffee. They were not bored with each other like the cowboy and his wife we had seen a few weeks ago in Smithville. These two paper readers were just relaxing with each other and had nothing to prove to each other by trying to have a lively breakfast conver-sation. It appeared that they might easily and freely discuss the events they read in the paper on the way home.

There were three or four couples at separate tables. And one couple obviously was taking one of their mothers out to breakfast. The mother was smoking as were several others in the Country Diner. It seems that rural people tend to smoke more than people in larger cities. Maybe they are like the farmer in the TV pickle commercial who bragged that his company made the best pickles in the world. "You know why we make the best pickles in the world?"the farmer asks, "Cause we ain't got nothin' else to do."This may be the reason rural people smoke so much. Maybe they don't have enough bowling alleys and movie theaters to give them some-thing else to da I'm going to look for some statistics on this subject.

Three really bedraggled people sat at one table looking as if life had been treating them roughly. They appeared to be a moth-er, a father and a son. Life had not beat on the son long enough to make its marks quite as deeply as it had on his mother and his father. The mother looked truly pathetic. Her hair was long and stringy, her mouth evidenced the need for dental work, and, her face was totally devoid of expression. No emotion, no sadness, no feeling at all, just blankness. It was as if life had wrung every ounce of hope and expectation out of her. I felt immediate sorrow for what was obviously a very unhappy unexpecting life. Her husband was apparently living a hard life as well. His hair and clothes were unkempt. He appeared to be a man who worked very hard physi-cally at whatever he did for a living. However, he was not to the point of despair where his wife obviously was. A very noticeable and, potentially, very embarrassing speech defect did not hinder him at all. He spoke often and freely at his own initiative to several of the other customers in the restaurant who appeared to know him well. I marveled at the spirit of this man who had not let an obviously hard life get him down. But I felt deeply for his wife who had apparently already given up.

We ordered our breakfasts. The cook came out to give the young waitress a hand and served our coffee and water. Betty ordered two scrambled eggs with link sausages and biscuits ($3.40). I ordered three eggs over-medium with one-half slice of country ham, grits, home fries and biscuits ($7.60). As we waited for the meal, we continued to marvel at the spirit of the little man who had every right to be spiritless. But he dauntlessly and cheerfully greeted his acquaintances as they entered the restaurant. And he seemed to know them all.

It was not a meat-n-three country restaurant. All the dinners listed on the menu were hamburger steaks, chicken strips, country ham, or steaks with sides of French fries, home fries or onion rings. It reminded me of the way I learned to cook when I was at Trevecca College working as a short-order cook at the Campus Grill. There were times when I was the only one working and had to do all the cooking, serving and dishwashing. It is the reason I lay claim to being the fastest cook in the Western hemisphere, if not in the whole world. And I can never complain when I see that service is a little slow especially when the workers are going about their jobs as fast as they can. Like here today.

While we waited one of the customers helped out by getting the coffee pot and serving several people fresh coffee. After a few minutes we spent people watching our breakfasts arrived, and it was well worth the wait. The eggs were cooked to perfection and the country ham could not have been better. The grits and the home fries were great additions. The fact that I shared them both with Betty was no reflection on the quality of their taste by any means. Perhaps I wanted to feel especially righteous since I was probably going to visit one of my early pastorates within the next hour. I need to report that our biscuits were not up to par with the rest of the breakfast, but they could have been. They were tasty but had not been cooked long enough to get them good and brown which I saw as evidence that the cook was pushing things in an effort to keep the wait time down for her Sunday morning customers.

Our bill came to $14.10 with tip. And at 9:50 a.m. we were on our way south again while the sun burned off the haze and made the day remarkably more cheerful. We passed by Henry Horton State Park where I had played golf with my friend Frank Sutherland in several tournaments sponsored by his newspaper, The Tennessean. A few minutes later we reached Lewisburg and turned left to stay on 31A and 431. Belfast was now only seven or eight miles away. Betty and I started talking about the people at Belfast whom we remembered. There had been several bachelors and spinsters in the church back in the days when we were there, and we wondered why that had been the case. Of course, there was no answer. One of the bachelors had been Paul Tate. He "caught the eye" of Betty's mother who had been a widow. She would attend church with us practically every Sunday driving all the way from Nashville. And not just to hear her favorite and only son-in-law preach, we conjectured. Paul remained a bachelor until he died in 1963. I think he was the only man who could have convinced Nannie (Betty's mother) to marry again.

Many of the Belfast men were just not inclined to marry. That said, Earl Glen, one of the almost confirmed bachelors, broke rank shortly after we moved to the First Presbyterian Church in Hendersonville. He brought with him Catherine Tate, Paul's sister. They asked that I perform the ceremony of marriage that very day. So Earl ("Preacher") and Catherine married in our Hendersonville living room in 1962. On that one day we depleted the number of unmarried members of the Belfast church by about 20 percent in one fell swoop.

We arrived in Belfast with time to drive around some. We saw the little manse that these good and loving people had built for us although we lived in it for only a couple of years. I hoped that they had forgotten our rudeness for doing so. We went to the one service station in town to borrow their restrooms. I bought a coke and some gum to "repay" them for the use of their facilities. Finally, we drove up to the Union Presbyterian Church. As we walked in we saw Gloria Rambo who had been a member of the church while we were there. There was no mistaking her. She looked just the same as she had over 40 years ago, at least to our eyes. Then we saw Sarah

Orr ("Kip" to everyone there back then) and again there was no doubt of recognition. After speaking with Kip for a few minutes Betty and I went in and spoke with Lloyd Coffee. He brought me up to date on his brothers Claude and Barry, all of whom I knew when I was there. Lloyd reminded me of my helping them put the hay in their barn one day. I am absolutely sure that Lloyd was being kind when he said I "helped" them. We spoke with Jerry Beech and Charles Miller, both of whom we also remembered as having been there during our two-plus years in Belfast.

We had pushed it a little close to the service starting time. We only had a moment to go down to the front and say hello to Julia McDaniel and Catherine Glenn (for whom I had performed the wedding service with "Preacher" Glen in our Hendersonville home in 1962). We agreed to talk more after the church service.

The service began with the organist playing the prelude which was followed by an "opening sentence" read from *Mark 1: 14 – 15* by the pastor, the Rev. Mr. Jim Coone. He then welcomed the congregation and "Grant and Betty Browning from the past" before making some announcements about upcoming church activities.

The pastor, wearing a black robe with a green sash and a large cross pendant around his neck, gave the prayer of invocation. He then invited us to stand and sing Hymn No. 1, *Praise Ye the Lord, the Almighty.* Then he led the congregation in a responsive reading of the scriptures from *Psalms 62: 5 – 12.*

I looked around and admired the sanctuary which had been newly built in 1989 because of a fire that destroyed the original church a year before. The new church was designed to seat perhaps 150 people. There were 17 in attendance today, including the Brownings. The church was comfortable. The burgundy upholstering on the beautiful dark oak pews matched the carpet on the floors. There was a simple dark wood cross about eight feet high behind the pulpit. Presbyterians always emphasize the empty cross rather than the Crucifix, the empty cross pointing to the risen Christ rather than the Christ still nailed to the cross. There were four narrow stained-glass windows on each side. Just to the right of the chancel area was a baptismal font made of oak. In front of the pulpit was a large *Bible* that was displayed open upon the Sacrament table, a light from the ceiling beaming directly down

upon it.And a candle on each side of the large *Bible* had been lighted by a young female acolyte during the prelude.

The pastor said that the "Call to Confession" and the
"Confession" would be changed today, coming after the sermon
rather than at this point in the service. He then asked for prayer
requests after noting some which had been printed in the bulletin.
He then prayed the "Pastoral Prayer" which was concluded with the
congregation praying the *Lord's Prayer* together.

The sandy-haired and bespectacled pastor, who appeared to be
in his early fifties, started to read the scripture lesson from *Jonah 2:
6 – 10; 1 – 5 and 10.* But before reading the passages he shared the
whole story of Jonah. He said that God wanted Jonah, the Prophet,
to go to the wicked city of Ninevah to warn them of their sinfulness. Instead, Jonah fled to Tarshish by ship. While he was on the
ship, a great storm came that made all of the passengers fear for
their lives. They decided that Jonah's fleeing from God was the
cause of the storm, God's wrath. Jonah agreed and told them to
throw him overboard to calm the storm.They did so and the storm
ceased. But God caused a great fish to swallow Jonah and he was in
the belly of the fish for three days and nights. At this point,the pastor read the scriptures which were the text of his sermon.

The scripture lesson said that when Jonah repented of his sins
God caused the fish to vomit Jonah upon dry land. The pastor
asked, "What do you think Jonah looked like when he came out of
the belly of the fish?" His clothes were probably ragged and
bleached out from the acids in the belly of the fish. And his hair
was probably ragged,full of sand and seaweeds. He probably looked
spooky was what the pastor was saying. But Jonah set out for
Ninevah which was a large city. Large enough it took three days to
walk across it. Jonah told the people that in 40 days their city
would be destroyed because of their wickedness. But the people of
Ninevah repented and God spared the city. Jonah became furious
at God. He was embarrassed because he told the people that their
city would be destroyed and now God had not done so.

The pastor emphasized God's words to Jonah, "How could I
not respond to them for they repented?" These words inspired the
title of the pastor's sermon, "God's Response to Repentance." The
pastor pointed out that Jonah's choice when in the fish's belly was

to either repent or die and that, likewise, we all must either repent or face eternal death.

The pastor spoke freely with no notes and walked easily around the pulpit area. He continued by saying that God allows U-turns and characterizing repentance as a U-turn. Repentance requires us to see what God wants us to see. It requires us to listen with intent to respond. Then he gave other instances in the *Bible* where God shows us how He responds to repentance. He spoke of Job's repentance and God's forgiveness. He also spoke of the story of the prodigal son who repented to his father after wasting his life in riotous living and sinning against him; the father forgave him and had a feast in honor of his return.

The pastor said that many people do not accept the absolutes of the scriptures and that one of those absolutes is that repentance is required for forgiveness. At this point he offered the "prayer of confession" which he had deferred from earlier. He prayed, "Praise to God for His plan of salvation, for the opportunity to repent and to know your forgiveness."

The pastor then announced *Hymn No. 262*. The organist said, "I will play it all through one time first." And she did before everyone sang "Thy life was given for me...What have I given for thee? ...Thou gavest Thyself for me...I give myself for Thee."

The pastor led the congregation in repeating the *Apostle's Creed*. Tithes and offerings were taken followed by the singing of the Doxology: "Praise God from whom all blessings flow...Praise Father, Son and Holy Ghost. Amen." Then the prayer of Thanksgiving was read responsively from the prayer in the printed order of worship. The benediction immediately followed. During the postlude the pastor walked to the rear of the church to greet his 15 parishioners and two visitors.

After the service I had the opportunity to visit a few minutes with the pastor and his wife. He had served 20-plus years in the military service and, upon his retirement, decided to go into "full-time Christian service." He received his B.D. in 1998 from a seminary in Louisville, Kentucky. After being ordained he had pastored two other churches before coming to Belfast. If he was anything like I had been, I thought, he was probably changing churches every time he ran out of sermons. I guess I ran out of churches which

would have me, and so I left the ministry in 1964 to "find myself."
I'm still looking.

After speaking with the pastor, Betty and I were joined for
lunch by Julia McDaniel, Catherine Glen and Sarah Orr. We drove
over to Henry Horton State Park and had a fine buffet lunch. The
lunch itself ended with a visit to the dessert bar at which I found
one of my favorites, bread pudding (unfortunately Betty's least
favorite). We visited with the three ladies and enjoyed talking about
times remembered from over forty years ago.

During the lunch conversation I learned that the church's
endowment had grown to about $3 million dollars and produced
about $300,000 per year in income. I told the three dear ladies a
story about a preacher who had quit preaching and took up farm-
ing. When a friend inquired about how the farm was doing, the
then-farmer said, "Well, it ain't doin' too good and if it don't get
better I'm goin' to go back to preachin'. I done it once and I ain't
too good to do it again."

I told our friends at lunch that, having heard about the endowment reaching three million dollars, I might finally "find myself" by
going back to preachin'. I done it once and I'll guarantee you I ain't
too good to do it again. If the Union Presbyterian Church's pulpit
ever becomes vacant again, I may talk with the Columbia
Presbytery to see if I could be ordained again without having to be
examined as to the orthodoxy of my beliefs. If such an examination
is required, I guess I'll just have to keep seeing if I can find myself
elsewhere. Betty thinks I ought to speed the process up a bit. She
would like me to "find myself" before my 72nd birthday.

Chapter 21

The First Unitarian Universalist Church of Nashville

February 2, 2003

I t had been an emotionally packed few days for me, more so than any similar period of my life that I can remember. First, my oldest brother who lives in Florida had been hospitalized. He did not seem to be doing well at all. And I worried because I was not able to go visit and perhaps stay with him until he regained his strength.

I could not go stay with my seriously ill brother because I had also been having medical issues, the second reason for my emotionally-charged life recently. I mention here again my surgery performed two weeks ago by my proctologist, Dr. Howerton on my Abscessed Anal Fistula. I capitalize the condition because to me it was serious. Really serious. Evidence of its seriousness to me was the language I had left for my family to help expedite matters of my non-funeral (my body was to be given to Vanderbilt Medical School with instructions for cremating any final remains). The fact that I had reminded my family about some of my beliefs and had provided them a file entitled *UGB's Funeral* was no indication that I was depressed. I had assured them that it was simply my age. I told them: my life is content and happy; my love and affection for my wife and my children was stronger than ever; and, I had a great appetite and "absolutely pleasurable bowel movements."

Any condition interfering with the items on that list was very serious to me. The last two items on the list were not as pleasurable as they had once been because of Dr. Howerton's discovery. He had prescribed surgery. The surgery was to sort of close off a little satellite type of anus just above my original one; the new one had been caused by the draining of an abscess in an embarrassing area of my anatomy. It's also embarrassing to others. While relating my physical problems to my friend Jim McCann, he told me that I was telling him more than he needed to know about the subject.

Because of this surgery I had been spending a lot of time nursing the posterior part of my digestive system by spending an inordinate amount of time sitting in tubs of hot water. While doing so I had plenty of time to brood over another concern which was bringing on more than a moderate measure of distress — a large, new real estate transaction. I had only become involved in the deal during the last few weeks, and I was having problems working out some of the details. At my age I find that problems breed problems. My wife Betty used to say, "Grant doesn't have a nerve in his body." She doesn't say that any longer. The older I get the more things like this real estate deal seem to affect me.

I actually decided to soak both ends of my body in the tub at the same time; I tried and almost drowned. Anyhow, if I had drowned I had already written my funeral service to help prevent any mounting distress on my loved ones. By the way, my "funeral service" calls for a gathering of family and friends to hear eulogies offered by friends — what I refer to as a "Lying Contest." We are a little short of a quorum of people for my funeral to take place because Betty will not prepare hors d'oeuvres for fewer than six or more than twelve. Betty and my two daughters have made firm commitments to come (if they are in town) which leaves spots open for three to meet the minimum of six. So, if you would be willing to come, please contact me. Betty is leaving *all* the final arrangements to me.

Another thing which had been bothering me was the actions of the "Texas Cowboy," as the Europeans refer to our present official occupant of the White House. He's pulled both guns at once, firing first at Iraq and immediately afterwards at North Korea. He may be right in that both these regimes may be a serious threat to the world. The world, however, would rather have a judge and jury make the final decision as to its fate rather than a cowboy and his handpicked posse. The thought of possible war was also proving to be bad for business, another reason why I had been trying to soak my head. Others think that war in these situations will be best for the world "in the long run:"

> *But I'm not in the long run;*
> *You see, I was born in 1931.*

*"Cowboy, don't make me need to soak my head
By filling the "Axis of Evil" full of lead."*

The final reason that life had been so emotion-packed had happened only the day before. I had awakened to the news that contact had been lost with the space shuttle Columbia during its re-entry into Earth's atmosphere after its sixteen-day perch at the space station. Only a few minutes later confirmation came that the shuttle had broken apart; it had been destroyed probably due to damage to the heat shield tiles that had occurred shortly after its original launch. It was one of a few such disasters in our space program. Another one had been the violent explosion of the Challenger shuttle shortly after its launch in 1986. Such tragedies are, of course, extremely hard on the families of those lost. But in a wider sense the whole nation, and much of the world, seemed to adopt the men and women who had been lost and a collective loss was felt for ourselves and all mankind. It seemed that the loss of each of the shuttle tragedies amounted to a "short step backward for all mankind." And there is an added sense of failure when space exploration goes awry because it is one of the noblest efforts of mankind. Except for those who wish ill to all American efforts, the world joined in the sense of loss because space programs are an effort to lift the sights and spirits of all peoples.

So I was not "on top of the world" as Betty and I started out on another blue road adventure. Partially because of recent physical and emotional burdens, I had decided not to travel too far on the blue roads today, but instead hoped to find a blue-road restaurant and a place of worship near our home. We left at 8:58 a.m. and drove east on Woodmont "Boulevard," if a two-lane road can technically be called a "boulevard." Webster defines a boulevard as "a wide, often landscaped thoroughfare." I guess residents of the boulevard might feel more important if we were living on a wide, landscaped thoroughfare, but we really do not. It should be wide to handle the traffic of those trying to miss the traffic somewhere else, but it is not. Perhaps dropping the "boulevard" from the name and calling it Woodmont Lane would make those passers-through go home some other way. At any rate, on our way east on the "boulevard" we passed the Sugartree development which is just next to our place.

"Our place" is a condominium project built expressly for those who did not care to or could not afford to spend the money it takes to own a house in Sugartree. The beautiful Sugartree development was the first successful cluster-home development in Nashville, thanks to its creator and developer Fred Webber. Webber has since created better and even more visionary planned housing developments in Nashville. He's my hero in the real estate business. When I grow up I want to do developments of the quality he has.

It was a beautiful day with clear blue skies. Just as we passed Sugartree, the vapor trail of a commercial jetliner marked its own path across the same sky in which the lives of seven brave citizens of the world had come to an end just the day before. When we brought our gaze back to Earth again, we felt saddened more by the recent tragedy. St. Andrews Episcopal Church was on the left just a few blocks from our home and we thought that it might be just too close, only a few blocks really, to be considered blue roading. We pressed on. As we approached Hillsboro Road, we passed on the left the Woodmont Baptist Church and on the right the Woodmont Christian Church. The churches seemed two great enterprises competing for the religious commitments of those they could attract for services. Like gas stations competing for customers loyal to a particular brand of liquid energy. A little farther along we passed the Universalist Unitarian Church, a congregation offering worshipers a sort of "unbranded" look at religion. Others would say, of course, that even an "unbranding" is a kind of "brand" of its own. While other churches say, "This is the way, walk ye in it," the Unitarian-Universalist church says that any way you embrace to bring energy and meaning to life and to make a positive contribution to the world is the right way for you.

Betty and I thought that we might like to attend services with the Unitarian-Universalists unless we found another compelling reason to attend elsewhere. Anyhow, I made an executive decision right there that the day's blue roading would simply be "one dimensional." We would both eat breakfast and attend church somewhere along Woodmont Boulevard or its natural extensions. Woodmont Boulevard, Thompson Lane and Briley Parkway are actually one continuous street, changing names only as it meanders through the different "boroughs" of Nashville.

We traveled on, and crossing over I-65, Woodmont became Thomspon Lane. We soon passed St. Edwards Catholic Church which I also hoped to attend one Sunday if possible. Next to St. Edwards are the "Country Squire Apartments" which my partner G.T. Scott and I developed around 1970. The development, designed by Gresham and Smith Architects, is still an attractive and well-kept complex even 30 years after we had built and sold it. We developed some apartments that don't look so good today, and I attribute that more to the poor design work than to perhaps any other factor.

We entered another area of Woodmont-Thompson Lane where the name changes to Briley Parkway. We passed the Aerostructures Corporation near the Metro Airport and wondered if the company, which specializes in making large wing sections of large jetliners, had possibly participated in assembling the wing structures for our tragically lost Columbia space shuttle.

Near the Aerostructures site is the International Plaza building which my company developed with the Joe Rogers Company more than 30 years ago. The large modern building, entirely encased with gold tinted windows and built on land we leased from the Airport Authority, was the first suburban high-rise office building in Nashville. The Rogers Company was the contractor for the building and became our partners. Later on, we sold our remaining partnership interest to them and it became their headquarters. It took a few of these good deals over our years to feed the habit of other bad, money-losing deals.

We spotted a Denny's Restaurant just beyond the International Plaza and decided immediately that it would be our blue-road restaurant for the day. Well, if Nashville can call Woodmont a "boulevard"then I guess we can call Denny's a blue-road restaurant. We walked in through a front door which had a sign, "Under New Management." Usually such a sign is an apology for the poor quality of the recent past management. On the positive side, such a sign says, "Give us a try." It seemed they were saying, "We've learned from our mistakes and have hired new people whom we think you'll like." And we did.

The service at Denny's was quick and courteous. As we were ushered to a seat near the middle of the recently remodeled restaurant, I spotted Francis Guess an executive with the Danner Company. Ray Danner, owner of the Danner Company, is the founder of the Shoney's Restaurant chain, which had fallen on hard times and had been sold to another food-chain operator. I went over to Francis and said, "I guess since the changes at Shoney's at least you don't feel you have to eat at Shoney's all the time." The always-polite Francis said, "This is true."

While speaking to Francis and his guest, I had a chance to see their two absolutely beautiful plates of scrambled eggs with melted cheese, sausage, bacon and potatoes. I made up my mind then and there what I was going to have for breakfast. When I got back to our table and saw the menu, I saw the same beautiful breakfast platter I had coveted at my friend's table fully laid out in a large gorgeous, mouth watering four color photograph. This restaurant actually duplicated in real life what the beautiful pictures in the menu depicted. Under the picture of what was going to be my breakfast was "All American Slam" ($5.79). I ordered it with toasted English muffin. Betty spotted a better deal for herself — the "Original Slam" which included two eggs, two sausage links, two slices of bacon, and two pancakes all for $2.99. Leave it to Betty to spot a bargain. I see traits of Betty's mother in her more and more. My brothers say that they see more of my dad in me all the time also. I guess that when we get older we look and act more like older people. Quite a revelation, huh?

I don't know why more restaurants don't have menus like Denny's. Every picture was so beautiful and appetizing that I actually wanted everything I saw, including the lunch and dinner selections.

The restaurant was about 90 percent full when we entered and remained that way all the way through breakfast.At one table two ladies sat with four little girls under six years of age. The ladies were young and attractive and I hoped that their husbands were out playing golf on a beautiful day. I just did not want to think that they were divorced and that these young women, girls really, were starting out on the hard life of being single parents. And so, for these pages at least, it shall be that golf it was! Their adoring husbands would be home soon to complete a beautiful day with their beautiful wives and children. The world could use a little good news today. And so there it is, read all about it: "Two beautiful families of four are deliriously happy ever after."

But Denny's was really a men's place. There were two tables with four men each and a number of tables with two men each, all no doubt on the way to the golf course on this beautiful Sunday.

A table in the far back corner held three adults and one child. The adults were white — a husband, a wife and a small elderly woman who was probably the mother of one of them. The couple was in their fifties and had with them a small black child of about two years of age. The child apparently was adopted or either these were foster parents. I was sure of this because of the parental way they were treating the child — disciplinary when necessary but constantly loving and caring for his needs. It was a beautiful site and another good news headline for the world today: "All racial barriers finally broken and all orphans adopted into loving families."

The food was even better than it looked in the picture. Betty's pancakes were so good she almost "forgot" to save me my requested test bite. My entire breakfast platter was excellent except for the English muffin; it was just slightly warmed as the English eat them, but this is America where all English muffins must be crisp, almost burned.

We finished breakfast and while paying for my check at the register I had a distressing conversation with an attractive female manager in her mid-twenties. I said, "You're pretty busy," and she responded with a smile, "Yes, and I've been going at this for 24 hours." I asked, "You mean you've been here 24 hours?" She looked up and with a hurried half-smile said, "I have worked three shifts at three different locations." Maybe that was how Denny's didn't have to pay overtime rates to their employees. Not to be a troublemaker but I certainly do hope that employee was properly paid for her dedication and hard work.

It was 10:15 a.m. as we left Denny's to return to the Unitarian Universalist Church. Halfway back I pulled into the new Krispy Kreme Donut place on Thompson Lane. One bite of pancake does not a breakfast dessert make. I went inside for a quick snack and, as I waited in line, I saw the full process of the donuts being automatically made — all the way from the mixing of the bulk batter, through the squeezing of the small donut shapes onto a conveyor belt that carried them into a warm chamber to slowly rise to regular donut size, through the machine guiding the donuts-to-be into the hot oil and turning them over at the halfway point to finish their cooking from the other side, and then in the end baptizing the freshly fried dough in a constant flowing stream of donut glaze.

I ordered one of the freshly glazed donuts. The waitress-technician used a stick to rescue one of the newly and sweetly baptized ovals before its entombment in the darkness of green and white boxes to be carried out in multiples by a steady line of customers.

My rescued dessert fulfilled its intended purpose in life in a matter of seconds. I devoured it and washed it down quickly with delicious coffee which was almost too hot to handle. The doughnut was as delicious as I had remembered Krispy Kreme being when I first tasted one over forty years ago. I could smell the millions of yeast spores reaching maturity and preparing each host doughnut for the conveyor ride of its short life. The doughnuts are like butterflies which spread their beauty and finish their intended purpose in life in a matter of a few short hours.

I was back in the car a few seconds later and noted Betty waiting more impatiently than patiently. She had seen right through my flimsy claim that the stop at Krispy Kreme was a matter of historic curiosity. She can always see right through me and it makes me feel so naked. I started talking about another subject quickly, "Think we should stop and get some gas?" My quick diversion worked. She said, "Oh, let's just wait 'til after church."

At 10:40 a.m. we walked into the Unitarian-Universalist Church through what seemed to be the back door and into a crowded room. The 100 to 150 people were all milling about and visiting loudly with each other. We were invited to sign the guest register. It was that obvious we were guests because I had on a coat and tie, one of two such dressed men in the entire church — including the choir director. I guess I could have passed myself off as a guest soloist or something. That could have worked unless I actually had to sing or something.

We selected a seat in the back far left side of the fan-shaped contemporary room. The high ceiling was accented by stone, redwood, and lots of irregularly shaped glass doors and windows. The seats, pews with no padding, were arranged theater style. The pulpit area was raised about 15 inches and had a cluster of plants at the very back along with two vases of fresh flowers. Candles stood on a table in front of the pulpit. The pastor, Mary Katherine Morn, was seated alone on the platform behind the pulpit. She was dressed in a skirt and a cream-colored sweater set. A piano was located to the left of the pulpit.

Before the service we met Jenny Martin whose name tag announced her as a "lay minister." After she told us what she did for the church, I said, "This sounds like you are sort of like a deacon." She smiled saying that she once belonged to the Baptist church. She was warm and gracious as she welcomed us to the church, taking the time to tell us about some of the different services and discussion groups of the church. Probably ascertaining that I was sort of the intellectual jock type (my imagination goes wild at times), she told us about the Sunday evening discussion group for men only. It was, she said, "usually over pizza and beer." Not that the discussion was about pizza and beer. You know what I mean.

At 10:48 a.m. a piano player began "warming up" or practicing. While the church gradually filled up now with about 200 people (most of whom were very casually dressed) I spotted another tie — another visitor, of course. The "warm up" piano player surrendered the piano to Susan Snyder as he then took the position of song director. He invited us to sing song No. 175, *We Celebrate the Web of Life*, which was a reminder of how we are totally connected with each other in all walks of life. Then we sang No. 134, *Our World is One World* through which we confessed together that "What touches one affects us all...What thoughts we think affect us all... Just like a ship that bears us all." The third song was No. 288, *All Are Architects*. The words of this song included: "All are architects of fate, working within the walls of time ... Build strong and sure with a firm and ample base... Todays and yesterdays are the blocks on which we build."

At this point in the service Becky Bowman rang a single chime on a bell and let it reverberate for a few seconds as sort of a "Call to worship" in which she invited us to "Open our minds and spirits." Then there was "the prelude," a contemporary piano solo entitled *By Way of Introduction* by Susan Snyder. After "some opening words" and the "Chalice Lighting" led again by Becky Bowman, the minister, Mary Katherine Morn, gave a sort of youth sermon. She was assisted by Ben Papa, the director of religious education. The sermon was entitled *Story for All Ages* and focused on how the World Wide Web (WWW) and the Unitarian Universalists (UU) are similar. She told us that in both instances the power comes from the people. "No one owns either and no one is in charge," she said. She noted that in both there was democracy and that all ideas were welcome; anything could happen on the WWW and in the UU churches.

Becky Bowman then came to the pulpit and welcomed everyone to the service and asked visitors to introduce themselves. One lady introduced herself as a member of the Bahà'i faith which she said was "a sister church" with the UU. I introduced Betty and myself as visitors who lived just a few blocks down the street.

The choir, composed of about 20 members, came out of the congregation to sing a well-rehearsed song with beautifully trained voices. The next part of the service was "Joys and Concerns" during which different members told of Joys or Concerns and lit a candle representing each. One concern was for a woman whose husband had died the previous week. Another was for someone's relative who might have cancer. Others included a family out of employment, a brother in the army leaving for Turkey, an anniversary of a father's death, a father who had died, two friends who might have to go to Iraq, a new baby who had been born, someone who had broken a hip, concerns about our government at this trying time, and many others. Two people asked for thoughts and prayers for the deceased astronauts' families.

After the offering the minister delivered her sermon on the *Webs of Life*. She wanted us to think about the ways technology had changed us. She read a poem that she received just the day before. Sort of hot off the press, from a fellow UU minister with whom she exchanges e-mail. The poem ended, "Now voyager, come home and be blessed, be blessed." She marveled at the speed and directness of possible contacts, such as the poem, with regard to the tragedy of only the day before. She focused mainly on the marvels of information technology. She told us that it was changing her life by allowing her to get facts quickly and to communicate with family and friends. The instant communication with the world had also enriched her life. She continued the sermon by commenting on how the WWW allows small pieces to be loosely joined together "in a landscape that has no limits and few rules." She marveled at how each Web connection exponentially increases our connections yet still brings us closer to each other. But she mourned the fact that many were still excluded from the information explosion.

The minister pointed out the sadness she felt in realizing that through the WWW both good and bad could be exponentially multiplied. She asked us a number of questions about the WWW: "Does it help or hinder us? Does it include or exclude and does it give us freedom or restrict us? Are we allowing the Web to be used to its fullest and best potential?"

The congregation then sang No. 207, *Earth Was Given as a Garden*. We sang that the Earth "was given for humanity…A tree of light and knowledge placed for our discovery."

After a brief "Candle Extinguishing" period the minister gave a brief benediction that ended with the words, "Go in Peace." As we left Jenny Martin invited us to meet with the minister and have a few minutes of fellowship over coffee and tea. Betty and I declined her warm offer "because Betty had an appointment" that afternoon. And she did. She was going to see the Vanderbilt and the University of Tennessee women's basketball game at Vanderbilt, yet another reason we had not traveled far on the blue road today. *Fifty-two Sundays on the Blue Road* was my project, not hers. Her project was to help the Vandy women win as many basketball games as possible and possibly make it to the finals or at least to the Final Four. There was not much hope that Vanderbilt would ever win it all; they never have. But Betty's project is to wave her black and gold pompoms and cheer them on toward victory. She's really charismatic in her religion. Know what I mean?

The Unitarian Universalists would allow Betty to have her religion as long as she allows those who cheer for U.T. to have theirs. We both like that. We believe in equal opportunity religion and pompom waving. But she would like to have a few more converts waving black and gold pompoms. She's tolerant but evangelical.

Chapter 22

Community Congregational Church
Naples, Florida
February 9, 2003

No, I did not ride the blue roads all the way from Nashville to attend church in Naples, Florida. But I came as close to blue roading in the sky as is humanly possible; I flew Southwest Airlines, a blue-collar (if not blue-road) way to travel. This airline's whole market strategy has been reducing the high cost of flying by reducing many of the frills associated with air travel. It has succeeded at both. The round trip ticket from Nashville to Ft. Lauderdale cost $230.00. I was meeting some of my wealthier friends in Naples for a few days of golf, and they paid two to three times as much to get cheese crackers rather than plain peanuts for an in-flight snack on competing airlines which they chose to patronize.

I let the cat out of the bag by admitting that I came here to play golf for a few days. For several years I had been meeting some friends in Florida during February for a week of golf. I had been really busy this year starting two new development projects, which had been quite demanding in terms of time. Also, recent minor surgery on a major part of my body had left me a little uncertain of my ability to swing a golf club. But my doctor removed all my excuses two days before I left, and I knew I just had to go. The real reason I had to go was a desire to secure my place on this trip for years to come. The tenuousness of my place was part of the reason why, at the ripe old age of almost 72, I had started two new real estate ventures. I am hooked on making these trips and staying in the beautiful beachfront condos of my wealthy golfing friends. But even though I have been warmly invited to come on these trips for years, I recognize that I am an outsider. The others who come are judges, lawyers or journalists — real professionals. I sell real estate. See what I mean? My spot may be lost at anytime by some legal maneuver regarding a mere technicality concerning my true golfing handicap that could definitely and easily be revealed as a result of investigative reporting by some unscrupulous newspaper people.

Because of my insecurity regarding my lack of tenure for such golfing outings, I had put myself back to work. I had to make some money — a lot of money. One of my business partners in Nashville says, "When you run with the big dogs, you've got to hike your leg real high." I'm definitely running with the big dogs when I come on the February trip. My friend, Judge Gil Merritt, is our genial host for the annual trip. Gil, a true legal scholar, is just now taking senior status as the Chief Justice of the Sixth Circuit Court of Appeals. He is always cordial in his invitation to me, but I am who I am. And I realize that I could be replaced at any time. Also, Gil is no spring chicken himself. While he is a few years younger than I am, his number could be called at any time and then where would I be? Get my drift? I need some insurance, thus my need to make some more money. Gil just purchased a new penthouse on the beach. He moved up several notches when he bought and remodeled the magnificent penthouse since our last outing. He and his wife Robin have done a truly beautiful job remodeling and furnishing it. It also has an unbelievable wrap-around view of the Gulf. Mega bucks! And I am addicted to the opulence. I'm going to have to go back to Nashville and dig up two or three more projects to get me to the point where I can buy my own place, just for insurance. It's my own social security plan. Pray for me. Like the country song says: "Oh, Lord, won't you buy me a Mercedes Benz. My friends all drive Porches, I must make amends." And like Tavia in "Fiddler on the Roof" I keep pushing the question: would it spoil some great eternal plan if I were a wealthy man and had a penthouse in Naples with a great wrap-around view of the Gulf?

Since we had arrived on Wednesday evening, we had played a lot of golf, eaten at several of Naples' finest restaurants and talked big — very big! We discussed at some length: the current problems with Iraq and Saddam Hussein, the problem of George W. Bush acting and thinking like a cowboy, the pros and cons of tort reform (particularly as it relates to healthcare situations), the human proclivity to violence towards other humans, the death penalty, the economy, the presidential election of 2004, ex-Vice President Al Gore, and the new majority leader of the senate, Senator Bill Frist.

Didn't I say we had been talking big? You see the additional pressure I am under?

There were only five of us here for the trip this year. In addition to Judge Merritt there was John Seigenthaler (who has won more awards for about everything then anybody), Wendell Rawls (who is a Pulitzer Prize winning journalist), Frank Sutherland (who is the editor of *The Tennessean* newspaper in Nashville), and me — little ol' me, the real estate salesman.

I had tried my best to act knowledgeable about these heady topics; I fear that I am transparent,however, and that they saw right through me. On the other hand, my lack of knowledge on most of these subjects might have been my best asset. I made all of them feel more important. I am sort of their schmoo. With my being around each of them can seem intellectually superior to at least one person. I'm feeling more secure even as I write these words. If I can make sure the basis for future invitations will be democratic, I will have a better chance. I can lobby during the coming year with each one separately on my behalf. Every salesman knows how to lobby on his own behalf.

When I told the four hard-ankle golfers that I was not going to play golf on Sunday morning I got all kinds of razzing from them. "The ex-preacher's got religion again," was a sort of chant I heard often around the golf course — mostly during my back swing. Sunday morning did finally come down on the not-too-sleepy city sidewalks of Naples, Florida. Naples' sidewalks are not at all sleepy in February when all of Nashville and half of the rest of the world descend upon it.

When Sunday morning arrived, I set out to find a blue-road restaurant and church to attend while my four friends continued their quest for bragging rights for the remainder of the year by playing one more round of golf at the Naples Grande Golf Resort. I left Gil's condo on Gulf Shore Drive at about 6:45 a.m. and drove north past the many fabulous gulf high-rise condominiums. Such condos fill my heart with absolute, undeniable and totally sinful envy to the point where it becomes pure lust. I also passed the unbelievably beautiful Venetian Villa Condos, which, although they are not located on the beach, have a subtle elegance about them. They rise unexpectedly on piers out of the inland waterway and were inspired by the beautiful villas throughout Venice, Italy. The condos seem to define what Naples, Florida is all about. Another of my wealthy friends, Charlie Martin, owns one of the villas. I had decided when I saw him golfing at Naples Grande that I needed to cultivate my longtime friendship with him, just in case I am "voted out" of my present group — more insurance. I had heard that Charlie had a magnificent yacht docked at the Venetian Villa. I told him I could easily change to yachting instead of golfing if a warm invitation was forthcoming. I'm a pushover, I guess.

After passing Charlie's place and his yacht with envy, I turned east onto Park Shore Drive until it intersected with Highway 41, also known as the Tamiami Trail (Tampa to Miami trail). I turned north onto the Trail and began to look seriously for a blue-road restaurant. A blue-road restaurant in Naples is probably an oxymoron. The whole area seemed to be broken out with opulence. But still, it has its share of McDonalds, Burger Kings and Wendys. And I passed several of them on Highway 41 as I drove northward past the truly spectacular development of Pelican Bay. On the way to Pelican Bay I passed the Perkins Restaurant. I had eaten breakfast here before and it had been truly outstanding. All of the breakfast items at Perkins had been almost as good as the Pancake Pantry in Nashville. I decided to push on in hopes of finding a new breakfast place to experience but I held Perkins in reserve just in case I couldn't find anything else.

I passed the Covenant Presbyterian Church and decided to keep it in mind if I ended up circling back to Perkins for breakfast. I passed another McDonald's, which helped me continue to claim the route as a semi-legitimate blue road. And the shopping centers! They seemed to have infested the whole area, like boll weevils. You know why there are so many shopping centers in Naples? It's because the people here ain't got nothin' else to do but spend their unconscionable amounts of money. Buying stuff at the shopping centers is their way of redistributing their wealth. It's their way of tithing to the poor.

A few miles further north I passed two similar looking churches on the right and decided to attend church at one of the two: The Christus Lutheran Church (which I decided was perhaps Hispanic) and the Community Congregational Church. The Lutheran Church had services at 8:00 a.m. and 11:00 a.m. The Congregational Church services were held at 8:30 a.m. and 11:00 a.m. I could make either the 8:00 a.m. or the 8:30 service a.m. at one of the churches. The only thing left to do was to find a breakfast place in the neighborhood.

I had driven less than a mile farther when I spotted a likely suspect: "Mel's Diner." The building was a new facility and was modeled after a 50s diner — lots of art deco architecture with its use of chrome-curved surfaces accented by multiple rows of multi-colored fluorescent lighting. It also was a play on a popular TV series of a few decades ago that had featured "Mel's Diner." I drove into the parking lot at about 7:20 a.m. There were only about twenty-five cars in the large inviting lot. The interior was expensively done even in its obvious attempt at replicating the features of the rather inexpensive "diners" of yesteryear. I was ushered immediately to a booth and given a menu. Immediately I realized that I would not be doing very much people watching as I waited for breakfast between cups of coffee because dividers located throughout the diner minimized my view of the other breakfasters. I was locked into a breakfast carrel and about all I could do was study my menu and the expressionless face of an otherwise fairly attractive waitress. And so I studied them both rather carefully. I studied the menu more carefully than the expressionless face because my hunger exceeded my curiosity about what was causing a could-be-attractive young lady to be not-attractive at all. The menu study revealed several interesting facts. I could get the "Country Benedict" breakfast ($3.99) or the "Country Omelet" ($5.29) with "biscuit" (singular) and "potato or three eggs with pork chop, potato, biscuit" (singular again). The printer obviously had run out of a supply of the letter "S." He could not make things plural after the "eggs" and the "grits" insertions. Of course, he had to use one in the grits to make a complete word but could spare no more for the biscuit.

With single-mindedness I chose the three eggs, pork chop, potato, grits and biscuit, in spite of the attractive offerings of county-fried steak, eggs burrito or "Smoked Kielbasa Scramble." My efficient, but uninspired, waitress responded to a query about the age of Mel's Diner with the conversation-ending answer of "about four years" as she walked away from my booth. With no expression, she had communicated non-verbally with me her preference of no more questions. Not that she was so very busy. She wasn't. She just had something else on her mind and it must have been something ugly because it was rendering her unattractive. If it was a money problem it was going to be exacerbated by the diminished amount of her tips. Lack of expression translates directly into lack of interest, and lack of interest is poor business when you are in a service business. Even with a headache a waiter or waitress should smile freely and often; the resulting generous tips might help the headache go away.

Alone in my cubical, I further studied the menu and found that I could buy things to help me remember my breakfast at Mel's. The memory aids offered included T-shirts, coffee mugs and golf shirts. I would rather remember a breakfast spot for a friendly waitress and eggs cooked to my order. And I will remember Mel's positively by the way my eggs were cooked perfectly, as ordered (over-easy with the whites done or over-medium with the yellows runny). But I will remember Mel's even more positively because of the excellent fried potatoes. They were prepared like those at the Pancake Pantry in Nashville, but maybe even better. They were deeply browned and crisped on the bottoms without being cooked dry all the way through. Such potatoes take a really hot, thick grill and a patient cook who will wait just a few more seconds until the desired doneness is achieved. The pork chop was good also — sweet, juicy and done.

The bad news? Mel's failed the biscuit test. The biscuit (singular) had not been baked long enough to give it the brown, crisp bottom and the rippling gold-brown top every biscuit (singular) deserves. Instead, it was a lonely, washed-out looking piece of supposedly country pastry masquerading as a biscuit. And it had been nuked! Eating a breakfast with one biscuit is like a bird trying to fly with one wing; it doesn't work. Especially when it has been nuked. I would almost rather see Mel patting his sausage patties flat in his armpit than see him micro-waving a biscuit. The nuked biscuit (singular) had to be pinched off bit by bit to make sure it lasted throughout the breakfast and to reserve one last piece for jelly as a one-bite dessert. It wasn't good enough to ask for another one from my expressionless waitress. It wasn't worth the bother. And since I was by myself I could not easily order some pancakes or French toast "for the table." Thus, the lonely and vapid biscuit was a definite negative about my breakfast at Mel's. It's a shame because the rest of the breakfast was very good. If you give Mel's a try, ask for two biscuits, double baked and not nuked. I wish I had. And a waitress without a headache.

As I left, I noticed the nostalgic 50s music collection that had been playing during my breakfast time here. It was appropriate and had helped create a warm, nostalgic atmosphere for the time I was there. When I left at 8:15 a.m., I noticed that now the parking lot was filling up. It appeared that by 8:30 a.m. it would be full.

I realized that the time meant that I would be going to the Community Congregation Church for its 8:30 a.m. worship service. I drove immediately to the church and followed a stream of cars into the parking lot. I entered the building along with several car parkers who had let their passengers out closer to the sanctuary. As I entered, I started to think that maybe I had found the fountain of youth. Suddenly I seemed young again. It seemed as if I was the youngest person there. I felt there was the distinct possibility that I might be carded, and so I started reaching nervously for my billfold to be sure my driver's license was available. As I walked in, the church was teeming with old people seemingly trying to emulate the community churches in Nashville that teemed with young people. There were activities going on everywhere. Groups were set up here and there to offer information about a part of the church: a fund drive; a non-bake sale; a fellowship dinner; and, a bookstore selling religious literature.

I moved quickly to a back pew on the far right side and claimed a seat. After I made my way through all the activity of the foyer, it was relaxing to have a seat. As I sat, I realized that it was a relatively new sanctuary. It was an attractive stucco building outside with vaulted, paneled ceilings and beams inside. There was one large screen about 10 feet by 10 feet to the left of the pulpit area and another over to the right, both of which were rendered practically ineffective because of the sunlight reflections from the windows. There were four stained glass windows on each side of the sanctuary. Another large stained glass window was centered above the choir loft with an additional one on each side of the pulpit area. The choir of twenty mostly consisted of women who were older, of course. Each of them wore a cream-colored robe with a blue sash.

Most of the congregation, about 400 people, was dressed in "Sunday dress" with about a third in "Florida casual" attire. I was Florida casual today. As the congregation gathered, John Davis played a classical piece on the piano as a prelude that ended with a flourished Crescendo. The congregation gave him a standing ovation. He was listed in the program as "Director of Music and Related Arts."

Immediately following the rousing prelude, a young man (kid like) came to the front to make several enthusiastic announcements. He was dressed very casually in wash pants and a blue shirt. And he looked to be in his late teens or very early 20s. It was later pointed out that his name was Jim Murphy and that he was the "pastor of youth and evangelism." He told about a dinner dance, a new-members class and about a new Wednesday night format. He said, as if speaking to teenagers, that last Wednesday had been an "awesome night". Then there was the announcement that it was Minnesota, Montana, Iowa, South Dakota, and Wisconsin Sunday; all members from those states were asked to stand and be recognized and honored.

Kid Pastor Jim then gave the invocation, which he ended with a hope that we all might "discover where we fit. Amen." The congregation stood and sang "Holy, Holy, Holy...early in the morning our songs shall rise to thee...God in three persons, blessed Trinity." If I could have only forgotten the kid, it would have been a very therapeutic service for me — a real dip in the fountain of youth. The congregation went through the familiar routine of everyone greeting the ones next to them and welcoming them to church. The sight of old people trying to move about and stretch stiff muscles across a straining distance to shake someone's hand soon helped erase from my mind the affrontment of the "kid pastor."

At this point I had no clue who was the pastor. Then a woman in a blue-gray robe with a dark blue sash appeared in the pulpit. She made some announcements and talked about the funeral arrangements for one of the members. I surmised that this type of announcement was made quite frequently both here and throughout this whole area. Florida is the place for old tired bones to warm themselves in the sun before moving on to their "final rewards." I later found that she was Pastor Judy Montgomery, listed as the

"Associate Pastor of Pastoral Care." She gave the "pastoral prayer" and prayed for forgiveness for our tendency to war and for our pettiness. She then asked all to silently present our own prayers to God as the piano played softly. Pastor Judy then led us in a version of the *Lord's Prayer* that used "debts" instead of "trespasses" when asking God for forgiveness.

John Davis, the music director and pianist, directed the choir. And while the choir sang a beautiful anthem the offering was taken. I had $3 or $20. I gave the $3 to make it more nearly equitable with the $5 which Betty generously gives. She would be so proud of me. The congregation warmly applauded the choir for an excellent rendition of a worshipful hymn and then stood to sing the *Doxology*, "Praise God from whom all blessings flow." During the *Doxology* the offering was presented to the pastor. The congregation sang *Great is Thy Faithfulness* after which the choir left its place behind the pulpit to join the congregation.

At this point another pastor appeared. He was listed as Pastor Michael Bickford. Michael appeared to be between 40 and 45. The title of his sermon was *The Marks of Faith-Service*. He read a rather lengthy scripture portion from *I Corinthians Chapter One*. He said that it was a letter from Paul to the people in the church in Corinth. Paul was telling the people that even though there is "but one Lord" there are many gifts. Some people are given gifts of wisdom, others are given knowledge while others are given the gifts of prophecy or tongues. But all these gifts are from the same God, the pastor proclaimed. "Some are to be apostles, others prophets and still others are to be teachers," he said.

The pastor then referred back to last Sunday's sermon that had focused on prayer. He said that if there is no prayer, there is no relationship. Then he said they had discussed discipleship, a maturing discipleship that must be followed if we follow Christ. The pastor told us that we tend to let the world, not God, determine our lives because the world largely determines our careers, our social lives and our work. He noted that we get too involved in tending to the details of our lives like the car, the laundry and all sorts of little things that wrap us up in the insignificant. The pastor then said that Irma Bombeck, the humorist, had listed things she would do differently if she had it all to do over again:

- *Invite people to her house even when the carpet was not clean*
- *Drive with the windows of her car down and not worry about her hair*
- *Say more often "I love you" and "I am sorry."*

The pastor worried that it was so easy to fall into undesirable traps in life. He then wondered if we were living the life God expected us to live. "How do we know?" he queried. He said that *I Corinthians* held the answer in its revelation of the gifts of the Spirit. "Not talents and skills," he said, "but gifts of God." He said these were the gifts of administration, evangelism, hospitality and giving. He continued by saying that Pastor Judy had the gift of mercy, and Pastor Jim had the gift of evangelism. I cringed a bit when he volunteered his own gifts as those of leadership and teaching. It reminded me of the man who was talking about the disciples who said, "I may not have the strength of Peter, the enthusiasm of James nor the wisdom of Paul, but when it comes to humility, I excel them all."

The pastor stated that when the body is healthy, every member of the body is healthy and that when we all play our parts, the church is healthy. When we understand our gifts, amazing things start to happen. He then spoke about a seventy-five year old who would do things differently if he could start over; the man had decided he would reflect more, risk more, and do more things that would live on after he passed away.

The congregation than sang "Blessed Assurance, Jesus is mine, oh what a foretaste of glory divine" followed by the *Alleluia Response* and the *Benediction*. During the postlude piano solo by John Davis, the pastor walked to the foyer to greet members of the congregation as they left.

Me thinks Pastor Michael was also politicking a little. I would have done the same if I had been in his shoes and wanted to be called Pastor Michael of the church. The senior pastor had retired five months before, and now a pastoral search committee was looking for a new senior pastor. The young Pastor Michael was apparently applying for the job along with several others the committee was considering. My personal feeling was that they would look for someone older, at least in his 60s; someone who understands what retirement is all about.

When I had entered the activity of the church that morning and had seen all the announcements of activities, fund-raisers and committee meetings, I immediately developed two theories about the frenzied beehive of activity. First, the people were so bored in their retirement that they got involved with anything to give them something, anything to do. Alternatively, the young whippersnapper pastors did not understand that these people were tired. They had raised money, built churches all their lives, and worked on all kinds of committees (both in and out of the church). They had finally retired and had come to Florida to get some well-deserved rest, but these young energetic pastors just couldn't see it. They were thinking up things to keep the poor, old, tired, retired people busy.

My bet was that the new pastor would be more nearly the average age of the congregation — at least 60-years-old. I'll let you know if I find out what happens before the fifty-two week period of this book's time line ends. Stay tuned to "The Last Days of Our Lives."

Chapter 23

First Presbyterian Church
Hendersonville, Tennessee
February 16, 2003

We had planned on leaving home at 8:30 a.m. this morning, but Betty was a little late. I actually did not notice until we were in the car that it was already 8:42 a.m. The whole 12 minutes we were late could not be charged to her however; I had been distracted reading the newspaper. The delay of game was a double foul and therefore no penalty would be assessed.

I had walked out early to get the newspaper. It was a gray, rainy day, a continuation of three days of solid rain in Nashville. The newspaper reported many flooded areas all around Nashville. Yet the miserable weather was not behind my absorption in the newspaper today. It was the possible, perhaps even probable, war with Iraq that caused the clouds to hang so heavily over Nashville — perhaps the wide world. A sagging economy, also casting a shadow over the country, added to the bleakness of the day. Never ending rain, the looming potential war, and the sad state of the economy was a triple whammy. A wet, gloomy bad news day.

The newspaper reports struggled with the question of why we were about to go to war with Iraq. To disarm Saddam Hussein's Iraq of weapons of mass destruction? To control Iraq's oil supply? To avenge the attempt on George W. Bush's father's life? To remove Saddam Hussein in order to allow us to establish a democracy in Iraq? I personally think the last reason the most compelling of them all. But perhaps they all had some measure of truth to them.

I believe that the best way to stabilize the economy would be simply calling off any threat of war and putting it all on the back of the U.N. Even if war did ensue under this scenario our economy would not suffer so greatly. We would not feel so alone, and thus would not feel so directly threatened by the overwhelming possibility of terrorism which would certainly be evoked by the go it alone "cowboy" approach.

Although the day was gray on all accounts, there was a bit of brightness to look forward to because Betty and I were going to visit old friends. Jan and Jim Wells in Hendersonville were having over a group of old school friends from our Trevecca College days of 50 years ago. Jan and Jim had recently been to Germany to visit their son and his family — especially the two grandchildren. And we would see plenty of pictures. The day would be brightened just by witnessing the pleasure it brought Jan and Jim while showing the pictures.

The city sidewalks of Naples, Florida had not been sleepy at all during my visit a week beforehand. Nashville's sidewalks were a different story on this Sunday morning; its sidewalks were sleepy and wet with the ongoing rain. As the drippy rain and Sunday morning continued to descend on Nashville, Betty and I made our way down Broadway toward the Cumberland River on the way to Hendersonville via the blue roads.

The streets at lower Broadway had overdosed on sleeping pills. This area of the city seems to hibernate, at least on Sundays, since the Titans began taking their long winter's nap after the NFL season — no tailgaters, no ticket scalpers. Councilman Ludye Wallace had wisely wanted the Titans' owners to name the stadium "The Coliseum at Nashville." Such a name would allow Nashville a bit of soft advertising mileage for the city whenever the stadium was mentioned on TV. But it wouldn't be mentioned today. No game today. No Billy Graham Crusade either. Someone recently asked me if I realized how the Titans games and a Billy Graham Crusade in the coliseum were alike. The answer? Both the Titans and the Billy Graham Crusade can fill the stadium with 67,000 excited people who, at certain times during both events, will stand simultaneously and shout, "Jesus Christ!"

I almost used the same expression when I spilled some of my Sunday morning coffee on my pants. I was trying to look especially nice because I was a little nervous. When Jim and Jan had invited us to Sunday lunch in Hendersonville I had decided to take the opportunity to visit the First Presbyterian Church of Hendersonville. The reason I was a little nervous was because I had been the pastor of the beautiful little historic church from 1962 – 1964 while in graduate school at Vanderbilt. Why would visiting the church make me a little nervous? Well, I've always felt a little ashamed for having left it after only two and one-half years. In 1961 they had asked if I was planning to continue in the ministry or to go into teaching, which I had considered. On my assurance that I had decided not to go into teaching, they graciously offered me the position of pastor. But in June of 1964 I had decided not to teach or continue the ministry and I left after having been there for such a short period of time.

Betty and I loved the time we spent in Hendersonville, but I had never had a conversation with any of those fine people about why I left the church or why I left the ministry altogether. "Should I tell them if they ask?" was my nervous question. Should I tell them that my beliefs had changed to such an extent that I felt I was unqualified to stay. I had vowed at my ordination that if my theology ever changed I would let it be known to the Presbytery. My beliefs had indeed changed, and I had felt obligated to tell the leaders of the Presbytery that I, therefore, would be leaving the ministry. But I had never discussed the matter with the people at the Hendersonville church. I hoped that these good people had forgiven my early departure from the ministry and that they had not thought too badly toward me. I also held onto something a professor had told me, "We would not be so concerned about what people think about us, if we realized how seldom they do."

Armed with the courage provided by that last thought, Betty and I pressed on toward a reunion of sorts today. I wondered if any of the people I knew would even be there. I was sure that most of them had passed on to their rewards, hopefully aided a little in that journey by a young pastor in his early thirties who had briefly been a part of their lives almost 40 years ago.

In the midst of this slightly nervous excitement we drove on out Gallatin Road toward Hendersonville, passing many churches along the way. This was real church country. Many, many choices. Here I was, again, breaking my own blue-road rules. I had a destination church already in mind. But I was also gathering ideas for future possible visits. The New Destiny Fellowship Church sounded interesting. We put it on our future "maybe list." A new church was under construction without a readily noticeable sign as to what church it would be, but a sign did read, "God At Work." Perhaps a Church of God?

Soon we were at the city limits of Hendersonville. We had taken

our time and did some good easy blue roading on a gray-blue Sunday
morning. We saw the Blue Goose Restaurant which was normally
open on Sunday, but it was closed for repainting. At 9:45 a.m. we
pulled into Mallard's Restaurant on the corner of Gallatin Road and
Saunders Ferry Road. It's sort of just across the street from the
Hendersonville Presbyterian Church. We noticed that the services
start at 8:30 a.m. and 10:30 a.m. Two services? I remembered when
I was the pastor there that I was joyful at having just 50 people to
warm the pews on a good Sunday. We had about forty minutes for
breakfast, and then we would attend the 10:30 a.m. service. I wondered
if the 10:30 a.m. service was in honor of the Titans.

Betty ordered scrambled eggs, bacon, biscuits and coffee. I
ordered three eggs over-medium and said not one word about my
requirements beyond the over-medium instruction. I also ordered
bacon, hash browns, grits and biscuits. There were no pancakes or
waffles so we were spared from the temptation of a breakfast dessert.

We sat in the middle corner of the non-descript blue-road diner
and had a panoramic view of every table in the room. One young
couple intently read selective portions of the paper as they waited for
their breakfast. A group of about 20 young people nervously chattered
away to our far right. They seemed to be on some type of organized
outing. The organizing was just getting them there. From that point
on it seemed to be total disorder. But they were having fun and
were all demonstratively happy. They sort of made the gray day a
little less somber.

One table away from us a man eating alone was finishing off his
breakfast with a cigarette which he was obviously enjoying more
than he had been while eating his eggs and pork chops. He wore a
black cap with "Buffalo Wild Wings" written in gold across the back
and a thin beige "Members Only" jacket with the sleeves pulled up
to his elbows in a sort of jock style. Obviously a regular, the cook had
come out to talk with him while our order was being processed by
an assistant. And he had also been speaking with the man whom I
thought was the owner of the restaurant. The owner was tall and
lanky but carried a little pot belly. His dress, a black shirt with blue
jeans and a Western-type belt with silver medallions, helped to accent
his curving portliness. Neither he nor I needed to call attention to this
part of our anatomy. He talked to my smoking table neighbor about

the Daytona 500 Stock Car race with great interest. Whomever he was pulling for would win his fourth race if he won at Daytona today. Both men certainly talked as if they were pit crew members of the driver they hoped would win.

As we waited for our food, I noticed that the plastic-coated top of the table had ads under it for local businesses. There were ads for GMAC mortgages, Michael T. Pickering Attorney-at-Law, McCloud's Lawn Care, a computer repair shop and many more businesses that were suddenly being delightfully covered by our breakfast selections. Our breakfasts were better than average, thanks especially to the eggs. My eggs were fried perfectly, apparently in a medium-hot skillet because they were slightly browned without being overcooked, just like I always try to cook them at home. The potatoes were just okay. Not great. They were the processed and pressed grated potatoes in a rectangular shape that had been deep-fried to resemble a Pop-Tart.

The biscuits were good, and I am pleased to say they had not been nuked. The waitress told me that they were held in a warmer drawer after being baked. And there were two of them. Even though I intended from the start to eat only one, I was pleased to have a back-up. It put me in a breakfast comfort zone that I prefer as a result of my childhood in West Virginia when my large family practiced bulk cooking. Actually, the extra biscuit turned out to be very important. I used the very last piece of the first biscuit to help push the last morsels of my "Pop-Tart" and eggs upon my fork, and it became a part of this last designer bite of my breakfast entrée. I, therefore, was forced to break off one piece of the second biscuit as a means of transporting a spoonful of jelly into my mouth — my one bite version of breakfast dessert. No pancakes or waffles here, remember?

I paid $11.21 for our breakfasts and left a $3.00 tip. I always wanted to be thought of as a big spender, especially by waitresses who work for less than the minimum wage outside of their tips. This big spender and his wife left at 10:15 a.m. to go on over to The First Presbyterian Church where we would later give a $5.00 offering. I said I was a big spender not a big giver. Anyhow, I can blame the $5.00 offering on Betty. Offerings were her department. Mine was tipping waitresses. Somehow I feel that $3.00 to a waitress would be as pleasing to a good God as $5.00 in the offering. This may be utter blasphemy to most preachers and I may have thought differently 40 years ago, especially since I counted on perhaps only 40 to 50 right-eous souls to financially support the church and pay my salary.

We walked into the historic church and felt immediately as if we had gone back in time. The sanctuary had been enlarged lengthwise, but it seemed to me that the same soft-mint color of paint was on the walls that Miss Sarah Berry had paid for in 1963. The enlargement had not affected the quaintness of the beautiful place of worship with its old original pews, now comfortably and thankfully cushioned. The floors were light, natural-colored oak. There was a comfortable center aisle with two smaller aisles on either side next to simple, tall windows. The tall, simple windows were of plain glass. Just simple, plain classic Quaker-like design.

The pulpit in the chancel area was slightly off center to the left and a simple empty wooden cross was hanging high at the back of a centered choir area. The congregation was a pleasant mixture of people from very old to very young. Most of the older people wore "Sunday-go-to-meetin' clothes" while most of the younger people were dressed more casually. Casual dress had been more or less typical in most of the churches we had visited so far with some few exceptions.

At 10:26 a.m. the church was three-fourths full and filling up rapidly. By 10:30 a.m. it was full and the organist began to play. The organ accompanied a flutist named Jennifer Abrock who played a worshipful prelude. The minister was listed in the order of worship as Tim Reynolds — not Reverend Tim Reynolds. Just Tim Reynolds. And that was the way he presented himself to the congregation throughout the service. He and the choir were dressed in dark blue robes with Kelly-green sashes. The choir consisted of five men and five women plus a director.

Immediately after the prelude the minister said, "The Lord be with you." The congregation responded in unison, "And also with you." He then gave a warm welcome to all, especially the visitors, "We are glad that you are here and hope that sometime during this service you will experience God!" Then he proceeded with several announce-ments about a mission trip and about an old-fashioned chili supper to raise money for the church. He petitioned for more "Acts" for the chili supper program:singers, dancers, storytellers, etc. to go with the lonely, singular, only one who had already signed up. He also asked for volunteers to make favorite chili recipes and cakes, pies and desserts to be sold at auction.

The service continued as Laura Gardner, listed in a flyer as the "liturgist" for this morning, led the congregation in the call to worship. After a congregational hymn, Laura led the reading of the printed "prayer of confession." The prayer asked God to forgive us for not being more open about our problems with each other and for God to help us to open up to each other as a community of brothers and sisters, as a community of forgiven sinners. Laura then read words assuring our pardon by God for confessed sins.

Next the pastor introduced the offering with a story. A female member of the Jake Woods' family had given the minister a check from Jake. Jake had been sick and unable to come to the church to make his offerings but the lady insisted that Jake wanted the church to have his support. Jake would have it no other way.

After the offering and a warm, spontaneous applause for the beautiful solo by the flutist, the pastor made some heartfelt remarks about the world situation. He said he had considered changing the entire sermon this morning in order to direct our attention to the potential war looming with Iraq. He wrestled for a few minutes with the problems facing us. Do we go to war and face the possibility of many being killed? Do we let Saddam Hussein go on with an inhuman regime during which hundreds of thousands had already been killed? He effectively pointed out the dilemma we faced, but ended his expression of concern by simply saying, "God is bigger than our problems."

Pastor Tim strapped a guitar around his neck and led a group of instrumentalists and singers in a contemporary gospel-type song entitled *My Glorious*. The words of the song were printed on an insert to the order of worship, and at the end of it the congregation joined in. The pastor later commented on the variety of music in the day's service between the flutist, the beautiful songs by the choir and then the contemporary gospel piece. It was "cool," he said, that the church had this variety of music in one service.

Next the pastor called the "young disciples" to the front for a children's sermon. He effectively lined them up and, one by one, coaxed each to fall into the arms of the others who were there to catch them. He then asked if they knew what they were doing in this little exercise. He answered his own question by saying that they were "practicing community" by catching a person as they fall, by catching each one as a united group. The piano softly played *Jesus Loves the Little Children of the World* as they left.

"The Prayers of The People" and "The Lord's Prayer" were next in the printed order of worship. The pastor noted some prayer requests in the supplement to the Order of Worship. And among those for whom prayer was being requested were Mavis Leslie and Virginia Duffett who had been good, faithful members of the church when I was pastor in 1962 – 64. These were the only names I recognized in the bulletin except that of John Martin, the son of Jim and Marg Martin. John, and his wife Susan, now teach a Sunday school class for grades 3 through 5. John had been in about those same grades when I had been pastor at the church. Of course, little Johnny was still about 9 years old in my mind. I had not seen him since 1964. He probably still thought of me as thin and still in my 30s like I had been while playing football in his side yard with his older brother Jimmy.

The congregation prayed together. The only difference between this service and a Methodist service in a church of similar size would be the difference in words used in *The Lord's Prayer*. In a Methodist church the congregants ask for forgiveness for "our trespasses" while Presbyterians ask for forgiveness of "our debts." I report this finding for those who would wonder. That's about it. Maybe Methodists and Presbyterians will merge one day if this great difference in the liturgy can be worked out.

After the reading of scriptures from both the *Old Testament* and the *New Testament* that were separated by a choir anthem, the pastor began his sermon which was taken from the *New Testament* scripture lesson from *Mark 2: 1 – 12*. The lesson is about a man who was sick of the palsy. He was carried by four men to the house where Jesus was. The crowd there was so great that the four men had to lift him to the rooftop, cut a hole and let him down into the house so that Jesus could minister to him. Jesus said to him, "Son, Thy sins be forgiven thee." Some of those present said that Jesus' words were blasphemy because only God could forgive sins. Jesus responded by asking them if it was easier to say "Thy sins be forgiven," or "Take up thy bed and walk," at which point Jesus said, "Arise and take up thy bed." And the man did, and he was healed.

The pastor, who spoke totally freely and effectively without notes at all as he moved all around the chancel area, said that the passage was not about illness caused by sin. He said illness and sin are not connected. He was more focused on the men who brought the sick man to Jesus — his community of support. He spoke of their great efforts to get help for their friend. They climbed the roof, cut a hole through the mud and the thatch, and probably had to go somewhere to get ropes to help let the man down to Jesus' feet. This, he said, was a real community of faith supporting each other.

Pastor Tim asked a member of the congregation whether it was Bonhoffer or Kirkegaard who said that, "The purpose of organized religion was to keep people from experiencing God." The man to whom the question was asked (identified by Pastor Tim as "our resident philosopher") quickly answered, "Kirkegaard." The pastor pursued his point; the church should really be a community of support, "We are all paralyzed at times and need the community to lift us up."

The pastor continued by telling a few stories of lives having been touched by the community of faith in the church. He told about a conversation which he recently had with a leader in the church. The man was touched that the people of this community had placed him in a position of leadership. This act of confidence in him on the church's part had strengthened him and made him a better man. The pastor also told about a group who had decided to leave the church a few years ago as a result of some dissention within the church. They had planned to leave as a group after Christmas. During the holiday season one church family was involved in a terrible wreck that killed some of them and left others seriously hurt. The church so rallied around this devastated family to "lift them up" and support them that the disillusioned group changed their mind. They decided not to leave after witnessing the true love and support the members of the church showed toward their own.

The pastor concluded his very effective sermon by stating that the mission of the church was to be so loving and supportive of each other, to be a true loving community fellowship, that others will say, "We have never seen anything like this." After a beautifully written "Affirmation of Faith," which tied directly into the need for community and fellowship, Pastor Tim invited Jennifer Bryant to the front to be received into the congregation by letter of transfer from the Central

Presbyterian Church of Atlanta and by renewal of her baptismal vows.

The pastor underscored that she did not need to be re-baptized, but that she wished to renew her vows of baptism. The pastor then ushered her to the back of the church where the baptismal font was located and repeated the baptismal vows which she affirmed. He then sort of vicariously re-baptized her by saying that her earlier baptism was reconfirmed by her actions on this day. He took her back to the chancel area and gave her some gifts including a membership certificate and a history of this church. The history of the church had been written by Powell Stamper, a leading member of the church "way back" when I was pastor here.

After the benediction and the postlude the handsome young Pastor Tim went outside to greet his parishioners. Betty and I were among the first to leave because of the advantage we had gained by sitting on the back pew. I gave Tim my card and shared with him that I had been the pastor here from 1962 to 1964; he warmly invited me to come back and talk to him about the history of the church. I think I will.

As we left, I felt that if I could have preached as well and as easily as Pastor Tim did that I might have sublimated my emerging theological positions and stayed on as pastor. Who knows? I might have been able to stay here all these years. I guess I could have hired Pastor Tim as my assistant — but not as a preaching pastor. He's too good. I always wanted to be the big shot and that would not have happened if Tim preached in "my" church. Actually if I were here, I don't think it would be good for me to have him in the same Presbytery. Maybe Memphis would not be too close. I would think about it.

I couldn't think about it right now, though. I had to start thinking about getting out of the parking lot. This preacher had really screwed things up at my church here. I now know I should have stayed; we certainly never had a traffic jam like this when I was here. What a mess! I wonder if they've started a search committee for a new pastor to clean up the traffic problem. If so, I'm probably their man.

Chapter 24

Mt. Paran Church of God
Atlanta, Georgia
February 23, 2003

*T*his had been a somewhat unusual and very busy week. One of my partners in a real estate venture and I had been working on the purchase of a very desirable piece of property which finally had closed on Thursday afternoon. My partner, our architect and I had also planned a trip to Birmingham, Alabama and Destin, Florida that weekend. We wanted to see a couple of projects which we felt could conceptually help fine-tune the final design on our development. We intended to leave Friday morning and come back on Sunday.

Friday morning my partner became ill and could not go on the trip, and therefore the trip was cancelled. So, Friday morning I drove south toward Pulaski on I-65 to check out another matter, and then on to Huntsville. In Huntsville I realized I was only a little over an hour from Birmingham, and that I could go there to see the project that had been on the agenda for the aborted trip. And so I drove on to Birmingham. The development there was beautiful, but it was not close enough to our own design criteria to be of help.

Before I began the trip back to Nashville, I called my longtime good friend Yousef Abbasi. Yousef had moved from Nashville to Atlanta about eight years ago. Since I was less than two hours from Atlanta, he graciously invited me to visit with him, his wife Tracy and their two beautiful daughters — Isabella who is seven and Hana who is three. It so happened that my wife Betty was on her annual trip to the gulf coast (with her dear friends Barbara Pate, Peggy Benson and May Lou Cook) and would be gone for the weekend. And as quick as that I had talked my way into a weekend visit with Yousef and his family.

Yousef and Tracy live in a fabulous 11,000-square-foot house in the St. Ives Country Club community located northeast of

Atlanta. Yousef owns over a hundred Hardee's restaurants in Georgia and Florida. He also has one of the most creative and energetic minds I have ever known, so I naturally always love being around him and getting the waves of energy emanating from his mind. I now know why his mind is always so active. It is very simple as I see it. He must keep having profitable ideas in order to pay for a fleet of very expensive cars and an enormously beautiful house, which is full of beautiful furniture and art. And then, of course, he has to make lots of money for his many friends. You see, Yousef is a check grabber. He is one of the most generous people I know. Someone once said the difference between being rich and being very rich is that when you are rich you can have everything you want, and when you are very rich you can have everything you want and you can see that your friends can have everything they want too. This is the way Yousef is. Therefore, if he is not already very rich, I am pulling for him to become very rich and for me to remain his friend. The crumbs falling from his table are bountiful and delicious.

I spent Friday night in the lap of luxury and in the company of my generous Arab-American friend and his family. Yousef had come to the U.S from Jordan to attend college in Missouri. After college he continued to live and work here. He was also able to help two brothers come to the U.S. later on. And about 10 years ago Yousef became an American citizen.

I assisted Yousef as a broker during the acquisition of his first chain of restaurants in Nashville. He moved to Atlanta about eight years ago shortly after he married Tracy. While we had kept in touch over the years, visiting back and forth over, this would be the first time I would be a guest in his home. I looked forward to spending time with him and getting to know Tracy, Isabella and Hana better. I initially planned on spending Friday only but, again, things changed. Yousef and Tracy insisted that I go with them to visit Yousef's brother Mohammed in Rome, Georgia. Mohammed is the franchisee of 15 Wendy's restaurants there. I decided to accept the offer which meant that we would drive back to Atlanta on Saturday evening and that I would go to church No. 24 somewhere in the Atlanta area on Sunday morning.

Now, the real clincher in my decision to spend another day

and night with these dear friends was the promise of a celebration. There would be a typical Muslim Eids feast at Mohammed's house in celebration of the end of a period of Islamic pilgrimages to Mecca. Saturday also happened to be the 27th which was the anniversary of Mohammed and his wife Sandra. What a treat it would be to visit a Muslim home on this dual occasion!

Yousef and Mohammed are Muslim, but are probably not gold star attendees at their respective mosques. When I was a child, we used to get a gold star after our name if we had a perfect attendance record for one year; neither Yousef nor Mohammed has received any gold stars for the last 25 years or so. I really do not know the main reason behind the gathering. It could have been their deep religious observance of the Feast of Eids or the 27th anniversary celebration, or the chance to eat some of Mohammed's famous cooking. I was certain of one thing — I was happy to be invited. And afterwards, I was even happier that I had gone.

Mohammed's and Yousef's friend, Ali Adabi was also at the gathering, along with his wife Melani and their two sons Joseph and Jonathan. Yousef, Mohammed and Ali all married American wives, all of whom were Christians before their marriage and have remained Christians during their marriage. Ali and Melani, I understand, are members of the Bridgeway Christian Church of Atlanta. The three marriages are cross-cultural, cross-religious and (apparently) functioning beautifully as of party time.

It was a truly warm and memorable occasion to witness as an invited participant. Mohammed, a warm and jovial bear of a man, was the chief cook and the life of the party. He obviously loved preparing traditional feast favorites of lamb and rice with pine nuts with a delicate yogurt sauce, a large rack of six stuffed and golden roasted chickens, and a beef tips and eggplant casserole in a marinara sauce. Yousef prepared a delicious salad with practically every vegetable known to man in it. We all sat around a large oval table like one large hungry, happy family and ate far more than we should in an effort to follow Mohammad's constant instruction of "eat more, eat more." And we did, and we did!

After we toasted Mohammed and Sandy's 27th anniversary, their son Yousef and daughter Amanda, who both work for their father while finishing college, took their leave of the festivities.

They went off to their own Saturday Nite Live activities and left the rest of us to finish too many dessert selections to be named topped off with coffee, cappuccino and lots of family stories and jokes. It was difficult to break up such a festive gathering of family and friends. But, slowly we did. At about midnight we began the drive back to Atlanta with the Abbasi children asleep two minutes into the return journey.

On the way back to Atlanta Yousef, Tracy and I made plans for the next day. I wanted to attend a church in Atlanta the next day. And I also wanted to come back to Atlanta in a few weeks to attend a mosque with Yousef if my schedule permitted. We decided that the whole family and I would go to breakfast at J. Christopher's breakfast, brunch and lunch place. Then Tracy and I would attend a service at the Mt. Paran Church of God, a church widely known by most Atlantans. Yousef would take Isabella and Hana back home to finish their night's sleep and hopefully give Yousef the opportunity to do the same for himself.

At 9:00 a.m. Sunday we all started out on the 10-minute ride to J. Christopher's in an Abbasi – Browning three car caravan. We went to Christopher's at 3294 Peachtree Industrial Boulevard, one of eight locations in Atlanta. The menu is a breakfaster's delight, with offerings under "The Griddle" section featuring pancakes, crepes, and French toast. The "Morning Star" section featured "Huevos Avocado," steak and eggs, and country ham and eggs. Then there were "The Skillet" selections — poached eggs topped with all sorts of combinations and, of course, a whole array of omelets.

I ordered country ham, eggs, potatoes, grits and biscuits. Yousef ordered a Spanish omelet, while Tracy copped out and only had turkey sausage and toast. The girls ordered the kids' meals pancakes decorated with smiley faces. Yousef laughed when I carefully ordered my eggs over-medium, and then proceeded to "scramble them" on my plate. My wife Betty does not approve of this habit either, Yousef. But since Betty was not there, I felt much more comfortable "table scrambling" my eggs only to be caught in this breach of table etiquette by my friend Yousef. He may be a part of an international etiquette spy ring crusading to establish and enforce a standard for how all breakfasters are to order and eat their eggs in public. But I will resist to the end any attempt to arrest my God-given West

Virginia right to "table scramble" my eggs.

Why don't these "do-gooders" busy themselves with something of international significance such as teaching the world how to properly prepare breakfast potatoes like the world leader, the Pancake Pantry in Nashville, does? It's a mystery to me. J. Christopher's does everything beautifully. The eggs were prepared perfectly, table-ready for custom scrambling, and the grits were properly seasoned and buttered with no need of table enhancement. The biscuits were superb. They were baked, sliced and custom grilled while the other breakfast items were being prepared. This is destined to become a world standard. But the potatoes! Send in the inspection team quickly! The hungry pilgrims of the world, many of whom rely on this international staple, deserve better oversight from the inspection team. This near world-class eatery could be lifted to the next level easily as a result of a little industrial espionage at 1296 21st Avenue South in Nashville, Tennessee, the home of the potato czar of the world. He poses as the owner of the Pancake Pantry. For ease of entry the spies need only stand in line for one to two hours with all the other potato inspectors from all around the world.

After eating breakfast and ignoring my potatoes, Tracy and I took two cars to the Mt. Paran Church of God located at 2055 Mt. Paran Road in Atlanta. How we got there only God and Tracy know. I merely followed her. That's my story and I am sticking to it because it is my only protection from the wrath of true blue-roaders around the world. I had not told Tracy beforehand that I travel only on the blue roads on my *Fifty-Two Sundays* expeditions. But then, of course, you cannot get anywhere in Atlanta except by freeways, and just barely then.

When we arrived, we were guided by well-placed parking attendants to a remote parking area from which we were then ferried by bus to the church. Part of the need for the bus came from ongoing construction. The church was in the process of building 25 million dollars worth of new facilities and, apparently, some of the parking had been displaced by the present construction of a new parking structure. A new sanctuary would be built during Phase II of the construction. Tracy and I sat in the balcony which provided a panoramic view of the sanctuary which seats 1,750 people. The 11:00 a.m. service had all the seats filled; there had already been two other services during the morning and another was scheduled for 6:30 p.m. It was one busy church with programs and services for every age group and every interest group.

Before the service began, a professional sounding female voice narrated "A Mt. Paran Minute" on two large screens located on either side of the pulpit area She presented in a most media-savvy manner many of the upcoming activities of the church, and when it was finished she signed off by saying, "This has been a Mt. Paran Minute" before giving her name just as they do on T.V. I was duly impressed.

After the "Mt. Paran Minute" a 100 voice choir wearing blue robes with blue and white sashes filed in. The service began with their beautiful well-trained voices singing *Let Us Come and Bow Down*. They were accompanied by two pianos, an organ, and an orchestra with drums, guitar, violin and a two-piece brass section. They were led by the director of the church's music ministry, Mark Blankenship. During the musical call to worship a few hands were raised in praise from the mixed crowd of black and white, young and old. The worshipers were dressed in as mixture of ways that mirrored the mixture of worshipers themselves. After the choir's call to worship there was a warm applause of appreciation by the congregation.

The next part of the order of worship was "Congregational Worship." The choir and congregation joined in singing, "I will worship with all my heart...I will follow you all my days...I will give you all my worship...I will give you all my praise." The entire congregation was standing with at least 75 percent of it waving their arms and clapping their hands with joy. The congregation remained standing while singing several songs including "You are great. You do miracles so great, there is no one else like You," which was repeated over and over many times. Perhaps 90 percent of the congregation now had their arms raised to wave as the musical director asked, "Would you raise your hands with me?" Mark's skillful direction tastefully created a worship mood for almost the entire congregation.

At this point, senior pastor Dr. David Cooper, who appeared to be in his mid-40s, came to the pulpit and softly asked, "How many of you need a miracle today? Lift your hands." About 50 members of the congregation raised their hand. The pastor then asked the elders and the ministers of the church to come to the front to anoint with oil "anyone who needed a miracle today." It appeared that 250 people came forward while the choir and congregation continued to sing, "You are great. You do miracles so great; there is no one else like you." Most of them knelt at the altar to be anointed. Those who could not get to the altar stood behind those kneeling and in the aisles while the ministers and elders anointed each one with oil. The minister said that there were miracles for those who were sick, for those who had financial problems, for those who were out of work, for those who needed forgiveness of sins, and for those who were tired and worried; a wide net was cast and many troubled seekers came forward to claim their miracle. The pastor prayed that all who came would be "helped, healed, redeemed, forgiven or made whole, in Jesus' name. Thank you, Father." When he finished the prayer the whole congregation applauded as if to congratulate the seekers who had gone forward for miracles as they now quietly returned to their seats.

The music director continued to effortlessly lead the choir and the congregation in singing, "We worship you, we worship you. Hallelujah, Hallelujah" over and over. Most of the congregation clapped to the beat of the tune with great feeling. "You are good, all the time, all the time. Yes, You are, yes, You are" was sung again and again as the pastor asked the congregation to greet one another with the words "God's been good to me." Most of the congregation warmly responded.

It was now 11:41 a.m. Another minister, tall and handsome, came to the pulpit to inform the congregation that the $10 million building campaign had been exceeded by $5 million. But then he asked them to raise another $10 million to complete the total $25 million needed for both phases of the construction program. Then Mark the Pastor of Music was introduced in a video tape presentation in which he spoke of the desire to make the new larger sanctuary as warm and intimate as the old one. He said that they did not want to lose the warm spirit which was obviously felt today in the existing sanctuary.

The offering was taken, and I gave the $5.00 standard which had been set at the beginning of the *Fifty-Two Sundays* pilgrimage. I really felt bad about the $5.00 today because it would not even pay for the shuttle bus to and from the parking lot. But a deal's a deal. During the offering there was a truly beautiful solo that was expertly timed and choreographed. It was performed by a very talented, very tall and handsome member of the choir and it was perhaps the most spirited and captivating song I have ever heard during any church service. Anywhere. It was simply wonderful. And my judgment was echoed by great, great applause by the congregation.

The sermon was next, and it was a fine sermon from any perspective. But it was destined to be a little anticlimactic after the beautiful emotional mood created by hundreds seeking miracles, the fabulous music by the choir, and the extraordinary song by the soloist. Pastor Cooper's sermon was entitled *Stop Doubting and start Believing* and he used *Mark 9: 14 – 29* as the scripture lesson and basis for the sermon. It was about a man who brought his son to Jesus to be healed. His son was possessed by evil spirits, and Jesus healed him to the amazement of everyone, including Jesus' disciples. While he told the story of the healing, the preacher encouraged the congregation, "You can say 'Amen' at any time." "Amen, Amen, Amen" came the response from the congregation, already emotionally spent by the earlier part of the service.

In the scripture lesson Jesus told the man that his son could be healed if the father could only believe. The Father said, "I believe, Lord. Help thou my unbelief." The pastor said the man was going through a crisis of faith when he said, "Help Thou my unbelief." The pastor stated that lack of faith kept the children of Israel from entering the Promised Land, and he emphasized that doubt can lead us to abandon our faith altogether. He noted that some people champion reason over revelation but warned that "God's ways are not our ways."

Pastor Cooper said that when things do not turn out the way we think they should we experience a crisis of faith. John the Baptist had a crisis of faith when he said to Jesus, "Are you the One who was to come or do we look for another?" The pastor assured the congregants that everyone has doubts at times but, he insisted, if we believe we can say to that mountain, "move" and it will be done. He received a few spirited Amens, but not as spirited as the Amens had been during the singing. He said that when we doubt we should ask, "What did Jesus say? What did Jesus say about prayer, about forgiveness, about truth?" The pastor said that Jesus bore witness to the truth.

At 12:33 a.m. the pastor declared, "This is the victory which overcomes the world, even our faith," and he said "the zip code of this truth is *I John 5: 4.*" He then spoke about the difference between an inherited faith and integrated faith. An inherited belief is the sort of belief you have when born into a Christian home while an integrated faith is the sort of belief you have when you make it your own. He told of when his wife became very ill when they were newlyweds. Her sickness put his faith to the test. He prayed, "God, heal my wife. My voice cries out to You." To the astonishment of everyone in the hospital he said that God healed her, and that he witnessed that miracle. He said when you can't see God's hand, trust His heart. At this point, as if on cue, the organ started to play softly. The pastor then did a creditable job of leading the congregation in singing *Hallelujah, Praise the Lamb:* "My heart sings this praise again, Praise the Lamb."

It was now 12:39 a.m. The pastor gave a short benediction, and the service was over. It truly was a great service. The service had ministered to the needs of the congregation in a most effective way. It was perhaps the most moving service that I had ever attended because it touched the hearts of the people, warmly and effectively. The pastor's sermon, though well thought out and very effectively presented by a great preacher, was not the high point of the service by any means. The heart of the service had been the music — the music opened the hearts of the people, leading many of them to seek help and forgiveness in the middle of the service. Sermons may still be considered a necessity for a worship service, but the centerpiece they definitely are not. At least not always.

Watch out preachers, here they come — music directors who become senior pastors! Brace yourselves preachers, or better yet, learn to sing as senior pastor Cooper has done. Will the next evolution of the sermon be a singing sermon? Followed perhaps by no sermon at all? Could be.

Chapter 25

Bethlehem Freewill Baptist Church
Ashland City, Tennessee
March 2, 2003

T here's a country song that says, "Some days are diamonds,
some days are coal." The day was neither a diamond nor a
piece of coal. It was just gray. It was not a bad day, nor was
it a good day — it was just a gray day. Not clear-cut black or white
on another scale — it was just so-so or gray. It was not particularly
cold; it was not particularly warm. The sun was not shining; it was
not raining except for an occasional drizzle. The day was just sort
of blah.

We left home at 8:19 a.m. Betty let me know that we were
only four minutes past our expected time of departure in a totally
indirect way. In the car she took my pad and pen and said, "Do you
want me to make some notes, let's see, it's 8:19." She just wanted
me to know that we were well within any reasonable person's grace
period. She might have even been hinting at the possibility that the
four minutes had been spent getting ourselves together and into the
car. In either case, she was proud of the timeliness of our departure.
Her lilted tone as she said, "Let's see, it's 8:19," gave away her pride,
and although she did not address it directly, she wanted it duly
recorded. So it was duly recorded in my notes. And now it is duly
and doubly noted here — recorded for posterity — that we were
timely leaving our house on this gray, overcast day.

As we departed, Betty and I informed one another of our
mutual observations that it was truly a gray blue-roading day. At
that moment I realized that I had not specifically told Betty that
her traveling with me on Sundays was by no means obligatory. Of
course, the trips were not obligatory technically because we had never
had that kind of arrangement between us. Just as on the blue-road
SCOLTA trips several years before, Betty was an invited guest. I
welcomed her on the trips, but she knew that she had not signed

249

on for the duration and was free to leave any time she became bored. It was the same on the current Sunday trips. I was always happy to have her with me, but I wanted to make it abundantly clear that she could bug out any time the day was too gray or any time she would rather just sleep in.

It was the 25th Sunday since I had started on this series of journeys and Betty had been with me on all but five of them. For three of those five trips, I was in another location. The other two times other reasons had made it seem best that I go alone. No gray-outs yet for her, but I wanted her to know that she was not accumulating "points" to be used for negotiating some future outing that I did not particularly want to go on. *The Fifty-Two Sundays* venture was not to be used by her to pile up pressure points for the future. So, no points were given or received on this truly stay-at-home type of day. She already had many points on her side of the ledger because she just naturally always does more for me than any marriage contract requires. I just didn't want to stack the deck any higher. I felt like a love slave already.

We drove across Briley Parkway until we turned north onto 41A toward Joelton and Pleasant View. While traveling in the area several weeks ago, I had noticed a particularly large number of Free Will Baptist Churches and now I had a clue as to why. The Free Will Baptist College in Nashville is planning to move in the near future from its West End location. Its new campus may possibly be located in the Joelton – Pleasant View area. In preparation for the eventual move the school had apparently been sending out student mission-aries to colonize the area with numerous Free Will Baptist churches. Enough so that the college's students will have plenty of congregations for practice sermons for years to come.

If the college moves to this area, they will not have the many readily available restaurants the students presently have to choose from at its present location — both as places to eat and places to work. But we did find one restaurant which was open for breakfast — The Pleasant View Café.

At 9:03 a.m. we entered the restaurant/community hangout for a good blue-road breakfast. Betty ordered two scrambled eggs with tenderloin, grits and biscuits. I ordered three eggs over-medium with country ham, hash-brown potatoes and grits. I also ordered one pancake "for the table" for our dessert. After ordering I read further in the menu; the Café is not a meat-and-three restaurant. They serve no fresh vegetables, and all its meats seem to be fried or grilled. Maybe with the college coming they will have enough help and customers to allow their menu to branch out a little.

Our breakfast arrived just as a man who looked liked Colonel Sanders of KFC fame was leaving. He looked just like the distinguished Colonel would have looked in his 50s. He apparently was also a charmer, just as the late founder of the KFC chain must have been. He had been "holding court" at a table where all the restaurant workers congregated as often as possible between serving their customers. And the service got noticeably better when the modern day colonel left. Our cups were filled two times after the dead ringer for the "finger-lickin' good" chicken king moved his franchise elsewhere.

Our breakfast was sort of like the weather today — not bad at all, just not noteworthy. But it could have been. My eggs were cooked perfectly and, to Betty's chagrin, I used the last bite of my biscuit to "sop" up the last bit of my self-table-scrambled-over-medium eggs. She said she was glad Miss Manners was not there to witness such a display of poor table etiquette. While it was indeed fortunate that Miss Manners was not present, it was unfortunate that another kitchen Nazi was in residence. His presence was evidenced by the nuked biscuit (singular) which came with my order, a double whammy against this blue road breakfast spot. Fortunately, the country ham was quite good. But had it not been for the pancake which I ordered "for the table" which was shared equally by the Brownings, there would have been no acceptable breakfast dessert. No second nuked biscuit was available to receive bites of jelly to sweeten our palates before we left.

We had some time to decide which Free Will Baptist Church to attend. There were several including Head's Free Will Baptist Church which was four miles off the main highway. It was a plain, nondescript brick building that sat on a curve in the road and had several added projections of various materials that gave the church a "growed-up-like-Topsy" look. It was only 9:45 a.m., and we had plenty of time left. So we drove toward Ashland City were there was another array of Free Will offerings.

On Highway 49 between Pleasant View and Ashland City Betty spotted a strange sight and insisted that we turn around and investigate. On a small, hard-scrabble farm-like situation sat some two hundred white plastic barrels with holes cut into one side of each one, obviously to provide some kind of ingress for some kind of critter, to be sure. But homes for what? I first blurted out to Betty, "I think they are beehives." The barrels were lined up row after row and spaced 15 to 20 feet apart.

"Guess again, flannel mouth," I said to myself a second later as I noticed rows and rows of roosters that stood statue-like either beside or upon each of the domiciles. It looked as if the rooster statues were some sort of "scarecrow" device to ward off predators and protect he occupants of these curious residences.

It turned out that the rooster scarecrows were real roosters. They had been tied to a stake in the ground on a short tether of some sort, just short enough to keep the roosters apart. They looked strangely artificial because they hardly moved at all. We knew that they were not artificial after two of them flapped their wings almost simultaneously. Some of the nest-houses, as we now identified them, were elevated on a pole six to eight feet off the ground which further fascinated us. In an attempt to satisfy our curiosity, we drove around a bit in search for a native of the area who could tell us what we had just seen. Luck was with us. A man at a self-auto wash place told us that we had just seen a farm that raises game roosters bred for cock fighting. He said that this sort of thing was done all over Cheatham County, which was the county we had chosen today for visiting a Free Will Baptist Church.

Ashland City is the county seat of Cheatham County, and this farm was conceivably within a stone's throw of the city limits. Since it is the nature of the breed to fight, the tethers were there to limit their free will to the lengths of their respective restraints. We would probably be at the Free Will Baptist Church we would attend in Ashland City before any one of the gamecocks could crow twice. And, unless those cocks suddenly got more life than exhibited by their scarecrow type demeanor, we would probably beat the first crowing of most of the sedated birds as well. Maybe that was how they kept them alive; they fed them Prozac up until fight day and then filled them with speed balls. We broke out of the tether of our seat belts and bolted into the Bethlehem Free Will Baptist Church in Ashland City at 10:25 a.m., with only five minutes to spare before the service began.

Several friendly members warmly greeted and welcomed us in the hope that we had moved into the area and were prospective members. They seemed a little deflated to hear that we lived in Nashville and had just stopped in for the worship service while on a Sunday drive. Earlier on our blue roading we had visited a Southern Baptist Church, a Missionary Baptist Church, and the Mt. Zion Baptist Church (which seemed to be a denomination all to itself) but this was our fist visit to a Free Will Baptist Church. The belief behind the prefix of "Free Will" to the Baptist name was interesting. Free Will Baptist churches follow the Armenian theological position that man has a free will to choose for or against God. "Regular" Baptists, on the other hand, more closely follow the Calvinistic theology which some say, more or less, limits the free will of those who have been born again. The "once in grace, always in grace" theology of "regular" Baptists is rejected by The Free Will Baptists.

We certainly thought that we had chosen this particular church over the many other possible ones as an exercise of our own free will. But perhaps, before setting down the foundations of the world, God had ordained that we were to eat at the Pleasant View Café, drive by to see the cocks whose free wills were restrained by tethers and Prozac, and then attend services at this church. I dunno. But I think the Armenians have the edge on logic with the free will thing. Besides, it just doesn't seem Godly for God to be mixed up in determining if I am going to order grits or not. But maybe I am making Baptists here into Presbyterians at this point. Here Presbyterians certainly out Calvin-ize the Baptists.

Freer than game birds, Betty and I chose seats on the far right side near the back. Surely God would not want to have a hand in such a choice. He obviously would have chosen for everyone to be in the pews nearest to the front and the "Amen corner." According to the strict Calvinists, God founded this Free Will Baptist church in 1847 and predestined that the new sanctuary would be built in 1970 and that the first hymn of this day would be *No. 336*. God may have done all this. I certainly had no hand in any of it except being here today.

When God built the church in 1970, He did a marvelous job and He had been helped considerably by the man who sat in front of us. His wife proudly announced to us that he "headed up" the building committee. The man may have felt he had no choice in the matter at all because I suspected that his wife may have helped God and him to take on the job. Maybe they all together decided on the beautiful laminated arches which formed the impressive cathedral ceiling. And somebody besides us chose the handsome light oak pews. Somehow, I just can't imagine God selecting the matching mauve carpet and seat padding. But true Calvinists, if pushed to the wall, would probably be forced to admit that nothing happens without God's permission at least.

A choir of seven men and seven women entered while the organ played the prelude. They were not wearing robes, which John Calvin may have said was God's choice in the matter. However, in this Armenian church this matter was the choice of the pastor or the deacons. The choir sang the *Call to Worship*. Their selection was *Draw Me Nearer*: "Draw me nearer...to Thy precious wounded side."

Pastor Corn then welcomed the congregation to the service, including the visitors. There were about 150 people present of all ages, and most of the adults were dressed in "Sunday Clothes" except for three of the four "ushers" who took the offering: one in a suit coat; one in a leather jacket; one in shirtsleeves; and, the last also in shirtsleeves with a plaid, lumberjack sort of pattern.

After the song *No. 336*, a member of the congregation was called on to offer a prayer from his pew. Then we all sang Hymn *No. 290*: "There's a new name written down in glory...and its mine, oh, yes, it's mine...with my sins forgiven I am bound for heaven, never more to roam." After the offering we sang *No. 295*, "I will sing the wondrous story...of the Christ who died for...how He left His home in glory for the Cross of Calvary."

During "A Time of Fellowship" it seemed as if the whole congregation came to welcome us again while the children were "dismissed." We then sang No. 285, *No one ever cared for me like Jesus*:
I would like to tell you what I think of Jesus, since I found in Him a friend so strong and true...I would tell you how he changed my life completely. He did something that no other

friend could do…no one else could take the sin and darkness from me…Oh, how much He cared for me.

Just before the sermon one of the choir members and the piano player performed a beautiful duet, setting the tone for the "Morning Message" by "Pastor Corn." Neither his full name nor the names of the other people assisting in the service were provided, either by announcement or in the printed order of worship. Their names were freely omitted by the free will of the Armenian Baptists, because if God had determined that my single biscuit that morning had to be nuked, He surely would have ordered that visitors to the church should and would know the names of those who sang the beautiful duet.

Pastor Corn read from *Ephesians 4: 17 – 24* wherein Paul told those at Ephesus to "put off the old man and put on the new man." Hs sermon was entitled, *The New Man.* Pastor Corn was a tall, semi-handsome, balding man appearing to be in his mid40s. He began the sermon by saying that through salvation God destroys the old man and we put on the new man, becoming totally new — not just sort of cleaning ourselves up. Paul had said that we are to be totally different, to be totally made over.

The preacher said, "You know what it takes to go to hell?" He answered his own question, "You do what comes naturally. To follow Christ you do not continue doing what you have always done. You must change — you must become new."

The pastor said that when he was 18-years-old he went to the Free Will Baptist College and Seminary and then took some graduate work. During this time one seminarian had been asked, "What are you going to be when you finish school?" The student had answered, "An old man." He then told about when he had eye surgery. He had become very aware of the handicap of not being able to see and needed someone else to drive him home after the surgery. This gave him the opening to say, "Without Jesus Christ we are blind."

"Do you live like you know Jesus?" the pastor asked. He was saying that knowing Him should make a *real* difference in our lives. He then shared a question which Lucy, in the comic strip "Peanuts," had asked Linus. She asked, "Do you think people ever change?" Linus replied, "Yes, I do. I've changed a lot." Lucy then retorted, "I mean for the better." Pastor Corn said that "real change for the better comes in cooperation with the Grace of God." A true Calvinist, you know, could have left the cooperation part out. The pastor also said that the *Bible* tells us that there can be a change in our nature and in our lives.

During his closing remarks the pastor asked us if we had changed. He pressed his point by asking, "If not, why not? If not now, when?" He then asked us to stand before he invited all those ready to have God make them into a new person to come forward to pray. The congregation began singing, "Have Thine own way Lord, have Thine own way, Thou art the potter, I am the clay." After a few moments a girl in her teens went forward to speak with the pastor. He said that the young girl wanted to join the church and be a part of its fellowship. While the young girl stood there, he said that the normal course of events would involve an official church meeting and "and all that stuff," but since they already knew the young lady he was going to ask the congregation if they wanted to invite her into this fellowship. "All in favor, let it be known by saying, Amen."

I wasn't sure if I was breaking a congregational rule which might require calling for a new vote on the young lady's membership, but I said "Amen" along with the rest of the congregation. I think I heard Betty cast an affirmative vote also. Regardless, by the time this book comes out the membership of that young, sweet girl will have passed the statute of limitations and no new vote will need to be called. Betty and I, however, might be indicted on a charge of stuffing the ballot box or voting out of our precinct. If called before a judge, I think I'll become a Calvinist and just say, "Your honor, I must have been predestined to cast that vote. I don't know what came over me." Anyhow, the outcome of this court session has already been determined. Case dismissed. Court Adjourned.

Chapter 26

The Belmont Church
Nashville, Tennessee
March 9, 2003

Whatever I ended up doing this morning, I was going to end up doing it alone. You see, I am a basketball widower. My wife, Betty, is something of a fanatic about Vanderbilt women's basketball — just like her longtime friend Billie Patton is fanatic about many things. That is, Billie really enjoys a lot of things. Think up something to do, and Billie is usually out front leading the parade with gusto.

Vanderbilt was playing basketball in Little Rock, Arkansas this weekend. Billie started the parade and Betty joined right in with her black and gold pompoms and the two of them (both in their 70s) took off for Little Rock with the enthusiasm of teen-agers. They had left Thursday morning at 8:00 a.m. in Billie's car, and they planned to be back Monday evening after Vanderbilt had surely won the Southeastern Educational Conference Crown.

I love the childlike enthusiasm Betty has for basketball and many other things. She's always a good sport and is always willing to go along with any adventure, as long as it does not require much walking. This particular restriction on her enthusiasm has only come about in the last few years after having had both hips replaced with artificial ones. Traveling in a car or on a plane for some new adventure? No problem. And so Betty and Billie have been in Arkansas since Thursday to cheer and wave their pom-poms and challenge the competency of the ophthalmologists who neglect the nearsightedness of all referees.

For three nights in a row, I enjoyed watching TV without Betty's sweet little way of questioning my taste in TV programming. She usually says something like, "Do you really want to watch that program?" In truth she is usually saying something like, "If you are not really into that program, there is a re-run of Prince Charles and

Diana's wedding." And, usually, I tell her it is okay; I wasn't really into the re-run of Tiger Wood's last 100 wins. Sometimes though I say that I'm really into something, and she goes off into another room to watch the royal wedding yet again. Either way I lose. I lose a little if I agree to watch the wedding again, because I really don't want to. And I lose a lot if I don't agree to watch the wedding again and she ends up going into another room because I like to have her with me watching something, whatever it is.

But the first night she was away I felt no guilt. I watched Tiger win again, watched the elephants try to make love, and just surfed through the channels looking for nothing in particular and finding lots of it. On the second night I had a great time watching all the "know-it-all" guests on CNN and CNBC argue about the right thing to do in Iraq — over and over, replay after replay. By the third night I wanted to hear Betty asking, "Do you really want to watch that program?" But she was still in Little Rock trying to get Vandy into the finals. Unluckily for her, but luckily for me, the eyesight of the refs had not been corrected by the time Vandy played LSU in the semi-finals and so Vandy lost. The good fortune hidden in the LSU win over Vandy? My comfort in knowing that by prime time on Sunday Betty would be sweetly asking again, "Do you really want to watch that program?" And I planned to say, "No, not really," regardless of what I am watching.

Since Vandy would not play Tennessee in the finals Betty and Billie did decide to come home. They had suddenly lost interest in hoping for a miracle cure to the myopia of the referees. But, they would be praying again for healing in a week or so when referee eyesight would indeed need to be tested by these two specialists again. Betty called to say they were on their way home, but she would not be here in time to go to breakfast and church with me on Sunday morning.

While playing golf on Saturday with my friend Frank Sutherland, we had decided to play again on Sunday at 12:50 p.m., the only tee-time we could get. Our tee-time meant that I needed to limit my blue roading to the sleepy city streets of Nashville again. At 8:45 a.m. I left home taking Hillsboro Road north toward Hillsboro Village. There, of course, I saw hungry souls freezing in the line to get into the Pancake Pantry; they may have been standing there since last Sunday for all I know. I passed the Belmont Methodist Church and saw several individuals rushing into the service in a way that made it seem they were already late. And so I knew it was too late for me there as well. I went in toward town on Music Square, East (known as 16th Avenue to old-timers) and found another hurrying crowd gathering for a service at the Belmont Church, one of the proliferating independent types of community churches in Nashville. This particular church had been perhaps the first one in Nashville to go in the community church direction. Pastor Don Finto had been its early leader and had started the church successfully after a Church of Christ had vacated the location. Some of the Church of Christ's members decided to remain and were the core of the current church's congregation. However, the nucleus of the new church had focused on making the new church different from the old one. For one thing, the church had instrumental music, lively music at that. I decided to attend the next service which would begin at 11:00 a.m.

Now all I needed was to find a restaurant for breakfast. There were a myriad of bagel shops and coffee shops all around this music industry/Vandy area. But I wanted a traditional breakfast with eggs and stuff. After driving around in this section of the city, I found Noshville, a breakfast/delicatessen on Broadway located between 17th and 21st avenue. This would be it. It had to be it if I was going to have eggs for breakfast because the area IHOP had closed during the last year in the name of progress — more parking for Vanderbilt!

Noshville bills itself as a New York delicatessen, and the menu explains that "Nosh" is Yiddish for "to eat." Its menu offers a whole array of "Thick" French toast, Grandma's Griddle Cakes, corned beef, bagels, eggs, omelets, bakery and deli offerings of pastries, and all sorts of lox, sliced nova, whitefish and pickled herring. I ordered, of course, three eggs over-medium, bacon and hash browns — and a cinnamon roll for "my table for two for one." They offered only toast or bagels to go with breakfast. I suppose I will have to let them get away with this oversight since perhaps the best breakfast place in town doesn't offer biscuits either. The constant line at the Pancake Pantry is the reason such biscuit oversights are accepted and validated in the minds of many Nashvillians.

Noshville had both male and female waiters. Was this a sign that I was eating in something other than a true blue-road restaurant? Could be. But I was there and quickly declared it a blue-road restaurant for one day. I was lucky and got an attractive, friendly, but no-nonsense waitress. She soon had my order and coffee on my table. I had to "doctor" up the coffee with three little creamers and two sweeteners to make it palatable. If that was New York coffee, then I have another explanation as to why I now consider myself a southerner. It was strong — very strong. But it became better than acceptable at the hands of Chef Grant.

As I waited for my breakfast, I noticed that the gathered crowd kept the place comfortably full of sophisticated-looking, inner-city dwellers. Fully a third of the breakfasters were reading a Sunday paper from somewhere. There were two bars, one for single customers and one for partiers. But the partiers were not yet present at the partying bar where alcoholic beverages are sold. Tennessee's "blue laws" prohibited the sale of alcoholic beverages before noon on Sundays in deference to those of the Christian persuasion. Will blue laws be considered unconstitutional if ever challenged legally? Probably so, unless new laws make it illegal to serve alcohol before noon on all seven days of the week.

I'm just glad the Jews and the Muslims have not lobbied for laws to prohibit the sale of pork before noon. At any rate, they could not stop me this day because bacon was already sitting sinfully on my plate before me. And it was *good*. It was all good except the toast, a compromise to begin with; it was wilted and limp. They evidently have not learned that making toast is simple, as my dad always said. My dad said that he learned how to make toast from my mother. You just put a couple of pieces of bread in the oven, burn them and then scrape them. I would have happily scraped the toast today if they had "burned" it a little and made it crispy.

The eggs were cooked just as I had ordered them, and I thoroughly enjoyed silver dollar-sized, hash-brown potatoes — golden brown and crunchy. And although the cinnamon roll was tasty, the Nazi Nukers had invaded Noshville and had brainwashed the kitchen staff. The roll had lost its original consistency and wilted under the nuclear attack. Still, I ate part of it and left part of it — and not just because it was ordered "for the table." Maybe they would send the rest of it to the poor people in China. In its staleness it might recover some of its original substance.

After breakfast I drove back by the Pancake Pantry. A loyal, if less sophisticated, crowd was still standing in an even-longer line, all bundled up against the 37-degree weather. Those in line were even greater fans of the Pancake Pantry than Betty and Billie were of women's basketball. Case in point: Betty and Billie were on their way home; the Pancake Pantry crowd was still in line, and would be again next Sunday.

I got to Belmont Church at 10:45 a.m. and had time to scout out an ideal seat in the far left side of the balcony. I had a view of almost the entire congregation, which was still visiting in a loud, lively and friendly way all over the sanctuary as I took my seat. The sanctuary appeared able to seat about 1,500 people. The blue seats on the soft green carpet were nearly full, while the band/orchestra gradually, one by one, took their place on the platform to "tune up" for the service which was held under a large, 10 x 12 foot projection screen. To the left of the pulpit area stood a large wooden cross flanked by two smaller ones. On the platform stood a simple plexiglass pulpit.

At 11:00 a.m. sharp, the band/orchestra began to play. It consisted of a percussion section (in a glassed off booth), a bongo drummer, three guitars, a violin, a xylophone, a keyboard and a clarinet. One of the guitarists and two vocalists led the congregation in singing. The first song was *Trading My Sorrows*, and the congregation, standing, began singing:

I'm trading in my sorrow; I'm trading in my shame, I'm laying this down for the joy of the Lord. Yes, Lord. Yes, Lord. Yes, Lord. I'm trading in my sickness; I'm trading in my pain for the joy of the Lord. Yes, Lord. Yes, Lord. Yes, Lord.

Most of the congregation clapped and waved. Some actually danced — not just moving rhythmically in place but actually dancing in the aisles and in the front of the pulpit. At least one couple performed disco steps, twirling around and around.

One mother had dressed her three young daughters, aged about three to six, all alike in lavender velvet dresses. The girls were learning early to praise the Lord in an exuberant fashion. Each of the "triplets" had a lavender flag. And the mother was unsuccessfully attempting to choreograph their flag movements as they had apparently practiced at home. The girls, to the chagrin of the mother, were content to run around waving the flags as they might fly a kite in the park.The mother wanted them to "grow up" and worship as she had instructed them. She persisted. But despite her best efforts, these little adults behaved like kids.

Another mother was apparently teaching her daughter to pray in a Muslim fashion. They sat on the first row and, periodically, mother and daughter would get on their knees and bend forward prostrate on the carpet, heads on the floor and hands stretched out in front of them. The rest of the congregation swayed and clapped in rhythm with the lively, gospel music uninterrupted (except for a few announcements) for about 45 minutes.

We were welcomed to the service by a man whom I assume was one of the assistant pastors. He was dressed in black pants with a long black Nehru shaped shirt — un-tucked. He announced that several young people would be baptized that morning, including an eight-year-old who had "been with the Lord" for three years. A female minister conducted this part of the service and asked the young people as a group, "Do you believe that Jesus Christ is God's own special Son? And will you be His special followers?" They answered "yes" and she then prayed a prayer. I was confused somewhat because the children were not actually baptized at this point but her prayer ended, "In Jesus name, in whose name we baptize them."

Several other lively gospel songs were then sung, including: "Lord, we've come here for You. Can we stay here forever, for You are awesome. Holy spirit, You are awesome." All the while, the "triplets"were still being trained to dance and wave by their diligent and devout mother. But it was easy to see that the triplets were winning on this day.

Next the congregation sang,"Our God is an awesome God. He reigns from heaven above, with wisdom and power and love" while the words to the song were presented on the large screen at the front. Then, "Lord, you are the only reason for the song of praise I bring to you..." and a large cheer mysteriously and spontaneously went up, over and over again, as the song continued. Finally, I saw that the young people were being baptized in a pool to the far right side of the pulpit. As each one was raised from the water an exuberant cheer would arise amid the words of the song.

As the congregation sang, "Here we are to worship. Here we are to bow down. Here I am to say, You are my God; You are altogether lovely, altogether lovely," a minister announced that the communion elements would be served. The senior pastor, Steve Fry, a tall, thin man dressed in suit and tie and with light hair and a graying goatee, read from the *Bible* to initiate the Lord's Supper portion of the service and said, "Let us eat and drink together." Without saying "This is my body and my blood" (which is usually said at this point in most Christian communion services), he began to sing over and over again, "Here we are to worship; here we are to bow down." And he continued to sing this refrain while the communion service progressed until finally all who wished to do so had participated.

Pastor Fry then called on a young minister named Rob (the black shirt) to pray with and over a young man by the name of Chris who was going into military service. After a prayer by the pastor, Chris' father also prayed:"Lord, I give you my son...We release him yet again, Lord, to the military and, more importantly, to the high commission of our Lord."

After the offering was taken and I gave my $5.00, a prayer was offered for all our servicemen and women and was followed by a song, "Thank you for blessing me. Thank you for loving me. Thank you for saving me." The song was repeated again, over and over, while the young children went to their classes. The departure of the children is usually a sign that the sermon is about to begin, and so it was. Pastor Fry read from *Philippians 3: 7* and he underscored the words, "That I may know Christ." He started the sermon by telling about when he turned 30. He had felt that the age of 30 would be the time when his ministry would be full. Jesus, John the Baptist and several other Biblical personages were 30 when the fullness of their time arrived. He and his wife had been taking a beautiful, seven hour drive up the California coast.And he felt as if all things were now just perfect. Out of the blue, his wife said, "I don't think you love me." He didn't understand why she would say such a thing. He asked:

(1.) *"Is it that we are not spending enough time together?"*
"No," she answered.
(2.) *"Am I romantic enough for you?"*
"Yes" she answered.
(3.) *"Then what's the problem?"*
"I don't know," she confessed.
(4.) *"If I don't know, how can I fix it?"*
"I don't know, I just don't feel it," she answered.

He said that he felt like a jerk of a husband. She was saying that "even though I have you, I really don't have you. Your attention is divided between me and your work." The pastor then said that Jesus has the same questions about us. He said some preachers want to bring more of the spirit of God to their congregations in order to be "successful."

The pastor then stated that he now enjoyed his wife Nancy just as she was — for who she was, and as she was, and not just because she was a good wife to him. He said it was appropriate to know God so that He could meet our needs, but we should want to know God as He is and to know who He is. He said, "I wanted to write a book about this — the character, and nature of God." But an editor had told him that such a book would not sell. People wanted to read about what God could do for them. He noted that when Jesus was tempted by the devil to "turn those stones to loaves of bread" Jesus said, "Man shall not live by bread alone but by every word that proceeds out of the mouth of God." Pastor Fry told us that while Jesus recognized our physical needs "We do not live by 'bread alone,' " but by the word of God as well.

He said that God helps us, but still there will be times of doubt. "It is then," the Pastor said, "that we need to know the character of God. If we know who He really is, and not just that He is a God who helps us, we will be sure that the land that is filled with giants will be of no real concern to us." He said God had helped us but that we tended to say, "But, God, I haven't done giants." His point was that if we know who God is, we are ready for all specifics, even giants.

The pastor effectively delivered his meaningful message with little or no reference to notes. And during his sermon a lone, devout female voice would intersperse his exhortations with, "Yes, yes, Amen."

At 12:30 Pastor Fry said, "I want to know Jesus for Jesus." And I said to myself, "I want to know if he sees the large clock just in front of him and if he knows that I have a tee-time at 12:50 p.m.?" The pastor apparently did see the clock, but felt some things were more important than tee-times. He pressed on and asked, "While all eyes are closed," for us to sing softly, "Jesus, I love You. Jesus I love You," over and over. Then he asked, while heads were bowed, "If any of you might have an issue with God?" He said, "Can you say, Lord, I don't understand, but I love You?" He led us in singing, "Oh, Lord, I trust in You. Oh, Lord, I trust in You," over and over. He said some may be in need of a rekindling and might say, "I have lost that fire." He said, "If you need a fresh fire sing: 'Thank you for saving me. Thank you for saving me. Thank you for saving me.'"

Again, Pastor Fry asked us to continue in singing these words over and over. He said, "Those of you who are stressed in your job, who have a financial crisis, or who have other issues and need some help, raise your hands." He asked the elders of the church and other ministers to go to those with raised hands to pray for them and with them. The congregation continued singing, "Thank you for loving me, thank you for loving me."

Then, the pastor invited all those who wanted to pray to stay and pray. He made a couple of announcements and, at 12:48 p.m., casually said, "See you next time."

I had two minutes to make tee-time. I worried that Frank might think I had taken my winnings and left the game since I already had $10 of Frank's money in my pocket from the game the day before. A miracle then happened. When I checked my phone messages after getting into my car, I found one from Frank. When Frank says, "It's too cold to play," it truly is too cold to play. One can believe that an "It's too cold to play" from Frank is not just a disguised preference to sleep in. And it was now very cold and raining. All I had to do was go home, build a fire and get ready to watch the wedding of Prince Charles and Diana again when my cheerleader comes back this afternoon.

I was soooo glad that Frank had called to cancel.

Chapter 27

First Christian Church (Disciples of Christ)
Sparta, Tennessee
March 16, 2003

*F*riday afternoon I played golf (rather poorly) with my friend Frank Sutherland at Richland Country Club. I played badly enough to lose $4.00 to Frank who loves to play whether he wins or loses. He reminded me that he was still $6.00 down to me for our golf this year. We play for $10,000 per hole because we like to act and talk big, but we discount that amount to $1.00 cash. We are not as big as we talk and act.

As soon as we finished, I rushed home to pack a couple of coolers with food for a visit with some members of my family who were meeting Betty and me at our cottage near Center Hill Lake. We were to meet my brother Joe and his wife Jetta, and my sister Margaret Jane ("Pixie" to the Browning family and "Mag" to her husband) and her husband Boyd Trump ("Pig" to the Brownings and "Sam" to Pixie). These two members of our family are big on nicknames. I don't know what my nickname is to them, and I don't want to know it because if it were complimentary they would have already told me.

I hurried after golf and met the four of them just as they arrived at Center Hill after a long drive from North Carolina and Bristol, Tennessee. Both Joe and Pixie have become real surprises as they have matured. My other siblings and I had always been in accord that Joe probably would not make it to adulthood, and that if he did he probably would be sitting in a prison cell. The reason we thought this was because of his fiery temper as a child. I never fought with another of my six other brothers or sisters, but I fought with Joe. We *all* fought with Joe, primarily defending ourselves from or retaliating against some devilment he had perpetrated which had sprung forth from his overactive mind. His wife Jetta said to me during this visit that it was a true wonder that Joe turned out well or even alive at all, given how all seven of us were "against him." I responded that children do not think of the big picture, rather they just react to the situation at hand. And with Joe we always had a situation on our hands — probably because of a vase which fell off a mantle and hit him on the head when he was very young. Our grandmother used this explanation to defend his early mischievous ways. Even in her defense of Joe, she tacitly agreed with the rest of us that we had a problem on our hands. How Joe has turned out to be the sweetest, most considerate and most generous of the children is a complete mystery to the whole family.

Pixie is almost as much a mystery as Joe, at least to me. She was the last of eight children and was spoiled rotten by our mother and daddy and our grandmother (who lived with our family from before I was born until she died). Pixie was the "runt" of the litter, barely topping five feet and thus was always overly protected by the rest of the family "because she is such a little thing." "Be sure and save the milk for Pixie," we were told so many times. I still do not know what milk tastes like because, out of guilt, I still always feel I should save it for little Pixie.

Trying to explain why she was being spoiled, the rest of us children would say that by the time Pixie came along Mother, Daddy and Grandma were simply worn out. Probably so, but we all just knew that she was going to turn out to be a worthless "little twit" (as I told her this weekend) — another misprognostication. How the little spoiled brat turned out to be a model wife, a model mother and a perfectly proud giant of a person, in the estimation of our entire family, and I am sure of all who know her, is a continuing question of all of us.

So we made predictions for both Joe and Pixie and were almost 100 percent wrong on both accounts. As for the other six siblings, we all turned out okay which was no surprise to anyone, because no one expected anything either good or bad from the rest of us. We were neither a surprise nor much of a disappointment because no one gave much thought to how we would turn out. All our future-gazing was spent straining and squinting into the futures of Joe and Pixie. The rest of us were just there. Since we worried so much about Joe and Pixie, we were all probably sort of worn out too and had no more energy or time to consider the future for the rest of us.

But here we were, the "menace" and the "spoiled brat" and their spouses, and Betty and I, at Center Hill for another all-too-short mini-reunion. We snacked, watched TV and talked about the miracles of Joe and Pixie until late. And then we retired only to wake up Saturday for more of the same. At breakfast I told them that the two of them almost ruined my life. I told Joe I didn't think I would ever forgive him for sneaking a feel of the breasts of my 14-year-old girlfriend one summer night while I drove all of us home from church camp. And Pixie gave me osteoporosis and denied me the pleasure of milk products for most of my life. Now I'm still trying to think of how I can get back at both of them. See what I mean? They still are probably the cause of most of my guilt feelings. They may even be the reason I left the ministry 40 years ago. After all, a minister should not harbor all these grudges. I just know it.

In spite of the fact that I was no longer a minister, I told them all that I was going to church Sunday morning and that I wanted them to follow me to Sparta, Tennessee on the blue roads. We would eat breakfast together and they would be well on their way back to East Tennessee and North Carolina. So, Sunday at 8:30 a.m. we left Center Hill and headed east on Highway 56 toward Smithville. As we crossed the bridge over Center Hill Lake, the fog lifted to where we could see the water below the fog and the trees above the fog. It seemed as if the mist were a large hula-hoop around the girth of the whole lake area. Though overcast, we could sense that a beautiful day was in the making. At Smithville we turned toward Sparta on Highway 70 S and arrived in the City of Sparta at 9:30 a.m. We only saw one restaurant that was serving breakfast. It was just off the square and was called the Sparta Grill. It was a "hole-in-the-wall" spot that doubled as a cab stand and restaurant. We were about as nervous about this combination as Bob Newhart had been while white-knuckle flying to Hawaii when the pilot announced over the PA system, "Welcome to Transcontinental Airline and Storm Door Company's flight to Hawaii."

The Sparta Grill seemed to be more of a cabstand than it did a restaurant. It was about 12' x 20' with a small kitchen behind a curtain which was no larger than most bathrooms. There were six stools whose "genuine naugahide" tops were now more covered with genuine duct tape than the other "genuine" material. Surely

Tom Ridge, the new homeland security czar, will investigate this establishment for reckless use of duct tape, a material declared critical in any national defense code-red alert. There were also three booths which could seat four small people the size of Pixie, but only in a real true hunger emergency.

This "restaurant" was dimly lighted by two single tube yellowing fluorescent lights hanging from the wooden-paneled ceiling. It was dingy and almost purposefully unkempt, looking as much like a garage as a restaurant. There were old coke bottles and liquor bottles arranged on a rack over the register, and just under the bottles was an assortment of pocketknives displayed on a cardboard in a mumblety-peg style. There was a red gas can peering out from under the front booth near an old kerosene heater, and two antique glass oil lamps on a dingy shelf over the heater. Also near the heater was a 17-inch color TV whose sound was competing for attention with the police scanner barking, "Was that an 81 on the last call?" "That's 10 – 4." I barely heard the scanner over the cartoons playing on the TV.

The floor was worn out and made no pretense of being clean. It was just there to give substance to footsteps. The lone cook-waitress said the place had doubled as a cabstand for more than 50 years. She verbally told us what she could cook for us for breakfast. She was the menu. Joe, Pig and I ordered three eggs each over-medium and hash browns, a side of bacon for Joe and me and a side of sausage for Pig. They did not offer biscuits so we agreed to have toast. It was either toast or pancakes.

While we waited for our food, our wives waited in a separate booth involved in their last few minutes of gossiping before we finished breakfast and our visitors would be headed back home. It was then that I saw a poster showing John Dillinger as Public Enemy No. 1 and offering a $20,000 reward for his capture. There was an old yellowing sign advertising "Brownfield's Little Liver Pills" and several pictures of movie cowboys of the past including Hopalong Cassidy, Roy Rogers and Gene Autrey. There were several calendars and baby pictures on one wall and a Sealtest milk clock on another.

Another area had a wrench set, a gumball machine, cigarette machine, two old hand saws and one fan belt just waiting for the unlucky motorist whose car needed to use this last and only one available. There were also two practically new dust busters. They must be practically new because they certainly had never been used in this place.

Joe, Pig and I agreed that this stand/restaurant reminded us of Silverstrushi's in Logan, West Virginia, our birthplace. Silverstrushi's served only hot dogs and hamburgers, but had the best hot dogs we had ever eaten — probably because of the "secret" meat sauce served on them and the perfectly steamed buns (a light towel filtered out just the right amount of steam). Only four or five people could get into this West Virginia "whole-in-the-wall" at one time and only by standing — no seats. It was always busy! Next door was Maw Murphy's Pool Room from where our mother had to go several times to pull Joe by ear out the backdoor. Didn't I tell you he was a rounder? Not one of the other three of the Browning boys would ever think of going into a den of iniquity like Murphy's. But Joe did. And he became a competitive pool player often going in there to win pocket and movie money.

After about twenty minutes our waitress/cook/cab dispatcher brought our breakfasts, and all at once. They all were good — very good. The over-medium eggs were beautifully done with the yellows left uncooked allowing Joe to mix his with the grated hash browns into sort of a breakfast casserole, West Virginia style. The potatoes were very tasty with the right amount of crispiness and yet soggy enough with grease to be tasty. The bacon was thick and especially crispy. Only the toast was below par. It was soggy. I guess it had lost its toastiness in the wait for all our breakfasts to be served simultaneously.

The check was $24.17. I gave the all-in-one attendant $30.00 and told her to keep the change as a tip. I felt like a big spender from the big city. As we left, we saw a poolroom right next to the Sparta Grill. I thought Joe was going to go in, rack-em up and challenge Pig and me to play for movie money again. Lucky for Pig and me the blue laws had kept this "Recreation Room" closed for Sunday.

After taking several pictures of each other we parted, four pilgrims heading back East and two sad pilgrims beginning to look for a blue-road church. I needed to pray for Joe — that he not fall back into his old ways. Remember the vase that fell and hit him on the head? It hit really hard. He may have a relapse at any time. Jetta was going to take him back to their mountaintop retreat in North Carolina and keep him out of trouble.

It was about 10:05 a.m. Just before going to breakfast we had seen a beautiful old Christian Church near the square which announced services at 10:45 a.m. We thought that this was a real possibility since we had not been to a Christian Church during the past 26 weeks of my "52 Sundays" project. Last week had been number 26, the halfway point. This week would put me on my homeward journey. But before finally deciding we thought we would drive around the area for twenty minutes of further searching. We saw the Sparta Church of God which announced a "Jews for Jesus" program on Sunday which would be forthcoming. Then we saw a Jehovah's Witness Church and drove in with the thought that this might be a good prospect but we found that the "Public Talk," which all Jehovah's Witness Churches call their Sunday worship services, had started at 10:00 a.m. It was now 10:23 a.m.

After a few more minutes of driving around, we decided to go back to the Christian Church near the square. We drove into its parking lot at 10:35 a.m., and we walked into the church while being warmly greeted and welcomed by several of the members. We sat on the back pew in the right-hand section of the church while wave after wave of members and ministers came to welcome us to the service. The first to greet us was a distinguished looking gray-haired man wearing glasses that I immediately identified in my mind as a successful lawyer or doctor who was surely an elder in this congregation. It turned out that my assumption about his position in the church was correct. He gave one of the prayers by a layman during the service. One minister, Bob Winger, introduced himself as a former pastor of 17 years. He was now listed as the "Pastor of Prayers." Russ Ragovin was listed as pastor. We assumed that his wife was the "third pastor" since we were told by one of the elders that they had three pastors here.

The church literature we received as we entered called this church, "The First Christian Church (Disciple of Christ)." It was in a handsome old historic building which had a simple, warm feeling of a rich heritage. There were two rows of wood pews in the rectangular sanctuary with white-coffered ceilings accented by dark rich wood beams and six Gothic hexagon shaped chandeliers. The pulpit area was set back into a stage-like setting with a lower ceiling, accented by word carvings above the inset area. There were handsome burgundy draperies concealing what appeared to be a baptistery in front of which was a wooden cross with golden-gilded accents. The pulpit was to the right of the congregation.

This congregation was mixed with young, middle-aged and senior citizens with the dress code as varied as the communicants, though the majority seemed to be dressed in their Sunday best. As the service began, the pianist (Lynda McCoy) began softly playing *Gathering Music*, after which the wife (assistant minister) of Pastor Russ gave words of welcome to all and especially to "the Brownings who are visiting from Nashville." She made several church announcements which were printed on a flyer which had been distributed to all upon entering the sanctuary. With three pastors, this church has enough firepower to get many things going as was indicated by the many listed activities such as board meetings, new membership class meetings, community-wide services and prayers, continental breakfasts, a candlelight dinner, an Easter egg hunt, a fashion show and several other activities.

Immediately after the announcements the congregation was invited to sing *No. 71, Victory in Jesus.* The words of the chorus were: "O' victory in Jesus, my Savior forever. He sought me and bought me with His redeeming blood. He loved me ere I knew Him and all my love is due Him. He plunged me to victory beneath His cleansing blood." Then we sang:"His name is wonderful... Jesus my Lord." These songs were followed by prayer by retired Pastor Bob Winger. He asked us to pray for our men and women in uniform, for our president and especially for those who will become martyrs, perhaps plagiarizing the Muslim terrorist concept. He also asked for other prayer requests and welcomed back Mrs. Miller, who had been very sick (followed by a warm applause by the congregation). We were asked to pray silently for our own special needs before the retired pastor prayed:"We lift these requests up to heaven where our Father sits in power and in glory." He continued, "Thank you that we have the power to be the greatest power on Earth, but we must be humbled, and our president must be humbled and the leader of the British Empire must be humbled...Bless our minister as he brings us Your message for today." Then he led us in the *Lord's Prayer* and used "debts" instead of "trespasses" as Presbyterians do.

Next the pastor's wife gave a sermonette to the children about the contents of her wallet which included pictures of loved ones and notes and thoughts from others. She concluded by asking, "What do you think God has in His wallet?" She said, "God's wallet would have pictures of all of you and lots of little notes of love because God has a really big wallet." Then she prayed a simple prayer, "Thank you God for all my friends in this congregation. Amen." Then she said, "Okay, off now to junior church."

Following the children's sermon a young attractive blonde teen-ager read the scripture for the day from *Romans 8: 28 – 34* which emphasized "If God is for us who can be against us?" after which Pastor Russ Ragovin, dressed in a business suit and wearing a mustache, gave the sermon of the morning entitled, *The Good News*. After a couple of introductory stories the pastor began delivering his sermon without extensive notes. He began by saying, "Nations by definition are selfish." He said they must seek first their own self-interests. Then he told of the many wars fought over religion and concluded that both Bin Lauden and Hitler's wars were about religion. He stated that Hitler blamed many of Germany's problems on the Jews and believed that it was God's will that Germany become a strong nation.

The pastor proclaimed that instead of God taking sides, we must take God's side. He indicated that in the *Bible* the Jews' problems came because they took on other gods. He then noted that Lincoln did not say that God was on our side but he quoted Lincoln as saying "If God is on our side, who can be against us?"

The pastor assured us that God sticks to His promises even though it seems sometimes that the answer is a long time coming. He then told of two neighbors in San Francisco during the Second World War. Both were Christians, but one was Japanese and one was Swedish. Both loved roses and had friendly competitions about who grew the best. When the war came, the Japanese family was sent to a concentration camp and the Swedish neighbor promised to take care of his neighbor's roses and business. When the war was over, the Swedish friend proved himself a man of his word — fresh roses from the Japanese family's garden welcomed them home to their perfectly kept house and also showed them that their business had been ably cared for during their absence.

The pastor said that God keeps His promises just as he did for Abraham and for Moses. He said there are no accidental children in God's world, only accidental parents. He declared that God has had a plan for all of us "even before the foundations of the world." "What is God's purpose for us?" he asked. "It is to prepare us for eternity," answered the pastor. Here the pastor faced the problems of predestination. He said that while God chooses us it does not mean that He does not choose others. This pastor, like all others, found it difficult, when explaining that God has known and chosen who will be saved, "from the foundations of the world," to also explain how the sovereignty and the love of God co-exists with the fact that some would be lost. The minister moved on rather quickly here. I always did, too. I understand completely about the dilemma here, Brother Ragovin. Let's hope that the parishioners don't push the questions any further on this point.

The pastor told a story about how a minister crossed the powerful King Henry VIII during a sermon and then rebuffed the king's instructions that he correct the matter in his next sermon. The minister refused in the face of the might of the king saying, "It is my purpose to do God's will," and he preached the same sermon, refusing to buckle under the king's ominous threat. Pastor Ragovin said that God wants us all to find His purpose in our lives and gave a general invitation for someone here today who was about to make the first step in finding Christ's will and purpose for his life. He asked us to stand and sing an invitational hymn. He came down from the pulpit and stood at the front while entreating any who would make the first step for Christ to come forward to pray. The Pastor's demeanor was plaintive as if he were pleading earnestly for someone, anyone, to come to allow him to pray with them. I always feel sorry for a minister who makes such an invitation and yet no one comes. It seems that they feel sort of like having failed to properly or effectively deliver God's message. No one came. The preacher accepted his failure to convince sinners to repent and change, and he seemed dejected.

The pastor then segued into a sure winner — Holy Communion. He invited all Christians to partake in this part of the service. He said: "We don't have rules about your theology for partaking in the Lord's Supper. If you believe in Jesus Christ we invite you to partake." One of the elders prayed a prayer over the Communion elements. The pastor then read the Communion Scriptures and had the bread and wine passed to the congregation. Most of the congregation responded to this invitation and so the pastor soon moved past the failure of the first invitation.

A woman elder in the church prayed a prayer for the offering which was next taken and Betty responded here with our usual $5.00 so that the pastor would feel he had successfully reached some of us about the need to give of ourselves to God. This was followed by the singing of the *Doxology*: "Praise God from whom all blessings flow." Following this the pastor prayed a standard Biblical benediction and the congregation responded by singing the *Congregational Benediction*. Amen. Amen. The service was concluded at about 12:00 p.m. Betty and I left with the good wishes of many for a beautiful remainder of the day and several warm invitations to return.

As we left I began remembering the 300 to 500 who had come forward to prayer at the Mt. Paran Church of God in Atlanta few weeks ago and felt it just wasn't fair. This minister deserved one or two to come forward today. From before the foundations of the world I wished God had ordained that at least one or two had been chosen to come into the fold as a result of this pastors' invitation this morning. It wouldn't hurt them any. Would it have spoiled some great eternal plan by allowing Pastor Ragovin to have been a happier man as a result of one or two sinners responding to his sermon and plea today? I don't think so. But who am I to question God's plan? But still I think out of respect for Pastor Ragovin's righteous efforts that he should have been rewarded with one measly little sinner.

I thought I heard an "Amen" from the area of the pulpit where the pastor was standing.

Chapter 28

First Presbyterian Church
Clifton, Tennessee
March 23, 2003

Saturday afternoon my golfing buddies John Seigenthaler, Frank Sutherland and I played golf. Phillip Margolin, the best-selling novelist and John's guest, completed our foursome. Frank and I were partners and played against John and Phillip. I told Phillip that we played for $10,000 per point, but that we discounted the losses to $1.00 per point if the losers paid up in cash. Frank and I won the match by seven points. On a non-cash basis, we won $70,000 each from John and Phillip. Since Phillip did not come across with the $7 cash, I can only assume that he still owes me $70,000. Be sure and tell him if you see him.

Phillip was in town on a promotional tour for his new novel, *Ties That Bind*, and Betty and I had gone to his book signing at the Davis-Kidd Book Store on the night before our Saturday golf match. Phillip graciously signed a copy of his new book and joked that while he normally charged $1.50 for autographs he would discount this normal charge for us down to $ .75 "this one time only." I realized afterward that I did not pay him for his autograph and therefore face a dilemma. I felt strongly that I should deduct the $ .75 I owe him for his signature from the $70,000 he now owes me for golf. But since I did not pay him cash for his autograph as he did not pay me cash for the golf bet, what formula determines the proper deduction? Should I deduct $ .75 and leave the balance he owes me at $69,999.25? Or should I use the non-cash golf formula and deduct $7,500 from the $70,000 and leave him a balance owing me of $62,500?

After sleeping on the matter and attending church I decided to use the more righteous formula in order to give Phillip the $7,500 offset from his golfing debt instead of the lesser offset of $ .75. My decision was greatly due to the pastor's sermon which was entitled *Grace or Grab?* I wanted to try to be gracious and not grab for the larger amount I am by all rights probably entitled. I know that Saint Peter will take note of my act of generosity and duly credit me with this unselfish act.

I purchased Phillip's new book and have read only the first few chapters and do not know what the title particularly refers to, but it may have had some influence on my choice of churches to attend. While considering which direction to take out of Nashville, I was drawn to the idea of driving down toward Clifton, Tennessee which is located about halfway between Nashville and Memphis. I have long historic ties to Clifton. It was in Clifton that I became pastor of the First Presbyterian Church while attending the Divinity School at Vanderbilt. In the fall of 1957, James Glass, the professor of pastoral subjects and fellow in charge of arranging temporary pastoral appointments, sent me to Clifton to fill a temporary vacancy at this Church. I continued going to this church every weekend for about two years until I became the "permanent supply" pastor at the Union Presbyterian Church in Belfast, Tennessee in 1959.

Betty and I traveled the 100 miles each Sunday morning during this two year period and formed some ties that, while still binding, had sadly loosened over the 44 years since we had last been there. Today the ties were binding enough to encourage us to once again make this 100-mile drive. So we left Nashville at 6:33 a.m. in order to have enough time to take the same route which we had driven over a 100 times while I was a student minister there. We took Highway 100 West. Six-thirty a.m. was our scheduled time of departure. Betty proudly informed me as we left that we had only missed it by three minutes.

It was a chilly 43° when we got in our car, and we hurriedly turned the heat up as we drove out of our driveway. The daffodils and the Bradford pear trees were all blooming cheerfully on this beautiful clear, crisp pre-spring day. The remainder of the trees were still bare of leaves which left us casually wondering how and why the different flowers and plants choose their own times to emerge from their winter's rest.

We listened to the news of the war with Iraq which was the only facet of this day casting a shadow on our spirits. Actually our spirits were uplifted by this truly perfect day to be traveling on the blue roads. But we feared that this war was going to cast dark and long shadows on national and international landscapes for a long time to come. Our leaders were beginning to warn us that this war would be much more difficult and costly in lives on the part of both the Iraqis and the coalition forces. The coalition forces came from the only countries to volunteer for active duty in this fight to oust Sadam Hussein from power: England, Australia and the U.S.

As we traveled west on Highway 100, we passed the Loveless restaurant which we had happily visited a few weeks ago and drove under the Nashville terminus of the beautiful Natchez Trace Parkway. We considered taking this Parkway route today toward Clifton but decided to follow the original path of our 100-or-so journeys on this pilgrimage of many years ago. Thus this beautiful day was filled with nostalgia as Betty and I tried to recall events and people from our past visits to Clifton, as we drove toward this town which rests on the extreme westerly edge of Middle Tennessee.

I particularly remembered the Hughes, the Hassells, the Lays, the Beckhams and the Fowlers. But I remembered that I had been most impressed when, at the age of 26, I first met Tom Frank Hassell. Tom Frank was perceived, at least by me, as being the titular head of all that happened in Clifton. He was the owner of the hardware store in Clifton which was just the "front" for the large family logging business in this part of the state. I remember him as a "mover and a shaker" in the church and the community. He was sort of like "Teddy" Roosevelt in my mind — a short and stout "rough rider" without the abrasive side of the former president, just smoothly forceful.

While Tom Frank was the outspoken "leader" of the community, Frank Hughes was perceived as the godfather of Clifton, and was taller, softer spoken and probably more deeply and historically respected. This quiet and taller scion of this wealthy and powerful family seemed more laid back than the brusque Tom Frank, but (like E.F Hutton) when he spoke, people listened. In tandem, the Hughes families and the Hassell families were definitely the undisputed leaders of this part of Wayne County and probably among the most influential in the entirety of this part of the state. And they were somehow historically related by a marriage which had enabled these two power towers to be merged into a single forceful power, both economically and politically.

Betty and I realized that most of the church and community leaders, whom we had known when we were there, were already deceased because we had been in our mid-twenties then and these leaders had already been in their 50s and 60s. But we were eager to visit Clifton this day and to see if there were any members remaining who had been there during the late 1950s.

We drove through Centerville which is the location of the First Methodist Church, the first church we had attended on this pilgrimage of "52 Sundays." After driving a little over an hour we stopped at the first restaurant we had seen that was open since we had left Davidson County. We had driven through Williamson and Hickman counties and were in Perry County when we saw the Dinner Bell Restaurant in Linden, Tennessee. At about 9:00 a.m. the small parking area was full, and we had to park in the adjacent lot of a business which was not open on Sunday. We walked in and seated ourselves near the door which gave us a panoramic view of what was obviously the breakfast-feeding trough for this part of Linden. The gang was all here and, if noise and laughter is any indication, the whole gang was enjoying their breakfast and their Sunday morning together.

There was no doubt that this was a true blue road spot. The whole atmosphere said, "We're country and proud of it." There were antique farm tools and implements displayed on the walls along with newspaper clippings about the successes of the local basketball and football teams. There were two rooms — one for the smokers and one for non-smokers. There was only one customer in the non-smoking room. Practically everyone in the smoking room was smoking but the Brownings. We chose to sit in the smoking area because we did not want to miss out on any of the fun the gang in this room was obviously enjoying. In this room were mounted deer-head trophies on one wall near the entrance to the restrooms which were proudly named "outhouses."

The "mature" waitress who was serving most of our room was in total command and gave the impression she could have held her own in the toughest late-hour bar in the state. She was friendly, efficient and totally self-confident as she approached us to bring our coffee and to take our order. She had such a strong presence that I forgot to give her my specific instructions about how to fry my three eggs. I was intimidated enough just to order them "over-medium, please" with country ham, hash-browns and biscuits. Betty ordered two scrambled eggs, bacon and toast.I ordered French toast "for the table."

We had time for "working the room" visually as we waited for our breakfast. There were two different tables with five men each, and we soon saw that these two tables were the focus of all the Sunday morning merriment. Nine of the ten men at these two tables had on hunting-type caps except for a state trooper who had on his official hat.All of the men were smoking and enjoying every puff as if they were flaunting the warnings of the Surgeon General on each pack of their Marlboros. These men all had to be smoking this brand because each one looked and talked as if he thought himself the embodiment of the Marlboro man, transfixed from Montana to Middle Tennessee. All, that is, except for one little squirt of a man who had to know most assuredly that he had no chance of pulling off this macho image. But somehow he was hanging in there, giving no quarters to his much larger and more ruggedly handsome Sunday morning Ponderosa partners. He was the Barney Fife of this part of Mayberry. His insignificant size and posture, however, did not keep him from talking as big as the biggest of the bunch.

Several of the men at these tables were wearing heavy, Afghanistan-type full beards — making them appear even larger and more imposing. The owner of one of the big beards had a deep, loud baritone laugh which filled the whole room constantly. I just had to wonder when our inclination toward prejudice is going to turn on men who wear their beards Afghani style, as if they did not wear them this way before 9-11. I certainly hope this will not be the case, but I wouldn't be surprised, especially since Tom Daschle had recently been declared almost-a-traitor for pointing out the failure of President Bush's diplomatic efforts to find a peaceful solution to the situation in Iraq. All liberals were once labeled "pinko commies." Would beard wearers now be called "Muslim terrorist sympathizers?" Maybe not, but clean shavers will certainly feel more comfortable in many ultra conservative groups for the duration. But, then, they always did.

One woman diner wore a T-shirt with the American flag emblazoned all over it. Maybe all men sporting beards could help offset the Afghan-leaning beard syndrome by wearing a flag T-shirt. One of the big beards had a beard so long it would have hidden most of any flag on the front of his t-shirt. I wondered how he managed to eat his sawmill gravy.

Our breakfasts, sans gravy, were soon set before us and I wished immediately that I had not let the waitress intimidate me into not specifying how I wanted my eggs. They were good but slightly overcooked for my taste. Fortunately for me, I have never seen an egg I didn't like. The hash-browns were gunky but with that unmistakable great greasy-country taste. The country ham was also good and country. The biscuits were good, but must have been far better when the same batch supplied customers about two hours earlier.

Betty's scrambled eggs were not scrambled at all after they hit the frying pan. They were mixed together, fried into a monolithic slab and served in a solid unscrambled state. Her breakfast was beautifully salvaged, however, by the French toast which had been ordered "for the table" and, as it turned out, was mostly "for Betty." I grabbed enough of one piece to witness that these fried, thick slices of golden-egged bread were superb.

While we were finishing our breakfast, a clean-cut giant of a man who must have stood 6'10" and could have weighed 400 pounds came in for breakfast. He was neatly dressed in a black suit with a purple shirt and wore a large ring with a large showy stone. He ordered a huge breakfast, almost as large as mine. When his food was brought to him he bowed his head and prayed for a full minute or more while wording his prayer with his lips. He looked to be a devout man who I thought might be a local minister. This giant Samson did not have his Delilah with him, but she had seen to it that his hair and his beard were neatly trimmed. I hoped this large breakfast would enable him soon to regain his full strength. Betty remarked how peaceful and satisfied he looked. I might have looked as satisfied if I had been able to eat another piece of "French" (freedom?) toast.

We left the Dinner Bell Restaurant about 9:15 a.m. and took Highway 13 a few miles before turning off onto Route 128 toward Clifton. This was a double duty, winding blue road through the woodlands of this part of the country, which were already showing the effects of the lumbering ventures of Tom Frank Hassell and his successors. In a few minutes we were in Wayne County and very soon saw the sign informing us that we were at the city limits of Clifton. A warm feeling of expectation slowly moved over me, just as it had done at other times when I had been away from home for a few years and was driving excitedly to a reunion with family and friends.

As we drove into town, the Tennessee River was on our right. We turned left through the "main street" of town and passed the building where I had visited Tom Frank in his hardware store which really seemed to me his excuse to go into town and hold court with the locals who revered him so much. Then, in less than a block, we saw the First (and only, of course) Presbyterian Church of Clifton. It is a stately old red Buick edifice which was built in 1854 with a majestic white steeple. We learned later that it had been remodeled in 1998. It was now 10:00 a.m. and we drove by to see that the worship service was at 11:00 a.m. We drove around the town refreshing our faded memories and found the Riverside Restaurant (with a prominent sign indicating it was open for breakfast) located on the banks of the river.

Just perfect, I thought, time to read some of the paper and have more coffee while we waited for the eleven o'clock hour. Only one other table was occupied when we entered and its occupants soon left as the waitress excitedly brought us menus. She was ecstatic to have two more breakfasters. In order not to break her heart, I added to our coffee orders an order of French toast "for the table" again. We read *The Tennessean* from Nashville which was apparently still the dominant paper here. But probably a few miles further west *The Commercial Appeal* from Memphis would be the paper of choice. I dominated in the choice of portions of the paper I wanted to read and also ate the dominant share of French toast this time before Betty could lift a fork. It was almost as good as the same item at the Dinner Bell.

But now it was about time for the 11:00 a.m. church bell to ring and Betty and I made our way to the church parking lot. We sat there for a few minutes to time our entrance at just about five minutes before the service would begin. As soon as we entered, we were warmly welcomed by several members who knew we were visitors immediately. Soon the word was out that I had once been a student minister here and several more members came to welcome us. Then, just before the service began, Dr. Michael R. Bradley who had been the pastor here for more than 22 years came to welcome us. Dr. Bradley, a handsome man probably in his early 60s, reminded me immediately of a Burl Ives who has been on a six month semi-diet, not that he had over-done the diet. Still his ample proportions were not a challenge to the size of the great balladeer. He wore glasses and the Burl Ives gray goatee and beard which had been as much a trade mark of Ives as had been his rich baritone voice and his grandfatherly portliness.

The service began as informally as Dr. Bradley and all the members were dressed.They were all following an obviously established tradition of casually dressing for church which was indicated by the sign in front of the church which read, "Come As You Are. Worship with Us." Dr. Bradley himself wore an open necked blue shirt with a Mr. Peepers light colored cardigan sweater as he made several announcements while standing at the front at congregation level. He then proceeded to the pulpit and, in so doing, announced that the worship service was beginning.

Betty and I were truly pleased to be back in this beautiful old church after 44 years of absence. It was obvious that this great old church had been remodeled but all the old had either been preserved or reconstructed as the original. There were two sections of original handsome oak pews seated on rich red carpet.The old dark oak wainscoting was kept and beautifully refinished. There were two ornate old oak pulpit chairs with green upholstering and an unoccupied choir loft separated from the other chancel areas by oak railing and green curtains.

To the left of the chancel there was the Sunday school register which said there had been 19 in attendance last Sunday and 24 today. There was a large cross at the center, and to the far right of the chancel was an old Sunday school type picture of a tranquil Jesus. There were two stained glass windows to the right and left of the pulpit area and three on each side of the sanctuary. The ceiling was the old pressed metal ceiling which had been duplicated in St. Louis from the original pattern of the 1854 ceiling.

There were about 35 people in church today including the organist and the pianist who played and sang the worshipful prelude to the service. Dr. Bradley read the call to worship from

Psalms 19: 1 -- 14 and then led us in singing *For the Beauty of the Earth*. "For the beauty of the Earth, for the glory of the skies, Lord of all to Thee we raise this our hymn of grateful praise." The pastor then prayed the "Pastoral Prayer" during which he especially prayed for our national leaders during this difficult time in our history. He then led the congregation to pray in unison the printed prayer of confession, after which he gave his assurance that God forgives those who truly confess their sins.

The pastor next read the scripture lessons for today from *Exodus 20: 1 -- 17, I Corinthians 1: 18 -- 25* and *John 2: 13 -- 22*. These lessons were followed by the Apostles Creed which was said in unison by the congregation followed by the hymn, *How Great Thou Art*: "Then sings my soul, my Savior God to thee, how great Thou art, how great Thou art."

The sermon for today by the pastor was centered on the scripture lesson from *John 2: 13 -- 22* where Jesus chased the moneychangers out of the temple. Dr. Bradley effectively and dramatically said, you could almost hear the "crack, crack" of the whip as Jesus was clearing the temple. He said that Jesus poured out the coins of the moneychangers and demanded that they cease making His Father's house into a market place. He noted that even today Jesus challenges us to do the difficult things. He said that Jesus then and now was and is "getting up in the faces of men" and telling them point blank to cease and desist doing certain things.

Dr. Bradley, whose day job is a professor of history at Motlow State College in the Manchester-Tullahoma area of Tennessee, gave us an interesting lesson in Biblical history during this sermon. Dr. Bradley lives in Manchester and commutes to this church on Sundays just as I did 44 years ago. On our commute here today, he told us, the money-changers probably thought they were doing the traveling pilgrims a favor by providing the "proper" currency, and selling their sacrificial animals for those who could not always easily bring their animals with them on their journeys. Of course they made a nice profit and thought they were entitled to do so because these were "convenience-store" prices, which we all expect to be higher. They were just like scalpers at a ball game. The price is always higher on game day.

From this lesson in history Dr. Bradley told the congregation that God leaves no part of our lives untouched whether it is social, personal or business — even our money. He said that the money-changers were there to exchange "pure Jewish money" for the travelers' unclean foreign money so that their temple offerings would be worthy. In overthrowing the tables and the money, Jesus was overthrowing the idea that some money and some people are better than others. This historian-pastor said that Jesus told us that money is neither good nor bad. It is what we do with it that categorizes it as good or evil. He said that money can be a *Grace or Grab* which was his sermon title.

Dr. Bradley noted that if we really put our minds to it, we can generally have everything we want. He quoted the scripture which says, "Ask and you shall receive." If we work hard we can have everything we want but not <u>ALL</u> of everything we want. He said that his father always told him, "Pigs get fat but hogs get slaughtered." My dad did, too.

Pastor Bradley said that after Jesus threw the moneychangers out of the temple and castigated them for their unholy practices that these same practitioners were probably right back at it again the very next day. But he said we should grab for the grace of God in every part of our lives. Striving for the things of life is necessary but we should also strive or reach for God's grace in all of our reaching.

This thoughtful and helpful sermon by Dr. Bradley was delivered forcefully and effectively from extensive notes. The notes indicated that his sermon had been carefully studied and crafted to bring to his parishioners thoughts and truths that often lay beneath the surface of the scriptures.

We had an opportunity to visit with the pastor and several of the people after the service and to re-connect bits and pieces of our collective histories. Another historian once said, "History is a bag of tricks we play on the dead." We know this is true because the histories constructed in our minds many years after the fact are (most of the time) like shadows cast onto the rugged cave walls of our minds from the real fires of actual life events of the past.

Our memories of 44 years ago are dim and, doubtlessly, our reconstructions are colored by looking through dim time-darkened glasses. Also, and sadly, most of those of whom we have remembrances have passed on off the stage and are no longer creating new memories. But the ones these old friends have etched on the fragile films of our minds are warm and pleasant — my "bag of tricks" which I have played on the people at Clifton who walked across the stage of my life. Pleasant tricks which I hope to play again and again over the next 44 years before Betty and I return here to visit again. And I hope Dr. Bradley will still be here teaching his Biblical history class on Sundays. Hope to see all 35 of you in 2048.

Chapter 29

First Seventh Day Adventist Church
Nashville, Tennessee
March 30, 2003

*I*t was Saturday, and thus "Fifty-two Sundays" should now, as of this day technically read, "Fifty Sundays, One Friday, and One Saturday on the Blue Road." A few weeks ago on Friday evening we had visited a Jewish worship service at the Congregation Micah located on Old Hickory Boulevard in Nashville. Today we decided to visit the Seventh Day Adventist Church at 2800 Blair Boulevard. I had passed by this church for years and had often seen members scurrying across Natchez Trace while I was probably going to the Pancake Pantry to wait in line far longer than these scurrying would-be worshipers would be in their worship service.

With the knowledge that I would be visiting this church, I had planned for this Saturday to eat breakfast at the Melpark Restaurant in the Melrose area of Eighth Avenue, South on Franklin Road, partially because it is not open on Sundays. The Melpark Restaurant has been a popular family restaurant for more than 20 years. But a new owner had been operating it for the last two or three years and I wanted to see if the new owners knew how to make biscuits.

Looking forward to trying the breakfast fare at Melpark, Betty and I left home at 8:31 a.m. It was one minute past our targeted departure time, but our late leaving on this morning was my fault. When I confessed my guilt to Betty, I could not help but remember a story my friend Bob Phillips liked to tell about a car accident involving his uncle and Miss Sally which happened in the late 40s.

Bob had often heard his uncle tell the story of this incident which occurred on a Thursday afternoon years ago and, after telling of the accident in which Miss Sally's 1929 Ford collided with his car, he would always say, "She hit my new Chevrolet with her car, but it was my fault." Someone would always ask how it could have been his fault when Miss Sally was well known for her terrible driving, weaving from side to side all along the road from her house to the grocery store, "What do you mean it was your fault?"

Bob's uncle would simply reply, "Because it was on Thursday."

"What's Thursday got to do with it's being your fault?" his sympathizers would ask.

Bob would always die laughing when he repeated his uncle's answer: "Because I knew Miss Sally always went to the grocery store on Thursday afternoon, and so I had no business being out on that road when I knew she was going to be there, and so it was all my fault."

We were one minute late when we left this morning, but it was all my fault because I never should have set a definite leaving time when I knew Betty was going to be late leaving anyhow.

Nevertheless, we left at 8:31 a.m. I may have felt a little like the announcer at a heavyweight boxing title match who was delaying the start of the main event too long by introducing one celebrity after another until boos started to rise heatedly from the crowd. Taking a hint from the crowd but still not being deterred from the program, the announcer said into the microphone, "And now before the main event of the evening the greatest operatic singer of all times, Maria Callis, will sing for us the *National Anthem*." To this, one totally inebriated and equally miffed boxing fan yelled out above the other rumbling of the crowd, "Maria Callas is a hog caller." (I cleaned this part of this story up a bit to avoid the editor's censorship). Without being shaken by the heckler the announcer simply replied, "Nevertheless, Maria Callas will now sing the *National Anthem*."

We were one minute late, but "nevertheless" we were on our way to a hopefully fine Saturday Sabbath breakfast. I use Saturday here as an adjective of Sabbath, but historians, Jews, and Seventh Day Adventists would say it is just a redundancy.

This redundant day was a truly beautiful looking and feeling day. The daffodils were in full bloom literally everywhere. The red-buds, weeping cherries and the dogwoods were now taking the place of the Bradford-pear trees which had provided Nashville with some of its first spring blossoms. A soft tint of green was beginning to be seen in the tops of the trees. And Bradford-pear blossoms were being pushed to the ground like snowflakes by leaves now taking command. The freshness of spring filled the air with soft breezes and fluffed up the scattered clouds that drifted by as if leading us to some springtime festival.

We passed several churches which were not holding worship services on the "true Sabbath," as some would rightfully call this day. However, one church, the Woodmont Bible Church, was "preaching" its gospel emphasis for today and for all of this week by proclaiming on its marquee-type sign "The Necessity of Baptism," something I have never really been clear about. I mean, I am not clear, really, on what most Christian churches truly believe about Baptism. But this church apparently was very clear on what they believe about baptism. I do know that many Christian churches really do not think baptism is absolutely necessary for salvation, but apparently the church behind this marquee is not at all ambivalent on the subject. Even so, this church obviously taught that baptism (probably by immersion) was essential for salvation.

In just a few minutes we drove into the parking lot of the Melpark Restaurant and seated ourselves near the far end of the open-seating area where we could have a panoramic view of all of the diners. Soon a bright ball of sunshine in the form of a super friendly, semi-attractive waitress brightly asked if we wanted coffee. We did, and ordered two cups. She disappeared and I began to call her "the friendly disappearing waitress." After about 10 minutes she reappeared with a double-barreled apology for having "forgotten" (her word) us. She said that for this mistreatment she would make an adjustment to our bill. We insisted that this would not be necessary and proceeded to order our breakfasts. Betty ordered two eggs scrambled with bacon, grits and toast. I ordered three eggs "over-easy/over-medium" in an effort to convey the idea that the consistency of the finished product was important to me. I also ordered one-half slice of country ham, home fries, grits, biscuits and "two pancakes for the table." I always add the "for the table" for the excessive parts of my order so as to not appear as a glutton. Fat chance! But I will keep up this longtime custom, nevertheless.

When we entered, the restaurant (which could seat 150 to 200 people) was only about 20 percent full. There was a mixture of people all nicely dressed in Saturday morning attire — a clean casual look. There were four well-dressed black families and two tables of two black men who were respectfully and quietly conversing about the war and other topics of interest to them. One neatly dressed wholesome looking man was reading *The Tennessean*. Two couples on each side of us were obviously regular customers because of "the usual?" questions posed by the disappearing friendly waitress. Then there was the "stalker." This was a tall, clean-cut man who was balding with gray hair around his ears and across the back of his head. He had a pleasant, but somber look, as he did every time we see him and we seem to see him a lot, always by himself. Betty asked, "Who is that man? I see him around a lot?" I said I didn't know, but that I thought he was a stalker. He always seems to wear a green causal jacket and just quietly keeps to himself and seems to converse with no one. "He's probably taking pictures through a miniature camera in his glasses," I said to myself, but not really. It just made me feel important that he seemed to want to be where we are. I wondered if he thinks the same thing about us.

The room was decorated in the style of the 70s with booths lined up side by side low dividers between them constructed of very dark four-by-eight sheets of paneling. This popular restaurant is located in a transitional area of Nashville which was improving economically year by year. The general character of the area is that of car dealerships, antique shops, tire dealers and service stations.

Time passes quickly when you are thinking of the secret places stalkers conceal their miniature cameras and what the cost would probably be for a new set of tires for my four-wheel-drive Jeep. Before I could get the price added up in my mind, our disappearing friendly waitress appeared with a whole array of plates up one arm and one hand freely waving my "for the table" pancakes. She said, "I'm not charging for the pancakes."

With a few more disappearing acts I could save enough to have my old tires balanced and forestall the heavy purchase of new tires. The pancakes were creating a "spare tire" around my waste, anyway.

All our food was good here, especially the eggs. Maybe it was the verbal "slash" I emphatically put between the words over-lightly and over-medium. These were perfect and allowed proper custom scrambling on my plate (as it seems all West Virginians do who are repatriated to mountaineer eating habits at breakfast time). The home fries were good, but mushy looking — almost like warmed slices of peeled baked potatoes. The country ham was a beautiful, succulent, tasty slab. Half of my two biscuits were excellent. Not one of the two biscuits, rather the bottoms of both. The bottoms were brown and crusty just as they should be, but the tops were almost unbaked and had a vapid,white doughy look and taste. They apparently had been baked too quickly at a high temperature on a lower rack in the oven. But they were not nuked, thanks to the continuing war on kitchen terrorism.

On the way out of the restaurant I saw Kermit Stengel and his wife. I have always admired the way Kermit seems to hang on to his real-estate holdings. I guess I am saying I admire (covet?) the apparent wealth which allows him to hold onto his real-estate assets. I have always wanted to hold onto all the real estate I have owned over the years, but I can never get the full cooperation from the banks that hold the mortgages. Maybe I'll start coming to Melpark more often, start stalking Kermit and see what banks he uses.

At about 9:35 a.m. we left the Melpark and drove to the Seventh Day Adventist Church at the corner of Natchez Trace and Blair Boulevard. At about 10:25 a.m. we entered the foyer of this church which is much larger than it appears from the outside. It looks relatively small from the street but opens up into a large sanctuary which appeared able to seat about 400 people.

As we entered, a friendly round-faced deacon greeted us, introduced himself as Tommy Hawkins and asked if we were from the visiting church, which led to the evolving information that there was going to be a special musical program presented by some young people from an Adventist church in Sumner County. While the sign outside indicated that the worship service began at 10:30 a.m., it soon became apparent that the period from 10:30 a.m. to 11:00 a.m. was sort of a membership/fellowship period. We, therefore, had about 30 minutes to visit around and get ourselves acquainted with some aspects of this denomination which were totally new to me.

I latched onto Tommy who was a warm, friendly and open ambassador for his church. I asked him what some of the distinctive features of his church were. He said first, of course, the most obvious difference between the Seventh Day Adventist Churches and other

Christian churches is the fact that they worship on Saturday — "the Sabbath." I asked, in a non-threatening way, how they were sure that Saturday was the last day of the week on the Sabbath and he replied that the Jews, the real historians of Biblical monotheism, had always regarded Saturday as the Sabbath.

I learned from some literature that the "Adventist" part of the name refers to some particular emphases which this denomination places upon their eschatology, or study of last things. They have specific doctrines which they trace directly to specific scriptures regarding the nature and the time of the second coming of Christ. Particularly, they believe in the purification of the Earth on which God shall establish "a new Earth" where the Christians who are taken up into heaven at the second coming of Christ will return with Him after 1,000 years to establish His reign in holiness and happiness. Most other Christians believe that the Earth will be destroyed completely at the second coming of Christ and that all God's children will be taken to heaven to live in paradise with Jesus forever.

Another difference, according to Tommy, was that the Seventh Day Adventists still practice foot washing, which is referred to in *The New Testament* as an act of brotherhood and humility, and as a way of remembering the love and humble sacrificial life of Jesus. He told me that this practice was customarily a part of the worship service once each quarter. "Just like the Lord's Supper," he added. This led me to the conclusion that this denomination places about the same emphasis on both foot washing and Communion services. Tommy further told me how this service is customarily observed. He said they wash each other's feet while segregated according to genders —all the men go into one room and all the women go into another. He said, "For example, neither you nor I would wash your wife's feet." His statement was a humble, simple attempt to convey the legitimacy and sanctity of this practice.

Betty and I settled ourselves on the second pew from the back on the right side of this sanctuary. (Someone had audaciously claimed the very back pew).There were three sections of oak pews which were "pickled" a light taupe/gray. The walls were a cream color with the bottom four feet painted a beautiful taupe color to match the color of the carpets and the pews. The pew seats had rose-colored upholstering. The sanctuary was fan shaped with the pew sections wider at the back and narrower at the front. There was a soft, cloth-formed swaddling over the baptistery pool behind the pulpit and the choir.

A handsome young man unceremoniously came to the front to make several announcements. Probably in his mid-30s, he introduced himself as Brian and wore a dark suit with a dark crew neck knit shirt. A young woman of about the same age came and stood with Brian to give an enthusiastic announcement about Vacation Bible School which would take place in July. "Which will be here sooner than you think," she warned.

The congregation was widely diverse; probably 25% of the congregants were people of color. According to Deacon Tommy the church has members from 22 different countries. This was partially emphasized when Pastor Jerry Rimer, a stocky dark-haired balding man in his early 50s, came to the front and announced that there would be two baptisms today. They were Eddie Armstrong and Frank Ansah, both of whom were black. The pastor said they would go and prepare for the baptism while the service progressed. The service then "officially" began with the call to worship which was initiated with a soft worshipful hymn played on the organ.

The invocation was given by Doug Faulkner, who was listed in the order of worship. Next a young black woman announced *Hymn No. 25, Praise the Lord, His Glories Show*. By the time this hymn was finished, the pastor was in the baptismal pool with the two men being baptized. As the pastor baptized each of these men, a chorus of Amens arose from the congregation. Then, the pastor prayed for the two who had been baptized and for any others in the congregation who still needed to be baptized.

Next Doug Faulkner announced that the offering would be taken and encouraged all of the members to be mindful of the church budget which had not been met by the last few offerings. Maybe our $5 would help. I felt maybe we should have given more to help and was inclined to do so, but did not follow the spirit. I know, "The road to hell is paved with good intentions." After the offering Dean Flint, who is listed in the bulletin as being in charge of Personal Ministries, prayed the pastoral prayer, after explaining that the pastor had to leave early for Chattanooga for a funeral. At this point the congregation was invited to kneel at their pews (no prayer benches) while the organ played a beautiful worshipful piece. Flint then prayed a short prayer for our servicemen "who are fighting for our freedoms." After the prayer the organ again played a beautiful punctuation to this simple prayer.

The worship program for the day, a substitution in place of a sermon, was the musical play entitled, *Kings, Dreams and Schemes*. The play, a well-written musical about the life of Daniel, was performed by "The Highland Church Juniors." The musical was introduced by a young man of color who read the scripture lesson from the book of *Daniel* in *The Old Testament*. Then the lights went off, and there was much disorder and nervous uncertainty as the 30 to 40 young people visiting from another church delivered their performance. They were all dressed in costumes reminiscent of the way people were believed to have dressed long ago. During the first upbeat tune the "cheerleaders" of the olden time put up the letters D – A – N – I – E – L, in "rah, rah, rah Daniel" fashion.

Then the next scene, to the song *What Will Happen to Him?*, showed Daniel being captured and taken before King Nebuchadnezzar. Daniel and his three followers would not eat the meat or drink the wine offered to them by the king because it was food and drink which had been offered to idols. The young people then sang another catchy tune to the words to the king, "Please don't think that we are rude, but we can't eat that meat or food." The point being made (in song) was that Daniel did not just go along with the crowd.

The king came to know Daniel and asked him to interpret a dream that was bothering the king greatly. After Daniel interpreted the dream for the king, Daniel was put in charge of running the kingdom. Then Daniel was called into a great banquet to read the mysterious writing on the wall while five young dancers performed for all the guests. After Daniel read the writing, he was elevated even further in the kingdom. Those whom he was over became jealous and set a trap for him. They had the king pass a law that no one in the kingdom could pray to anyone except the king because they knew that Daniel prayed daily to God.

Therefore, according to the king's decree, when Daniel was caught praying to God he was cast into the lions' den. And, to the astonishment of the king and everyone, Daniel tamed (to the song

Kitty, Kitty) the lions to where they were gentle as kittens. Then these young people sang a catchy song about the men who tricked the king into throwing Daniel to the lions thinking that Daniel was becoming "a little feast to the king of beasts."

The next song was *Glory to the King of Daniel* and they sang, "God needs Daniels today" and "Will you dare to be a Daniel?" The musical ended with "Dare to be a Daniel for all the world to see. We will be like Daniel, we will be like Daniel." This upbeat ending had many in the congregation applauding enthusiastically with a chorus of "Amens" coming from all over the church.

Lights. Fade in. Benediction by Doug Faulkner. Postlude by the organist. And this service ended. The well-written play, with its extraordinarily clever and creative music, had the character of the hit musical "Jesus Christ Superstar." It surely has been or will be performed by professionals on a larger stage.

I was truly sorry that I did not get to hear Pastor Jerry Rimer give a sermon, but maybe I got a better or even truer feeling about this church by witnessing this little musical and, perhaps more importantly, by talking with Deacon Tommy Hawkins about the Saturday Sabbath and the foot-washing services. The tradition of worship here at this church is based on a mission to strictly follow the teachings of the Bible and the example of Jesus in both their lives and worship services.

C h a p t e r   30

St. Edward's Catholic Church
Nashville, Tennessee
April 6, 2003

etty got so caught up in reading a romance novel by one of her favorite authors last night that she forgot to turn our clocks forward an hour (you know, the "spring-forward" day on the daylight savings program). Fortunately, she was taking a trip to Atlanta to see the "Final Four" of the NCAA Women's National Basketball Championship and, just like a kid, she was so excited that she woke up well before her normal two-hour prep time for any day's activities (of course, to be fair, this also includes 30 minutes of exercise which she does religiously every morning). Even if she receives a phone call she keeps doing her leg raises while she talks, or she goes through the house looking for things while she does her arm exercises. I love this about Betty — she always does what she is supposed to do — that is, except for refraining from eating chocolates which is entirely too much to expect from her.

Anyhow, in her excitement she woke up automatically in anticipation of her trip to Atlanta with her pompom pals. However, her own personal black and gold Vanderbilt pompoms were neatly stored away on the top shelf of our storage closet for the remainder of this season. The Lady Commodores, her favorites, had lost to Texas Tech in the Sweet Sixteen a couple of weeks ago. I don't think she'd picked a new favorite yet, but it probably would not be Tennessee because of the strong rivalry between Vandy and Tennessee. I am sure she felt a little guilt for not being able to pull for Tennessee, our own state university's perennial powerhouse, but she just couldn't. Just like she couldn't refrain from eating chocolates, she could not pull for Tennessee.

When she got up at about 5:30 a.m., she woke me and told me that she had failed to set the clocks forward. It was really now 6:30 a.m. and she only had one hour and forty-five minutes to get ready to leave at her appointed departure time of 8:15 a.m. Her exercises were a little more hurried — as if going a bit faster for 30 minutes would cut some time off the full 30 minutes she exercised anyhow. When Betty exercises, she holds onto a bed post to stabilize herself, and the bed shakes just enough so that any further efforts on my part to remain asleep are not worth the bother. So, I got up to begin planning my day. Bathroom first. The paper had not yet arrived so I just read another chapter in Phillip Margolian's new novel *Ties That Bind*. Sorry Phillip, but that's where I do all my light reading.

Next, take my medicine, including Metamucil. For God's sake, folks, I'm almost 72. Pleasurable bowel movements are one of few purely biological functions that still have their original amount of satisfaction. So why risk it? Go for the gusto, I say. I took a double dose hoping for the Doublemint formula for pleasure. Next, I put out my golfing clothes for the day. Frank, John, Jim and I were going to play golf at 1:50 p.m. and so I needed to be prepared to go from wherever I went to church directly to the golf course. Next, of course, I put on my church clothes. No sweat here, because I almost always wear the same thing, except for today. Today I switched from cools to hots in my choice of sport coats.

Betty was ready to leave at 8:15 a.m. on the dot. Not really a miracle that she was not even a few minutes late today, you all. Remember? She was going to a basketball tournament! I took her luggage, put it in her car and wished her the very best time she could possibly have with Vandy not being one of the Final Four. And she was off, excited as a high-school sophomore who had just gotten her driver's license. I went back into the lonely confines of our "doublewide" to read some of the paper which had just arrived. Someone at The Tennessean forgot to set his clock forward, also.

The day's golfing plans sort of helped me set my agenda. Breakfast and church would be somewhere nearby. I had wanted to go to another Catholic church and had decided a few weeks ago to attend St. Edward's on Thompson Lane. I had heard about St. Edward's Father Breen who is considered one of the most progressive priests in the Dioceses of Nashville — as well as one of the most respected and loved ministers in the city.

I am not a member of the Catholic Church. I guess I am not much of anything anymore but I still hold my membership at

Trinity Presbyterian Church in Nashville, thanks to the liberalism of the late Dr. Tom Barr. Dr. Barr agreed to not ask me any technical questions when our family became members there after I left the ministry in 1964. Though not a Catholic, I presently serve on two boards under the Diocese of Nashville including the Diocesan Properties board which manages low-income properties as part of the Catholic Church's social outreach efforts to assist low-income people. I have been on this board for about 30 years and have jokingly called myself the board's "token protestant." But all these years I have truly been impressed with the liberal policies of the Catholic Church in this regard; I am not aware of any Catholics who have been invited to serve on Presbyterian or Baptist boards. Also, the other Catholic board I sit on has a member of the Church of Christ as a very active board member.

I wanted to go to another Catholic Church, sort of in keeping with my "equal time" concept. I had been to three Methodist churches, two "regular" Baptists and two irregular Baptist (Missionary and Free Will) churches, and three Presbyterian. Now halfway through my "Fifty-two Sundays" program, I was aware of the need for "balancing my books" across the next few Sundays. So, Father Breen's St. Edward's Church was going to be it, and this would be the second time my blue roading allowed me to stay on my extended home street of Woodmont-Thompson Lane.

When I left home at 8:57 a.m., it was beautiful — a gorgeous day. The sun brilliantly lit the blossoms of the many dogwood and redbud trees all along this part of town. The blossoms of the Bradford pears had now all turned to their delightfully delicate spring-green freshness. All the birds sang happily. It was creating the mood of "God is in His heaven and all is right with the world," as we used to say. But the war in Iraq was keeping many of us from repeating this expression of total good feeling.

In a matter of just 18 minutes this beautiful day completely changed. It started raining heavily just as I spotted a Shoney's restaurant on Thompson Lane near Nolensville Road. The lightning and thunder of an angry God was now surely reminding us that certainly all was not right with the world. I thought of all that was wrong: the war, the suffering, the prejudice and the many other aspects of non-rightness of the world crowding in on us like the dark clouds of the present thunderstorm. So I determined to go into Shoney's and drown my sense of wrongness filling the world this day in some of Shoney's intoxicating morning solutions, served up in abundance at their sinful breakfast bar.

I bought a newspaper and prepared to withdraw from the world and eat a sumptuous breakfast. I made a mistake in buying the paper because I was unable to forget the war for a single minute. Even now in the midst of the raging battle, congress and the world courts were waging a separate war about how reconstruction monies would be controlled and who would have the biggest say in the after-war politics. Surely all of this was sufficient cause for me to over-eat. And I did, and all that I ate was very good — almost great. As a matter of fact, it was all great except the hash-brown potatoes. They were hash but not brown, even though they were greasy good — just enough of an imperfection to keep my breakfast from being perfect.

I ordered three eggs over-light/over-medium (which I found is allowed even when ordering the breakfast bar) and country-fried steak smothered with gravy. The crunchiness of the steak was enhanced by the delightfully smooth gravy-sauce. My eggs were cooked to order and came with an offer from my very friendly, efficient waitress to have more cooked for me if these were not just right. The biscuits were absolutely perfect. They were crisp and golden brown on the tops, and the bottoms were ready for slicing and eating separately — the tops first, then the bottoms — the tops with butter, the bottoms with jelly.

Perhaps the best touch of all was my very own individual pot of coffee served on my table, hot and ready whenever I was ready. Why not this touch everywhere? I'm going to pass the word. And I'm going to pass the word also about the sugared French toast on the bar. It made me truly appreciate the ready pot of coffee that allowed me to dunk each bite of this crisp Frenchy sweetness with a swig of coffee without any fear of having to eat the next bite without this ever-ready accompanying pot of morning nectar.

As I was finishing my last gluttonous bites and denying the adverse caloric effect which they would doubtlessly have on my body, I read in the paper about how the Iraqi leaders were denying in the media the presence of the coalition forces now in occupation of Baghdad International Airport (which was only yesterday called Saddam Hussein International Airport). Both these denials would have absolutely no effect on reality. I was already gaining weight at that very moment, and the last Iraqi military plane had doubtlessly landed at this newly named airport for the war's duration.

There was another reminder of the war as I finished my breakfast and read the paper. Three young, attractive black women came in for breakfast dressed in clean, crisp battle fatigues with the inscription "U.S. Army" emblazoned on their left breast pocket tabs. Then there was the story of Jessica Lynch who had just been liberated from hospital captivity a few days earlier, and was now recovering in a U.S. Army hospital in Germany. I hoped that the war would be over soon enough to keep these three soldiers home or that, even if they had to go, they would not be sent to the front lines. I hope all the women of the world appreciate this prejudice of mine, which I am sure is held by a large majority of both men and women around the world. All women should be kept out of harm's way in wars so that they can go on having babies so that men can have someone to kill in the next war — or something like that.

By 10:10 a.m. I was leaving this Shoney's which had been all freshly painted to create a pleasant atmosphere which complimented my delightful morning blue road breakfast experience. I found myself hoping that the new owners who had purchased this chain could recapture some or all of the aggressive cleanliness that had been the case in Shoney's during the Ray Danner days. I remember when Ray would go into a Shoney's and, if it was not up to his standards of service and cleanliness, he would close the restaurant. He would apologize to all the customers there and make their meal complimentary. He would tell them that no one should pay for a meal in a dirty restaurant. I would have to pay my check today, even by Ray's standards. I was happy to pay $10.35 plus tip before visiting their very clean restroom and then driving the few blocks to St. Edwards.

It was now raining hard, and I wondered if many would be attending this morning's service. The church sign said there were three services each Sunday: 8:00 a.m., 10:30 a.m. and 12:00 p.m. A lay assistant announced that Father Breen would be celebrating the Mass this morning and I wondered if he was the only priest for all three of the day's services. As I was writing these words, I called my friend John Seigenthaler, a close personal friend of Father Breen, to ask if he knew if Father Breen would have celebrated the Mass at all three of today's services. John called the church and learned that Father Breen, indeed, had been the only priest to officiate at the three services. This thought wore me out completely. I remembered how a single service at 11:00 a.m. (surely God's own anointed time of worship) used to leave me totally drained back when I was a minister.

The rain apparently had no effect on attendance because this beautiful new sanctuary was full. The four sections of pews, each seeming to hold about 200 people, were completely filled, and extra chairs had been placed at the end of each aisle. The warm, friendly feeling of the congregation as I entered was a reflection of the warmness of the architecture and the beautiful detailing of the landscaping at the entrance. This array of red brick buildings was constructed to give the garden effect of a compound rather than that of a massive institution. The vaulted ceilings and beams were a soft white, fading into pleasant green walls and on down to the contrasting Kelly green pew cushions. The pews were solid light oak. The entirety of the interior was comfortably accented by a section of stained glass in a contemporary style of multicolored panels of glass accented by dark oak trim. Behind the chancel were two vertical rows of more traditional panels of stained glass in rectangular shapes, with one oval panel at the top between the two rows.

The congregation was truly mixed as to age groups, style of dress and ethnicity. I sat beside a Japanese couple, and I saw several African-American people scattered throughout the congregation. Most of the congregation were respectfully, yet casually, dressed with fewer than 10 percent wearing suits or jackets. The 12 person choir was also casually dressed. All the crosses in the church were draped with purple sashes, and the Crucifix centered behind the chancel area was completely covered with a purple cloth (which a Catholic friend informed me would probably not be removed until Easter Sunday).

A member dressed in a large Easter bunny costume wandered around the church to the delight of the children, especially when the bunny stopped to pat their heads or chuck under their chins. Most members reverently genuflected and made the sign of the

cross before entering their pew section. One gregarious soul accidentally broke this sense of humility and reverence by laughing,
waving, and speaking to his fellow pew mates as he perfunctorily
made the sign of the cross. Just then a loud clap of thunder echoed
overhead as if to rebuke his carelessness, and as if to say it was time
for the bunny to go in its hole and for the worship service to begin.

Several announcements were made by lay members of the
church about the congregation's health ministry. John Clark
announced a blood drive and said all donors would receive an
umbrella. Becky Doyle announced a blood pressure clinic at which
members could also get their cholesterol and blood sugar checked.
After these announcements, Steve Mullin, a lay lector according to
the church bulletin, announced *Hymn No. 193* as the "entrance
hymn." The congregation stood and sang "I want to walk as a child
of the light" during the procession of several worship assistants, and
followed lastly by Father Breen.

Father Breen is a princely man of the cloth in both looks and
actions. He was dressed in "purple vestments," and was obviously
revered, respected and loved by the congregation. He took his time
in the procession and followed far behind the others as he made his
way to the chancel. He took the opportunity to wave at and briefly
speak with various church members, as much like a politician as a
priest, as he made his way slowly to the chancel. When he arrived
at the front of the sanctuary, he told us in his rich bass voice that
we all should be grateful for this day. He said it was only raining
here while just a little further north there was ice and snow — "just
another reason we should be grateful today." He said, "Let's pray a
prayer that wherever we go that we may take the light of Christ
with us. By our presence may we make a difference and may this
be our sincere prayer in the silence of our hearts."

Father Breen then asked everyone "to be hospitable and welcome
those around you." The whole congregation responded, especially
those in the back rear section, because everyone within reaching
distance shook my hand and said, "Good morning," each in his own
way. I like this approach better than the custom in several of the
churches we had visited where everyone was instructed to say, "The
peace of Christ be with you," and to which you were instructed to
respond, "And also with you."

The pastor then prayed for God to help us change our selfishness
into true self-giving, and "that we may help change the darkness
around us into the blessings and light of a blessed Easter. Grant this
through Christ our Lord. Amen."

Steve Mullin, the lector for this service, offered the first scripture
reading from *Jeremiah 31: 33 – 34* where God said He would "make
a new covenant with Israel and the house of Judah...I will put my
laws within them and write it upon their hearts. I will be their God
and they shall be my people...I will forgive their sins and remember
them against them no more."

Following this reading there was a beautiful solo backed by the
voices of a small but well-rehearsed choir. After this solo Steve
Mullin again read from the *Bible*, this time from *Hebrews 5: 7 – 9*
which reads in part: "When Jesus was in the flesh He learned obedience from what He suffered." This scripture lesson was followed by
a song by the choir, then Father Breen ceremoniously held the bible
high over his head before lowering it to read from *John 12: 20 – 23*,
where Jesus tells of His coming time of suffering and His glorification.
After reading this scripture, the priest raised the *Bible* back up and
kissed it in another sign of reverence for the Word of God.

At this point Father Breen came down to welcome the visitors
to the congregation in a very personal way. He asked: "Do we have
anyone from out of town? Raise your hands." Someone said, "From
Texas." He said, "Well, Texas tried hard last night. Maybe next year
they'll go all the way, right? Glad to have you here. Leave an abundant
offering, hear?"

Father Breen then spoke in reference to the earlier announcements about the dangers of diabetes. He said he knew of people who
had to have their feet cut off because of the disease and he urged
everyone to take advantage of the free tests offered by the church in
the interest of the good health of the whole congregation. He said, "I
want you to be as healthy as you can in body, mind and spirit." Then
he asked if there were any birthdays to celebrate or any other celebra-
tions. Several people spoke about their causes of joy and the pastor
congratulated them all in a personal and humorous way. The whole
congregation warmly responded to the interest the pastor showed.

Next Father Breen announced that one of the deacons would
give the homily for this service and noted how this deacon recently

had undergone painful by-pass surgery and was recovering very nicely. Then, just as the deacon was slowly walking to the pulpit, the pastor said, "Don't keep us waiting," and the whole congregation responded with a roar of laughter.

The deacon read some scripture, and then gave a short description of "this holy season." He said, "We, like the Apostles, would wish that every Sunday would be Palm Sunday, then sleep through dark Friday." But he said we can't because, "He who hung the clouds and the sun is now transfixed to a cross of wood with nails." He said that the Roman soldier said: "He that is called Jesus Christ is dead," but, he continued, "We know that He will rise and come again...Jesus will keep His promises. He is coming back." This deacon prodded the congregation, "Let us, with Jesus, save the world from disaster and war." He then concluded by saying, "On Easter try to remember that Easter is more than ham and potato salad. Amen."

Father Breen then led the congregation in a recitation of the Apostles' Creed and prayed a prayer of several parts while, after each part, the choir would sing: "Lord, hear our prayer." He next announced the offering and said to this congregation: "Please be generous." During the offering, the choir then sang a beautiful arrangement of "The Old Rugged Cross" and then they sang the song that says, "Jesus walked that lonesome valley. He had to walk it by Himself." And I felt constrained to give our usual $5 for the offering. Betty was not here to do it with me, so lonesome Grant did it by himself.

The pastor announced that the day's mass was celebrated in the memory of Ed, a member of the congregation, and his late wife of 58 years who had passed away 2 years ago. He said that Ed has been a faithful communicant at St. Edward's for many years, and he praised him for his forethought in writing plans for his own funeral to take the strain off his surviving family when he dies. I wanted to stand and announce that I, too, had written my funeral service. And I have a place for eulogies which I call the "Liars Contest," and have been assured by Betty that she will award an extra egg roll to the winner. But I didn't say anything because I didn't want to take anything away from Ed.

The priest prepared the bread and wine praying: "Sanctify

these simple gifts of bread and wine." As the priest spoke almost all of the congregation knelt on the prayer benches. He said:"We pray that in the great mystery that these gifts will become the body and blood of Christ." Then he read the Biblical account of "The Lord's Supper" and ended by saying: "This do in remembrance of Me." Then he prayed for Ed and his departed wife and said we should all look forward to the day when we can all be together with, "Mary, Joseph and all the saints," followed by the song "Forever and ever. Amen. Amen. Amen."

Next, we stood and the people sitting on either side of me persisted until they held my hands during "The Lord's Prayer."Then the pastor served the bread and wine to the "Eucharist ministers" who were listed in the church bulletin. They, in turn, filed out to parts of the congregation where the communicants in turn filed past to be served the bread and the wine. Some dipped the bread in the cup themselves and ate the bread and wine, while others opened their mouths and invited the Eucharist minister to place the wine soaked bread in their mouths. When all had been served, the Eucharist ministers drank the remainder of the wine. All the while the choir sang, "I am the Bread of Life."

The choir then sang *America the Beautiful*. Then, while still seated, Father Breen said, "It is time to be grateful and faithful and I want to say thank you for making this church to be special." Next he prayed a simple benedictory prayer and concluded by saying: "Remember to be special to your family and friends. Amen." The choir then sang the recessional hymn, and Father Breen went to the foyer to greet his parishioners. On my way out I interrupted him briefly to say that our mutual good friend, John Seigenthaler, sent his regards. It was obvious that the name "John Seigenthaler" got the good Father's attention.They had been in school at Father Ryan together during the 1940s.

On my way home after the service, I called John to give him a return greeting from Father Breen. John then told me a story about a chance meeting between himself and the then priest-to-be, when in 1961 he met Joe Pat Breen in Rome. "Joe Pat," as John called him, was in Rome finishing his priesthood training while John was there as administrative assistant to Attorney General Robert Kennedy. At the chance meeting "Joe Pat" said he would love to meet Robert

Kennedy who, of course, was also Catholic. John invited him to go immediately to the hotel so that he could introduce them. From the hotel lobby John called Bobby Kennedy's room and told him that young Father Breen would like to meet him. The attorney general said, "I am naked but tell him to come on up. I am waiting for my doctor to give me a B-12 shot."

As young Father Breen and John entered the room, there was Bobby Kennedy — totally naked and leaning over a table while a doctor prepared to stab him in the butt with a syringe. While still bent over the table, Bobby extended his hand and said laughingly, "Hello. I'm the attorney general of the United States." John said that, of course, this story has been retold many times over the years because of the uniqueness of the situation, and because young Father-to-be Joe Pat Breen was proud to have met the third best-known fellow Catholic in the world at that time — after only the Pope himself and the president of the United States.

After this service I was to have met John and Frank Sutherland and Jim Neal to play golf today, but we canceled our game because of the rain. The rain probably saved me a considerable amount of money because my game had been slipping. Both John and Jim each had won $16 from me just this past Friday, a record-high winning in our foursome (although Frank and I each had won $15 from John and Jim a few games back). Perhaps I have been spending too much time in church. I don't know, but it seems to me that a good God would reward the efforts of the righteous. While I don't expect God to send the bears out of the hills to eat those who would strip me bare on the golf course, as He had done to those who mocked the prophet of old, I don't see how it would hurt God's eternal plan to help keep my game intact during the remainder of my "Fifty-two Sundays." It would seem that God could help me keep my swing intact until I could actually practice golf instead of observing the religious practices of true seekers after His will.

Do you suppose God would consider it a threat of any kind if I said I might have to consider reducing my $5 Sunday offerings if my golf losses continue to add up? I should have asked Father Breen, but then I guess priests are a little biased in favor of God. Maybe I will make a test of it. I might reduce my offering to $4 next Sunday if my game continues to slide and my losses continue to rise. Those of you who talk to God regularly please keep this a secret from Him, okay? I don't want to prejudice my case before the fact. I mean, you can go ahead and talk to God all you want, but just don't mention what I am thinking about my Sunday offerings. Okay?

C h a p t e r   3 1

Jesus Name Pentecostal Church
McMinnville, Tennessee
April 13, 2003

S ometime during the past few days Siegfried and Roy brought
their marvelous disappearing Vegas act to the Hurricane area
of Center Hill Lake again on their semi-annual tour. They
had been here in late fall and magically turned our house in the
woods into a house with an acceptable view of Center Hill Lake.
Then, just this past week, they one-upped their disappearing Bengal
tiger trick by making our view of this beautiful body of water disappear
altogether. They do this through a clever combination of photosyn-
thesis and chlorophyll which was first introduced on the world
stage by Mother Nature, who still laid claim to the intellectual
rights attached to this perennial vanishing and disappearing act.
Siegfried and Roy be hanged. I'm a real believer in protecting all
international intellectual property rights. From now on I'm going
to give Mother Nature top billing for this truly fascinating and
beautiful show.

Mother Nature outdid herself this year. She made the lake
completely disappear from view by sliding it behind a beautiful
screen of delicate green leaves painted on millions of trees all at
once. She made it look oh so simple, if totally unbelievable. She was
aided in this unbelievable, almost instantaneous, act by a slight of
hand distraction that simultaneously drew our attention to the
appearance of delicate dogwood and rosebud blooms all over the
area. The fabulous combination of early spring colors easily took
our minds away from the disappearing muddy hues of
winter/spring lake water. With the spring splendor holding our
attentions, we truly did not even notice the lake view disappearing,
nor did we care if the reversal of this Vegas-type phenomenon would
not happen again until the next show begins sometime during the
next fall/winter show tour.

Betty and I took our friends, Jan and Jim Wells, to see this show again this year. We also invited Jim's brother Earl and his wife JoAnn to witness it with us this season. JoAnn and Earl live in Knoxville, while Jan and Jim live in Hendersonville. We were to arrive at about the same time from three different points of origin — at about 5:30 p.m. However, a strange and all too frequent thing happened today. Betty was late getting home for our planned departure time of 3:30 p.m. which would have allowed us to miss much of the early evening traffic which was just peaking at 4:15 p.m. when we finally got away. To be fair, Betty was working on a project with some friends and was delayed, probably through no real fault of her own. My friend Don Sheffield says, "It's always something. It ain't never just nothing." So it seems to be the case with people who are punctuality challenged.

I took our tardiness in leaving with what, I must say, was gracious acceptance of the inevitable, as I am learning to do. Maybe I'm finally growing in grace, or maybe it's those new purple pills Dr. Shaw has prescribed, or perhaps Betty has just worn me down. Regardless of how it is credited on the great scoring card in the sky (or on my blood pressure charts in my doctor's office), I am better today than ever before. Grace, medicine and the Zen torture of the drip, drip, dripping of the cyclical wheel of Betty's timeliness challenged proclivities have made me more relaxed about the whole problem of spousal punctuality.

Anyhow, through the miracle of the cell phone we were able to keep in touch with our guests. While we were delayed in rush hour traffic, we talked them through our elaborate security system, and had them light our propane gas grill to have it ready to pop hamburgers on soon after our arrival. With the goodies that each one brought we had a delightful evening — eating, visiting and watching the up-to-the-minute happenings in the war with Iraq. The next day we had breakfast at the lake house and then drove all around the areas of Smithville and McMinnville shopping for trees (the area is known widely for its plethora of plant nurseries). Afterward we played golf at the River Watch Golf Course located between Smithville and Sparta. This course only had nine beautiful holes open, and so we only played nine holes. My score was terrible, but I have definitely found the way to shoot my age (play a nine-hole course).If my golfing buddies in Nashville had played with me today, I would have had to sell our lake cottage to keep out of debtors' prison — because they all demand cash for golfing debts.

Sunday morning I left Betty to entertain our guests and set out toward McMinnville to continue my odyssey — a Sunday morning wayfarer searching for different blue road breakfast places and churches. I left our one-time lake view home at 8:45 a.m.and drove south on Highway 56 through Smithville and toward McMinnville. I drove around McMinnville for about 25 minutes looking for both a good restaurant and a church to attend. Of course, I saw several Methodist, Baptist and Church of Christ churches. Then I saw the "Jesus Name Pentecostal Church," and decided that it would be my church of choice today unless another one grabbed my attention before 11:00 a.m. which was when its service would begin.

It was now time to find a good place for a fitting breakfast. After driving around and seeing several choices, what looked like a true blue road restaurant just beckoned to me — Patsy's Burger Queen and BBQ Restaurant. I stepped inside to verify that they were serving breakfast and knew instantaneously that I was in the right place for a true blue road morning experience.

I seated myself, as was the custom here. Anything else would seem pretentious — no hostess, only a cook and a waitress. You were sort of on your own. I sat next to a wall lined with several pieces of country music memorabilia. One sign indicated, with great pride, that McMinnville was the birthplace of the late country music superstar Dottie West. There also were proper recognitions of the coal miner's daughter, Loretta Lynn and the king, Elvis Presley. There was a smoking section and a non-smoking section. The smoking section was in the front, obviously planned this way so that the waitresses could join the coffin nail drivers while waving off raised hands requesting more coffee, at least long enough to allow the waitress a quick puff or two.

This non-descript facility had apparently "jes growed up like Topsy." There obviously had been no architect; if there had been one, he surely was no longer in business unless they give out awards for "Most Unstructured Facility." It was designed with four bar seats near the cash register and the dairy dip machine for "good ol' boys like Bubba," who was holding court there as I walked in. You know

Bubba. You've seen him everywhere — overweight, scraggly beard, John Deer ball cap, and full of conversation and advice for everyone. This Bubba was telling about how he almost went to jail for something which wound up costing him $150. He was telling this and other events in his life to any of the other three at the bar who would listen. Of course you had no choice but to hear if you were anywhere in the restaurant.

Bubba announced, to no one in particular, that he had "something to do at 10 o'clock but thought I would come back over here and kill a little time." In this sentence he revealed that he had already been here sometime earlier before the present session. Bubba always found something to talk about. When there was a little lull in the conversation because no one was left at the bar, he said to the waitress at the ice machine behind the bar, "Something wrong with your ice machine?" He apparently hates the sound of silence.

Finally, someone new came in, sat at the bar and gave Bubba a fresh start with a whole new array of subjects to talk about. He seemed versatile and customized his conversation to his new captive. In the meantime, two women in separate booths were eating, smoking and visiting verbally with each other — booth to booth. Soon Bubba's newest captive escaped, and Bubba joined the two women in conversation, he at the bar, and they in their respective booths. It was surely the meat n' three version of TV's sitcom *Cheers* "where everybody knows your name."

Bubba continued, of course. Now he was telling the two women how he had won $150 at "Powerball," just the same amount the judge ordered him to pay. Bubba said he won the $150 in some town in Georgia, but he could not remember the town's name. Eureka! Another subject to be pursued for awhile. "I don't understand why I can't remember the town's name, but it's south of Chattanooga," he said. And then Bubba became mobile. He left his perch at the bar, coffee cup in hand, and continued his one way conversation with the two women. One of the women had been joined by a man with a gravelly, whiskey soaked sounding voice, long hair, and a cane that helped him walk. He had tattoos on both arms, and I concluded that he had been in a motorcycle accident. Profiling, I know. We all do it, but I guess it's only profiling if we write or speak our thoughts. In his loud, deep gravelly voice, he talked as if every word required such force that pain accompanied reception. He said, painfully, "You don't have to be crazy to live in this town, but it helps."

Bubba now sat at a table somewhat closer to the booths with the women and the Hell's Angels survivor. At 9:40 a.m. he encroached on the territory of this scattered threesome and said, "I think I'll kill a few more minutes before I leave," and then continued with his discussion of different aspects of the Georgia lottery. He still could not remember the town's name where he bought the $150 winning ticket. He said, "I can't afford to play as much now since I am not working." Then he justified his new gambling situation by hopefully saying, "But one ticket is as good as 100 if you hit it, right?"

Finally at 9:45 a.m. Bubba said, "See y'all later," and he was on his way to his 10:00 a.m. meeting. I was hoping it was a job interview and that he would get the job, and that he wins the big money on the one ticket he will surely buy this week. I had a feeling that he would share it with his friends. Bubba was a big talker, but I had come to like him in the short time I had spent in the restaurant. I felt a little lonely as my big talking 275 pound friend left. As he said his good-byes, the gravel-voiced cyclist simply said, "Dude." Now the whole place was his alone, and he took over with his painful fog-horn voice. It made my throat hurt just to listen to him. He walked toward the kitchen with the help of his cane and bellowed, "Hey, y'all ain't got no lemon back there, have you?" They did, but he kept talking louder and louder, as he was now competing with a song by the Everly Brothers. He kicked it up another notch, and the Everly Brothers song was history.

The crippled Angel was the king of the domain. Now he was the greeter of everyone who came in. "How are you?" he croaked to a new arrival who said, "Just right, thanks," in a pleasant voice coming out of a pleasing smile. What a contrast in voices, I thought. I tried to emulate the soft-spoken newcomer as I quietly ordered my breakfast: "Three eggs over-easy/over-medium, bacon, hash browns, biscuits and French (freedom) toast, for the table." It was prepared quickly and just as I ordered it, especially my eggs. I ordered my hash browns fried on the grill, à la waffle house, and they were almost as good as those served at these hundreds of restaurants located primarily at interstate locations.

After enjoying every bite of my breakfast including several bites of the freedom toast, I left the rest of this breakfast dessert for the poor people in China. I hoped to find a blue-road church nearby, hoped that Bubba's meeting at 10:00 a.m. went well, and hoped I would see him again sometime. I am sure I could find him at Patsy's BBQ, where everybody but Grant surely knows his real name. And I'll bet they're always glad he came.

I left Patsy's at 10:15 a.m. and drove around to further investigate possible churches to attend. There were several old historic churches in the downtown area, but they were all Presbyterian, Methodist and Baptist and others, which I considered. But by 10:40 a.m. I decided to attend the Jesus Name Pentecostal Church, just about one block east of Highway 56 at the 70S By-Pass. It was on the eastern edge of a strip shopping center housing mostly local tenants and offices. The building was a traditional structure of red brick with white trim and a Baptist-like steeple. At 10:50 a.m. I entered the sanctuary which had two sections of pews with a center aisle. The oak pews could perhaps seat 200 people if they were willing to be very friendly.

The 12-foot walls were painted white up to the ceiling which was also white. The windows were a residential double-hung type and were covered by a sheet of rigid rippling plastic which was tinted yellow (giving the sanctuary a mild jaundiced tint). There was a Baptistery behind the pulpit area with a wallpaper type mural attempting to give the illusion of a waterfall flowing into the Baptistery.

When I first entered, a very young youth group was already singing, as if to "warm-up" for the service to begin. A young girl, perhaps five-years-old, had a microphone comfortably in her hand, and she was singing with great confidence the song's solo parts. In sort of a young Brenda Lee voice she sang, "I am a Christian, a mighty, mighty Christian." I could easily imagine that in 15 years she could burst onto the country music scene in Nashville, the new Dottie West. Her singing accompanied by pre-recorded music had a toe-tapping, hand-clapping beat to which most of the congregation rousingly responded.

The next song (also sung to an unprofessional quality tape) had yet another budding star singing the solo parts with confidence equal to the first soloist. This soloist was "much" older, however. He must have been seven-years-old, and I imagined that he could have been the brother of the young blooming Dottie West. He sang with full voice, "With my mouth I will praise the Lord, all day long," over and over again, and the congregation was simultaneously entertained and uplifted. In an orange T-shirt that hung down over his blue jeans, he was a truly future potential replacement for Alan Jackson. He even had a young Alan look and presence.

The pastor came back to the back pew, introduced himself and welcomed me to the service. He knew I was a visitor — I had on a sport jacket. He told me that another group would be singing a few songs. This was a group of about 15 teenagers all dressed in matching black T-shirts. They sang and danced a simple choreographed routine during which they would all take two steps right and clap and then two steps left and clap. The congregation got caught up in the syncopated rhythm of the song, moving and clapping along with this group who were obviously enjoying this time of doing their thing in the house of the Lord. They sang, "Shout with the voice of praise," and then another song in which a teenage girl with long blond hair and a white blouse sang the solo part, "My Jesus, my Savior. I sing for the joy and the glory of your name. Nothing can compare with the promise I have with you." All the while the pastor cheered them on shouting, "Praise God. Praise God. Thank you, Jesus."

The pastor said that he wanted us all to come back to church this evening because, "God gave me a message and gave me the illustrations to use. You need to hear this message tonight. The title God gave to me is 'The Trash Man.' " Then he said he wanted us all to give a "love offering" to our preacher this morning, and it was just at this moment that I became aware that we were not going to have a sermon from the pastor during this service. Well, anyhow, I gave my $5 before I heard the sermon from the guest preacher. I suppose I had faith that it would be worth the price Betty had put on all worship services we were attending this year. While the offering was being taken, the pastor led us in singing "Oh, how I love Jesus ...because He first loved me."

The pastor then got very serious and said to his congregation "Now we come to the most important part of this service — the preaching of the Word." He said that our visiting preacher was

317

bringing us a message from God and, "I don't want us running in and out of the church while our preacher is preaching today. Mommas get hold of your babies and let's keep them still, and let's pay attention to our guest preacher today."

The young preacher who wore an olive shirt and tie (but no coat) came to the pulpit and said he had enjoyed the volleyball yesterday and all the eating. He said, "When church people get together they just have to eat, and we have done a lot of it since I have been here." He complimented the singing and dancing of the young people. He said, "They do it and have fun in the bars so why not in church? Amen? Amen." The congregation agreed with him and said, "Amen. Praise God. Amen."

He then read the scripture from *Genesis 1: 1 – 3* and *II Corinthians 1: 3*. He prayed for God's guidance as he preached His word to His people. The scripture lesson was when God came to the Garden of Eden after Adam and Eve had sinned and God called for Adam. He said that God wanted to communicate with Adam, even though Adam had sinned against Him. This handsome young preacher, who appeared to be in his mid-30s, said that communication is necessary in any relationship. He noted that when Adam sinned he broke his relationship with God because Satan caused the rift. Satan put doubts in Adam's mind and caused the estrangement. But God came looking for Adam to re-establish communication.

This young preacher then noted that God was not obligated to come looking to reconcile with Adam. "When god called to Adam, it was out of mercy. When God speaks, mercy comes out." The visiting preacher said his sermon was titled, *When Mercy Speaks.* He pointed out that when Adam sinned we were all, as his descendants, a part of this sinfulness, and therefore we all deserve death. Therefore, if we receive salvation it is because of "God's mercy." The pastor sat behind the visiting preacher and cheered him along all the way with his "Amens" and "praise the Lord" and "you're right preacher."

The young preacher, encouraged by total vocal support from the congregation which followed their pastor as cheerleader, continued with his point that we owe everything to the mercy of God. "It is by the mercy of God that I am alive, that I can talk and pray and raise my hand as I do now. When God speaks cancer is healed, the alcoholic is healed," he declared. He said, "Mercy speaks and Lazarus was healed. Without mercy I am nobody." The preacher said that he had this message from God when he came yesterday, but God pointed out *Exodus 25: 17*. It is where God instructed the Hebrews to build a "mercy seat" with two cherubim who looked down on the gold mercy seat. They did not look at each other but looked instead at the mercy seat. The preacher inferred from this that "they did not see eye to eye, just as we don't always see eye to eye or we don't always agree, but we don't have to always agree, but we must always look at the mercy seat — look at the mercy of God."

The young preacher really struck a chord with the pastor when he said, "We must always look at the mercy and not at the fault of others." The pastor immediately jumped to his feet and said, "Yes, preacher, that's right brother. You're right on." An attractive and barefoot teenage mother with her newborn baby was walking in and out of the sanctuary during the sermon and the pastor's cheering. Other youngsters also were not kowtowing to the preacher's request that this activity not take place today, "out of respect for our visiting preacher."

The barefoot mother was on her way back to her seat as the youthful preacher concluded his sermon by saying, "How many people want mercy to be spoken here today? Someone here needs mercy today." The pastor then came to the pulpit to welcome any who wanted to come forward to pray for God's mercy. No one came, but the pastor said that two people were going to be baptized today and maybe there would be others who would want to join them. While the pastor got into his baptismal clothes, a soloist sang "Sometimes when we are weary we stumble and fall, but one drop of His blood covers it all."

While the two new believers were baptized, most of the congregation gathered near the baptismal pool in such a way that those of us in the pews could not see (sort of like when a Titan makes a touchdown). But we all knew full well when one was baptized by the applause and the "hallelujahs" echoing around the sanctuary. After both individuals had been baptized, the pastor returned once again wearing his pre-baptismal clothes and asked: "How many of you heard the word today? Let's go out and apply it to our lives." He then walked to the back of the church and unceremoniously said: "See you tonight. You are dismissed."

This pastor and champion cheerleader had dismissed us but fully expected us to be back at 6:00 p.m. that same night when he would deliver the sermon which he felt God had directly given him for all of us. I knew I would not be coming back because I would be back in Nashville. I was going to miss the message from the God of the universe about "The Trash Man." But this did remind me that I had to go load the trash up at our lake house and take it to the dump on my way home. Maybe God, in His own mysterious way, had spoken to me on the subject. Amen? Amen.

Chapter 32

Christ Episcopal Church Cathedral
Nashville, Tennessee
April 20, 2003

This was Easter Sunday, a triumphal day in all of Christendom when Christians around the world celebrate the resurrection of Christ from the grave after his crucifixion on dark Friday 2,003 years ago. While risking sacrilege by mentioning it in the same paragraph, I must say that it also was something of a triumphal day in the Browning household. Perhaps for the first time during our 50 years of marriage we were early in leaving before our designated time of departure. Easter Sunday played a major part in the victorious procession to our car on this 32nd of our *Fifty-two Sundays on the Blue Road*. Betty knew that if we were late for church this morning we might have to stand, and her two almost new artificial hips are real incentives for timeliness in such situations.

When our short celebratory procession ended at her little Lexus EX 3000 (which she almost worships) the chancel clock on her private mobile chapel read "8:27 a.m." She pointed at the three-minute lagniappe of time we would have this morning almost as proudly as Christ's disciples must have pointed at the empty tomb on their day of victory. Betty's choice of music for the pre-Easter service time in her mobile chapel was the sound track from Chicago. She can almost worship at the music and words of this dominant "Up with Women" theme, but it makes me a little nervous when women confess how they killed their significant others for such heinous offenses as popping their gum. I don't chew gum anymore.

The day was slightly overcast as we made our victory lap down Woodmont Boulevard. We had the streets practically to ourselves even when we were passing the Cathedral of the Incarnation when the early worshipers leaving the 7:00 a.m. mass made their way across Broadway on their way hopefully to a fine Easter brunch — somewhere.

I had decided that we would go to some larger church this morning to witness a larger number of people worshipping on the day which is the focal point of the Christian faith. Easter, as a matter of fact, is the reason that Christians worship on Sunday rather than on the "real" Sabbath of the seventh day on which the *Bible* tells us God rested after the six days of creation and commanded His followers to do likewise. After the resurrection of Christ, however, Christians began worshipping and resting on Sunday, or the first day of the week instead of the seventh day.

We wanted to hear the triumphal music of a large choir and a powerful organ which would more likely be found in a larger church. The Cathedral of the Incarnation was definitely a possibility, but we drove on toward downtown Nashville in search, first, of a place for breakfast. Betty suggested one of the downtown hotels as a likely place, and while the newly remodeled Hermitage Hotel was a possibility it was sadly not open for breakfast yet. On our way to checkout the Hermitage we passed the Christ Church Cathedral located at 900 Broadway. This is an old gothic Episcopal church with a deep rich history in the City of Nashville. We had been to a couple of special events here in the past, but never a worship service. And since we had not visited an Episcopal church yet on our "Fifty-two Sundays" tour, this one jumped to the top of the list. The search was not over, nor would it be, until we found a breakfast place and discussed our possible choices over breakfast.

Betty's mobile chapel with its supple leather chancel bucket seats moved on. We drove around and witnessed again the sleepy sidewalks as this Sunday morning slowly came down, but not as slowly as most Sundays, because Easter had brought out a few more denizens of the depths of downtown. Still, nothing much was open for business and until some restaurants, coffee shops and groceries open in this area, the residential character of downtown will languish. This is the chicken and the egg conundrum, however, because such businesses cannot open prosperously until the residents who look for these services have moved in.

The tour bus lines were in business. The Gray Line Tour buses were out at 9:00 a.m., and were where Vince Gill and Amy Grant would probably have been walking had they been downtown, and where the Titans would be playing, hopefully for their conference championship next fall. The tour bus drivers surely point out where the Nashville Sounds baseball team hopes the city fathers will see fit to build them a new home on the site of the present thermal plant — anything to keep the sound of silence out of the bus! The driver has a job to do, and on these early tours I am sure the first assignment is to keep the ticket holders awake. "And there's the Ryman Auditorium," he doubtlessly says, "birthplace of the Grand Ole Opry."

We followed a tour bus around James Robertson Parkway inside of which the driver probably droned on and on about the State Capitol being built in such-and-such year. And just about then I had an inspiration. We would get off this boring tour and go to the Farmers' Market located on Eighth Avenue within sight of the Capitol. "I am sure there will be something open for breakfast there," I said jubilantly to Betty. And I was right, but just barely.

At about 9:15 a.m. the food-court restaurants were just beginning to get ready for the lunch crowd. But someone in this place has to serve breakfast to these workers preparing for lunch, right? Right. And there it was — Magpie's Deli. And they had a large hanging banner announcing that all those who labor and are heavy-laden could rest a spell and have coffee and a biscuit sandwich before going back to preparing food for their very own customers (the ones they hoped would be coming in soon from their Easter Sunday services).

The Asian owner-worker was there promising that he could prepare anything to suit anyone's palate. And most of his customers were taking their food away in to-go boxes, probably back to their own booths. We ordered our usual breakfasts. For Betty, two eggs scrambled with bacon and biscuits. For me, three eggs over-easy/over-medium with country ham, hash browns and biscuits. And for the table, two pancakes. He said it would be a while. No problem. We had the Sunday *Tennessean* and our coffee. The sun was shinning beautifully. All was right with the world. So why fret?

This one-man operation was an energetic pleasant round-faced man, perhaps from Thailand. Our breakfasts came out seriatim. First was the table's order, the pancakes. Not just as we had planned, but, again, no problem — we would just eat our breakfast dessert first — one for Betty and one for me — large, light, and fluffy pancakes with one mini-tub of syrup for each one of us. We continued to read the paper.

Betty was reading about Vince Gill's ex-wife Janis who had recently married Roy Cummins, her handsome horse trainer and ten years her junior. She was making a musical comeback and an overall comeback from a devastating time in her life. She said that she was okay now. She now has about $10 million to spend without checking with Vince, and her five-year confidentiality agreement ends in June of this year. Oh, boy! Bet Vince and his new wife Amy Grant will be nervously reading all the tabloids then and, also, Janis has an autobiography coming out soon. Suppose anything written during the five-year quiet period but not released until after the five-year timeline will be exempt?

By now my order had arrived. My three eggs were easy/medium but not "over." They were cooked "sunny side up" but had been cooked with a lid over the cooking surface because the whites were done and the yellows runny just as the over-easy/over-medium order would have produced. The country ham was on the biscuit, but that was okay, too, but there was only one biscuit. Thankfully, it was perfectly baked with a delightful golden brown crust on both top and bottom. Finally, Betty's order came and it was obvious his method of scrambling left something to be desired — sort of bowl mixed then fried as a monolithic egg pie rather then scrambled or just cut into pieces. But everything was tasty, except the hash browns which did not come until the very end.

It was not until I was leaving that I saw that this young Asian had created a veritable Easter miracle by what he accomplished with what he had to work with. He was cooking our entire breakfast on a portable 10 by 12 inch residential type griddle/electric grill. This explained why our breakfast came out in a series rather than all together.

Between one of the breakfast courses, we read an article in the paper about the small country churches struggling to hold on. The featured church was the Beech Grove Community Cumberland Presbyterian Church, which now had only 30 members and no children. It was about in the same circumstance as the First Presbyterian Church in Clifton and the First Baptist Church of Charlotte. The Union Presbyterian Church in Belfast, Tennessee had only about 15 in church the Sunday we were there, but it is not struggling financially because of the $3 million they have in an endowment fund.

This article made me feel sort of guilty for choosing to go to a large Cathedral this morning instead of going to one of these small churches where our warm bodies would be more appreciated than our $5 contribution. But then the small ones are always so disappointed when they discover that we have not recently moved into their community, and are not prospects for membership since we are only visitors from the big city.

As we left the Farmers Market, we saw a biracial family sitting at the only other occupied table in the food court. The mother was white, the father was African-American, and the three young sons (ages from three to six) were a true mixture of the two parents. There was an African-American janitor walking around with a broom, a bottle of Windex and a roll of paper towels. We saved him some effort by being good "do-bees," and using some of Betty's hand cleaning liquid to clean off the sticky syrup residue on the table. I was embarrassed to leave our table in such a mess. It had looked like three little boys between the ages of three to six had just finished eating here, too.

I walked over to the Tennessee Bicentennial Mall located just next door. It was brightly lit by the fullness of this bright sunny day. This part of the mall gives a walking history of the state that greatly emphasizes the Civil War. Neither Betty nor I had been here before and we determined that we would return someday soon to make a leisurely visit.

Now on to church. The late service at the Cathedral was at 11:15 a.m. but Betty said we should get there at 10:45 a.m. in order to get a seat, what with her artificial hips and all. Then, too, I wanted to get my usual perch at the back right section so that I could observe the whole congregation. And so it shall be written that the Brownings entered this awe-inspiring cathedral at 10:45 a.m. and took their seats just where they wanted them as the sanctuary filled rapidly. The old handsome oak pews with their ornate extended pew ends, with carved oak clusters gave the impression that much time, money and planning had gone into every detail of this edifice.

This entire cathedral had been built to create a feeling of awe and expectation on the part of worshipers. The carved limestone and granite pillars create a sense of substance and strength, and they support the beautiful arched rich wood ceiling areas which flow from one area to another. Of special interest to me were intricately wood carved parts of the chancel area, together with the sculptured statues of saints and Biblical characters. There were numerous stained-glass windows throughout the cathedral, both at the pew level and high up in the arched ceiling area, and above the ornate carvings in the chancel area which was painted in a soft green pastoral color.

By 10:50 a.m. the cathedral was almost full, and the altar boys were finishing lighting the chancel candles. The congregation was a total mixture of young and old, trending toward the older. There was a wide variety of styles of dress from the very casual to the Sunday best of others. Some women even wore rubber thongs for shoes, and one nicely dressed man had on a tan suit with tan jogging shoes. Several women wore very stylish Easter bonnets. A tall slender, yet voluptuous, teenage girl sitting immediately in front of us had her stringy hair pulled up on top of her head and was dressed in a delightfully revealing tight black blouse and a low hip hugging blue skirt. She spent the entire service worshipping her teenage boyfriend who was dressed in Docker jeans, a checked blue and white shirt, and tennis shoes.

At 10:52 a.m. the brass section of several pieces began playing music before the service, which continued until the church bells started ringing at 11:07 a.m. And they continued to chime until 11:10 a.m. They were sort of frantically telling or warning us that something tragic or important had happened or was about to happen. This was not unlike the dinner bell which would ring on my Uncle Noah's farm in West Virginia when either some emergency needed attention or dinner was ready.

At 11:10 a.m. all the seats apparently were full and latecomers were scavenging for seats. At 11:15 a.m. the long procession began from a room to the right of the chancel. Some 75 to 100 choir members, altar boys and priests wound their way all the way to the back of the right aisle, across the right side of the back, and then up the middle aisle to the chancel. They were led by a tall gaunt verger dressed in a simple black robe over a burgundy vestment of some sort, and the altar boys were swinging canisters of burning incense which gave off a (to me) noxious odor.

There were several church leaders wearing priestly vestments of various degrees of ornateness. They were followed by the last one, the bishop, who wore the most regal vestments of white with gold trim in generous proportions. He wore a miter, or a pointed hat, of white and gold and carried a silver shepherd's crook or crosier which he touched to the floor as a cane as he proceeded to the chancel.

The tall thin verger in the black robe acted as sort of a floor manager or director of the service. He moved about the chancel area ushering the chancel participants to their appointed places. With at least 75 participants in the pageantry this simple vested verger, who is a trained layman, may well have been the single most important person in this service. Each of the others only had to do his one or two things. It was the verger's responsibility to see that everyone was at the right place at the right time. He was to this service what a director is to a movie or a stage production.

After the verger had all the chancel participants safely on their marks or in their proper places, the 50+ voice choir led the congregation in singing *Hymn No. 175, Hail Thee, Festival Day*, of which the refrain was "Hail Thee festival day! Blessed day that art hallowed forever, day whereon Christ arose, breaking the kingdom of death."

Following this hymn there was the singing of the *Gloria* followed by the "Collect of the Day," a prayer read from the *Book of Common Prayer*, page 222.

Next on the order of worship, the scripture lesson was read by a female layperson from *Acts 10: 34 – 43* followed by a hymn printed in the multi-paged order of worship. Then a priest read from Paul's letter to the *Colossians 3: 1 – 4* and then another hymn from Page 207, "Jesus Christ Is Risen Today, Alleluia."

At this point the Bishop of the Diocese of Tennessee, The Right Reverend Bertram N. Herlong, and a group of chancel participants, ceremoniously proceeded down to the middle of the center aisle and read the Gospel from *Mark 16: 1 – 8* which gives the account of the resurrection by "Mary Magdalene, and Mary the mother of James and Salome" after which this group proceeded back to the chancel.

The bishop then went to the pulpit for the sermon. As bishop he is the senior priest at all Episcopal churches in his diocese and, as such, gave the sermon and was the celebrant of the Eucharist for this service. His first words were *That's Impossible*, the title of his sermon. He said that everyone, even Peter said, "That's impossible," referring to the idea that Jesus (who was crucified and then buried) rose again from the dead. "Yet," he said, "This is what all Christians believe." The bishop continued, "Some say that Jesus was sort of a divine secret, and he pulled it off." But this minister said this was not the case. God actually sent His son to actually die. He was saying that this fact affirms Jesus' true human nature, that it was not some sort of charade that Jesus died and was buried.

The bishop said that if Jesus did not really suffer it would mean that, "The Christian life would be beyond living." He emphasized that, "He became like we are, so that we, through His grace might become like Him. Jesus did not come to tell us to do what is humanly impossible." He said that Jesus told us to go the second mile, to turn the other cheek and to "love one another as I have loved you." He then told a story of when, as a young priest, he was a chaplain in a parochial school. He was talking to a student who had gotten himself into some difficulty when the future bishop asked the student, "What do you think Jesus would do?" to which the boy in trouble answered, "Sir, Jesus would never have gotten Himself into a mess like this."

The bishop continued his sermon by declaring that the church is the continuation of the resurrection. He said: "A new life with possibilities of a life through grace is like to that of Jesus Himself. God's love will strengthen, empower, and enable us to follow Him." He continued his brief but pithy sermon by emphasizing that if the resurrection is possible, then truth is possible and a creative and loving community is possible. He told us that onetime in his early ministry he was crossing a new bridge early in the morning and when he got to the top and broke out of the mist, he saw the light on the other side. He said this gave him a glimpse of how God's light breaks through to us. He concluded by saying, "Crossing God's bridge is not going from life to death. It is going from life to life. Jesus did it, and when He did, he made the impossible possible for us."

After the sermon the congregation read the *Nicene Creed* which is to me the theological equivalent of the *Apostles' Creed,* which is used frequently in many Christian churches. It was followed by "The Peace" in the order of worship, during which time all visitors were welcomed by those around them. Then the priest during this part of the service welcomed the bishop who had given the sermon this morning. He also told us about the fabulous new pipe organ which would take eight to ten weeks of "tuning up" before it could officially be used in the worship services this fall. He called for the offering at this time and Betty brought forth her $5. I thought either we should give much more to help pay for this very expensive church and the new organ or nothing at all since any church which was obviously this wealthy did not need our money. Of course we compromised and placed the $5 in the plate while self-consciously trying to hide the niggardly denomination which we contribute to this act of worship.

This was followed by "The Holy Communion" as printed in the order of worship. After several readings of the liturgy for the Eucharist, the priest prayed a long liturgical prayer which ended with prayers for members of the congregation (called by name) who were ill, for our nation and for the members of our armed forces, and for "all who have died in the peace of Christ, and those whose faith is known to you alone." This was followed by the *Lord's Prayer* which says in part, "Forgive us our sins as we forgive those who sin against us."

The order of worship instructed all who wished to receive Holy Communion to proceed at the instructions of the ushers up the center aisle to the altar where they were asked to either stand or kneel. All the communicants drank from the common cup as they participated in this service of communion. The Episcopal Church differs in their beliefs at this point from those of the Catholic Church. The Catholic dogma is that at the time of consecration by the priest the bread and the wine miraculously are transported into the actual body and blood of Christ, while maintaining their appearance only of bread and wine. This dogma is called transubstantiation. The Episcopalians and Lutherans believe in consubstantiation which means that the bread and the wine contain the substantial presence of the body and blood of Christ, while physically remaining bread and wine. Other Christians think of the bread and wine as symbols of the body and blood of Christ which they use to remember the sacrifice of Christ's body and blood for the sins of mankind.

As the communion service was proceeding, Betty and I saw it was now 12:30 p.m. At the rate this service was going it would not be concluded before 1:00 p.m. and I had a tee time with my regular golf group at 1:40 p.m. The question "What would Jesus do?" was being squarely put to me. Of course, my first answer was that Jesus would never have gotten himself into a mess like this in the first place. Okay, but now that I was in it what do I do? I decided that the righteous thing would be to keep my promise to be on the tee at 1:40 p.m. And so it was.

After the golf game was over, I had grounds to believe that I made the wrong decision. I lost about $10 each to Jim Neal and John Seigenthaler. Had God punished me for ditching before the communion service was over? Surely God would not do that for a measly $20 bucks, especially since John and Jim apparently had not gone to church at all this day.

Maybe the answer to this question can be found in the scripture which says that God would rather we be cold or hot for in His word if we are lukewarm God says, "I will spew you out of my mouth." Maybe Jim and John were cold for not going, but I was lukewarm in the eyes of God for going to church but not fully participating until the very end. It doesn't seem right, now does it? But if God is God, He can make the rules anyway that pleases Him. Anyhow, I don't like it. I don't know whether to enter my protest to God for the spewing thing, or to take my complaint directly to Jim and John for getting five strokes from me for each nine at Richland and who (in addition) had turned God against me for missing only a few minutes of a worship service which had already been winding down anyhow.

Maybe I am just being paranoid. But please pray for me just in case it's God and me and the lukewarm thing. Maybe we should try giving $10 next Sunday. I'll discuss it with Betty. Maybe an extra $5 bucks could save me $20 in my next golf match.

Chapter 33

Church of God of Prophecy
Gallatin, Tennessee
April 27, 2003

*T*he clock in Betty's car (a.k.a., her mobile sanctuary) read 8:30 a.m. on the dot when Betty and I got into it this morning. For me, it was the perfect beginning to what promised to be a great day. In actuality, I thought, the day might turn out to be a total mess, but at least it was beginning just right. We had agreed the night before to leave at 8:30 a.m., and here we were sliding into the supple leather bucket seats of Betty's traveling temple to begin our period of mobile meditation on a timely basis. The reading of 8:30 a.m. on her chancel time-metering mechanism was like a vocalist getting in tune through the use of a pitch pipe before singing. Golfers believe that they can't par every hole unless they par the first one. Leaving at 8:30 a.m. on the dot started us out in tune; and we, therefore, parred the first hole of the day's course.

My old golfing friend, Ray Danner, is known for his promptness. And when I say promptness I mean right on time, every time. Always. Every time. Precisely punctual — never early, never late. If the tee time is 8:30 a.m., he will be standing on the tee, his driver in hand and a ball on a tee, ready for his first shot at 8:30 a.m. Not 8:29 a.m. And not at 8:31 a.m. He was the very busy chief executive officer of a company that operated several hundred restaurants, and he was known for saying, "Boys, it's wasteful to be early, and it's disrespectful to be late," as he nervously addressed his golf ball at the appointed time. Every time.

Ray is always nervous, too. He always wants to play a perfect game, and for him that means starting on time, parring every hole and finishing on time. I always feel like I am a little more of a realist than Ray because of my knowledge that any golf game I play will be played with many imperfections. Therefore, it is never quite the disappointment to me when a few errant shots occur during a round. But Ray never can accept anything but perfection. That's probably the reason that he is a very, very wealthy man, and I am not. He drives himself as relentlessly in everything as he does in golf.

One day, as Ray was playing on the old Richland course in Nashville, he hit an errant shot into the water on a par three, which had a wrought iron railing on a bridge crossing a stream that fed the lake in front of the green. Swept up in great anger after having missed the shot, this diminutive determined golfer forthwith proceeded to the bridge. With tremendous force, he slammed his rebellious six iron across the wrought iron railing — which, of course, broke the iron and propelled the shard of the shaft completely through his right leg. Needless to say (as I proceed to do precisely that), that particular day did not turn out to be a perfect day for Ray. You can rest assured, though, that it started out perfectly on time.

When we began this 33rd Sunday morning on the blue road precisely at 8:30 a.m, I knew Ray would be very proud of us. It was up to us to avoid hitting any errant shots and, to avoid by all means, "breaking any clubs in a fit of anger." If we did, we would jump back very quickly as we swung. For our blue roading choice of the day, we swung onto Woodmont Boulevard and then turned east onto Harding Road to head toward Hermitage Avenue and Lebanon Road.

The sun was shining beautifully, and it was obviously beckoning to many Nashvillians at a relatively early hour for even a Sunday morning. Betty's early morning devotional minutes were spent listening to the soundtrack of "Chicago" again, her pitch pipe for getting tuned up every morning. I used the cell phone to talk with my afternoon golfing partners, being sure that they were mindful of my Ray Danner type admonition to be timely for our 1:50 p.m. tee time.

We leisurely drove out Lebanon Road in a relaxed blue roading mood. After all, we were leaving on time and had no need to rush — benefits of Ray's requirement already. Shortly after crossing the Wilson County line, we turned north onto Highway 109 which leads to Old Hickory Lake and, eventually, to Gallatin. Soon after we crossed a bridge over the neck of the Cumberland River and Old Hickory Lake, we were inside the Gallatin city limits and began to look for a good breakfast place that would help us keep the beautiful day in tune.

We passed an intersection leading to a Jehovah's Witness Church and recognized it as a possibility for us. Their "public talk" began at 10:30 a.m. I was eager to find out why they refer to what others refer to as a "sermon" as a "public talk." We were to attend our 33rd church today. There were only 19 left as we began the countdown toward No. 52. Fifty-two different churches in one year. That might be a record. Suppose Guiness has a list of any such things as this?

During the countdown I wanted to attend as many different places of worship as I could and Jehovah's Witness would certainly be one of them. Maybe today. But, again, first things first. Don't sing out of tune. We needed to find a breakfast place, and we did. We passed the Church of God of Prophecy on our left as we headed toward the town square of Gallatin. Soon after, we found the Three Sisters Family Restaurant located at 207 South Water Avenue, about a block off the square. It was now 9:40 a.m. The service at the Church of God of Prophecy, we noted, was at 10:45 a.m. We had not been to a church of this denomination. We could spend a leisurely 40 to 50 minutes eating breakfast and still make the 10:45 a.m. service. Both decisions were made just that simply, just at that moment.

We entered the Three Sisters at 10:42 a.m. and seated ourselves at the first table on the right, which gave us a panoramic view of this "meat'n'three" family restaurant. The restaurant obviously catered to the working people near the town center. They opened at 4:30 a.m. and close at 2:30 p.m., figuring most of the town square people would be headed home to this county's burbs soon thereafter. This was a true blue road restaurant, even though it catered to the "city folk" of Gallatin for the most part. It catered to their blue road, country-cookin' appetites. After all, Gallatin is a country town, and proud of it. And the Three Sisters contributes to Gallatin's country roots and the pride taken therein.

This restaurant was started about twenty years ago by (You guessed it!) three sisters according to our friendly waitress, Rene. She was thirty-years-old, the mother of a seven-year-old son, and lived about 12 miles away in the small community of Bethpage. She was a wealth of information and talked freely with us between fresh coffee refills, smacks of gum between her teeth, and her easy smile. She told us that one of the three sisters had died. One of the surviving sisters was on the premises but not actually at work. She was just having breakfast on the way to church. She worked four days a week, while the other living sister worked one day each week.

One couple eating as we entered caught my attention. They were both smoking, as most of the patrons were. The wife was demure and attractive, but the husband was tough looking. He wore very dark glasses, a ball cap, and a ponytail protruding through the hole created by the cap and its adjustable strap. He looked like he could be mean, but he may have only been sad. He was trying to make some type of statement to the world which his wife was not involved in. She appeared to be just going along to get along.

Betty ordered two eggs scrambled with bacon and wheat toast. I ordered three eggs over-easy/over-medium, country ham, grits, biscuits, and French toast for the table. Also, coffee for both of us — decaffeinated, of course. After all, we are both 71 years of age. Our eggs were cooked just as ordered, and the country ham was succulent and tender. But the biscuits were wilted. The cook in the restaurant didn't look like an S.S. trooper Nazi, but he had access to a nuke machine or my name is not Ulysses Grant Browning. He looked like a good ol' boy. But you can never tell. He may be a member of a neo-Nazi group that is hoarding machines of mass destruction for biscuits everywhere.

Across from us sat a character. A woman in a pink dress who was reading a paperback novel was wearing glasses and hanging a cigarette from her lips in a "go-to-Hell" fashion. Her hard image softened considerably a few minutes later when a person we thought might be her daughter joined her. At that point, her cigarette was suitably placed between her two forefingers like a proper lady and the seamy paperback was shuffled out of sight to her lap.

Another couple sat with their backs to the front window with their faces toward the middle of the room. They were both attractive and in their early 40s, but looked as if they felt twenty years older after what was probably a hard living Saturday night. Soon another couple joined the original Saturday night revelers. The new breakfasters appeared to have barely made it. By the way all four were dragging heavily on their cigarettes, it seemed as if they were desperately attempting to jumpstart their metabolic systems and cast off the Saturday night demons.

At a table up front an attractive trim-looking, left-handed

brunette young woman sat with a handsome son who appeared to be about four-years-old. I always have great sympathy for young people who are divorced and are setting out in the world to make it on their own — especially when there is a child involved. Therefore, I decided that she was not divorced at all but was just taking her nephew out for a Sunday breakfast. Her sister was working at Wal-Mart this morning and her sister's husband was in the Marines serving a tour of duty in Iraq. And he's coming home soon; they just got word that he would be home in two weeks. He would be just in time for the wedding of his son's attractive and attentive aunt, a woman who took valuable time off from planning her wedding in order to entertain her nephew who plans to be a Marine like his father when he grows up. Now, I feel better about the situation. I hope you do, too.

In the middle of the room there seemed to be a community table. At that table, our gum-smacking informant told us, the regulars hold court from the minute the restaurant opens at 4:30 a.m. until closing time at 2:30 p.m. A few minutes after we arrived, an attractive and tall couple left this insiders' table while a short garrulous black man in a white T-shirt and a white painter's cap postulated some idea that he felt all in the restaurant needed to hear. And we did, but just barely. I could not quite hear all that he was saying, and I felt I should stand up and say, "Shorty, would you please repeat that? I could not hear what you were saying because of the popping of Rene's gum," because I knew he intended everyone in the house both to hear what he was saying and to agree with him. Our informer told us that Shorty came in several times a day to vacuum the carpet and do a little general cleaning. When he does, he does not pay for his breakfast. She said that if he comes in the morning and pays the cashier for his breakfast, they know he will not be coming back to clean again that day. When he has another job to do on that particular day, nothing needs to be said. He just pays for his breakfast and they know. Shorty paid for his breakfast as he left today. Goodbye, Shorty. See you tomorrow.

After Shorty left, there were only two men left at the community table and the conversation ceased. I don't know if they did not like each other or if they didn't know each other, but not a word was spoken until two others came to the table and began the party anew.

The two non-talkers were animatedly engrossed in everything being discussed from that point on. They were going strong when I gave Rene a $20 bill and told her to keep the change from a $14.35 check. Five dollars and 65 cents ($5.65) went to my undercover agent who masquerades as a waitress at the Three Sisters. I'll share my informant with you if you need to know any dirt on the politicians who eat lunch there every day. You know, who's doing whom in county government. "Me and Rene" are a real team. She tells it, and I write it. But that's another book — the paperback kind that the smoker in the pink dress was reading before her daughter came in. The working title is the "Three Sisters of Sumner County."

At 10:25 a.m. we left the inspiration for my next literary work and directed our blue road mobile sanctuary southward a few blocks to the Church of God of Prophecy. As we entered into this stationary place of worship, we were met by Howie Cantrell, a friendly hospitality greeter who said: "Make yourself to home. And I mean that in every respect." And we did by claiming our rightful place at the far right part of the very back pew. From that location I could see the whole congregation of about 90 to a 100 souls today. Last Sunday there had been 126 worshipers for Easter Sunday according to the bulletin given to us by friendly Howie as we entered. The bulletin also identified the pastor as Gary L. Riley.

The church was a smallish, traditional Baptist-looking edifice. It sort of partially shared a parking lot with a commercial facility next door, but hopefully not for long because, as the pastor would say later in the service, "The Lord is blessing us and helping us expand our parking lot this very week. Glory be to God. Amen? Amen."

Soon after we were seated, the pastor's wife came to welcome us and she was followed very soon by Pastor Riley, who was greeting practically everyone person by person as he worked his way back to us. Lastly, a handsome young black man in a beautifully tailored sport coat and tie came to welcome us to the service. We came to sense that he was sort of an assistant pastor from the active part he played in the service.

The sanctuary was neat, clean and decorated simply with white 12-foot ceilings and walls of white down to the four-foot Luan paneling wainscoting which circled the rectangular room. The carpet and the seat pads were of a matching light blue. There were eight colonial residential-sized chandeliers with teardrop light bulbs in each one. Around the walls were banners of different colors between the mini-blind windows. Some of them read, "Jesus Is Lord," "Praise Jesus," "Lift Up The Name of Jesus," "Lord of Lords," "King of Kings," and "Worthy is the Lamb."

Pastor Riley had answered my question as to the origin of the word "Prophecy" in the church's name by telling me that it had been added to the church's name in 1923 after the "regular" Church of God and this group parted ways over some minor points of church polity.

A woman in a red dress unceremoniously went to the pulpit area and said, "I think we'll take the offering first." Good idea, in case someone leaves early. Then she read the scripture lesson from *Matthew Chapter 16* starting at *Verse 15* where Jesus asked Peter, "Whom do men say that I am?" Peter then answered, "Thou art Christ, the Son of the living God." Then Jesus said, "Blessed art thou ...Peter, for upon this rock will I build my church." She read this scripture in a flat rural Tennessee voice, but with clarity and conviction. Afterwards, she made a commentary on this scripture and her belief that Jesus was coming back soon.

When she left the pulpit area, the keyboard player took the lead of the service, backed up by the organist, drummer, electric guitar and the left-handed pastor also playing a guitar. The other members of the "Praise Team" were three women singers and the handsome, nattily dressed African-American singing with the three women. The loquacious keyboard player easily took the lead by saying, "Good mornin'. How y'all doin'?" He then asked us all to stand up and shake someone's hand which sort of intimidated us into shaking every hand around us within shaking distance.

The praise leader then led the congregation in a spirited singing of "God Is Good," which was repeated over and over for about five minutes and was accompanied by shouting and clapping. Several members of the congregation had tambourines whose jingling added to the rhythm of the singing. The next song was *Victory In Jesus* which also lasted for about five minutes. It started with the words, "I heard an old, old story how my Savior came from glory. How he gave His life on Calvary to save a wretch like me...He sought me and bought me with His redeeming blood."

The praise leader gave a sermonette between each song in an

endeavor to keep the spirit of the congregation building. After *Victory In Jesus* he said, "I got the victory. Devil you don't got the victory. I got the victory through the blood of Jesus." "Hallelujah. Hallelujah.Hallelujah.Praise the Lord," from all over the congregation during the breaks between the songs. The next song was *Nothing But The Blood of Jesus*, "No other fount I know, nothing but the blood of Jesus," again repeated over and over. "Hallelujah. Hallelujah. Yes, Lord. Yes, Lord," was heard as the song wound down.

The words "Holy, Holy, Holy" were flashed on a large screen over the pulpit as the congregation began singing "Holy, Holy, Holy is the Lord God Almighty. Praise Him, praise Him, praise Him." Then they sang "Holy Lord, Holy Lord are you." He said that Isaiah had a vision of angels crying out, "Holy Lord, Holy Lord." He also said, "If the angels who fly about and do all kinds of cool stuff and a lot of other things I don't know about, how much more we should especially sing, 'Holy Lord. Holy Lord.' "

The response to this song, in the words of the pastor, was "Thank you, Jesus. Thank you, Jesus." And it was repeated by many in the congregation, over and over. The praise leader asked us all to, "Close your eyes and raise your hands and promise to give your all."

At 10:25 a.m. the pastor came to the pulpit for the first time and said, "Aren't you glad you came to the house of the Lord today? Aren't you glad that we can come to give something back to the Lord today instead of just asking for God to keep doing something for us?" Next, the pastor dismissed the children to their children's worship and gave a sermonette on how important this time is in the life of the children because it is a time during which the spirit of God can move into their lives to make them into His true children. "We have a good group of children. Amen? Amen," the pastor said. He then welcomed everyone to this service, "We're glad you came. Amen? Amen. Praise the Lord."

The pastor then invited Sharon and Lee forward to dedicate their new child, Bethany, to the Lord. He talked for several minutes about the value of parents recognizing the need to start their children out right in the church. He invited the grandparents and the two sisters of Bethany forward. This pastor then read some scripture about how Hannah had Solomon and dedicated him to the Lord. He spent several more minutes talking about this to the congregation and to the family in front of him. He continued until about 11:55 a.m. with the dedication service. Next he gave a pink rose to the mother and explained the meaning behind the rose color, a red rose to the father and explained the meaning of a red rose, and a white rose to Bethany and spoke about the symbolic purity and innocence of the white rose.

Finally, this dedication service of about 25 minutes began to come to an end; it was just about noon and the sermon had not even begun yet. Betty looked at me sympathetically with regard to the looming encroachment upon my afternoon tee time. It seemed as if the pastor was paying no attention to the clock. He seemed to be ponderously repeating dedication ideas over and over. We could not figure out what was going on. Why was the pastor going on and on, over and over the same thoughts? He prayed a long prayer for everyone in the family and then, finally, he took Bethany into his arms. If Bethany had not started crying, we would have still been there at 10:00 p.m. on Monday night (the point in time that I am writing these words).

After the applause at the end of the dedication, he said, "I know the time is late this morning, but this is not wasted time. This is not wasted time. All life is precious unto the Lord. I believe that life begins at conception. Not just when the baby comes out of the womb. Amen? Amen...Now we're not going to go into a message this morning." And there it was — the word we were waiting for. The pastor was not going to give a sermon this morning. But he did invite us to come to the church that evening for a service during which he was going to have a program and video on the tribulation.

After mentioning several requests for prayer, the pastor offered a short prayer and concluded the service. He made a floor mistake by not telling the congregation that there would be no sermon. I am sure that people would have gotten more out of the several sermonettes during the dedication service had we known that, indeed, they would be his day's sermon. It seemed to me that the pastor knew all along that he had prepared no sermon this morning and was stretching the other parts of the service to fill the time. It was not "wasted time," as the pastor said, it was just stretched time. And that's okay.

But me thinks the pastor planned no sermon for today. A wise man once said, "Blessed is the man, who, having nothing to say, refrains from giving the world evidence of this fact." At the least, the pastor had nothing else to say this morning, but he provided us with abundant evidence of this by "playing the clock" and stretching a potentially beautiful five-minute child dedication service into 30 minutes. He even got into a mini-sermonette against abortion.

Midway through the dedication service, I thought I was going to fly right into the face of Ray Danner's saying — "It's wasteful to be early and disrespectful to be late." Although I was not going to be early for my tee time, I was in real danger of being late. It might have been better if I had been late. I ended up losing another $15 to my golfing friends. Friends? With friends like this, who needs enemies? Amen? Amen.

Chapter 34

First Church of Christ Scientist
Nashville, Tennessee
May 4, 2003

y golfing group had dinner last evening at Richland
Country Club after we had played golf in a foursome,
Frank and I against Jim and John. Frank and I won eight
bucks each from our opponents, and we waited patiently to collect
our $8 until we could have all our wives witness the ceremony and
the crossing of our palms with the booty. The dinner party also
included Gil Merritt, who had just recently taken senior status as a
Federal Appeals Court judge, and his wife Robin — partially
because it was Diane Neal's birthday. It was just another excuse to
get together, celebrate and talk big.

We talked really big during this evening together because Gil
was leaving the next day for Iraq. He had been tapped by the Bush
administration to head up a group of legal scholars and lawyers
which had been assigned the formation of a temporary legal system
for the transition period in Iraq and which, hopefully, might be the
launching pad for a permanent judiciary system. So, we were talking
big about our friend's big assignment, celebrating Diane's birthday,
honoring today's golf champions, and bemoaning that golf on
Sunday seemed unlikely because of threatening rain and that
Baghdad had no golf courses at all. Saddam must have been a very
high handicapper. Maybe we could find an oasis in Saudi Arabia
where some Saudi prince had performed a Muslim miracle by
changing oil into water — at least enough to water a Jack Nicklaus
designed golf course. Gill would find one if there was one within
flying range of his single engine plane.

When Betty and I got up Sunday morning to go blue roading,
the weather, indeed, was threatening. There was no actual rain yet
though so our Sunday golf game was on hold. We would wait and
see after church what the weather was like. At 8:30 a.m. we still

had not left for our Sunday trek. Betty had gone back to sleep and had not gotten up until 8:00 a.m. this morning. But a Sunday miracle happened. She was ready and in the car at 8:38 a.m. We were on our way — the 38-minute miracle! And Betty thought it could never be done. She looked great; maybe better than she looks when she spends two hours getting ready.

Up until today I had just sort of meandered around Middle Tennessee for the most part and found the churches we had visited, many times by sheer accident as we relaxed our way around in Betty's chapel on wheels. But now I was faced with another blue-road conundrum. Was I to just keep slithering around the hills and valleys in this area visiting churches as I found them? To do so meant giving up, at least partially, on my goal of as much diversity as I could find during the remaining approximately one-third of my projected 52 different churches in as many Sundays on the blue road. The conflict in my mind was the choice between spontaneity and diversity. I was just then deciding to bend a little more than I had intended at the beginning by starting to pre-select as many different churches in the remaining one-third of the balance of the year as possible. This would dilute some of the "no destination" rule of blue roading, but it would give us an opportunity to observe a greater variety of religious worship services in this area.

Betty and I traveled east on Woodmont Boulevard and then turned north onto Hillsboro Road, passing the Christian Scientist Church on Hillsboro Road near Interstate 440. When we passed this church at about 8:42 a.m., we noticed that worship services would start at 10:30 a.m. and that there was a lonesome black Jeep sitting in their parking lot — the only car there. I drive a Jeep — a 1990 Cherokee Loredo. It is thirteen-years-old now, and I'm going to try for twenty-six. Some of my friends have accused me of some sort of reverse snobbery for driving such an old car, but the truth is closer to the fact that I'm a tight wad when it comes to cars. I hate to buy new cars. Maybe it was the lonely Jeep at the Christian Scientist Church parking lot that sealed the deal, but I sort of decided then and there that this would be the church we would attend today. I had determined back in the deep recesses of my mind that I wanted to visit a Christian Scientist church during this year and realized this might be my best chance.

But "for the nonce," as my friend Jim Neal would say, we would just wander around the back streets of Nashville in search of a blue road restaurant. We drove on in toward town on Hillsboro Road and turned onto what was known as 16th Avenue South before it was changed to Music Row East as some sort of sop to the country music industry which always claimed that the Nashville city fathers had treated the industry as a "red-haired stepchild"from the beginning. Naming 16th and 17th avenues as "Music Rows" had not revived the spirit of the country music industry. But it had raised my spirits high enough for my partners and me to build the multi-storied City Executive Building (now called The United Artists Tower) in this area many years ago in an attempt to ride the crest of the new wave of music-city pride. The wave never developed for us, and this misjudgment of the tides almost washed us out. Even though this building, after a succession of owners, is now apparently experiencing smooth sailing, it sends a cold chill up my spine to realize that it almost caused my economic ship to rest in Davey Jones' locker.

But today we sailed smoothly on toward a rendezvous with some blue road restaurant. We passed the location of the once very successful Shoney's Restaurant on Demonbreum Street whose former owners were all now casting their nets in other waters around the world. But slowly out of the ashes another restaurant was emerging and serving breakfast, recycling the building after several years of vacancy. Another day I wanted to try this new restaurant to see if the new operators could make this location work since the Country Music Hall of Fame moved to their new site downtown. But not today.

We drove on toward downtown on Broadway and turned south onto First Avenue which becomes Hermitage Avenue within the distance of a few blocks. Near the beginning of Hermitage Avenue we saw the Hermitage Café which is near the old General Hospital. It is a nondescript, open looking café with lots of window space. We decided that our search was over for today and so we went in with considerable trepidation on Betty's part. She wasn't sure but what this might be a coke-in-the-bottle (with a straw, please) kind of a spot.

Country music was blasting as we entered and continued for most of the time we were having breakfast.The layout was just like a Waffle House Restaurant, with the breakfast bar separating the open cooking area from the single row of tables all along the window-walls. The cooks wore neat white chef's coats and hats, and the place looked generally clean except for the carpeted floor, which was...not appetizing. Because of this Betty considered the coke for breakfast idea, which she had inherited from her mother when she was not so sure about the cleanliness of a restaurant. But after a few minutes her stomach and mind became coordinated enough to allow her to order a ham-and-cheese omelet with home fries and wheat toast.

I ordered, without trepidation, the special for today — country-fried steak with gravy, three eggs over-easy/over-medium with biscuits. With regard to my egg order, our worldly wise, peroxide blond waitress gave me an "I know what you mean" nod of her frizzy-haired head. She gave the impression that she would be more comfortable serving drinks in some tough bar than she was serving specially ordered eggs to some not-too-hip Sunday morning breakfasters.

Our waitress, with yesterday's blue eye shadow, was dressed in a red smock-like waitress shirt which covered a multitude of sins, or more accurately, the results of sins of pleasure such as a bulging tummy and rippling love handles. And she looked as if she could hold her own, and indeed she may have, in a rough barroom brawl caused by a missed drink order or in a café where some customer's eggs had not been cooked perfectly to order. I made up my mind early not to complain at all about anything this morning. Know what I mean?

As we patiently waited for our breakfasts to arrive, we saw this establishment's wall of fame which consisted of 20 to 30 auto-graphed pictures of country music photographs, including Goober, Waylon Jennings, Lori Morgan, George Jones, Brenda Lee and Verne Gosdin. Our warden/waitress would stop every time she passed her workstation at the counter/bar for a long, deep drag on her coffin nails. A man sitting next to Gertrude (my derivative name for our waitress) wore a three day old T-shirt with "Cope" emblazed across the back that rode up his back like a defective window shade to reveal a grizzly and hairy back every time he bent forward for a large bite of sausage and gravy. I could sense that, with every bite of breakfast our "Coping" blue boy took that resulted in this shade action, Betty wished a new wish that she had ordered a Coke with a straw.

Our breakfast came before Betty was able to change her order for which I was grateful. I think I was justifiably afraid of what Gertrude might say or even do in response to any act of dissatisfaction from anyone in her bar. As it turned out, Betty enjoyed her breakfast for which I was very grateful. I don't know if she had the proper respect for what I perceived of Gertrude's propensities. I am not so sure it was fear of Gertrude, or if my breakfast was actually good. Guess I'll never really know, but I thought my eggs were perfect, probably just because the cook feared not cooking the three eggs just as Gertrude had ordered them. And the potatoes were great! They were prepared by peeling the potatoes and boiling them and refrigerating them before being sliced very thin on the large blade of a grater. The potatoes were then fried in oil on a hot grill. But don't try this at home. These people are professionals.

While we trembled in fear of offending Gertrude as we ate, we saw a young couple eating at a small table located in the front left area of the restaurant. We surmised that they were new sophisticated urbanites who make their digs in the new in-town loft apartments and condos, just like in the big grownup cities. After the young couple left, one of the cooks said that they came every Sunday and sat at the same table. "They never come on Saturday or any other day — just Sunday," the cook observed. Building a tradition, I thought. The beginning of a story to tell their grandkids: "When we moved into our tiny loft apartment back in '03 we had to practically, but gently, move the sleeping street people off their cardboard mattresses in front of our warehouse loft to make our way to the Hermitage Café. We went there every Sunday for 56 years, every Sunday, only on Sunday. And we sat at the same table. Not really because we wanted to but because we thought Gertrude, our blond bombshell waitress for 17 years, told us to sit there. We were afraid to try to sit anywhere else. By the time Gertrude retired, we had already established this as part of our tradition. And we always ordered the same thing. Tim ordered..." as they continued ad infinitum telling of their Hermitage Café tradition to anyone who would listen. And we were there early to witness its beginnings.

A sign at the front in the serving area read:"No self service. No exceptions." It was obviously put there by Gertrude. Nobody, but nobody, was to mess around in her domain.As we prepared to leave after paying our bill, we left a larger than normal tip, partially out of appreciation for Gertrude's exceptionally good service and partially out of fear that if we did not, she would follow us to the car, jerk me out and rip my liver out.

Before going to our car, I, with great trepidation, asked Gertrude if they had a restroom. She pointed to a door which read, "Out of Order." She said, "But it ain't out of order." Betty and I used this surprisingly clean facility (only one, unisexual). It was then that we realized that somehow we had been accepted into the club. It was probably because we were clean and dressed for church that our verbal application had been accepted. I felt if I had come in dressed as I dress on other days the "Out-of-Order" sign would have applied to me, and I would have had to seek healing for a burst bladder at the Christian Science Church we were going to attend. I would love to hear the story of when the young, tradition building couple was first told that the facilities "Ain't out of order."

With great relief for both our urinary systems and for feeling that Gertrude's acceptance of us meant she would not be following us to the car in order to berate the character of our dearly departed mothers because our tip was a piece of something we would not want in our hands let alone our mouths, we continued our Sunday morning blue roading. I wanted to see if the black Jeep was still parked in the parking lot of the Christian Science Church. It was and that made me feel sort of at home. Any little thing helps when you are going into an unfamiliar setting.

At 10:25 a.m. Betty and I entered the First Church of Christ, Scientist, (the official name of Christian Science Churches) located at 2911 Hillsboro Road. This red brick church with its white steeple looks just like any number of Baptist or Churches of Christ buildings around Middle Tennessee. The interior was attractive, simple and sedate. There were two rows of pews with white ends, dark oak seats and trim.The pew cushions were burgundy to match the burgundy carpets in the aisles. The remainder of the floor was of simple composition square tiles. The walls were an elegant taupe with tasteful white and soft green accent trim work.The ceiling was about 24 feet high and the windows were nearly 12 feet tall with textured opaque glass in individual panes.

At 10:29 a.m. the organist began playing soft prelude music prior to the actual beginning of the service. At the left of the chancel area these words were written on the wall:

"Ye shall know the truth and
the truth shall make you
free" – Jesus Christ

To the right of the chancel were these words:
"Divine love always has met
and always will meet every
human need." – Mary Baker Eddy.

Mary Baker Eddy had been born in New Hampshire. Suffering some early tragedies in her life, she founded the Christian Science religion after she felt that she had found healing while reading about how Jesus healed one of His followers. This experience began her in-depth study of the scriptures that focused on the search for the principles of divine healing. Her teachings, contained in *Science and Healing, With Key to the Scriptures*, were published in 1875. In this book, the core of the teachings of Christian Science, she explained principles of divine healing in its broadest forms, including the healing of physical, mental and spiritual diseases. All diseases were caused, according to Eddy, by separation from truth, love and light — all of which were manifestations of God.

At 10:30 a.m. there were 29 people in the sanctuary as the service began. Sunday school was conducted at the same time for children and young people up to 20 years of age. The majority of the people in the service were older adults, all dressed in "church clothes." The service began with the singing of *Hymn No. 304*. An attractive woman, appearing to be in her mid-40s and neatly dressed in a light blue two-piece suit, introduced this first hymn, "The words of the first hymn are by our beloved leader Mary Baker Eddy." She read some of the words before the congregation joined in singing the hymn. The words she read were: "Shepherds show me how to go o'er the hillside steep, how to gather, how to sow, how to feed thy sheep. I will listen for thy voice lest my footsteps stray. I will follow and rejoice, all the rugged way." I later identified this woman as the "first reader."

I learned that there are two readers elected by the membership to read from the scriptures and from *Science and Health* during every service for a three-year term. Usually there was one man reader and one woman reader, but during this service there were two women readers. Reader No. 1 said, "I shall read from the scriptures," and she read from *Psalms*. She then read from *Luke* where Jesus met Zachaeus who was a short rich man who had to climb a sycamore tree to see over the crowd and see Jesus. The first reader then led us in a period of silent prayer followed by the *Lord's Prayer*. This reader, after being joined by the second reader, read the *Lord's Prayer* while the congregation and the second reader read (what I saw as) Mary Baker Eddy's interpretation of each part of the prayer. It went as follows:

Our Father which art in Heaven
Our Father – Mother God, all harmonious
Hallowed be Thy name.
Adorable one
Thy kingdom come
Thy kingdom is come; thou art ever present
Thy will be done in Earth, as it is in heaven,
Enable us to know, as in heaven, so on Earth,
God Is omnipotent, supreme

Give us this day our daily bread;
Give us grace for today; fold the famished affections
And forgive us our debts as we forgive our debtors
And love is reflected in love
And lead us not into temptation, but deliver us from evil
And God leadeth us not into temptation, but delivereth
Us from sin, disease and death
For Thine is the kingdom, and the power
And the glory, forever.
For God is infinite, all power, all life,
All truth, love, over all, and all.

The first reader commented early in the service that the entire service would, and always does, follow this format. There would be scripture readings read by the first reader, and the words of interpretation by Mary Baker Eddy would be read by the second reader. The first reader indicated that this way there should be no misunderstanding of what God wished us to hear and understand today.

The readers (especially the first reader) used very precise diction as she carefully read every word, yet she seemed to remove any interpretive inflection from her voice in an attempt to let God speak directly through the actual words without undue assistance from the reader. It reminded me of my early blue roading days on our vehicle which we named SCOLTA. On board SCOLTA I had my secretary-assistant put a file cabinet containing information on every state in the union. Betty, who had signed on dutifully as my first mate, agreed to read to me from this material upon request without INFLECTION. This was very important to me. This was MY TRIP! I had planned it all, had set the mood and I wanted Betty to read words only. No inflection, in order to minimize emphasis on what she thought might be important or interesting to see. This was information I did not want conveyed by her. If she let me know what she wanted to do or see, I could see two distinct possibilities for discord: (1.) If I did not follow her wishes, I would feel guilty for not having done so, or (2.) if I did follow her wishes, there was a good chance that we would wind up in some museum or art gallery, thus spoiling my true blue roading mood.

The readers were obviously trained to let the words of scripture and Mary Baker Eddy speak for themselves and to allow the congregation to assimilate these words into their lives with as little coaxing from the readers as possible. They both would make excellent blue road material readers for any owners of SCOLTAs seeking to let the travels speak for themselves without unwanted assistance from traveling companions.

The service continued with the singing of *Hymn No. 92*. Again, the reader read some of the words of the hymn first. Some of the words in the hymn were, "Happy is the man who knows his master to obey, whose life and labor flows where God points out the way."

The order of worship next came to "Notices" (announcements in many churches). The first reader told us about the Wednesday evening services which consisted primarily of testimonials from members about how God's healing was working and had worked in their lives. We were also told of the Christian Science Reading Room downtown which is open from 10:00 a.m. to 2:00 p.m. every day.

After the announcements a third woman sang a beautiful solo. It was now 10:50 a.m. and there were 51 people in the sanctuary participating in this service. According to the order of worship, the next part of the service was an "Explanatory Note" which was printed on Page 2. It was a note from Mary Baker Eddy that read:"Friends: The *Bible* and the Christian Science textbook *(Science and Health)* are our only preachers. We shall now read scriptural texts and their correlative passages from our denominational textbook; these comprise our sermon.The canonical writings, together with the word of our textbook corroborating and explaining the *Bible* text in their spiritual import and application to all ages, past, present, and future, constitute a sermon undivorced from truth, uncontaminated and unfettered by human hypotheses and divinely authorized."

And thus the service followed.The first reader read the "Golden Text" which was on the subject of "Everlasting punishment." The Golden Text was from *Psalms 94: 14 – 15.* "the Lord will not cast off his people, neither will he forsake his inheritance. But judgment will return unto righteousness: and all the upright in heart shall follow it." This text was followed by a responsive reading of the scriptures from *Isaiah 59*, which was then followed by the "Sermon – Lesson," which was read by the two women.The second reader, a woman dressed in a soft green suit, read from the *Bible* and the first reader, who was the one dressed in blue, read Mary Baker Eddy's words from *Science and Health* which was first published in 1875.

After this Lesson – Sermon, the offering was taken to which Betty contributed our $5. And I will bet the whole $5 that you would find that $5 listed before the day is over on a list of donations in Betty's office which might save us somewhere between $1 – $2, depending on the amount of our income this year and the amount of other deductions Betty can accurately record. There will doubtlessly be fifty-two $5 church contributions over the same number of Sundays. God will not be pleased with the amount, but the IRS will be impressed with the neatness of fifty-two $5 charitable deductions duly listed and annotated.

After the congregation sang *Hymn No. 356*, the first reader read "The Scientific Statement of Being and Correlative Scripture" which the order of worship stated are read at the end of each Christian Science service. Mary Baker Eddy would be proud that I accurately record them here now:

"There is no life, truth, intelligence,
nor substance in matter. All is infinite mind
and its infinite manifestation, for God is
all-in-all. Spirit is immortal Truth, matter is mortal
error. Spirit is the real and eternal matter
is unreal and temporal. Spirit is God,
and man is His image and likeness.
Therefore man is not material; he is spiritual."
Science and Health 468: 9 – 15

"And the correlative scripture:
Behold what manner of love the Father
hath bestowed upon us, that we should
be called the sons of God; therefore the
world knoweth us not, because it knew
him not. Beloved, now are we the sons
of God, and it doth not yet
appear what we shall be: but we
know that, when he shall appear,
we shall be like him, for
we shall see him as he is. And
every man that hath this hope in him
purifieth himself, even as he is pure."
I John 3: 1 – 3

The reading of these words is sort of the *Apostles Creed* of the Christian Scientists and is reminiscent of platonic philosophy and Gnosticism in the early centuries of the Christian church, both with their dualism of good and evil, matter and spirit and light and dark. Mary Baker Eddy is elevated to the level of a Prophetess in the minds of Christian Scientists in the practice of their worship services, if not in church polity or theology.

Many equate this church with the "power of positive thinking" movement in vogue in different cultures and at different times in the world, but there seems to be this slight (members of this church would say "great") philosophical difference. Those of the "Positive Thinking" persuasion believe that the mind has the power to change and bend the physical world to make it serve us better. On the other hand, Mary Baker Eddy definitely teaches that the physical is evil and not real, and that healing and positive change is not ordered or forced by our minds. She teaches that the positive, good and truth are the only actualities, created by God. They are not "improved" by the power of our minds. It is only as we recognize and let our lives flow along with the truth and love and healing that is always there that there can be healing and forgiveness, which brings us to the fullness of life in God through Christ.

Now, I've done it. I've gone to philosophizing and theologizing. This is not blue road talk at all. Back on track, I say that the Christian Scientists have found an interpretation of *Bible* teachings which make their lives more meaningful. For them, pain and suffering, sin and evil, are the absence of God and good. This seems to me to provide a resting place for a lot of guilt on the part of those whose lives have even an average amount of pain. It, of course, can all be explained, but it is a significant problem just like predestination is a problem for Presbyterians and transubstantiation is for Catholics.

My significant problem for Sunday was rain foretold by dark clouds which was surely going to bring sadness, if not pain, into my life this afternoon. For Mary Baker Eddy, the clouds, the rain, the golf, and the golf clubs are unreal, and, therefore, the basis of pain and suffering. Boy is she ever right. All golfers agree.

Chapter 35

Jehovah's Witness Kingdom Hall
Gainesboro, Tennessee
May 11, 2003

*T*rivia question: When is blue roading better done on a major highway than on a back road? My answer (and you can print this in the trivia books): When traveling on the major highway is more leisurely accomplished than traveling on a back (or blue) road. And when is that possible? It is now possible on most of Tennessee SR840, which may eventually will be a circumferential major thoroughfare around Nashville. Currently, however, it is not totally complete and, thus, it is practically not used at all. As a result, it is more easily used in leisurely driving than the more heavily used back roads. The distance may be longer and it may take more time than other routes, but today's 840 (the parts of it that are completed) is certainly a leisurely "blue road" drive.

Betty and I went to our cottage on Center Hill Lake Saturday afternoon and traveled on 840 as far as it could take us before turning off toward the lake. It was a truly beautiful drive through what was to us a new look at perhaps some of the last undeveloped rolling farmlands in Middle Tennessee — no service stations, no motels, no nothing. Yet. The communities through which it winds are braced for the onslaught of development and traffic in the next few years. But for now, the answer to the trivia question, "What color is Tennessee Route 840 in 2003?" is "blue." Only blue roaders would know what you were talking about in the first place, and only blue roaders who have traveled over 840 this year would recognize it as true blue.

Here we were blazing a limited access four-lane trail across this part of the state just like pioneers blazed trails across this area hundreds of years ago. Well, almost "just like." At the least, we were early travelers and some of the fortunate few to see it in its infancy. I felt just like a modern day pioneer, or probably as close as I will get to a modern day pioneer in my lifetime. Sort of sad, isn't it? But not in Betty's books. She's happy the pioneering days are over. She appreciates the necessity of the early efforts by pioneers but wants no part of any trek unless a temperature controlled bubble bath waits at the end of it (and perhaps even one or two interspersed along the way).

But, I digress. We went to Center Hill at twilight on Saturday, or "eventide" as proper ladies of the court might say. No tea and crumpets, but we did have iced tea and our favorite catfish dinner at the Rose Garden Restaurant in Silver Point, Tennessee, near our lake cottage. And we watched TV and read for most of the evening before finally going to sleep at about midnight. The pleasant twilight drive, the leisurely blue road dinner and the quiet relaxing evening turned out to be, indeed, the calm before the storm. There are those who would say that God allowed a ferocious storm to blow in upon us Saturday night. It was as if there was a Jonah that God wanted cast overboard. Had there been anyone among us with a name that even started with a "J," Betty and I would have taken him to the lake's edge and sacrificed him to the great fishes in Center Hill Lake. One of our Center Hill neighbors who was also fearing the storm may have sacrificed a Jonah (or a John or even a James) to the large-mouth bass of the lake, because the tempest subsided in a couple of hours and a tranquil calm and freshness greeted us with a beautiful sunny dawn.

Betty was a little sleepy from the disturbance of the storm but she "shook herself" like Samson and regained her strength sufficiently enough to allow us to leave at 8:10 a.m., a full five minutes before my requested time of departure. Will miracles never cease? Last week she was in the car and ready to go after only 38 minutes of prep time. This morning's miracle established her victory over the devil clock, and we watched her digital dashboard clock as it jubilantly displayed the numbers 8:10. I wondered if it were a real conquest by my chronologically-challenged companion, or merely her eagerness to be one of the first to see a regurgitated Jonah or John on the swollen banks of Center Hill Lake. I did not want to dash her hopes. Because she thinks most of the *Bible* is allegory, she has never been consumed by its details and did not know that the great fish's stomach contents would not be visible for sinners and believers alike until acid tested for three days and nights.

We did travel the few hundred yards necessary to see the rising waters of "our lake" at Hurricane Marina. The water had cut off the "boardwalk" from the shore to the dock where our boat is kept. And the lower parking lot was covered by 10 to 15 feet of muddy water. This storm, and the many others of the past week, had wreaked havoc upon the midsection of America to be sure. The newscasters said that the week's storms were more devastating than during any week in U.S. history.

Storms cause damage in many ways. The cost in loss of life is tremendous and the cost in property damage is in the billions annually. Then there is the psychological burden heaped upon those subjected to the wrath of the storms. One church in Jackson, Tennessee was destroyed for the third time in its history this week. The third time!! Many of its parishioners no doubt asked, "What was God thinking when He allowed this to happen again?" Members asked their pastor, "Why did God allow this to happen again, pastor?" He probably gave the traditional answers about how God's ways are not our ways and that "God works in mysterious ways, His wonders to perform." I was glad that I was not the one being called upon to help those whose faith had been tested this week. It was things just such as this which had made me feel unfit to continue as a minister and caused me to demit the ministry in 1964. I realized then that I did not have enough faith for myself, let alone enough faith to offer helpful answers to those whose hearts were hurting. Better no answer from me at all than one which might prove hurtful or harmful to the ailing faith of my parishioners. As a realtor I just buy and sell properties. I don't explain disasters; that's way above my pay grade now.

About all my pay grade allowed me to answer this morning was the first question a friendly waitress asked me at the Hurricane Dock Restaurant, "Are you going to have breakfast?" Without a single doubt I answered a positive, "Yes." And it was easy for me to order three eggs over-easy/over-medium, country ham, hash browns, biscuits, gravy and coffee. And Betty's faith gave her the assurance that this establishment could prepare her scrambled eggs, bacon, wheat toast and coffee. One reason we ordered our breakfasts to our specifications with great assurance was my additional order of two pancakes "for the table." This is the answer to a lot of "what ifs" at breakfasts. What if my eggs are not cooked right, the ham tough, or the biscuits spongy? Not to worry. The pancakes on the way were a form of breakfast insurance.

We did not need the insurance after all. Everything except the hash browns was just as my faith allowed me to hope they would be. When I ordered my eggs, "over-easy/over-medium," our waitress let me know with a high sign with her left eye that she knew exactly what I meant. And she let the cook know exactly what I meant, which communicated to the cook, "Look, this guy is particular about his eggs, so pay attention." And he did. They could not have been better. The insurance was great too. But we bought far too much of it. Betty and I shared one of the two large delicious fluffy pancakes and saved the other one to feed the fish. Especially the one who will lose three days of calories on Tuesday after having regurgitated a Jonah, James or John.

While we finished our breakfast, a younger couple came in and sat on the screened porch. Betty and I were sitting in the open double doorway leading onto the porch which allowed us the best of both worlds — the freshness of the fresh morning-after-the-storm air and the interior view of the restaurant. At 8:15 a.m. we were the first customers there this morning. Not much lake traffic since the dock area is limited to access by boat. The only other people in the dining room were the manager and the owner, both older females about our own age. They always sit at a round table in the center yet near the entrance of this boat-dock restaurant, which has a nondescript boat-dock motif. It is always clean and orderly. For God's sake, it should be; the owner sits there most of the day and sees to it that it is.

I wondered one thing. Should I tell these people about their hash browns? I could help them very easily. Just bake more potatoes then you need every night and refrigerate the leftovers. Then the next morning slice them, peelings and all, and put them on a very hot grill very briefly to brown crisply and "presto," their inferior hash brown problem would be gone. This would turn what I saw as their only negative into an asset immediately. What do you think? Should I tell them or not? Let me know. Vote yes or no by sending your e-mails to ugb@comcast.net.

With tip, our breakfasts totaled about $20.00 and after paying our check, we were on our way to find a Jehovah's Witness Church. I had seen Jehovah's Witnesses in Sparta and Cookeville in the past and also knew there was one in Gainesboro which I had not seen. I wanted to attend one of their services to add to the variety of different churches I would visit over the next three to four months.

We took Highway 56 toward Gainesboro and then turned east onto Highway 70 toward Cookeville. During the drive, we were reminded of the storm that pastors were doubtlessly having to preach and pray about, or around, today. There was evidence everywhere that the weather forecasters had been right about the strength of the last night's winds.

By 9:25 a.m. we were in Cookeville looking for the Jehovah's Witness Church which I had seen before; but after failing to find it where I thought it was located, we started driving around only to find ourselves at 9:41 a.m. on a different road headed toward Gainesboro — and we soon passed the point of no return. We would now need to go to a Jehovah's Witness Church in Gainesboro which I knew would be easier to find. I had found that most Jehovah's Witness Churches meet at 10:00 a.m. for their "Public Talk" service.

We drove up to the Jehovah's Witness Kingdom Hall at 9:59 a.m., walked in and went directly to their sparkling white, clean restrooms. While I was in the restroom an announcement over the intercom by the day's leader said, "Y'all take a seat now. Y'all take a seat." I sort of rushed things in the restroom a bit, if you know what I mean. We went in to take a seat as directed (while everyone else was doing the same) in order to be seated as unnoticed as possible, but we were not successful in this effort. In a congregation of only about 75 souls, two new faces are easily spotted and several of the people seated around us introduced themselves and welcomed us to this service.

We were seated in moveable office-like chairs, which were lined up as pews in two sections, with an aisle down the middle. The chairs were upholstered in a cranberry-colored fabric which matched the tones in the carpet on the floor and some bits of cranberry trim in the pulpit area where four faux columns adorned the back wall. The nine-foot walls were a textured white and accented by a faux finish below the chair rail. There were no windows.

The leader who told us all to take our seats announced the topic for today, "A local congregation under Christ's leadership." And he announced that we would sing song *No. 34* entitled, *A Local Congregation.* We were handed a hymnal with oversized print that was open to Page 34. Some of the words were, "God Jehovah has a people who delight to bear His name...To God's loyal congregation we will show loyalty...Give it our steadfast allegiance... Loyally we will help our brothers."

After the hymn the leader offered a simple prayer which began, "We approach you, Jehovah God." He prayed for the members of the congregation to be steadfast and loyal followers in Jehovah's Kingdom. Then the leader introduced the speaker who would "give our talk for today." I was, and still am, curious as to why they refer to their "public talk" which most Christian Churches call sermons. I suppose it is because they have a different concept of ministers or pastors than traditional Christian churches. They truly believe in the concept of the "priesthood" for all believers (except they would never refer to themselves as priests, pastors or reverends). They believe that all Jehovah's Witnesses are Jehovah's Christian Witnesses, and as such, they claim to be the end of a long line of Witnesses of Jehovah's from many centuries preceding even Christ.

These seekers believe that Jesus Christ was sent as Jehovah's ransom of mankind from Satan's grasp. They say that Jehovah's holiness demanded a high price to be paid for disobeying Him and that His son was the only sacrifice worthy to pay the ransom. They believe that Satan was cast out of heaven in 1914 (I don't yet know why this year was significant) and this same Satan and his evil system must be defeated. Then, and only then, will Christ establish His reign of 1,000 years upon the Earth.

Ten of the members are chosen as elders of each congregation and have the responsibility of running the affairs of the church. The speaker for today had actually been sitting in front of us. He had introduced himself and given us the open song book before we knew he would give the "public talk" today.

In his early remarks the speaker, a nattily dressed man who was about 5'8", noted that Jesus Christ was Jehovah's chief loyal Son. And he said that Jehovah listens to his loyal followers and answers their prayers. The loyalty of Jesus Christ to Jehovah was an example of how we should also be loyal followers of His. Throughout his talk, the speaker referred to a long series of scripture verses which he felt proved that Jehovah expects and demands loyalty of His followers. He referred to *Acts 5: 38* through which he indicated that Jehovah has given His holy spirit to those who obey Him. He then told us that Esau was not loyal to Jehovah while Jacob was loyal and, because of this, Jacob became the ancestor to Jesus Christ.

Everyone in the congregation was neatly and respectfully dressed in his Sunday best, as if it would be a sign of disloyalty to Jehovah if they did not at least show this amount of respect. The speaker said that Moses was such a loyal follower of Jehovah that God dealt with him "face to face." He then indicated that the loyalty of Moses was the total reason he had such a high standing with Jehovah. He told us that Baleem *(Numbers 22: 12)* was disloyal, and he displeased Jehovah. Phineus, on the other hand, was loyal to the point that he killed two fornicators with his javelin *(Numbers 25: 8 – 11)*.

The speaker said that we too must be loyal to Jehovah's "arrangement," which He has set up through Jesus Christ. He said that no elder would want to cause strife in the congregation. It seemed that the speaker was speaking of specific evidences of strife within this congregation and that such strife was itself a sign of disloyalty to Jehovah. He said that to be loyal is to be like Moses. Then he read from *Romans 12: 3* which he said indicated that to be loyal is to be humble and willing to submit to the congregation. He continued this thought by saying that we cannot be loyal if we fail to cooperate with "the elder arrangement" of the congregation. He insisted, over and over, that all the followers of Jehovah must be submissive to the leaders of the congregation. He read from *Isaiah 32* which he indicated was a lesson not to develop a critical or negative attitude regarding any little imperfection in the congregation. Next, he read from *I Peter 3: 8* which teaches us to be likeminded in brotherly affection.

In the concluding moments of his speech, the speaker said, "Loyalty is submitting to the theocratic order. This we must do if we are Jehovah's people." He emphasized that Jesus Christ was our leader and that, being engaged in spiritual warfare, we must, "act as a group, united, close-knit and compact." With his final words he said we should all be like Jesus Christ, Jehovah's most loyal son. The congregation gave him a warm round of applause at the conclusion of his remarks.

The original ("take your seats") leader then came back to the pulpit to conclude the service. He told of a member who was in the hospital and in need of prayers. He ended this part of the meeting by announcing that the Watchtower Study Period would begin almost immediately and that "we will have another talk next Sunday." And with these words the service ended unceremoniously.

There was no offering taken and, from what I understand, there is never an offering taken. I wonder if the IRS could possibly be aware of this and would suspect anything if we recorded our usual $5 gift today, even though it remained safely tucked away in Betty's billfold.

Betty and I tried to slip out unnoticed, but we were caught in the act and had to confront several of whom we thought were the church elders. They had gathered at the back as if taking the names of those who were ditching after today's public talk about loyalty. We had enough momentum leaving so we were slowed only a little as we ran the gauntlet of the elders and made our way to the car. We were almost childlike with giddy feelings at having successfully avoided being cross-examined as to who we were, where we were from and, most of all, why we were leaving so early.

I could have said that we were leaving because we thought we were coming to a Mother's Day service and had been disappointed when mothers were not honored at all today. But that would have been prima facia evidence that we knew almost nothing about Jehovah's Witnesses. Later that afternoon I found on the Internet that they do not celebrate even Christmas and Easter, believing them just pagan holidays out of the past which were assimilated into the Christian calendar.

We headed back to Nashville after the bolt to our car in order to celebrate Mother's Day with our two daughters. They were preparing a special Mother's Day dinner for Betty. They are loyal daughters with whom Betty works very closely every day in our family real estate business. I just hope they can always keep that spirit of love and loyalty in spite of the pain that I sense might be being felt today in the Kingdom Hall in Gainesboro. The speaker, indeed, was "preaching to the choir" today in his talk because he seemed to feel that some of the soldiers in Jehovah's army were breaking ranks. He was attempting to rally the remaining troops back to a solid Christian army for Jehovah. He had made a reasoned and clarion call for a deeper sense of loyalty in the life of his congregation. If the warm applause meant anything, it seemed that almost all, if not the entirety, of this congregation heard his call.

Chapter 36

The Church of Jesus Christ of Latter Day Saints
The Mormons * Nashville, Tennessee
May 18, 2003

*A*t 8:29 a.m. this morning we were seated in Betty's car looking at her clock and I said, "Do you think we should record this morning's departure as a minute early or 14 minutes late?" Betty answered defensively to me, "You said we were to leave at 8:30 a.m. this morning so we are one minute early." I did not press the point vigorously that at the end of our departure planning conversation on the evening before I had said, "Make that 8:15 a.m." Betty needs the momentum of striving for punctuality. But I just could not help but be amazed that Betty, who hears absolutely everything I say and can quote it back to me verbatim 20 years later, did not hear my amendment of our departure time last night. I guess it is some sort of natural selective audio voyeurism that just automatically kicks in when defensive measures are called for. The power of the creative mind constantly amazes me.

So at 8:29 a.m. on a cloudy, overcast day with patches of drizzling rain, we left our home on Woodmont going toward Green Hills with a planned objective for this 36th Sunday on our schedule of fifty-two. I had planned to go to the Mormon Church on Hillsboro Road in Green Hills. I had been speaking with Lynn Ellsworth whom I had met more than 30 years ago soon after he moved to Nashville. I learned back then that he was a Mormon and, I suppose, had come to Nashville as part of his religious commitment to share his faith. Lynn is still a handsome and youthful looking man who, over the years, has impressed me with his drive and creativity. He was the first in our area to build the outlet malls now scattered almost everywhere. And nowadays Lynn is the first to really bring new loft-type condos to the Nashville area on a large scale.

When I decided to go to a Mormon service, I spoke with Lynn and he offered to invite me to visit his church in Green Hills. I had planned to await his personal invitation, but I decided last night to go ahead and put this church on my schedule because of developing circumstances in my life.

Some friends had invited Betty and me to Falls Creek Falls later on this afternoon for a three-day "golfing" trip. Our wives were calling this trip something else, but I am sure that Roy, Jim, Earl and I were planning three days of golf, "The Lord willing, and if the creek don't rise," as the saying goes. But, indeed, I knew that the creek might rise as all creeks have been doing during the heavy rains of the past two weeks. And I suppose men of faith would say that if the creeks do rise, then it is not God's will that we play golf. Frankly, I don't think He cares one way or another. I hope if He cares about anything, it is mostly about the hurt and suffering going on now in the Mid-East. Anyhow, I hoped Roy and Earl were praying for sunshine since they are men with more faith in God's concern about the details of our lives than Jim and I.

Rain or shine, and golf or no golf, we planned to leave early that afternoon. As a result, I needed to go to a church near our home in order to be able to coordinate our schedule with the others. Therefore, the Mormon Church was moved up on our schedule before Lynn could personally take us to his church as his visitors.

But to make this Sunday complete we first had to find a good place for breakfast. We thought about the "Bread and Company" in Green Hills which had started opening on Sundays and was beginning a breakfast menu, but I decided to give them a few more weeks before putting them to the test. So, still looking, we drove out toward Brentwood to find a place to eat and on the way we passed our old "home place," 1432 Tyne Boulevard. We sold our home there more than two years ago and moved into the "doublewide" condo (two condos combined into one) that serves as our present home until we build a new one. Passing 1432 reminded me of another rainy season a few months after we had sold this house during which the whole basement flooded. I felt so badly that I felt I just had to solve this problem for the new owners at a cost of about $25,000. Ever since this incident heavy rain tends to leave me a little depressed. And it doesn't take a shrink to tell me why. The sprinkling rain on our windshield caused a minor sinking spell as we passed this house which I had built and which had been our home for about 35 years. With a salute in our hearts we rushed on past what will always be a shrine to an important part of our lives.

Soon we were in Maryland Farms in Brentwood searching for a place for breakfast and found "Dimple's Deli." They were now open for breakfast, and so we went in and laid claim to one of their largest booths so that Betty could spread out her paper and join several others who were getting their morning news along with their morning meal.

After claiming our booth, Betty and I went to the "Order Here" station and finally coaxed a young attendant to take our order. She wasn't rude. She just wasn't there. She was about sixteen-years-old and had absolutely no expression either in her voice or on her face. She didn't even look bored, which she may well have been. She just seemed sort of non-communicative, both facially and verbally. When she finally did respond to a question after a lapse of time, we were reminded of the response delay from TV correspondents in Baghdad being asked questions from New York or Atlanta. You know — the long second or two before the transmission reaches there and before an answer comes back. Well, this is just how it was with our breakfast correspondent. We felt she was in Baghdad while we were in the Dimples in Brentwood. Finally, our transmissions were made, received and expressionlessly recorded. Betty ordered the "Breakfast Special" — two scrambled eggs, bacon, wheat toast, home fries and coffee. My order took longer because I felt like I was asking, "Hello, do you hear me?" with each part of my order. In desperation, I finally just ordered three eggs over-medium, bacon, hash browns, biscuits and coffee. My long distance attendant had discombobulated me to where I forgot to order a waffle "for the table." I thought she might ask at any moment, "Do you want to pick it up here or in Baghdad?" Of course, I knew she would ask neither this question nor any question. She didn't ask anything and barely responded to anything.

After our order was delivered by a young Iraqi teenage soldier we discovered part of the problem. The young attendant actually was not in Baghdad, she was in love with another young worker. The object of her affections was slicing thin meat piles for lunch. She actually smiled at him twice while we ate. They were coquettish smiles directed only at the object of her affections; but we were happy, nevertheless, to see them. She's far too young to be in Baghdad.

Our breakfasts were quite good. Not great. Betty's was sort of cold. Maybe hers did come from Iraq. Her wheat toast, obviously from the good ol' U.S.A., was warm and crisp. My breakfast was better. The eggs turned out far better than they had a right to because I had not transmitted enough info to get them this good — perfectly cooked as if ordered from a five-star chef. The biscuits were also good, brown on both tops and bottoms. Crusty, too. Only my bacon and hash browns needed help. The bacon was limp. And the home fries were cold and almost not there at all — only four or five small pieces of cubed, unpeeled fried potatoes. I was already regretful that earlier I had been frustrated to the point of failing to order a waffle for dessert.

While we ate we saw a nice looking man eating his breakfast alone and reading the morning paper. I hoped he did not have to eat all of his breakfasts alone, and I felt this probably was not the case when I saw that he was wearing golf shorts. I surmised that he had left his sweet significant other sleeping in bed while he went to play golf. Now he was just going to finish breakfast, recognize that golf was rained out for the day, and was going back to spend the rest of the day with "sweet thing."

There were two young couples, each with two children under three years of age, just leaving as we began eating. They looked semi-happy but frazzled and bedazzled with armloads of responsibility almost spilling out onto the floor as they tried to leave. It made me very tired just to think of the next 18 to 20 years of juggling from arm to arm and from school to school they faced. I was sort of glad they were leaving — less of a chance I would step on one of the bundles of joy as I went back to the serving line for more coffee. They were everywhere! Wheh! I thought I would request prayer for both moms and pops if an opportunity to do so was given in church this morning.

A young couple was contentedly eating and reading the paper when I noticed how the woman reminded me of Nicole Kidman in "Eyes Wide Shut." Specifically, how she looked in the scene when she looked up and over her glasses which were resting lowered on the tip of her nose. This movie had been a bust, but the simple image of Nicole looking up from writing a note had given me a basis for looking forward to her understated parts in future movies.

We were nearly finished when we saw our friend James Buck come in for breakfast. He is the young man who came to Center Hill with Betty and me several weeks ago to help out with some minor problems at our cottage. He had then stayed over Saturday night with us, gone to breakfast with us, and also visited the Trinity Missionary Baptist Church in Cookeville with us. I told Buck, as we call him, that we were going to a Mormon Church today and that I would send him a copy of the Trinity Missionary Baptist chapter to my *Fifty-two Sundays* when we got back home. Maybe I should have invited Buck (and his brother Robert who had come to breakfast with him) to join us again, but they were just beginning to eat. Besides, I didn't want Buck to think I was trying to convert him to something. Actually I think Buck is one of these people who, like my dad, are better by nature than most others are by grace. So we went on alone and, at 9:57 a.m., we entered this Mormon Church located at the corner of Hillsboro Road and Castleman Drive in Green Hills.

We sort of "ran the gauntlet" upon entering (as we had done the previous Sunday when leaving the church we had visited). Fifteen to twenty young men and women were lined up on both sides of the center aisle and acted as a greeting line. Each one shook our hands and welcomed us to their church. We proceeded to our pew at the far back right of the sanctuary. This church was a traditional red brick building with a steeple, similar to many Church of Christ buildings in the area. As a matter of fact, it had once actually been a Church of Christ until the congregation moved on to a larger facility. And just before the Mormons moved here, the Covenant Presbyterian Church had made it their home for several years. So this Mormon church looked much like many others we had visited over the past few months. The 20-foot ceiling was supported by beige colored walls with a greenish tint. The columns along the walls, the chair rails, and the window trim were all white. The carpet was a soft green and the oak pews were covered by emerald green cushions. The panes of the tall arched windows were crinkled opaque glass.

As we entered, the organ played *How Great Thou Art* and other recognizable selections. When we were seated, there were only about 40 people already there, but it was slowly filling. It seemed that there were more people than just Betty who had a problem fighting the clock. People were still coming in as the "chorister," Meg Embody, directed the congregation in singing *No. 85, How Firm a Foundation*, a standard hymn in practically all-denominational hymnals. She stood to the left and directed the singing by waving her arm and hand as if the congregation were a choir. We remained seated during the singing which was a switch, especially from the community churches which almost always keep their congregations standing for the first 20 to 30 minutes for the sing fests that open each service.

There were several young men seated in the chancel area of the church along with Bishop Scott, the service leader today according to the printed order of worship we had received. Most of the younger men were dressed in shirtsleeves with ties. The Bishop was a husky man with gray hair and glasses and wore a bluish-gray suit.

The congregation numbered about 100 at 10:06 a.m.; predominantly younger people — younger people with lots of children. This congregation apparently did not believe in shipping their children off to junior church at all. There were children all over the church, just being children. A few minutes into the service they were fidgeting around all over the pews. The philosophy here seemed to be to teach the children about the worship experience early. The ones I saw, however, were mostly rejecting the teaching efforts of their elders in this congregation.

After the first hymn a young woman quietly led us in prayer — too quietly. It turned out that the microphone had not been turned on, but this was corrected as the bishop came to the pulpit to welcome visitors and to make some announcements. He told the members that the mold in the basement would be solved in a few days. He said it was going to be sealed in acrylic. The bishop also told the members about their new church building which would be under construction soon. He said it would be on the "Hermitage Plan" and would have large palladium windows and a steeple. Other "Ward Business," as listed in the order of worship, included a singles meeting at a member's house and a car wash at McDonald's next weekend.

Immediately after these announcements the bishop told us that we would sing *Hymn 175* titled *Sacrament Meeting*, as we prepared for the "Administration of the Sacrament" as printed in the order of worship. Some of the words of the hymn were "O God, Eternal Father, who dwells amid the sky, in Jesus' name we ask thee to bless and sanctify, if we are pure before Thee, this bread and cup of wine, that we may all remember that offering divine." After this hymn the covering over the sacramental table was removed, and a prayer was offered by a young man wearing a white shirt and tie. Five young men, three in shirts and ties and two in suits, came forward to serve the elements. The bread was small broken pieces on a small tray and the wine was served in demi-glasses, and both were served rather unceremoniously by the five young men who passed the trays among the aisles. When the cup was taken, its contents were immediately swallowed by the communicant, the empty cup placed back in the tray, and the tray passed on. Even small children who were three-to-four-years-old participated in this sacrament.

After this part of the service, the covering was reverently replaced over the remaining elements and the service proceeded. The bishop then called the names of several women in the congregation in order to recognize them for their accomplishments in the church. He referred to each one of them as "sister" as he announced their awards. One of them was a young girl who may have been eight-to-ten-years-old and, as part of her recognition, she was invited to the pulpit by the bishop to recite "one of the articles of faith."

The Mormons, or The Church of Jesus Christ of Latter Day Saints, was started by Joseph Smith in the state of New York in 1830. Joseph Smith felt he was led by God not to join any of the other churches of his day and was eventually led to "restore" the Christian faith in its original purity. Mormons strongly claim to be Christians, but not Protestants. They believe that Joseph Smith, led by God, wrote the Book of Mormons as God's revelation to "Latter Day Saints." Smith, therefore, is seen by Mormons to be a prophet, just as Isaiah, Jeremiah and Abraham are seen to be prophets. As a result, Mormons believe that the Book of Mormons is further revelation from God through His prophet Joseph Smith and, thus, the Book of Mormons is an inspired book of God just like the Bible. It does not replace the Bible just as the *New Testament* does not replace the *Old Testament*. Instead, the contents of the Book of Mormons are God's additional words to "Latter Day Saints." This is the major point of separation between other Christians and Mormons.

The Mormons have no professional clergy. In a sense, every member carries the responsibility to share their faith with the world and needs no priest or pastor to direct them. Different members take on leadership positions from time to time but without compensation. The bishop, demonstrating this concept, announced that there would be three "speakers" today. The speakers were identified in the order of worship as Mike Koch, Anne Marie Davies and Sean Davies.

Mike spoke first. A burly man perhaps in his early 30s, he wore a white short-sleeved shirt with a short-sleeved sweater and a tie. He had very heavy, dark hair and wore glasses. He began, "I have tried to come with a good talk for today, so please bear with me." He then proceeded to tell us that we show our love to our Heavenly Father through obedience. He said that we show our obedience through making and keeping covenants, through our praying, through baptism, and "through following the promptings of the Holy Ghost." He assured us that the Holy Ghost would warn us three times when temptation came to keep us away from evil.

This first speaker continued by telling us that we show our obedience to the Heavenly Father by keeping the Sabbath day holy and by following His commandments. He emphasized that Jesus said that the greatest commandment is that we love God the Father with all our hearts, and that the second is for us to "love thy neighbor as thyself." Mike said that if we show God we love Him it will be easier for us to show others.

The next speaker was Anne Marie Davies, a short woman who appeared to be of Asian parentage. She stated that she and her husband Sean (who would be the third speaker today) have three children. She shared that fact as she began a discussion about the need for us to teach our children the right path to follow. The best way, she told us, was to set a good example. Then she told us of some of her experiences in teaching children in Sunday school. She also related some of her experiences in praying with her own children. She said that her young daughter had learned that we should pray for others and, on occasion, had reminded her parents when they did not pray for her by saying, "Mom and dad, you forgot to pray for me." After this speaker, but before her husband, the order of worship called for *Hymn 142* entitled

Sweet Hour of Prayer, which sort of served as the conclusion of Anne Marie's discussion about teaching our children to pray by praying with them.

Sean Davies, the last speaker, was a tall, rather handsome young man with glasses and a goatee. He wore a white short-sleeved shirt with a tie. He was a real contrast to his diminutive wife, Anne Marie. He said his talk would be about "a prayer for adults." He said that we are "backpacking" Christians who need to learn which things are important for us to take in our backpacks as we travel. Following the "backpacking" concept, he said that we all need good maps in our travels and that a good mapmaker puts on the map things that will last forever — not trees that die or little rocks that might be swept away. Instead, the good mapmaker marks the way with large mountains and rivers. He said we must teach our children about the fundamental truths — the mountains and rivers. If we don't teach them well, they will lose their way. They will fail. He said that God gave us a plan, a map, and that we must have faith in that plan.

Sean then told us that we must teach our children the joy of fellowship — the love of church. This third speaker for today said, "I love my children and must apply this same love to others in the church." This father of three then dramatically and effectively said, "Let me finish by bearing my testimony to my children." He then very deliberately turned toward his wife Anne Marie and his three children and said, "I want you to know that I love this church and the Farther and Jesus Christ." With this effective testimony, his speech ended.

The congregation was directed in the singing of the closing hymn, *No. 6, The Redeemer of Israel*. Some of the words to this hymn were: "Redeemer of Israel, our only delight, on whom for blessings we call, our shadow by day and pillar by night, our King, our deliverer, over all...We know He is coming to gather His sheep."

With a simple benediction offered by a young woman this service was over. Betty and I left immediately to hurry home and begin the final packing for our afternoon trip to Falls Creek Falls. But before I finished my packing for the three-day respite, I made some calls to clear my calendar and also made some notes on the service we had just attended. Those notes included the following observations:

1.)   *This is a church which has a lot of young adults who have a lot of young children.*

2.)   *This is a church which obviously emphasizes the concept that if we teach our children early the ways they should go they will likely not depart from it.*

3.)   *Their worship service is very simple and informal without any significant amount of ritual, even during the administration of the Sacrament of the Lord's Supper.*

4.)   *Their emphasis on the "priesthood of all believers" puts its stamp on the simplicity of their worship service.*

5.)   *There was no offering taken and, presumably, this is not a part of their worship service, just as an offering was not taken at the Jehovah's Witness service last week. This means that we have saved $5 for each of the two last Sundays.*

6.)   *Since this congregation is building a new church I wonder if they are going to move and, if so, if I should make any move to see if they will be selling this great piece of property, or if I should just forget it since my good friend Lynn Ellsworth, as a member here, probably already has it all locked up. According to the Mormons it is a sacrilege to even think of the matter today. Maybe tomorrow then...*

Chapter 37

Newsong Christian Fellowship
A Foursquare Gospel Church * Brentwood, Tennessee
May 25, 2003

*B*etty and I had spent three days of the previous week with friends in a great getaway cabin located near Falls Creek Falls State Park. We played golf and all sorts of board games (at which I lost every time). I hate games that reflect in any way on my lack of intelligence. At any rate, I got my "lead" to attend Newsong Fellowship in Brentwood, Tennessee from Genevieve DeSha, the champion of the boards. She was the champion game player on the trip.

I had gone on this retreat for relaxation and had ended up humiliated by my attempts at scrabble and other such games, but I did get the "prospect" of a new and different church to attend. The term "prospect" reminds me of the story about the teen-ager who had sex with a widow in his church and then told a buddy that he felt compelled to confess his sin to the priest. After his confession, the good Father said that the young confessor would have to "confess all" before he could receive forgiveness. "Who was the woman?" the Father asked.

"Oh, I can't tell you that," said the young sinner.

The Father persisted. He asked, "Was it Widow Brown?"

"No."

"Was it Widow Jones?"

"No."

"Was it Widow Smith?"

"No."

The Father then said, "You go and think about this whole situation; when you come back truly contrite enough to confess your sin completely, I will then forgive you. But not until then."

The grieving young sinner went back and met with his friend who immediately asked, "How did it go? Did the Father forgive you?"

"No, he didn't," he replied rather cheerfully.

His buddy then asked, "If the Father did not forgive you, why are you so happy?"

The young carnal offender revealed his reason for happiness, when he said elatedly, "Because I just got three new prospects."

I had lost all the board games, had played miserable golf and even been accused of cheating by one of my playing companions after moving my ball away from a fence — apparently, too far away from the fence. To this day, I am sure that I have not been forgiven by this new high priest of pastime golfing etiquette. So why wasn't I dejected? Because of the "new prospect" which was a church of a denomination I had not heard of in years. I thought that the Foursquare Gospel Church (started by Aimee McPerson in the early 1900s) had perhaps died out, but discovered today that just the opposite was the case. It is alive and well and flourishing.

Betty and I left at 9:07 a.m. on this morning, missing by only seven minutes our target departure time. No sweat, because the new prospect was located in Brentwood only 15 minutes away. The problem would be getting to Richland for a golf tee time at 1:40 p.m. Not really a problem here either because of our good planning. We took two cars and dropped mine along with my golf paraphernalia at Richland which was located about halfway between our home and Brentwood. Then we headed to Brentwood to find a blue road breakfast place. Fat chance. Brentwood is not blue road; it is blue silk stocking, if anything.

It was raining rather steadily as we left, so I reasoned that golf was probably going to be cancelled and that we could just sort of take a leisurely look at everything this morning. We'd probably have to make a major compromise on a blue road breakfast place today and end up settling for a donut (or bagel) and coffee at Starbucks or Atlanta Bread Company. Even though I hold tremendous artistic license as the author of this work, I had difficulty imagining the addition of this burden to my working manuscript of *Fifty-two Sundays on the Blue Road*. Starbucks, a blue road restaurant? Now that's a real stretch. With the power of the pen, I have changed Fridays and Saturdays into Sundays, water into wine and boulevards into blue roads, but Starbucks into a blue road restaurant? Surely some higher authority, a high priest of the pens, would say, "Whoa there, good buddy, that's totally disallowed in blue road writing."

Now in Brentwood, Betty and I tried to position ourselves near the area of Brentwood where Newsong was located. We tooled down Mallory Lane, a blue road sounding name but definitely not a blue road under a conservative interpretation of blue roads. However, no one has accused me of being conservative since my early days at Trevecca College in the late 40s and early 50s. And so, in the true liberal tradition, I declared Mallory Lane as one of our blue roads for this morning. There were shopping centers, furniture stores and some well-known restaurants (none of which were open for breakfast). I was on my way to a shopping center in which I knew there was a Starbucks and an Atlanta Bread Company, both of which were open for breakfast. Bagel breakfasts! I was ready to bite the bullet (or bagel) and call it a blue road breakfast. A man's gotta do what a man's gotta do.

As I write these words, I am perhaps overly nervous about journalistic ethics because, at least partially, of last night's dinner discussion. Betty and I had joined the Sutherlands, the Seigenthalers and Jim Neal (Dianne was in Europe touring with girlfriend buddies) for dinner at the Richland club. John Seigenthaler and Frank Sutherland particularly had discussed the poor oversight of *The New York Times* over their young star reporter Jason Blair who had just been exposed for a total lack of journalistic ethics. In light of the lack of editorial oversight over Blair, I was sweating the possibility that Frank and John might feel an ethical duty to reveal my tendency to incrementally alter the truth to fit my journalistic purposes.

I was really sweating the possibility of their exposing me for coloring Mallory Lane blue and for calling Starbucks a blue road restaurant (an unforgivable twisting of the truth). My defense was already in place. Twenty years ago Mallory Lane had actually been a blue road and, as such, it is grandfathered in as a blue road. Also, any restaurant within 500 yards of a blue road may be called a blue road restaurant. And since Starbucks was in a shopping center site facing Mallory Lane...

Just then, yet another blue road miracle saved me from possibly being detected as a journalistic fraud, to say the least, and from a poor substitute for a fine blue road breakfast, to say for sure. There it was. Right on the grandfathered blue road Mallory Lane in the middle of Cool Springs, like a star appearing in the East to save my budding journalistic soul — the sparking "5th and Diner" restaurant. What a find! It's a miniaturized version of Mel's Diner in Naples, Florida. It had a neon sign that read, "Breakfast." And there was absolutely no question that it was open on Sundays because of the parking lot that swarmed with activity.

We did find a parking spot and Betty went on in and found that there would be a 20-minute wait — shades of the Pancake Pantry, until today the only other place we had to wait for a table during our previous 37 Sundays of breakfasts. We took our paper in and prepared to wait by reading, but we were summoned to our table after only a ten-minute wait. It could have taken us longer than that just to read the menu. It was absolutely filled with tempting selections, but we had other business today and so we speed-read the menu. I ordered three eggs and started to say "the usual" but then realized that this would not compute with our obviously bright waitress. It would sort of be like the woman driver who suddenly turned left without signaling and ended up in an accident. When called an idiot by the other driver she replied, "Well, if you were so smart you'd know that I turn here every day."

Realizing that our waitress did not witness our ordering every Sunday, I specified that my eggs should be cooked over-easy/over-medium and completed my order by specifying chicken-fried steak, hash browns. Of course, I ordered French toast "for the table."

Now I could have gone back to my newspaper, but I had some more reading to do on this very appetizing menu. It offered 16 different appetizers, 15 different versions of hamburgers, and 20 other sandwiches to choose from for lunch in addition to many salads and a great selection of soups and desserts. For dinner they offer entrees of liver, pot roast, ribs, fish, fried chicken, pork chops, shrimp, meat loaf, and several "blue plate specials" — move over Pancake Pantry!

The décor was that of a diner in vogue in the 50s. The floor was handsome black and white small squares in a checkerboard style, and the ceilings were red, white and chrome with sweeping curves of art deco everywhere instead of corners. Everything was geared to the rock-'n-roll craze of the 50s and movie stars of the same era. There were pictures of Elvis, Marilyn Monroe, Frank Sinatra and James Dean. Rock-'n-roll music played constantly and the place was full of families and kids. Kids everywhere. But not in an uncomfortable way — in a wholesome way. Two dads and two moms sat across from us with their two sons who were dressed in gray and green baseball uniforms. They were obviously on their way to little league — some suburbanites' version of church, you know. And the boys could hardly contain themselves.

Another young couple fed their baby breakfast from a Gerber's jar. This scene was just across from a picture of *Our Gang* meeting outside their club house with the sign reading, "E N T R A N S E." I didn't see anything special about calling attention to their entranse until Betty pointed out that it was spelled with an "S" rather than a "C." How's a fellow to know?

Our perky, friendly, and freckled waitress wore a crisp, short white uniform that was trimmed in blue with delicate touches of red. She soon brought our breakfasts and, to save a few words in reporting on its quality, everything on our table was either great or excellent. The only thing on the entire table which did not earn the mark of excellence was the French toast. It just did not measure up to the delicious French toast at the Dinner Bell restaurant in Linden, Tennessee or the superb French toast fingers at Shoney's. But to be sure, 5th and Diner will be one of the spots where we choose to stand in line for breakfast for a long time to come.

It was 10:35 a.m. and almost church time. At least, it was so long as you were not a rabid Titan's fan, a Sunday activity for next Fall that already was beginning to loom on the annual horizon. The papers and the other media outlets were full of news about the team — the possible starting line-up, which Titans would make it and those who might not, who had been arrested for DUI during the past few days, and who had broken his hand while playing golf. The last two were obviously a bad drinker and an even worse golfer. But, I digress.

The second worship service of the morning at the Newsong Christian Fellowship Church was scheduled to begin at 11:00 a.m. The first one had taken place at 8:45 a.m. When Betty and I walked into the foyer, I immediately realized that I had been in this building several years ago before it was a church. I had visited Jim Van Hook in this building when he operated Brentwood Music out of it in 1994 – 95. Shortly after that time, Jim sold the business to another company while keeping the ownership of this building. He moved the new company to another location shortly thereafter and then leased this building to Newsong which Newsong has since purchased. The small congregation had mushroomed in both size and spirit since that time.

The informality of the church was obvious when we first walked in. A Starbucks-looking coffee bar dispensed several flavors of coffee to those waiting for the first service to end, which it finally did at about 10:57 a.m. This should have been a warning to me about the length of the services, but at the time I was not aware that the first service had begun two hours and 12 minutes ago. Betty and I took a seat as soon as enough of the early marathon worshipers had exited the auditorium (I learned that they prefer not to call it a sanctuary out of concern that the term might adversely affect their sense of freedom in worship.) We sat as near the back as we could and estimated the room would seat about 500 people.

This building had been effectively changed into an informal place of worship with its high warehouse-type ceilings and block walls. The individual burgundy-tinted seats were connected into pew-like rows on the green-carpeted floors. Four prominent banners across the pulpit area announced something of a theme for this church. They read:
 – *Reach Up To God*
 – *Reach In To One Another*
 – *Reach Out To Christ's Body And To The World*
 – *Reach Forward To The Future*

Again, we were in the minority by far. Mostly young people were both leaving and coming and they were all (100 percent, no less) casually dressed. There were no coats and ties. Zero. A young blond woman in a black pantsuit with a knee length jacket and a red blouse began leading the music. She was supported by four back-up singers and a band consisting of drums, keyboard and three guitars. The first song was *You Are Good* and the words flashed upon a large screen over the stage (not "chancel") area. The congregation sang: "We worship you for who you are for You are good...You are good all the time, all the time" over and over. It was 11:02 a.m. and this service was not yet half-filled. One young man in the pew in front of us was drinking a bottle of orange soda with one hand and, as a result, had difficulty waving and clapping along with the music. The majority of the congregation was exuberantly singing and swaying rhythmically to the beat of the music.

Scott Weaver, who was listed in the church literature as the head of "Administration, men's ministry," came to the pulpit at the end of the first song and declared that it had been the "wettest and coolest spring in Nashville in my 20 years here," obviously a recognition of the heavy rain pouring down outside. Then he welcomed the visitors of this service and called on ushers to give each visitor a "packet." He said, "I want all members to stand and all visitors to remain seated." He said to the members, "You know the drill." And we were trapped like a deer in the headlights of a car. It was obvious we had no hiding place. The obedient and enthusiastic young ushers swarmed over us with welcoming words. I'm not sure but we may have been the only visitors there. It surely seemed like it.

Next we were encouraged by the worship team to sing "Forever." Some of the words were, "For the life that's been reborn, His love endures forever...Forever God is with us — forever...God is faithful forever. God is strong forever, forever...Sing praise, sing praise... forever." In the front, one member of the worship team stood at pew level giving exuberant sign language to a section of hearing impaired members during the entire service. I could hardly keep my eyes off her because she was so enthusiastic.

At 11:20 a.m. the church was two-thirds full and the blonde song leader now also acted as a cheerleader, "How many are prepared to give your all to worship this morning? Raise your hands." She then asked everyone to join in singing over and over and over: "I will worship — I will worship with all my heart. I will praise you with all my praise. I will give you all my worship and all my praise ...I will give you all my worship and all my praise." One attractive woman to our right and toward the front was the most fully involved in the music that I had even seen. With full and free movement of her arms and hands along with total rhythmic body movement, and head language, she was giving her all to worship as requested by the leader. For a short period during one of these songs she kneeled to the floor and prostrated herself there in prayer with seemingly total self-abandonment.

At the end of another song Dale Evirist, the senior pastor,

came out and further led the cheers and applause before saying, at 11:37 a.m., "You may be seated." He was a middle-aged man of average size dressed in black pants with a seaweed green shirt which was the kind not requiring being tucked in. The worship team and the band then left their spots indicating that their part of this service was over. Now it would be up to the senior pastor. But first things first — the tithes and offerings. While the offering was taken, the minister made announcements. Betty deposited her $5 into God's storehouse, the Newsong Fellowship branch. One of the most exuberant female worshipers took a respite in the form of a coffee break and brought a cup back to her seat in order to tide her over. She knew something about the length of the service which we did not know, at this point.

With great fanfare, including recorded music and pictures on the large screen, a man dressed in missionary-type fatigues came out and brought us "Greetings from Kenya." He read, rather poorly, his report from mission work in Africa. He said that he had read the report better at the early service. After the report the pastor commented that "our team was in Nairobi during the height of the terrorist threats there."

Pastor Evirist then said we would now "dismiss our kids so that they may go to their classes," before asking the ushers to pass out pledge cards, "to raise $600,000 for our celebration room." The celebration room is apparently used for weddings, stage productions and other like events.

Then the pastor introduced a ten-minute skit. Well-written and well-acted, it was about a young man brought into a Christian fellowship through the persistence of his girlfriend who gradually became an integral part of the group, mostly through the attention of "Bubba" one of the group who had two refurbished Nash Ramblers — a real love of the young man.

The pastor then came back at about 11:50 a.m. and read from *Ephesians 2: 19 – 22.* He then said he was going to talk about the "Power of Family." He said: "The church is family in macro form and the family is the church in micro form." He pointed out that this belief was the reason the church did not call its meeting room a "sanctuary." He said he felt strongly that whatever you do in your living room you should do here and vice versa.

The pastor then shared a story about how he and his family recently went to a funny movie. They had all laughed and laughed together with all the others in the movie theatre, but when it was over the laughing camaraderie disappeared and the moviegoers walked out "like zombies," neither talking nor looking at each other. He said that is "not how it happens here at Newsong. Here we stand around and talk and enjoy each other's company like a family. But there are those who do not join in this fellowshipping. They are disconnected." The pastor said that if you were not connected, you were not receiving all you could receive. He pointed out that the scripture lesson says "you are no longer strangers." He felt that these words gave us a word picture of what our church should be like, the picture of a family.

The pastor next declared, "I'm not going to live my life without a close friend. It's dangerous." He followed this by saying, "Try to live for God on your own and you'll find that it won't work. We are meant to live in community." He said that even with "the nut cases" in the church there was much more healing than hurt. He said our country is so much on the move that the people were many times a "mile wide and an inch deep." He suggested that this was especially dangerous for kids. Then he warmly told how his sixteen-year-old son had a visitor the previous night whom he had known for 10 years, and how they had grown together, and how they are real friends with genuine common interests. He said, "Until you have walked and talked with people a long time you don't know love and commitment." He even indicated that an evangelist who does not live in a real community is dangerous.

The pastor spoke freely with few notes and moved easily about the platform area to establish a direct rapport with the congregation. He said that he did not want to know how good a speaker a potential pastor would be. Instead, he wanted to know how he treated his family, friends and employees.

It seemed that the first 30 minutes had just been an introduction to the sermon because at this point the pastor began to speak about the ten points in the "Power of Family."

I.   *Fathered Together*
II.   *Founded Together*
III. *Fitted Together*

IV.   *Flowing Together*
V.   *Feeding Together*
VI.   *Focused Together*
VII. *Favored Together*
VIII. *Fighting Together*
IX.   *Fruitful Together*
X.   *Finishing Together*

The pastor began going through the whole ten set of alliterations. The first two said that we have a common Father and that Jesus Christ was the cornerstone of the foundation of the church. When he got to III he said that we must become a part of a real congregation. He noted that Tim and Christa Ashworth were connected and fitted together. He asked them to come forward. He said they were connected both here and in Texas and were going back to Texas to work in one of their ministries called "Apartment Life." He noted that most apartment parking lots were full on Sundays, indicating that this was a great un-churched group of people that Tim and Christa were going to serve.

Number IV was an illustration of how tributaries flow together to form a mighty river. He said that when the Psalmist said, "Behold how good it is for brethren to live together in harmony" it was the "flowing together that is important for us to be a mighty force together." He said that Number V, "Feeding Together," was the most important because he said, "I have never known of an isolated person who is full." He then added, "They may be full of it but not really full." Numbers VI and VII simply say that we must be "Focused" together as a family to do God's work in the world and that only as we are truly together can we be "favored" by God. He stressed that God wanted to bless us, but He could not do it in isolation.

In Number VIII he told how "Fighting Together" was important when we needed a friend to stand up with us and for us. It was also important when we needed a friend who was willing to listen to the battles we were fighting.

Frankly, numbers IX and X got away from me. Now this preacher was really good. Everything he said was interesting and very well said, but after an hour of any sermon I develop a severe case of ADD (attention deficit disorder). I've had it all my life. I'm sort of like the young boy asked what he was going to be when he grew up. He answered, "I'm going to be a preacher."

"Why?" asked his adult questioner.

The boy replied, "Because I have decided I'm going to have to go to church all my life and I've decided it is harder to sit in a pew and be quiet than it is to stand up and holler."

Pastor Evirist had been "hollering" quite effectively, I might add. But at Number IX my ADD kicked in and, like the young boy, it just became hollering to me. Then he announced that he had come to his last point, Number X, "Finishing Together." I wrote these words in my note pad: "Okay, pastor, I'm ready if you are. Now let's all as a community finish together. Okay, on the count of three, let's stop. Okay, 1 – 2 – 3. Okay, pastor, it didn't work that time since you are still going, I must have jumped the clock. Now all together again. Ready to finish? Okay, now let's all finish together this time 1 – 2 – 3. Okay, pastor, now on 10 this time 1 – 2 – 3 – 4 – 5 – 6 – 7 – 8 – 8 1/2 – 8 3/4 – 9 – 9 1/4...Aw, come on now, pastor, you're not really trying – 9 1/2 – 9 3/4 – 10. Well, brother, I just finished with the rest of the congregation, now you finish when you can." It was 1:00 p.m. Betty and I closed our minds and I closed my note pad. And we prepared to bolt at the first opportunity — the very minute Pastor Evirist realized that the rest of us had already finished. I was ready now for even golfing in the rain, which three of us did. The only one who did not join us will not be named, but his initials are James F. Neal.

C h a p t e r   3 8

Buddhist Meeting
Nashville, Tennessee
June 1, 2003

By a new Browning declaration, the Christian Sabbath begins at sunset on Saturday and ends at sunset Sunday. Thus, our 38th Sunday on the blue road began on Saturday evening with a gathering of a few friends wishing Frank Sutherland a happy 58th birthday. We assembled at Jimmy Kelly's restaurant because none of us had been invited to the large wedding taking place at Richland club. There was simply no room for us in the inn, so to speak. Just a few hours earlier, Frank and I had finished a round of golf, and I had just presented Frank with his birthday gift — by "letting" him beat me for the very first time by one stroke. Folks, that's my story, and I'm sticking to it. Putting the "letting" in quotes is the closest I will come to admitting anything else, and altering my "facts" is the closest we will get to changing my story at this time. More revelations may come to me later, but for the time being that is it. Nothing more. Nada.

Anyhow, fast forward to sunset at Jimmy Kelly's. There were 11 of us:Delores and John Seigenthaler, Lady and Tom Jackson,Jim Neal (his wife Dianne was still on a trip to Europe), Frank Sutherland and his wife Natalie, his mother Fontelle and son Daniel, and, Betty and I. It was almost like the Last Supper except there were only 11 people, none of whom would I consider very righteous, except for Fontelle. And I'm not totally sure about her, either. She surely bears the mark of the beast on her somewhere since it is reported that she gave birth to a Billy Goat Gruff in 1945. (That's an inside joke, folks.) That was right at the end of World War II. Rumor, and some other spurious documentation, has it that the only way she could get the busy doctor to circumcise Frank after his birth was by giving the doctor a pound of "black market" rationed butter. Still another rumor has it that the same doctor was saved from a liability suit filed by Frank against him by the statute of limitations. The suit allegedly charged that the doctor during circumcision maliciously cut off far more than civility allowed, adversely affecting Frank's self-image to this day. And that's all I have to say on that subject. Except that, if I were Frank, I'd challenge the statute of limitation law on the grounds that he never had any idea he would live as long as he has.

Jim Neal helped us end this party (as he always does) by saying, "Well, boys and girls, it's time for me to go home." Jim's not a party starter, nor is he a party pooper. But he has no peers in his ability to bring a party to a close. So with Dr. Neal's benedictory and party-ending words, we were free to disperse to our homes and to begin our individual ways of spending the rest of the Christian Sabbath.

Betty and I chose to spend our Sunday morning by attending a Buddhist meeting, which I had found on the Internet. It meets at the Bongo Java restaurant located on Belmont Boulevard in the Vanderbilt University/Belmont University area. Rita Frizzell (whom I contacted through the Internet) had informed me about three meetings which the Buddhist community in this area holds each week. The first was on Sundays at 11:00 a.m., which we would attend today. This meeting is described in their literature as a meeting of "Basic Meditation and Dharma Study." The second meeting of the week was on Tuesdays at 7:00 p.m. at Morgan House which is a part of the Universalist Unitarian Church located on Woodmont Boulevard. This meeting is for "traditional practice, Tibetan chanting and dharma study for practitioners." The third meeting was held on Thursdays at 7:00 p.m. at Rita Frizzell's home and was for "deeper dharma study." Attendees were invited to "bring any refreshments you'd like."

Rita is apparently part of the glue that holds this fledgling (only 15 years old) Buddhist community together. It seems that she was at one time the wife of a Baptist minister. In a telephone conversation with her, she recommended that Betty and I go to the 11:00 a.m. Sunday meeting and so, at 9:15 a.m. on June 1, Betty and I left to have breakfast and attend this Buddhist meeting. We drove toward Hillsboro Road, turned toward downtown, and then turned right off Music Parkway toward Belmont Boulevard where it bends and gives way to Belmont University. Immediately across from a new student activities center, currently under construction, was the Bongo Java Restaurant. It is in an old residence which had been converted to its present use years ago, and it makes no pretense to be anything other than a funky coffee house which also serves a variety of items to keep its clients coming back there throughout the day. No alcoholic beverages are sold. The building has a large wooden porch/deck protruding out from the front of "this old house" and, at 9:20 a.m. there were numerous patrons gathered to drink coffee, read their papers and generally mix with others in this collegiate community.

The walkway to the restaurant was unkempt and littered with unfinished cigarettes and the plastic wraps from many varieties of oral pleasurements. The interior was somewhat cleaner but rest assured that cleanliness here was not next to godliness by any means.

We encountered the coffee bar as we first entered. Several people were already in line for coffee, and some were ordering breakfast.They displayed a large selection of muffins, scones, bagels and sweet rolls of several descriptions. Overhead, a menu board written in chalk offered several selections of "green eggs" and other breakfast items. Green eggs just don't do it for me. I can't get past the sound of "green eggs" this early in the day.

Betty ordered a combo of fried-egg sandwiches on toasted English muffins while I ordered the "grand slam" breakfast, which turned out to be sort of an egg soufflé congealed sufficiently to allow it to be cut into fingerlets and smothered in spicy marinara sauce. It came with ham (warmed lunch meat,you all), hash-brown potatoes and wheat toast. As always, I ordered dessert "for the table" which was a waffle covered with bananas and strawberries. Betty really liked her twin egg sandwiches and I thoroughly enjoyed the hash browns and the waffle. But the ham and the egg soufflé (or whatever they call it) was too un-American for my tastes. Betty probably would have liked it really well. But it was too much like quiche to suit me. Does that prove that I'm manly, or what?

Betty and I acted like regulars at Bongo Java by inviting ourselves to join a young blond woman in her late 20s who was eating a bowl of cereal with strawberries and reading the paper. She sat at the only table in the room large enough to both eat and read the paper at the same time, and Betty had brought her paper for this occasion. When our semi-attractive tablemate finished her cereal, she excused herself, moved over to a computer stand, and logged onto the Internet for a little surfing.

Around the room there was a curious combination of customers. A single man in his late 30s sat on an old faux leopard skin sofa reading a paper and drinking coffee. Another woman sitting alone at a small table appeared that she was grading papers. I determined that she was a teacher, perhaps at Belmont. I wanted the man on the sofa to meet this professor with soft brunette hair and sad eyes — and for them to live happily ever after. Maybe they will if they keep coming to Bongo Java and give fate a little helping hand.

Several people around the room were using laptop computers plugged into outlets around the wall. These customers appeared to have already had their coffee. I wondered how the restaurant could make any money off these tables unless there was an hourly rate for their use.

By now I had invited a group of four in their 40s and 50s to join us at our "reading table." One of them read a book while the others shared a paper — three men and one tall, attractive blond woman. One of the men, the oldest, looked exactly like Cheech Moran who played Kevin Costner's partner in the movie "Tin Cup." I am still not sure that it wasn't Cheech himself. But I'll never know. Somehow I can never get myself to ask a question which would satisfy my curiosity in a situation like this. I guess I don't want these "stars" to know I am impressed by who they are, or something like that.

Most of the people in this restaurant were well past student age. I guess they just wanted to be in a cool place, or they did not want to stand in line at the Pancake Pantry. Maybe they feel it is uncool to go to Starbucks where the yuppies were. These customers were more likely to be student hangers on, professors who liked to hang out, or music industry people who like the individualism and the "artiness" of Bongo Java more than the slickness of Starbucks.

An older woman (60s) who was very thin wore a sweat shirt and shorts, although I thought she ought to have had sweat pants on to hide her much too skinny legs. And then there was this other tall, thin, bald man who looked as if he must be auditioning for character roles in the grade-B movies often filmed in Nashville. He looked like a 6'3" Kojak. Then just as Kojak sat down another middle-aged man with a beard came in and sat on the leopard sofa. He could not keep his eyes off Kojak. Then again, neither could I. But Bluebeard kept slicking his hair back over and over in hope that the 6'3" would-be movie star might notice him. Kojak may have been writing his own movie to star in because he was constantly making notes in a spiral notebook. My Lord, I thought, I hope he is not writing a book called *Fifty-two Sundays* and is already on his 40th Sunday.

Our waitress and the other employees in the restaurant appeared to be college students and were (to different degrees) trying to push the envelope of acceptable hippie-like attire. Is the term "hippie" even still used? If not, what is the new word for this attitude and look? Was it hip-hop? At any rate, our waitress was dressed in very tight tan hip huggers with a heavy metal belt swagging well below her hips and large earrings. Her companion at the coffee bar was similarly dressed and had a nose piercing with a chrome tack accent. I saw no tongue hardware.

It was now 10:50 a.m., and so Betty and I slowly made our ways upstairs to the room where the Buddhists were gathering. None of the people who came to the meeting upstairs had also had coffee or breakfast downstairs in Bongo Java. As we entered the small theater room upstairs, a middle-aged man asked if this would be our first time to meet with this group. When we said it was, we were given an information sheet entitled "Padmasambhaua Buddhist Center." It seems that this center in Nashville is one of twenty centers around the world started by two brother Lamas Buddhist meditation masters. I noticed that all the others in the room had their shoes off and Betty and I still had ours on. Then I read in the literature that the "protocol" is to "please remove your shoes before entering the dharma room." I removed mine. Betty didn't.

Betty and I sat on the back two seats in this tiny theater which may have had room enough for 30 people. There was a small stage with a sound system and microphones in place for performances, and there was a lighting system to be used for small productions. Rita Frizzell had set up a small Buddhist altar consisting of statues and candles on a burgundy cloth covering a very low table placed in the center of the room. As the meditators entered, they folded their hands and went through a simple ritual of humbling themselves before the altar. They would prostrate themselves by bowing a couple of times before finally taking their seats. Then some sort of recorded chant in Tibetan signaled the start of the meditation period. When it ended, Rita, who was seated at the front and faced the other 15 or so of us, welcomed everyone to the meeting by saying, "Good morning to all. Thank you for coming. We are a Tibetan meditation group." Rita is a tall, trim blond woman in perhaps her early 50s and was dressed in black pants and a burgundy sweater. She sat cross-legged in the traditional Buddhist style, which I could not do even if I were the most devout practitioner.

Rita explained that the meetings were always opened with breathing exercises. She instructed everyone to close their left nostril with the index finger of their left hand and said, "And we then breathe out our anger for a few seconds. At this time if you have any anger toward any situation or toward anyone just let it go." Then she directed all of us to close our right nostrils in the same manner and to breathe out all of our attachments or any strong desires in an effort to release us from the "things" and situations around us. She then told us how to breathe out of both nostrils and concentrate on breathing out all our misconceptions about life and the world. Everyone, including Betty, went through these exercises. Everyone except the writer of these words, that is. Betty's a real sport. She gets right in with all the different groups and sings their songs, recites their creeds and prays their prayers just as if she were a new convert. I just couldn't risk the nose exercises with a sharp writing instrument in my hand, which was allowing me to take the notes that are the basis for these reflections on the meditations. Betty had us covered, however.

Before this meditation period began, we had been given meditation guides and, at this point, our leader pointed us to Page 4. This was a prayer asking the energy in the universe to enter this room, and asking us to realize the energy which was already in our lives and was ready to be discovered. The prayer was in the Tibetan language and the form of a peaceful and relaxing chant. There were now 21 people in the room, two-thirds of which were men (the first time in 38 weeks that men have outnumbered women in the religious gatherings we had attended). Stragglers kept coming in as Rita directed us to Page 5 which she said was the Sumadma which helps to relax and quiet the mind. She said that we should all repeat this three times and in a singsong fashion. The group (including Betty) repeated the chant. As Betty joined in, I could recall hearing her years ago during a Christian youth gathering around a campfire singing in almost the same voice the words, "Kum Ba Yah. My Lord, Kum Ba Yah. Oh, Lord, Kum Ba Yah." We, too, would chant these words over and over again. I felt that these Buddhists were doing the same thing by creating a relaxing, reflective mood, just as if singing "Kum Ba Yah" around a campfire with marshmallows roasting on a straightened coat hanger or forked stick.

This part of the chanting had been totally familiar to me, but at the end of the printed Tibetan chant, in which Betty gleefully participated, all the individual Buddhist practitioners began individual chants (while some were handling their prayer beads). The manner of the individual chants reminded me of a sound which I had heard for only a few seconds months ago when a lone woman spoke in tongues in a Pentecostal Church. The sound I would never have forgotten from that day was now being reproduced by some 15 to 20 voices at once during this Buddhist meditation experience.

Rita produced a light "gong" sound by hitting a brass dome with a drumstick-like instrument to signal the beginning of another part of the service. She said "Our teachers like the great Buddha are teachers...they don't tell us that they have found the absolute enlightenment. They teach us how to find our own enlightenment." She said that one of the ways they taught us was to focus on the breath because it was always with us. "Breathing deeply helps us relax our mind which brings a calming to us," she told us. With the sound of the "gong" she signaled a period of 4 to 5 minutes during which we were to simply concentrate on our breathing in and breathing out and to feel its relaxing effect.

As I breathed with all the rest, I was like a kid in church. I peeked and looked around this theater. I saw the evidence of some of the other uses the theater is put to, including a poster announcing past performances of the "Vampire Monologues" by Jeremy Chiles. The period of breathing exercises was ended by the sound of the "gong" again. I continued breathing nevertheless.

Rita then told us that for the past few weeks the group had been reading and studying together *Comfortable With Uncertainties*.

The book had been written to help us become more comfortable with life's uncertainties. The chapter for today was entitled "Turning Arrows Into Flowers," just as the great Buddha did 2,500 years ago. This chapter listed some problems we face in life. The first one our attention was pointed to was "seeking pleasure." She said when we have pain we seek what can help us blot out the pain — a shopping spree or an alcoholic drink or some other escape mechanism. Unfortunately, we find that the pain persists and is even worse after these unsuccessful "seeking pleasure" remedies are over. We have just postponed the pain. With the sound of the "gong," she asked us to think of times we had followed this method of escape from pain.

While we were going through this exercise, I saw signs of one man's attempt to obliterate pain by momentary pleasure. It was evidenced in the tattoos which were all over his arms and down to his wrists. I imagine the pain he was "escaping" when he went on this spree will be with him for a long time. (I'm sorry teacher. I know we were supposed to think of our own situation. And I was trying — till I saw my friend in front of me reach up to adjust his beautiful earring and saw the evidence of his spree and was distracted.) The "gong" ended the exercise before I could get to my own pain-ending sprees. Guess I'll have to do it as homework.

Rita then read of situations which cause us to tighten up like the loss of a job, a girlfriend or a boyfriend. She said we first try to recreate the exact same situation by trying to get a job, girlfriend or boyfriend, just like the one we lost. But we can't. It will never be the same. She said we should just relax, try to accept the situation, and go from there. And from there, maybe find a different way to go. At 11:45 a.m. the "gong" sounded again as she directed us to take a few minutes to think about these situations in our lives.

With the next "gong" Rita told us about how "strong emotions" get us into more pain, just as our evasive "pleasure seeking" efforts do. She said that, when we have been hurt, we don't have to build on that emotion. The emotion is made worse by delving into why some person hurt us like they did. This just exacerbates the pain. We would be far better off by breathing in and out and just "letting it go" without building on the story and the pain. Another "gong" gave us a few minutes to think about situations like this in our lives.

Again, I broke the rules. I looked at a black woman sitting

Buddha fashion on the floor in an aisle while following Rita's every direction. And there was the "beige man" (beige pants, beige socks and beige shirt) who was 100 percent into everything — a good meditator reaching toward Nirvana. The "gong" sounded the end to yet another 4 to 5 minutes of my writing instead of meditating.

Rita next said that another problem we all faced was a "fear of death," but she hurriedly explained that in this situation what we were actually experiencing was a fear of life. Now, I don't quite know about this one Rita. I was willing to think about it later, but she wanted us to think about it right then. "Gong," and we were thinking again.

Rita then told us that the Dali Lama said that true happiness can only come in what we do for others and not in what we do for ourselves. With this thought she asked us to think of others we know who may need our help. After a Tibetan chant and three "gongs," and with hands and heads bowed in the classical style of Buddha, this meditation period was over.

Rita brought us back to reality by making some announcements, including the visit the two great leaders of this branch of Buddhism would be making to Monterey, Tennessee at the end of June. She urged all to attend. Lastly Rita told us something which made us feel right at home. She said that there would be an offering plate at the door as we went out. This gave Betty and me an opportunity to participate in a way which had been offered to us as part of almost every religious service we had attended, except during the Mormon service and the Jehovah's Witness services. (These two may be just like membership in the Augusta National Golf Club where the Masters Tournament is held each year. The Augusta Club does not have monthly dues. It just adds up the expenses at the end of the year, divides it by the number of members, and sends out equal statements to all members. Maybe the Mormons and the Jehovah's Witnesses just send out statements also.) Anyhow, feeling right "to home" after being asked for a donation or an offering, Betty proudly deposited our $5. Once again, we went away realizing how very much alike most of us are. Amen? Amen. "Gong!"

Chapter 39

St. Bartholomew's Episcopal Church
Nashville, Tennessee
June 8, 2003

*T*oday was affirmative action Sunday by my choice of a church to attend. Most Episcopalians I know would not fully appreciate the "affirmative action" reference being applied to my choice to go to St. Bartholomew's Episcopal Church. "Equal opportunity" might be a little more palatable, but I don't think so. At any rate, I was doing some sort of equalizing when I decided to visit another Episcopal Church. We had been to two Catholic churches, three Methodist churches, three Presbyterian churches, three Assembly of God churches, several types of Baptist churches, and a wide selection of others. We had been to only one (regular) Baptist Church, one Church of Christ Church, and only one Episcopal Church. Therefore, it was obvious that some sort of "religious equal opportunity" or "affirmative action" needed to be a factor in my decisions regarding which churches I should attend during the next twelve to thirteen Sundays before my 52nd Sunday was upon me.

My arbitrary affirmative action for this Sunday had been decided upon early in the week, and I determined it was time to be fair to the Episcopalians. Or maybe my decision to attend an Episcopalian service was actually an act of fairness toward all the other churches which had been subjected to my unsolicited visits during the past several months. Regardless, it was the Episcopalians' time again. I swear I can hear the Catholics, Methodists, and Presbyterians saying, "Fair is fair." Whatever. I was settled on visiting the Episcopalians again this Sunday.

I know someone is asking, "Okay, now I understand your choice of this particular denomination today, but how did you choose St. Bartholomew's?" Perhaps you don't want to know the answer as badly as I want to tell you but, at any rate, here it is. On

Easter Sunday morning, Betty and I had attended Christ Church
Cathedral which is the crown jewel of this area's Episcopal churches in size (probably), tradition (definitely), and history (definitely).
While the pomp and pageantry of the Easter service had been what
we had wanted to witness on Easter, now we wanted to visit the
most "liberal" Episcopal Church (in terms of liturgical practice)
that we could find in the area — and all indicators pointed to
St. Bartholomew's.

During the middle of last week I played golf with John
Seigenthaler (John had won rather handily which I am sure he
would wish to have recorded) and Fred Detwiller. Fred is a member
of Richland club where we play (as well as The Golf Club of
Tennessee, I was happy to find out later). Fred's regular group was
not playing that day, and he joined John and me. Aside from being
a good playing companion on the course, I found Fred to be a real
resource for information on the Episcopal churches in this area.
Now that's an interesting matter in its own right. Fred is owner of
the Det Distributing Company in Nashville whose products are
several brands of beer and bottled water. At dinner after golf, I told
Fred and his wife Katherine that I had at one time (pre-1964) been
a Presbyterian minister. Now get this. Fred is about 71-years-old
and he said, "Would you believe I am studying to be a priest?" Say
what! Yup, that's what he said. He's taking a prescribed course of
study directed by the bishop and the Episcopate which will lead to
his eventual ordination to the priesthood.

So, here the four of us were: an ex-preacher/real estate salesman
and his wife having dinner with a soon-to-be priest/beer distributor
and his wife. We talked about the ministry, the priesthood and
about a potential future book entitled *Fifty-two Sundays*. From time
to time and as a result of his future new life as a priest, Fred will
find himself assigned by the bishop to fill in at vacancies in the
Diocese. "I'll bet he knows a lot about all the Episcopal churches in
the area," I thought. What better source could I find to get a bead on
an Episcopal Church which would be as different from the Cathedral
as possible? Without a moment's thought Fred said we should go to
St. Bart's (also known as St. Bartholomew's) in Nashville.

St. Bart's is apparently in the tradition of the few — apparently
very few — charismatic Episcopal churches to be found anywhere.

There was a time when a wave of charismatic worship was, strangely enough, being experienced in both Episcopal and Catholic churches. This was an unexpected and unusual phenomenon in that both of these traditions have a very strong liturgical order of worship which, in and of itself, does not encourage spontaneity. And charismatic worship, by its very nature, does not find an inviting breeding ground in overly structured situations.

Future Father Fred told me that whatever the present level of charismatic activity there was in the area's Episcopal churches, St. Bart's would lead the pack. So, with this information from soon-to-be Father Fred, we easily chose St. Bart's for today's religious service. I called and found that they have two worship services each Sunday — 8:45 a.m. and 10:30 a.m. Which service to attend was also an easy decision. Betty and I could never make it on a voluntary basis to a service before 10:30 a.m., and we by far prefer 11:00 a.m. (except in the cases when the service goes for two hours or more).

So, while St. Bart's was an easy choice, where to have breakfast was another matter. We were running out of different places to have breakfast in Nashville. Again, I think that freedom of religion laws should require all restaurants which open Saturday must also be open on Sunday. Jews and Seventh Day Adventists unite! Also breakfast loving Sunday Christians unite! Let's force those who serve breakfast to Saturday worshipers to also serve breakfast to Sunday seekers of the truth and the light.

But until the light shines upon the Supreme Court and we are led to true Sunday morning breakfast equality, we will have to be more and more diligent in finding righteous restaurant owners who feed the flocks on Sunday morning. I had a network of friends and relatives out scouting, and this week it paid off in a secret report from our daughter, Beverly. She called and clandestinely whispered, "Pssst. I have just heard that the Sportsman's Grill is now open and serving a great breakfast on Sundays." It was almost as if she were telling us of a speak-easy which was open. "Just knock three times and tell them Beverly sent you."

We left home at 8:31 a.m. according to Betty's notes in my book. She didn't even force the record to read 8:30 a.m., which I gave her permission to do as an act of charity on my part and in recognition for her considerable improvement of late in her timeliness. It is like she is now able to openly admit to the world her problem — "Hello, my name is Betty and I'm a timeaholic." As she wrote proudly and confessionally in her own handwriting, she said loudly and clearly, "We left at 8:31 — beautiful sunny day — 72 degrees." The chancel accessories provided by her mobile worship vehicle give her all these verities as she languishes in luxurious leather lounge chairs no matter where she worships day by day.

The Sportsman's Grill is located at the intersection of Harding Road, highways 100 and 70 going west toward Bellevue out of Nashville. It's called Sportsman's Grill because one needs to be a real sports driver to negotiate the three merging lanes to visit this establishment. Deftly, I engaged the Lexus' supercharger, sliced between other racers merging from other courses, and then (nearly slamming into the curtain wall near the entrance) skidded into this new pit stop for breakfast.

We acknowledged the waving of the checkered flag as we entered unscathed to join the others who were already safely parked in the infield. As I stood there admiring my own racing for life victory, I felt strangely attracted to the idea of ordering a glass-bottled quart of milk and drinking it down completely and immediately.

Safely inside, we soon were relaxed in this watering-hole cum breakfast-hole and reading the new six-week-old breakfast menu. I'm a speed-reader of menus and soon ordered a breakfast fit for the king of the road. Of course, I ordered three eggs over-easy/over-medium with hash browns, grits, gravy, bacon and biscuits. What'd you expect? And Betty ordered two eggs scrambled, bacon and wheat toast, right? Right. And I ordered pancakes for the table, right? Right. And coffee by the pot, ready for us when we were. Now that's real service, sports fans.

Before I could drink my milk and take a victory lap, our young model, err, waitress and her assistant served us fine looking meals. And these meals not only looked great, they actually were great. Betty said her breakfast compared favorably with breakfast "at the 213 Club." By that, she meant the breakfasts I cook at home. She will never admit that anyone cooks breakfast any better than I do. She may not be truthful, but she's definitely not dumb. It's her version of social security since a great deal of our social lives these days is sitting at home at 213 Westchase Drive eating hardy home-cooked breakfasts. I could hardly blame Betty for crowding the center line a bit here this morning because the breakfast was outstanding. The eggs, biscuits, bacon, potatoes were all well-prepared, and (just as ordered and wished) the biscuits were crispy on the bottoms and well baked on the tops. And the large portions of bacon were thick and crisp. If I were grading I would give an A-. Why the minus? Well, the syrup for our dessert pancakes was not up to my standards. But remember, my standards have been set awfully high by the Pancake Pantry which has the best syrup in the world. A-? We're grading on the curve, folks.

As we enjoyed our breakfasts, we watched two men sitting at different tables each of whom surely weighed 500 pounds. It made me realize that after 9-11-03 when my *Fifty-two Sundays* time is over, I will have no further excuse for pampering myself at Sunday breakfasts like this. The King of the Road was becoming the Wimp of Willpower. If I had been drinking tea with tealeaves, my fortune would have read that a rigid diet was forecast. Our beautiful blond waitress may have had as much influence on this thinking as the two 500 pound bookends surrounding us. This young lady possessed a classical beauty which Betty and I quickly defined as beauty which reveals itself even when there is no effort to project it. The Scandinavian-looking beauty wore her blond hair on the top of her head, just thrown up there to get it out of the way. She had adorned herself with a non-descript white T-shirt and blue jeans. She had absolutely no reason to look beautiful. But there she was, against all odds, looking like the breakfast goddess of all the blue road eateries we had visited. This place will do very well. Good food and good looks. What a combination!

We were served so well and so efficiently that it was only 9:30 a.m. (The world doesn't know about this new breakfast spot yet. Should we tell them? Or should we keep it a secret?) St. Bart's was only minutes away. What to do? We decided to make our final pit stop back at 213 before going on to St. Bart's. A full, delicious meal with the love of your life served by a really beautiful young woman and a comfortable pit stop in your very own bathroom is about as close to heaven (or Nirvana for the Buddhists) as one can get at the age of 71 1/2.

After lounging in Nirvana for about 30 minutes, Betty and I

were back on the city's blue roads on the way to visit our church of choice. Next Sunday the new nearly Father Fred would be feeding his first flock at another Episcopal Church in Nashville, and I wondered if I should go hear him give his very first sermon. It should be a great one because he has worked on it for months. I'd have to think about visiting a third Episcopal Church in my series. Another thing I would have to think about was my discussion of trading some of my old sermons for some of Fred's beer. How many cases should one sermon be worth? I'm afraid Fred may try to negotiate me down to six packs. Once I get the amount fixed, I'm going to switch my trade to bottled water. Don't tell Fred, but I really don't like beer. Also, water sometimes sells for more per bottle than beer, so I would be getting a better value. Can you believe that?

Refreshed, Betty and I entered St. Bart's on Belmont Park Terrace at 10:24 a.m. This church was an unimpressive, rather unattractive brick structure on the outside which belied the warm, attractive sanctuary inside. Soaring 50-foot beamed ceilings supported by concrete pilasters and brick walls, punctured by narrow rectangular stained glass windows, gave the inside a feeling of strength and character. The chancel area was accented by long, rich wood panels from which a suspended wooden cross was projected. As we entered, there was much visiting going on among the early arrivers. As newcomers arrived, we did not witness many of them genuflecting before the cross as they took their pew seats, which is the custom at most Episcopal Churches.

At 10:28 a.m. some lay worship assistants in white robes lit the candles in the chancel area, and some of the robed assistants chatted freely with other members of the congregation standing in the aisles. This congregation of many young people numbered about 200 at this time. Several were walking down the aisles with white Styrofoam cups of coffee that were being gulped down just prior to the beginning of the service.

At the same time, a processional entourage was beginning to form under the encouragement of the assistant rector, although without a great deal of early success. After a few moments and a few humorous words from the leader (I could not hear him but those who could laughed happily at his remarks), the procession began with a triumphant sound of music that came from the choir loft at the rear of the sanctuary. They sang, "Hail thee, festival day! Blest day that art hallowed forever. Day when the Holy Ghost shone in the world with God's grace." As the procession of twelve entered the chancel area, each bowed reverently before the altar and the cross before dispersing to their assigned places in the chancel area.

Drums from the elevated choir loft introduced the next hymn. Among the 200 or more worshipers singing were many young people, most of whom were casually dressed. Some were wearing shorts and sandals. The fewer than half-dozen men in coats were older, but not as old as the two first-time visitors sitting at the right of the very back pew section. A group of five sitting in the row immediately in front of us were dressed alike in a fashion indicating that they were, or thought of themselves as being, a sort of musical (perhaps rock) group. Each of the five wore black pants, a black T-shirt, and mix-and-match black jackets. The tip off was their hairstyles. All of them had dark or black hair individually streaked with gold, purple or orange highlights. The young, muscular young man sitting nearest to us wore a "message T-shirt." The message was about the number of abortions taking place annually in the U.S. and ended by imploring the reader to join in the effort to bring a stop to this practice. This whole group of young people enthusiastically joined in the spirit of this service by raising and waving their hands during the more exuberant songs sung by the choir and the congregation.

After the scripture lesson was read from the *Old* and *New Testaments*, the Revered Thomas McKenzie came to the front and center of the chancel area. This dark-haired priest began in a relaxed and personal mode. He said, "Morning All." After the congregation responded to this personal greeting, the assistant rector began his sermon. (The rector, according to printed information we received as we entered, was on leave while he dealt with some "personal issues" under the direction of the bishop.)

Father Thomas, as they called the assistant rector, said that he had been talking about the Holy Spirit for the past four weeks and the same topic would be continued today. He said that he had recently been in Mexico. One night while he was in a certain area, he saw thousands and thousands of stars, more than he had ever seen before anywhere. He said his experience was almost like being in a planetarium such as the one in New York at the Museum of Natural History, which I personally have visited several times. He said that the planetarium shows the expanded universe with its trillions and trillions of stars. Father Thomas was really into the expanded universe and the trillions discussion and moved about with his arms waving and flapping frantically as he tried to coax us into seeing the immensity of the universe through his words and body language.

As he walked around the chancel area freely, he spoke without any notes at all. As I admired this facility he had with words and gestures, he began telling us about how amazed he had been (as he stood in the planetarium in New York) with the God who had put all this together. Excitedly, he flapped about the chancel area almost as if he might at any moment take flight toward the extremities of the universe which he was describing. The magnitude of all this creation was exhilarating to him, as all could see. "But," he said, "the amazing thing is that the God who created all of these trillions of stars and planets inhabits it all — the stars, Earth and Mars and everywhere."

Now Father Thomas soared with the eagles. He said, "He is there and He knows it all. He knows of the other life forms in the universe because he is there." Father Thomas then brought his message from the extremities of the universe right down to where we live. He told us that through the miracle of Pentecost, the God of the universe comes and inhabits us. This young priest then emphasized even further that the Holy Spirit has come to us lives IN US, not in churches or buildings, but IN US. He said, "The Holy Spirit lives in us and knows us and loves us." Yet even though the Holy Spirit may dwell in us, many ask, he said, "Why do I not always FEEL the presence of the Holy Spirit?"

"Why?" Father Thomas asked. He said it was because most of our Christian lives were about "Me." He said, "It's Me working, Me praying, Me, Me, Me." Father Thomas kept pressing the point that it was the God of the whole universe who is in each individual, but that we had lost the sense of the majesty of this God of the entire universe living within us. He was inferring that if we felt the wonder of this miracle, we would not be so consumed with the Me of everything. He said that, "The God within us is worthy of worship, and I pray that we will renew our sense of awe and wonder." He continued by asking, "Why do we need the sense of awe?" He said the answer was because (1.) it produces joy and (2.) it produces love.

The priest then concluded his Pentecost sermon by admonishing the congregation to, "Pray with me that we may renew our sense of awe and wonder." Then Father Thomas prayed a short concluding prayer: "Holy Spirit you are more present in this place than I am; and you are present in all the universe. Amen."

After the sermon the priest led the congregation in their confession of faith through the words of the *Nicene Creed*, which in the view of most Christians is approximately the same as the *Apostles Creed* (also used in the Episcopal churches in some instances). As the confession of faith was repeated by the priests and the congregation, the priests faced the altar and the cross thereby presenting their backs to the congregation.

The next part of the service was the "Prayers of the People." It was led by the priest and during it many members of the congregation knelt, although a few chose to remain seated. In this prayer the priest covered all the bases. He prayed for the priests and the bishops, the missionaries and all who serve the heavenly Father. Next, he prayed for "all of us," for the sick and for a lengthy list of individual names. He went through the list name by name. Finally, he prayed for St. Bartholomew and prayed for God to "guide us to do your will." He mentioned that the church was going through trying times because of some problems in the life of the rector who was being counseled by the bishop to help him deal with some "personal issues." The priest then asked all to pray, privately and quietly, for all those people and situations as well as for their own personal needs. "The Confession of Sin" was the next in the order of worship and the priest asked God to "forgive us for our sins in word, thought and deed."

After the prayers and confession Father Thomas asked the congregation to greet one another and to welcome any visitors sitting near them. Then the good father came down from the chancel and walked partway up the aisle, being as informal and friendly as possible, to officially welcome all the visitors in the service here today. While down on the congregation's level Father Thomas made several announcements regarding upcoming events, including one about a group whitewater rafting trip scheduled for the next month. Another announcement regarded an upcoming seminar about how to come closer to God.

The offering was next, during which a man with a beautiful baritone voice sang *Singing Alleluia* while being accompanied by drums and a fabulously played classical guitar. During this part of the service several women stood (while the congregation as a whole remained seated) to praise the Lord exuberantly by moving and swaying to the music and freely waving their arms heavenward as if reaching up to God. Some of the "rock group" in front of us joined in this particular form of worship.

Just before the Eucharist several musical introits led the congregation to prepare their minds and hearts for the communion table. Then there were the words of the institution of the Lord's Supper. The worship assistants in the chancel area partook of the sacrament first. The congregation was then invited, row by row, to come to the altar to eat the bread and drink of the cup. The communicants had the choice of drinking directly from the cup or dipping the bread in the chalice of wine in order to partake of both elements simultaneously.

During the concluding moments of the service and while the congregation sang the last hymn, a single attractive blond young woman stood with her arms stretched heavenward to praise God. Gradually, additional women stood one after another to join her in exuberant praise. The priests and other chancel assistants had no reaction to these six or seven women who were now setting the tone for this part of the service.

The service was soon over, and Betty and I were on our way home, and we were also still enjoying this beautiful late spring day. I thought about what we had just observed in this worship service. This was the first time I had ever witnessed the charismatic type of praise and worship practiced in a church which follows a rich liturgical tradition and an elaborate printed order of worship (thirteen pages), which normally allows for little or no deviation. Nevertheless, there it was — worshipers not bound by the unwritten code of conduct which tacitly exists in more liturgically-oriented services. I am sure that these elements of free worship had been a part of these services here before, but it still seemed as if the priests did not know how to respond to these unconventional acts of worship.

They did not encourage it like most ministers in the less liturgically-oriented churches tend to do. In the Pentecostal churches and Churches of God, the pastors actively encourage free expressions of praise and many times join the rejoicing themselves.

Here today there had been no encouragement at all from the chancel area, but the women were not dissuaded from their vigorous rejoicing. The music somehow gave rise to these free acts of worship. I also noticed that these free worshipers were not giving a "Praise the Lord, Preacher" or an "Amen Father, Tell it Father" during the priest's sermon. Perhaps if these free worshiping members verbally supported the priest during his sermons, they would (maybe, just maybe) see a self-conscious priest begin to slightly raise his own arms in praise during the singing. I'd love to see a bishop or archbishop in full vestments swaying rhythmically to the music and waving his arms joyously. It could happen, but I fully believe that in most Episcopal churches there will need to be a lot of "Amen, Father," "Preach it, brother," and "Yes, Lord" during the priests' sermons before the priests will join the praise lines to dance up and down the aisles. That's a big "Amen" there, brother.

Chapter 40

Moslem Mosque
Nashville, Tennessee
June 13, 2003

Today did not start out as a "holy day" in any sense of the word. It was Friday the 13th — a day when superstitious people avoid black cats, step ladders and doing any serious business at all. I must be becoming superstitious because I had been shying away from any serious business on this day. I certainly had not intended to do ANYTHING serious today, but sometimes things just don't work out the way we plan. After a busy day yesterday I had intended to take about six days of rest. (Extrapolating on God's instructions for all His followers to rest on the seventh day — one out of seven — my goal was to rest for six days and do a little work on the seventh).

So, today I had intended to start my six days of rest, but business hangovers from yesterday (Thursday) pushed in on me and crowded my schedule in an ungodly manner. You see, I had intended to make Friday my "Sabbath" for this week in honor of my choice to attend the Mosque on Nolensville Road at Elysian Fields Drive. The Muslims do not necessarily refer to Friday as their "Sabbath" as such, but it is their chosen day to assemble at Mosques around the world to worship. Friday is the holiest day of the week for Moslems because, among other things, they believe that it was on a Friday that God created Adam and that it will be the last day, the judgment day.

My six days of rest did not get off to a great start because of the "bleeding over" of my one day of work. I rushed around all morning hoping to at least start my recognition of the Moslem "Sabbath," as I will continue to refer to their choice of day to assemble at an appointed hour to pray and worship. Soon I realized that my busy "Moslem Sabbath" morning had so pressed in upon me that it was not until after 12:00 p.m. that I got free to begin concentrating on this, the 40th of my *Fifty-Two "Sundays."* The mosque I had decided to attend today began its service at 1:00 p.m.; therefore, I only had about 50 minutes to go somewhere for breakfast/lunch since I had been too busy for either of these meals up until this time. I have come to consider eating a very important part of whichever Sabbath I am adopting as my own for any particular week. With both a restaurant and a Mosque in mind, I took Thompson Lane toward Nolensville Road and then drove east on Nolensville Road.

I was running late, and I did not have Betty with me to blame. What to do? I had to find someone to blame because I always claim to be punctual. The closing attorney who handled one of my business items yesterday? That's it! It is his fault that I am running late. He caused me to need to run around finishing binding together some loose ends from yesterday. And, with that, Betty was off the hook. She had decided not to go with me today, although not in any direct way. It just never developed that she would go with me since it was in the middle of the day Friday, always a busy day for many people, and especially so for those in the real estate business.

So, Betty was working in our office while I was pursuing my attempts to uncover the age-old mysteries of how and why people are different in so many ways while being so very much alike in so many others. Betty was making a living for us while I was attempting to become famous as an author who (through 52 different observations) will show the similarities and differences of most of us in such a clear way that all people on Earth will forever cease fighting with each other, will come to see each other as true brothers and sisters, and will come to love one another. Betty was not at all sure I could achieve my goals in the manner in which I was proceeding. She thought that the best way to keep us from fighting each other was for her and all others to work hard and be sure that we all have plenty to eat and a few comforts of life. That way, we will have no need to fight and steal from each other. Women seem to have such a simple way of looking at life. It takes men like me with a grand vision of life to really see the big pictures of life.

Don't you think?

Therefore, while Betty was taking little baby steps toward doing her part, bit by bit to see that she and I have plenty to eat, I was taking giant steps toward world peace. But even with my approach I would have to eat first so that when I went to the Mosque at 1:00 p.m. hunger pangs would not interfere with my grand vision of reality. So, I kept my eye peeled for a likely eating spot where I could get some blue road food quickly. I wanted to at least be timely for my very first time attending a Moslem prayer and worship service. I thought I might have to settle for some KFC fried chicken and call it country, knowing it would be good and fast. But would it be country? Is all fried chicken country because it is chicken or because it is fried, or both? The beginning of these thoughts might be the basis for another book. For certain, such weighty questions needed to be answered.

Just as I was considering this possible topic for my second book I came to "Norman Couser's Country Cookin." I had eaten there on one occasion many years ago, but had forgotten about it. It was located only one long block away from the Mosque I would be attending today. It was country, to be sure, but would I be able to be served and to eat in fifteen minutes? It was 12:30 p.m., the parking lot was full of cars, and people were streaming into this country feeding spot. I developed a plan right there on the spot — I would put pure old unadulterated capitalism to the test.

I stood in line for five minutes before being seated. At 12:35 p.m., seated with a menu, I flagged my waitress down. I explained to her that I had to be served and finished eating in 15 minutes. I gave her $5 and said, "Can you help me?" She assured me that she could, so I gave her my order immediately. I had the choice of "Country Meals" for $5.80 or "Highbrow Meals" for $6.25. One basic difference between the country meals and the highbrow meals was that the first one was $ .45 cheaper than the second one. The other basic difference was that the country meal came with dark-meat chicken and the highbrow meal came with white meat. Since I had already passed myself off as a big spender with my $5 experiment in capitalism, I splurged and bought myself some class for $ .45 more. What a bargain! For less than half a buck I bought myself some class. I had wanted some all my life and especially since I had been listening to Betty's soundtrack for the movie "Chicago" on which Catherine Zeta Jones sings, *Ain't Nobody Got No Class?*

Within two minutes my highbrow, classy white-meat fried chicken, mashed potatoes, green beans, corn muffins, and iced tea

were sitting before me. Somehow, I really felt that this accommodation by my waitress was a combination of capitalism and
compassion on her part. I saw in her eyes a glimmer that spoke to
a delight in being able to help me which went beyond the value of the
$5 bribe. And all the food was good, down to the last bite of finger-
lickin' excellent (not "finger-lickin' good" as in the old KFC ads)
chicken. It was both thoroughly cooked and crispy.

Within ten minutes I was finished with my meal. I gave my
waitress $10 and asked her to please pay my tab and for her to keep
the change. So, with my $5 bribe added to the leftover change, I
had tipped my waitress almost 100 percent.And it had been worth
it because for a total of $15 my whole day was now back on track.
I walked out of the restaurant still eating one of the delicious semi-
sweet corn muffins as my dessert. I had 10 minutes to get to the
Mosque which was located only 200 to 300 yards away.

At 12:55 p.m. I walked into the Mosque which was located at
the edge of a strip shopping center. This Mosque was in a storefront
building which could well have been a rent-all center or a carpet
store in the not too distant past. It still had the large glass storefront
windows quite similar to the Mid-Eastern food store just next door.
You've seen thousands of them all around the country. They're used
at pet shops, hardware stores, flower shops and hundreds of other
establishments. Now add a Mosque and you'll get the picture of
this setting for today's worship service. As I was walking in, I was
joined by several Middle-Eastern looking men (non-discriminatory
profiling, I hope) who hurried to get the best spot on the floor. I
started to say "to get the best seat in the house," but in this case the
best seat was synonymous with the best spot on the floor. There
were no chairs at all, except one lonely chair at the front behind a
simple wall which was the seat of the Immam — the religious
leader of the Mosque.

I took my usual spot at the back-right section of the room and
propped myself up against both walls in the corner while coveting
the folding chair at the front reserved for the Immam. This man
was an employee of the Mosque hired by the president and the board
of trustees of the Mosque, usually through interviews, references
and ads placed in Islamic publications. In my view, the position is
sort of comparable to a senior pastor in some Christian churches

(like Baptist and Presbyterian) which hire their own pastors/ministers. Other Christian churches (such as Catholic, Episcopal and Methodist) have ministers appointed by a bishop.

Before I entered I had removed my shoes, as did every worshiper who entered. Soon, the shoe racks were filled and shoes were then stacked all over the foyer area, pairs on top of pairs. When I first entered there were about 40 people already seated at various places around the room, some already in the act of worshiping and praying. My section of the room was filled mostly with young boys who seemed to prefer the support of the wall as I did. Those already involved in worshiping were standing, sitting, or bowing from a seated position and touching their heads to the floor in an act of submission and humility before Allah.

The room was the size and shape of a double bay showroom/warehouse facility. Each bay had been about 25 ft. by 50 ft., and thus the entire room was approximately 50 ft. by 50 ft. Two columns in the middle of the room were there for support and to allow the division of the room by previous or future tenants. The back wall was of concrete block and the other walls were constructed of drywall. The walls were painted white and the room was well lighted by recessed fluorescent lights which were about 12 feet from the floor. The room was covered with carpet that was almost a Kelly green.

As everyone came in, they faced the block wall in the back of the room which roughly faced eastward toward Mecca. All Moslems are asked to face toward Mecca wherever they are when they stop to worship and pray. The focal point of the room was a gold-colored, metallic-looking dome which was supported by carved 4' x 4' wood columns typical of many porch columns in modest American-style houses. The columns were connected by partial walls about five feet tall covered with a material that simulated brick panels. At the back of this focal point were inscriptions of words in Arabic. This area reminded me very much of the Ark of the Covenant focal points in most Jewish Synagogues.

Men and boys were milling about and walking in and out as 1:00 p.m. arrived. By this time there were about 100 men and boys in various stages of their prayers and worship. At 1:00 p.m. sharp the Immam, who had been seated in the coveted (at least by me) chair, introduced a man who came and faced the simulated brick wall. He quoted some words from the Koran in sort of a chanting or singsong fashion, which lasted for about one minute. Then, the Immam, speaking in Kurdish, gave what seemed like a sermon (which I later confirmed indeed it was) as men and boys came and went.

As they came in, the men would first stand, then put out their hands in an act of supplication with palms up. They would then bow and repeat the supplication before bowing again. After the second bow each man would kneel or take a seat on the floor. From this position each would prostrate himself on the floor by touching his face to the floor in an act of submission to Allah. Then each worshiper would stand again to repeat the entire process.

At their daily noon prayers all Moslems repeat this act of worship four times, except on Muslim Holy Days (Fridays) when the proscribed number of four is reduced to two. On Friday, however, there is the addition of the sermon. In Islam, listening to the sermon equates to two of the normal acts of humility and submission practiced during the prayers. Most Christian sermons that I have heard over the years would probably rate a credit reduction of all four prayers because they are usually twice as long and, thus, twice the load on my attention deficit disorder.

The Moslem religion began during the lifetime of Mohammed (570 – 632 A.D) who lived in Mecca in Arabia. Mohammed's objections to the neglected poor of Mecca turned the leaders against him. Mohammed began having revelations from Allah and teaching them to the people of Mecca. His revelations make up the context of the Koran. The Koran teaches that the great prophets of God, including Abraham and Moses, were indeed messengers of God. It also teaches that Jesus was a prophet sent from God. Thus, the religion of Islam is connected by this monotheistic umbilical cord to the Judeo-Christian tradition.

Islam teaches five pillars of faith: (1.) the confession that there is but one God and that is Allah, whose messenger is Mohammed; (2.) prayer (five times a day); (3.) a pilgrimage to Mecca by all Moslems at least once in a lifetime; (4.) fasting during the holy month of Ramadan; and, (5.) giving (they are taught to give two-and-a-half percent of their assets each year, plus other offerings.)

The Khuta (or sermon) of the Immam who spoke in Kurdish

gave me no chance to get my two credits for this time of worship because I could not understand or gain from his teachings during the approximately 10 – 15 minute sermon. However, the second speaker (the assistant Immam whose name I later learned was Fadi Ezzeir) spoke in English, and I got most of my credits restored here because I heard and understood most of what he said. He later told me that both he and the Immam spoke on the same matter today in order to be sure that one of the sermons would be understood by everyone.

Immam Fadi is a part-time, unpaid assistant leader of this Mosque who makes his living as part owner of a donut shop. He gives liberally of his time to the Mosque, both in the worship services and in his role of working with the young people. Immediately after the 1:00 p.m. service he was deeply involved as the leader of a Boy Scout troop. This open faced man, with his beautiful smile and his warm welcome to me after the service, convinced me of his sincere desire to help these young people to find the will of Allah and his desire in helping them to live productive, loving lives.

While speaking during the service Immam Fadi immediately turned his words and attention toward the young people, many of whom were helping me hold up the walls we were leaning against. This assistant Immam said first of all, "I am glad to see many younger men at the house of Allah." He said very clearly that his remarks today would be directed to these young people. He said, "I am talking only to the young men up to 27-years-old." This Immam said that when most of us look at teen-agers today we have a negative attitude. He said that the way young people tend to dress and their seeming lack of direction appears to cause this feeling of negativity. He said, "Brothers and Sisters, we of the older generation bear part of the responsibilities for the way our young people look and act."

Next Immam Fadi said that these young people must start taking strong initiatives. A few more times he said, "Brothers and Sisters," before following these words with admonitions as to how we should relate to and encourage these young adults in our midst. "Brothers and Sisters," "Brothers and Sisters," he kept saying until I felt for a moment like saying "Brother Fadi, there are no sisters here to hear these words, in case you hadn't noticed." Speaking with him afterwards, I saw that he was a man with a warm sense of humor, and I mentioned the fact that there were no persons of the female persuasion in the Mosque today. And of course, I was right but only in the sense that the men and women were physically separate in the Mosque. The women and their female children were in another room with a closed-circuit television system bringing the entire service to them also.

By the middle of Immam Fadi's sermon the main room of the Mosque was full, and this assistant leader told me later that he supposed there were about eight hundred worshipers there today. After I had been sitting for about 40 minutes, I became very restless. The position I was being required to assume while sitting on the floor with my back to the corner of the room began to cause me to have cramps in my legs. It seemed by now that there was no new position that I could assume which would give me any relief. And I was not alone. I saw the young men sitting near me shuffling around and occasionally standing up and assuming the positions of prayer. A time or two, I questioned whether they were going through the stages of the Moslem prayers or were attempting to change positions for relief from a tiring sitting position. It probably at times was a bit of both.

I wanted to stand and stretch so badly, but I knew that I would be self-conscious about what would certainly be seen as an awkward attempt to accomplish their prayer positions. My plight reminded me of the story about the man who asked his friend if he knew why the members of a fundamentalist church do not make love standing up. The answer? If someone saw them it might be seen as awkward attempts at dancing. I, therefore, applied the yoga-type meditations which I recently learned at a Buddhist meeting to work through my pain. So, I may well be on my way to becoming a Buddhist. Naw, not really. I'm too old and too stiff to begin learning the traditional cross-legged positions. I like sitting a lot, but only on my own time schedule and preferably in an overstuffed Lazy Boy recliner. I don't believe I could pass the physical to become either a Moslem or a Buddhist.

By now the sermon of the assistant Immam was nearing the end. He had spoken pointedly and freely and without notes of any visible kind for about fifteen minutes. His sermon had absolutely nothing to do with my restlessness today. But I will not lie to you; a Barcolounger would have helped me enjoy it far more than I did. He spoke of Rambo and other characters such as Arnold Schwarzenegger as Hollywood concepts which young people would be ill-advised to try to emulate in their lives. Maybe that's my problem in not being able to sit comfortably on the floor for long periods of time. Maybe my body emulated that of Arnold the movie star too much to allow me the flexibility required to be a good Moslem or Buddhist. Maybe I'm just too muscle bound; you suppose?

At any rate, the service was now nearing an end and everyone in the Mosque formed long lines. They stood shoulder to shoulder and foot to foot and pressed in tightly toward the Eastern wall of the Mosque facing Mecca while they went through a series of prayers and responses from the members. Finally, they were all bowing in a prostrate position again with their heads touching the floor in a final act of worship and submission to Allah.

Just at 2:00 p.m. this service was over, and the crowd left quickly, most of them going back to work. Immam Fadi told me that it is difficult for Moslems in the U.S. to worship on Fridays because it, of course, is a busy workday here in the U.S.A. In Moslem countries Friday is their Holy Day and they do not work on their "Sabbath," just as most Christians do not work on Sundays. This unpaid Immam said that most of the members here today probably did not take a lunch hour yesterday so that they could take a double lunch hour today in order to attend the service. Come to think of it I didn't see any really overweight people at the Mosque. Dieting would not hurt me any for sure, and the exercise of the Moslem prayers was definitely a plus in this direction also. Immam Fadi said that someone once asked what must one do to become a Moslem. The answer was, "Take a bath and bear witness that there is no God but Allah and that Mohammed is His messenger."

I hereby state unequivocally that there were 800 or more (mostly Kurdish) Moslems bearing witness on this day that there is no God but Allah and that Mohammed is his messenger. I also do hereby state unequivocally that I took a long, hot bath as soon as I got home to loosen up my Rambo-type muscles which had definitely been stretched far too much today. Maybe I'm halfway there. I'll ask my new friend Immam Fadi what he thinks.

Chapter 41

Sri Ganesha Temple
Nashville, Tennessee
June 22, 2003

*I*t was a perfectly beautiful spring-like day as we left home at 8:35 a.m. on the 41st of our *Fifty-two Sundays* pilgrimage. The temperature was 70° and was expected to rise to 82° by late afternoon. In spite of today being a perfectly golfable day, there would be no golf on this delightful day for poor little ole me. Saturday while getting ready to play golf, I had opened my Jeep, pulled my clubs out and rested them on my car while I went to get a cart in order to return and transport my clubs. When I got back to my car after about five minutes, my clubs were gone — stolen right at our clubhouse in full view of everyone. I wondered if this could be the work of the al-Qaeda terrorist network. Could they now be attacking the very core of our social fabric by disrupting our golf games? Doing so would create a feeling of social disconnect which could surely cause our whole social order to crumble and deteriorate into total anarchy.

I am going to suggest that our homeland security agency pull out all the security forces from our airports and put them all around our country clubs to protect our Calloways and our Pings and our whole way of life. It seems only reasonable for our country to put all its resources where the real problems lie. If my memory serves me well, there has not been a real incident of terrorism at an airport in more than a year while my clubs were stolen only yesterday. And I'll bet that a careful investigation would reveal several hundred sets of clubs stolen only yesterday all across our country from sea to shining sea. Now what would that tell you about the new focus of terrorism?

I'm also going to request that Tom Ridge, our homeland security czar, introduce legislation which will provide funding for new golf equipment for all the victims of this new wave of terrorism.

"Keep America playing"is my suggested theme. I'm also going to try to get Tiger Woods to be the spokesman for this new effort to save the American way of life. Let me hear from you. Show your support of my initiatives to thwart the heinous efforts of international terrorists to destroy America the beautiful — which is, of course, now more symbolized by our beautifully manicured fairways than it is by our golden fields of grain. Please send your supportive e-mails to ugb@comcast.net. No negative criticizing e-mails from any egg-sucking pinko al-Qaeda sympathizers, please.

Today was a real test for me, I already knew. I needed to find solace from my recent devastating loss; and therefore I was, indeed, fortunate that for today I had already planned to attend a Hindu temple for my worship service. Hindus believe that the inner spirit is strengthened by prayer and meditation which enable us to diminish our attachments to material things. I was really attached to my Big Bertha driver and my Calloway irons, so I guess I'll start with my Odyssey putter first. I wasn't too attached to it anyhow, and as an amateur in the meditation field, I imagine that detachment efforts would find greater results in dealing with items a little less desirable. Then, I could move up to my furtive three iron, and on up until I reached Nirvana by being totally detached from this diabolical game.

There are obviously two paths to Nirvana for golfers. One would be arriving at total perfection in the game. Total perfection would manifest as par being achieved every time the game is played. Or would perfection be eighteen *under* par? Except, of course, on par 5's where an eagle would be perfection and on par 3's where holes in one would be perfection? Nirvana on this path is an always receding goal.

What all of this means is that Nirvana can truly only be achieved via the second path of totally detaching oneself from this hellish game. Maybe the most desirable legislation to defeat the devil and the terrorists would be a bill outlawing this national distraction. This would remove this terrorism target immediately and definitely improve the spirituality of this great segment of society. It would also assist us in learning to speak the King's English again by removing the great temptation to revert to the four-letter street-speak in which most golfers have become so very fluent that English has almost become their second language.

On my way to my visit to the Hindu temple the morning after the al-Qaeda invasion of my personal life, I realized that I would need some good blue road nourishment to physically fortify myself. I had planned to visit Joe's Diner in Bellevue. Joe's Diner is located on Old Hickory Boulevard which is the same street as the temple. I had been assured by some friends just two days earlier that Joe's was definitely open for breakfast and definitely open on Sunday. But it was not! Aren't there any verities anymore? We drove all around this area Sunday morning and came out with five other possibilities for breakfast: two bakeries (where we could get sweet rolls and coffee), McDonald's, Burger King, or Mrs. Winner's (all three of which serve a semblance of breakfast).

We chose Mrs. Winner's because of the name. It just sounds more like a blue road name. (This was similar to a choice we had made years ago while traveling through New England vowing to keep on the blue roads and stay only in bed 'n' breakfasts or country inns. While in Boston we stayed at a Holiday Inn so that I could at least hold on to the "Inn" part of country inns). In this case I felt I would have a difficult time convincing my readers that I had done the best I could to find a blue road restaurant if I announced that I had had breakfast at McDonald's or Burger King. I rejected the bakeries because I could not get my blue road staple of eggs there. So, Mrs. Winner's was the winner. But we were the losers. The egg McMuffin and the bacon, egg and cheese biscuit at McDonald's are always great. Blue road or no blue road, I always enjoy these breakfast treats.

We had never had breakfast at a Mrs. Winner's, and we almost did not today. It was the poorest choice we had made in 41 Sundays. We both ordered scrambled eggs, bacon, hash browns, grits, biscuits and coffee. I also ordered a bacon, egg and cheese biscuit for the table, and most of it and most of Betty's entire breakfast stayed on the table. The eggs appeared to have been reconstituted from dried or powdered eggs, and the bacon was paper thin and limp. The triangle-shaped hash-brown potatoes were unappetizing looking and fairly devoid of taste. The grits were almost good but were probably dragged down a notch or two by association with the other inferior offerings. The biscuits were great, just as they are at almost all fast-food outlets because almost all of them use the incredibly good frozen biscuits which have come on the market in the past few years, and which are now available for retail at all major food stores.

So, here's the situation. Feel comfortable going into Mrs. Winner's for breakfast for their coffee, their biscuits and jelly (in the messy plastic tubes) and maybe even for their grits. Forget the rest until further bulletins. Maybe they'll see the light and see that anything worth doing is worth doing right. The plastic and Styrofoam at Mrs. Winner's are no different from the same items at Burger King and McDonald's, except there may be a few more annoying plastic barbs on the Mrs. Winner's forks. The barbs simply reminded me at every bite that this was fast food — but not fast food at its best. The menu boasted that this was the home of "Classic Southern Fried Chicken." Maybe their breakfast should be billed as "Classic Northern Breakfast Food," and it is probably not even this, but for certain it is not classic southern breakfast food. And there was no southern music (a.k.a., country music) being played on the sound system. It was just some annoying and agitating music.

"Wow!" Mrs. Winner's must be saying. "Let someone steal some simple-minded southerner's golf clubs and all of a sudden he becomes an acerbic food critic." Better luck on the draw next time, folks. Maybe the next time I feel violated I'll end up at your competitor's restaurants.

Betty and I left Mrs. Winner's at 10:00 a.m. before our negative attitude was detected, or we might have been unceremoniously thrown out on our behinds for not appreciating the efforts of those who do at least try to serve Sunday morning pilgrims something to help them make it through the worship hour. So we shook the dust off our feet and headed toward the Sri Ganesha Temple. The previous week I had driven up to this unusually ornate temple which has a distinctive Indian flavor. There is a sign which instructs visitors to call for an appointment. After several attempts and always reaching a recording, a priest finally called me back to say that Mrs. Babu who handles tours was not available and that I should call Dr. Mani, the chairman of the board of the temple.

Dr. Mani answered my call immediately. He cordially invited Betty and me to attend the worship service at the temple at any time. He said that if we came on this Sunday he would be available to give us a tour. He hurried to say that Mrs. Babu would be a far better tour guide but that she was in India and would not be back in time to greet us.

Dr. Mani, a Nashville physician, said that if we could arrive by 10:30 a.m. (30 minutes before the worship service) he would meet us and introduce us to some of the aspects of the temple and of the worship service. So, after blue roading around the area for about 20 minutes we drove up to this fascinating structure which was designed by an architect from India in consultation with local architects. The temple as it exists was finished in 1991, while a previous structure on this site now houses the six Hindu priests who are from India.

Dr. Mani said that the temple operates under a not-for-profit corporate charter. He was the chairman of a board of 11 trustees who oversee all aspects of the temple including the interviewing and the hiring of the priests. He was obviously very busy when we arrived, but he soon took the time to show us around. He introduced us to some of the basic tenets of the Hindu religion and some of the aspects of the architecture and art in the temple and how these join together in their worship experience.

Hinduism is one of the oldest living world religions and has perhaps more than 500 million followers. The Hindus believe that only Brahman is the unchanging essence of everything which exists. Brahman cannot be anthropomorphized, or described in human terms. He is the "ground of being" to put Him in the contemporary Christian theological concept of Paul Tillich. Nothing exists outside Brahman. In many ways, this concept of Brahman is similar to the monotheism of the Judeo-Christian concept of God — the immutable, unspeakable creator of all that is. And, in a sense, the three aspects of Brahman are not totally dissimilar to the Trinity in the Christian religion. In Hinduism Brahman is seen in three manifestations: (1.) Brahman, the creator, (2.) Shiva, the destroyer of ego, and (3.) Vishnu, the redeemer and preserver. The Hindus go even further and worship many lesser gods who are emanations or stepping-stones to the immutable Brahman. Again, perhaps this is not too far removed from the position of the prophets and saints of Christendom who have been used by God to illuminate the path to the eternal One.

Dr. Mani said that Hindus do not spend much time worshiping Brahman because His work of creation is finished. Hindus, therefore, concentrate on worshiping the emanations of Brahman in Shiva and Vishnu. This temple is named for the son of Shiva who is worshiped "as the remover of all obstacles, and as the god of wisdom and success." Dr. Mani showed us the many statues of elephant heads throughout the temple, because the elephant has become the symbol of the strength and wisdom of the Shiva part of the godhead. There are 10 incarnations of Vishnu. One is the sustainer and protector of the universe, another is the goddess of prosperity who represents the blessings of health, wealth, courage, victory, fame, fortune, family, peace and happiness which are sought by all human beings. Another of the incarnations of Vishnu represents selfless love and total surrender to God while still another represents universal brotherhood and the equality of all humanity.

The worship experience at this temple revolves around Sri Ganesha, the remover of obstacles and the embodiment of gentleness, strength, wisdom and peace. At the 11:00 a.m. worship service that began with the ringing of a bell, Dr. Mani provided the two oldest people present with the only two seats we saw in the temple worship area. We were placed in the center of the temple which had a granite path leading to an enclosure at the end of which was a larger black granite head of an elephant — the focal point of this entire service. The beginning of this service was the act of carefully and lovingly washing Ganesha, over and over, for about 20 minutes. The priests gently bathed this figure with water, then many other different liquids such as milk and orange juice, and then more water. While Ganesha was washed gently and softly, the worshipers sang and chanted in Sanskrit which is an ancient language like Latin or Yiddish. Dr. Mani said that more and more of the younger people do not speak or understand this ancient language and, as a result, that some temples are using more and more of the modern languages of worshipers in various parts of the world. In more conservative temples, only Sanskrit is used — just as only Yiddish is used in Orthodox Jewish Synagogues.

The central part of the temple containing the large black granite Ganesha was surrounded by walkways with altars to the many manifestations of Shiva and Vishnu. The worshipers would fold their hands reverently and bow toward the altars, and many would touch the altars and prostrate themselves and touch their heads to the floor in total humility and submission before this particular emanation of Shiva or Vishnu. There was only one other Anglo-Saxon couple in the temple this morning as far as I could see, and they were participating peripherally in this worship service.

We noticed that all the men were dressed just as all other Americans would be dressed at any casual affair. T-shirts and pants were the order of the day. We had all removed our shoes on the lower level of the temple and were now sitting around the shrine to Ganesha. The women were dressed in traditional long-flowing saris. The children were dressed as you would expect to see any children of this area dressed at a picnic or ball game – just totally relaxed casual clothing.

At the beginning of the washing of Ganesha there were about 50 people involved in this worship experience. Through the entire service, there was chanting and singing from worship books which had been passed around. The singing or chanting would be led by one person or another interspersed around the worship area. As others would come in, some would make the short pilgrimage around the temple genuflecting before the shrines while others would come in, sit and join immediately in participating in the service of bathing Ganesha. After about 25 minutes of bathing Ganesha a curtain was pulled, and we were told that the priests would now be dressing Ganesha. During this period of about 20 – 25 minutes the worshipers continued singing and chanting while the privacy curtain was closed.

During an earlier part of the service Dr. Mani went to a locked offering box-vault into which worshipers had been placing offerings of money. He took the money away while people continued to come in and make offerings. Some worshipers brought baskets of fruit to particular shrines and left them there. Dr. Mani later said that this was a symbolic gift which was always given back to the worshiper at the end of the service.

During the entire service a man dressed in olive colored pants and a nice knitted T-shirt sat just in front of us. He was one of the worshipers located in different areas of the temple who took leading parts in the singing. Our neighbor kept perfect time with four fingers of one hand nervously beating against the other. He enthusiastically entered into all parts of the service. They would call him a lay leader in most Christian services I enjoyed seeing the completeness of this man's worship experience. I saw through his movements, singing and expressions the deeply-felt worshipful mood of this man, just as I saw the moods of most of the others sitting in worshipful postures.

Dr. Mani said that Hinduism is not evangelical. He said it is a way of life. It has no one great founder like Christianity, Buddhism or Islam. It just developed out of the lives and teachings of many wise and devoted seekers of truth over thousands of years. The young white couple I met later answered my question, "Are you Hindus?" by saying, "You don't join the Hindus. You are a Hindu if you say you are a Hindu." There is no vow to be taken, no tithes to be paid, no litmus test as to how devoted you are or how many times you go to the temple. You are a Hindu if you say you are without any "sign up" rolls or membership obligations.

During the service people moved in and out at will to perhaps go to the restroom or to attend to a child or for any number of things, including making again the pilgrimage around to the other shrines. All the figures at the shrines were dressed in ornate regal dress with many flowers and gold and bejeweled ornaments.

At 11:48 a.m., a family of four came in and joined in the worship. Then another large group came in and just hung around the periphery, visiting animatedly with each other while the worship of Ganesha was still proceeding. At 12:00 p.m., a priest pulled back the curtain to reveal with flair the ornately and freshly dressed Ganesha, who was covered with garlands of beautiful fresh flowers — a custom which is repeated every day.

One of the priests came out to the area of the worshipers and was saying something to which someone would respond and the priest would go to them and a discussion would proceed. I learned later that the priest was asking if anyone had any special prayer requests. The priest would repeat the names of those needing prayer — name by name —before asking if any others had any special requests. Then the priest returned to the area of Ganesha to offer the prayers.

By now it was about 12:10 p.m., and there were about 200 people who had gathered during the last hour. Children were running and playing everywhere. A very festive occasion was blossoming. At 12:15 p.m. a bell was rung by one of those who had requested special prayers for someone or something. At this point everyone stood as if expectantly waiting for something to happen. The priests faced the altar in prayer. Then the priests turned toward the congregation and walked among them with different chalices — one with a candle, one with water and others with rice and raisins. The priests were asking all to touch the chalices or to take some of the water, rice or fruit.

One priest came by me, and he held out the chalice to me, but I declined to touch the chalice just as most non-Catholics would not partake of the Eucharist in most Catholic services. But this priest would not be denied. He persisted and put the chalice in my direction again. Again I refused saying "No thanks." He then thrust the bowl toward me and said, "Touch the bowl." I felt obligated to do as he requested because, as I told one of the worshipers later, I was afraid he had to get 100 percent participation or he would lose his job. I touched the chalice, and his countenance beamed just as an evangelical Christian might do if he had just won a new convert to the Lord.

I know that Hindus are not evangelical, but I wondered if I had made the first step toward Hinduism by touching the chalice. Some took raisins and rice from the cups or had small amounts of the water from the bowls dipped into their hands from which they ceremoniously drank, wiping the remainder over their heads in a sort of baptismal motion. All of this was remarkably similar to the celebration of the Lord's Supper in Christian churches everywhere.

Since I did not partake of all the offerings during this part of the service, I suppose I am not a full-fledged member of this Hindu community, but I certainly did feel that I communed with brothers and sisters from a tradition which was foreign to me until this morning. And Betty made her $5.00 contribution here just as she had at all religious services which allowed offerings to be a part of the worship experience.

Dr. Mani then stood at the front to make several announcements about activities and invited everyone to join them for lunch on the bottom floor of the temple. Betty and I went through the serving line and then joined Bill and Lisa Patterson, the two other Anglo-Saxon people we had seen at the worship service. We enjoyed talking with the Pattersons who had been attending services at this temple for about seven years. I plan to visit with them more later to discuss the path which led them to begin worshiping at Sri Ganesha.

Dr. Mani, the Pattersons and all those we met today made us feel totally welcome. A whole new approach to worship had been revealed to me, and my eyes and mind were now definitely opened to the efforts of this great number of Hindus in the world. For thousands of years members of this tradition have turned their minds and hearts toward something greater than themselves in an effort to become better citizens of the world through a feeling of love and brotherhood toward all mankind.

In a brochure entitled "A Description of Hinduism" I later read: "Hindus say that all religions are different paths toward the same goal of God — realization, and that God incarnates from time to time to proclaim spiritual wisdom to humanity."

I certainly know that my personal horizon has been expanded and that my thoughts of the brotherhood of all mankind have been strengthened. And I probably helped a humble, persistent priest keep his job by touching his bowl.

Chapter 42

Wolf Creek Baptist Church
Silver Pointe, Tennessee
June 29, 2003

"When I was just a boy, I was so ugly my ma and paw had to tie a pork chop around my neck to get the dog to play with me." This was a story that my "story of the day" funny man Don Sheffield had told me recently. Don will often call and say, "Here is a story I knew you would appreciate today." He knows that I am always ready to hear a good story. I almost tried the pork-chop concept this weekend. Betty and I had tried and tried to get some folks to go with us to our cottage at Center Hill Lake to play with us. We first had tried several couples who did not pan out. I guess they were steak people instead of pork chop people. Then Betty had tried to get a group of her lady friends to go with us by promising them everything — including that I would be there to do all the cooking and play the part of boat captain for any water activities. No luck. Excuses, excuses. We had not been able to get anyone to play with us even while tying every pork chop in Kroger's around our necks.

I had about given up by the time I played golf on Thursday with Jim Neal, John Seigenthaler and Jim Sanders. I asked them to go with me and play golf at the new River Watch Golf Course which is located on the banks of the lake between Smithville and Sparta — a really juicy pork chop for golfers. Not much luck here either. More excuses. Jim Sanders was going to a high school reunion in Johnson City and playing golf with his old high school football pal, Steve Spurrier. John was going to some political function for Governor Phil Bredesen. But Jim Neal nibbled just a bit on the golf pork chop, and deftly I set the hook by also promising him I would fry pork tenderloin for breakfast. So, with a pork chop and a pork tenderloin tied around my neck, Jim agreed to go with me. And I thought I had no friends!

Jim's wife Dianne was in Texas visiting her folks. With Dianne gone, Betty was off the hook. Now Jim and I could rough it. No shaving or bathing required. Just hang and talk big and talk a lot. And if you weren't there you were fair game.

I almost lost Jim when I told him I would be going to church Sunday, Number 42 on my list of 52. Not that Jim is opposed to church or anything. It was just that it might change the way he would have to pack — you know, like bringing a razor and a comb and stuff like that. I recovered nicely, however, by telling him that he could drive his own car the 65 miles to our lake place and then, after breakfast on Sunday morning, he could go on back home. So Jim confirmed his commitment and I went to the grocery to buy pork chops and tenderloin, and a few other things to have around my neck if his friendship wavered.

We got to our cabin at about 5:15 p.m. on Friday and had some refreshments which I had hung around my neck to further set the hook. After relaxing a bit we went to the Rose Garden for a catfish dinner, and afterwards we decided to drive the 15 – 20 miles to the River Watch Golf Course. We got there just at dusk. We wanted to see the second nine holes which they had just completed. A security guard told us it had just opened that very day, and so we felt we were in luck, having been a little worried whether or not the construction period had been completed.

After driving around a bit, we headed back to our cottage while planning our golf schedule for the next day. We were tooling along at about 55 mph when BAM! A full-sized deer suddenly jumped out into the road and attacked my right front headlight. A 55-mph collision. We stopped to check the damage to both my car and the deer as soon as I could find a place to pull over. My front fender and lights had been maimed, but the deer, which I had been sure was dead in the road, was nowhere to be found. I guessed he was waiting in the bushes somewhere looking for another car to attack. Suppose he thinks he's a dog. All of this reminded me of the "killer rabbit" that jumped into President Carter's boat and attacked him years ago. Maybe this deer thought I was President Bush and Jim was Vice President Cheney?

We knew that the confrontation with the deer had not been a total victory for the deer and felt sure that his headlights had been knocked out of line a bit, too. Not wanting another deer attack, I drove a bit more cautiously during the rest of the trip back to our cottage.

After watching TV a while Jim took one of the "chops" which I am sure helped me reel him in and took advantage of what I had promised would be lots of time to sleep. We both slept about 9 – 10 hours. I woke up a bit earlier, took the pork tenderloin from around my neck and fried it in small crispy pieces, as I had remembered Jim had eaten at my house before and particularly liked. I also baked biscuits (frozen Pillsbury, you all) and fried potatoes. I made gravy from the tenderloin pan leavings. A really beautifully ripe cantaloupe helped round out the breakfast. There was plenty of coffee, and plenty of pear preserves which make a great breakfast dessert when combined with crusty biscuit tops or bottoms.

After resting a while after the hard work of eating this country breakfast, Jim and I left to go to River Watch to play golf. On the way we stopped at the Rose Garden to see Betty and my daughter Beverly. They were waiting for our other daughter Barbara and her friend Dave to join them for a boat ride on this beautiful day. Jim and I then went on to the golf course. As soon as we drove up to the Pro shop, we knew our golf game was in jeopardy. The parking lot was totally full of cars. The most we had ever seen before at one time was 10 to 15 cars, but today it looked like a CarMax parking lot.

Not to be deterred so easily, we walked into the trailer (the club house was still not completed), which serves as the pro-shop and inquired about playing possibilities. Now we were deterred. There were two tournaments being held there today. The first one was the area Chamber of Commerce. We offered to join. No luck. And then in the afternoon the new lot owners were going to play. Jim's law firm has done some legal work for some of the owners of this beautiful course, and his firm has taken three lots in lieu of a fee. But Bill Ramsey, an attorney for the Neal and Harwell firm, still had not completed all the work to get the lots recorded.So, because Jim's law firm was not legally an owner, we were foiled again. Rats!

Jim and I consoled each other by saying, "You know, it would be awfully hot to play golf today anyway." We jumped back into Jim's air conditioned mobile cigar fumidor and headed back to our cottage to play golf vicariously through the televised coverage of the PGA players in the FEDEX-St. Jude's Classic (being played in

Memphis) and the Seniors U.S. Open. We hadn't watched for an hour before both of us were sound asleep again. Finally Jim pulled himself off his temporary napping place, made his way to his weekend bedroom and sacked out for a long summers' nap. Another big bite at the sleep "chop" dangling around my neck. I pretended to still be watching TV golf until he was gone and then I, too, fell into a deep sleep. I was awakened by hungry boaters who came in and caused me to again pretend to be watching golf. After they scavenged for a snack, they were on their way back to Nashville.

Finally after a good two hours of rest and meditation, Jim and I both were awakened just in time to see the end of Saturday's golf. Now we voted to just snack also on baked pork loin, salad, and a baked Mrs. Smith's apple pie. They're great! And I'm not being paid a fee by Mrs. Smith for this endorsement. But I'd be happy to accept one if they feel at all inclined. After our supper-snack and a couple of hours of TV Jim and I both sacked out again at about 9:00 p.m. Jim claims he read for a good hour while in his bedroom, but I make no such claims. I slept soundly again until about 6:00 a.m. Sunday morning — another good night's sleep. I wondered if we had a sleeping sickness. But it was great!

I had told Jim that we would need to leave at 9:00 a.m. on Sunday in order for us to have breakfast at Edgar Evins Marina and for me to get back to the West End Church of Christ at Silver Pointe. I had thought of visiting here several months ago but chose instead to go to a sister Church of Christ called Silver Pointe Church of Christ. I wanted to see what difference there would be between the two. I had noticed that the people at the West End church seemed to dress to the nine's when I saw them going to church, while the Silver Pointe members were just the opposite. And these churches were located only a couple of miles apart.

Jim and I actually left at 8:40 a.m. to go to breakfast at the marina which was located 10 to 12 miles away. We got to the restaurant at about 8:55 a.m. and found ourselves a table in this newly remodeled boat dock, which is by far the biggest and best on the lake. The best, if you like things nice and neat. If you like things old, rickety and rustic you'd probably choose Hurricane Marina where we keep our boat. It's a good thing we left early because even though there were only three to four tables of customers, it took them at least 15 minutes to even recognize us and then only after we waved our arms as if we were on a life raft and fearful of drowning. "Oh, I didn't notice you," our waitress said. I felt like Mr. Cellophane in Betty's favorite movie "Chicago." The character says "Mr. Cellophane should have been my name. You can look right through me and never know I'm there." When her eyes adjusted to my congenital invisible condition (which actually was so pervasive that it even also helped hide Jim from view), she finally came to take our order.

This must have been the very first hour of the very first day on this job — or any job — for this very sweet un-waitress. She had the obtuseness of the sometime-waitress Phoebe on the popular TV sitcom Friends. Phoebe is apt to ask "Who ordered the sliced chicken sandwich on wheat toast?" to which a customer would say, "I didn't want chicken. I wanted sliced ham." Phoebe would reply, "I'm sorry. We don't have wheat toast, would you like white toast on your chicken sandwich?"

I ordered three eggs over-easy/over-medium, hash-brown potatoes, country ham, grits, biscuits and coffee. And pancakes for the table. Jim ordered sausages and milk, his eye already on the pancakes which were "for the table." After about 15 minutes our waitress returned and said, "We don't have grits." Then five minutes later she came and said "We don't have hash browns." Only after some probing as to what else I could substitute did she finally say "We have home fries." I said, "Please bring me some of those. I think they're in the same family."

The breakfast was just okay. The eggs were cooked just right. The biscuits were nuked, and the country ham looked and tasted like shaved ham. The pancakes were good, but the syrup served in a miniature casket was a negative. The computer took entirely too much of the waitresses' time. It did not give them time to study the relationship of hash browns to home fries. I told Jim I wanted to pay the check and would deduct it from my income for tax purposes since my report on the meal would be in my *Fifty-Two Sundays*, and he verified the $25.40 expenditure for my IRS files.

Jim left to go back to Nashville, and I hurried out and on toward church to pray for our sweet waitress whom I shall always call "Phoebe." Maybe I'll also pray that they throw away the computer. Maybe that would help her.

I rushed to the West End Church of Christ only to find that it was closed. I waited for a while, walked up to the door and saw no signs of life. The sign at the road read:

Sunday School 10:00
Worship Service 11:00

There was no other sign telling pilgrims that the "pastor is on vacation." Nothing. Now I had 12 minutes to get to another church. I had seen the Wolf Creek Baptist Church just a few miles back toward the Evins Marina and had noticed that they held services at 11:00 a.m. I had seen definite signs of life there — several cars and pick-up trucks. At 10:56 a.m. I drove up, parked in the shade and then walked into this simple white frame church. Sunday school was still in progress and Carl Halfacre was still teaching his class. The reference board at the front read:

Enrollment   63
Today   38
Last Sunday   42

Offering
Today $679.25
Last Sunday $547.00

A small foyer separated the sanctuary from the outside which gave me an opportunity to spot an empty pew to the back left of the church. I slinked in while Brother Carl finished his Sunday school lesson. There were 23 people here at 10:58 a.m. No one wore a coat and,for the very first time, I was not wearing one either. I had made a correct guess before I entered and left my blazer in my Jeep. There were eighteen pews — nine on each side. Brother Carl unceremoniously said at the end of his lesson, "That's all I have for today."

Before dismissing the class, Brother Carl Halfacre told everyone to remember the cookout on the 12th of July, and with a wave of his arm the Sunday school hour was over. Before the worship service began, Pastor Herb Leftwich came and introduced himself to me. I knew he was the pastor because he had on a coat and had just arrived.Then Carl Halfacre and his wife came to welcome me also.

Brother Carl went back to the pulpit area, strapped on a guitar and began getting the choir of ten together. There was another guitar player, a piano and an organ — quite a musical team for a congregation which would only number 40, including all the musical assistants.

At the front behind the choir were two pictures, one of the *Last Supper* and one of Christ praying. A stark wooden cross in the middle separated the two pictures. The sanctuary had 12-foot ceilings with recessed fluorescent lighting. The pews had red cushions, and the walls and ceilings were stark white. The pastor walked to the front and asked us all to stand and sing the Doxology "Praise God From Whom All Blessings Flow." Then we were seated and asked to sing *Will You Meet Me Over Yonder?* which was a song from the songbook, *Mulls Singing Convention No. 4.* Some of the words were: "Will you meet me over yonder and with happy millions dwell? Will you meet me over yonder where we will never say farewell?"

At 11:10 a.m. Pastor Herb remade the announcement about the cookout on the 12th of July from 4:00 p.m. to 7:00 p.m. Brother Carl, who seemed to do everything at the church, seemed to be in charge of the cookout too. He said this cookout would be a part of the outreach of this church and they hoped to reach some of the people "up on the lake." Next the pastor took prayer requests from the congregation. At the end of his thoughtful and beautiful prayer he said, "Take us and use us and take us and hide us behind the cross of Jesus...Amen."

Next we sang *Hymn No. 100, When I Wake Up To Sleep No More.* The whole church sang these songs in four-part harmony just as if they had been rehearsed by the whole congregation. This singing was done as if it were a gospel singing, where all parts are well known and sung for worship as well as for entertainment. Following this song the offering was taken. Standing in for Betty, I placed our standard $5.00 in the shiny gold-plated offering plate. Animated organ music played during the offering.

No. 302 was the next choice of the song director. It was *I Know My Savior Is There.* Some of the words were "When I am heavy laden, laden, when my friends are gone...I'll just keep on smiling, keep on smiling through my tears, for I know my Savior is there." Then the next song, *I Want to Know More About My Lord,* was sung and, just as it was finished, someone in the congregation asked, "Brother Carl, can you do *No. 242?*" The answer was "yes" and we sang, *I'll Have a New Life.* The refrain was: "I'll have a new body, I'll have a new life."

At 11:33 a.m. the choir left the pulpit area and joined the congregation, although two members stayed and sang a duet and a solo. The duet was *I Thank God for the Lighthouse,* and the solo by the pianist was *One Joyful Morning You'll Find Me at Home.*

At 11:37 a.m. it was now all up to the pastor. He said, "I heard a little funny this week, and it has nothing to do with what I am going to talk about today, but I still want to tell it to you." He said a third-grade teacher asked her class what they did the past weekend.

One little girl said I went to Sunday school and learned how Jonah was swallowed by the whale. The teacher was incensed that young people would be taught such as this and asked the little girl, "How do you know Jonah was swallowed by a whale?"

The third-grader answered, "I don't now, but I'll ask him when I get to Heaven."

The teacher pressed: "What if Jonah is not in heaven?"

The little believer said, "Then you ask him."

Of course, the congregation roared with laughter, and the little story had done its job, regardless of whether it had any relation to the upcoming sermon or not. The pastor then read the scripture from *Luke 15: 11 – 24* which is the story of the prodigal son. He then said, "I want to talk to the parents today. No two children are alike." He went on to say that he sees this all the time in his work. I assumed immediately he was a teacher or a principal. He told of how children of the same parents were different, and hurried to say that it's not the parents' fault. But he said the story of the prodigal son tells us how we are to deal with situations like this.

The story is about two sons and their father. The younger son demanded his inheritance from his father, and the father split the shares of his estate between his two sons. The younger spent all his money and soon found himself broke and working in another country feeding pigs. He finally "came to himself" and went home to apologize to his father and beg to be forgiven. He also asked to be received not as a son but as a servant. The Biblical story tells, of course, how the father received him openly as his son and forgave him.

The pastor then stopped and asked Brother Carl to "lead us in a word of prayer." Among other things Brother Carl (the go-to man of this church) prayed that God would "Bless Brother Herb as he brings us the message for today...Amen." Now Pastor Herb picked back up on how children were different and, within a very few minutes, he was into his preacher's voice as he told how the older brother was blind to the weakness of the younger one. The pastor said that the younger (the prodigal) was "just a sorry type of boy...a trifling, no count, self-centered individual." This son demanded that he be given his share of the money. By now the pastor was on a preacher's plane as he walked around the pulpit twirling his glasses.

Next the pastor said there was a time when we have to turn our children loose. A woman in front of me was shaking her head in an "Amen" fashion. Someone else said, "Uh huh." Pastor Herb said there comes a time when a young man has to make decisions for himself. He said it was not the father's will that the son leave, but it was his "permissive will." "Children are not always going to make the right choices," he said repeatedly. He said it was like Moses when he smote the rock instead of touching the rock as God had commanded him.

The pastor followed up by saying:"God will not make you do His will." But he said that God's household will not have rebelliousness. He noted that the younger son had become a "royal pain." The pastor then observed that the younger son was probably doing things in his household that were forbidden and the father probably said, "I am sorry, son, but you'll just have to leave." He continued this by saying, "The father said no, and he meant no, just like my father did." "This is the way I believe it should be. The last time I checked," Preacher Herb said, "I was paying the taxes, paying the bills, buying the groceries."

"Kids will test you," he warned. They will say, "I don't want to be an odd ball. I want to be like everyone else." He said that kids know when we are worn out, but that we must be firm and consistent time after time. Brother Herb said,"My father wasn't perfect but he was strong and consistent." The preacher declared he believed the father of the prodigal had the strength to be uncompromising and unyielding in the right things. But when the prodigal came back home, his father did not then say to him, "I told you how things would go, so don't come crawling back to me." The pastor said the father in the scripture did not try to hurt the son just because the son hurt him. The scripture says that the father had compassion, mercy and forgiveness. Pastor Herb told the fathers here today, "Daddies, there is nothing wrong with hugging and kissing your children." The father in the scripture reinstated his son, put on his best robe, and killed the fatted calf in honor of his son's return home.

Pastor Herb asked:"What would have happened to that boy if he said 'I don't have no home to go to?' "

He concluded his remarks by saying,"Let me assure you today that God loves you and wants you to return to Him." He then told us to stand and sing *No. 174, Heaven Is My Home.* The words of this song are: "Coming home, coming home. Lord, I'm coming home. Coming home, coming home, never more to roam. Lord, I'm coming home."

At 12:25 p.m. the pastor invited Tanya to come to the front because she wanted to move her church membership to Wolf Creek. He said, "All in favor raise your right hand. All opposed same sign." There were no objections, and so Pastor Herb invited all the members to come forward and extend to Tanya the right hand of fellowship.

Having had no vote, I felt I was not expected to welcome Tanya into this fellowship. So, I slipped out to my car and left while feeling that Tanya had made a good choice. I also hoped that she would be a good church worker because Brother Carl Halfacre needs some help. It seemed that he was as busy as the preacher. The pastor had probably found out that if you really need something done you should look for someone who is too busy to do it and he/she will get it done. And in my opinion, Brother Carl was too busy. So, Sister Tanya, I too welcome you to the fellowship of Wolf Creek Baptist Church, and I know I speak for Brother Carl and all his family. By the way, can you help with the cookout on the 12th of July?

Chapter 43

Heavenly Host Lutheran Church
Cookeville, Tennessee
July 6, 2003

"*H*ow do you spell 'relief'?" "R – O – L – A – I – D – S" was the way this commercial of years ago asked and answered its own question. An Alka Seltzer ad simply went, "Plop, Plop, Fizz, Fizz. Oh, what a relief it is. Alka Seltzer."

On July 4, 1776, the forefathers of our nation determined that the American colonies needed relief from the oppression of the British crown, and they risked their freedom and happiness by signing the Declaration of Independence. But the relief they sought was not so simply achieved by a "Plop, Plop, Fizz, Fizz." This declaration cast the fledgling and almost unmanageable colonies into a war for relief from the crown — the Revolutionary War. This war had been in the making for several years prior to 1776, and it would not be concluded finally until 1783. But the celebrating began early-on for July 4, 1776, the day the members of the Second Continental Congress signed the Declaration of Independence and demanded relief from British oppression.

Americans today spell their 4th of July relief in many diverse ways — ball games, picnics, concerts and fireworks. Our family goes to the lake at Center Hill. And even there different members of our family celebrate this, and all lake occasions, in different ways. Some of us like to go for long, boring boat rides in the hot sun on the lake. Others like to play silly little board games, such as Scrabble. Still others like to sit, eat, and watch exciting and challenging golf games on TV.

All of us spent the better part of the holiday pleading our case before the sovereign Master of the Universe. It was overcast, and while some prayed for the clouds to clear out, I prayed for rain. Dark clouds would do. Even the most enthusiastic boaters don't like to be on the lake during a storm. Too many Jonahs here for that. So, we tried to heap a guilt trip on God. Either way He was going to make someone unhappy — like two opposing high school football teams praying for victory.

Their team won. We went for a long boat ride. What a way to celebrate and be happy! I DON'T UNDERSTAND IT AT ALL. You see, I am the one who had been to a worship service for 42 consecutive weeks now. I wondered if it would have hurt God to allow a threatening little cloud to keep hanging around. We had enjoyed enough rain in the area for a while, but just a little cloud would have done the job for me. Then I could have celebrated the Fourth by sitting with my golf buddy and talking big about the many golf matches being televised that day — no fireworks required.

Sunday morning I kept the faith and followed through on my plans to attend a Lutheran church. I had not attended a Lutheran church during this series of Sundays, and time was running out. I had a choice of going to Tullahoma, McMinnville or Cookeville. There was a Lutheran church in all three of these Middle Tennessee cities. Cookeville was the closest location, and the choice was made.

Maybe as a result of my Independence weekend sacrifices, Betty dutifully got up early with me. We left our cottage at 8:15 a.m., as I had requested. We drove north on Highway 56 until it merged with I-40 going toward Cookeville; we got off I-40 ASAP. We drove around the back roads looking for a good country-cooking place to eat before going to church. Back and forth, back and forth, crossing I-40, then back again we went several times until we came to South Willow Avenue. The Heavenly Host Lutheran Church was located at 777 South Willow Avenue, and so we turned south onto South Willow. We drove for several miles looking for a breakfast spot and then turned around feeling that a Cracker Barrel or McDonalds might have to be the choice, but just then we saw a sign for the South Willow Grill at 1115 South Willow Avenue. This restaurant was located in the same complex as a motel which apparently serves many tourists who are going to the Burgess Falls State Park. It is also a gathering place for the many fishermen who seem to congregate here.

When we parked in the parking lot, which serves both the motel and the restaurant, a friendly, cheerful fisherman with his coffee cup in hand greeted us as if we were fellow fish people. He said, "Mornin', folks. What part of Nashville y'all from?" Now, Nashville is only about seventy-five miles away, and yet this pilgrim fisherman was asking us this question as if he had just seen friends in another country thousands of miles from home. We told him where we live, and he said, "I'm from Donelson." I entered into the conversation and asked him what brought him to Cookeville. He said, "I'm in the fishing tournament. It's tonight. I'll fish all night tonight." Here it was 9:00 a.m. in the morning, and this exuberant fisherman (who was probably no more than 60 miles from his home) had already been here one night getting ready for his fishing tournament. He was so excited he could hardly contain himself.

This fisherman was as excited as the man at a public lecture about sex. The lecturer said that sexual desires and habits of people vary extremely. To demonstrate this he asked, "How many people have sex once a day?" A few raised their hands. "How many once a week?" More people raised their hands. "How about once a month?" Now, again, fewer people responded. He then asked, "How many have sex once a year?" A small man in the back excitedly jumped up and raised his hand and said, "I do! I do!" "Thanks for responding," the lecturer said, "but why all the excitement?" The little man, as exuberantly as the fisherman, almost unable to control his excitement, said, "Tonight's the night! Tonight's the night!"

I was excited for the fisherman because of the contagiousness of his excitement. We left him pacing in the parking lot looking for someone else to tell about his fishing tournament that night. We went inside and took a table near the window so that we could see our excited fisherman. There he was, still walking and talking. There were six people besides us who were there for breakfast at this time. Our friendly waitress should join up with the fisherman. She pranced up and asked us if we would like some coffee. She looked so happy when we said that we did. "Cream?" she cheerfully asked. "Yes, please," we said, smiling back. "Coming right up and I'll take your order," she said, as if she had just hooked a big one.

Soon we ordered. Betty decided on a meat and cheese omelet with grits and wheat toast for $4.99. I ordered three eggs over-easy/over-medium. Surprised? Then I ordered country ham, hash browns (after learning that the home fries would be deep fried), grits, biscuits and gravy, and then French toast for the table —

$11.95. While we waited, I read about the Friday night "All You Can Eat Catfish" – $6.95. I guess our happy fisherman had told them that he would catch plenty for everyone. How else could they keep the price so low?

This dining room was a typical motel dining room, vintage 1960. It had one large area with a half wall divider that essentially dissected the room. The tables all had dark green oilcloth coverings and vinyl cushioned chairs in complimentary colors. The menu was a typical motel menu with steaks and sandwiches for lunch and dinner. They served "meat and threes" Monday through Fridays for $4.50. Our friendly 40-something waitress wore white tennis shoes and black shorts with a red T-shirt sporting the name of the restaurant. She looked ready to go fishing right after her shift.

Betty's omelet was not very good, and it looked even worse — flat and greasy. My breakfast was excellent. My eggs were cooked just as ordered. The biscuits were nice and brown on tops and bottoms, and the gravy was good and country, as was my fried country ham. My grits and hash browns were just okay. Betty ate most of the French toast to make up for the fact that her omelet was almost inedible.

Just as we were getting ready to pay our bill and leave, some more fishermen came in, also animatedly talking about the upcoming fishing event. And our fishing friend from Donelson was still telling anyone who would listen about the excitement that night. I wanted to tell him about the fishermen inside having breakfast, but he was having too much fun greeting the public outside.

It was now 10:00 a.m., and the service at the Lutheran Church was set to start in half an hour. We drove around awhile and visited the county square while awaiting the worship time. At 10:25 a.m., Betty and I entered this church which was right in the midst of a building program. The chancel end of the sanctuary had been totally removed for construction of an elongated sanctuary extension. As a result, the chancel area was covered with black plastic paper and other temporary construction measures to keep out as much noise and dust as possible.

The order of worship we were given named "Rev. Roger Paavola" as the pastor of this church. The Lutheran Church was started by Martin Luther, a German priest, who broke from the Roman Catholic Church in the early 1500s. Luther had studied law as a young man, but later turned to religion, entered a monastery, and became a priest in 1507. Early in his priesthood he began to differ with official positions of the Catholic Church. These differences culminated in his posting of his famous "The Ninety-Five Theses" on the church door in 1517. Luther was trying to help reform the church and had no intention of leaving his Mother Church, but this publication of his differences eventually led to his being declared a heretic and the eventual formation of the Lutheran Church.

The Lutheran Church is the largest church to come out of what became known as the Protestant Reformation. It is especially strong and dominant in Germany and in the Scandinavian countries where it is the largest religious body. Lutherans maintain two sacraments: baptism and The Lord's Supper. One basic difference between the Lutherans and the Roman Catholics is that while Catholics believe that during the institution of the sacrament the bread and wine "become" the body and blood of Christ, Lutherans (and Episcopalians) believe that the elements simply "contain" the spiritual presence of Christ.

The order of worship in this Lutheran church and the Episcopal churches I had attended were quite similar, almost identical in liturgical terms. One difference, however, was that while the Eucharist is served at each and every Episcopal Church service, here the congregation served The Lord's Supper only on the first and third Sundays of each month.

There were 80 to 90 people present at this church's second service today. The members were about evenly divided between those who were dressed in "Sunday attire" and those who were casually dressed. The casual dress here, however, was the "Belle Meade casual" type — no blue jeans or "relaxing at home casual" clothes. There were no members in the choir today. The place for choir members was located to the back left side of the sanctuary, perhaps because of the construction proceeding in the front section of the church. Church literature reported that last Sunday there had been 93 people in the 10:30 a.m. service and 56 in the early service. It also said the offering was $2,553 last Sunday.

Just before the service began, a nice looking man wearing a dark blue suit with a white shirt and light blue tie went to the front.

He said that the vicar had been in an automobile accident and would not be here this morning. A "gasp" went through the congregation before this spokesman continued by saying, "He's okay but I'll be doing the service today," and he led us right into the service.

The first part of the order of worship was the "Invocation Hymn," *Forgive My Sins, O God*. Some of the words were: "Forgive my sins, O God, I pray, for I have gone astray." After this hymn the worship leader, who was not named in the order of worship, led the congregation in three sets of printed responsive readings including the Kyrie and the Introit. The next part of the service was the Hymn of Praise, *God Himself Is Present*, followed by the "Prayer of the Day" which also was printed for both the leader and the people to read responsively.

The order of worship then listed under "Word" a scripture reading from the *Old Testament, Ezekiel 17: 22 – 24* followed by the *Epistle, II Corinthians 5: 1 – 10* and the *Holy Gospel, Mark 4: 26 – 34*.

The reading of the scriptures was followed by the *Apostolic Creed*, or the *Apostles Creed* as the leader called it. The creed reads in part: "I believe in the Holy Spirit, the Holy Christian Church." The original creed read: "the Holy Catholic Church" from which the Lutherans separated during the 16th century.

The next part on the printed order of worship was the "Sermon Hymn" which was then followed most appropriately by the "Sermon." The lay leader who was standing in for the vicar today gave the sermon. I wondered if the vicar had given the lay leader his sermon notes, or even (perhaps) his written sermon, because this speaker read this sermon for today based on the Gospel reading. He first said, "Good morning" and the congregation did not respond, and then he went right into the sermon by saying that on this fourth Sunday after Pentecost we were in a period when we speak of growth.

The speaker paraphrased the scripture lesson which likened the Kingdom of God unto the sowing of seeds. He said that the first parable of the Kingdom of God was like the sowing of seeds, some which fall onto rocky soil, some into thorn patches and some onto fertile ground. The second parable, the one about the mustard seed, was next. He said that this seed is so small it is barely visible and, it is an annual seed that must be planted each year.

The speaker spent more time on this second parable. He said that the mustard seed is a slow growing seed and that this does not fit well in our modern society when we like INSTANT everything, especially gratification. The speaker said that this attitude often creeps into our churches. He said pastors often compete to have the largest or fastest growing churches. He said that the real question is not how fast are we growing, but are we following "The Great Commission?" He noted that the Kingdom of God does not always proceed as we expect. Our sermon reader said that the church had grown very much here, but he noted that we set ourselves up for guilt and disappointment if the church does not grow just as we expect it to.

The speaker said that it is not enough to have the seed, protect it, and store it. We are commanded to sow it and let God provide the growth. It is our job to sow the seed in our part of the garden, and leave it to God to see that it grows.

The sermon was over in 10 minutes. Now this man has real promise of becoming a fine vicar. He was not like the preacher who preached on, and on, and on.A man arrived late for the service and asked someone if the pastor had finished his sermon yet. The disgruntled and tired member said "Yes, he's finished, but he still won't quit." This substitute today both finished and quit at the same time.

Next in the order of worship was the "Prayer of the Church" which the leader and the people read responsively and it was followed by the *Lord's Prayer.*

The offering was taken next, and I really wondered if we should cut our offering because the pastor was not there or double it because of the time saved by the lay leader (who had definitely tacked at least 15 minutes onto my golf surfing for the afternoon).

I know the good people of this congregation wished the vicar a speedy and complete recovery, but I would not be at all surprised if the congregation didn't insist that he take plenty of time to recover. But I guess, really, it would be better for him to return next Sunday because 10-minute sermons are addictive to almost all church goers everywhere.

Chapter 44

St. Vincent DePaul Catholic Church
Nashville, Tennessee
July 13, 2003

T his week was the 44th week in my pilgrimage of "Fifty-Two Sundays." I was becoming more and more conscious of the countdown in regard to the number of remaining Sundays that would complete my year of visiting 52 different churches in the same number of weeks. I began asking more and more questions of friends and associates about other religious groups I might want to include in my visitations. With only nine weeks remaining, I wanted my visits to include as much variety as possible. With this thought in mind I asked my friend Frank Sutherland, the editor of *The Tennessean* newspaper to introduce me to his religion editor.

Frank introduced me via telephone to Brian Lewis, and within a few days we had agreed to meet for lunch to discuss my project. Brian is a young tall, handsome African-American who moved to Nashville from an assignment in the Midwest and familiarized himself quickly with the religious climate in Middle Tennessee. He proved to be a valuable asset, zeroing in on some prospects for me to visit in the next few weeks.

Brian had been raised a Baptist, but he had joined the Catholic Church during the past couple of years. His personal experience itself assured me that he was aware of the diversity in our area's religious cultures. During our discussion Brian told me about St. Vincent DePaul Catholic Church in Nashville which is located near the campus of Fisk University and Meharry Medical College, both of which are primarily African-American institutions of higher learning. St. Vincent, he told me, was also attended mostly by African-Americans. Brian also said that this Sunday the choir from the St. Augustine Catholic Church in Memphis would be singing at St. Vincent during the 11:00 a.m. service. He said they would be singing primarily Gospel songs. This did it for me. I could not resist

445

going to see and to hear how Gospel singing would mesh with traditional Catholic liturgy.

This morning Betty announced, "It is really 8:29 a.m. and I am ready to leave." She said it rather triumphantly, and she had every right to do so because I was still in my bathroom and was at least 10 minutes from being ready to leave. I had been razzing her pretty good lately about her battles with the clock. But she didn't razz on me at all when 10 minutes later I walked with her to the car, because she is not the type of person to rub it in. So with nothing more said, I told her that we were going to St. Vincent's for church and that we would look for a restaurant in the area.

We first drove to the Metro Center area of Nashville, which is the most commercialized part of this general area, and began driving around but were unsuccessful in quickly finding a good blue road restaurant which was open for breakfast on Sunday. The day was partially overcast as we wandered around in the Clarksville Highway and the Trinity Lane areas, but to no avail. Finally, we headed back to the Metro Center area where the only possibilities for breakfast were McDonald's, Sonic, Burger King and Pralines.

The choice of Pralines was simple given the competition. We walked into the restaurant at about 9:20 a.m., seated ourselves near the hardy looking breakfast buffet, and immediately began helping ourselves. They offered a full menu for us to custom order our breakfasts, but we decided that we would just graze the double area buffet. We helped ourselves first to some pastries, primarily mini-Danish and pecan rolls. We then moved on to the fruit bar which was an extension of the main part of the bar. We each chose some cantaloupe and then proceeded on to the more serious part of this breakfast buffet.

By now our table for four was pretty well covered in breakfast choices for only two, and we had not completed our greedy grazing yet. I dipped out a bowl of what I thought were very thin grits which turned out to be cream of wheat. I began wondering immediately if the managers/owners of this establishment were misplaced northerners who knew nothing about our taste for grits in the mid-south.

Just past the should-have-been-grits area was the serious southern breakfast territory. I pried open a biscuit between my thumb and my two forefingers and smothered this biscuit receptacle with sawmill gravy, and I placed another undamaged biscuit on my plate to go with my other breakfast fixins'. Next were the hash-brown potatoes, which sort of resembled a container of straw. The eggs were in a separate container. There were two types of eggs, scrambled and omelets. The scrambled eggs were far too dry and lumpy, and the cheese omelets were flat mini-cheese omelets which Betty actually took because she thought they were cheese blintzes. We both then helped ourselves to the sausages and bacon.

Actually the food was better than it looked, but I have never seen an egg that I didn't like. Betty thought the pecan roll was outstanding. The biscuits needed some help, except for the one under my tasty gravy. It never knew the difference. It neither needed to look nor taste like a good biscuit because it was simply the palette on which the gravy was transported to my mouth. The other biscuit merely stood by as a sleepy sentry, and it was never disturbed. The bacon, sausage and coffee all were as they should be — crisp, then chewy and then hot. Our breakfast buffets cost $9.00 each plus the tip for a total of $22.00. For that price, we had an acceptable simulated country breakfast at Pralines at 2025 Metro Center Boulevard. It was slightly better than acceptable, but beggars did not dare to be choosers this morning. After all, our other choices were Burger King, Sonic and McDonald's.

Oh, what the heck! I might as well fess-up and tell you that Pralines was not a blue road restaurant at all. It is the coffee shop in the Maxwell House Hotel. For us to eat a blue road breakfast in a hotel is almost unforgivable. No wonder they served cream of wheat instead of grits. What do they know? It is almost as bad as traveling on the interstate system and calling it blue roading. But now that I have confessed that my choice of Pralines was not in full compliance with my self-imposed guidelines for blue roading, I feel much better about the whole thing. Well, not the "whole thing," because of the thing about the cream of wheat and grits. Betty and I both agreed that we had not eaten cream of wheat in more than 50 years and would probably not eat any more in the next 50 years if we could help it.

When we left Praline's, it was about 10:15 a.m. and the second service of St. Vincent was to begin at 11:00 a.m. Since we had already broken faith with blue roading for this day, we slipped onto the interstate and slipped back off again at 28th Avenue in order to head for 18th and Jefferson, the general area of the Fisk campus and St. Vincent DePaul. At 10:30 a.m. we were parked in the shade near the church and reading the paper, which Betty always takes with her for just such occasions as this.

As we sat there in the shade awaiting the end of the first service and the beginning of the second one, we both read the story about a man named Jim who had befriended a young blind boy who always sat in a booth at Jim's favorite breakfast place and listened to gospel music on the radio while his grandmother pulled her shift at the restaurant. Jim had become a real father figure to the boy over the past few months. Betty and I discussed the fact that doing so had taken real sacrifice on the part of Jim, the kind which most of us are unwilling to make. We all could do more of this, but we just don't. I guess we're all just too selfish and lazy to help out in situations like this. I wish I had what Jim has to help me get more involved and be of more help in really needy situations. Maybe next year when I have finished with this important task of visiting 52 different churches...

At 10:45 a.m., with my conscience now bothering me about the very little I do to help others in real need, Betty and I entered St. Vincent to claim our seats at the very back of the right hand section of this sanctuary. This church and school had been founded in 1932 as a Catholic mission and had been run by the Franciscans since 1942. It is the only remaining Catholic school that is still operated for blacks, according to an historical marker in front of the church. The pastor, a white Franciscan, wore a simple black (or very dark brown) robe with a rope belt with three knots on the one sash to indicate his vows of poverty, chastity and obedience. He was standing in front of the church in order to welcome the members of the visiting choir group as they disembarked from their bus.

This attractive sanctuary was constructed of pine-paneled walls and a vaulted ceiling supported by pine laminated beams. There were two rows of pews with a center aisle. The 15 rows of pews on each side were designed to seat a total of about 300. The chancel area appeared to be constructed of stucco and cut stone with a simple wooden crucifix elevated at the center. On each side of the sanctuary were the simplest, yet most beautiful stained-glass windows I have ever seen. It appeared that they had been slowly and lovingly crafted over many months of time, perhaps by some artistic Franciscan monk in some secluded monastery.

At 10:50 a.m. the choir, dressed in gold robes trimmed with burgundy and blue stripes around the collars, began to sing. They sang and swayed with choreographed movements which kept time to the syncopated beat of the music. There were about 100 people in the pews as the choir finished their first song. Then the African-American priest who was listed as the parochial vicar came to the chancel area and said,"Good morning. Please join us in singing the processional *Hymn No. 302.*" This hymn was *I Just Came To Praise the Lord.*

After this hymn the parochial vicar, wearing vestments of two shades of green with white trim, again said, "Good morning." He continued, "Now y'all know we're to have church this morning, right?" Then the microphone went out and the vicar said, "Y'all know I'm going to have a hard time keeping up with this, this morning, don't you?" while pointing toward the choir. And the whole congregation roared with laughter. By now it was 11:05 a.m. and there were about 250 people in the congregation, mostly African-American; there was only one other Caucasian couple other than Betty and me. Most of the men in attendance wore dress-up casual clothes while the women wore mostly "Sunday clothes." This congregation had a healthy mixture of all ages with perhaps too few as old as Betty and me (which seems to be the case in almost all churches we have attended).

A middle-aged woman in a multicolored dress went to the chancel and read the *Old Testament* scripture from *The Book of Amos.* She was followed by another woman in a bright red suit who read the *New Testament* lesson from *Ephesians 1: 3 – 14.* The vicar then read from the *Gospel of Mark 6: 7 – 13.* This lesson was about the time that Jesus sent out the apostles two by two. Jesus told them to take no money, food nor extra clothes.

The pastor followed this reading of the Gospel by saying:"We get into trouble when we don't order our steps in the name of the Lord." Several in the congregation responded by saying, "Amen, that's right. Amen." The vicar said, "My mother said God never promised you a rose garden."

"Amen."
"All right."
"Amen."

By now the vicar had warmed to the congregation, and the congregation had definitely warmed to him. He was walking down the center aisle preaching easily without notes. When he was about one-third of the way up the aisle, he stopped and said, "But before you go out into the world make sure that Jesus calls you or sends you." Then he turned toward the choir and said that as beautiful as this music is "We don't come to the church for the music. We come for Jesus' sake."

He noted that when the disciples were sent out that they were sent to heal the sick. Then he gave this bit of a warning — that while there certainly is a lot of pain and suffering in the world, not all will be healed when we pray for them. He said, "I had my mother on fifty prayer lists but she died anyway." He further warned, "We are all going to have pain and suffering. We are going to have problems in our families and in our marriages." Then he said a few things which I could not clearly hear since he had no microphone, but obviously those near him in the aisle could hear because they enthusiastically said, "Amen. Amen. All right. Amen."

I could not hear all I wanted but felt like the man in a story who was sitting far back in a meeting hall while a visiting evangelist was preaching exuberantly to a very enthusiastic crowd. Suddenly almost everyone in the hall stood up shouting and cheering and our man joined right in. His friend, tugging on his jacket asked, "What did he say? What did he say?" to which the man of our story answered, "I don't know, but just look at the *way* he said it." I felt like joining in amen-ing with this congregation at St. Vincent today because, in spite of the fact that I could not hear all he was saying, I was totally impressed by the way he was saying it.

This vicar carried the enthusiasm right home to the congregation through his sermon which had been initiated by this talented visiting choir from St. Augustine's Church in Memphis. The vicar led the congregation in proclaiming their faith in the words of the Apostles' Creed. This was followed by a prayer led by a woman who prayed while the congregation responded sequentially by saying, "Lord, hear our prayer." The final part of this prayer was, "We pray that all people will learn to treat each other as brothers and sisters." And the congregation again said, "Lord, hear our prayers." At this point I especially wanted to say a big "AMEN."

It was now only about 11:25 a.m., and the priest had already preached his sermon. He then called for the gathering of the tithes and offerings. By now the sanctuary was totally full. Does this vicar know how to work a crowd and a room or what? If he had called for the offering 10 minutes earlier he would have denied about 50 souls the opportunity to worship in this very important way. And it is especially important to this church since it is $70,000 below the budget in giving so far for the year, according to some earlier announcements. And now they are only $69,995 short since Betty worshipfully placed her $5 in the basket. I know they had not budgeted her $5 because we had not even heard of St. Vincent until just a few days ago.

During the offering the choir sang a rousing gospel song with a very talented soprano soloist to hit the highest notes, which she did just as Betty's $5 settled into the extended basket. When this soloist finished, there was a full round of applause with many "Amens" from the congregation. After the applause died down, the vicar asked the soprano to come to the center of the chancel, and he embraced her in a big bear hug to the total delight of the congregation. Didn't I say this man of God knows how to work a room?

The Eucharist was next, and it is always the focal point of Catholic services. After the words of the institution of the sacrament, the congregation, standing, sang "Ah-Amen, Ah-Amen, Ah-Amen, Amen, Amen." The vicar then led the congregation in praying *The Lord's Prayer* during which time most of the congregation prayed with both hands extended in a supplicatory manner, palms turned upwards. Then, as a part of the celebration of the Eucharist, the vicar invited the whole congregation to visit in fellowship with others in the sanctuary for a few minutes. This part of the service proceeded like a family reunion with members visiting members everywhere. I even got into the act by walking several pews forward to greet my old friend Jerry Shelton with whom I had served for years on the board of a not-for-profit corporation which provided housing for low-income people. My hat was off to the vicar for allowing me to work the room for a few minutes.

451

The vicar then began distributing the elements of wine and bread by serving the choir first. He announced the "Communion Hymn" which was *The Gift of Finest Wheat*. It was sung as, row by row, members went to partake of this sacrament. Most of those communing today drank from a common cup.

After communion the choir sang some snappy Gospel songs with much clapping by the congregation and more finely choreographed in-place dancing by the choir. All this was brought to a crescendo with the congregation standing and clapping enthusiastically along with the choir.

Then the white Franciscan pastor in the dark robe reappeared to give thanks to the choir and to encourage the congregation to come back in the same numbers and with the same enthusiasm every Sunday. Some announcements were made, and some awards were given to some young acolytes. Visitors were encouraged to stand and introduce themselves; the Brownings chose to remain anonymous (except to my friend Jerry).

Now at the end of the service, with all the housekeeping announcements completed, the choir began singing again and within seconds they were really rockin'. The piano exuberantly pounded out the tunes as the choir and the congregation together swayed and clapped in unison, as if the congregation had just had a one-hour lesson in how to really get into enjoying a worship service St. Augustine style.

I just hope St. Vincent DePaul does not have St. Augustine choir withdrawal symptoms next Sunday. It could happen in many congregations, but I believe the parochial vicar of St. Vincent will have his very own brand of Methadone ready to feed to his flock. It may even be in the form of a simple announcement that, "the budget deficit miraculously and suddenly dropped by $5 last Sunday." God works in mysterious ways His wonders to perform.

Chapter 45

Sherith Israel Synagogue
Nashville, Tennessee
July 20, 2003

*H*ere it was Saturday again, and Betty and I were leaving our house at 7:54 a.m. to have breakfast and then attend a Sabbath service at a reformed Jewish synagogue. Of course, Saturday is the seventh day of the week. It is therefore the day that all Jews, and some Christians, maintain as their day of rest following the words from the book of Genesis where God rested on the seventh day of creation. *Genesis 2: 3* also says, "God blessed the seventh day and sanctified it."

Christians have sort of been double dipping on this matter for some two thousand years. At least today most Christians blend both Saturday and Sunday into a type of quasi-cultural/religious, 48-hour Sabbath. And the powers that be in Western culture have performed their own form of sanctification of this two-day weekend. Christians started worshipping on Sunday in memory of the teaching that it was on the first day of the week that Jesus was raised from the dead. Then, for good measure, they more or less maintained Saturday as a type of preamble to their day of worship.

"Give them an inch and they'll take a mile" is surely the case here. The Bible clearly says that God worked at creating the heavens and the Earth for six days and rested on the seventh only. See what I mean? Christians in Western civilization have adopted what might well be called a Judeo-Christian Sabbath. Watching golf, college football and stockcar races and shopping at the Home Depot make up the Christian preamble to their Sunday worship. These days more and more Christians worship far more fervently on the 50-yard line of professional football games than they do in more traditional places of worship on the second day of their extended Sabbath.

Jews aren't too shabby at reversing the field of play either. Westernization of the weekend Sabbath is addictive. Most

American Jews, as well as Christians, seem to take full advantage of this elastic Sabbath period. But the Jewish community would have all the childlike rights to pose and point a collective tattletale-shaking finger at Christians while saying, "But they started it." And they would be right. It certainly was the early Christians who changed Saturday into Sunday and then culturally acquiesced in the plot to make a "one-size-fits-all" weekend out of Saturday and Sunday.

Christians and Jews alike have adopted the 40-hour workweek as if it is a sacrosanct protector of the "one size fits all" religious weekend. The Jewish-Christian labor coalition has successfully lobbied our lawmakers to force the overtime work laws to penalize the capitalist infidels who would dare to tread on the holy ground of this 48-hour God and Jesus blessed expanded Sabbath.

I must admit that I love the weekends. They certainly give me a measure of relief from my tendency to feel guilty for playing golf on Saturdays and Sundays. Actually my list of playing partners is comprised of Catholics, Jews, Protestants and Muslims. So it is natural that the recognition of the Muslim holy day of Friday is gaining acceptance in our regular foursome. I can well imagine all four of us joining the protest marches if there was a groundswell movement for the acceptance of a 72-hour weekend in the name of religious tolerance.

Maybe there should be a law that would make a requirement of each person who makes use of the two-day or three-day weekends. Perhaps we should all be required each year to attend at least one worship service of each religion whose traditions have made these days of rest possible for us. If we fail in this way to ratify the validity of each of the religions which give us 52, or even 104, extra days of rest each year, maybe we should be required to do 52 to 104 days of community service for each violation. Or maybe give up our rights to overtime pay. Wow! What ways to assure a great measure of religious tolerance these concepts carry with them!

I had planned to go to another Jewish Synagogue today, perhaps to assure my 52 weeks of overtime pay (in case I should ever actually work on Saturday.) Also, I knew doing so would provide some relief from my guilt for enormous amounts of goofing off on this holy day for Jews without proper recognition of the tradition which supported my lifetime of savoring Saturdays.

I had already attended a reformed synagogue some months earlier and wanted now to attend an orthodox Jewish service. There is only one such synagogue in Nashville — Congregation Sherith Israel located at 3600 West End Avenue. My friend Perry Moskovitz who is a member of Sherith Israel said that we should meet him at 9:45 a.m. in order to observe some particular part of their service which would begin at 10:00 a.m.

In order to meet Perry on time, we decided to leave home by 8:00 a.m., and we were in our car at 7:54 a.m. I'm so proud of Betty I could pop. She is apparently enjoying a full recovery from her life-long problem of poor morning punctuality. Pray for her that she does not lapse back into her bad habits after our 52-week pilgrimage is over.

I had discovered that Bread and Company on Hillsboro Road was now open for breakfast every morning. I go there some mornings for a scone or a Danish and coffee. But now they were open for a full breakfast. They have an omelet station where they prepare eggs to order including Eggs Benedict, omelets of all descriptions, and eggs fried to order (even over-easy/over-medium). So, about five minutes after leaving home we were inside this bakery which also is an upscale delicatessen that provides a whole array of gourmet recipes prepared for customers to either eat-in or take-out.

This restaurant is a bakery which has developed and redeveloped its original concept since first opening several years ago and, as a result, is rather dysfunctional. In one area you order gourmet foods, and in another is the breakfast bar with cooks preparing egg entrees, waffles and French toast. Yet another area offers the breads and pastries, and the next area houses a gourmet coffee bar. Now all you have to do is queue up in still another line to pay for your selections. You see, the space was just never designed for all these varied offerings and so the whole operation is awkward. But they built it, and in the crowds came. They come ready to have their palates tantalized and their pockets raided.

The young, the middle-aged yuppies and the pretty people come in by the droves to purchase calories which are then washed down with a selection from a whole array of gourmet coffee drinks, while seemingly happily being fleeced at the end of the last line. I was fleeced of $8.95 for one loaf of delicious cranberry-nut bread which came to about $ .75 for each slice of this specialty. Baaaa, baaaah, baaa.

Two hungry sheep on a 52-Sunday pilgrimage joined the herd of yuppie sheep this morning as we lined up only mildly bleating, and we shifted from hoof to hoof waiting to be shorn of some of our discretionary funds. Betty felt we had enough disposable assets to order an omelet with bacon, cheese, broccoli, spinach, tomatoes and mushrooms. I finished the spending spree by ordering three eggs over-easy/over-medium with bacon, potato casserole and two scones. Just before I entered the final sheering line to pay the cashier, I ordered French toast for the table, which was a very small silver top table in the center of the restaurant. With hardly a bleating complaint, I paid $40.63 for everything including the loaf of bread — a mere pittance for the same fare in some parts of New York City and apparently becoming nearly the same in West and South Nashville.

I was so hopeful that this breakfast place would be exceptionally good, and therefore I had respectfully waited a couple of weeks after they officially opened the egg island. Apparently we should have waited longer. Betty's omelet was filled with beautiful items and this entrée looked delicious; but, alas, it was not. It was rather disappointingly bland. My eggs and bacon were good, even though my eggs were slightly under cooked even though I coached the young cook as she prepared them. The potato casserole just does not make it as a breakfast item, perhaps for lunch with a sandwich but definitely not with eggs and bacon. Maybe in a couple of weeks they will get the message and offer real breakfast potatoes.

The French toast was superb, but the maple syrup overpowered this delicacy with too much maple flavoring (either natural or added). My advice to the chef here is to make a visit to the Pancake Pantry for a little industrial espionage on a couple of items such as their hash-brown potatoes and their syrup. One visit is all it will take.

We left Bread and Company at 9:00 a.m. with enough time to drive around a bit and even make a pit stop back at our house before going to the Sherith Israel Synagogue. Along the way we were reminded of the Metropolitan elections which were only a couple of weeks away. Of course, there were candidates' signs everywhere, but the biggest sign of all was blacktop pavement. Fresh pavement everywhere was a sure sign, and it read, "Vote for the incumbent who is doing away with all the potholes."

We drove smoothly on the practically seamless asphalt for only about three minutes and then parked on Bowling Avenue. Soon we were walking up to meet my friend Perry Moskovitz who had invited us to go with him as his guest to this Saturday worship service of the only Orthodox Synagogue in Nashville. Perry had been a lifelong member of this synagogue which holds strictly to the ancient beliefs and practices of the Jewish people.

Perry's mother and father had both been members of this congregation since they first immigrated to Nashville. His mother came to this country from Hungary in 1914 when she was fourteen years of age. She spoke no English and wore a sign written in English telling those who would help that she was coming to live with relatives in Nashville, Tennessee. She moved into a storeroom over the Jacobs Dry Goods Store located at 225 Hermitage Avenue and worked for her relative for one dollar a week. She worked 14 hours a day, six days a week, for this precious dollar.

Perry's father came here from Poland in 1912 when he was eighteen-years-old and became a shoemaker at the Blue Ribbon Shoe Store located at 12th and Broadway. When he was thirty-six, he bought the Jacobs Dry Goods Store after Mr. Jacobs died and changed the name to the Moskovitz Dry Goods Store. Perry lived in the back of the store with his brothers and sisters, and later the family moved the store to 2604 Lebanon Road.

When Perry's mother and father were married in 1919 the Sherith Israel Synagogue was called the "Fifth Avenue Synagogue." It sat right next to the Ryman Auditorium. When the Grand Ole' Opry began, Perry said that many times country-music fans would come into services at the synagogue thinking they were entering the Opry House.

This orthodox synagogue moved to its present West End site in 1951/1952. This congregation then was made up mostly of Jewish immigrants from Eastern European countries, just as his parents had been.

Perry and his family are part of the approximately 50 % of the Orthodox Sherith Israel congregation who are not strict observers of every aspect of Orthodox Judaism. The Moskovitz family keeps kosher in their home and follows the dietary laws such as not eating

pork, shellfish and other scavenger seafood such as eels and catfish.
The strictly orthodox contingent, on the other hand, will not eat in
restaurants where the food is not kosher. Members of this group
also adhere to the practice of walking to the synagogue on the
Sabbath. I felt a rush of shame when I suddenly realized that this
50% were potential clients of a housing development I was helping
develop just a block away from the synagogue. Pray for me in case
this commercial thought was sacrilegious so close to the time when
I would be a visitor in their worship service.

Perry drove up and parked in front of the synagogue, a sure
sign that he was part of the less conservative part of this congregation.
He provided Betty and me each with a yarmulke, or skull cap, to be
worn in the service. All who attend there are required to wear a
covering for their heads. Also Perry told us that Betty would have
to sit in one of two sections reserved for women on each side of the
synagogue, which are separated by partial walls from the mid-section
reserved for men. Betty sat very near to where Perry and I were sitting, but was separated nevertheless by an aisle and the partial wall.

My friend Perry very carefully helped me follow and understand the various aspects of the worship service. He told me that
the new Rabbi, Rabbi Merdinger, who just succeeded Rabbi Posner
about eighteen months ago, was a young man with a law degree
from Harvard who decided to become a Rabbi after practicing law
for a short time. Perry said this Rabbi was in his early 30s and was
just getting adjusted to this congregation, but he had been well
received and was greatly respected. He was married and had a six-
month-old child.

Perry told Betty that she should be very careful not to touch the
Rabbi. The Orthodox Rabbis are not to touch women at any time
unless they are part of his own family. If he is even accidentally
touched by a woman, he must go through a rigid period of ritual
cleansing. This part of the orthodox tradition is one of the most puz-
zling parts to me because of the matriarchal aspect of Judaism, which
basically defines Jews as those who have been born of a Jewish
mother. There are other tests of Jewishness, but this one is the litmus
test of Orthodox Judaism. However, after this one matriarchal beginning point of Jewish life, Jewish males become the only gender which
has any authority or voice in orthodox Jewish Synagogues.

This service was the Bar Mitzvah for a young boy who had just turned 13 — the age of responsibility in Judaism. This young man had a major part in this service as he read from the printed liturgical order of worship, and was guided and coached by the cantor, the member of the congregation who has many responsibilities in guiding these worship services. A young man may choose the Sabbath which is nearest to his birthday to have his Bar Mitzvah. "Bar Mitzvah" means "Son of Jewish Law", and on a young man's 13th birthday he may officially become a son of the Jewish Law.

This worship period proceeded with the reading of the pre-scribed service for this day with the Bar Mitzvah candidate reading some of the cantor's part of the service. There was no music at all during this service, even though music had been an integral part of the worship service at the reformed synagogue, the Congregation Micah, which we attended a few months ago. In this orthodox service almost all the men wore a Talith, which is a scarf or a shawl type of covering draped over their shoulders and arms. Only unmarried men or young boys do not wear the Talith in the worship services.

The young man whose Bar Mitzvah was celebrated on this day started reading in Hebrew from the prayer book on Page 421, the SHEMONEH ISRAEL-AMIDH, as the cantor carefully watched over him. He read about the patriarchs, God's might, the holiness of God's name, and the holiness of the day. Following this was a part invoking God's blessing in restoring the temple service. We were able to follow his Hebrew readings with the parallel readings printed in English in the prayer book.

Next this young man, who was accepting his personal respon-sibilities before God, read a prayer of Thanksgiving thanking God for His power and miracles evidenced in our lives every day. He then read a prayer for peace.

The next reading was of the "Full-Kaddish" which is a sort of benediction similar to the Christian benediction:"May the words of our mouths and the meditation of our hearts be acceptable in Thy sight, O Lord, our Shepherd our Redeemer." These words preceded immediately the removal of the *Torah* from the Ark. This is the most ceremonial and apparently the most significant part of this worship service. The *Torah* is a carefully hand engraved scroll of the first five books of the *Bible*.

The Ark is a focal part of the synagogue where several copies of the Torah are kept. They are very ornately covered, and they are various sizes. Perry told me that some of these had been gifts to the synagogue from someone, sometimes in memory or honor of a deceased relative. He said handcrafted copies may cost as much as $50,000 each. Each one may take months or years to produce because each one must be totally error free — no erasures. If a mistake is made at all, the writer must go back to the very beginning of that part of the scroll and start over.

The ceremonial removal of the *Torah* and the loving, careful, way in which it was uncovered and then carried in celebration around parts of the synagogue was a beautiful and worshipful experience. As the cantor and others participating in the service gently carried the uncovered *Torah* around in a proud elevated fashion, it reminded me of a proud father showing off his firstborn son to his friends and relatives. As they passed up and down the aisles the members of the synagogue would reach out and touch the *Torah* with their hymnal or their Talith and then kiss the object which had touched the *Torah*. These acts of respect are carefully taught in the laws which are printed in a part of the prayer book.

The acts of the cantor and the Rabbi are very carefully prescribed. On Page 421 at the beginning of the SHEMONEH ESREI – AMBAH, the prayer book says that the reader should take three steps backward and then three steps forward. Then it says the reader should remain standing with both feet together as the reader recites devotedly without interruption in any form. The person praying is told to pray audibly so that others can know this person is praying, but only loud enough that only the person praying can truly hear. These instructions refer to laws numbers 61 and 90 for the details of these instructions. These laws tell how the person praying should bend their knees at the word "blessed" and bow at the word "You" and straighten up at the word "Hasheem." I was very interested in these instructions because it was in these instructions that I first found the explanation for what had seemed peculiar types of movements by orthodox Jews praying which I had previously only seen on television.

After the reading of the selection of the *Torah* for today, the cantor read the various prayers from the book of prayer. First was the "Prayer for the OLEH." This was the prayer for the young man whose Bar Mitzvah was today. Then there were the prayers for newborn children and their mothers, and a prayer for sick people. This prayer asks God to speed recovery to the two hundred and forty-eight organs and the three hundred and sixty-five blood vessels in the sick.

Following these were "Prayers for the members of the Israel Defense Force," prayers for those Jews of the Diaspora, prayers for teachers and students of the *Torah*, and finally prayers for the members of this congregation. There was a prayer for the welfare of the U.S. government, the president, vice president and the cabinet, and a prayer that this government would always be kindly disposed toward Israel.

There was a prayer for the welfare of Israel, and a prayer for God to send the promised Messiah. Finally, there was a prayer and blessing on the return of the *Torah* to the Ark.

At one point during this service there was a delightful respite from the seriousness of the prayers and readings from the *Torah*. This was when all the very serious participants in this service held hands in a circle and danced, around and around, while singing a sort of happy Bar Mitzvah to the new man in their midst who had just reached the age of responsibility. Pieces of candy were thrown into the dancing circle, and Perry told me this signified everyone's wish that this would be a sweet and happy year for him. It was obviously a joyous occasion that this young man would not soon forget.

Before the *Torah* was returned to the Ark, it was again held in a celebratory fashion and worshipfully paraded around the synagogue. Finally, it was back in its exalted place in the Ark at the center of the chancel area.

Finally, Rabbi Merdinger announced that he would be giving a sermon on the subject of the question of whether or not it is ever right to kill. Essentially he said that there are times when our hearts tell us it is right or alright to kill. He did go on to say that the final verification of the rightness and wrongness of any act, and especially the act of killing, can only come from God. He said that only God knows and sees the real intention of our hearts.

One of the members of the congregation interrupted the Rabbi at this point, and asked the Rabbi how his statements on this subject meshed with other statements in the scriptures on this subject. This question obviously flustered the Rabbi momentarily. It apparently was very unusual for a member of this congregation to ask a question in the middle of a Rabbi's sermon. My friend Perry said that this had never happened in all the years he had been worshiping there. The man asking the question, I was told, was an immigrant from Russia where, perhaps, this type of open discussion was more common. When he saw that the Rabbi was taken aback momentarily, he pulled his Talith over his head in a gesture of embarrassment as if to hide. The Rabbi graciously insisted that this man not be embarrassed, and the sermon proceeded, but I frankly do not remember much else the Rabbi said.

Our host Perry Moskovitz told us it would be appropriate for us to leave after the sermon. There had been a preamble to the service which we had attended, and there would be a postlude service with more prayers and readings, but the Bar Mitzvah part of this service was over.

Maybe they took an offering during the prelude or the postlude, but Betty and I left without contributing our $5 to this congregation. Maybe if they need a new *Torah* sometime in the future we can sneak our $5 in the back door by giving our donation to Perry. This way they will only need 9,999 additional such generous gifts to get the job done. Shalom.

Chapter 46

Christ Church
Nashville, Tennessee
July 27, 2003

I had no one to blame but myself this morning when I left for my Sunday morning excursion. Betty was not going with me today because she was staying at the hospital with our daughter Beverly who was facing some pending surgery just as soon as her doctors could arrange for an operating room. At least, that is what they said,but I was betting that they would not be able to make the arrangements until Monday morning. I was also betting that they weren't trying very hard. Of course, they had to act as if they were trying, what with their signatures affixed to the Hippocratic Oath and all.

Actually, Beverly had to interpret the intentions of three different doctors who were attending her. First, there was her internist to whom she had gone when she first experienced stomach pain and other symptoms. He then referred her to two different surgeons who had decided to do a tandem surgery act on her. She was going to have some gall stones removed orthoscopically by Dr. Wallace McGraw, who had performed the same procedure on me about ten years ago. And as soon as the first procedure was finished, Dr. Louis Garrard was going to perform laparoscopic surgery to remove her gall bladder.

Beverly is in the property management business. Several years ago young Louis Garrard, then a medical student, lived in one of the apartments which she managed. He did part-time work for Beverly for a time to help work his way through medical school. When he walked in and introduced himself as the surgeon who was going to remove her gall bladder, he asked her if she were sure she wanted her former maintenance man operating on her.

Both her surgeons said that her problems were genetic, which meant that I am probably the one who was the cause of her present problems. Betty hasn't had gallstones. So, although I left Betty behind to bear the responsibility of watching after Beverly, I could not leave my guilt behind for passing onto my children such defective genes. My great grandfather was one mountain man from West Virginia whose name was Anderson Hatfield, alias Devil Anse Hatfield. If these doctors knew Beverly had inherited the genes of the patriarch of one side of the Hatfield – McCoy feud of about a century ago, they may have refused to operate on her at all. After all, this great, great grandfather of Beverly's just may have started this feud just because someone may have stolen one of his pigs. Careful, doc. We don't know how either she or I may react if you make a slip. Know what I mean?

Trying to forget what my reaction might be if either surgeon made a mistake, I started turning my thoughts to food. It worked magically. I was driving out Nolensville Road when I spotted the International House of Pancakes (IHOP, of course). At one time there was one of these near Vanderbilt University where I had eaten many times, but now this is the only one in Nashville to my knowledge. I decided I wanted to revisit some of the breakfast tastes which I began remembering immediately when I saw their sign.

I walked in and was seated quickly even though the restaurant was practically full. After reading their menu I asked the waitress if I could customize my order rather than "go by the book." She assured me I could, and so I ordered three eggs over-easy/over-medium, two pork chops, hash browns, biscuits and gravy, three pancakes. And coffee, of course.

As I waited for my order, I did my usual people watching and spotted a handsome young couple with a daughter who was about two-years-old. Both the young father and mother were strikingly and wholesomely good looking. He was about six feet, two inches tall and so handsome that his casual carefree shorts, T-shirt, sandals and almost unkempt hair seemed to provide a rugged frame for his not too pretty, but all-American handsome features. His wife reflected a similar picture as a young woman so beautiful that all her relaxed moods and clothing could not hide a classic beauty. Her dark hair, moderately high cheek bones, dark eyes and her light olive skin were like a magnet to my eyes. Their politely active daughter was definitely going to have fabulously beautiful features when the genes she had obviously inherited were fully developed about twenty years down the road.

While watching the three of them (just after their food arrived, but before they ate), I saw them almost automatically join hands and quietly, but openly, voice a prayer of thanksgiving for their food. So beautiful was this simple scene that when my food arrived, I felt their prayer was efficacious enough to cover the meal of this voyeur at the next table. My food was diversion enough that I now focused my eyes on my handsome pork chops and my perfectly beautiful pancakes.

As I ate, I began to realize that all of the people in the restaurant were completely normal, with the exception of the "movie stars" at the table next to mine. My waitress was nominally attractive, and the customers were a mixture of whites, African-Americans and Hispanics. I saw no Jesse Venturas, no Dennis Rodmans, no fat people and no skinny people. No one was oddly dressed — no tongue hardware, no cowboy country-western sequined outfits, and no stiff looking "suits." The clientele here was not homogenous by any means — just normal and different people out for a pleasant Sunday breakfast.

My Sunday breakfast ($13.48, plus $3.00 tip) was definitely above normal. Great eggs fried perfectly and absolutely delicious, and truly handsome pork chops. I did ask my waitress to take my biscuits and gravy back, but only because I always want to cover my biscuits with gravy my very own way — I want to keep one biscuit clear of the mess so that I can use part of it as a backstop for my eggs if they became unruly and cannot be politely coaxed onto my fork. The hash browns were good. Not perfect, but good. The pancakes here challenge those of the Pancake Pantry, but the Pantry's syrup definitely puts IHOP's pancakes in second place.

I was missing Betty who had been my breakfast and church buddy during most of my Sunday morning pilgrimages. As I left the IHOP, I continued south on Nolensville Road and turned west onto Old Hickory Boulevard. I had decided to visit Christ Church which is located at 15354 Old Hickory Boulevard. This is one of several churches now referred to as Christ Church in Nashville. There is the Episcopal Church located at Ninth and Broadway, and another Christ Church which is located near Franklin which is nominally or parenthetically Presbyterian. Today's Christ Church is Pentecostal, both nominally and parenthetically. Neither church seems to proudly acknowledge its denominational affiliation.Both seem to want to be considered more or less non-denominational, community-type churches. I do not know whether most of these community churches are growing so rapidly because they are community churches, or whether they become community churches because they are growing so fast and are assimilating so many varied types of people.

Several years ago my company was employed to be the real estate agency for the Woodlands development which is located immediately across Old Hickory Boulevard from this church (which was only called Christ Church even back then).While I had witnessed from across Old Hickory the impressive activity and growth of this church, I had never visited it, and I decided today that it should be one of the 52 churches I would visit this year. When I drove up, I was immediately intercepted by a series of parking assistants who moved me ever upward, circling around the hillside on which this church sits. I passed massive excavation and blasting sites which were the beginnings of the new expansions of this already enormous church facility.

Higher and higher we went, and I soon began to be grateful for the activities of shuttle buses which were moving people to their cars from the earlier services, and others from their cars to the church who were on their way to attend the 10:30 a.m. service. It was now about 10:15 a.m., and I had flashbacks of the Mt. Paran church of God in Atlanta several months ago when efficient shuttle buses ferried worshipers to and from worship. At all of these community-type churches, the people-moving arrangements are every bit as efficient as the shuttle services at the Nashville Airport.

Soon I was walking down the down staircase, while exiting worshipers were dutifully taking the up staircase. All was going well, and I soon understood why. In the middle of the service one of the pastors narrated a video which was shown on the three large screens placed at the front of the sanctuary. This video followed an arriving and departing bus and gave simple instructions regarding how to exit the church after the service. There is absolutely no way to operate church programs of this magnitude without paying attention to these practical matters. This church had learned this lesson very well.

I was in awe as I walked into their enormous sanctuary which was comparable in size to the other rapidly growing community churches I had attended prior to this service. This whole growing phenomenon is mind-boggling. Twenty-five million dollar building programs overlap each other all the time in most of these churches. Just then I reached into my pocket and pulled out a folded $5 bill which Betty had given to me before I left home, almost like a mother giving her child lunch money before sending him off to school. I immediately wondered if she put it into my pocket to be sure I had money so that I could participate in the offering part of the service, or if she did it to be sure I didn't get carried away in the excitement and do something crazy like giving $10 instead of $5. She knows that a $20 contribution on my part would not be totally out of the question except that she rarely lets me out of the house with little more than lunch money. If she could have seen the obvious costs going into this new construction program, she would have tried to dissuade me from going alone today. Of course, her only concern was fairness. I can just hear her saying, "It wouldn't be fair to give more than $5 since we had given all the other churches this same amount, now would it?"

This sanctuary appeared to be able to seat 3,000 – 4,000 people with its large wraparound balconies which tier down to the main level at the left and right of the sanctuary. There was a large semi-circular pulpit-choir area with a beautiful drawn curtain while the stage was being set. It was now 10:20 a.m. and the sanctuary was about 50% full. Most of the worshipers were nicely casually dressed. Very few suits or jackets were worn by men, but at least half of the women were dressed in their "Sunday clothes."

I sat in the back balcony with a panoramic view of most of the sanctuary. At 10:37 a.m. nothing was happening except more and more people gathering. Then at 10:38 a.m. the multi-piece band/orchestra introduced the beginning of the service with a rousing introduction of the song *This Is the Day the Lord Hath Made* as the curtain dramatically opened simultaneously with the cheerful voices of the 75-plus member choir. These talented and trained singers were dressed in emerald-green robes with white collars and red trim.The congregation was standing and waving and clapping along with the leadership of the choir. The senior pastor, L.H. Hardwick,

Jr., who is a gray-haired senior citizen, came to the pulpit with cheerful words of welcome and the invocation.

The next song was *I Am Thine, O' Lord*, with the well known words, "Draw me nearer, nearer, precious Lord, to Thy blessed bleeding side."

All the pastors here wore dark business suits, which stood in contrast to about 50% of pastors in the other community churches. I also did not see nor sense the freedom here to bring water, coffee or cokes into the sanctuary, which I had seen in about half of the mostly younger community-type congregations. It seems the more charismatic these community churches, the less free the ministers are to dress casually and the less free the members are to dress and act as if they were attending a rock concert. I haven't seen any Miller Light in any of the younger, more casual churches yet, but I would not be too surprised.

At the singing of the song O, *Ancient of Days*, the choir was into a swaying motion as they sang and clapped three times in a choreographed series of movements and synchronized sounds. By now the sanctuary was about two-thirds full as the choir and the congregation were totally in sync with their singing, swaying, clapping and waving of hands in a joyous and worshipful mood.

Next there was a rousing solo, with support from the choir, which had a storyline of a man on a plane reading the *Bible* and having the opportunity of witnessing to the man sitting next to him. When he came to the part where he told his fellow passenger about how Jesus came to die for our sins, almost the entire congregation was on their feet cheering and shouting as if the Titans had just won the Super Bowl.

The senior pastor came back to the pulpit while the people were still cheering and waving, and he said, "Look out, Brother Paul, I'm about to preach." Brother Paul Russell, an associate pastor, was apparently the one assigned to give the sermon for today. But, instead, the senior pastor, who founded this church, introduced Phillip D. Goldsberry, who was listed as pastor, and asked him to say a few words. This handsome youngish articulate pastor said that he wanted to follow-up last week's remarks entitled, *A Time to Share*. He said that God had built the laws of sowing and reaping into the universe. He said if you sow radishes, you will reap radishes.

If you sow sparingly, you will also reap sparingly, according to God's ordained laws.

I thought Pastor Goldsberry was beginning a sermon, but he tricked me. He was introducing the offering. But, not to worry, my $5 was ready and folded in my pocket so that it could easily be mistaken for a $20 bill as I dropped it into the plate. But by now I am sure all the ushers are aware of the fact that when someone actually is giving a $20 or larger bill they are sure that the denomination shows. Shucks, my usher probably thought I was only giving $1.00. From now on I'm going to be sure the number 5 on my offering shows. I would think even Betty would be embarrassed if someone thought we were only giving $1.00 per Sunday.

During the offering, a saxophone player from the band-orchestra played a jazzed up version of the hymn *Crown Him Lord of All*. It was so inspiring that I wanted to put another $5.00 into the plate, but I knew Betty would reprimand me for showing partiality in our giving. I am sure that many members and some visitors who were less conscious about showing partiality were inspired by this rousing instrumental solo to dig a little deeper before the usher got to them.

Linda Hillard, the church administrator, who was responsible for the video showing the best way to get to the shuttle buses after the service, came to the microphone to welcome a group of teens who were visiting from a Baptist church somewhere in Kansas. I thought it was a good thing Christ Church is only parenthetically of the Pentecostal persuasion, or most Baptist ministers would have guided this group to the Bellevue Community Church which seems to be parenthetically associated with the Free Will Baptists.

Bill Stoner, a layman, read the scripture lesson for today and the text was projected on the large screens for participation by the congregation who read parts of the scripture lesson responsively. This was followed by a member of the choir singing a lengthy, animated and moving solo which soon had many in the congregation on their feet shouting praises and waving their arms and hands, while the choir forcefully and effectively backed her up.

As it turned out, this solo led to another solo by the male pianist, who was ably supported by a female trio from the choir. This solo was continuing the theme that there could be healing in our midst today. These two solos became the focal point of the entirety of the remainder of this service. The pianist-soloist who sang while playing the piano himself began asking those who needed healing of any kind today to stand for prayer. As he continued playing and singing along with the trio, the people who stood were met where they were by members of the congregation who came to pray with them. Scattered among the congregation there were 25 to 30 people standing, praying, and being prayed for by others.

I sensed that this was turning into the type of service which I had witnessed at the Mt. Paran Church of God in Atlanta. Some of the same elements were in both services. I thought immediately that the word was getting around about the effectiveness of this approach to moving people. Who knows? It may have even started here first and then spread to Mt. Paran. One thing for sure, this type of service will soon spread to community-type churches everywhere.

Soon the Associate Pastor Paul Russell came to the pulpit and, following the mood that had swept over this congregation, said, "We need healing more than we need anything. We need healing more than we need a sermon." This was the key to the remainder of this service. I sensed that he was beginning to let us know that there would be no sermon today. As the choir and the trio continued to sing healing songs in the background, Pastor Paul said he wanted us all to stand and asked anyone who needed healing of any kind to come forward and pray at the altar.

This pastor said that today he had had a friend — a Catholic priest — who had come to the earlier service for healing and renewal. This electrified the congregation. A Catholic priest coming to this church for healing and renewal was some kind of verification that God was working here. Pastor Paul then singled out Brother James Smith who was in the congregation and said to him, "Brother Smith, the Lord is going to heal you completely, both physically and mentally," as several members of the congregation gathered around him to pray for him.

The invitation to come to the altar to pray continued as the choir now sang, "I need, you, Lord," over and over while perhaps 150 people gathered along the 100-plus-foot altar to pray. By now it was impossible to tell who had come to pray and who had come to pray with those in need of healing. Now the pastor said the expected words (at least by me), "I'm not going to preach a sermon this morning." He was saying the Lord was working his own way this morning and he (the pastor) was not going to interfere. I felt this was a wise move and had felt the same way at the Mt. Paran Church when the pastor, however, did go on to preach a sermon which had seemed anticlimactic after the hundreds who had come forward in response to a call for those "who needed a miracle."

The pastor now addressed the entire congregation again and said, "We are all ministers. We don't have to be preachers to be ministers." He then said that he wanted the whole congregation to "group together, where you are in groups of no more than four." He then said he wanted the members of each group to exchange names and to exchange needs and pray together for one another. It worked. Now there were small clusters of people throughout the sanctuary and audible prayers were ascending from each group. I saw two groups cheating because they had groups of five and six. But I didn't tell on them.

At 11:49 a.m. the prayer groups were still going strong while all the pastors circulated and prayed among the small groups, and while the choir sang *I Will Worship You.*

When I left at 12:00 p.m. the prayer groups were still going strong throughout the sanctuary. I followed Sister Linda's instructions and made my way along with hundreds of others who were now leaving without a benediction and without saying, "May I?" Or, "Amen." As I left to board the shuttle, I saw the only reference to this church's parenthetical denominational connections. In the lower foyer there was a poster giving information and pictures of different members under the heading: "Christ Church — Pentecostal, 1991 – 1992."

Maybe the Baptists took another exit.

On my shuttle there was a minister and his family leaving early to beat the rush to our cars. He was a pastor from Cleveland, Tennessee on sort of a busman's holiday. He probably had heard of the great success of this church and had come to learn what he could. I know he learned that a lively music program is perhaps the most important thing in a service like this. More people by far were moved and excited during rousing songs by the choirs and the soloists than they had been during the sermons.

I hope he learned when to preach a sermon and when to save it. Perhaps for a Sunday when the music fails to excite the people, then they can just relax and go on to sleep.

Chapter 47

St. Ignatius Antiochian Orthodox Church
Franklin, Tennessee
August 3, 2003

*B*eauty certainly is in the eye of the beholder. While one may see only beauty in the Grand Canyon, another can just as easily see only ugly scars on the face of the earth caused by devastating erosion linked to raging flood waters over millions of years. This overcast Sunday morning could have been viewed by one set of eyes as very depressing and gloomy. To another set of eyes, specifically my own, this overcast day seemed to draw a soft picture in which the contrast between the sharp edges of bright sunlight and the dark shadows of shade had been erased. The light clouds were not heavy or dark enough to create another darker set of contrasts. Instead, the clouds were like a filter that allowed only enough soft light through to pleasantly merge light and dark, sun and shadows. The soft filtered light was just enough to reveal the lifting of a misty fog. The trees halfway up the slopes of the ridges were just beginning to release their grip on the sleepy, milky wisps of visible moisture, and those wisps were unexcitedly moving toward their midmorning nuptials with the clouds which softly awaited their union.

Wow! How did I come to see a semi-sloppy gray morning in any way, but ugly on this day?

The eyes of this particular beholder were obviously peering through filtered lenses created by the realization that I was going to breakfast and church this morning with my wife of almost fifty years. Now, this is the same wife with whom I have been attending many religious and nonreligious functions during these fifty years. The only difference was simply that the fifty-year milestone had been in the forefront of my attention recently; we had been talking about going on a cruise through the Panama Canal later this year as a way to celebrate the occasion of our marriage fifty years ago.

The filter of fifty years of marriage to my high school sweet-heart caused all the images I saw today to seem softer and more touching. Thus this Sunday morning was, perhaps, more beautiful than usual in the eyes of this beholder as we left our home at 8:00 a.m. The two possible choices of church services to attend today were both located in the Cool Springs-Franklin area. One was the Weigh Down Worship Center in Cool Springs which is also called the Remnant Fellowship. I had called their telephone numbers several times. While their voice mail message sounded very pleased to receive the call and grateful that the caller had found out about them, they still had not returned my call with more information as to their service times.

The second choice for a service today was the St. Ignatius Antiochian Orthodox Church on Peytonsville Road in Williamson County. We drove by the Weigh Down Worship Center and, finding no signs giving information about service times, we decided to move on toward St. Ignatius.

We drove out toward Peytonsville Road, crossed I-65, and drove into Truckstops of America which had a meat-n-three type restaurant called Apple Creek. We observed their breakfast buffet as we entered to take a seat at one of the truckers' booths — you know, the ones that have telephones for the good buddies of the 18-wheelers to check in at home. I guess these phones will gradu-ally be eliminated because of the proliferation of cell phones among Americans today. The point has come where a cell phone is almost more of a necessity than the CB radio. 10-4?

Now if you do not know how to respond to the 10-4 question, you probably will not understand why it is generally smart to stop at a truck stop if you are hungry, but I will educate you. Truckers are known for their ability to sniff out good places to eat, and their CBs allow them to spread the word. Guess that when CB radios go the way of dinosaurs the truckers will have to find another way to communicate about good eating spots. Maybe this particular need to mass communicate will ultimately be the salvation of the CB radio afterall.

We nixed the buffet and chose to order from the menu instead. Betty ordered creamed chipped beef on toast and hash-brown potatoes. I ordered three eggs over-easy/over-medium with sausage, hash browns and biscuits and gravy. And then pancakes for the table, of course. The total tab was $20.27 plus tip. While our breakfasts were being prepared, I checked out a sign which I had noticed as we entered the restaurant foyer. It called attention to a 9:00 a.m. worship service in the TV room which is reserved for truck drivers. It was now about five minutes 'till 9:00 a.m., and so I went to check it out. It is a "Trans-denominational Ministry" which is sponsored by TruckStop Ministries.

I went upstairs to the TV area and looked in. There were three rows of chairs neatly lined up with about five chairs per row, making room for about 15 people. The TV was still on because it was still not yet 9:00 a.m., and the chaplain whom I met said that these truck stops allow the Truckstop Ministries to turn off the TV only between 9:00 a.m. and 10:00 a.m. each Sunday morning. When I walked in, this chaplain greeted me hopefully because he apparently thought momentarily that I might be a prospect for his service. Dressed to look very much like a truck driver, this sturdy looking chaplain wore work pants and a short-sleeved white shirt with "Truckstop Ministries, Inc." monogrammed over the shirt pocket. His nametag identified him as the chaplain for today.

With a cherubic face and a gentle smile, this chaplain greeted me and then told me about Truckstop Ministries, which he said had been founded by a former truck driver in 1981. The founder and former trucker was now the Rev. Joseph H. Hunter, and his organization now puts out a newsletter giving locations and information about their ministries located in truck stops across 29 states. The chaplain at this truck stop (Exit 61 off I-65) said that three chaplains shared the ministry's work at this location; this day was his assignment. He said that some days a small number of men and women come to the service, and he said that the chaplain may stay around for a while after 10:00 a.m. when the TV officially goes on in order to talk one-on-one with any who wish to talk.

After Betty and I finished breakfast (which should not be receiving the highest marks from truckers in the future), I stopped by again to see how this truck-stop congregation had assembled. Well, if it had been an orthodox Jewish service it would have had to be dismissed. Orthodox Jews do not hold services unless there are ten males present. There was one lonely trucker there —

a congregation of one. And unless we count the chaplain also, this service would not have met even Webster's definition of a congregation — "an assembly of persons who meet for worship." Nevertheless, this dedicated chaplain was standing behind the pulpit facing a single pilgrim just as if he were facing a fully legal congregation by any definition.

This picture was sad, yet inspiring. This chaplain doubtlessly would have had his spirits buoyed if all 15 seats had been filled. An SRO crowd would probably have made him feel that God was working in mighty and mysterious ways. But notwithstanding his substandard congregation (both by size and by most definitions), the picture of this dedicated chaplain with his smiling face shining as he faced a lone seeker was inspiration to me and will remain so for a long time. It was a picture of someone whose simple faith leads him to this humble task of sharing his message and beliefs to someone, anyone, who would stop and listen. I almost felt that I should go in, take a seat, and try to act as much like a truck driver as possible. 10-4?

I am ashamed to say, however, that Betty and I moved on by resisting the urge to do something simple and perhaps uplifting to someone else. I wonder if St. Peter gives any credit for good intentions. I know we are told that the road to hell is paved with good intentions, but surely my sympathetic thought (along with my storehouse full of this and other good intentions) is better than a warehouse full of evil intentions. We moved on because I wanted to report on a legally assembled congregation so that my unbroken string of 46 Sundays would surely continue unchallenged by Webster's Dictionary, by Orthodox Jews or by *Ripley's Believe It Or Not.*

So, we continued on our pilgrimage for the 47th consecutive week of attending a different religious service. We drove about three miles on further out Peytonsville Road in search of the St. Ignatius Church. About twenty years ago I had helped develop a condominium project, and our advertising campaign for the project tried to make a positive out of a negative. The negative? The property had very little street frontage, and it was very low and almost out of sight from passing traffic. The main ad said that the development was "secretly hidden away at 147 Woodmont Boulevard. Look for it. You'll find it." And so it was for the St. Ignatius

Antiochian Orthodox Church. We found it off the main road, sitting down low and almost hidden away. It was an attractive, modest enclave of buildings clustered low on a neat five-acre plot in a mostly rural setting. It was bordered on one side by a small, neatly cultivated and maintained blueberry farm. I missed it on the first pass but later found it — primarily because I was looking for it, just like in my condo advertising.

After driving around the area to find Peytonsville (the name given to this road on which we were traveling), we headed back toward St. Ignatius aware of the fact that we could just as easily have missed the metropolis of Peytonsville as well had we not been looking for it. I think I'll give the area the rights to my condo ad. It fits really well.

At 9:50 a.m., we pulled into the almost hidden St. Ignatius Church and parked in their almost paved parking lot. Actually, we parked on the grass just off the someday-to-be-paved-but-neatly-graveled parking lot. Watching several men enter the church wearing jackets, I immediately made an executive decision to put on my blazer over my buttoned up T-shirt. At 9:55 a.m., we were seated near the back right corner and ready for the service to begin.

This church was started about 15 years ago by the V. Rev. Fr. Gordon T. Walker, who is now the pastor emeritus. The V. Rev. Fr. Stephen Rogers is the current senior pastor, and Fr. Robert Sanford is the associate pastor. This congregation has a rather unique history in that most of its members have come from other, and many times completely different, Christian traditions. Father Stephen and about seventy-five other members of this congregation came from other traditions with a trail leading many of them through the campus crusades of many years ago. As a group they sought for a tradition that had the theology and historical verities of the original Apostolic Church, and after a long and careful search they chose the Antiochian Orthodox Church.

Father Stephen had been a Southern Baptist early in his life, and he attended a Methodist seminary before becoming a part of the Antiochian Orthodox Church. He was later ordained as a priest in this tradition. One would have to attend both a Southern Baptist Church and St. Ignatius over a relatively short period of time to get the full impact of the force of the decision this group of religious pilgrims made to go from one extreme part of the Christian tradition to the other. The Southern Baptists shun a formal liturgy like the plague. In contrast, one visit to St. Ignatius will convince almost anyone that the Antiochian Orthodox tradition follows the most formal liturgical order of worship found in any church in Christendom.

Some Episcopalians lightly refer to the high church liturgy followed in the most formal Episcopalian churches as being filled with "bells and smells." Crocodile Dundee, in the movie of the same name, responds to being threatened with a small knife by unsheathing his oversized Bowie knife. He says, "That ain't no knife. This is a knife." Likewise, the Antiochian Orthodox Church could well say to most Episcopalians in reference to the formality of their liturgy, "That ain't no bells and smells. This is bells and smells."

The Antiochian Orthodox Church was once part of the early church in what is now known as Syria. Antioch, Jerusalem, Alexandria and Constantinople are the early churches which became known collectively as the Eastern Orthodox Church, or the Greek Orthodox Church. The branch of the church that later developed in Russia also came to be known as a part of the Eastern Orthodox tradition. The separation of the Roman Catholic Church from the Eastern Orthodox bodies began during the First Ecumenical Council in 325 A.D. According to Eastern Orthodox leaders, the final separation came in 1054 A.D. when the Roman Catholic Church separated itself from these Eastern churches. The final rift was basically over different interpretations of the Trinity.

The sanctuary at St. Ignatius was a simple, "A" frame-type stucco structure with a wooden ceiling. Part of the modification to this structure was the protrusion from the top of the building of a gold painted dome which had been accented with a simple cross as is typical of many Eastern Orthodox churches. The pews were individual moveable seats. At the entrance, a large *Bible* on a stand was kissed by most of those entering the space before they proceeded to their seats. There was a single circular stained-glass window at the top of the chancel area. At the beginning of the service the priest walked up the center aisle from the rear while the entire congregation turned facing the back, just as we are accustomed to doing at a wedding as the bride enters. As the priest walked up the aisle with the Bible, the members would bow respectfully just as the priest approached their section of the aisle. There was then a period of bowing and chanting over and over that lasted for a few minutes as Father Stephen recited some of the beginning parts of the liturgy.

After a few moments Father Stephen announced that there would be a service of baptism for two newborn children of members of this congregation. One at a time, the priest took the children to the chancel area and then beyond the icon screen into the most sacred part of the chancel area. He held each child high with its back to the congregation and presented each child as a gift to God.

Father Stephen and Father Robert wore turquoise and gold brocaded robes, while several other participants wore white and gold vestments. There was a small balcony at the rear where a choir was seated. This choir bore a great part of the responsibility for keeping the liturgy flowing smoothly by tying various parts of the service together with beautiful a capella music. Their beautiful voices were aided only by three notes played on a piano as a sort of a pitch pipe at the beginning of each musical part of the service.

During a lengthy prayer by the priest, the choir led the congregation in a beautiful melodious, "Lord, have mercy"at the end of each of the many parts of the prayer. After the prayer, a young man in a black robe read the epistle, *Romans 15: 1 – 7*. During the entire first twenty-seven minutes of the service the congregation remained standing. Then, after the reading of the scripture, we were seated for about one minute before we were back up again as one of the priests read the gospel, *Matthew 9: 27 – 35*. He read this scripture in a chanting fashion.And then we were seated again — Betty and I happily so.

At this point Father Stephen welcomed visitors. He then announced that he had just come back from a church conference in Miami at which the delegates voted to make the Antiochian Orthodox Church autonomous. He stressed that this was not an acrimonious division over some theological matter, but only to enable the American Antiochian Orthodox churches to be more quickly responsive to uniquely American customs and therefore relevant to its members.

Father Stephen then gave a ten-minute sermon based on the scripture lesson from Matthew, where Jesus healed many people including those who were blind and one man who had been possessed by an evil spirit. He said that we live in a world of sickness, disability, disappointment and tragedy, and that we as Christians are not immune to these problems. As he spoke without notes, he asked, "How can sickness, pain and death be in the world created by God? Why, God, do you allow these things to happen?" He said that sometimes we are prone to wonder if there are two Gods.

Pastor Stephen said that we live in Western culture where most Western Christians believe that sin and disease are passed on to all generations, and that one of the great church schisms has come from these differences in belief. He said that the Orthodox Church does not hold to the Western church's belief of sin and disease as being a part of the fall of Adam. This senior pastor said that in the Eastern Orthodox tradition, "Sin is our separation from God. It is not a disease." He said that Adam broke communion with God, and then all creation came crashing down upon us.

Because of our separation from God, he told us, we are all born into a universe which is corrupted. Only in reconnection with God is there to be healing, he declared as he spoke freely — moving about, never standing close to any pulpit or lectern. He continued by saying that in Jesus the human and the divine were united and that through Jesus the human and the divine are reunited in our hearts. He declared that, "Christ has made possible our ultimate union with God." Then he told about an ice storm several years ago when the power went out. After the power was interrupted, his home became colder and colder. He said that it was still his house, but that it was cold and disconnected. When the power was reconnected, however, his home really became his home again, as he knew it and loved it. He was saying that the universe is our home, but it is not really and fully our home until we are reconnected to God through Christ.

At 10:47 a.m. the sermon was over and we were standing again. There was the ringing of the bells and the spreading of incense in the chancel area at the beginning of the Eucharist. After the dedication and blessing, the priests marched up and down the aisles with the bread and the wine as Father Stephen chanted the names of the different families and people for whom this mass was being said. At about the midpoint of the celebration of the Eucharist, the congregation greeted one another to show forgiveness, brotherhood and unity. This was followed by a choral institution of the *Lord's Supper*. At 11:07 a.m., the bread and wine still had not been served to the congregation.

Next, the congregation recited the *Lord's Prayer* and the *Nicene Creed*, which is similar, yet with some minor differences, from the *Apostles' Creed*. During all of this time, there was much chanting and bowing and making the signs of the Cross. Each time the sign of the Cross was made (in broader and bolder strokes than in the Roman Catholic services), the communicants would reverently bow.

Father Stephen then invited all baptized Orthodox Christians to come and partake of the bread and the wine. He invited all visitors to come and partake of only the bread from the loaves which had not been consecrated. This bread was served by separate servers from those who served the church members. The communicants filed out row by row to the altar to be served. The bread was hearty loaves baked by different members of the congregation on different Sundays. Some of the members came back to their seats reverently holding the bread in one cupped hand while covering it with the other hand, as if it were a delicate bird which might fly away. One man walked back to his seat with one hand in his pocket as if he were at a Titans' game and eating his bread as if he were eating a delicious hot dog. He looked hungry, as if he would have liked a second helping.

During this service we sat next to a lovely, considerate woman who was most courteous and helpful to Betty by helping her follow this complicated, detailed liturgical service. When this thoughtful woman came back to her seat, she brought back with her two pieces of bread which she offered to Betty and me. Betty readily accepted, and I politely rejected with a "No, thank you." I wondered if she told the priest she needed two extra pieces of bread for two crippled old people who could not leave their pew. I also wondered if she brought them from table number one or table number two. At any rate, I was impressed by the thoughtfulness of this dear lady and felt badly afterward about not accepting her offer. I realized that I was mentally splitting theological hairs by not accepting her kind and thoughtful gesture. I was ashamed of my nervousness in not accepting what I could have construed as a part of communion of friends, or just as a piece of bread, or a make believe hot dog as did at least one of the communicants. It would not have hurt any-one or anything if I had popped a piece of the bread in my mouth, at least from my revised theological perspective.

The offering was taken, and so we did participate in this part of the Eucharist celebration. I actually dropped the $5 in the plate. At 11:28 a.m., Father Stephen pronounced the benediction which was followed by several announcements, including one about the "coffee hour" which would immediately follow the service. He then shared a story about one of the church children of whom he had asked the question of what good things we all get from this church. The young girl had answered, "Cauliflower." She had been mishearing the pastor's invitation Sunday after Sunday when he invited every-one to the "coffee hour."

At 11:30 a.m., we left this service. I thought about the extreme differences in the worship services I had witnessed this morning. The first service was by the barrel-chested, gently smiling trucker-chaplain who was in his monogrammed white short-sleeved shirt with his chaplain's badge identifying him; it had been held for one lonely trucker at the truck stop. The second, of course, was the high church service we had just left; it had generous portions of "bells and smells" and bowing and chanting by a gaggle of priests and assistants in ornate vestments before a well-dressed congregation of 200 to 300 worshipful souls.

When thinking about these two extremes, I wondered if the diversity of the gene pools embodied in the peoples around the world is perhaps the human race's greatest strength and safety against the possibility of some dreaded disease destroying all human life on this planet. And just maybe the diversity exemplified by the extremes of the two services I witnessed this morning was a real sign of strength in the Christian religion. Perhaps the checks and balances inherent in the diversity of theological interpretations and liturgical differences can help keep all worshipers aware that it is foolhardy and arrogant to be so perfectly certain that the chaplain is right, or that the priests are wrong, or vice versa.

The question remains whether one liturgical form or the lack of one is the best way for all human beings to worship. We could all be hearing "cauliflower" when what is really being said is "coffee hour." God, I hope so. I never have really liked cauliflower.

Chapter 48

Trinity Church
New York City, New York
August 10, 2003

T wo years ago, immediately after the 9-11 World Trade Center tragedy, when asked what Americans could do to help New Yorkers Mayor Rudy Giuliani responded candidly, "Come to New York and spend money." Our family (my wife Betty and I, our two daughters Barbara and Beverly) had made annual trips to New York for theater shows, shopping, and dining in New York's newest and finest restaurants as revealed by our research. Continuing this tradition, we had scheduled our trip for early October, 2001 in order to beat the horrific Christmas shopping crowd. Then came the horror of 9-11, and tourist traffic to New York almost came to a standstill. We, along with millions of other would be visitors to the Big Apple, felt nervous and apprehensive about the risks involved in going to New York City. But then Giuliani made his aforementioned plaintive appeal to all Americans to come and spend money in NYC. We took his directives to heart; Betty decided that we would not change our plans. She rallied the Browning spending cavalry, commandeered four airline seats, and we invaded New York City on a mission.

Our mission was to spend money. We deployed our crack spending troops and, in a matter of only a few days, we had the economy of New York City on the mend. We were fearful, however, of a recurrence of the recession immediately following the removal of our super-spending brigade after our tour of duty. We expected to see the headlines of the *New York Times* fearfully asking, "WILL ECONOMY SURVIVE BROWNING WITHDRAWAL?" This headline never actually was printed, probably at the request of a mayor nervous of the fear factor which might sink the city into an even deeper depression if word of our retreat back to Nashville was leaked to the media.

We have been called upon periodically since 9-11-2001 to return with a new infusion of discretionary spending to keep this great city's economy rebounding. Duty had called us to return two weeks ago, but our daughter Beverly's emergency surgery had delayed our money mission by one week. We rescheduled for one week later, again without announcing the change in our plans for fear of any negative effects the ill health of one of our spending leaders could have on NYC's economy which was still slowly recovering. Thank God it wasn't Barbara who became ill. Barbara is widely known as one of the great free spenders of all time. New Yorkers dearly love her and her kind. Even word of a slight rash on her credit card signing hand could be a crushing blow to this city's rebounding tourist industry's hopes.

We wanted to keep the news of our arrival in New York as quiet as possible. Too much fanfare about our arrival could possibly send the wrong message that New York is still not strong enough to survive without the periodic infusions from the Brownings' disposable spending coffers. We flew in practically unnoticed and alighted from our economy seats disguised as ordinary tourists. Little did our fellow travelers know that we were on an important mission of mercy. We had purposefully not asked for any special fanfare or dignitaries greeting us at the airport, and it worked out just as we planned. We actually carried our own luggage and arranged for our own transportation from the airport to our hotel.

When we checked into our hotel, the room clerk had obviously been let in on the secret nature of our trip because she acted as if she did not know who we were. She even told us that our rooms were not ready yet. Was this a ploy to further downplay the secret importance of our visit by acting as if we were just like the others waiting in line? I could not be sure if it was to shield the sensitive nature of our visit, or if the management had been instructed to get us to the spending front lines as soon as possible. At any rate, when she told us our rooms would not be ready until after lunch we were immediately cast into the middle of our spending mission.

The four of us crowded into a cab like common tourists and headed immediately to the Gotham Bar and Grill, one of our regular places in New York to eat great food and spend great amounts of money at the same time. And we did a lot of both over the next few hours. I feel that I should say a word of warning to my readers. PLEASE DO NOT TRY THIS AT HOME.

Remember, we are professionals here. Spending money in New York is in our field of expertise. We have honed our skills at spending lavishly over many years. And then, of course, we had Barbara with us; she is genetically the best qualified spender I have ever known. She has had a black belt in spending since we took her to Europe in 1964 when she was only seven-years-old.

Not only are we seasoned professionals in the field of spending in New York, but we could probably make the first team in most cities of the world except New Delhi. (We have not yet visited there. No wonder they are struggling there). So, our advice for amateurs to not attempt these spending sprees at home is not just because we are professionals in doing this almost everywhere, but because if ordinary people exhibit these spending traits at home, they are likely to be declared incompetent and put in restraining devices. Know what I mean?

For the next few days we did what we had been asked to do. We spent money. Lots of money — going to Broadway shows, eating at some of the city's finest restaurants, and, of course, shopping. We rode to all of them from multiple points of origin by taxi. The cab industry would probably be the first part of the economy of New York to feel ill effects after our departure.

On one of my cab rides back to the area of "Ground Zero," where the terrorists of 9-11 struck, I saw the sister churches of Trinity and St. Luke's. We had seen these churches soon after 9-11-2001 on our original 2002 errand of mercy to New York. At that time, they had still been digging out of the smothering cover of dust that shrouded this part of the city. The two old historic brownstone Episcopal churches date from the early days of our nation's history. I decided during a visit to Trinity on Friday that this would be the church I would visit for my 48th week on my 52-Sundays pilgrimage.

Betty and I left our hotel room at 7:30 a.m. and passed up the temptation of the beautiful and delicious looking breakfast bar at our hotel, determined to do some New York taxi blue roading right in the middle of Manhattan. We walked to the front of our hotel and saw this sleepless city taking sort of a catnap at this hour. The sidewalks were by no means sleeping, but they were "resting their eyes" for this brief period. Instead of having to stand out like a hitchhiker trying to flag down a cab for a ride, there were eight or ten of them lined up ready to take us where we pleased. Well, almost. The first two cabbies obviously had not gotten the word that I am a big tipper here on a mission. They said they were only interested in fares to the airport.

We (the financial salvation of this great city) felt a little dejected after having been rejected by two of its newly immigrated citizens. But before we could sink too low, another immigrant cabbie, a strapping six-foot-two-inch man, walked up to us with a big smile and said, "Where do you want to go?" And by his tone I knew he meant to say, "Get in. I'll take you wherever you want to go." It seemed almost as if the mayor had secretly dispatched this driver to be sure that we were well cared for, perhaps in hopes that we might extend our stay.

Before getting in his cab I said, "First I want to ask you if you have had your breakfast." With a friendly, though quizzical, look on his face, he told me he had eaten earlier. He hurriedly assured me, however, that he would still take me anywhere I wished. As he started driving he said, "I must say, this is a little unusual." This was when I felt constrained to let him in on my secondary mission while I was in New York. I told him how we start out each Sunday morning in search for a good blue road restaurant where we could have a good Country breakfast before going on to church somewhere. I told him that I wanted him to take us to breakfast and to stay with us and then take us on to church. And I told him the whole story behind the *Fifty-Two Sundays* idea.

Immediately after having met our taxi driver, I felt he not only got the idea but that he embraced it himself. He told us he knew exactly what we were looking for — a neighborhood restaurant which catered primarily to New Yorkers. A neighborhood restaurant in New York would be as close to a country restaurant as we would be able to find in *THIS* city. He told us that his name was Tupea Miltia, but said we should call him Mike.

A native of Romania, Mike had immigrated here almost seven years ago. He said that he had been 48-years-old and newly divorced when he first arrived. He confided that his divorce had been very difficult for him and that he came to this country to just get away from the bad memories. This tall handsome man had obviously been hurt deeply by this sad event in his life. He also said that he had not been back to Romania since coming here, but that he was thinking that he might return soon.

Mike told us about the jobs he had worked since coming here. He was now about 55-years-old and spoke English beautifully. But at first he could not speak English at all, and he had to take a job in an auto repair shop changing oil for only $3 per hour. It was then that he came to realize that he had to learn to speak English. He went to night school to study our language as his second language. And (here comes the reason he now speaks English so fluently), he married his teacher.

This new citizen of our country was apparently an extremely happy man. When I asked him if he liked being here he said, "Are you kidding me? I have a new land, a new job, a new wife and a new life." We talked incessantly from the time we met about his life in Romania and his happy new life here in New York.

After driving around for about 15 minutes Mike pulled up across the street from the Chelsea Galleria Restaurant at 72 Seventh Avenue. When we walked into the restaurant, it was clear that Mike had understood what we were looking for. Here was, if not a mom-and-pop operation, a neighborhood or family (they do have families in New York, don't they?) restaurant right in the Chelsea area of New York City.

Betty ordered Eggs Benedict and, after a little coaxing, Mike ordered two scrambled eggs and bacon. I ordered three eggs over-easy/over-medium with bacon, hash-brown potatoes and a toasted English muffin. There are no buttermilk biscuits even in a family restaurant in New York, but Mike said that his wife bakes the frozen kind for him which is almost the standard these days even in Nashville. I asked the waiter, "I suppose you don't even know what grits are?" He assured me that he did not. After I described grits to him, Mike seemed interested in the idea of having his wife prepare some grits for him at home. Maybe Mike hails from the southern part of Romania.

After finishing our very tasty, almost country, blue road breakfast, (even the delicious waffle which had been ordered for the table and shared by Mike and me), we re-boarded the taxi (we had kept the meter running during breakfast) and headed for Trinity

Church. It was now about 9:00 a.m., and the service at Trinity was scheduled to begin at 10:00 a.m.

With almost an hour to spare before church, I decided to enhance my tax deduction qualifications for part of this trip by having Mike drive around some of the side streets as we meandered southward on Manhattan toward Trinity Church, which is located in the Wall Street area. I wanted to take some pictures of New York brownstones to help me tweak some design features with the architect we had employed to design some brownstone-type houses we were building in Nashville. Also for tax purposes, I suppose I should go ahead and tell my readers that these cluster houses are on West End Avenue at Craighead in Nashville. They are called West End Close. Now, that should be enough help to save a few lousy bucks from my tax bill.

I took several pictures for further documentation for my tax write-off and to show to our architect. We were particularly interested in new ideas for entrances, balconies and flower boxes. We spent about 30 minutes on this project, and then it was time to move on toward Trinity Church. This historic Episcopal Church is the sister church to an Anglican church in London which aided in the establishment of this New York parish in 1697. The present building, a handsome church featuring Gothic Revival architecture, was erected in 1846 and is on the national register of historic structures.

This beautiful edifice near Wall Street on lower Manhattan is like an oasis in the asphalt-concrete jungle of world commerce. It is surrounded and shadowed by many extremely tall buildings, of which the twin towers of the World Trade Center were the tallest before being destroyed on 9-11-01. For several weeks afterwards this beautiful green, restful sanctuary-oasis had been covered with several inches of thick dust from the fallen behemoths of international trade. For weeks it had been impossible to have worship services there. The heavy rancid dust had ruined the prized old pipe organ, which would not be fully replaced until late 2003.

The Reverend Daniel Paul Matthews is the present rector and the vicar is the Reverend Samuel Johnson Howard, who was listed as the celebrant of the mass for this 9:00 a.m. service today. The Reverend Gayanne Silver, we read, was to be the preacher/deacon for this same service. This handsome, awe-inspiring edifice must put awful pressure on the priests/pastors to perform well in their appointed capacities. Hundreds of years and hundreds of tons of beautiful carved stone look down upon those who would serve here. The large cut stone pieces were carefully sculpted to create beautiful massive columns, which reach to the top of the approximately 75-foot ceiling and form the basis for an intricate worshipful canopy over the entire sanctuary.

The pews which the priests and pastors face are the same seats on which many famous leaders of our land have worshiped for more than seven scores of years. The graves in the peaceful park-like cemetery, just outside the beautiful windows, include the remains of the likes of Alexander Hamilton and many captains of industry and finance who helped make our country what it is today.

At 9:55 a.m., there were only 15 people in the pews awaiting something special to happen in this very special place. At 10:00 a.m., there were 30. All the worshipers here today were casually dressed. I had on the only coat in the sanctuary, but I still did not feel overdressed because of the awesomeness of this sanctuary. After a brief and rather truncated processional by the priests and several worship assistants, the congregation stood to sing *Hymn No. 410, Praise My Soul, The King of Heaven*. The worship group who made up the procession was a politically correct assembly of worship leaders; there were three white men, one white woman, one African-American woman, and one African-American man.

After the reading of the Epistle from the *Ephesians (Ephesians 4: 25 – 5: 2)* and another hymn, the woman preacher/deacon Rev. Gayanne Silver walked one-third of the way down the center aisle, stopped there with an assistant, and read the *Holy Gospel (John 6: 37 – 51)*. After the reading of this scripture, she raised the large, ornate copy of the scriptures high over her head, in a presentation fashion, and said: "The Gospel of the Lord," to which the congregation responded, "Praise to You, Lord Christ."

Immediately following the reading of the scripture, the Rev. Gayanne Silver proceeded directly to the pulpit to give this morning's sermon. It was the second sermon by a woman that I had ever heard. The first had been by the young female at Congregation Micah, a Jewish Synagogue in Brentwood, Tennessee several months ago.

This preacher started her sermon by telling how, when she was very young, she would dress up very carefully and put all sorts of make-up on. She said she remembered very clearly how very much she wanted to look like her mother. Then she segued to the scripture lesson from *Ephesians*, where Paul instructs all of us to "be imitators of God, as beloved children."

This preacher/deacon talked about the impossibility of actually imitating God, but went on to say that we can, however, imitate God "as loving children." She then told how in the sixth chapter of *John*, Jesus said He was the Bread of Life. Then there was the story of how Jesus fed the 5,000 with the loaves and fishes of a young boy. This preacher followed that story with another about a group of children drawing a picture of Jesus feeding the 5,000. One young child simply had drawn a big box. When she was asked what the box was for, the youngster answered, "For the leftovers." This pastor then said that the lesson for all of us was that by sharing what we have, all will be fed and cared for, and plenty more left over.

She then said that Jesus used the metaphor of the bread and said, "I am the bread of life." She said that during the sacrament, at the point of the consecration, the bread becomes the body of Christ and the wine becomes the blood of Christ. She stuck to her script and read most of her sermon. She was right to be very careful as to what and how she spoke on this subject, because this has been the point of much discussion and heated debate and dissention in both private and public church councils for hundreds of years. This is one of the great dividing issues in all of Christendom. She concluded her 10-minute sermon by saying that in communion the body of Christ becomes the body of the real community of believers.

The sermon was followed by the recitation of the *Nicene Creed* after which an African-American woman from the congregation prayed *The Prayers of the People* while standing in the center circle with a microphone in her hand. The first part of the printed prayer concluded with: "We pray for the Episcopal Church in the United States and for Frank, our presiding bishop, and for Mark, Catherine, Don and Herbert — the bishops of New York." I noted particularly how this prayer so informally spoke of the church leaders by their first names only. This prayer continued for "George our president, George our governor and for Michael, the mayor of New York." No respect of persons here either. She prayed for those who had been attacked by terrorists in Indonesia, for our armed forces in Iraq and for the visitors in this parish today. Suppose the mayor had tipped them off that we were possibly coming to visit here this morning? Mike, our friendly cabbie, must have called Michael Bloomberg, the current mayor, just after he left us at the church door.

This prayer also included the words: "Grant a good use of leisure to members of this parish, that they may return refreshed to do the work you have given them to do." I felt this was perhaps as much an announcement about why so few people were here today, as it was a prayer for those who were summering in the Hamptons or the Poconos.

After prayers by both the layperson and the celebrant, the Rev. Gayanne Silver came back to the front to make several announcements and to invite the congregation to greet one another, which was difficult to do since we were so scattered throughout this large sanctuary. We just did a friendly wave at everyone and sat down.

The next part of the service was the Holy Communion. The printed order of worship stated: "In the Episcopal Church all baptized persons are invited to receive Holy Communion. Members of other Christian churches who receive Holy Communion in their own churches are invited to share in receiving the body and blood of Christ." At last Sunday's service at the Antiochian's Orthodox Church, only Orthodox members had been invited to partake of the consecrated bread and wine.

The offering was listed as part of the Holy Communion service. We participated in this with our $5 offering, but please don't tell anyone it was only $5. We don't want the people of New York to feel sorry for all our sacrificial spending on their behalf. Heck, we probably could have put in another $5 easily, but it's the principle, not the money, remember?

The Rev. Gayanne Silver sort of "set the table" for the communion service. Then the "Celebrant," the Rev. Samuel Johnson Howard, acted as the official "headwaiter" as had our headwaiter who had ceremoniously "raised the cover" from our restaurant entrée selections the night before. The celebrant said the official prayers, read the scriptures, and made the official invitation for communicants to come and dine at the Lord's Table. Many of those who participated in this communion service drank from the common cup, while others allowed the priest to dip their bread in the wine and then place it in their mouths.

Approximately 30 of the 50 people present in the sanctuary at the beginning of the communion service went to the altar all at one time to partake of the bread and the wine. It was near the conclusion of this simple service at which there were few "bells and smells," as in some very high church Episcopal services. The simplicity here had even reached the oval office at the White House and leader of the free world when, during prayers, they simply called our president "George." Just one George among other Georges. I liked that. And now I feel constrained to invite all my readers to just call me Grant.

At 10:55 a.m., this service was over, and we were soon out on the street and supporting the tourist industry again. We all too easily hailed a cab to take us back to our hotel to finish our final packing and leave for the airport to begin our trip back home.

We are already saving our money for the next time our services and our discretionary dollars are needed to jumpstart NYC's economy again. We're looking for new recruits to assist us on future efforts to help New York rejuvenate their economy. We found one new prospect while having dinner at Daniel's the last night of this season's NYC rescue mission. A godfather-looking diner at the table next to ours was drinking his Dom Perignon over ice. Now, this kind of spender we can really use in our rescue efforts; don't you agree? Please contact us if you know any others who are equally qualified, either to be lavish wealthy free spenders or to just act that way while in New York City.

Chapter 49

St. Andrews Church (Episcopal)
And
The Family of God at Woodmont Hills
Nashville, Tennessee
August 17, 2003

*T*oday was a doubleheader, and there was no rain. We had decided to go to two, possibly three, churches this morning, and so we left our house at 147 Woodmont Boulevard at 7:15 a.m. We were going to attend the 7:30 a.m. service at a church called (until very recently) St. Andrews Episcopal Church before going on to breakfast at about 9:00 a.m., and then on to at least one more additional service before noon. The St. Andrews Church is located at 3700 Woodmont Boulevard on a site almost as secretly hidden away as our present home at the Westchase Condominiums. This church is located only five or six blocks from our own Woodmont address.

The reason for my quandary as to what to fully name St. Andrews is why we had decided to make this service the first part of our double, or possibly triple, header for today. The General Convention of the Episcopal Church had been held very recently (July 30 – August 8, 2003) in Minneapolis. This convention had ended only nine days ago, and at least two very divisive issues had come before the delegates there. The first involved the passing of a resolution acknowledging that some Episcopal churches were blessing same-sex unions. The second involved the passing of a resolution approving the election of an Episcopal bishop who openly lives in a homosexual relationship.

Now these two issues would likely be difficult ones for any religious gathering. But the Episcopalians had approved both of the resolutions, and as a result this religious body had been shaken to its foundations — which brings us to my interest in St. Andrews. St.

Andrews had received considerable media attention as one of a number of individual Episcopal churches not taking either of the Convention's resolutions lying down. Soon after the convention took its stand on these issues, St. Andrews took immediate action. They quickly blacked out "Episcopal" from both of their signs, and now the signs which two weeks ago read "St. Andrews Episcopal Church" show up as "St. Andrews Church." In addition to the black-out of "Episcopal" on each sign, they had put out black ribbons as if someone or something had died. I guess I just wanted to attend the funeral or at least the wake.

I also felt that this might very well be the beginning of a new Christian denomination, and I wanted to be an eye witness to part of its beginning. I had already visited my full quota of Episcopal churches, including the Trinity Episcopal Church located near Wall Street in New York City just last Sunday. In order to keep from over-visiting one denomination, I hereby declare that I am taking St. Andrews at their blackened-out word. For the time being at least, I declare that I visited a religious body today that is different from Episcopalian. At least in their minds, and also by their public actions, they are separated from the main body of the Episcopal Church. They say that they have not left the Episcopal Church rather that it has left them. That's what they all say. The Democrats and Republicans, too.

Father Ray Kasch, the rector of All Saints Episcopal Church in Smyrna, Tennessee, believes that leaving the Mother Church — even over substantial issues — is not the answer. In a pastoral letter he wrote:

"Schism is rarely if ever the solution. Look at church history and see what a temporary fix it is. The Methodists left us because we were too liberal and the Nazarenes left the Methodists because they were too liberal and the Nazarenes created new branches because the old one became too liberal. It never ends."

He is one of many church leaders who fear that the most conservative Episcopal churches will pull out and form a whole new denomination. So maybe I did not attend a wake today at all; maybe it was the birth and baptism of a new infant church.

At any rate, Betty and I entered chapel at St. Andrews at 7:25 a.m. and took a seat near the back. This chapel was attractive, modest and residential in scale. Only two women were in the sanctuary at that time, and they were seated in a small pew section to the right of the chancel area. They invited us to join with them, but we declined — I always like my view from the back.

The Rev. James M. Gull is the rector here, but he was attending another church meeting at Monteagle. I'm sure he will be at many such meetings during the next few months. The celebrant for this morning's service was Cantor Dedmon who fills in for the rector frequently at this church. As the service began, on the right side, there were three women and one tall, handsome and bespectacled African-American man wearing a white robe over a longer black robe and assisting Cantor Dedmon during this service. The cantor was alone on the other side and faced the communicants directly across from him. They read responsively back and forth from the *Book of Common Prayers*. Sandra Cohran was listed as the organist and choirmaster of this church, but she was not here. There was no music at all during this service — just as in Orthodox Jewish services.

At this point, while this service would not qualify as a religious service according to Orthodox Jewish law, it certainly would qualify as a service according to the Truckstop Ministries — such as the one I witnessed last week where one chaplain led one lonely trucker to worship. This priest, dressed in a white robe with a green sash, began a discussion of the convention ten days ago when the ordination of the gay bishop had been acknowledged.

Next, the celebrant read the scripture: "Where two or three are gathered in my name, I will be in their midst." I suppose they use this verse a lot at the early services here which is apparently not well attended. By 8:00 a.m., there were only eight people plus the two worship directors and the Brownings. The 10:00 a.m. service was much better attended, we were told later by a member when we were leaving. He said it was "real high church with bells and incense spread around everywhere." He was inviting us to come to what he was saying would be a far more impressive service.

At this point the cantor said he was going to read, "A pastoral letter to the Clergy and People of the Episcopal Diocese of Tennessee" from "The Right Reverend Bertram Nelson Herlong

D.D. Tenth bishop of Tennessee." His words discussed the two resolutions of the convention. He said that the resolutions at the convention were not doctrine, and were not mandatory for people who
believe contrary to the passed resolutions. He said that while many
would leave the church, "I beseech you not to do so...We...must not
let the actions of one convention deter us from what we believe
God is calling us to do...I ask for your prayers for our diocese and
people. May God have mercy on us all."

After several minutes the people moved to the pews in front of
us for the Holy Communion part of the service. The order of worship
reads: "Visitors and guests who have been baptized and have been
admitted to communion in their own churches, who recognize the
real presence of Christ in the Eucharist, whose conscience permits,
and who are duly prepared to make their commitment are invited
to receive Holy Communion in this service." The two caveats were
(1) a belief in the real presence of Christ in the elements and (2) a
clear conscience; the second of these two should pretty well omit
most visitors who can pass the litmus test of number one.

Now there were nine communicants, plus two visiting pilgrims.
As the service proceeded, the cantor read the *Gospel*, "He who eats
my flesh and drinks my blood abides with me and I with him." The
cantor continued with the service, all of which is a part of the Holy
Communion, including the *Nicene Creed*, the *Prayers of the People*, the
assurance of pardon, and the fellowship period during which time the
communicants greet one another as brothers and sisters in Christ.

At this point in the service the cantor, with great care, put on a
ceremonial robe over the one he had worn to this point to signal the
real beginning of the Eucharist. Then the offering was taken and the
Brownings worshiped with our $5 offering. That's $2.50 each, right?

Now the consecration of the bread and wine began with the
ringing of bells as the priest said, "Holy, Holy, Holy, Lord God of
Hosts. The whole world is full of Thy glory." The priest, facing the
altar with his back to the congregation, held the bread high over his
head and ceremoniously broke it as he read the words of Jesus:"This
is my body which is broken for you." After the consecration of the
wine, all nine of the communicants went to the altar. But Betty and
I did not commune. I was stuck on the conscience qualification
thing. Most of those who communed did so by drinking from the

common cup. The priest partook of the elements last and then reverently covered the remaining wine and bread, placing them on the table away from the altar.

After the benediction Betty and I got in our car and witnessed a WSMU-TV truck setting up for the 10:00 a.m. service. I suppose they too felt that they might be witnessing and recording a part of history — the making of a new denomination over some very sensitive issues facing the Episcopalians. Many other churches are facing these same issues which seem far more important to local churches than strictly theological issues such as the nature of Christ and the Trinity, both of which had divided the church as the result of decisions of great church councils of the past.

Betty and I had a family council in the car at 8:40 a.m. as we left St. Andrews. We debated the great issue of where we would have breakfast. Would it be at the Waffle House or the Cracker Barrel? Both were located in the I-65/Harding Place area near our choice for church for the second half of our twin bill of worship services this morning. There's no way to lose at either of these breakfast places. I threw my vote in with Betty's in order not to have a family schism, and we went forthwith, with great anticipation, to the Waffle House.

At 8:52 a.m. we walked into the Waffle House and ordered immediately. We wanted to attend the 9:45 a.m. service at the Family of God Church at Woodmont Hills. But first Betty and I were going to break bread and eat eggs at one of our perennially favorite breakfast spots. This is a place where atmosphere is totally sacrificed, but the quality of the food is sacrosanct. Betty ordered scrambled eggs, bacon, grits, raisin toast and coffee. My order is the same yesterday, today and forever. My order never changes if the restaurant offers my choices. Here they do, except the Waffle House never offers biscuits. But their toast is always outstanding, as is every single item they offer. I ordered three eggs over-easy/over-medium, bacon, hash browns, grits, toast, coffee and a waffle for the table — total for both orders $15.47 plus tip.

The Waffle House gets far more of my breakfast business than any other single place — even more than the Pancake Pantry. I would take all my business to the Pantry except that it only has one location and its waiting line is too long. The syrup at the Pantry and its unequaled hash-brown potatoes are the only two edges the Pantry has over the Waffle House. But these same items at the Waffle House run the Pantry a close second.

We ate quickly here, mostly with weekend casual yuppies. You know, the pretty or would-be pretty people all dressed in their clean shorts, T-shirts, tennis shoes or flip-flops, and their ball caps or sun visors. Several were reading their papers, looking over their sophisticated-looking half-glasses. Our worldly-wise waitress, calling everyone "darlin,' "was generally taking command of the whole restaurant and barking out her orders loud enough for everyone in the restaurant to hear. God, I love eating here. There is real atmosphere in the total lack of atmosphere here. Its squeaky cleanliness and openness isn't country and certainly isn't blue road ('cause they're almost always at interstate exits), but it suited me perfectly on this doubleheader Sunday. And we finished quickly enough to *Get Me to the Church on Time*, as the song in the musical *My Fair Lady* goes.

At 9:40 a.m., we walked into the Woodmont Hills Church. We were greeted by a friendly man whom I only know as Cliff. Cliff had serviced our Rollins Security System for twenty-five years and had just been laid-off after twenty-seven years of working for them. He was a great help to me by identifying some of the participants in this service who were not named in the church literature we were given.

I wondered if this church was on the verge of separating itself from the Church of Christ. It was certainly in the parenthetical group. The "Order of Worship" literature identified this church only as "The Family of God at Woodmont Hills." And only parenthetically is the Church of Christ referred to on the sign at the front of the property.

This church holds worship services every Sunday at 8:15 a.m., 9:45 a.m. and 11:15 a.m. This sanctuary appeared to seat 1,200 to 1,500 people in its new auditorium type of building with the exposed metal structure ceilings. They had blue metal chairs lined up and attached in an auditorium-type pew arrangement. Almost everyone was dressed in casual clothes as had been the case in all the community-type churches we had attended. And if this is not a real community church, it seemed to be headed in that direction.

As the service began, a worship team of six vocal musicians (led by a man dressed in slacks, a blue open-collared shirt and no tie) led us in singing "At The Name of Jesus Every Knee Shall Bow Down" which was sung over and over, with much clapping of hands and some waving of arms. The clue that this church may have some connection with the Church of Christ was the absence of instrumental music, but what a difference between the music here and the music at the Silver Point Church of Christ. The music at Silver Point really needed help, but here today I soon forgot that no musical instruments were helping with the singing.

The songs kept coming over and over — just like the community churches spreading rapidly around Nashville. The lyrics were repeated over and over as the congregation followed along by reading from the large screens placed on either side of the platform area. Among Churches of Christ, the scriptural basis for not using musical instruments in worship is that neither Christ nor the apostles specifically instructed their followers to worship with instrumental music. I am certain that more than one of the members here had asked the leaders to help them find the large video screens mentioned by the apostles in the New Testament.

Some members of the praise and worship team helped to set the tone for the congregation by waving their arms in worshipful exuberance as they sang. And more and more people got the spirit from the leaders, and soon the congregation began to follow this spirit as the service progressed.

At about 10:00 a.m., a woman read a passage of scripture about the blood of Christ, and this was the beginning of the sacrament of the Lord's Supper. As the elements were served, only the prayer team sang the communion songs, *Fairest Lord Jesus* and *My Jesus I love Thee*. Now at about 10:10 a.m., the communion part of this service was over — quite a contrast with the highly ritualistic serving of the Lord's Supper in the St. Andrews Episcopal Church we had experienced earlier this morning.

Soon, without notice or announcement, two youngish looking men appeared on the platform. They were dressed like the worship team leader — slacks and open-necked, long-sleeved dress shirts. They pulled stool-like chairs and metal lecterns toward the center of the stage and began their "sermon." It was a team act. One of the team was identified later (by my friend Cliff) as Rubel Shelley who is the senior pastor. He appeared to be about thirty-five years old.

The second man was John York who is a more recent addition as pastor, and he appeared to be a few years younger than Rubel. I learned later that John teaches some classes at David Lipscomb, a church-related university in Nashville.

Rubel read the scripture lesson from *I Corinthians 3: 16 – 17* which reads: "Do you not know you are God's temple?" John then said, as he sat on his stool with his left hand in his pocket, "The Woodmont Hills is the Temple of God, but most of us don't think of it that way."

They bantered back and forth, commenting on a quote projected on the large screens. The quotation said that most people think of the church as a formal, ritualistic, stodgy, and boring time together. One of the pastor team said that the church really is, or should be, a nurturing place. He said you don't just come up out of the water in baptism with all your questions suddenly and miraculously answered. He told us that after baptism the Holy Spirit closes the gap between the life of God and ours. He stressed that the Spirit of God comes and lives in us, and this is the beginning of the fruits of the Spirit: "The beginning of our life being made divine."

One of the preachers said that we become less and less controlled by things about us through God's Spirit, and that we become more and more controlled by the Spirit of God. The other one told us, "The scripture is the record of God's activity in history prior to us, and so we must start with the scriptures and allow them to be a guide to our lives." He said that there are some thorny issues in our day and time. Here he indicated that the role of women in the church is one of those thorny issues. These pastors were apparently leading this congregation to see that things and times change. Noting some specific things in the scripture told to individuals, the pastors told us that we must see that the scripture is not to be interpreted as being an exact description of how we should act from that time forward.

Pastor Rubel said that at one time all women wore hats to church. Now almost no one does. He said also that at one time a man with hair as long as Co-Pastor John's would have had to get a haircut before he could take a leading part in a church. Laughing, both agreed that things had changed in that regard as evidenced by John's being on the sermon team even with his long hair.

Pastor Rubel continued by saying that while the scripture says, "Greet one another with a holy kiss," today the custom was to greet one another with a handshake. He said we let common sense tell us what customs were for specific times and places. One of them asked, "But what about homosexuality?" Pastor Rubel said that the *Bible* says that homosexuality is wrong, but then he asked, "Could this be like the greeting one another with a holy kiss? A custom of another time and place. Could God's opposition to homosexuality have been only for a time and situation in the past?" He answered this question in the negative because human sexuality was part of the original divine plan — not one which was designed for only a few years time span.

The pastors together agreed that homosexuality was wrong, not just because of a command from God, but because heterosexuality was part of God's eternal plan. Dressed in a yellow open-neck shirt, Pastor Rubel said, "I am not homophobic." He insisted that regardless of how vehemently we oppose homosexuality we must express our beliefs lovingly and respectfully, and not as if we have a chip on our shoulder. Pastor Rubel said that Jesus ate with sinners and that he was criticized because of this. They were saying that sinners of all categories were welcome here where they could be ministered to along with all the rest.

These pastors said that some say women should not serve communion. They agreed that when Paul talked about women's roles in the church, it had been for a specific time and place in a specific social setting. Things had changed. "Paul didn't even have communion trays back then, so how could he say that women should not serve communion trays?" one of them asked.

Pastor Rubel said, "John and I don't always agree on how things are to be done, and we don't just hide our disagreements and act as if there are really no differences." Then he asked, "So which one of us are you to follow if we should disagree? Are the members to follow only one and split the church?" He declared that this would not happen because, "we are following the Spirit of Christ."

Maybe so. But just suppose what would happen if John began insisting on performing gay marriages? Or what if Pastor Rubel wanted to hire a new assistant pastor who was openly gay and living in a homosexual relationship? And what if these things actually took place? Could they then continue the spirit of love and tolerance for one another? Probably not. And this is sort of where St. Andrews

Episcopalian, a.k.a. just "St.Andrews," is today.

Betty and I did not split over whether we should give another $5 to this church since we had already given at the other church today. But a couple of things could have caused a schism in our marriage (possibly a divorce) if I had insisted that Betty follow my lead. No. 1 on that list — if I had decided to give half of our assets to these churches today, I probably would be sleeping in the guest bedroom tonight.

No.2 on that list of ways to develop a real rift in our marriage — if I had pursued my thought of possibly visiting a third church today. Betty had been a bit drowsy during the Rubel and John show this morning. When this show was over Betty drew the curtain on any more church services today. I graciously acceded to her wishes, however, and our marriage survived this morning's doubleheader.

Truthfully, I was a little sleepy myself. But don't tell Betty. You see, I get more personal points with her if I let her think that my curtailing the plans to visit a third church this morning was a real sacrifice on my part. I need all the points I can get. She's way ahead of me. I want us to live happily ever after.

Chapter 50

Primitive Baptist Church
Franklin, Tennessee
August 24, 2003

T he selection of churches to attend was more and more difficult the closer I came to the end of my fifty-two weeks of visiting different churches. There were several different churches I still hoped to attend before the year's worth of church-visiting came to an end, but I had decided to ration myself. No more, and no less, than fifty-two Sundays of weekly religious services. I would not stretch it to fifty-three nor stop at fifty-one — just fifty-two weeks of attending a different religious service each week.

At this point it was apparent that my hope to attend some particular churches or religious services was just not going to work out. I definitely had wanted to visit one of the "snake handlers" services. Of course, "snake handlers" is not the official name (nor is "holy rollers") of charismatic churches whose religious services often include snake handling or speaking in tongues.

Many of the "holy rollers" and "snake handlers" churches get their authority for speaking in tongues and handling snakes from *Luke 16: 16 – 18*. In this part of the *New Testament* Jesus tells his disciples:

> *He that believeth in me and is baptized shall be saved, but he that believeth not shall be damned. And these signs shall follow them that believe; in my name they shall cast out devils; they shall speak with new tongues; they shall take up serpents; and if they drink any deadly thing, it shall not hurt them, they shall lay hands on the sick, and they shall recover.*

Obviously, these words give the authority these groups rely on when their worship includes snake handling, speaking in tongues, drinking poison and faith healing. But the obvious dangers, at least to nonbelievers, have caused many states to pass laws prohibiting such practices. Such laws come close to breaching the constitutional barrier regarding the separation of church and state. The state says that its responsibility to protect lives is threatened by religious practices which potentially threaten the lives and health of its citizens. Of course, the churches say that the state is denying them the right to practice their religion in the manner set forth by God. State laws prohibiting snake handling primarily outlaw the use of dangerous animals in public places.

All of this has caused churches which still practice snake handling to do so clandestinely. They have more or less gone underground and do not readily allow visitors easy access to their services. I have not been able to gain access to one of these services because of this situation.

I also had wanted to attend an Amish service somewhere near, and I had contacted several people (including one person who was friendly with some of the Amish bishops in Middle Tennessee) to explore my options. The Amish live simple, private and separate lives; they do not relish exposure of their lives to the "outside world." One bishop told my friend that while he could "not keep you from visiting because they never tell people they cannot come to church, but that he and the church would rather you didn't write anything in a book about them because it already has been done and no one ever does it correctly." Because of this unfortunate set of circumstances, I would probably not be able to visit an Amish service during my self-limited fifty-two week period.

Today, I had to decide whether to go to the Remnant Fellowship in Cool Springs or to a Primitive Baptist church in Franklin. I thought I would decide after a full breakfast, and so we drove toward the Cool Springs/Franklin area. "8:29 a.m.," Betty proudly pointed out to me while tapping gently on the dashboard clock of her car. Clearly, we were leaving before 8:30 a.m. It was a beautiful and clear day. The external thermometer in Betty's car reported a pleasant temperature of 74 degrees. My car doesn't even have an internal thermometer, much less an external one. Guess I'm deprived, but I'm trying to make my 1990 Jeep last until the year 2015. Somehow I figure — if my car can make it, maybe I can too.

We drove out the semi-blue road Hillsboro Road until we

reached Franklin and then turned left onto Highway 96 toward I-65 and Murfreesboro. Of course, there were several restaurant options where the blue roads met the red roads. I decided to try Steak 'n Shake Restaurant. I had visited one a few weeks ago and tasted the best hamburgers ever. This was my chance to see how they did with breakfast.

At 9:03 a.m. we were seated in this 1950s diner type restaurant. Both the floors and walls were covered with black, gray and white tiles that were beautifully clean and sparkling. It also featured red fluorescent signs and chrome tables matched with red and black vinyl chairs. At any other time I could imagine the sounds of Elvis coming out of all the speakers, but this was Sunday morning. The four couples present (including us) were barely awake, and so we were spared any blaring intrusion into our peaceful moods by Elvis or his like at this morning hour.

After looking at the menu for a few minutes, Betty ordered the cinnamon swirl French toast — $2.50. I ordered three eggs over-easy/over-medium, bacon, hash browns, gravy, biscuits and two pancakes — $11.60. Coffee for both of us. Now we had a little time for people watching.

Three separate tables held two couples and a woman with her seemingly well-mannered but developmentally-challenged son. One of the couples was a squeaky clean pair — fresh T-shirts, shorts and walking "tennis shoes." Both wore very clean ball-type caps and were obviously prepared for a relaxing Sunday. It did not appear that they would be going jogging because they had already showered. Instead, it appeared that they were ready for blue roading or some other civilized Sunday activity aimed at ignoring, if possible, that jogging was even an option at all.

The second couple appeared really tired or bored. They looked really clean and fresh, but maybe they had taken warm tub baths which had left them in their overly relaxed or lethargic mood. Maybe they should have taken a cold shower to awaken them, or perhaps they were fully awake but had just become so used to each other that ignoring one another felt comfortable. They did not appear to be angry at each other, or at anyone else. He was just reading the paper while she was just gazing off into space — not even wondering how she could get some excitement into her life. Maybe she could no longer realize that her life could have some texture and color to it. Perhaps her marital brain had not absorbed anything except boredom for so long that it could no longer recognize marriage as anything beyond the same old textureless, blandness she had come to know so completely — just like the man Betty and I had read about in today's paper. He had been blind since he was three-and-a-half years old. His sight had been restored, but his brain had not yet been retrained sufficiently for him to see differences and features clearly enough to recognize his own wife and family. I do hope this is truly not the case for the paper reader's bored wife this morning. I do hope she sees and recognizes her husband. Perhaps she was just too tired from a big Saturday night party to show any emotion at all this morning.

My level of excitement increased measurably when our breakfasts arrived. We were served by a friendly waitress whose uniform was color coordinated with the black and white tiles on the floor and walls. The breakfast visionary part of my brain — honed to a perfect 20/20 by many years of participatory observation — immediately knew that someone in the kitchen knew how to do breakfasts (as well as hamburgers) by the beautiful textures and colors of our breakfasts.

The golden-brown, dark-brown and yellow streaks of the cinnamon swirl French toast caused my 20/20 sight to transfer immediate information to other parts of my brain, making it almost impossible to resist reaching over immediately and stealing a taste from Betty's selection. Sometimes looks can be deceiving, but not this time. The taste was just as the texture and colors advertised — "Excellent French Toast Here."

The grass is not always greener on the other side; Betty's breakfast was different from my own, but not better. Our waitress said, "Here are your eggs, cooked just slightly less than over-medium." Immediately after I tasted them, I wanted to burst out in jubilant song as Professor Henry Higgins had done about the achievement of his student Elisa Doolittle in *My Fair Lady*: "She's got it, she's got it, by Jove I think she's got it." Our attractive waitress had trained the auditory part of her brain to truly hear and register the words "over-easy/over-medium." She had obviously translated these sounds into her own instructional words for the cook, and the cook had listened to her — perhaps because the sex portion of his brain was fully developed — and, voila! Perfect eggs cooked just as I had ordered. The bacon, the hash-brown fried potatoes, the gravy, the biscuits and my short stack of pancakes were all just as I had hoped. Boy! The cook had it bad. He's definitely in love with our waitress, and I was fortunate to be here smelling the flowers and tasting the candy.

Another couple came in and sat just across from us, and they were ready for some breakfast flowers and candy, also. My 20/20 vision was not at all needed to conclude that they were true breakfast lovers, too. The ample proportion of their girths gave full evidence of that fact. I wondered if these two new breakfast lovers and the Brownings, who were just now finishing, should not be going to the Remnant Fellowship for church this morning. It was my understanding that they offered assistance in weight management.

During the past fifty weeks, I have gained about twenty pounds which I directly blame on the fine breakfasts sampled every week before each different worship service. I am not at all sure that my journey has not been more directed by my love for fine Sunday breakfasts instead of my desire to visit fifty-two churches in one year. I don't mean to brag or anything, but if I were to become a boxer today I would definitely be required to fight in the heavyweight division. Now that this fifty-two week worship service pilgrimage is coming to an end, I fear that my cover for eating fine Sunday breakfasts is also going to be blown away. And I desperately needed to get back to my real fighting weight in the light-heavyweight division.

The Remnant Fellowship reportedly has a "Weigh Down" program to help breakfast offenders like me. Think I'll check it out — but not this morning. Their service started at 9:30 a.m., and here it was 9:40 a.m. We left the Steak n' Shake with a smile on our faces and a "weighty' cloud over our heads on this otherwise perfectly cloudless day.

The Primitive Baptist Church located in Franklin at Hill Road had only one weekly service according to their church sign, and it begins at 10:30 a.m. on Sunday mornings. Betty and I had plenty of time to drive around beautiful historic Franklin before this service would begin. I was in the middle of developing a small housing project in Nashville located on West End Avenue at Craighead, near the historic Richland area. I had been considering looking for a similar development site along the same lines here in Franklin, and I was happy to have a few minutes to cruise the streets near the old historic square for some possible locations.

At 10:25 a.m., only five cars were parked near the Primitive Baptist Church as we drove up just before service time. They had no visible parking lot. The cars were simply parked on the grass on the Hill Road side of the building, and it was clear that they were not expecting a large crowd on this beautiful Sunday. We parked on the grass just as the others had done but still felt a little guilty for doing so. Apparently they have so few cars parking here that there was no threat at all of tire marks; the beautiful green grass would be unharmed by the five or six cars parked here for less than two hours each Sunday throughout the year.

The sign at the front of the church announced Elder J.B. Fentress as the pastor. We met him right away. He is about six-feet in height and has gray hair. With a friendly smile, he welcomed us as we reached the top step before we entered the church. He introduced himself and apologized in advance for the small number of people who would be in attendance on this day. We talked for a few minutes and found that we were both seventy-two years of age. But he was nine days older than I am. Betty, at seventy-one, may well have been the youngest person in attendance at this service today.

There were 15 super-senior citizens, including the Brownings, gathered here this morning. This was either 12 or 13 more than required to assure divine presence according to the scriptural formula. Elder Fentress readily assured us that the quorum had been met as he quoted Jesus, "Where two or three are gathered together in My name, there I will be in their midst."

This simple white-brick church had been there for about forty years according to Elder Fentress. The sanctuary was a neat rectangle finished with simple sheets of simulated wood paneling, indicating that the ceiling was 10 feet high. There were five fluorescent light fixtures and one lonely ceiling fan located over the pulpit area. There were eight pews on each side of the aisle, each padded with avocado colored cushions. Just behind the pulpit was a baptistery with a picturesque wallpaper mural of a grotto that created a natural looking scene for baptisms. The windows were self-stained with a brownish yellow cast coating which was applied unevenly and gave a days-end type of glow to the room.

There was no piano. I understand that is the case in all Primitive Baptist churches — no instrumental music. Elder Fentress wore a white short-sleeved shirt that revealed tattoos on each arm. He began leading the singing with the assistance of one of the members. He asked us to "turn to Page 495 and sing *A Light at the River.*" The chorus of this song went: "There is a light for me at the river guiding my soul across the dark foam, down through the valley past the dark shadows. Jesus my light will carry me home."

After the first song, the song leaders asked the congregation for requests for the next songs. A septuagenarian woman requested Number 426 — *Leaning on the Everlasting Arms.* All of us in this service could readily relate to this song, without a doubt. At our collective or average age of about seventy-five to eight, we all felt the need to lean on something in order to be "safe and secure from all alarm."

Pastor Fentress, who had been pastor here for the last 19 years, then took a request for number 346, *I'll Live on Somewhere.* Some of the words were, "When this life is o'er, and I'm not here no more, in a happy home never more to roam, I'll live on somewhere." Next we sang, also by request, number 377, *My Latest Sun Is Sinking Fast.* The central theme of this song is given in the words, "O' come angel band, come and around me stand. O' bear me away on your snowy wings to my immortal home."

I could not join in this song too enthusiastically because I'm just like the little boy and his friends who were caught gambling by the preacher. The preacher scolded the boys and asked, "Don't you want to go to heaven?" All the other boys answered affirmatively, but this one lad started backing away and shaking his head, "No." The preacher then grabbed the boy, shook him and asked again, "Are you sure you don't want to go to heaven when you die?" The boy's face brightened considerably and he said, "Oh, yes, reverend. I just thought you were making up a load to go today." Now if there is a better place to go after I die, I surely want to go there, just like the little boy. But I am not at all interested in going today.

The next song request also pursued the notion of going to heaven. It was No. 368, *Twilight Is Stealing.* This one is about voices coming from "A mansion filled with delight, smart happy home so bright." I think they might do well to remove the brownish yellow tint from the windows.

One good thing about going to a church where the average age is almost four score is that standing while singing is almost totally out of the question. We kept sitting and singing, request after request. We remained sitting and sang number 373, *Does Jesus Care?* The answer, of course, is yes: "Oh, yes, I know He cares...When the days are weary and the long nights dreary, I know my savior cares."

The next requested song was number 73 from "the little book." So from a smaller paperback songbook we sang *I'll Fly Away* with its hopeful words, "When I die, hallelujah, bye and bye, I'll fly away." Then just before the sermon we sang number 58, "Because He Lives ...I can face tomorrow, because He lives all fear is gone, because I know He holds the future."

Elder Fentress had told us earlier that Primitive Baptists believe in foot washing as part of their worship services, but he said these services were only on the third weeks of May and October. He said that when Jesus told His disciples to "do this, as oft as you do it, in remembrance of Me" He was speaking about the washing of feet as well as the Lord's Supper. Since Jesus did not instruct them as to how often to do it, each individual Primitive Baptist Church decides when and how often to have these two sacraments as part of their services.

Before his sermon Elder Fentress mentioned that several sick people known to the congregation needed the prayers of the people of faith. Brother Fentress named several individuals and then said that one of them in particular was very, very sick. So sick was he that Brother Fentress' faith had been stretched to the limits. He said of this poor soul, "I don't think he will be back with us, unless he gets better, but I don't think he will, but I'll keep praying that he will get better." Then Elder Fentress said, "Brother Paul, will you lead us in prayer?" This dear brother prayed, "Dear Lord we pray for all the sick and hope they will come back...and I believe they will." He may have had more faith then the pastor. Probably not, but he did know that this congregation needed to keep as many members alive as possible. They have no Sunday school here as a place to nurture and bring along new young members. It appeared that those members present today were the "last of the Mohicans."

Pastor Fentress, after the prayer, said that we all needed to remember our soldiers on foreign soil. He followed this by saying, "9-11 told us that we need to get back to God." This was one of the two times I can remember 9-11 even being mentioned or referred to during the fifty weeks of my pilgrimage.

At 11:05 a.m., Pastor Fentress actually began his hour-long sermon. He said that he wanted to talk with us today about preachers. He started out by saying, "Man cannot call a preacher. God has to call a man to preach." He read about the prophet Isaiah in *Isaiah Chapter 61*: "The Spirit of the Lord God is upon me; because the Lord hath anointed me to preach good tidings." The pastor then asked, "What are these good tidings?" He immediately answered, "That Jesus died for us to forgive us of all our sins."

Brother Fentress then proceeded to cover the subject of preaching from Adam to Paul. He told us that when Adam sinned a war began between God and Satan for the souls of men, then Jesus died to forgive our sins, and preachers are called to tell this story. He then told us that Isaiah was called to preach good tidings to the broken hearted, and that while we are often sad and broken hearted, God will not put on us more than we can stand. "So what about suicides?" he asked. He simply said that these are those who do not turn to God for help.

He then began talking about Moses and the children of Israel in the wilderness, how Moses took the credit for bringing water from the rock and that God, therefore, did not let him go into the Promised Land. "As a preacher Moses tried to claim too much credit for what God had done," said Elder Fentress.

He moved on to Paul and Timothy where Paul tells Timothy to preach the Word. "Be instant in season and out of season." Next he quickly covered the story of the *Prodigal Son*. This preacher then said, "There are so many things to say this morning that I'm not going to get to, but I want to talk about Peter when he preached at the house of Cornelius."

Elder Fentress then talked about Judas and the apostles who were called to "preach to the lost sheep of Judah." He told about the woman at the well who was so impressed by the spirit of Jesus that she went to her friends and asked them, "Is this not the Christ?" Pastor Fentress apparently was categorizing her as a preacher. Then he went back to *Isaiah 58* where the prophet said "Cry aloud and spare not." The elder here was saying that in preaching, "We can't keep from stepping on toes, but preachers must tell the truth even if it hurts."

This sermon then told of Jesus and the two thieves on the Cross, one of whom spoke words in defense of Jesus — like preachers should do. He spoke about Peter again when Jesus asked Peter three times, "Peter, lovest thou me?" When Peter answered that he did, Jesus instructed Peter, "Feed my sheep." This pastor said that God expects preachers to feed His sheep as His children.

Pastor Fentress continued by preaching about all the gifts of the spirit. "Some are called to be preachers, some pastors, and some evangelists, and so forth," he noted. He quickly said that he himself could not quote great portions of scripture like some preachers could, but that the acceptance he had found to his sermons in different situations was evidence that he had the gift of preaching. In his concluding remarks he offered additional evidence of his calling to preach,"I've never gone into the pulpit afraid that I would not have something to say." I don't doubt that in the least. It was now 12:05 p.m., and this good brother had preached about preachers and preaching for about an hour. He had covered both the *Old* and *New Testaments* in exhausting what the *Bible* had to say on this subject.

He pretty much exhausted Betty as well during the process; I had to pinch her several times to help keep her awake. I hope Brother Fentress took no offense if he happened to see her nodding off because she did it to me a time or two some forty years ago when I was also a pulpit professional. I didn't feel badly toward her even then because I often had to pinch her to keep her awake during some of the best movies. That's why I call her "Snuggles." She just loves to snuggle up and take little naps. She just hadn't had her nap since breakfast, Brother Fentress, that's all. First, I want to thank you for so cordially welcoming us to this service today. Second, I am sure Betty wants to thank you for the sweet little nap.

Chapter 51

The Remnant Fellowship
Nashville, Tennessee
August 31, 2003

Today I made one easy choice and one hard choice as I came to the second to the last Sunday during my 52-Sunday pilgrimage. The first and easy choice was where we would go for breakfast during the first leg of our journey. To the best of my knowledge there were only a very few Sunday breakfast locations left in Middle Tennessee which we had not visited during the past year. One of the few remaining locations to be visited was the Cracker Barrel — a true blue road restaurant which has several locations scattered around Nashville where the blue roads intersect with the interstate system. And it was a must to visit if I was going to adequately cover at least the weekend breakfast eating scene in this area.

Another real possibility for breakfast today was Monell's which is located in the old historic Germantown area of North Nashville at 1235 Sixth Avenue, North. My family and I had eaten lunch at this down-home cookin' restaurant several times over the years, but it apparently had only recently opened for breakfasts on Sundays. So, the choice was simple; since the Cracker Barrel had multiple locations to serve as options next Sunday (our last Sunday), we easily chose Monell's for today.

Many times the new menus or new serving times tried out by restaurants, even very good restaurants, do not work out. I did not want to risk this possibility. I called and, indeed, confirmed that Monell's served breakfast from 8:00 a.m. to 10:00 a.m. on Sunday mornings. Since I had also already made the much harder decision as to which religious service we would attend today at 10:00 a.m., Monell's 8:00 a.m. opening time would be just about perfect for us.

Well, to be honest, breakfast at 8:00 a.m. at Monell's or any other place is not perfectly perfect with me. I really do not enjoy committing myself to meetings of any type before about 10:00

513

a.m. You know, just in case I want to roll over in bed for another short 40 winks before I decide I have fully run out of sleep. Now, please remember, I am seventy-two years old. One of the simplest, sweetest perks of the "golden years" which I have given myself is the pleasure of awakening slowly and gently, without the aid of some artificial awakening device such as the nerve-jangling sounds of an alarm clock.

Somewhere back in my youth when I was about nine or ten years of age Mrs. Bachtel, my school teacher, taught me a little ditty which surprisingly I remember even to this day. It goes: "True culture, to be true, must first be unconscious of the process that induced it; but, before it can be attained, one must be more or less, under a law, until he becomes a law unto himself, and does spontaneously and unconsciously, what he once did consciously and with effort." I have never been able to arise in the mornings before 8:00 a.m. without considerable conscious effort. So this morning we were forced to use the uncivilized and culturally unacceptable artificial method of the alarm clock to be sure we were ready to leave before 8:00 a.m. At 7:52 a.m. we were, still sleepily, documenting by Betty's digital car clock that we would probably just barely make the 8:00 a.m. seating at Monell's.

The 8:00 a.m. seating was important to us so that we could leave by about 9:00 a.m. to make our chosen 10:00 a.m. worship service. You see, Monell's is different. All the food is served family style, or perhaps more accurately stated, "country family style." I feel truly sorry for those readers who may need this explanation. Anyhow, here it is: the guests are seated at large open tables; the food is passed around in large bowls or on platters; and, each person helps himself to as much or as little of the numerous items as he wishes. No such thing here of ordering "two scrambled eggs, please." While you will almost certainly be served scrambled eggs, it is up to you to say "when."

At 8:01 a.m. we walked into Monell's which is located in a handsome historic home in what was once a very affluent section of Nashville. We joined a table of eight men who had apparently set their clocks one minute earlier than ours. These eight men were the only other pilgrims who had chosen Monell's as their breakfast place this morning. They were a lively group of businessmen who were associates in a national wholesale produce alliance. They were all very much awake and warmly welcomed us to this open table. The table was completely filled a couple of minutes later by a family of three — a man, his wife and their one-year-old daughter. This newcomer was associated with the Dell Computer Company and its Nashville division.

Soon the food started to flow. First, the biscuits and gravy. Move over Beacon Light and Loveless. Here comes a new competitor for the best biscuits in the area. And, without doubt, Monell's wins for the best combination of biscuits and gravy by my score sheet. But I definitely am a man of the moment. I am very much like the man in the country music song who says something like, "Your kisses are better, but hers are here." Still, I truly believe Monell's would easily win a face-to-face taste-off with this true country combo.

It was time to loosen our belts and tuck our napkins under our collars because the rest of the beautiful bowls and platters of food arrived. The large bowls were filled with scrambled eggs, fried new red potatoes, cheese grits, fried apples and corn pudding. A humongous platter of crisped thick bacon, sausages and center-cut pieces of country ham followed. Finally, a large platter arrived with delightfully light medium-sized pancakes — just the right size for our breakfast dessert, but not for a single item entrée.

Now this was a real breakfast. It was like the ones we had back in West Virginia when my grandmother lived with us. She was the daughter of Anderson ("Devil Anse") Hatfield who was the patriarch of the Hatfield clan made infamous by the Hatfield–McCoy feud during the latter parts of the 19th century. My grandmother learned to cook for the whole clan, and this was how it was done — a table full of great country food for breakfast. Not to worry about any waste because there was never any waste; what was not eaten for breakfast was recycled for dinner. Dinner, back then, was what city folks called lunch. Lunch, back then, was food packed in a sack or packed in coal miners' black lunch boxes. Any time you ate around noontime at a table it was "dinner." Only in a sack or box was it "lunch." I wanted to go back to Monell's for lunch today (Sunday dinner, you all) to see if they properly and wisely recycled this delicious food. It's an art, you know — how to take leftovers and make them look new and different.

The fried red potatoes needed a little help. This was an item which was a little more country than we even had in West Virginia. I just really prefer some browned crispiness in my breakfast-fried potatoes, and it is almost impossible to fry new red potatoes and get them to be crispy. The cheese grits were a little thin for easy handling on a plate. I had a little trouble eating this very tasty item with my fork, and it would not puddle deep enough to allow it to be successfully eaten with a spoon. This may have been what our friendly waitress meant when she said that the chef was having a bad day.

We all felt we wanted to come back to Monell's when we could be assured the chef/cook was having another "bad day." We would even all agree to bring our own mini-bowls for the cheese grits and our own doggie bags for anything they were not going to recycle, for whatever you choose to call the noon meal. Somehow today, even in much of city life, the noon meal on Sunday is often and easily referred to as "Sunday dinner." Maybe it has something to do with the volume of food served. It's just hard to refer to a small salad or a half-sandwich as dinner, yet easy to refer to a large country meal served at lunchtime as Sunday dinner.

Surely this was a "brunch" rather than breakfast if the volume of food has any bearing on what we call these meals. Certainly we had all eaten enough for both breakfast and lunch at this one very fine meal. And the conversation was easy and delightful among a mixture of people from different walks of life. Wish I had my book already published. I believe I could have sold eight to ten copies to these breakfast lovers who indicated they were always looking for good breakfast places. *My Fifty-Two Sundays* certainly could point them to a few.

At 9:00 a.m. we paid our bill (which was $12.00 per person plus tax and tip) and began to make our way to where we were going to church this morning. The choice of church service had been difficult because there were only two services left for us to attend if we were to keep our total number to fifty-two, one full year's worth. There were so many churches which I would like to visit. Maybe I should have been more selective earlier and limited myself to only one or two from any one group or denomination. But I am not a historical revisionist. I have been where I have been, and that is that. Now I had only these last two Sundays to complete my full year of one church service each week, except, of course, for the Sunday I attended two services during one morning.

After much deliberation I had decided that we would go to the Remnant Fellowship. It is located on the Weigh Down Workshop campus — forty acres located at 308 Seaboard Lane in the Cool Springs area of Williamson County near Nashville. I had been intrigued for weeks by what I saw as a symbiotic relationship between the Weigh Down Workshop and the Remnant Fellowship. They are located at the same location and share some of the same facilities.

The Weigh Down Workshop was started by Gwen Shamblin, a dietician. She developed the diet called "The Weigh Down Diet" in the late 1980s. This diet became popular in the 1990s in secular circles as well as in Christian churches all over America. She taught dietary moderation as a Christian principle. At times, her program was facetiously called "The Weigh Down with Jesus Diet." Soon after that time she also started the Weigh Down Workshops. The Workshops soon spread to thousands of locations across the country and began attracting hundreds of thousands of men and women — primarily from a wide group of Christian churches across the country.

Gwen's infectious enthusiasm for her diet combined with her physical beauty made her a true guru for multitudes of diet-conscious and religiously-oriented people from every state. As time passed, her message and workshops were increasingly colored by her Christian concerns. In 1999, with financial resources gained from her diet workshop profits, Gwen started the Remnant Fellowship at the same location of her Weigh Down Workshop address in Cool Springs. I had first been attracted by a small tasteful sign at the front of this property. It had a cross superimposed over the words "Weigh Down Workshop." I called to get information and found by way of an enthusiastic recording that they, indeed, held religious services. I soon found that their main service was held at 10:00 a.m. on Sundays and that they gather at the Weigh Down reception areas at about 9:30 a.m. for fellowship before the service begins.

Betty and I arrived at 9:50 a.m. We walked in with two attractive, definitely not overweight, women who happened to be mother and daughter, but who truly looked like sisters. They directed us to the restrooms and pointed us to the auditorium which was in reality a complete sound-video recording studio that was also used for the

Remnant Fellowship worship services. One thing which we noticed immediately was that they were serving coffee and donuts as refreshments during their fellowship time.

We were still so well fortified with servings from Monell's that these temptations were easily resisted, and the Brownings went straight in to find a backseat with a good view of all the possible activities this morning. As we were seated, we were met and welcomed by Patrick Stites who was with his very attractive wife and their beautiful baby. Patrick gave me a brief history of the founding of this church and its relationship to Gwen Shamblin and the Weigh Down Workshop. He told us that Weigh Down is a for-profit corporation, which allows the Remnant Fellowship, a church started by Gwen Shamblin, to worship in the workshop's facilities.

Patrick also told us that this service would be "Web cast" to 130 other Remnant Fellowships around the country today and that we would be hearing the voices of some members from other locations during this service. He also went to the office and brought us a copy of "THE NEW JERUSALEM" which was copied from the Remnant Fellowship's web site. This was a document of seventeen pages presenting the biblical, ideological, and theological basis of this new church under various headings such as: "THE SOUND OF THE TRUMPET," "FUNDAMENTAL AGREEMENT: THE *BIBLE* IS GOD'S WILL," THE POWERFUL DELUSION," "THE CHURCH HAS ALLOWED MULTIPLE GODS," "WHAT MUST WE DO TO BE SAVED?," and other topics including "WHY REMNANT?"

Soon the service began with the leader asking us all to pray and to "Bow down as low as you can." Everyone in this place, except the Brownings and one other conspicuous soul, followed the leader's instructions. Many were prostrate on the floor with their head and hands touching the floor during this opening prayer.

As soon as this prayer by one of the worship leaders ended, the congregation went into a musical introduction of the service by singing, *I Surrender All.* The worship team was a group of about eight people on the stage, two of whom played guitars while the others led the singing. The words to the songs were displayed on one of the two large screens on either side of the stage. The opening song continued: "All to Jesus, I surrender all. All to Thee my blessed Savior, I surrender all."

Several cameras taped this service to allow it to be watched simultaneously all over the country. There was an orchestra of six instruments in addition to the two guitars on the stage. I had learned early that Gwen Shamblin and some of the other members of the Remnant Fellowship had been members of the Otter Creek Church of Christ in Nashville before founding this new church in 1999. One of their members told me that the Church of Christ emphasized the restoration of the "form" of the early church when they were formed in the 1830s. This same member told me that the Remnant Fellowship was founded to restore the "function" of the early church. He was saying that such things as instrumental music or non-instrumental music were a matter of form only, and that this body's emphasis on function and content allowed instrumental music and other differences in worship services as God's Spirit led them.

We were next asked to stand and sing. We sang *Joyful, Joyful, We Adore Thee* with most of the members moving rhythmically, waving their arms and clapping throughout the song. Even the smallest children, who could barely as much as stand, joined in actively with these singing sounds and motions. The exemplary conduct of the children from age two through the teenage years was perhaps the most remarkable aspect of this service for Betty and me. Literally every one of these children participated in this service almost as adults. Each and every one of them sat through the entire service without fidgeting around at all. They sat straight up in their chairs, bowed reverently and sang enthusiastically. We could hardly believe our eyes that every child in this service behaved in such an admirable way during this entire service. Betty and I both could take a lesson from the children.

After this song, Gwen Shamblin took over the service from the worship team. An attractive and tan blond, she wore a stylish black sleeveless dress and a white necklace that appeared to be made of pearls from where we were sitting in the back. She sat confidently on a tall barstool with her legs crossed, as she had been while she was participating fully in the spirited music during the opening moments of this service.

Gwen, almost regal on her stool-throne, announced that Rusty Henry from the Marion, Ohio fellowship would give his testimony by audio transmission to the Nashville Remnant Fellowship. Rusty began speaking to us, while a large picture of him and his wife was projected on a large screen to the left side of the stage. He gave an effective testimony as to what the Remnant Fellowship had meant to him and his family, and then said that "I stayed up until 1:30 this morning asking God to let me know what to say to you today." He spoke for a few minutes from *Psalms 119: 52 – 64* before ending his testimony by saying that all Remnant Fellowship members "should be bold and not bashful about our message."

Next, Gwen introduced Ted from the Nashville congregation and told us that he wanted to share something with us. Ted, a handsome young man, said that he surrendered to God at age 28. He said, "I was really involved in the life of a church, and on the outside it seemed I was 'there,' but I was not." After he found out about the Remnant Fellowship he came to find, "the real peace which God brought to me." Ted continued, "In my old church I did not have that humility. I did not wake up in the morning and ask God, "What can I do for you and Your people?" He said that now there is "total death to my pride." He quoted from *Matthew 7* where Jesus said, "Ask and it will be given to you." He assured us all that God can give us anything and He "can give you the same spirit and heart that Gwen has." He concluded by saying, "I charge you, Remnant Nation to ask God for that life, that heart that (Gwen and her husband) have." His last words were, "Love you guys. Praise God! What a day!"

Earlier Gwen had tried to get Marcus Francis on the line without success. Now he was on the line for all of us to hear his testimony while a picture of this handsome African-American and his family was projected on the large screen. His first words were, "Praise God! What an opportunity to praise Him today." He then told of how he and his wife had tried to lose weight and how they had found their way to Remnant Fellowship nineteen months ago. They had lost weight and had learned how to eat. He said, "I learned that if I love God, I will obey God." He then noted we have all sinned and come short of the glory of God, before going on to say, "But that is past sin." He was refuting the idea that says we must sin every day and emphasizing that through a life in Christ we can live above these sins.

Marcus and the other speakers this morning kept referring to "The Remnant Nation." He said that in the Remnant Nation God is trying to find those who are pure in heart. He witnessed that most of us have been taught that we will always sin,"but that is not what God's word says." He said,"If you are overweight, great! God can help you take this weight away and the other weights in your life away. We can have freedom from sin!" His concluding words were, "I love you guys and...sorry I took so long."

Next there was a message from Elizabeth in Columbus, Ohio. She said that this was her first time to watch a Web cast. After a few personal greetings to people she had seen in this congregation during the Web cast she concluded, "Love you guys so much and can't wait until I see all of you."

Now it was time for the morning's sermon. Gwen, still sitting on her stool with her large *Bible* in her lap, began to speak. She first read several scriptures including *Ezekiel 18: 1 – 24* which, she said, gives us the rules for a righteous life. She said, "Many of you may have come from an infamous background and have committed shameful acts, but if you turn from your wicked past then none of this will be remembered against you. Get a new heart and a new spirit and repent and live."

Gwen, who is considered by many of her followers to be a prophetess, then had us listen to a recorded song which included these words, "I don't care who you are or where you are from or what you did, as long as you love me." She indicated that this song would be played again during communion. Then just before communion was served, Gwen told about how Solomon messed up within Zion when he married another wife. She then informed us that some people in this fellowship had also done wrong and had been corrected. She invited those who had not been able to see blind spots in their lives to, "bring your hearts back to God as we listen to this song again."

Communion was then served as the song played over and over, repeating: "I don't care who you are, where you are from, or what you did, as long as you love me." This was the only introduction to the communion service. There were no words such as, "This is my body. This is my blood." Young people in their early teens passed the trays of bread and wine among the approximately 200 very young, very trim people here today for this service. And in just four or five short minutes this part of the service was over.

Following communion Gwen asked everyone to bow down again for prayer, "O, Father, O, God, we love you and pray that you will come down and be with us. We pray for Zion, for exiles, for them to return home...It matters not what we have done in the past...Father you are way too generous, wider than the sky. God please see our love and make us white as snow." She then reached for, while still prostrate on the floor, a list of people for whom prayer had been requested. She made individual mention of these names and needs including one couple who, "needs to sell their home." She ended this prayer with, "We pray for Phoenix and Beaumont (referring to two of the other Remnant Fellowships), Amen."

After this "pastoral prayer" Gwen said, "Kent wants to share some things with us." Kent, another handsome young man, came to the stage for his testimony with his whole family, including his very pregnant wife who was one week past her due date. He told about how they had been in another church "not on the sidelines, but we were in the game, if you will, but we knew something was wrong." He said they had been in three churches. He named the first one as the Disciples of Christ. He charged that "This church did not teach 'once in grace, always in grace' but they lived like it." Then he said he also had been a Baptist where they *actually* taught this belief. The third church was a "Full Gospel Church where the full emphasis was primarily on themselves and their feelings."

Finally Kent said, "We came here and Gwen used her gift to help us see. Three years ago today really marks what we call our new birth. That was when we were reborn." He praised Gwen and Martin (her husband, I supposed) for their being here. He declared, "I am eternally grateful to God and to Gwen for laying down the truth." He further testified that he and his wife had changed for the good emotionally, spiritually and physically. "And we have lost weight," he proudly proclaimed.

After this testimony Gwen asked us to stand and sing a song that Michael, who I believe is her son, had written. This lively song had many words from *Old Testament* scriptures with each being introduced and ending with "Hey, ya. Hey, ya," in a lively and bouncy, almost rap, style. The infectious beat of the song had almost everyone clapping and waving and dancing in place at their seats. Then two young men came to the front of the room and did a choreographed, merengue-type dance, to the beat of this song for about five minutes. The song ended with the words: "Hey, hey, I love this place. Here comes the truth so here I'll stay."

In a happy and relaxed voice Gwen then casually said, "You are dismissed." But most of those present were following the last words of this song and were here to stay for a while longer. By now it was 12:15 p.m. Betty and I did not dare look at ourselves because we just knew we had already turned into pumpkins at the stroke of twelve noon after two hours of service. We knew we looked like pumpkins to this group of spiritual weight watchers. We felt certain that we were at least thirty years older than the oldest member here and undoubtedly outweighed the largest of them by at least fifty-pounds.

As we walked out, we were both tempted to help ourselves to the boxes of donuts. They looked as if they had not been touched by the members of the church during the social hour which had preceded this service. Maybe they do not eat these donuts here at all. Perhaps this was Gwen's way of strengthening the willpower of the members here by helping them to face up to sinful desires right here on holy ground. This attractive and charismatic leader of spiritual resistance to temptation is building a veritable fortress against sinful self-indulgence for her followers. And her followers sing, "Here I will stay."

Chapter 52

The Bahá'i Faith
Nashville, Tennessee
September 6, 2003

There are always some mixed emotions at a journey's end. Of course, there is a measure of happiness which comes from the completion of a journey. You are there. You have arrived at your destination. You've accomplished your mission. Congratulations!

Yet, there also are unmistakable feelings of sadness — just as there are many times at the end of the day as the sun dies in the West. The day is over. The trip has ended. The adventure has come to its conclusion. The questions begin to press in as you near home. Did I take full advantage of this opportunity? Did I forget anything? Should I have stayed a little longer? Will I ever travel back along these same paths again?

As we left our home at 8:12 a.m. on this beautiful summer morning the comfortable feeling I always have at the beginning of fall was, for the moment, overshadowed by the feeling of sadness caused by the end of summer. This season truly has been my favorite season ever since fall no longer meant the end of a summer of fun and freedom; while still in school the end of summer had meant the beginning of a year of working hard at school and days upon days of rigidly controlled schedules.

Today was also the end of my journey spanning fifty-two weeks during which I had visited at least one different religious worship service each week. Along the way I had stopped to visit different restaurants as well and, sadly, had gained the extra twenty pounds to prove it. This day would be the last — both for worship services to visit, and, alas, for blue road breakfast places to visit. Now, by no means does this mean that I will not be visiting both these types of Sunday destinations again, soon and often. But this program is over. I had arbitrarily limited the scope of this adventure to the number of fifty-two. Some of my friends and literary mavens have suggested that I should have limited it further. One respected critic said that I perhaps should reduce the scope, and thus the size of this book, by changing the title from "Fifty-Two Sundays" to a "Month of Sundays" and reducing the number of chapters from fifty-two to thirty or thirty-one.

How can I possibly do this? Already I realize there are restaurants and churches which I will have to exclude from this book. One of these restaurants has been one of my favorite breakfast destinations for many years, and also for many of my friends of this fast-paced, hard-charging generation. How can I possibly omit McDonald's with their time saving and palate satisfying Egg McMuffins and bacon, egg and cheese biscuits? They have been the salvation for travelers on the red, green and blue roads for more than two scores of years. But we are faced with difficult decisions almost every day, and today would be no different. As a matter of fact, the choices we would make today would be *more* difficult because there would not be any possible corrective opportunities next week. There would be no next week. These choices today would be final and I had debated the possible selections all week long.

I had sort of "saved" three breakfast places during the year to allow them to fit in when my selections for breakfast places would begin to be limited: McDonald's, Waffle House, Cracker Barrel. The reason for "saving" these three was the guaranteed presence of at least one of these three chains somewhere near any church I might decide to visit on any particular Sunday. I "spent" the Waffle House coin from my piggy bank of restaurants a couple of Sundays ago. Today I decided to draw the Cracker Barrel deposit out of savings and spend it on Sunday No. 52. There was just no way I could fail to include this truly blue road restaurant. It might have been an unpardonable sin in the minds of blue road travelers. Actually I guess I made this choice nearly a year ago when I deposited the Cracker Barrel in my savings account.

I had announced my selection to Betty just last night. She, of course, applauded this decision. The Cracker Barrel had been one of Nannie's favorites while she was alive. Nannie was Betty's mother who truly had delighted in traveling. Although she really had been a world traveler, nothing seemed to make her happier than our simple weekend trips to blue road restaurants. We still celebrate her birthdays on the 18th of August each year by gathering at some fine gourmet restaurant to toast her venturesome spirit, her love of travel and her love for her family. Next August I am going to suggest a Cracker Barrel for breakfast instead. We can toast her with a cup of coffee at one of her favorite blue road breakfast destinations.

At 8:30 a.m., Betty and I pulled up to the Cracker Barrel located on Charlotte Pike near I-40, west of Nashville. This is only one of 482 Cracker Barrel Old Country Stores spread throughout 41 states. The chain had been started in 1961 by Dan Evins in Lebanon, Tennessee. He started the first one with a small group of hometown friends, and it became the prototype of a concept providing the traveling public with down home country food and a comfortable atmosphere. While traveling around the country in the mid-60s with his family, Evins had been unable to find such a restaurant. He set out to provide an alternative to the fast food establishments which had been offering meals meant to be "swallowed down in three bites with a squirt of catsup."

The first stores were restaurants attached to small general stores, complete with a potbellied stove and a checker board. Such an establishment was similar to the one my dad and grandfather had back in Cow Creek, West Virginia. Cow Creek was a suburb of Barnabus, which had a population of nearly 50 — say about 47 or 48. There you could come for your gasoline, your overalls, your nails and your shotgun shells. You could also get your lunch if you liked bologna and cheese, either on crackers or light bread. You could stay all day, and most folks (mostly men) did on rainy days.

As we walked into the store on Charlotte, we noticed that the checkerboard is still on the front porch along with the comfortable rockers ready for the overflow crowd. The gas pumps are gone, however, and they now warn you to come in with only your stomach empty. And that's a good warning — to go in hungry — because everything on the menu is tempting. On the lunch and dinner menu they offer chicken n' dumplins, Sunday fried chicken, meatloaf, country-fried steak, roast beef and gravy and a large variety of vegetables: mashed potatoes, corn, green beans, fried apples, turnip greens, pinto beans, fried okra and macaroni and cheese. Then they have a whole assortment of biscuit sandwiches: country ham, sausage and fried pork tenderloin. And gooood country desserts!

But it was 8:30 a.m., and we wanted breakfast. Here they serve breakfast "All Day, Every Day." This suited me just fine. No disappointments, such as when you arrive five minutes too late at some places. We took several minutes looking over the menu. There were the Traditional Breakfast, the Old Timers' Breakfast, the Sample Breakfast, the Country Morning Breakfast, the Cracker Barrel's Country Boy Breakfast and many more. I selected the Sample Breakfast of three eggs over-easy/over-medium, which came with potato casserole, grits, apples, country ham, sausage, bacon and biscuits and gravy. $6.59! Wow! And Betty ordered the French Toast Breakfast with bacon, $4.69. Her order gave me the true comfort level I needed because I felt I could trade her out of a piece of her French toast, perhaps with some of my grits and biscuits and gravy. Now that's a fair deal if I ever heard of one.

Our friendly, mature and efficient waitress kept our cups filled with hot coffee while we waited for our food to be prepared in a kitchen where biscuits are obviously never handled by nuke Nazis. Any time of the day, they are always the right consistency, just as you would hope they would be. As we waited, we saw the very large stone fireplace which has replaced the old potbellied stove of years gone by. Here, in the large rooms, are the oak tables and chairs and walls lined with old pictures and memorabilia such as old plows, guns, clocks, Coke and Orange-Crush signs. And then there are the stuffed deer heads and the bobcats. Old stuff everywhere. Enough to keep your attention while you wait for your food.

Soon, very soon, our entire breakfast order was served all at once — a pleasant change, in and of itself, especially with such a large order placed by this breakfast connoisseur. But why not a very large breakfast today? It would be the last of these treats for a while. I had purchased my newly added twenty pounds primarily with my credit card and fifty-two breakfasts. Suppose they'll credit proportionately back to my credit cards in direct relation to the pounds that I will try to shed over the months to come?

My breakfast was almost perfect. Our friendly professional waitress paid attention and got my eggs just right. My sausage and country ham were succulent, and the thick bacon slices were appropriately crisp. The potato casserole was the best of this type of recipe that I had eaten, but I still prefer the hash browns à la the Pancake Pantry in Nashville. My half-orders of grits and gravy and biscuits were country good. I used my other half-orders to barter for a slice of Betty's French toast which I had for dessert. The texture and taste of this breakfast dessert were almost as good as the perfect French toast we had eaten at the Dinner Bell in Parsons, Tennessee. I preferred the syrup they served there to the pure maple syrup at the Cracker Barrel — to each his own. And I would like to own my very own Cracker Barrel, or at least a sizable block of their stock, so that I could just hire away one of their best cooks to come and cook our own private down home meals. But, then, my girth, my Lord, my girth!

As we left, we noticed that we were not alone. There were plenty of patrons here with generous portions of physical pulchritude. We paid our bill and made it through the general store part of this establishment, which had been planned to relieve patrons of any extra money they may have remaining as they leave. We resisted their tempting offerings of pancake mixes, jams, jellies, honey and a whole array of candies. The candies remind many of us of older and simpler days when salt water taffy, chocolate covered peanuts, and orange slice candies were about all the goodies offered in the old general stores.

We walked out of the past and climbed into our horseless carriage which was waiting to take us to the last worship service of the yearlong journey after having taken us to so very many interesting and different worship services. But now, another decision. I had wanted to visit with the Amish, the Scientologists, the Society of Friends, and also a service where snake handling was a part of the worship. And also I wanted to visit a service of the Bahà'i faith.

For various reasons I had found that I would not be able or allowed to attend several of these services which I truly wanted to visit. I had also feared that I would not be able to attend a worship service of the Bahá'i faith. However, on the Friday before my 52nd Sunday, Mrs. Ziba Ferdowsi told me that there would be a prayer and devotional service at the Bahá'i Center in Nashville at 10:00 a.m. on Sunday. While I had hoped to have the opportunity to join those of this faith in a full worship service, this week was the conclusion of my 52-week journey and so I decided I would attend here this Sunday in order to be able to include a service of this religion in my 52 Sundays.

I had very little knowledge about this faith until a few weeks ago when I started reading about it during some of my research. Because of my readings, I had begun to see how members of this religion view themselves as occupying a unique place in the history of world religions. The followers of this faith see themselves as playing a unifying role among the major religions of the world. Their beliefs and history lead them to feel they are directly connected to Judaism, Christianity, Islam, and other world religions.

The Bahá'i faith began in the mid 19th century with most members of the religion dating the founding of their religion to 1844 in Iran. This was a time in Christian history when the Millennialism movement was at a very high pitch. Many Christians were convinced that the end of the world was at hand and that the second coming of Christ was imminent. At this same time, this Millennialism movement in Iran was being carried to the people by a prophet-evangelist man who was simply called the Bab. The Bab pointed the Moslems of his day to the Messianic and Messianic-type teachings in Judaism, Christianity and Islam. And he said that Jesus was the Messiah prophesied in Jewish literature. Moslems regarded Jesus as a prophet in the line of Abraham and Moses and Mohammed (who came after Jesus) as the last of the prophets from God. Now the Bab, as the John the Baptist of the Moslem world, proclaimed the imminent return of the Messiah. Bahá'u'lláh, who had been a Persian nobleman, was a close follower of the Bab and became known as the "Father of the Poor." The Bab was executed for heresy and for being a rebel. After the Bab's death, Bahà'u'lláh announced that he was the "Promised One" whose coming had been foretold by the Bab.

Bahà'u'lláh then became the leader of this new faith which became known as the Bahá'i faith. After his ascension to this leadership position, he was either imprisoned or in exile for more than forty years for his heretical views. But his followers grew rapidly and began to spread his teachings. He taught that God the Creator had revealed himself throughout history through many messengers and prophets. He declared that these messengers were Abraham and Moses (Judaism), Krishna (Hinduism), Zoroaster (Zovoasterism), Buddah (Buddhism), Jesus (Christianity), Mohammed (Islam), the Bab and Bahà'u'lláh.

The Bab had taught that all of these different messengers delivered different and important messages from God for specific peoples and for different periods of time. Building on this foundation, Baha'u'lláh's message was one of unity of all mankind. He taught that there was only one God and only one human race. He believed that all the world religions have been revelations from God for different times and in different places. He was saying that at the founding of the Baha'i Faith, mankind had come of age and that this new message of unity and peace had been sent through this prophet-Messiah for this "New World Order."

There are approximately six million Baha'is today scattered across the globe. They have grown from five million since 1991. Today we were to visit with a small group of them during their 10:30 a.m. service. At 10:20 a.m., Betty and I walked into this Baha'i Center which had been built "about fifteen years ago" according to one of their members. It is a neat, unpretentious building which has several classrooms off a central gathering room. The central gathering room also leads to the worship center where we gathered for their prayer and devotion service. It is a moderate-sized room able to seat about a hundred very close friends. The room has nine sides (making the room almost circular) that are reflected in a dome of the same configuration. The nine sides honor the nine prophets of God throughout history, the founders of the world religions.

As we entered, we were cordially met by several of their members. Everyone seemed in a relaxed mood, slowly moving toward this Sunday morning worship-devotion time together. From the beginning they assured us that this would be a very informal meeting. We met a handsome, hospitable and very helpful member whose name is Derek Streets-Anderson. He made sure we met several of the members as they came in to take a seat. He is a Caucasian account executive with a media company in Nashville, and he introduced us to his wife who appeared to be African-American.

Some of the teachings of this faith emphasize gender and racial equality. And this meeting was a true example of cultural diversity. The leader of this devotional period was Tracy White, who appeared to be in her twenties. She said that she was substituting for an older member who was sick today. She welcomed us and told us that this service would be in two parts. The first would be a formalized program of study which would be followed by a time of open testimonials and prayer during which, she said, "You might want to share a poem or something or just say what is on your heart."

This faith has no paid priests, ministers or highly-trained religious leaders. The casual, informal room added to the easy relaxed mood created by the adherents to this faith. There were windows at a height of about seven feet off the floor and skylight windows in the dome. There was a simple lectern, a band-like keyboard, and a TV monitor on a shelf-stand which also housed an audio system and speakers which would be used for musical accompaniment during parts of this service.

There were twenty-eight people, including six children, in this room when Tracy began the service. She turned on a soothing recording of running water sounds which played while different members came forward to read from printed material which Tracy had given them. The first was a prayer of abdu'l-Baha, the son and successor to the leadership position in Bahà'i after the death of Bahà'u'lláh:

> *O God! Refresh and gladden my spirit.*
> *Purify my heart. Illumine my powers.*
> *I lay all my affairs in Thy hand.*
> *Thou art My Guide and my Refuge.*
> *I will no longer be sorrowful and grieved;*
> *I will be a happy and joyful being.*
> *O God! I will no longer be full of anxiety,*
> *nor will I let trouble harass me.*
> *I will not dwell on the unpleasant things of life.*
> *O God! Thou art more friend*
> *to me than I am to myself.*
> *I dedicate myself to Thee, O Lord.*

There were several other prayers, read mostly by women in this service, one of which included these words about the central message and mission of this faith:

> *"O Thou kind Lord! Unite all. Let the religions agree and make the nations one, so that we may see each other as one family and the whole earth as one home. May we all live together in perfect harmony."*

Midway through the service two young women sang a duet without accompaniment; they both closed their eyes while they sang. The title was Hallelujah, Hallelujah To The Ancient of Days. Then after four more readers, Tracy turned on the recorder and played a song in the contemporary gospel mode about faith: "As ye have faith, so shall your power and blessing be."

The leader of this service said, "This is now open prayer time. You can come and say what is on your heart." An attractive woman came and read a poem. She was followed by another who read from the teachings of one of the leaders of this faith who told us to "beware, beware, lest ye offend the feelings of someone, even if he be an evildoer."

A man who appeared to be of mid-Eastern descent chanted a prayer while remaining in his seat. The prayer I assumed was in Arabic, and he expressively raised and lowered his hands, turning his palms upward at different points in his prayer. It was a beautiful sight. Even though I could not understand a word he was saying, he prayed so fervently with his expressive hands that I was convinced he felt he was in direct communion with God.

Next, a man who may have been Jamaican gave a short testimonial which I could not understand because of his heavy accent. He was followed by an African-American woman who wore a turban and sang with a marvelously talented and sweet voice. Her beautiful acapella song concluded with the words, "Nearness to Thee is my home."

The leader, Tracy, and another young woman sang with recorded accompaniment a song which was asking for the presence of God: "My spirit is longing for Thee...shine down on us with the light of truth... Holy Spirit, come to us this day." This soft contemporary Christian song continued: "Show your power, make your presence known... Holy Spirit come and fill this space...Let it fall on me completely."

Two more women gave short readings before Tracy concluded this service. She said, "I want to thank all of you for coming and hope you felt the Holy Spirit. I know I did." Then she made some announcements — including one about a meeting that would be held here on Saturday at 7:30 p.m. during which representatives from several different faiths would come together in a service "commemorating 9-11."

Before we left, the small devout middle-Eastern man said he wished all of us would offer a healing prayer for someone he was concerned about and for some others who also needed prayers. Tracy asked this sweet-spirited and concerned man if he would offer this prayer. Then, in what was probably his native tongue, he chanted his prayer in the same tone that I had heard at the Kurdish Mosque a few months ago. Again, without understanding a word of his prayer, I could feel the intensity of his desire to present the needs of those he was praying for to a God whom he was convinced heard his sincere humble prayer of supplication.

Derek (who apparently missed most of this service to help take care of his three-year-old son) met us to give us some informative literature about this faith — which was now his new faith. He had grown up in three different Christian churches and now apparently felt more at home here. He feels that within the Bahá'í faith both Judaism and Christianity find a meeting ground that provides a comfort level with the other world religions.

As I left this service, I basked in the genuine friendliness of Tracy, Derek and the others from this morning. I also was hearing over and over again in my mind the haunting, rhythmic cadence of the little middle-Eastern man. He had reverently, humbly and comfortably presented the needs of his friends to the Creator of the heavens and the Earth. His humble prayer did not at all seem to be an obsequious meeting on his part with the Almighty God, the Creator of the Universe. Instead, it was apparent that he felt comfortable and that he knew God was intently listening to his every, prayerful word. He appeared as if he knew he was speaking to someone who cared and wanted to help. His relaxed, expressive hands — palms turned upward — told it all.

Eschatological Musings

September 14, 2003

*E*schatology is the branch of theology dealing with last things or the final events of world history. The literal meaning is tweaked here just a bit. The "Eschatological Musings" referred to are my last thoughts about the fifty-two week journey detailed in the previous chapters. I like to use the term 'eschatological' because it is one of the few terms I still remember from my days of studying theology and because it is an impressive word which rolls so rhythmically off my tongue that I even enjoy repeating it (Es-cat-a-logical). To be honest, I suppose some part of me wanted to make use of it in order to impress my readers with regard to my theological background.

My desire to impress reminds me of the joke about a man who confesses to his priest that he had sex five times the night before. The priest asked him to confess who the women were. The communicant responded that there was only one woman, his wife. The priest said, "My son, these acts of love were within the holy bonds of matrimony, and you do not need to confess this at all." The man, his chest swelling with pride says, "I know, Father, but I just *had* to tell someone."

In some ways, this entire work falls into the context of just having to tell someone what I found during the past year of visiting many different religious services. Is this not the case with all authors of books, songs or poems? We all just have to tell someone about our discoveries.

Friends who knew about my fifty-two week commitment of exploration have asked what the best or most unusual service I attended was. Such questions are truly difficult to answer. In each service I found things of interest because in each one I was witnessing each group's different efforts to communicate with and to worship God.

Of particular interest was how the small (sometimes very, very small) churches hold on when one might think it time for them just to give up, perhaps by merging with another church of the same faith. Why do they keep holding on? Almost always, history is the key. An obligation is felt by the members to hold on out of respect for their forbearers who had worshiped as a part of the church many years ago. People hold on because Great Aunt Sally was baptized in the very same church scores of years ago, or because once upon a time Uncle Cedrick, who was a pillar of the community and the county's most successful notary public, worshipped in this sanctuary. Or perhaps the great-grandson of George Washington visited this very church 50 years ago and "sat right over there in the very next pew where you are sitting." Everywhere I went I could almost see and hear the ghosts of history calling out "HOLD ON. HOLD ON."

While most of the smaller churches visited were found traveling the blue roads in rural Middle Tennessee, one of the ten smallest churches in terms of attendance was Trinity Episcopal Church in New York City. With the exception of this church in New York, New York, another in Atlanta, Georgia and a third church in Naples, Florida, all the other churches visited were located in Nashville and in Middle Tennessee.

At the beginning of the journey I felt that we would hear much more about 9-11 than we actually did. It was only mentioned in two or three churches. There were only a few announcements in the church bulletins asking members to "Pray for victims of 9-11." There were prayers for our soldiers in Afghanistan and Iraq after unfolding events led us into war with these two countries. One church announced upcoming meetings for discussions about Judaism and the Muslim religion. During those meetings I imagine considerably more was said about 9-11 and terrorism, the Muslim religion, and the overall situation between the Israelis and the Palestinians and how that situation influenced the individuals who had committed the 9-11 atrocities.

We visited six world religions during the year. We attended services with Orthodox and Reformed Jews at their Synagogues, with Muslims at a Mosque, with Buddhists at a small, makeshift place of worship, with Hindus at a beautiful traditional Temple, and with Bahà'is at a Bahà'i Worship Center. In addition, we visited more than 46 Christian Churches including Mormons, Jehovah's Witnesses and Seventh Day Adventists. Most of the other Christian Churches were Catholic, Greek Orthodox, Episcopal, Methodists, Church of Christ, Presbyterian, Cumberland Presbyterian, Nazarene, Church of God, Assembly of God, Pentecostal, Lutheran, Christian, Congregational and four different Baptist denominations. The four different Baptist groups were Southern Baptist, Free Will Baptist, Missionary Baptist and Primitive Baptist.

The rest of the Christian Churches attended were ones in the general category of Community Churches. I call most of these "parenthetical" churches because many times these churches have indirect relationships with other denominations. Community Churches, however, choose to downplay that connection, apparently in order, to broaden their appeal to a wider range of Christians.

Community Churches fascinate me more than any other single group and several common elements can be identified in most of these congregations. The strongest common element is the use of contemporary Gospel music, often referred to as Christian or Gospel rock, which is lively and moving. In most of the Community Church services the words of the rhythmic songs are displayed on large video screens. These video screens allow the worshipers' hands to be free for clapping, waving, keeping time and participating in the infectious beats of the songs. The singing and clapping are often accompanied by differing degrees of in-place dancing. The congregations usually are led in this moving musical worship by worship teams of highly talented musicians.

The use of music in the Community Church services allows for categorizing most of these churches as charismatic in a general sense — not necessarily, however, in the more specific sense of speaking in tongues and other more unusual practices. These practices are found in churches which have traditionally been referred to as charismatic. It might surprise one to learn that some Catholic and Episcopal churches are referred to as charismatic by their own leaders, primarily because of the use of more lively and expressionistic forms of worship. These forms of worship even include, in some instances, speaking in tongues.

Another common characteristic found in Community

Churches is an emphasis on youth. Most of the congregations are made up largely of singles and young families. The makeup of the congregations perhaps lead to another common characteristic: these churches are, for the most part, quite informal. Not only do the members dress informally, but so do the ministers and worship leaders. In one case the minister had taken the casual dress code to the point of wearing tennis shoes. But the informality goes even further; the worshipers often carry coffee, soft drinks or drinking water into the services.

These Community Churches also tend to downplay the identifying doctrines which are definite points of emphasis in the mother churches from which they have sprung. The messages are simple — believe in the Lord Jesus Christ, confess your sins, and live a dedicated Christian life.

Other common aspects found in Community Churches are that ministers with dynamic personalities lead most of them and that almost all of them are experiencing rapid growth. They tend to worship in new, large, and often very expensive facilities or to be in the planning stages of developing such facilities. Those who have new facilities usually are already planning expansions to accommodate the many varied church-sponsored activities which occupy much of the free time of the members

Unfortunately I was unable to attend all the services which I would have liked to have visited during the fifty-two weeks of visitation. One in particular was The Friends (Quaker) Church in Nashville. This congregation had just sold their building and had not yet relocated to a new place of worship. Then there were denominations which prefer not to be in the public eye and do not openly welcome visitors, particularly those who might think of themselves as writers. An Amish group indicated that, while they would not turn anyone away from services, they preferred that I not visit if the intent was to write about their service afterwards; I respected their wishes. Also, some churches which practice snake handling prefer not to have unknown visitors for fear of being reported to the authorities. There are laws in some states which prohibit the use of wild animals in public meeting places.

The most interesting places of worship I visited were the places with the most interesting people. This makes sense because

I was basically watching people. I suspect the most interesting people to me probably would not be the most interesting people to you had you traveled the same paths with us. A few of my most interesting people illustrate my thinking on this point. I will remember forever the beautifully expressive hands of a small swarthy man as he prayed in a language which was foreign to me. His hands open in supplication were the true expressions of a simple fervent prayer. His whole demeanor was of a man speaking to one he knew to be the God of the universe with full and complete confidence that this same God of the universe was indeed listening to him.

Another person who stands out in my memory was a young father, dressed in clean but modest work clothes one Sunday morning, feeding his beautiful young daughter in "airplane bites." While I watched them walking out hand in hand, my mind was captivated not only by what I had seen but also by what I could not see. Where was the woman that would have completed this family? I could not help but imagine all sorts of scenarios of where she might be before settling on one which seemed most appropriate for a good Sunday morning story.

There is the image of an elderly lay member of a church, substituting for his pastor, walking to the back of the church while being led by cherubic little acolyte girls, giggling as they tried to keep their flickering candles alive. And then there is the image of a humble preacher in a small town church who struggled with stuttering. He stopped at a point during his sermon to ask God for help in delivering His message to the people who had come that morning. And at the end of the service the same humble spirit asked God for forgiveness because he had lost a scripture lesson he felt God wanted him to share.

I shall never forget the courage of another man with a noticeable speech impediment. I watched him in a restaurant while he spoke without shame, freely and openly, to everyone as if he was the most eloquent man on earth. Nor shall I ever forget the sad nothingness in the eyes of a well-dressed "cowboy" I noticed in another restaurant. His blank stare seemed to block out the whole world, starting with the wife who seemed invisible to him as they sat waiting for breakfast.

I will always remember the contrasts I witnessed on this journey. On one morning at a truckstop, I took note of the hopeful, earnest eyes of a truckstop lay chaplain wearing a simple white T-shirt and a chaplain's badge which he wore proudly as he shared his faith with a lone truck driver. Then, within a span of just a few minutes, I found myself taking note of a distinctly different environment of worship. I was attending a church with several priests and worship assistants dressed in ornate priestly vestments. They ministered to a crowded church full of reverent and worshipful communicants whose formalities were in response to the traditional liturgical movements of the priests.

Still another image of contrasts comes to mind. An aging minister in his liturgical vestments approaches his pulpit slowly, his steps uncertain being assisted by a cane. The memory continues as this pastor ministers formally to his small group of followers. This scene is contrasted with the image of a very large and very informal Community Church and a youthful senior pastor who was enthusiastically exhorting his large congregation to go into all the world and preach the gospel. Another contrast in these two churches: the old hymns of one church and the contemporary gospel songs of another. And yet underneath the contrasts, each minister was doubtlessly ministering to his respective people as he felt God was leading him.

During the last week of my 52 weeks I went to a Saturday evening service sponsored by the Bahà'i Center in Nashville. The service was a commemoration of 9-11 with eight different religions represented: Jewish, Christian, Muslim, Buddhist, Hindu, Zoroastrian, American Indian and Bahà'i. The representatives of each of the religions prayed, often with both hands folded as in the famous picture of the famous "Praying Hands." In some cases the languages in which they prayed were unfamiliar to me. But with each prayer I had no question that all of these participants, regardless of their faiths, believed that they were praying to the same God to which the others were praying.

Religions and denominations differ in ways of worship. They differ in the language used during prayer, the songs they sing if they sing at all, in the way they baptize or receive adherents, in the way they commune with one another, in the scriptures they read, in the texts they emphasize and in the types of places in which they gather to worship. There are basic underlying beliefs, however, which link all of these differing groups into a single and united family of mankind. Each of these religions believes that we are all the creations of one God bound together under that God.

At the end of the day, the worship services I attended during this year left me with the distinct feeling that all worshipers believe they are communing and praying to the one God and creator of all mankind. The fact that each religious tradition approaches the acts of communion and prayer from a different set of cultural traditions, and emphasizes varying aspects of the Creator's will, is a difference of degree and not a difference of kind. At the very least, the worshipers engaging in worship seem to be doing so with the thought and hope and prayer that they are worshiping the Almighty God who created them.

I believe that we should all give each other the benefit of doubt. Perhaps we, as good Americans (if not as good Christians, Jews or Muslims) should agree that other religions and denominations will be presumed innocent of all heretical charges until they are proven guilty of praying to the wrong God and in the wrong way.

This concludes my eschatological musings on these matters. To once again quote my philosophical hero Forest Gump, "and that's all I have to say on that subject." And as "Mr. Cellophane" says in the movie Chicago, "I hope I have not taken up too much of your time."

Printed in the United States
26142LVS00002B/196-204

9 781583 850626